CAPTIVE COSMOPOLITANS

CAPTIVE

COSMOPOLITANS

Black Mariners and the World of

South Atlantic Slavery

MARY E. HICKS

Published by the

OMOHUNDRO INSTITUTE OF

EARLY AMERICAN HISTORY AND CULTURE,

Williamsburg, Virginia,

and the

UNIVERSITY OF NORTH CAROLINA PRESS,

Chapel Hill

*The Omohundro Institute of
Early American History and Culture
is sponsored by the College of William and Mary.
On November 15, 1996, the Institute adopted the
present name in honor of a bequest from
Malvern H. Omohundro, Jr.*

Cover illustration: "Braïa dos Mineros à Rio-Janeiro."
By Maurice [Johann Moritz] Rugendas. In Rugendas,
Voyage pittoresque dans le Brésil, liv. 3, Moeurs et usages des Indiens et des Européens
(Paris, 1827), 289. Digitized by HathiTrust.

Library of Congress Cataloging-in-Publication Data
Names: Hicks, Mary E., author.
Title: Captive cosmopolitans : Black mariners and the
world of South Atlantic slavery / Mary E. Hicks.
Description: Williamsburg, Virginia : Omohundro Institute of
Early American History and Culture ; Chapel Hill : University
of North Carolina Press, [2024] | Includes index.
Identifiers: LCCN 2024033113 | ISBN 9781469671468 (cloth ; alk. paper) |
ISBN 9781469671475 (EPUB) | ISBN 9781469680828 (pdf) |
ISBN 9781469671482 (ebook other)
Subjects: LCSH: Enslaved persons—Brazil—Salvador—Social conditions—18th
century. | Enslaved persons—Brazil—Salvador—Social conditions—19th century. |
Enslaved persons—South Atlantic Ocean Region—Social conditions. | Merchant
mariners, Black—Atlantic Coast (Africa, West)—History. | Merchant mariners,
Black—Brazil—Salvador—History. | Merchant mariners, Black—Legal status,
laws, etc. | Slave trade—Brazil—Salvador—History. | BISAC: HISTORY / United
States / Colonial Period (1600–1775) | SOCIAL SCIENCE / Black Studies (Global)
Classification: LCC HT1127 .H53 2024 | DDC 382/.44091821—dc23/eng/20240820
LC record available at https://lccn.loc.gov/2024033113

For Bonnie & James

"*They say that men who have seen the world, thereby become quite at ease in manner, quite self-possessed in company.*"
—Herman Melville,
Moby-Dick; or, The Whale (1851)

"*In the world I am heading for, I am endlessly creating myself.*"
—Frantz Fanon,
Black Skin, White Masks (1952)

{ ACKNOWLEDGMENTS }

Those of us who have the immense privilege of writing books know that we craft them alongside the inevitable unfurling of life. It is an enterprise of many years, with many starts, stops, and detours along the way. My time writing this book has coincided with the joy of knowing, learning from, and being challenged by a great many people, without whom this book would not have been possible. Leslie Schwalm introduced me, a curious undergraduate at the University of Iowa, to the history of slavery and sparked my interest in African influences in the Americas. Michel Gobat helped me develop an interest in Latin America, and Kevin Mumford, Shelton Stromquist, and Jeffrey Cox nurtured my knowledge of the discipline of history and encouraged me to keep going in academia, though I had little knowledge of the path that lay ahead.

I arrived at the University of Virginia as an enthusiastic but naive graduate student, with little precedent for what postgraduate studies looked like. Needless to say, I relied on my brilliant, kind, and patient adviser Brian Owensby for more than just academic support. As I hurried to figure out what being a scholar meant, alongside many others who already seemed to innately understand the contours of academic life, Brian's gentle but challenging guidance not only opened my mind to the possibilities of Latin American history but gave me the confidence to think I could become a part of the field. This project was conceived at the University of Virginia and greatly inspired by the rich cross-regional dialogues between Africanists and Latin Americanists there. I was fortunate to experience the mentorship of Joseph Miller in the final years of his career. His encyclopedic knowledge of the history of slavery, his care for the historian's craft, and his intellectual fire all left a lasting impression on my life and work. The steady insightfulness of Roquinaldo Ferreira helped guide me through archives across the globe and prompted me to change course at a critical juncture in my research. I also learned a tremendous amount from Tom Klubock, whose theoretical sophistication indelibly shaped my graduate career. I had many other inspiring teachers at the University of Virginia, across many disciplines, who provided excellent models for the kind of rigorous, forward-looking scholarship I endeavored to produce. These connections continue to shape the ways I think about race, freedom, bondage, and the making of the modern world. The support of my peers Anne Daniels, Jared Staller, Cody Perkins, Elizabeth Kaknes, Chris Cornelius, Emily Senefeld, Lauren Turek, John Terry, Nir Avisser, Tamika Nunley, Ryan Bibler, Trevor Hiblar, and Evan Farr continues to motivate my scholarship. Generous funding by the Jefferson Foundation proved to be invaluable in allowing me to undertake the extensive international research required for this project. A fellowship from the Ford Foundation enabled me to complete my dissertation and was essential to the writing of this book. The wonderful community of Ford Fellows also provided a warm welcome to the profession during my first years as a professor.

In Portugal, the helpful staff at the Arquivo Histórico Ultramarino, the Torre do Tombo, and the Arquivo Histórico da Marinha Portuguesa directed me to rich archival sources and answered my questions. The staff at the Arquivo Nacional and Arquivo Histórico do Itamaraty curated research spaces that became a welcome refuge amid the bustle of Rio de Janeiro. In Salvador da Bahia, the resourceful archivists of the Arquivo Público do Estado da Bahia carried out their work with warmth and humor, inviting researchers from near and far to become part of a capacious community premised on a shared love of Bahian history and culture. I was immensely fortunate to be one of them, alongside local researcher Urano Andrade, who explained the ins and outs of the archive, and Case Watkins, my American compadre and fellow Bahianist for life.

As a new professor at Amherst College, I was lucky to have two departmental homes. My colleagues in the History Department, Vanessa Walker, Ellen Boucher, Adi Gordon, Frank Couvares, Rick Lopez, Jen Manion, Trent Maxey, Ted Melillo, and Sean Reading, all provided advice and support—reading drafts of my work, talking through questions, and helping me find new directions. My colleagues in Black Studies provided a community that managed to be nurturing and intellectually inspiring in equal measure. The friendship and guidance of Rhonda Cobham-Sander, John Drabinski, Rowland Abiodun, Khary Polk, Olufemi Vaughn, Solsiree del Moral, and Dominique Hill were transformative. As I sought to experiment with forms of disciplinary knowledge beyond history, the insights and generosity of my Black Studies colleagues opened up completely new ways of thinking about my research materials. Their knowledge enabled me to more seriously ponder the implications of African epistemologies in Brazil and decisively altered the trajectory of my work. Many other colleagues at Amherst College and in the Western Massachusetts area wrote alongside me, provided encouragement, and greatly enriched my time there: Amelia Worsley, Yael Rice, Raphael Sigal, Yu-ting Huang, Krupa Shandilya, Ingrid Nelson, Tom Zanker, Shirley Wong, and Rafeeq Hasan. I am also very thankful for the excellent support of Karla Keyes, Carey Aubert, Robyn Rodgers, Tracie Rubeck, and Dee Brace.

During the writing of this book, I spent a pivotal year at Harvard's Hutchinson Center under the directorship of the always engaged and engaging Henry Louis Gates. With their generous support, I learned so much from my fellow fellows and will forever be indebted to their insights: ZZ Packer, Kinitra Brooks, Robyn D'Avignon, Michael Ralph, Christopher Ouma, Romeo Oriogun, Peter Hume, Pablo Herrera Veitia, Shirely Moody-Turner, Matthew Morrison, Akua Naru, Jessica Welburn Paige, Lakeyta M. Bonnette-Bailey, Reighan Gillam, and David Bindman. Also, many thanks to Alejandro de la Fuente and Tamar Herzog for inviting me to share my work with students and faculty in the History Department, and Krishna Lewis for her kind leadership. Cornel West remained incredibly generous with his time and knowledge during my year there.

Writing in the pandemic era has also entailed fashioning makeshift intellectual communities. I have tremendous gratitude to Christopher Willoughby for organizing a wonderful virtual writing group, alongside Kathryn Olivarius, Carolyn Roberts, Wangui Muigai, and Jonathan Lande. I am very appreciative of the many conferences, departments, and programs that invited me to share and workshop portions of this manuscript. My thanks extends to Sven Beckhart, Sophus Reinhert, Tatiana Seijas, Gregory Mixon, Adam Bledsoe, Oscar de la Torre, Zephyr Frank, Trent Masiki, Marc Hertzman, Christopher Dietrich, Nicole Eustace, João José Reis, Luis Nicolau Parés, Toby Green, Adriana Chira, Carlos Silva Jr., Natasha Lightfoot, Michelle Commander, Keisha Blain, Rachel O'Toole, Matt Randolph, and many others who were kind enough to provide comments.

Completing this project at the University of Chicago has given me the privilege of working alongside a number of formidable scholars of Latin American and Black Atlantic history. I've had the pleasure of sharing my work with colleagues and students and have always looked forward to their astute and meticulous feedback. Thanks to Brodwyn Fischer, Emilio Kourí, Mauricio Tenorio-Trillo, Dain Borges, Rashauna Johnson, Amy Dru Stanley, Leora Auslander, Benjamin Lessing, Victoria Saramago, and Gabriel Franco. I am also permanently indebted to the diligent and thought-provoking comments offered by the readers of this manuscript: James Sidbury and Mariana Candido. Working with the talented editorial staff at the Omohundro Institute,

Nicholas Popper, Emily Suth, and Kathryn Burdette, has been an amazing experience. And a special thanks to James DeGrand for producing the beautiful maps for this book.

Many of my enriching professional relationships have allowed me to craft the book I had always envisioned, but it is my family that has ultimately sustained me. My parents, James and Bonnie Hicks, always, no matter the obstacle, gave me the courage to take hold of my future and see the world. With their love, perseverance, and ingenuity, they taught me the art of making a way out of no way. In their day-to-day lives, they showed me the myth of boundaries and borders and the imperative to make home wherever you are and with whoever is near. Many thanks to my brother, Jason, for his endless positivity; my aunt, Bea, for her tenacity; and my uncle, Redmond, for his wisdom. I am hugely grateful to Kenny, Holly, Bob, and Joann for their loving support throughout my life. And finally, the greatest thanks to my partner, editor, and biggest supporter, Alec Hickmott. I have learned about the discipline of history from him as much as anyone. This book would have been impossible without his daily jokes and our wide-ranging conversations. As we have grown together as people and thinkers, I can only hope that I have lived up to all his biggest dreams for me.

{ CONTENTS }

{ LIST OF ILLUSTRATIONS }

FIGURES

MAPS

TABLES

{ LIST OF ABBREVIATIONS }

ACML   Arquivo Central da Marinha-Lisboa

AHI   Arquivo Histórico do Itamaraty

AHU   Arquivo Histórico Ultramarino

CU   Conselho Ultramarino

ANRJ   Arquivo Nacional Rio de Janeiro

ANTT   Arquivo Nacional da Torre do Tombo

APEB   Arquivo Público do Estado da Bahia

BNRJ   Biblioteca Nacional Rio de Janeiro

BNA   British National Archives

FO   Papers of the Foreign Office

HAHR   *Hispanic American Historical Review*

Voyages   *Voyages: The Trans-Atlantic Slave Trade Database,*
www.slavevoyages.org

WMQ   *William and Mary Quarterly*

CAPTIVE COSMOPOLITANS

The Sea Is History

Where are your monuments, your battles, martyrs?
Where is your tribal memory? Sirs,
in that grey vault. The sea. The sea
has locked them up. The sea is History.
   —Derek Walcott, "The Sea Is History"

On the day of June 7 [1830] escaped from the alley of Guindaste no. 15,
a slave named Fernando of the Mozambique nation . . . [while] in the
service of the canoes and boats of Mineiros' Beach, where he always had
the custom of denying his owner [and] saying that he was free . . . today
if he is found in São Matheu or in Bahia . . . it is believed he would travel
with a [fraudulent] title of manumission and work as a Mariner.
   —Fugitive slave announcement, *Jornal do commercio* (Rio de Janeiro),
   Jan. 19, 1833

In 1830, the well-heeled readers of the *Jornal do commercio*—Rio de Janeiro's premier periodical—learned of the travails of an African sailor named Fernando, whose dramatic flight from slavery was detailed in a series of announcements (*avisos*) published over three years. These fragments laid bare a life lived in motion. Born in Mozambique before being enslaved, displaced from his homeland, and forcibly transported to Brazil, Fernando was an *escravo ladino,* or acculturated and Portuguese-speaking captive, who labored as a "shipman and sailor" in the thriving port located on Guanabara Bay. Fernando had—at least according to his owner—proclaimed himself to be in possession of a "title of free status."[1]

At first glance, Fernando appears a confounding figure to encounter in the archive. In part, his life defies our archetypal visions of an early-nineteenth-century slave society defined by stark dichotomies between mastery and slavery, domination and submission. Though his owner scoffed at Fernando's impudent habit of "denying" him, the captive seaman's insistence that his lived experience of self-possessed independence contradicted his legally

1. *Jornal do commercio* (Rio de Janeiro), Jan. 19, 1833, 4; ibid., July 28, 1830, 2.

constituted enslaved status suggests a very different experience of early modern slavery. On the bustling littorals of the South Atlantic, African and creole men dominated the ranks of maritime laborers. In the very moment of the transatlantic slave trade's apex in Brazil, amid the intensifying exploitation around them, some of these men were able to chart an independent path. Though Fernando was compelled to move in order to satisfy the interests of his owner, his working life as an *escravo de ganho,* or wage-earning slave, could become a source of empowerment and self-making. As the *Jornal do commercio* acknowledged, the mariner had engaged in the entrepreneurial act of contracting himself out for pay to various ships arriving in his home port. Fernando would have worked side by side with Brazilian, European, and African-born seamen, both free and enslaved, laboring in an environment that afforded him the opportunity to craft a life that was not completely determined by his enslaved status.[2]

This was the maritime world of the South Atlantic: at sea and in port, the thin line between acting free and being free was one that could be transgressed in an instant. The veracity of Fernando's declarations of freedom likely went unquestioned in a space defined by a maelstrom of race, class, and status. On Brazil's sprawling waterfronts, free and enslaved, native and foreign born, wealthy and powerful, as well as destitute and desperate rubbed shoulders daily. Fernando moved among a diverse array of merchants, passengers, mariners, artisans, petty traders, and newly arrived captive Africans. The social fluidity of such an environment enabled Fernando's bold assertions as well as the self-conceptions and actions of many others like him who carved out lives in the often ambiguous interstices between slavery and freedom.

The labors of Fernando and his peers were indispensable to preserving and perpetuating slaving commerce. Their lives became a defining feature of the transatlantic trade at the heart of the early modern South Atlantic. As a study of European merchant capitalism and colonialism told from the perspective of enslaved mariners, *Captive Cosmopolitans* explores the lives of the Atlantic world's most mobile and culturally dexterous group of laborers. Focusing on the aquatic-oriented world of Salvador da Bahia in the eighteenth and early nineteenth centuries, *Captive Cosmopolitans* argues that such men exemplified a radically distinct experience of enslavement. For this exclusively male and urban maritime workforce, slavery demanded constant motion, in contrast to the spatially bound agricultural labor that defined servitude in Brazil's

2. Ibid., Jan. 19, 1833, 4. "Creole," or *crioulo* in Portuguese, refers to people of full African descent but born in the Americas.

hinterlands. Within the waterfront spaces of colonial and imperial Brazil, slaveowners did not rely on physical captivity or the cultivation of "social death" to exert control over their bondspeople. In the South Atlantic, slavery was defined less by the arduous nature of work to which one was assigned than by the instrumental use to which one's owner put one's labor. As ancient Roman writer Varro concluded, the enslaved were "speaking tools" (*instrumenta vocales*), both objects and subjects whose fungibility made them ideal "vessels" for their owner's will. Profiting from the labor of one's human property did not always require absolute forms of control or domination. Utility rather than degradation guided owners' often limited supervision of their maritime bondsmen. Maritime slaves in the South Atlantic existed in a world punctuated by exploitation, violence, and, at times, horror. But these elements did not completely define the experience of captive cosmopolitan mariners. Though slaveholders endeavored to make their bondsmen mere instruments, the enslaved in turn exploited their own instrumentality to create forms of autonomy.[3]

In centering these maritime historical actors, *Captive Cosmopolitans* pushes historians to imagine an Atlantic order centered on subaltern commercial and cultural exchange where the enslaved had access to a number of possibilities for social and economic advancement. These prospects remained firmly intertwined with the commercial imperatives of the transatlantic slave trade, however. Slave societies such as Bahia, where Fernando escaped to, were far from cloistered. They were defined by the constant circulation of people, materials, and ideas. Enslaved mariners' cosmopolitanism emerged from a mosaic of cultures, languages, religious beliefs, and ethnic identi-

3. Sandra R. Joshel, "Slavery and Roman Literary Culture," in Keith Bradley and Paul Cartledge, eds., *The Cambridge World History of Slavery*, I, *The Ancient Mediterranean World* (Cambridge, 2011), 214–240, esp. 215; Fernando A. Novais, *Portugal e Brasil na crise do antigo sistema colonial (1777–1808)* (São Paulo, 1983), 107. For a theorization of enslavement as social death, or the process of severing socially recognized kinship and communal ties independent of one's owner, see Orlando Patterson, *Slavery and Social Death: A Comparative Study* (Cambridge, Mass., 1982), 5. For critiques of social death as a permanent condition, see Jessica Marie Johnson, *Wicked Flesh: Black Women, Intimacy, and Freedom in the Atlantic World* (Philadelphia, 2020), 3; James H. Sweet, "Defying Social Death: The Multiple Configurations of African Slave Family in the Atlantic World," *WMQ*, 3d Ser., LXX (2013), 251–272. On slavery as premised on spatial confinement, see Stephanie M. H. Camp, *Closer to Freedom: Enslaved Women and Everyday Resistance in the Plantation South* (Chapel Hill, N.C., 2004). On slavery as premised on dehumanization, see David Brion Davis, *Inhuman Bondage: The Rise and Fall of Slavery in the New World* (New York, 2006), 2–4.

ties that suffused South Atlantic maritime milieus. Men such as Fernando navigated this kaleidoscopic world by traversing aquatic sinews that held together a system of discrete ports linking Africa to the Americas. And because slaveholders utilized the minds as well as the bodies of the enslaved, Black mariners' cosmopolitanism became a crucial technology for the forging of new financial instruments, the securing of commodified captives in Africa, and the forming of new cultures and communities in Bahia. Operating in the liminal spaces between master and slave, Africans and the Portuguese, captive cosmopolitan mariners were integral to commercial life and economic exchange in the early modern Atlantic world.

SALVADOR DA BAHIA:
A BLACK ATLANTIC PORT CITY

Though Fernando had fled bondage, he had escaped to one of the most active slave-trading ports in the Atlantic world: Salvador da Bahia. Geography and place were crucial to his "watery liberation." His attraction to another urban center of pulsating maritime commerce—and the benefits it conferred—was hardly surprising, considering his previous experiences in Rio de Janeiro. When Fernando arrived in Salvador, he would have witnessed a port city often described as breathtaking in its beauty. But the entrepôt's picturesque appearance belied its status as a voracious consumer of enslaved men, women, and children who had been disembarked from the coasts of Africa. As a thriving hub of colonial and then imperial commerce, Salvador was situated in the Baía de Todos os Santos, or Bay of All Saints, an expanse of water named in honor of the day it was first encountered by European navigators in 1501. The port received a staggering 1,730,070 enslaved individuals from Africa over a period of nearly three hundred years. And though most arrivals would ultimately be transported to rural plantations and mines, slavery left a profound mark on the city. The turbulent sea that surrounded it gave birth to an urban world defined by stark disparity and hardship alongside ostentatious displays of wealth.[4]

The spatial organization of Salvador expressed these powerful inequalities. Located on a sharp bluff, the elevated "upper city" conveyed the political and economic power of the mercantile elite, who moved easily through per-

4. David W. Blight, *Frederick Douglass: Prophet of Freedom* (New York, 2018), 34. Numbers for total number of enslaved individuals landed under Portuguese and Brazilian colors are from *Voyages*, http://www.slavevoyages.org/tast/index.faces.

fumed gardens and elegant facades. Submerged in the "lower city," the urban poor and enslaved toiled alongside unscrupulous merchants and rugged seamen while slavers disembarked ailing captive Africans onto fetid, winding streets, detaining them in dilapidated buildings lining the waterfront. The two spaces—tethered together only by a steep road too perilous for horses or oxen to traverse—were joined physically and metaphorically by enslaved labor, as Africans strained under the weight of the goods and people they ferried back and forth between the upper and lower portions of the city. As they did so, the fruits of enslaved labor in Salvador and on the sugar and tobacco plantations that surrounded it accrued to a Bahian elite, who maintained their lives in splendor.[5]

Because trade was the lifeblood of Salvador da Bahia, waterborne commerce permeated every facet of life. The built environment, the composition of the population, as well as the productive lives of its residents were all dependent on the port's relationship to an increasingly interconnected Atlantic Ocean. Salvador was not just a place in the Atlantic but an Atlantic *place*. Life there remained tied to the ebbs and flows of Atlantic commerce and politics, which connected the city to an array of geographically and culturally distant ports, particularly in West Africa and Europe. Indeed, most of the city's population lived by oceanic trade and transportation, including merchants, ship captains, and seamen as well as a sizable number of auxiliary laborers such as sailmakers, stevedores, and ironsmiths. After its founding in 1549, the oceanic entrepôt quickly became the heart of the Portuguese empire, the second most prolific importer of enslaved Africans in the Americas and the busiest port in the South Atlantic. Salvador's aquatic orientation reverberated through its inhabitants' lives for the next three hundred years.[6]

The port also featured a deepening reliance on Black maritime workers in all branches of navigation. Beginning with the dawn of Portuguese navigation in the Atlantic during the fifteenth century, Black waterborne mobility underpinned that imperial project of oceanic exploration and settlement. African and creole seamen not only provided the physical labor that was necessary

---

5. [François] sieur Froger, *Relation d'un voyage . . . de M. de Gennes (1695–1714)* (Amsterdam, 1715), 129, quoted in Pierre Verger, *Trade Relations between the Bight of Benin and Bahia from the 17th to 19th Century,* [trans. Evelyn Crawford] (Ibadan, Nigeria, 1976), 68; Verger, *Notícias da Bahia–1850* (Salvador, Brazil, 1981), 16–33.

6. The concept of an Atlantic *place* is borrowed from Alejandro de la Fuente; see de la Fuente, with the collaboration of César García del Pino and Bernardo Iglesias Delgado, *Havana and the Atlantic in the Sixteenth Century* (Chapel Hill, N.C., 2008), 223.

to man the central machine of Portuguese commerce and power in the early modern world—the oceanic sailing ship—but also furnished sea captains with the critical skilled labor—including navigational, commercial, and medical expertise—that was necessary to make long-distance sea travel a reality.

Even on the slaving vessels of the South Atlantic, whose primary purpose was to replenish the labor force supporting plantation agriculture in Salvador's hinterlands, Black mariners formed an indispensable nucleus of oceanic crews. Slaving ships' effectiveness in this endeavor, however, was not guaranteed; nor were the ships an anonymous technology of larger, inevitable historical processes. They required labor, management, and expertise to accomplish their task. In this regard, captive cosmopolitan labor was central. By 1775, an astonishing 90 percent of all mariners in Bahia were Black, including the sailors employed on transoceanic vessels, 40 percent of whom were African born, or *preto,* and 35 percent of whom were enslaved. Ships navigating to the Mina Coast, Angola, and Benguela were especially likely to employ African and enslaved sailors. These vessels were "accustomed to equip with a small number of 4 or 6 white sailors, supplying black captives with the rest of the majority that go." Bahian slavers' dependence on enslaved and freed African labor continued well into the nineteenth century. Between 1811 and 1839, at least 35.5 percent of all mariners laboring on the slave trade were African born, an additional 10.3 percent were men of African descent, and 27.1 percent of all seamen traveling to the African coast were enslaved.[7]

African maritime laborers were integral to every space that constituted the commercial South Atlantic: West African coastal communities, slaving ships traversing the Atlantic, and Brazilian port cities such as Salvador. Within these key nodes of an emergent South Atlantic system, Black mariners' cultural, commercial, and intellectual knowledge suffused Portugal's imperial project. As intermediaries between merchants and enslaved Africans, West African potentates and ship captains, they ensured the successful operation of a budding merchant capitalism that was enmeshed in transatlantic slavery.[8] Shipowners

---

7. AHU, CU, Bahia, caixa 47, documento 8812, July 3, 1775, "Mapa geral de toda a qualidade de embarcações que ha na Capitania da Bahia e navegam para a Costa da Mina, Angola, e Benguela." The percentages from 1775 derive from a total of 1,096 registered sailors. The "Mina Coast" was the Portuguese moniker given to the coastal West African region stretching from Elmina to Lagos.

8. This echoes Joseph C. Miller's depiction of Luso-Africans in Luanda as a "special case of the general class of African traders who brokered exchanges between the African and European worlds" (Miller, *Way of Death: Merchant Capitalism and the Angolan Slave*

and slaving merchants turned to enslaved and freed men of African descent to man oceanic vessels as servants, cabin boys, sailors, cooks, coopers, carpenters, medical practitioners (barbers and *sangradores*), and pilots. In ways similar to other marginal groups that the Portuguese crown viewed as expendable subjects—including orphans, convicts, exiles, New Christians (converts of Jewish ancestry)—enslaved Black mariners were relied upon to populate distant imperial settlements. In the sixteenth and seventeenth centuries, sea captains' efficacious and inexpensive employment of African interpreters, pilots, and slaves aboard Portuguese ships enabled the development of Iberian trading routes to West Africa and Asia. Inspired by these early precedents, Bahian merchants worked to conscript not only Black mariners' labor but, crucially, their unique skills. Without their efforts, the volume of Bahia's slave trade would not have surpassed that of every other Atlantic port city save

---

Trade, 1730–1830 [Madison, Wis., 1988], 249). The emphasis on figures who straddle cultural boundaries has a longer history in the literature on the Portuguese empire than it has for the rest of the Atlantic world. Brazilian historical sociologist Gilberto Freyre penned the term Lusotropicalism to define the multicultural, and distinctly benign, form of Portuguese imperialism in Africa and the Americas. His emphasis on the incorporation of the colonized and enslaved through processes of hybridization and "interpenetration," or the addition of foreign cultural forms into dominant Portuguese ones, influenced a generation of scholars. Revisionists, particularly neo-Marxist historical sociologists of slavery trained by Florestan Fernandes, rejected Freyre's emphasis on the Portuguese's harmonious paternalism, arguing instead that slavery and colonization operated as brutal systems of profit extraction. A resurgence in the literature on Atlantic creoles, cross-cultural brokers, and early modern intermediaries on the edges of the Atlantic basin has returned to some of Freyre's major themes, initiated by Philip D. Curtin's *Cross-Cultural Trade in World History* (Cambridge, 1984). Some notable interpretations include: Alida C. Metcalf, *Go-Betweens and the Colonization of Brazil, 1500–1600* (Austin, 2005); Robert W. Harms, *River of Wealth, River of Sorrow: The Central Zaire Basin in the Era of the Slave and Ivory Trade, 1500–1891* (New Haven, Conn., 1981); George E. Brooks, *Eurafricans in Western Africa: Commerce, Social Status, Gender, and Religious Observance from the Sixteenth Century to the Eighteenth Century* (Athens, Ohio, 2003); Roquinaldo Ferreira, *Cross-Cultural Exchange in the Atlantic World: Angola and Brazil during the Era of the Slave Trade* (New York, 2012); Toby Green, *The Rise of the Trans-Atlantic Slave Trade in Western Africa, 1300–1589* (Cambridge, 2012). On Gilberto Freyre's theorization of the particularities of Portuguese colonialism, see Freyre, *Casa-grande e senzala: Formação da família brasileira sob o regimen de economia patriarchal* (Rio de Janeiro, 1933), trans. by Samuel Putnam as *The Masters and the Slaves: A Study in the Development of Brazilian Civilization* (New York, 1946); Cláudia Castelo, "Gilberto Freyre's View of Miscegenation and Its Circulation in the Portuguese Empire, 1930s–1960s,"

Rio de Janeiro. Black mariners' stories are thus pivotal to reappraising the maritime Atlantic dynamics that irrevocably altered the economic and social landscape of colonial and imperial Brazil.[9]

BLACK MARITIME MOBILITY

Slaveholders and merchants' utilization of and dependence on the mobility of such mariners raises fundamental questions about the nature of Atlantic slavery. Paul Gilroy's 1993 text *The Black Atlantic* remains a seminal theorization of Black mariners' contributions to the transcultural and ideologically radical roots of the modern world. In *The Black Atlantic,* eighteenth-century sailing vessels are deployed as a metaphor for a movement-based politics that defines, to a significant degree, the modern Black experience. Gilroy explains that on ships "sailors [moved] to and fro between nations, crossing borders in modern machines that were themselves micro-systems of linguistic and political hybridity." The figure of the Black sailor becomes the locus of the

---

in Warwick Anderson, Ricardo Roque, and Ricardo Ventura Santos, eds., *Luso-Tropicalism and Its Discontents: The Making and Unmaking of Racial Exceptionalism* (New York, 2019); Lilia Moritz Schwarcz, *O espetáculo das raças: Cientistas, instituições e questão racial no Brasil, 1870–1930* (São Paulo, 1993), 248. On the historical materialist perspective, see Roger Bastide and Florestan Fernandes, *Brancos e negros em São Paulo* (São Paulo, 1959); Fernando Henrique Cardoso, *Capitalismo e escravidão no Brasil meridonal: O negro na sociedade escravocrata do Rio Grande do Sul* (São Paulo, 1962); Otávio Ianni, *As metamorphoses do escravo: Apogeu e crise da escravatura no Brasil meridional* (São Paulo, 1962). For a longer discussion of the debate between the patriarchalist and neo-Marxist schools, see Jean M. Hébrard, "Slavery in Brazil: Brazilian Scholars in the Key Interpretive Debates," *Translating the Americas,* I (2013), 47–95, esp. 51–56.

9. C. R. Boxer, *The Portuguese Seaborne Empire, 1415–1825* (London, 1969), 312; Timothy J. Coates, *Convicts and Orphans: Forced and State-Sponsored Colonizers in the Portuguese Empire, 1550–1755* (Stanford, Calif., 2001); Alfredo de Albuquerque Felner, *Angola: Apontamentos sôbre a colonização dos planaltos e litoral do sul de Angola* (Lisbon, 1940), 333; Roquinaldo Ferreira, "O Brasil e a arte da guerra em Angola (séculos XVII e XVIII)," *Estudos historicos,* XXXIX (2007), 3–23; Green, *Rise of the Trans-Atlantic Slave Trade;* A. J. R. Russell-Wood, *A World on the Move: The Portuguese in Africa, Asia, and America, 1415–1808* (Manchester, U.K., 1992), 106–107. Only a handful of studies of Salvador da Bahia employ an Atlantic framework and seek to interpret the urban center's history through locating and explaining its connections to an expansive maritime world. Those historians who have emphasized the vital role that seafaring life played for colonial Brazil have tended to focus on connections between Angola and Rio de Janeiro, an oceanic trade propelled by a very differ-

cultural, intellectual, and ideological hybridity that defined the Atlantic world. Drawing on the works of Marcus Rediker and Peter Linebaugh, Gilroy argues that the early modern Black sailor was an antislavery and anticapitalist radical who spread contagious ideas throughout the communities of the Atlantic Basin. For the Africans serving in the British navy, the "experience of slavery was a powerful orientation to the ideologies of liberty and justice." A number of pathbreaking works have advanced Gilroy's claims, illuminating the radical consequences of Black movement during the era of transatlantic slavery by revealing the variegated ways that people of African descent created counter-geographies and, in the process, counter-modernities through rebellious mobility. More generally, scholars have assumed the movement of enslaved people to be antagonistic to the power of slaveholders and slave societies.[10]

Enslaved people's movement could be, however, a double-edged sword. As historians have shown, slaveowners and their state allies asserted control of the circulation of the enslaved within both urban and plantation spaces to reify their own socioeconomic power and the hegemonic status of slavery

---

ent merchant community and labor force. In Salvador, ethnic, environmental, cultural, and economic particularities coalesced to form a uniquely West African–oriented Atlantic community; its intimate, bilateral connections to the Bight of Benin were separate from but acted as a parallel to the southern Rio de Janeiro–to–Luanda circuit. For studies of connections between Rio de Janeiro and Angola, see Mariana P. Candido, *An African Slaving Port and the Atlantic World: Benguela and Its Hinterland* (Cambridge, 2013); Ferreira, *Cross-Cultural Exchange in the Atlantic World;* Jaime Rodrigues, *De costa a costa: Escravos, marinheiros e intermediários do tráfico negreiro de Angola ao Rio de Janeiro (1780–1860)* ([São Paulo], 2005); Miller, *Way of Death;* Manolo Florentino, *Em costas negras: Uma história do tráfico atlântico de escravos entre a Africa e o Rio de Janeiro, séculos XVIII e XIX* (São Paulo, 2014). Exceptions to the paucity of maritime histories include Walter Hawthorne, "Gorge: An African Seaman and His Flights from 'Freedom' Back to 'Slavery' in the Early Nineteenth Century," *Slavery and Abolition*, XXXI (2010), 411–428; João José Reis, Flávio dos Santos Gomes, and Marcus J. M. de Carvalho, *The Story of Rufino: Slavery, Freedom, and Islam in the Black Atlantic*, trans. H. Sabrina Gledhill (Oxford, 2020); Rodrigues, *De costa a costa;* Beatriz Gollotti Mamigonian, "José Majojo e Francisco Moçambique, marinheiros das rotas atlâticas: Notas sobre a reconstituição de trajetórias da era da abolição," *Topoi*, XI, no. 20 (January–June 2010), 75–91; Luiz Geraldo Silva, *A faina, a festa e o rito: Uma etnografia histórica sobre as gentes do mar (sécs. XVII ao XIX)* (São Paulo, 2001).

10. Paul Gilroy, *The Black Atlantic: Modernity and Double Consciousness* (Cambridge, 1993), 12, 13. Camp has emphasized the enslaved's resistive geographies that were subversive without endangering slavery's hegemony. Julius S. Scott states that enslaved and free Black mariners connected "ports, plantations, [and] islands" to each other through a

more generally. In these instances, bondage was defined by "compulsory mobility."[11] As key agents in assuring the movement of goods and people, the enslaved provided the logistical means for plantation colonies to profitably function. This was particularly the case in the many port cities scattered throughout the Atlantic Basin.[12]

The unique experiences of African mariners in the South Atlantic—men who partook in condoned, regulated movement as well as subversive, clandestine circulation—suggest the necessity of both frameworks for understanding the vexed nature of enslaved people's mobility. In the eighteenth and nineteenth centuries, movement by captives could at times challenge—but more often affirm—the project of transatlantic slaving. *Captive Cosmopolitans* shows how the movements of enslaved mariners were essential in constructing transatlantic human, political, and commercial networks that existed independently of their owners' interests. In Bahia and the South Atlantic more broadly, however, these individual acts of mobile self-fashioning only sporadically weakened the dominion of transatlantic slaving; more commonly, the work and initiative of Black mariners enshrined its hegemony and stabil-

---

"seething mobility"; collectively, they constructed a clandestine "transnational geography of struggle." Scott's methodology involves tracing the seaborne movements of people in order to recover submerged intellectual and social histories of covert and "subversive networks" forged through the webs of commerce and maritime mobility that animated the region. Providing insight into what one observer in 1791 called the "unknown mode of conveying intelligence amongst Negroes," Scott argues that forced movement enabled the enslaved to create autonomous translocal networks that allowed them to construct their own communities animated by distinct political and intellectual principles that undercut colonialism and slavery's hegemony. See Camp, *Closer to Freedom*, 7–8, 48–51; Scott, *The Common Wind: Afro-American Currents in the Age of the Haitian Revolution* (New York, 2018), xi, 2–14.

11. Denying a simplistic and straightforward link between mobility and freedom, Rashauna Johnson argues that both forced and regulated mobility sustained racialized plantation slavery as planters relied on the enslaved to provide transportation to slave markets and gang labor throughout the city of New Orleans. At the behest of owners, the enslaved also delivered produce to market, fortified ailing infrastructures, and provided provisioning, entertainment, and other services for residents. Other forms of precarious movement, such as forced exile and refugee status, disempowered people of African descent in the port city. See Johnson, *Slavery's Metropolis: Unfree Labor in New Orleans during the Age of Revolutions* (Cambridge, 2016), 3.

12. The literature on Atlantic port cities has demonstrated that locales situated within the nexus of early modern transatlantic trading, translocal interactions, commodity flows, and interwoven merchant communities often required some measure of mobility by both

ity. The tensions inherent in captive cosmopolitans' lives and work expose the relational and at times fragmented nature of power in early modern slave societies and the Janus-faced character of agency for the enslaved. Even as they achieved personal objectives, their use of porous maritime spaces could in fact solidify slavery's power. As Joseph Miller has noted, in the South Atlantic, the very same people who became the "casualties" of merchant capitalism were also its agents. Black mariners were no exception.[13]

CAPTIVE COSMOPOLITANISM

This paradox reveals itself most clearly in the simultaneous experience of captivity and cosmopolitanism for seamen of the South Atlantic. Eschewing the word "slave," Portuguese merchants favored the term *cativo* to describe the commodified men, women, and children they trafficked from African coasts. Categorizing the enslaved as "captives" did not necessarily reflect a state of physical imprisonment. Instead, it signaled their status as prisoners of internecine wars in their native homelands who had been subsequently sold to foreign merchants. Though by the eighteenth century such terminology reflected a legal fiction rather than the actual mechanisms of enslavement in West Africa, it underscored the processes of deracination at the heart of Atlantic slavery.[14] As

---

the free and enslaved. This very mobility potentially enabled a diverse array of marginal individuals to enhance their own social status. See Ernesto Bassi, *An Aqueous Territory: Sailor Geographies and New Granada's Transimperial Greater Caribbean World* (Durham, N.C., 2016); Mariana P. Candido, *An African Slaving Port and the Atlantic World: Benguela and Its Hinterland* (New York, 2013); Gibril R. Cole, *The Krio of West Africa: Islam, Culture, Creolization, and Colonialism in the Nineteenth Century* (Athens, Ohio, 2013); Hilary Jones, *The Métis of Senegal: Urban Life and Politics in French West Africa* (Bloomington, Ind., 2013); Franklin W. Knight and Peggy K. Liss, eds., *Atlantic Port Cities: Economy, Culture, and Society in the Atlantic World, 1650–1850* (Knoxville, Tenn., 1991); Robin Law, *Ouidah: The Social History of a West African Slaving "Port," 1727–1892* (Athens, Ohio, 2004); Kristin Mann, *Slavery and the Birth of an African City: Lagos, 1760–1900* (Bloomington, Ind., 2007); Randy J. Sparks, *Where the Negroes Are Masters: An African Port in the Era of the Slave Trade* (Cambridge, Mass., 2014); David Wheat, *Atlantic Africa and the Spanish Caribbean, 1570–1640* (Williamsburg, Va., and Chapel Hill, N.C., 2016).

13. Miller, *Way of Death*, 245. For more on the paradoxes of enslaved people's agency, see Walter Johnson, "On Agency," *Journal of Social History*, XXXI (2003), 113–124; Camp, *Closer to Freedom*, 1–2.

14. The legally justified capture and trade of non-Christian prisoners in "just wars" dated back to the medieval Portuguese Reconquest. By the eighteenth century, West Afri-

"captives," enslaved and freed mariners were cosmopolitans by compulsion, not choice, unlike other mobile inhabitants of the Atlantic. Their worldliness sprang from the violent experience of enslavement, communal dislocation, and forced migration from Africa to Portugal's American colony Brazil. There, the imperative to acquire new language skills and cultural understandings was driven by the chaotic and desperate aftermath of personal displacement and the obliteration of communal and familial ties. Finding themselves severed from existing forms of belonging and selfhood, African bondsmen placed in maritime service employed their vital cultural and physical labor to connect distinctive worlds of the Atlantic and reestablish social connection.

Insinuating themselves into new social worlds after enslavement required mariners to adopt culturally hybrid behaviors and perspectives. More recent interpretations of cosmopolitan Black life hearken back to an earlier generation of scholarship on New World creolization, which a number of historians have argued was both a necessary tool and a consequence of early modern imperial expansion. Ira Berlin was the first to emphasize the "linguistic dexterity, cultural plasticity, and social agility" of the Atlantic's first generation of Black inhabitants. Frequently, however, the historical literature on Black "Atlantic creoles"—individuals defined by their savviness, cultural hybridity, and multiple (at times cross-cutting) loyalties—appear as bookends in the story of the rise and fall of the early modern Atlantic system. In the South Atlantic, cosmopolitan Black mariners shaped the operation of the slave trade at almost every historical juncture. They facilitated the emergence of the transatlantic slave trade in the sixteenth and seventeenth centuries while playing integral roles in the fractious politics of the Age of Revolutions and subsequent emancipations by living as people who, by "experience or choice, as well as by birth, became part of a new culture."[15]

------

cans could be enslaved via a variety of mechanisms, including warfare, kidnapping, raiding, judicial punishment, and debt bondage. See Sherwin K. Bryant, *Rivers of Gold, Lives of Bondage: Governing Slavery in Colonial Quito* (Chapel Hill, N.C., 2014), 11–13; Nancy E. van Deusen, "Seeing *Indios* in Sixteenth-Century Castile," *WMQ*, 3d Ser., LXIX (2012), 205–234; Alida C. Metcalf, "The Society of Jesus and the First Aldeias of Brazil," in Hal Langfur, ed., *Native Brazil: Beyond the Convert and the Cannibal, 1500–1900* (Albuquerque, N.M., 2014), 29–60, esp. 38–40; Jared Staller, *Converging on Cannibals: Terrors of Slaving in Atlantic Africa, 1509–1670* (Athens, Ohio, 2019), 47–48.

15. For more on the idea of Atlantic creoles, or a group of men and women who, as cultural and linguistic chameleons, facilitated the early modern transoceanic trade by "employing their linguistic skills and their familiarity with the Atlantic's diverse commercial practices,

With an ability to operate in the disparate cultural milieus of West Africa and Bahia, Black mariners wielded a degree of cultural power and influence uncommon for those who had first arrived in the Americas in chains. They were prized by slaving ship captains not only for their physical labor but also for their chameleonlike ability to adapt to new surroundings and apply culturally specific medicinal, linguistic, and navigational knowledge to facilitate their ship's passage and profitability. As transatlantic merchant capitalism in Bahia and West Africa produced an insatiable demand for maritime labor, circumstances required that enslaved mariners master the ability to live "in translation." In many of the Atlantic world's bustling metropolises, enslaved and free people of African descent developed cosmopolitan sensibilities to blunt the ravages of enslavement and empire. As Ifeoma Nwankwo has noted, the pervasive movement and displacement that characterized early modern life enabled people of African descent in the Americas to generate an ideal of rooted cosmopolitanism that was distinct from the sort usually associated with powerful European imperialists. Implicit in this historically and culturally specific form of cosmopolitanism was a sense of belonging in an expansive Black world defined by movement and rootedness, difference and belonging, and attachments to both the local and the global. For Black mariners in the South Atlantic, cross-cultural encounters at sea produced layered forms of subjectivity as forces of both coercion and desperation compelled their cosmopolitan strategies.[16]

---

cultural conventions, and diplomatic etiquette to mediate between African merchants and European sea captains," see Ira Berlin, *Many Thousands Gone: The First Two Centuries of Slavery in North America* (Cambridge, Mass., 1998), 17–39; see also Berlin, "From Creole to African: Atlantic Creoles and the Origins of African-American Society in Mainland North America," *WMQ*, 3d Ser., LIII (1996), 255–256; and Jane G. Landers, *Atlantic Creoles in the Age of Revolutions* (Cambridge, Mass., 2010), 4–14. Africanist scholars argue that those born on Atlantic African littorals had a predisposition to adaptation and cultural openness long before their first encounters with Europeans. See Joseph C. Miller, "Retention, Reinvention, and Remembering: Restoring Identities through Enslavement in Africa and under Slavery in Brazil," in José C. Curto and Paul E. Lovejoy, eds., *Enslaving Connections: Changing Cultures of Africa and Brazil during the Era of Slavery* (Amherst, N.Y., 2004), 86–87; Berlin, "From Creole to African," 251–288, esp. 254 n. 8; Landers, *Atlantic Creoles*, 8.

16. Stuart Hall, "The Question of Cultural Identity," in Hall, David Held, and Tony McGrew, eds., *Modernity and Its Futures* (Cambridge, 1992), 310; Ifeoma Kiddoe Nwankwo, *Black Cosmopolitanism: Racial Consciousness and Transnational Identity in the Nineteenth-Century Americas* (Philadelphia, 2005), 158–163; Lorelle Semley, *To Be Free and French: Citizenship in France's Atlantic Empire* (Cambridge, 2017), 10; Jones, *Métis of Senegal*, 4; Natasha

SLAVING CAPITALISM FROM BELOW

Cosmopolitan Black mariners, as exceptional figures among the multitude of actors involved in slaving commerce, provide a radically new window for understanding the history of capitalism in the early modern Atlantic. By dint of their legal status, such sailors were capital who moved capital. Simultaneously objects and subjects, they were sometimes conscripts and other times willing participants in the project of merchant capitalism that had reduced them to slavery. Narratives of transoceanic merchant capitalism commonly focus on the agency of well-capitalized European actors, including merchant houses and families as well as royally chartered monopoly companies. Integral to this portrait is the assumption that the role enslaved people played in the development of transatlantic capitalist relations was either as human com-

------

Lightfoot, "'So Far to Leeward': Eliza Moore's Fugitive Cosmopolitan Routes to Freedom in the Nineteenth-Century Caribbean," *WMQ*, 3d Ser., LXXIX (2022), 61–88. A number of works on the historical experience of "cosmopolitanism" have departed from the early modern European notion of being a "citizen of the world" to focus on non-Europeans, the colonized and the enslaved. Pablo F. Gómez explores the healing cosmopolitanism of Black intellectuals in the seventeenth-century Caribbean, whereas Rashauna Johnson has coined the term "confined cosmopolitanism" to explain how enslaved individuals' status and social and geographic position tied them to expansive global geographies at the same time it "contained" them according to their owners' will. My term, "captive cosmopolitanism," draws on the concept of "subaltern cosmopolitanism," first articulated by sociologists of contemporary working-class immigration who highlight the subversive potential of border crossing and the global economic imperatives for developing a cosmopolitan sensibility as a consequence of globalization from below. As such, enslaved and freed Black mariners' movements were compelled by commercial motivations. They transgressed boundaries but also constituted them through their professed allegiance to Portuguese imperial sovereignty on a shifting basis. See Gómez, *The Experiential Caribbean: Creating Knowledge and Healing in the Early Modern Atlantic* (Chapel Hill, N.C., 2017), 9–10; Johnson, *Slavery's Metropolis*, 4–7; Leigh T. I. Penman, *The Lost History of Cosmopolitanism: The Early Modern Origins of the Intellectual Ideal* (London, 2021), 1–8; Minhao Zeng, "Subaltern Cosmopolitanism: Concept and Approaches," *Sociological Review*, LXII (2014), 137–148; Vinay K. Gidwani, "Subaltern Cosmopolitanism as Politics," *Antipode*, XXXVIII (2006), 7–21; Boaventura de Sousa Santos, *Toward a New Legal Common Sense: Law, Globalization, and Emancipation* (London, 2002); Pnina Werbner, "Global Pathways: Working Class Cosmopolitans and the Creation of Transnational Ethnic Worlds," *Social Anthropology*, VII (1999), 17–35; Walter D. Mignolo, "The Many Faces of Cosmo-polis: Border Thinking and Critical Cosmopolitanism," *Public Culture*, XII (2000), 721–748.

modities whose value underwrote the expensive plantation enterprise or as a source of coerced labor used to power the productive mining and agricultural economies of the Americas. In both of these formulations, there is little room to appreciate enslaved Africans' and their descendants' *willing* associations with the expanding commercialism that defined both transatlantic slaving and the maritime Atlantic.[17]

Captive cosmopolitans' importance to the history of slaving capitalism in the South Atlantic took a number of forms. In Bahia, slaveowners, merchants, and ship captains crafted a racialized market for maritime labor. Slaveholders contracting their bondsmen to nearby ships marketed enslaved African seamen's experience, expertise, ethnic identity, and acquired linguistic skills to potential employers. Placing a premium on the market value of culturally hybrid mariners, slaveholders commodified the very cosmopolitan knowledge that the enslaved perceived as an asset to affirm their own autonomy. On a day-to-day basis, however, slaving ship owners and captains relied on devalued captive labor, which enabled them to reduce transportation costs and enhance the profitability of slaving voyages. Vessels engaged in the transatlantic slave trade paid seamen of African descent—including those who had been freed or born free—lower wages than whites, significantly dropping the initial capital outlays required for voyages. Racialization and enslavement as instruments of capitalist accumulation were defining features of the early modern Atlantic world. In this sense, Bahia was emblematic.

17. See Sven Beckert and Seth Rockman, eds., *Slavery's Capitalism: A New History of American Economic Development* (Philadelphia, 2016); Edward E. Baptist, *The Half Has Never Been Told: Slavery and the Making of American Capitalism* (New York, 2014); Beckert, *Empire of Cotton: A Global History* (New York, 2014); Daina Ramey Berry, *The Price for Their Pound of Flesh: The Value of the Enslaved, from Womb to Grave, in the Building of a Nation* (Boston, 2017); Robin Blackburn, *The Making of New World Slavery: From the Baroque to the Modern, 1492–1800* (London, 1997); Walter Johnson, *River of Dark Dreams: Slavery and Empire in the Cotton Kingdom* (Cambridge, Mass., 2013); Stephanie E. Smallwood, *Saltwater Slavery: A Middle Passage from Africa to American Diaspora* (Cambridge, Mass., 2007); Lorena S. Walsh, *Motives of Honor, Pleasure, and Profit: Plantation Management in the Colonial Chesapeake, 1607–1763* (Williamsburg, Va., and Chapel Hill, N.C., 2010). For an analysis of the evolution of Atlantic capitalism, see Mark Peterson, "Capitalism," in Joseph C. Miller et al., eds., *The Princeton Companion to Atlantic History* (Princeton, N.J., 2015), 71–79; Peter A. Coclanis, *The Atlantic Economy during the Seventeenth and Eighteenth Centuries: Organization, Operation, Practice and Personnel* (Columbia, S.C., 2005).

More exceptional, however, was the degree to which exploited enslaved and freed mariners were able to insinuate their own prerogatives into the workings of transatlantic trade. *Captive Cosmopolitans* reveals that the decentralized structure and organization of slave-trading commerce between Bahia and the Bight of Benin enabled enslaved African and creole mariners to actively generate commodity trades between the two regions as small-scale traders of their own volition. Bahia's slave trade, anomalous in the Atlantic, entailed the assembly of diverse, small-scale investments—mostly in goods rather than currency—that were often purchased on credit with the promise of monetary returns. Investment in such voyages was organized around familial and patronage ties, which allowed maritime laborers as well as the slaves of Atlantic merchants to participate in long-distance commerce through their personal connections with wealthy elites. In order to secure the loyalties of enslaved maritime laborers, merchants employed techniques to both coerce and obtain a measure of consent. The Bahian slave trade was perhaps the most vibrant and ruthlessly effective of all Atlantic slaving routes in part because of how it incorporated the desires and financial strategies of subaltern people—including, ironically, the enslaved themselves.

Despite their consistent proximity to the horrors of slaving, enslaved mariners did not categorically resist colonialism or merchant capitalism's hegemony in the South Atlantic. African and creole sailors were able to exercise a measure of personal and economic agency in the Bahian slave trade precisely because they were pivotal to ensuring the slave trade's perpetuation and profitability. On slaving ships, captive cosmopolitans performed the mundane duties common on all sea vessels—hoisting sails, pulling cables, swabbing decks, navigating currents, and repairing weathered hulls. Enslaved Black mariners, however, also acted as a front line between the enslaved men, women, and children held in cargoes and the white captains and officers who navigated the ship. Mediating between enslaved commodities and wealthy transatlantic merchants, African sailors translated, negotiated cooperation, defused tensions, administered food, and managed the quotidian routines of captives as ships crossed the Atlantic Ocean. Their essential role in preserving enslaved people's physical bodies—which declined in profitability if marred by corporal punishment, sickness, or suicide— underpinned the financial viability of slaving voyages.

This, above all else, was what defined the experience and central paradox of captive cosmopolitan Black mariners' relationship to transatlantic slaving. Their work helped sustain, as one observer put it, a "commerce in . . . human flesh and blood." But in doing so, they became agents of Atlantic capitalism.

Enslaved and freed Black seafarers leveraged their ties to global trade to limit their own marginalization and secure greater autonomy from their owners. By inserting their own material demands, enslaved and freed sailors were able to pioneer a transatlantic market for West African commodities. They established informal and at times illicit trading networks in African-produced textiles (*panos da costa*) and palm oil (*azeite de dendê*), which were pivotal in introducing African material culture to the New World. By negotiating directly with African traders and potentates on the West African coast, they incorporated a diplomatic dimension into their labors. As they traversed imperial boundaries, captive cosmopolitans engaged in contraband trade with British and French merchants and jumped ship in foreign ports. Enslaved Black seafarers enjoyed levels of economic mobility unprecedented for other enslaved Bahians; many were able to purchase their freedom and, in rare cases, become independent transatlantic traders in goods—and, in even rarer cases, enslaved people.[18]

Black mariners utilized the commercial wealth provided by their involvement in the transatlantic slave trade to establish households of their own in Bahia. Often alongside their wives, they became patrons who owned slaves and forged ties of dependency with other African inhabitants in the city. Their elevated status revealed the extent to which they successfully converted cultural capital into social and economic capital. As an emergent class of freed Africans with access to prestigious foreign goods, powerful forms of medical knowledge, and households with substantial numbers of dependents, slaves and heirs, they became the pillars of an ethnically diverse African community in Bahia. Like so many in the Atlantic, their own chances for freedom, self-determination, community formation, and mobility were secured through the profits and power derived from the enslavement of others. Ultimately, the condition of captive cosmopolitanism, or coerced cultural flexibility in the service of rapacious merchant capitalism, upends triumphalist narratives of modernity and highlights its violent, rather than enlightened, birth. The integrative forces of early modern globalization required subalterns to generate new, hybrid ways of being in the world. And the benefits of such cosmopolitanism often accrued, not primarily to themselves, but to the wealthy and the powerful. Their hybridity propelled, rather than forestalled, the devastating

18. Malyn Newitt, *The Portuguese in West Africa, 1415–1670: A Documentary History* (Cambridge, 2010), 156. On the diasporic journey of dendê, see Case Watkins, *Palm Oil Diaspora: Afro-Brazilian Landscapes and Economies on Bahia's Dendê Coast* (Cambridge, 2021).

commodification of a growing number of people in a slaving enterprise that had enveloped the South Atlantic.[19]

THE VIEW FROM THE MARITIME SOUTH ATLANTIC

Though they labored in one of the most racially integrated environments in colonial Brazil, Black mariners' experiences remained distinct from European, white Brazilian, and even indigenous shipmates. Unlike their peers, most had experienced the transatlantic "way of death" as enslaved people who had previously been held in slaving ship cargoes. Nearly all of Bahia's Black seamen laboring in Bahia's transatlantic slave trade had been born in Africa and arrived in Salvador in chains. Rendering the emotional complexities of their particular circumstances is difficult: their trauma is all but absent from the written historical record, as is any indication of their feelings about laboring in the service of the same ship captains that had once torn them from their homelands. Their experiences of the slaving ship likely mirrored those of other captives. The fear of natal alienation and the loss of a socially defined self suffused the first maritime journeys of such captive cosmopolitans. Like those destined to live, work, and die on the plantations of rural Bahia, they could not reverse their experience of the Middle Passage. Even for those who returned as mariners to their African birthplace, its terrors could never be expunged. Nor were captive seamen able to recover membership in communities into which they were born.[20]

In their new roles aboard slaving vessels, Black mariners faced a unique set of vulnerabilities and challenges. The decks and holds of slaving ships were dangerous, physically demanding laboring spaces where enslaved and freed

19. Edmund S. Morgan, *American Slavery, American Freedom: The Ordeal of Colonial Virginia* (New York, 1975), 5.

20. Miller, *Way of Death*, 314–315. The slaving vessel is the space through which many contemporary historians have come to understand early modern West Africans' experience of an Atlantic maritime world that linked Africa to the Americas. Smallwood has worked to describe—and comprehend—the essential destruction of humanity that accompanied slave ships' "one-way route of terror." This particularly spatial metaphor demonstrates how Akan captives conceptualized their forced oceanic journey as a passage into a "dangerous supernatural . . . watery realm." She argues that the experience of "saltwater slavery" entailed a physical and existential journey so wrenching that it "stretched their reckoning to the limits." Survivors of the Middle Passage, such as Olaudah Equiano, termed the ship's hold "this hollow place." See Smallwood, *Saltwater Slavery*, 22–25; *The Interesting Narrative of the Life of Olaudah Equiano, or, Gustavus Vassa, the African* (New York, 2004), 36.

seamen operated among a world of unspeakable pain, violence, and human tragedy. Death haunted transatlantic slaving voyages even as mortality rates for both captives and seamen declined in the nineteenth century. A single multi-week voyage could easily end in catastrophic losses, either from accident or disease. As Black mariners negotiated their complex relationships between merchants, captains, crews, and captives, the specter of their own mortality followed them to sea. In 1830, for instance, on a ship traveling from Mozambique to Rio de Janeiro, five captives held in the cargo perished alongside sixteen "slaves in the service of the ship."[21]

Working in such an environment—exploited, vulnerable, and enslaved— might have put Black mariners in the South Atlantic in the vanguard of rebellion against slavery. Indeed, many scholars of the North Atlantic have asserted that sailors constituted the quintessential early modern proletariat.[22] Though enslaved African mariners in Bahia shared characteristics with both commodities and proletarians, they did not fall neatly into either category. The cultural and commercial dynamics of the South Atlantic—particularly the intense interactions between the coasts of Africa and Brazil, coupled with the unavailability of free manual labor—distinguished that maritime world from that of the North. Although English sailors often interpreted their status aboard Atlantic sailing vessels as akin to "slavery," they were not legally enslaved. And whereas the tars of the North Atlantic routinely found themselves dissatisfied with their maritime existence, alienated by paltry wages, harsh discipline, and the inherent dangers of seafaring, enslaved seamen in

21. AHI, Coleções Especiais, Comissão Mista, lata 12, maço 4, pasta 1, Papers of the *Eliza*.

22. A rich tradition of scholarship analyzing maritime life in the early modern period has done much to unpack the complex and conflict-ridden social and labor relations that underpinned the deceptively romantic depictions of seafaring life. The work of Marcus Rediker has explored what was crucially modern about the Atlantic sailing vessel, focusing on the cutting-edge technologies used to construct and navigate it and the increasing economic power wielded by Atlantic merchants both at sea and on land. Such characterizations are not entirely transferable beyond the distinctive world of the Anglo-Atlantic, where the emerging battles between labor and capital defined British domestic politics as well as characterized the relations between common sailors and shipowners at sea. See Rediker, *Between the Devil and the Deep Blue Sea: Merchant Seamen, Pirates, and the Anglo-American Maritime World, 1700–1750* (Cambridge, 1987); Peter Linebaugh and Rediker, *The Many-Headed Hydra: Sailors, Slaves, Commoners, and the Hidden History of the Revolutionary Atlantic* (Boston, 2000); Rediker, *The Slave Ship: A Human History* (New York, 2007); Emma Christopher, *Slave Ship Sailors and Their Captive Cargoes, 1730–1807* (Cambridge, 2006): Niklas Frykman, *The Bloody Flag: Mutiny in the Age of Atlantic Revolution* (Oakland, Calif., 2020).

the South Atlantic were in a fundamentally different position. For captive cosmopolitans, the opportunities afforded by such maritime life frequently outweighed its hardships, and such work was likely viewed as far more attractive than many land-based alternatives.[23]

This element of enslaved labor in the South Atlantic explains one of the more confounding elements of slavery on Bahian routes: the relative alienation of such Black mariners from the ascendant currents of abolitionism in the larger Atlantic Basin. Several scholars of the North Atlantic have examined the particularities of Black seafaring life, emphasizing that mobility granted sailors the agency to create channels of long-distance communication and provided opportunities to fashion emancipatory political claims within even the most hierarchical slave societies.[24] Similarly, the dynamics of maritime life in Salvador enabled Black seafarers to construct advantageous social and informational networks that, at times, facilitated the development of antislavery legal arguments. This was particularly the case in the wake of a 1761 royal edict that made Portugal a free-soil territory and stimulated instances of maritime *marronage* and a number of innovative legal arguments. In dialogue with Black residents of Lisbon and with the help of mutual aid networks of Black Catholic brotherhoods that spanned the Atlantic, mariners forged new visions of manumission premised on access to favorable legal jurisdictions through mobility and the assertion of their vassalage to Portugal's crown. The era of free soil presented new possibilities for enslaved mariners, who faced

23. On the bilateral connections between Africa and Brazil, see Luiz Felipe de Alencastro, *The Trade in the Living: The Formation of Brazil in the South Atlantic, Sixteenth to Seventeenth Centuries,* trans. Gavin Adams and Alencastro (Albany, N.Y., 2018); José Honório Rodrigues, *Brazil and Africa* (Berkeley, Calif., 1965). According to Philip D. Morgan, one English mariner in the seventeenth century proclaimed, "All men in the ship except the master . . . are little better than slaves." See Morgan, "Introduction: Maritime Slavery," *Slavery and Abolition,* XXXI (2010), 313; Christopher, *Slave Ship Sailors,* 3.

24. W. Jeffrey Bolster, *Black Jacks: African American Seamen in the Age of Sail* (Cambridge, Mass., 1997); David S. Cecelski, *The Waterman's Song: Slavery and Freedom in Maritime North Carolina* (Chapel Hill, N.C., 2001), xvi; Charles R. Foy, "Ports of Slavery, Ports of Freedom: How Slaves Used Northern Seaports' Maritime Industry to Escape and Create Trans-Atlantic Identities, 1713–1783" (Ph.D. diss., Rutgers University, 2008); Foy, "'Unkle Sommerset's' Freedom: Liberty in England for Black Sailors," *Journal for Maritime Research,* XIII (2011), 21–36; Scott, *Common Wind;* Morgan, "Introduction: Maritime Slavery," *Slavery and Abolition,* XXXI (2010), 311–326; Alan Gregor Cobley, "That Turbulent Soil: Seafarers, the 'Black Atlantic,' and Afro-Caribbean Identity," in Jerry H. Bentley, Renate Bridenthal, and Kären Wigen, eds., *Seascapes: Maritime Histories, Littoral Cultures,*

the choice of whether to reject their owners' will and petition for freedom in alliance with a larger Black community or to remain in slavery until they could individually convince owners to manumit them.

Such choices remained complex, dynamic, and ambiguous, especially because shipboard life was overwhelmingly constrained by the dictates of the transatlantic slave trade. Ultimately, most Bahian seamen did not develop an unequivocal abolitionist stance as Black mariners did in the North Atlantic. As Britain began its military suppression of the slave trade in 1807, Bahia's African and creole mariners were increasingly swept up in violent transimperial conflicts over property and sovereignty at sea. Black mariners, imperiled rather than empowered by this development, were likely to lose either their lives or their investment property, the latter of which was liable to confiscation by the Royal Navy. A number of mariners even found themselves imprisoned on the West African coast as a result of military assaults on the now-illegal trade. Unlike the liberty promised by Portuguese free soil in the same period, the quality of freedom conferred under the auspices of British abolitionism in West Africa proved unappealing to most enslaved seafarers.

Taking the view from the South Atlantic also reveals the multitude of ways in which Black mariners helped to produce intimate and durable linkages between the politics, economics, peoples, and cultures of Salvador with those of the Bight of Benin.[25] *Captive Cosmopolitans'* centering of the maritime South Atlantic challenges a body of scholarly interpretation that has characterized the development of the African diaspora as a unidirectional phenomenon.

---

and Transoceanic Exchanges (Honolulu, 2007); Michael J. Jarvis, *In the Eye of All Trade: Bermuda, Bermudians, and the Maritime Atlantic World, 1680–1783* (Williamsburg, Va., and Chapel Hill, N.C., 2010); Linda M. Rupert, *Creolization and Contraband: Curaçao in the Early Modern Atlantic World* (Athens, Ga., 2012); Rupert, "Marronage, Manumission, and Maritime Trade in the Early Modern Caribbean," *Slavery and Abolition*, XXX (2009), 361–382; Kevin Dawson, "Enslaved Ship Pilots in the Age of Revolutions: Challenging Notions of Race and Slavery between the Boundaries of Land and Sea," *Journal of Social History*, XLVII (2013), 71–100.

25. For more on the South Atlantic as more of a unified space of human interaction than territorially contagious northern and southern Brazil, see Alencastro, *Trade in the Living*, trans. Adams and Alencastro; C. R. Boxer, *Salvador de Sá and the Struggle for Brazil and Angola, 1602–1686* (London, 1952). Pierre Verger's definitive work, *Flux et reflux de la traite des nègres entre le Golfe de Bénin et Bahia de Todos os Santos, du XVII au XIXe siècle* (Paris, 1968), first advanced the theory of a two-way commercial exchange between Salvador da Bahia and the Bight of Benin. It was translated into English by Evelyn Crawford as *Trade Relations between the Bight of Benin and Bahia from the 17th to 19th Century.*

Indeed, the notion that African people, ideas, and cultures moved from east to west is based on a presumption that informs most foundational theorizing of Black diasporic experience.[26] The prevalence of African sailors on the slave-trading route between Salvador da Bahia and the West African littoral reveals, however, the extent to which mutual influences circulated between these two regions and the vital role African and African-descended people played in diffusing them. In the eighteenth and early nineteenth century, mariners took multiple journeys between West Africa and Bahia in their lifetimes and acted as crucial vectors for exchanges of all kinds. Although there is a rich and influential literature on the circulation of Africans between the Bight of Benin and Bahia, many studies focus on the mid- to late nineteenth century, within the context of the homecoming of freed West African *retornados*, or returnees, from Bahia in the xenophobic backlash against Africans following the Malê revolt in 1835. The continuous movement of Africans between these two regions had much deeper roots and, in fact, dated to the very beginnings of the slave trade.[27]

26. Michael A. Gomez, *Exchanging Our Country Marks: The Transformation of African Identities in the Colonial and Antebellum South* (Chapel Hill, N.C., 1998); Gwendolyn Midlo Hall, *Slavery and African Ethnicities in the Americas: Restoring the Links* (Chapel Hill, N.C., 2005); Sidney Wilfred Mintz and Richard Price, *The Birth of African-American Culture: An Anthropological Perspective* (Boston, 1992). For the opposing perspective, see J. Lorand Matory, "The English Professors of Brazil: On the Diasporic Roots of the Yorùbá Nation," *Comparative Studies in Society and History,* XLI (1999), 72–103.

27. Edna G. Bay and Kristin Mann, eds., *Rethinking the African Diaspora: The Making of a Black Atlantic World in the Bight of Benin and Brazil* (London, 2001); Lisa Earl Castillo, "Between Memory, Myth, and History: Transatlantic Voyagers of the Casa Branca Temple," in Ana Lucia Araujo, ed., *Paths of the Atlantic Slave Trade: Interactions, Identities, and Images* (Amherst, N.Y., 2011), 203–238; Castillo and Luis Nicolau Parés, "Marcelina da Silva: A Nineteenth-Century Candomblé Priestess in Bahia," *Slavery and Abolition,* XXXI (2010), 1–27; Manuela Carneiro da Cunha, *Negros estrangeiros: Os escravos libertos e sua volta à África,* 2d ed. (São Paulo, 2012); J. Lorand Matory, *Black Atlantic Religion: Tradition, Transnationalism, and Matriarchy in the Afro-Brazilian Candomblé* (Princeton, N.J., 2005); Luis Nicolau Parés, *The Formation of Candomblé: Vodun History and Ritual in Brazil,* trans. Richard Vernon (Chapel Hill, N.C., 2013); Jerry Michael Turner, "'Les Brésiliens': The Impact of Former Brazilian Slaves upon Dahomey" (Ph.D. diss., Boston University, 1975); Milton Guran, *Agudás: Os "brasileiros" do Benim* (Rio de Janeiro, 1999); Lorenzo D. Turner, "Some Contacts of Brazilian Ex-Slaves with Nigeria, West Africa," *Journal of Negro History,* XXVII (1942), 55–67; Pierre Verger, *Os libertos: Sete caminhos na liberade de escravos da Bahia no século XIX* (São Paulo, 1992).

Strong transatlantic connections forged through Black mariners' circuitous movement would have profound ramifications for cultural life in the city of Bahia. Studies of African enslavement in Brazil specifically, and the Americas more generally, have highlighted how enslaved peoples re-created, to varying degrees, Western African religious practices, aesthetics, language, and ethnic identity.[28] These cultural histories of diaspora have demonstrated with increasing detail how African precedents inspired enslaved people's dynamic strategies, actions, and ideas throughout the Atlantic and have enriched our understanding of historical processes of creolization. In Bahia, African-derived influences played a particularly important role in creolization, or the creation of new or hybrid cultural forms generated as the enslaved adapted to American social and material environments. The maritime dimensions of African re-creations are crucial because waterborne mobility was a vector for other kinds of material and cultural exchange. Bahian mariners remained critical to cultural creolization as they infused and reinforced African-derived ideas and material cultures among the community of enslaved West Africans residing there. Their cosmopolitanism did not emerge from latent traditionalism or even a mere necessity for survival. Instead, Black maritime agents utilized African-derived cultural and intellectual resources out of creativity rather than habit, drawing on valuable West African precedents as they forged new material, medical, and religious worlds in Bahia in the context of enslavement and its afterlives.

28. For instance, John Thornton, in his pathbreaking study of the fundamental influence of enslaved Africans in transforming Atlantic cultures and societies, has argued that kinship ideology, languages, and aesthetics were the most established forms of African culture in the Americas (Thornton, *Africa and Africans in the Making of the Atlantic World, 1400–1800* [Cambridge, 1998], 183–213). In addition, James H. Sweet's *Domingos Álvares: African Healing and the Intellectual History of the Atlantic World* (Chapel Hill, N.C., 2011) and Parés's *Formation of Candomblé* have brilliantly traced the how African precedents informed diasporic iterations of spiritual worship, religious congregation, and ritual healing. For other examples of this trend, see Mariza de Carvalho Soares, *People of Faith: Slavery and African Catholics in Eighteenth-Century Rio de Janeiro*, trans. Jerry D. Metz (Durham, N.C., 2011); Curto and Lovejoy, *Enslaving Connections;* Curto and Renée Soulodre-La France, eds., *Africa and the Americas: Interconnections during the Slave Trade* (Trenton, N.J., 2005); Toyin Falola and Matt D. Childs, eds., *The Yoruba Diaspora in the Atlantic World* (Bloomington, Ind., 2004); Sweet, *Recreating Africa: Culture, Kinship, and Religion in the African-Portuguese World, 1441–1770* (Chapel Hill, N.C., 2003); João José Reis, *Slave Rebellion in Brazil: The Muslim Uprising of 1835 in Bahia*, trans. Arthur Brakel (Baltimore, 1993); Parés, *Formation of Candomblé*, trans. Vernon.

While this book contributes to scholarship on the history of the African diaspora, it is also an intervention in the history of the Atlantic world more broadly. As it fuses the insights gleaned by theorizations of the African diaspora with those of the Atlantic world historiographies, in the words of Edna Bay and Kristin Mann, "a new paradigm for understanding both begins to emerge." By tracing discrete cohorts of enslaved African arrivals to specific historically and geographically defined American contexts and African locales as well-defined starting points, instead of focusing on ahistorical, overgeneralized "traditions," scholars can gain key insights into the motivations and actions of the enslaved. As both African diasporic subjects and Atlantic actors, captive cosmopolitans bridge the divide between Atlantic and diasporic literatures.[29]

ARCHIVES AND PARA-ARCHIVES
OF THE BLACK ATLANTIC

For all its devastation, the transatlantic slave trade from Bahia produced a relatively ample trail of textual evidence in the eighteenth and nineteenth centuries. The perspectives of marginal Black mariners are more elusive than those of powerful slave traders, however. In analyzing the lives of a mostly enslaved population, this study adopts a prosopographical, or collective biographical, approach to the Black Atlantic, weaving together individual histories to create an assemblage of actors that illuminates the contours of Bahia's complex maritime social and commercial world. By tracing historical subjects' actions and, less frequently, their words, *Captive Cosmopolitans* uncovers the complicated motivations of men faced with a variety of wrenching choices.[30]

Reconstructing the scattered remnants of African and creole men's lives from archival sources required consulting voluminous slaving ship papers, official letters and reports, travel accounts, and a range of legal texts, particu-

29. Mann and Bay, *Rethinking the African Diaspora,* 15–16.

30. For biographical treatments of the Black Atlantic, see Lisa A. Lindsay and John Wood Sweet, eds., *Biography and the Black Atlantic* (Philadelphia, 2014); Lindsay, *Atlantic Bonds: A Nineteenth-Century Odyssey from America to Africa* (Chapel Hill, N.C., 2017); Rebecca J. Scott and Jean M. Hébrard, *Freedom Papers: An Atlantic Odyssey in the Age of Emancipation* (Cambridge, Mass., 2012); Sweet, *Domingos Álvares.* For a related "micro-historical" approach to Black Atlantic history, see Ferreira, *Cross-Cultural Exchange in the Atlantic World;* Lara Putnam, "To Study the Fragments / Whole: Microhistory and the Atlantic World," *Journal of Social History,* XXXIX (2006), 615–630.

larly lawsuits (*processos*), petitions (*requerimentos*), wills (*testamentos*), and property inventories (*inventários*). Bahian ships' papers recovered by British antislaving naval forces during the era of suppression (1811–1839) also form a major body of textual evidence for illuminating the experience of life at sea and provide a robust demographic portrait of the city's maritime laborers. British forces captured fifty-one vessels during this period and not only collected any paper documentation they held aboard but often also recorded the testimonies of any involved parties, including enslaved and freed seamen. The coldly rational and deceptively transparent numbers contained in ships' muster rolls (*matrículas*), accounting ledgers, and administrative correspondence by slaving merchants provide only one part of the story. Such documentation enables a reconstruction of Black mariners' movements at sea, but not all dimensions of their lives.[31]

31. The demographics of the trade are drawn from a combination of the matrículas from fifty-one voyages that originated from Bahia and were captured by British antislaving forces stationed in Sierra Leone, West Africa, or the coast of Brazil between 1811 and 1839. Matrículas commonly identified sailors by name, occupation, legal status, racial identity, place of birth, age, and pay. Some records also include parentage and marital status. The records from detained ships are housed at the British National Archives, Papers of the Foreign Office, in the Mixed Commission Documents for the Court in Sierra Leone. A second set exists at the Arquivo Histórico do Itamaraty in Rio de Janeiro, Comissão Mista Collection. The third collection is housed at the Real Junta do Comércio, Fábricas e Navagação collection in the Arquivo Nacional in Rio de Janeiro and holds the papers and legal petitions of Brazilian vessels seized before the official formation of the Mixed Commission Courts in 1817. The first two archives housed portions of the papers of slaving ships adjudicated in Britain's bilateral Mixed Commission Courts, which, over the course of fifty years, condemned 600 vessels. Some years featured a disproportionate number of captures; other years, none at all. The result is an uneven, but significant, sample of Bahian slaving ships. In 1812, for instance, 46 ships sailed from Bahia to the African coast; 10 were captured by British antislaving forces, meaning the sample of ships' papers included in this study for the year 1812 was very representative. One year earlier, only 2 ships were captured out of a total of 33 that sailed, making the sample for that year less statistically significant. These papers represent one of the most extensive collections of slave traders' activities during the period. Numbers for total number of ships from *Voyages*, http://www.slavevoyages.org/tast/index.faces. For more on the Mixed Commission Courts and British naval suppression of the transatlantic slave trade, see Leslie Bethell, *The Abolition of the Brazilian Slave Trade: Britain, Brazil and the Slave Trade Question, 1807–1869* (Cambridge, 1970); Jenny S. Martinez, *The Slave Trade and the Origins of International Human Rights Law* (Oxford, 2012); Siân Rees, *Sweet Water and Bitter: The Ships That Stopped the Slave Trade* (London, 2009); Padraic X. Scanlan, *Freedom's Debtors: British Antislavery in Sierra Leone in the Age of Revolution* (New Haven, Conn., 2017).

Recovering enslaved mariners' voices, emotional responses, and considered strategies is partially enabled by their engagement with diverse legal authorities. They testified to sympathetic colonial scribes and hostile British authorities alike. Though mostly illiterate, freed and enslaved people of African descent achieved a measure of legal personhood in the Portuguese legal sphere. This entitled them not only to testify in court proceedings but to negotiate contracts of purchase, sale, and debt, record them with notaries, and draw up wills and inventories. Many of these proceedings were formulaic, precluding spontaneous or more complex reactions to questions or situations. As African and creole mariners stood before legal authorities, however, they offered glimpses into their perspectives on family, property, the value of their labor, their relationships with owners and shipmates, the nature of liberty, and their perceived ties to Portuguese imperial vassalage. And though they articulated their oral testimonies as individuals, their words must be understood as coproduced, collective viewpoints that were representative of, and embedded in, larger Black communities with whom they shared frameworks for interpreting the world around them. The mobility of their labor meant they accessed multiple streams of information and engaged legal institutions across jurisdictions. Archival research across the boundaries of nation and empire stitches together lives marked by fluidity and disconnection. As such, these dense legal documents reveal fragments of complex life stories. Some were marked by profound upward social mobility and transformation; others, by irrevocable tragedy.

Examining this textual record suggests historians' ability to identify a multitude of voices and experiences between the silences of slavery's archive. In the South Atlantic, Portuguese colonial administrative norms and cultures helped create a robust documentary record of the laboring, religious, and social lives of enslaved and freed Black mariners. In the process, they generated wide-ranging textual remnants detailing Black life in Bahia. Scholars have questioned the transparency and neutrality of archives, viewing them as sites not only of domination but of violence and illegibility for enslaved historical subjects. To be sure, social historians who rely on the authority and comprehensiveness of documentary evidence to establish the quotidian realities of historical subjects must remain cognizant of the distortions produced through the archive as a locus of colonial power. But, as Michel-Rolph Trouillot has argued, how and why historical sources entered an archive is just as crucial to understanding their significance as their contents. Traces of enslaved lives appeared in archives under a variety of circumstances. While the gaze of slaveholders, merchants, and officials remained powerful, enslaved and freed mariners in the South Atlantic—rather than turning from the disciplining power of white authorities—frequently sought to engage colonial bureaucracies, however violent, to textualize their perspectives. The theorizations of "the Archive of Slavery" as a monolithic entity limit historians' ability to attend to enslaved people's strategies and experiences while often inhibiting an exploration of their inner lives. Silence and dehumanization, although pronounced in Portugal colonial archives, was not definitive.[32]

Many historians of colonial Latin America have crafted their own divergent understandings of archival practices to access sources that can articulate more than elite power and perceptions.[33] Scholars of Africa, Latin America, and the Black Atlantic have long insisted that archives do not fully capture the richness and complexity of Black expression. In line with such work, *Captive Cosmopolitans* traces a multitude of expressive forms. Enslaved and freed people of African descent in Bahia produced oral and textual forms of knowledge, but they also treated the material and metaphysical world as sites for their intellectual production. Their manipulation of aquatic environments,

32. Marisa J. Fuentes, *Dispossessed Lives: Enslaved Women, Violence, and the Archive* (Philadelphia, 2016), 7; Michel-Rolph Trouillot, *Silencing the Past: Power and the Production of History* (Boston, 1995), 49–53. For Saidiya Hartman, "The archive is, in this case, a death sentence, a tomb, a display of the violated body, an inventory of property, a medical treatise on gonorrhea, a few lines about a whore's life, an asterisk in the grand narrative of history." The image of the tomb evokes one of the preeminent themes of this body of literature. See Hartman, "Venus in Two Acts," *Small Axe*, XII, no. 2 (June 2008), 1–14. A list of deceased captives who perished on a transatlantic voyage only to be memorialized exclusively through their monetary value and the sign of ownership, which was burned onto their flesh before they disembarked from the African coast, is emblematic of the same epistemic violence that characterizes anglophone archives. See APEB, Seção Colonial e Provincial, no. 568–1, "Termos dos Cativos Mortos 1810–1811."

33. Scholarly work on litigation by people of African descent in the era of slavery and emancipation has been incisive about this point. See Carlos Aguirre, "Working the System: Black Slaves and the Courts in Lima, Peru, 1821–1854," in Darlene Clark Hine and Jacqueline McLeod, eds., *Crossing Boundaries: Comparative History of Black People in Diaspora* (Bloomington, Ind., 1999), 202–221; Bryant, *Rivers of Gold, Lives of Bondage;* Kathryn Burns, *Into the Archive: Writing and Power in Colonial Peru* (Durham, N.C., 2010); Sidney Chalhoub, *Visões da liberdade: Uma história das últimas décadas da escravidão na corte* (São Paulo, 1990); Adriana Chira, *Patchwork Freedoms: Law, Slavery, and Race beyond Cuba's Plantations* (Cambridge, 2022); Ferreira, *Cross-Cultural Exchange in the Atlantic World;* Alejandro de la Fuente, "Slave Law and Claims-Making in Cuba: The Tannenbaum Debate Revisited," *Law and History Review,* XXII (2004), 339–369; de la Fuente, "Slaves and the Creation of Legal Rights in Cuba: Coartación and Papel," *HAHR,* LXXVII (2007),

one dimension of their intellectual lives, gave rise to intergenerational techniques of navigation and fishing. In purchasing and circulating West African commodities such as panos da costa (textiles) and dendê oil, enslaved seamen created new forms of material signification that can be interpreted only by employing an interdisciplinary methodology. *Captive Cosmopolitans* draws at times from a range of other methodological traditions, including ethnohistory's use of contemporary ethnography, archaeology, and oral tradition, as well as Africanist mixed methods that utilize historical linguistics and environmental and material analysis to recover preliterate pasts.[34]

In doing so, *Captive Cosmopolitans* seeks to identify and explore slavery's *para-archives*—the repositories of enslaved consciousness that exist outside the textual but are parallel to and can be read alongside it. By imagining where traces of the consciousness of enslaved mariners might have been inscribed—particularly in the material world—this work can allow historians to move beyond the limits of traditional archival records and to challenge the problem of narrative posed by colonial sources. By combining commercial and cultural

---

659–692; Keila Grinberg, *Liberata, a lei da ambigüidade: As ações de liberdade da Corte de Apelação do Rio de Janeiro no século XIX* (1994; rpt. Rio de Janeiro, 2008); Grinberg, "Freedom Suits and Civil Law in Brazil and the United States," *Slavery and Abolition,* XXII (2001), 66–82; Ariela Gross and Alejandro de la Fuente, "Slaves, Free Blacks, and Race in the Legal Regimes of Cuba, Louisiana, and Virginia: A Comparison," *North Carolina Law Review,* XCI (2013), 1699–1756; Brian P. Owensby, "How Juan and Leonor Won Their Freedom: Litigation and Liberty in Seventeenth-Century Mexico," *HAHR,* LXXXV (2005), 39–79; Owensby, "Legal Personality and the Processes of Slave Liberty in Early-Modern New Spain," *European Review of History,* XVI (2009), 365–382; Bianca Premo, *The Enlightenment on Trial: Ordinary Litigants and Colonialism in the Spanish Empire* (Oxford, 2017); Frank Trey Proctor III, "An 'Imponderable Servitude': Slave versus Master Litigation for Cruelty (Maltratamiento or Sevicia) in Late Eighteenth-Century Lima, Peru," *Journal of Social History,* XLVIII (2015), 662–684; Danielle Terrazas Williams, *The Capital of Free Women: Race, Legitimacy, and Liberty in Colonial Mexico* (New Haven, Conn., 2022).

34. Greg Carr, "Translation, Recovery, and 'Ethnic' Archives of Africana: Inscribing Meaning beyond Otherness," *PMLA,* CXXVII (2012), 360–364; Robyn d'Avignon, *A Ritual Geology: Gold and Subterranean Knowledge in Savanna West Africa* (Durham, N.C., 2022); Kathryn M. de Luna and Jeffrey B. Fleisher, *Speaking with Substance: Methods of Language and Materials in African History* (Cham, Switzerland, 2019); J. Cameron Monroe, *The Precolonial State in West Africa: Building Power in Dahomey* (Cambridge, 2014); Akinwumi Ogundiran and Paula Saunders, eds., *Materialities of Ritual in the Black Atlantic* (Bloomington, Ind., 2014); Jan Vansina, *Paths in the Rainforests: Toward a History of Political Tradition in Equatorial Africa* (Madison, Wis., 1990).

history, textual records, and ethnographic insights, *Captive Cosmopolitans* historicizes the emergence of a culture of commercialized material expression by Salvador's Black inhabitants. Uniting textual sources located in archives with diverse paratextual traces of knowledge can bring a previously opaque evidentiary world to life in new ways.[35]

BOOK ORGANIZATION

Captive Cosmopolitans traces the evolving experiences and pervasive influences of African and creole mariners in Salvador da Bahia and the larger South Atlantic world from the advent of the Portuguese empire to its variegated afterlives in the late nineteenth century. Chapter 1 charts the long history of a South Atlantic commercial system that depended significantly on the skilled labor and cultural brokerage of Black mariners. Beginning with the earliest explorations of the West African coast in the mid-fifteenth century, Portuguese captains and merchants employed both free and enslaved African mariners who acted as interpreters, sailors, *grumetes,* canoemen, and trade auxiliaries aboard slaving vessels. From West Africa, the practice of employing Africans as maritime laborers diffused throughout the Portuguese empire, including to Brazil. In Bahia, productive aquatic activities were overwhelmingly performed by enslaved people. Black mariners became central to the infrastructure underpinning the growth of plantation agriculture in the region while the increasing demand for enslaved labor in Salvador established an African-influenced economic and cultural environment that afforded avenues toward manumission as well as crushing deprivation and exploitation.

Focusing on the eighteenth century, Chapter 2 contextualizes Bahian traders' growing commercial success on the Mina Coast after the 1721 construction of the São João Baptista de Ajudá fort in Ouidah. Driven by an exploding demand for enslaved laborers in rural Brazil, merchants, ship captains, and Black mariners successfully contested the economic and military hegemony of the Dutch by turning weaknesses into strengths, taking advantage of the interimperial nature of West African trade. They learned to navigate the tumultuous nature of West African politics and warfare by moving their slave-trading activities eastward over the course of the eighteenth and early nineteenth centuries. Within the ports of West Africa, African-born enslaved

35. The problem of deciphering voice and the conundrum of locating agency of oppressed historical subjects is not unique to histories of slavery. See John Beverley, *Subalternity and Representation: Arguments in Cultural Theory* (Durham, N.C., 1999).

seamen procured necessary provisions—including food and medicine—acted as interpreters, and managed enslaved men, women, and children held in cargoes. Citing extant legal petitions and ship manifests, this chapter argues that enslaved sailors drew on medieval Iberian precedents that permitted sailors to secure a *caixa de liberdade,* or "liberty chest"—a unit of space within a ship's cargo to house their personal trade goods. Enslaved and freed Black mariners utilized this trading privilege to engage in oceanic trade for their own benefit, supplementing their paltry wages with modest trading profits. Furthermore, enslaved and freed sailors forged temporary financial partnerships with fellow crew members and residents of Bahia, enlarging the number of investors in the transatlantic slave trade. This legitimized transatlantic slaving as an avenue of economic possibility across a broad swath of the city's population. By the early decades of the nineteenth century, the decentralized nature of Bahian slaving had produced a number of socially and economically ascendant captive cosmopolitan careers.

Chapter 3 provides an exploration of life aboard slave-trading vessels in the South Atlantic during the first three decades of the nineteenth century. This chapter illuminates experiences of daily life, labor, and confraternity among crew members as well as the interactions between enslaved and African sailors and captives in the cargo. Crucially, ship captains and royal bureaucrats often preferred African sailors to European ones because of the former's perceived linguistic and cultural expertise in dealing with African people on the coast as well as aboard slaving vessels. Taking advantage of this predilection, enslaved and free mariners utilized their mobility to earn wages, purchase manumission, and exercise a level of self-determination not often associated with the condition of enslavement. Slavers' dependence on the skilled labor of mariners of African descent paradoxically facilitated both the growth of Bahia's transatlantic slave trade and the social and physical mobility of individual enslaved mariners.

Chapter 4 turns to the transatlantic legal networks crafted by enslaved mariners and free Black Catholic brothers in the wake of the 1761 free-soil law that granted manumission to any enslaved individual who stepped foot on Portuguese land. Revealing a rich intellectual tradition of theorizing "freedom" through legal discourse, the chapter delineates the movement-based tactics of those escaping Brazilian sea vessels through the Portuguese "sanctuary" port of Lisbon. Enslaved mariners' and their metropolitan allies' engagement with and interpretation of legal principles—particularly their own lay theorization of jurisdiction, liberty, and imperial subjecthood—resulted in the articulation of what I term *jurisdictional consciousness,* a spatially grounded legal imaginary. Through a close reading of legal petitions authored by dozens of enslaved mariners, this chapter illustrates how they escaped to advantageous legal jurisdictions. Informed by their understanding of the political geography of the Black Atlantic, such mariners were able to draw on the material and legal resources of African brotherhoods in both Lisbon and Salvador to launch their legal claims. By the early nineteenth century, mariners had diffused knowledge of this emancipatory law to other enslaved inhabitants of colonial Brazil, facilitating the maritime marronage of an increasing number of enslaved Africans in Bahia and prompting a crisis of slavery in the colonies.

This moment did not become a watershed. Chapter 5 explores a period of historical transition—the rise of abolitionist sentiment and antislavery military action in the larger Atlantic world—that coincided with a resurgence in the economic vitality of Bahia's slave trade. As revolutionary democratic abolitionism swept across other Atlantic slave societies, enslaved Black mariners were put in a new position of vulnerability. Revived by the 1789 Haitian Revolution, Bahia's sugar economy demanded the importation of ever-greater numbers of enslaved Africans. By 1811, however, British suppression of the transatlantic trade in captured Africans created a new interimperial conflict. Abolition at sea, despite its theoretical promise of liberty, heightened the physical peril of Black mariners as they became reconfigured as potentially subversive actors aboard newly criminalized Bahian vessels. British suppression of the slave trade threatened both the lives of enslaved mariners and their investments aboard slaving vessels. In one of the great ironies of the age, captive cosmopolitans experienced the rise of abolitionism as a moment of danger as much as one of possibility.

The final two chapters analyze how African and creole mariners transformed the South Atlantic slaving ship into a site for the dissemination of African culture and knowledge in the Americas. Chapter 6 analyzes how African-derived medicinal knowledge deployed by slave ship barbers and sangradores (bloodletters)—particularly botanical pharmacopoeia and bloodletting—became the most common form of treatment on Bahian slaving vessels. Because Africans comprised nearly 90 percent of all Bahian slave ship medical personnel in the early nineteenth century, their medicinal practices became part of a larger body of healing knowledge in Bahia. This chapter also argues that African medical practitioners laboring in the Bahian slave trade were part of an expansive transatlantic circulation of medical knowledge and materials centered on and facilitated by the trade in human beings. Ironically, the deadly Bahian slave trade became a site of medical knowledge exchange that offered a space open to African medical practitioners' creativity, knowledge, and agency. In their appropriation of both European and Amerindian remedies for their therapies, African medical practitioners working aboard slaving ships remained crucial in sustaining the longevity and profitability of the transatlantic slave trade by maintaining low mortality rates among enslaved Africans. In turn, these skilled mariners reaped significant monetary rewards, receiving better salaries and investing in cargoes at higher rates than their fellow African crewmates.

Chapter 7 traces the small-scale trading practices of African mariners who pioneered a transatlantic commercial circuit in symbolically potent West African commodities to Bahia, particularly dendê oil and panos da costa. Venturing onshore in West Africa, they passed on these objects to their wives and lovers, who labored as ambulant vendors (*ganhadeiras*) and shop owners in Bahia. This commodity trade in West African goods was unique in the Atlantic world. An illustration of enslaved people's commercial ingenuity, mariners became central to a transoceanic circuit of commodity exchange that stretched from the African interior to the plantations of rural Brazil. In highlighting this development, this chapter emphasizes African material culture as a site of intellectual production by tracing how West Africans in Bahia introduced novel ideas about aesthetics and materiality to Brazil. In turn, transatlantic trades in panos da costa and dendê oil fostered the upward economic mobility of enslaved and free Africans residing in Bahia, creating commercial and social links that generated a class of transatlantic traders who were born in Africa but enslaved and freed in Brazil—and who gained a modicum of wealth and prestige by catering to the consumer tastes of the city's free and enslaved African population.

As *Captive Cosmopolitans* shows, African and creole mariners spent their lives in the spaces in between: between continents, between statuses, and between cultures. Their seamless movement through vast oceanic environments was mirrored in their metaphorical boundary crossing. The ability to operate across distinct social, cultural, and political spaces provided mariners with a means to survive—sometimes even flourish. Their protean subjectivities, forged between Africa and Brazil, enriched and empowered a handful of slaving merchants and slaveowners on land. Their movements were far from transgressive, and their labor, investments, and intellectual contributions shored up a transatlantic commerce in captive Africans. West African merchants and potentates controlled the flow of commodified captives for sale to foreign captains, but the commercial agency of enslaved and freed mariners remained ambiguous in both its human and historical consequences. Whereas the former group, entrenched in their natal communities, used the spoils of the transatlantic slave trade to empower themselves locally, the latter group's participation in the world of South Atlantic slavery was enacted in a far more precarious context. Many Black mariners already had been displaced from homelands, severed from ties of kin and community, and alienated from recognizable forms of language and culture. From this position of exclusion and exploitation, they attempted to insert themselves into the webs of patronage that structured Salvador's social landscape. They joined Catholic associations, constructed new social ties with workmates, and acquired languages beyond their mother tongues. Doing so meant submitting to seignorial authority in exchange for protection and perhaps the promise that one day they would become patrons themselves. Such vertical ties of solidarity became one of the few avenues for social rebirth available to Black seamen.[36]

The view from the South Atlantic offers us a markedly different portrait of the era of transatlantic slavery. Unlike the groups of rebellious slaves across the Atlantic world who pierced the seemingly invulnerable facade of slaveholder authority in the early nineteenth century, Bahia's African and creole mariners engaged in cooperation much more commonly than in violent contestation to achieve their objectives. They fashioned their own transatlantic networks of knowledge, goods, and rumor as a means of acquiring autonomy, social power, and self-fulfillment. These acts only strengthened the hold that transatlantic slaving had over the city of Salvador. By tethering their own commercial aspirations to those of slaving merchants, they helped to legitimize transatlantic commerce in slaves, ensuring the trade's longevity and prosperity. Commercial alliances were not always initiated by powerful merchants as a means of co-optation. Sailors, both enslaved and freed, independently asserted their own prerogatives, seeking to participate in the poorly capitalized but lucrative slaving ventures for which they labored. Insisting that they, too, should be able to reap the benefits of transatlantic commerce, they learned that doing so was one of the surest means of converting oneself from object to subject, from slave to freedman. The wealth accrued from hawking an assortment of West African goods could purchase manumission. For some, trading privileges could lead to a respectable life of propertyownership in slaves and land. For the very few, transatlantic exchange supported the formation of extensive networks of cultural and social power within Bahia's African community. If individual mariners could not transform the slave society they inhabited into a more

36. Joseph C. Miller, *The Problem of Slavery as History: A Global Approach* (New Haven, Conn., 2012).

egalitarian one, at least they could transform their place within it. As their complex life stories detail, the salience of liberal democratic and anticapitalist ideology was much less pronounced in the South Atlantic. Their ambivalent participation in the transatlantic slave trade meant that Black mariners harnessed commercial networks to achieve their ultimate aims: rebuilding social connections, securing personal autonomy, and cultivating a sense of cultural prestige within Bahia's West African communities. These achievements, more than liberal notions of personal independence, defined their sense of freedom. *Captive Cosmopolitans* tells such men's stories.

The Origins of a Black Maritime South Atlantic

Black mariners were integral to seaborne travel from the very dawn of Portuguese exploration of the Atlantic. The majority of Portuguese vessels navigating that vast ocean, no matter their size, employed at least one Black laborer in some capacity. As the Portuguese settled the Atlantic rim, colonists hoping to traverse the watery surrounds of Salvador da Bahia in the seventeenth century would likely have put themselves in the hands of a navigator of African descent. Portuguese imperialists were notorious for their orientation to water. As Brazil's first historian, the Franciscan friar Vincente do Salvador, noted in 1637, the Portuguese penchant for maritime transportation and coastal settlement around the globe gave the impression that they were like crabs—always scuttling over beaches. A 1690 map representing Olinda, one of Salvador's neighboring port communities, offered an early depiction of the realities of canoe-based travel in Brazil's coastal channels. Black watermen were shown ferrying Portuguese passengers throughout the settlement, with their labor providing a vital commercial link between town and plantation. In the coming centuries, European settlers would remain dependent on the labor and expertise of Black mariners to solidify Brazil's colonial economy.[1]

From its earliest moments, Portugal's waterborne Atlantic empire relied on two factors: an unrelenting trade in enslaved Africans and the subsequent predominance of Black maritime labor. At sea and on land, the tenuous nature of early Portuguese expansion required the conscription of the diverse physical and intellectual capacities of African people as well as the consolidation of ties of loyalty and cooperation with African interlocutors. African maritime brokers were emblematic of both objectives. Their linguistic, commercial,

---

1. Luiz Felipe de Alencastro, *The Trade in the Living: The Formation of Brazil in the South Atlantic, Sixteenth to Seventeenth Centuries,* trans. Gavin Adams and Alencastro (Albany, N.Y., 2018), 11; James Lockhart and Stuart B. Schwartz, *Early Latin America: A History of Colonial Spanish America and Brazil* (Cambridge, 1983), 229; AHU, Cartogràfica e iconografía, caixa 15–Pernambuco, no. 886, "Carta topográfica do porto de Pernambuco," 1690.

and navigational expertise drove innovations in commerce and aquatic travel, enabling Portugal's status as an ascendant early modern imperial power.

Although a number of histories have noted the presence of African-born seafarers in Portugal's early colonization of various Atlantic littorals, few have foregrounded the contributions of such men to the constitution and operation of the Portuguese empire itself. As this chapter shows, Black mariners played an essential role in establishing Portugal's outsized presence on both sides of the Atlantic. Their environmental knowledge provided one of the keys to transoceanic colonialization. Unlike terrestrially expansive empires, Portugal's maritime empire was defined by small colonial enclaves connected via waterways that eventually constituted the South Atlantic as a coherent commercial space.[2] The coalescence of a network of maritime ports, commodity markets, and plantation-based agricultural enterprises, however, depended in part on the skills and ingenuity of Black people enlisted to enable emergent merchant capitalist relations. These early African cosmopolitans, both free and enslaved, fulfilled demand for skilled maritime labor on both sides of the Portuguese Atlantic in the service of this accelerating commercialization. In turn, they fomented a transatlantic circulation in techniques of nautical navigation and extraction from West Africa to the expanding colony of Brazil, particularly its northeastern shores.[3]

2. Alencastro, *Trade in the Living,* trans. Adams and Alencastro, 11–16. For more on the contributions of African seafarers to Portuguese commerce, see George E. Brooks, *Landlords and Strangers: Ecology, Society, and Trade in Western Africa, 1000–1630* (London, 2018); Brooks, *Eurafricans in Western Africa: Commerce, Social Status, Gender, and Religious Observance from the Sixteenth to the Eighteenth Century* (Athens, Ohio, 2003); Walter Rodney, *History of the Upper Guinea Coast, 1545–1800* (Oxford, 1970); Robert Smith, "The Canoe in West African History," *Journal of African History,* XI (1970), 515–533; Peter C. W. Gutkind, "The Canoemen of the Gold Coast (Ghana): A Survey and an Exploration in Precolonial African Labour History (Les piroguiers de la Côte de l'Or [Ghana]: Enquête et recherche d'histoire du travail en Afrique précoloniale)," *Cahiers d'études africaines,* XXIX (1989), 339–376; Robin Law, "Between the Sea and the Lagoons: The Interaction of Maritime and Inland Navigation on the Precolonial Slave Coast (Entre mer et lagune: Les interactions de la navigation maritime et continentale sur la Côte des Esclaves avant la colonisation)," ibid., 209.

3. Early iterations of Portuguese merchant capitalism relied on the efficient transportation of luxury goods by oceanic merchants operating under the patronage of the crown. In West African trading posts, merchants initially focused on acquiring gold, ivory, and spices in exchange for Iberian cloth and horses. This commerce evolved into a dedicated trade in enslaved people. They were soon joined in their transatlantic merchant ventures by English,

In time, African pathways of labor and expertise came to define the aquatic landscape of Salvador da Bahia. By the beginning of the eighteenth century, a once-inconsequential trading outpost had blossomed into the seat of Portugal's imperial power in the South Atlantic. Central to the port city's rapid commercialization was the ascent of a vibrant maritime culture that facilitated the smooth movement of people and commodities between the bustling urban center of Salvador and the city's agriculturally productive hinterlands. Though waterborne mobility endowed enslaved individuals with the ability to subsist and cultivate relatively independent laboring lives, it also provided the infrastructure necessary for a colonial slave society. In a number of ways, the emergent South Atlantic system and the aquatic-oriented provisioning grounds of Bahia bore the marks of Black mariners' intellectual work. This paradox—of Black mariners making an imperial world premised on a trade in enslaved Africans—would become even more salient in the arduous deepwater journeys of the South Atlantic.

MARITIME BEGINNINGS OF
THE SOUTH ATLANTIC SYSTEM

From the unlikeliest of lands, an early modern South Atlantic system was born. Though a small territory composed of arid plains, rocky coastlines, and verdant hills occupying the southwestern corner of the Iberian Peninsula, Portugal was also uniquely situated as a meeting place between the Atlantic Ocean and the Mediterranean where numerous maritime trade routes intersected. In the middle decades of the fifteenth century, however, Portuguese mariners—supported by a combination of royal patronage and private capital—precipitated a radical reorientation of trading networks from markets in the Mediterranean, the Levant, the Black Sea, and North Africa toward the West African coast. This pivotal period drew the economically fledgling,

---

Dutch, and French merchants. By the mid-sixteenth century, Portuguese merchants began to push their investment capital into productive agricultural enterprises, first in the Atlantic islands and then in Brazil, with merchant communities in other European empires following suit in the Caribbean and North and South America. A trade in luxuries was supplanted by a more extensive commerce in goods for mass consumption, such as sugar, coffee, tobacco, rice, and others, and private investment replaced state-sponsored trading monopolies. See Peter Coclanis, ed., *The Atlantic Economy during the Seventeenth and Eighteenth Centuries: Organization, Operation, Practice, and Personnel* (Columbia, S.C., 2005); Malyn Newitt, *The Portuguese in West Africa, 1415–1670: A Documentary History* (New York, 2010), 76–77.

politically fractured polity of Portugal into the untraversed and perilous waters of the Atlantic. Various agents of the Portuguese empire, including merchants, sailors, and soldiers, approached West African territories previously only accessible through trans-Saharan caravan networks controlled by Muslim traders. Marshaling the seafaring technology of the caravel—first perfected in the relatively shallow and calm waters of the Mediterranean—merchants in particular found waterborne transport advantageous for conveying commercial goods cheaply and efficiently, spurring the discovery of new sea routes to regions imagined as particularly wealth-laden, such as West Africa, India, and China. These explorations initiated a process of disenclavement, as Portuguese seafaring brought previously isolated, distinct communities and cultures into direct contact with one another for the first time in the course of mercantile negotiations.[4]

Before the rise of Portuguese Atlantic exploration in the fifteenth century, the riches of sub-Saharan Africa had trickled into the medieval markets of Lisbon. Gold and slaves trafficked from the Akan region across the arid Sahel and Sahara by Muslim Wangara traders entered Europe through Seville, eventually circulating throughout Iberia. Spurred by the search for the elusive source of West African specie and looking to bypass exorbitant Muslim-controlled trading networks, the Portuguese crown sponsored a number of royal voyages that ventured south along the West African coast. Sporadic and opportunistic slave raiding on the Mauritanian coast turned to more peaceable trade after the 1440s, in the wake of Portuguese mariners' thwarted ambitions to secure captives from Gorée and other Senegambian littoral communities through force. As Portuguese settlers abandoned violence as a means to achieve commercial ends on the West African coast—largely due to its ineffectiveness—they turned to the mobilization of local cultural go-betweens or brokers to facilitate trading arrangements. In the following decades, the search for gold deposits complemented a growing desire to procure captives for domestic purposes in Iberia. Captains aggressively worked to identify willing local African potentates with whom to trade as they ventured down the coast; at their sides were often African *grumetes* (native assistants) charged with facilitating negotiations.[5]

---

4. Brooks, *Landlords and Strangers*, 60–62, 121–141; André Donelha and A. Teixeira da Mota, *Descrição da Serra Leoa e dos rios de Guiné do Cabo Verde, 1625* (Lisbon, 1977); John Thornton, *Africa and Africans in the Making of the Atlantic World, 1400–1800* (Cambridge, 1992), 14.

5. Brooks, *Landlords and Strangers*, 129–130; Toby Green, *The Rise of the Trans-Atlantic Slave Trade in Western Africa, 1300–1589* (New York, 2012), 78; João Paulo Oliveira e Costa,

Reaching the Senegal River in 1445, Portuguese mariners endeavored to convert sporadic commercial exchanges into durable trading relations. By this period, the Portuguese crown sought to exploit potential new sources of revenue by establishing royal commercial prerogatives for transatlantic trading. When Portuguese mariners and soldiers constructed small trading fortifications—called *feitorias*—along the West African coast, they did so with royal backing under the guise of trading monopolies. These settlements were the first nodes of South Atlantic commerce, initially focused on trade in "rich," or luxury, goods—gold, ivory, and spices—in exchange for Iberian cloth and horses. Portuguese merchants and adventurers who had been lured along the coast of West Africa by the prospect of acquiring rare specie encountered local lineage heads eager to secure beneficial trading relationships with outsiders, or "strangers," an arrangement that would endow them with comparative advantages in their communities. Seeking to control the flow of luxury goods into West African locales, these men cultivated simultaneous commercial and political alliances with Portuguese visitors through ties of intermarriage and barter, resulting in the rapid expansion of slaving in the region as men, women, and children were delivered to the hands of foreign traders in exchange for iron, textiles, and other commodities. By the second half of the century, Portuguese merchants trafficked one thousand enslaved Senegambians from Arguim annually.[6]

Initially, the crown restricted settlement on the West African coast by Portuguese merchants. Establishing regular commercial relations with commu-

---

José Damião Rodrigues, and Pedro Aires Oliveira, *História da expansão e do Império português* (Lisbon, 2014), 54–56. Six main routes characterized the trans-Saharan slave trade, including one from Ghana to Morocco, a second from Timbuktu to Tuwat, and a third from the Niger valley through Hausaland. See Paul E. Lovejoy, *Transformations in Slavery: A History of Slavery in Africa,* 2d ed. (Cambridge, 2000), 25–26; Aurelia Martín Casares, "Free and Freed Black Africans in Granada in the Time of the Spanish Renaissance," in T. F. Earle and K. J. P. Lowe, eds., *Black Africans in Renaissance Europe* (Cambridge, 2005), 247–260. On the idea of go-betweens as central to colonization around the Atlantic world, see Alida C. Metcalf, *Go-Betweens and the Colonization of Brazil, 1500–1600* (Austin, 2005); Susan Sleeper-Smith, *Indian Women and French Men: Rethinking Cultural Encounter in the Western Great Lakes* (Amherst, Mass., 2001); Yanna Yannakakis, *The Art of Being In-Between: Native Intermediaries, Indian Identity, and Local Rule in Colonial Oaxaca* (Durham, N.C., 2008).

6. Newitt, *Portuguese in West Africa,* 76–77; Brooks, *Landlords and Strangers,* 27, 135–140; Green, *Rise of the Trans-Atlantic Slave Trade,* 83.

nities on the Upper Guinea coast, however, required a terrestrial presence and increasingly complex forms of trading organization. After the Portuguese settled in the Cabo Verde Islands around 1460, merchants' voracious demand for enslaved Africans to populate burgeoning plantations and textile workshops led to an expansion of slave trading on the rivers of Senegambia and Upper Guinea. Expanded slaving on the West African coast allowed for the diversion of a small flow of captives to Iberia on Atlantic waters, bypassing older, trans-Saharan caravan networks. Portuguese mariners' and merchants' movement along the so-called "Guinea" coast culminated in the 1482 construction of São Jorge da Mina Castle, a trading fort in Elmina, forming the first territorial base for the trade in gold extracted in nearby Axim, which navigators had first reached eleven years earlier.[7]

Despite the crown's efforts to maintain fiscal control over Lisbon's emergent oceanic mercantile class through the distribution of royal trading monopolies to favored subjects, many traders on the West African coast continued to elude royal oversight. Such men were considered "renegades" by officials in Lisbon. The earliest intermediaries between West African coastal trading communities and Portuguese merchants and military leaders were *lançados* and *tangomaos:* predominantly New Christian Portuguese traders (*cristão novos,* or recent converts of Jewish ancestry) and their offspring, who integrated themselves into Western African communities during the fifteenth century through permanent residence and intermarriage with local women near the Gambia, Cacheu, Geba, Grande, Nuñez, Pongo, and Sierra Leone Rivers. New Christians submitted to the authority of the local African potentates who hosted them, often disavowing the crown's directives. Lançados and their Luso-African descendants were liminal figures in both West Africa and Portugal. They often adopted cultural signifiers that set them apart from both groups, including the embrace of European-style dress and the pioneering of Crioulo, a combination of African grammar and Portuguese vocabulary.

7. Green, *Rise of the Trans-Atlantic Slave Trade,* 88–89; Rodney, *History of the Upper Guinea Coast,* 74–77, 98–99; Ivana Elbl, "'Slaves Are a Very Risky Business . . .': Supply and Demand in the Early Atlantic Slave Trade," in José C. Curto and Paul E. Lovejoy, eds., *Enslaving Connections: Changing Cultures of Africa and Brazil during the Era of Slavery* (New York, 2004), 29–55; Elbl, "The Portuguese Trade with West Africa: 1440–1521" (Ph.D. diss., University of Toronto, 1986); Paul Trevor Hall, "The Role of Cape Verde Islanders in Organizing and Operating Maritime Trade between West Africa and Iberian Territories, 1441–1616" (Ph.D. diss., Johns Hopkins University, 1993); Herbert S. Klein, *The Atlantic Slave Trade* (New York, 1999), 5–9; Lovejoy, *Transformations in Slavery,* 24–45.

Through their close ties to local African communities, they were able—along with their commercial allies—to dominate a profitable interregional Atlantic trade in kola nuts and other commodities in the Senegambia region.[8]

Over time, quotidian contacts on land within and around the nuclei of Portuguese trading communities produced a growing group of African-born, culturally dexterous individuals who bridged West African and Iberian trading networks. A diverse range of local West African laborers, healers, traders, and mariners circulated through coastal feitorias, conducting the building, cooking, healing, and trading that animated daily life. As resident populations settled on the periphery of minuscule Portuguese settlements, they generated cultures that fused elements of European and African origin.[9] Ira Berlin has argued that lançados and their descendants were among the first of many groups of Atlantic creoles, chameleonlike men and women who facilitated the early modern transoceanic trade by "employing their linguistic skills and their familiarity with the Atlantic's diverse commercial practices, cultural conventions, and diplomatic etiquette to mediate between African merchants and European sea captains."[10] The newly fomented identity category of creole (crioulo) suggests the degree to which the Portuguese imperial project was

8. Brooks, *Eurafricans in Western Africa,* xix-xxii, 50–67; Green, *Rise of the Trans-Atlantic Slave Trade,* 125; Rodney, *History of the Upper Guinea Coast,* 76–90; Philip J. Havik, "Kriol without Creoles: Rethinking Guinea's Afro-Atlantic Connections (Sixteenth to Twentieth Centuries)," in Nancy Priscilla Naro, Roger Sansi-Roca, and David H. Treece, eds., *Cultures of the Lusophone Black Atlantic* (New York, 2007), 41–73; Brooks, *Landlords and Strangers,* 178–179.

9. Brooks, *Eurafricans in Western Africa,* 51–53; Newitt, *Portuguese in West Africa,* 78–82. As one Portuguese captain noted, "Among these blacks there are many who can speak our Portuguese language. They dress as we do, as do many black women of the advanced kind . . . these blacks, men and women go with the [lançados] from one river to another, and to Santiago Island and other places" (Brooks, 55).

10. The Portuguese term *crioulo* carried both racial and cultural connotations as individuals of African descent born in the Americas were denoted by the neologism, though the creoles to which Berlin refers were African born. Linda M. Heywood and John K. Thornton, inspired by Berlin's concept of a unified Atlantic creole culture, framed their discussion of creolization in Central Africa on "cultural synthesis" and the creation of new cultural forms. See Ira Berlin, *Many Thousands Gone: The First Two Centuries of Slavery in North America* (Cambridge, Mass., 1998), 17–39; Berlin, "From Creole to African: Atlantic Creoles and the Origins of African-American Society in Mainland North America," *WMQ,* 3d Ser., LIII (1996), 255; Heywood and Thornton, *Central Africans, Atlantic Creoles, and the Foundation of the Americas, 1585–1660* (New York, 2007).

suffused by forms of African cosmopolitanism linking Europe and Africa during the fifteenth and sixteenth centuries.[11] During the fifteenth century, mercantile success on West African coasts entailed cultural mediation and flexibility by both Portuguese traders and their African interlocutors. The nascent waterborne commercial networks forged by cosmopolitans in the 1440s would expand southward in the coming centuries.

PORTUGUESE VESSELS, AFRICAN SEAFARERS

From the beginning of Portuguese maritime exploration on the West African coast, ships employed or enslaved Africans to establish and solidify commercial relationships in the region. Enslaved watermen (especially fishermen and ferrymen) of African descent had been present on the waterways surrounding Lisbon and in southern Portugal as early as the thirteenth century, a continuation of the widespread use of enslaved mariners in the Mediterranean dating to antiquity. As the Italian navigator Alvise da Cadamosto explained, African interpreters had long been employed on Portuguese ships to facilitate communication with newly contacted peoples. In 1455, he related that every ship he encountered carried an interpreter brought from Portugal "who had been sold by the lords of Senegal to the first Portuguese to discover this land of the blacks." Already Christianized and speaking Portuguese "well," African interpreters employed by Portuguese captains "had them from their owners on the understanding that for the hire and pay of each we will give one slave to be chosen from all our captives." In addition, "each interpreter who secured four slaves for his master was to be given his freedom." Ship captains drew these men primarily from the ranks of enslaved inhabitants in Portugal, many of whom would have arrived in the kingdom as a result of trans-Saharan traf-

11. Though scholars have criticized Berlin and others' exclusive emphasis on the Euro-African encounter, which elides the vibrant contacts between distinctive African communities long before the arrival of Portuguese traders, the unprecedented political and economic upheavals on West Africa's Atlantic littoral during the period left an indelible mark on maritime communities. For critiques of the concept of Atlantic creolization, see James Sweet, "Reimagining the African-Atlantic Archive: Method, Concept, Epistemology, Ontology," *Journal of African History,* LV (2014), 147–159; Joseph C. Miller, *Way of Death: Merchant Capitalism and the Angolan Slave Trade, 1730–1830* (Madison, Wis., 1988), 86; Miller, "Retention, Reinvention, and Remembering: Restoring Identities through Enslavement in African and under Slavery in Brazil," in Curto and Lovejoy, eds., *Enslaving Connections,* 86–87.

fic that was caught up in the raiding and warfare on the Upper Guinea coast unleashed by Mandinka horsemen who targeted Banyun and other groups.[12]

As early as the 1440s, African mariners had been contracted for local coastal (*cabotage*) voyages. But by the beginning of the sixteenth century, a growing number of enslaved African seamen who were hired out by Iberian owners labored on the route from Guiné (the Portuguese designation for the Upper Guinea region) to Lisbon. On the caravel *Santa Maria das Neves* that sailed between Lisbon and Gambia in 1505–1506, Black mariners comprised seven of fourteen common sailors. And as São Tomé—an Atlantic island off the Bight of Benin first inhabited by Portuguese settlers in the 1480s—became one of the earliest large-scale importers of enslaved Africans to work on the island's sugar mills, an expanding population of enslaved and free African people labored on slaving vessels navigating between Guiné and the island. Though no systematic records exist that detail the composition of these early slave ship crews, navigators from other European nations noted the distinctiveness of Portuguese vessels' use of enslaved Africans as sailors. A Frenchman in the sixteenth century observed that, when attacked by French or English pirates, Portuguese captains were eager to prevent enemies from boarding their vessels "because their whole crew consists of slaves, and, coming to close quarters, they fear lest they be betrayed by their bondsmen who are not only Moors and infidels but all kinds of Barbarians." The employment of such men drew on metropolitan precedents in which early long-distance voyages from Portugal relied on impressment of local fishermen and convicts to man large vessels. On the West African coast, the labor of mariners could be compelled by enslavement instead of penal sanctions.[13]

Portuguese merchants soon learned to exploit the seafaring skills of other indigenous groups with expertise in oceanic or riverine navigation, fish-

12. A. C. de C. M. Saunders, *A Social History of Black Slaves and Freedmen in Portugal, 1441–1555* (Cambridge, 1982), 71; Joan M. Fayer, "African Interpreters in the Atlantic Slave Trade," *Anthropological Linguistics,* XLV (2003), 281; Brooks, *Eurafricans in Western Africa,* 42. On the Western Atlantic coast, politically decentralized coastal communities tended to be the victims of others' slaving. Internally, they practiced bondage; however, quite distinctly from the commercialized Iberian model, the labors of bondsmen and -women, as well as clients, was concentrated domestically as their efforts augmented production capacities of households. See Brooks, *Landlords and Strangers,* 34; J. D. Fage, "Slaves and Society in Western Africa, c. 1445–c. 1700," *Journal of African History,* XXI (1980), 289–310, esp. 298.

13. Saunders, *Social History of Black Slaves and Freedmen in Portugal,* 11–12; Stuart B. Schwartz, *Sugar Plantations in the Formation of Brazilian Society: Bahia, 1550–1835* (Cam-

ing, and trade. In 1508, one of Portugal's earliest explorers, Duarte Pacheco Pereira, detailed oceanic fishing practices along the Malagueta Coast. Near Ilha da Palma, Pereira noted local people were "great fishermen and go two or three leagues out to sea to fish, in canoes which, in shape, are like weavers' shuttles." He also explained that shipboard trade was common: "The negroes of all this coast bring pepper for barter to the ships in the canoes in which they go out fishing." In addition, Pereira described the impressive indigenous maritime fishing traditions of the Ahanta people near Cabo de Tres Pontas and at Axim, which was the first center of the gold trade. Likewise, to the east within the estuaries of the Niger, communities such as New Calabar and Bonny were home to local navigators who deployed

> the bigger canoes here, made from a single trunk, [which] are the largest in the Ethiopias of Guinea; some of them are large enough to hold eighty men, and they come from a hundred leagues or more up this river bringing yams in large quantities . . . they also bring many slaves, cows, goats and sheep.[14]

These formidable vessels housed a wooden-enclosed world, as crewmen slept, ate, and lived on them in a shipboard fraternity. Portuguese traders soon came to appreciate the craft of canoe building on the West African coast, which required considerable ingenuity. Many navigators favored the dugout canoe for oceanic and riverine fishing as well as for long distance commerce and warfare on several points along the Mina Coast.[15]

Early modern traders' desire for localized expertise led to the proliferation of coastal populations of African individuals who, for religious, military, or commercial reasons, acted as mediators, negotiators, or cultural translators between communities that were alien to one another. Often these groups coalesced around riverine or oceanic locations, including commercial or

---

bridge, 1985), 14; A. F. C. Ryder, "An Early Portuguese Trading Voyage to the Forcados River," *Journal of the Historical Society of Nigeria,* I (1959), 294–332. For more on the recruitment of Portuguese seamen, see C. R. Boxer, *Portuguese Seaborne Empire, 1415–1825* (New York, 1969), 13–14, 52, 57, 114, 211–215.

14. See Duarte Pacheco Pereira, *Esmeraldo de situ orbis,* ed. George H. T. Kimble (London, 2010), 110, 113, 116, 121, 122, 132.

15. Smith, "Canoe in West African History," *Journal of African History,* XI (1970), 518. Smith argues that, in crafting a canoe, builders constructed the vessel from a singular tree trunk and hollowed it with ax and fire, shaping the exterior into a tapered hull. Navigators had used this boat-building method since the Neolithic period (ibid., 515, 519).

missionary outposts. As the earliest cohort of captive cosmopolitans in the Portuguese Atlantic world, such figures swiftly became crucial to the operation of coastal commerce. Black mariners not only provided information pertaining to the languages and customs of potential trading partners but educated Portuguese navigators about maritime environments—currents, winds, water depths, and coastal geographies—that had to be mastered before trading could even take place. They also constructed and repaired ships. In doing so, they not only facilitated European merchants' trade on the West African littoral but were also key to the integration of African coastal communities into the burgeoning mercantile networks of the Atlantic world.[16]

In the sixteenth century, Portuguese captains increasingly contracted with African grumetes to capitalize on indigenous marine knowledge while anchored off the West African coast. As the predecessors to later cabin boys and sailors who would, in the following centuries, labor on Bahian slaving ships, these nautical men and women served dual roles on both Portuguese and Luso-African vessels. They attended to the maritime labor required on ships while acting as sailors and shipwrights. In addition, they assisted foreign merchants' efforts to access trade on the Upper Guinea coast by utilizing their connections to local communities. Defined by their membership in a range of power association and kinship groups, these African intermediaries were, according to the historian George E. Brooks, "prized for their intimate knowledge of winds, tides, currents, reefs, bars at river mouths, and the labyrinths of interconnecting rivers, marigots, and mangrove swamps." Grumetes were often locally recruited from elite families or hired out by their Portuguese owners, if they were enslaved. Many came from Lebou, Niominka, Papel, and Biafada ethnic groups, which were already heavily engaged in riverine and maritime navigation at the time of Portuguese arrival on the coast. Few details pertaining to their daily lives survive.[17]

Portuguese-African maritime collaborations enabled trade of all kinds on the Upper Guinea coast. In the late fifteenth century, lançado merchants regularly drew on the indigenous maritime expertise of local Biafada maritime traders, who traveled in dugout canoes to conduct a riverine and oceanic trade in kola. During this period, African interpreters and seafarers also aided the Portuguese in creating navigational maps of the coast. In the 1560s, a Cabo Verdean trader named André Álvares de Almada attested, "These blacks,

16. Brooks, *Landlords and Strangers*, 125, 136.

17. Brooks, *Eurafricans in Western Africa*, 52–53; Brooks, *Landlords and Strangers*, 124, 136–137.

especially the Banyun, are very quick to learn. Both men and women work for our people, and they travel with them to the other rivers as *grumetes* . . . to earn money, as confidently as if they had been born and brought up among us in full security (of life and liberty)." West African grumetes' strategy to acclimate to Portuguese language and custom while laboring on sailing vessels made them indispensable to the coastal trade. Some of these individuals were the decedents of lançados but successfully incorporated themselves into Banyun, Biafada, and Mandinka trading communities, settling near the north bank of the Cacheu River. Beyond the beaches and rivers of West Africa, merchants based in Cabo Verde took advantage of the cultural expertise of the growing manumitted Black population, deploying them on commercial expeditions to procure new slaves in the West African interior. In addition, populations of free seafarers residing on the coasts of West Africa—either through coercion or voluntary contract with Portuguese merchants—found their skills eminently transferable to Portuguese sailing vessels.[18]

The Luso-African circulation of navigational and commercial knowledge was also part of the region's rich history of waterborne travel. For hundreds of years before the Portuguese arrived, African mariners relied on seasonal currents and weather patterns by moving south along the coast from October to March, before they returned to evade the southeastward Guinea current once the rainy season began. The many rivers, streams, marigots, and lagoons that marked the Upper Guinea landscape, such as the Casamance, Cacheu, and Geba, linked inland communities to the Atlantic coastline as local traders circulated through the region in small crafts. Attentive to the aquatic orientation of West African trading cultures, the Portuguese developed relations with Papel mariners residing on Bissau Island in the 1570s, who later became sailors on Portuguese vessels alongside the Niominkas, Balantas, Bijagós, and Mandinkas.[19]

Exploiting the maritime expertise of local populations was essential to Portuguese efforts to forge a monopoly in the trade of lucrative gold exports from Elmina. The challenging maritime environment of the Mina Coast, a Portuguese commercial designation for the strip of coast stretching from Elmina to Lagos, initially impeded Portuguese captains' ability to access the

18. Brooks, *Eurafricans in Western Africa*, 50, 53, 54; Brooks, *Landlords and Strangers*, 125; Green, *Rise of the Trans-Atlantic Slave Trade*, 114.

19. Brooks, *Landlords and Strangers*, 14–16, 23, 136; Brooks, *Eurafricans in Western Africa*, 44, 80–81; Walter Hawthorne, *From Africa to Brazil: Culture, Identity, and an Atlantic Slave Trade, 1600–1830* (Cambridge, 2010), 10.

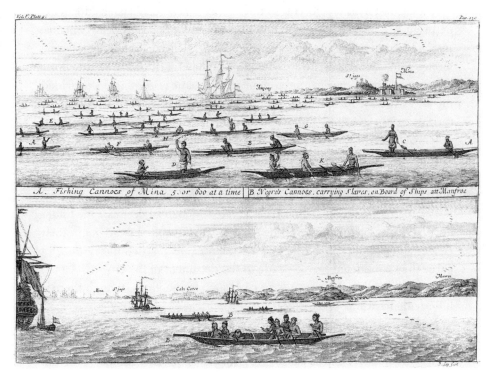

FIGURE 1. *"A. Fishing Cannoes of Mina 5. or 600 at a Time, B. Negro's Cannoes,
Carrying Slaves, on Board of Ships att Manfroe." Engraved by [Johannes] Kip.*
In *[Awnsham] Churchill and [John] Churchill, comps.,* A Collection of Voyages and
Travels . . . *(London, 1732). Canoes on the coast of Elmina, 1678–1712. Rare Book
Division, The New York Public Library. New York Public Library Digital Collections*

coveted trade in gold. Shore landings from the sea were difficult for even the
most experienced of mariners, in large part because of the powerful surf that
often destroyed European longboats. Local canoemen, however, were able to
navigate the turbulent seas, leading many Europeans to extol their skillfulness.
The French slave trader Jean Barbot called canoemen there "the fittest and
most experienced men to manage and paddle the canoes over the bars and
breakings." Portuguese traders and other Europeans began contracting the
services of canoemen to ferry goods and people from ship to shore as well as
provisions and trade goods along the coast.[20]

20. Smith, "Canoe in West African History," *Journal of African History,* XI (1970),
517; Gutkind, "Canoemen of the Gold Coast (Ghana)," *Cahiers d'études africaines,* XXIX
(1989), 339–376.

Mina Coast mariners leveraged their fishing and oceanic navigational expertise to abet the ferrying activities now in demand by European captains. Just as enslaved interpreters performed the vital intellectual labor of mastering foreign tongues to facilitate cross-cultural commerce, the intellectual efforts inherent in African navigators' command of aquatic environments provided the infrastructure for fledgling Portuguese enterprises overseas. During the early decades of the gold trade, captains paid free canoemen in goods to transport articles of trade from São Jorge da Mina Castle to awaiting vessels miles offshore. Local canoemen also conducted small-scale trade with European mariners outside the dictates of Portugal's mercantile trade. As laborers identified by their navigational dexterity and fierce autonomy, canoemen leveraged their expertise to advance their own private commercial desires. One trader noted, "It was customary for Mina fishermen [canoemen] to go out in their canoes and contact ships from Portugal before they reached the castle. Out at sea they conducted private trade to the detriment of the crown." A 1529 *regimento* (royal law) attempted to curb such transactions, though there is little evidence it was successful.[21]

Portuguese merchants and overseas representatives of the crown continued to rely on the expertise of West African seafarers as their imperial ambitions grew. This could, at times, take on the form of fulsome admiration for African maritime contributions. Astonished by the navigating and swimming prowess of local populations on the Mina Coast, Portuguese visitors imagined Africans and their descendants as preternaturally disposed to maritime life and labor. As Alvise da Cadamosto put it, "From this I conclude that the blacks of that coast are the greatest swimmers which there are in the world." Marked by Portuguese captains as distinguished seamen and swimmers on the West African coast, Africans soon began to populate vessels traveling all over the globe. As Portuguese navigators stretched the realm of their trade and settlement west across the Atlantic to Brazil and east toward India, China, and Japan at the end of the fifteenth century, they drew on an available pool of African seafarers to form an integral part of the labor force on such deepwater journeys. Vasco da Gama's voyage to India in 1498 was home to one enslaved servant of the pilot, João de Coimbra, who escaped the vessel when it anchored in East Africa. In 1511, a slave ship that traveled to Brazil from Africa recorded employing two Black seamen, one free and one enslaved. By 1578, enslaved

21. David Birmingham, "The Regimento da Mina," *Transactions of the Historical Society of Ghana,* XI (1970), 7, quoted in Gutkind, "Canoemen of the Gold Coast (Ghana)," *Cahiers d'études africaines,* XXIX (1989), 344.

FIGURE 2. *Detail of the arrival of the Portuguese in Japan, painted for a Namban Byobu–style screen. Sixteenth century. Afro-Portuguese mariners at work on the masts of a ship traveling to a Japanese port. Porto, Museu Nacional Soares Dos Reis (Art Museum) (Photo by DeAgostini/Getty Images)*

mariners were acting as Portuguese translators in China, as well as shipboard servants and nurses. As Japanese painted screens from the period suggest, they numerically dominated sea crews arriving in Asian ports.[22]

Throughout the early years of colonization, African and Black seafarers remained crucial to broader Portuguese imperial ambitions. In 1600, a British administrator noted that African sailors were commonplace throughout the Portuguese maritime empire, observing, "The Portugals send yearly eight ships to the great empire of Prester John [Ethiopia], which also furnishes

22. As Cadamosto argued, "The blacks of that coast are the greatest swimmers which there are in the world." See Newitt, *Portuguese in West Africa,* 69; see also Kevin Dawson, *The Undercurrents of Power: Aquatic Culture in the African Diaspora* (Philadelphia, 2018),

them with many sailors." The ships traveling between India and Lisbon also frequently employed enslaved and free African sailors. This phenomenon was at least partly a question of labor supply. In the sixteenth and seventeenth centuries, Portugal faced a continuing dearth of seasoned sailors to man their vessels, with a 1620 census estimating that only 6,260 "able-bodied" seamen inhabited the country.[23]

The labor required for maritime empire building was a perilous business. Portuguese sailors were reluctant to serve on royal vessels traveling to Goa, in large part because of the route's reputation for deadliness. Royal vessels also had a penchant for providing insufficient provisions and withholding wages on round-trip journeys, which could take anywhere from eighteen months to five years. Often Portuguese seamen perished on the return leg of a round-trip voyage, requiring *naus da Índia* (Indiamen) to procure enslaved sailors when anchored in Mozambique. In 1712, officials at the Casa da Índia stressed sea vessels' reliance on African labor, noting that many returning ships would not have completed their voyages "but for the continual labour of the Negro slaves in them." In a similar vein, the viceroy of India explained in 1738 that, on the naus da Índia, "All the seagoing personnel now in Goa, including officers, sailors, gunners, pages and grummets, scarcely amount (excluding the sick) to 120 men, which is just about the number required to man a single homeward-bound Indiaman." During the monsoon seasons, "no Kaffirs have come from Moçambique and there is a shortage of them here ashore, so that they will not be available to sail as deck-hands to do the hard work as they usually do." There is scant surviving information about the quotidian experiences of enslaved mariners laboring on Indiamen routes, though anecdotal evidence suggests that African sailors acted as helmsmen and performed menial tasks such as operating pumps during storms. As a

---

11, 15; Hall, "Role of Cape Verde Islanders," 192; Alexander Marchant, *Do escambo à escravidão: As relações econômicas de portugueses e índios na colonização do Brasil, 1500–1580* (São Paulo, 1980), 24. Several dozen Indian and African servants accompanied Gonçalo Teixeira Correa to China in 1630. See Don J. Wyatt, *The Blacks of Premodern China* (Philadelphia, 2009), 41; Timothy Brook, *Vermeer's Hat: The Seventeenth Century and the Dawn of the Global World* (London, 2007), 103; Kenneth David Jackson, *Sing without Shame: Oral Traditions in Indo-Portuguese Creole Verse* (Amsterdam, 1990), xi; Kano Naizen, "Namban byobu" (1593–1603), Museu nacional de arte antiga, Lisbon.

23. Mar. 10, 1600, London, *Calendar of State Papers,* Colonial Series, *East Indies: China and Japan,* II, *1513–1616,* Great Britain, Public Record Office, ed. Noël Sainsbury et al. (London, 1862), 104.

sign of the often dire conditions for mariners on vessels destined for India, when Dutch corsairs took the *Santiago* in 1602, the enslaved mariners aboard requested that the Dutch take them on their ship to serve, refusing to remain on the Portuguese vessel.[24]

The skilled, multilingual enslaved seamen who toiled on Portuguese ships navigating to Asia disrupt our familiar images of the nature and mechanisms of early modern African slaving. Such men were omnipresent features across the urban, maritime-oriented nodes of the Portuguese empire, embodying a subaltern cosmopolitanism upon which Portugal's global commercial ambitions increasingly depended. In Asia, the Americas, and Africa, enslaved and freed seamen's cosmopolitanism was driven by the dual imperatives of imperial expansion and Atlantic slaving. Because of their entanglement in these projects, however, mariners on Portuguese vessels were subject to serial dislocation, disconnection, removal, and forced mobility. As a slave labor regime emerged and expanded in coastal Bahia, the number of captive cosmopolitans in Portugal's Atlantic orbit would continue to climb over the seventeenth and eighteenth centuries.[25]

A WATERBORNE IMPERIAL FRONTIER

While enterprising Portuguese merchants assisted by African maritime brokers infiltrated circuits of trade in Asia and Africa, on the other side of the Atlantic, a royally sponsored fleet commanded by Amerigo Vespucci in 1501 made landfall in what would become the colony of Bahia. Irregularly punctuated by serene inlets and bays, Brazil's northeastern coastline featured a bay measuring 50 kilometers wide and occupying an area of 750 square kilometers that came to be named by settlers as Baía de Todos os Santos, or the Bay of All Saints. It was there that ambitions for the new colony of Brazil were initially concentrated. Surrounding these lands were rolling hills and bluffs (*tabuleiros*) lush with vegetation. Early arrivals to the Portuguese colony would have discovered nearly 100 islands, including the largest of all,

24. Boxer, *Portuguese Seaborne Empire,* 114, 211–215; A. J. R. Russell-Wood, *The Portuguese Empire, 1415–1808: A World on the Move* (Baltimore, 1998), 38; Geoffrey Allen and David Allen, *The Guns of Sacramento* (London, 1978), 9, 20–21, 26; Stefan Halikowski Smith, *Creolization and Diaspora in the Portuguese Indies: The Social World of Ayutthaya, 1640–1720* (Leiden, 2011), 19.

25. Mariana Candido, *An African Slaving Port and the Atlantic World: Benguela and Its Hinterland* (New York, 2013), 12–13; Heywood and Thornton, *Central Africans,* 5–7.

Itaparica, located on the southern side at the harbor's mouth. The shoreline within the Bay of All Saints was interspersed with the mouths of numerous rivers and creeks, including the Paraguaçu, Jaguaripe, and Subaé, connecting the Atlantic to a riverine network that stretched 600 kilometers into the interior. In the centuries that followed Portuguese contact, this landscape provided not only a wide variety of natural maritime resources that would facilitate intensive sugar cultivation by the *senhores de engenho* (sugar plantation owners) but also a range of aquatic subsistence strategies that fed the area's growing population of enslaved and free poor.[26]

Lacking in precious metals that enticed merchants elsewhere, the city of Salvador was founded as a precarious settlement to initiate small-scale trade in exotic brazilwood (*pau Brasil*). Absent the same densely populated, trade-oriented regions the Portuguese had found in India and West Africa, their colonization of the Bay of All Saints represented a major evolution in strategy. Instead of establishing trading networks for the exclusive purpose of commerce in Bahia, the crown encouraged large-scale agricultural enterprise conducted by a permanent class of settlers. In the centuries that followed the area's discovery, this water-oriented landscape would become home to widespread sugar cultivation by enslaved Africans at the behest of elite senhores de engenho.[27]

The salience of Portuguese seafaring expertise—a body of knowledge indebted to African maritime labor—was far from immaterial to this endeavor. The Portuguese seaborne empire depended on both the development of navigable maritime routes and the building of sailing vessels that could traverse both the deep waters of the open sea and the shallow waters close to land.[28]

26. B. J. Barickman, *A Bahian Counterpoint: Sugar, Tobacco, Cassava, and Slavery in the Recôncavo, 1780–1860* (Stanford, Calif., 1998), 9; A. J. R. Russell-Wood, "Ports of Colonial Brazil," in Franklin W. Knight and Peggy K. Liss, eds., *Atlantic Port Cities: Economy, Culture, and Society in the Atlantic World* (Knoxville, Tenn., 1991), 196; Luís Henrique Dias Tavares, *História da Bahia,* 10th ed. (Salvador, Brazil, 2001), 46.

27. Boxer, *Portuguese Seaborne Empire,* 25–33; José Damião Rodrigues, "Patterns of Settlement and Religious Imperial Agents in the Portuguese Empire," in Paul Christopher Manuel, Alynna Lyon, and Clyde Wilcox, eds., *Religion and Politics in a Global Society: Comparative Perspectives from the Portuguese Speaking World* (Plymouth, U.K., 2012), 15–32, esp. 15–16.

28. In the beginning of the fifteenth century, the Portuguese became the first to employ the three-masted ship. Commonly, vessels during this period featured one large, square sail to harness wind power, accompanied by two smaller square sails on the foremast and bowsprit to steer the ship. These three-masted ships required fewer crew members to navigate, necessitating few provisions, which made long-distance voyages more feasible. Portuguese

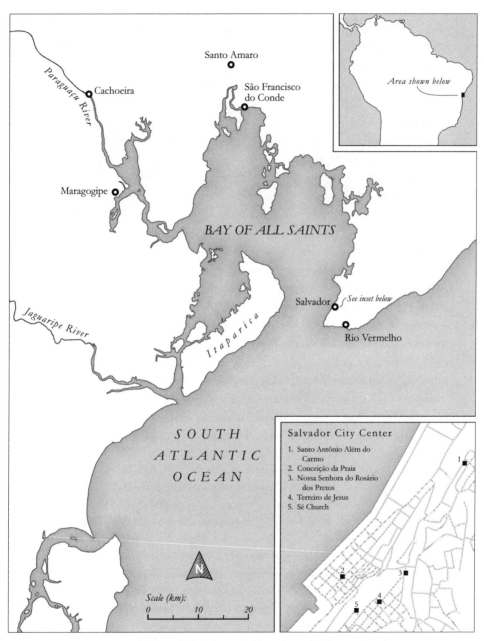

MAP 1. *The Bay of All Saints—Bahia. Drawn by Jim DeGrand*

In addition to improvements in ship technology, mastery of the South Atlantic required knowledge of the currents and wind patterns that governed that body of water.[29] Mastery of oceanic currents, winds, and weather structured new settlements in Brazil as advantageous waterways determined patterns of trade and colonization in the newly forming South Atlantic zone.

From the founding of the colony onward, Brazil's Black population was an important—and frequently overlooked—part of the development of such coastal settlements. And nowhere was this more the case than in Salvador da Bahia, a city that would eventually become one of the most populous, wealthiest, and busiest ports in the Atlantic world. South Atlantic trade was the lifeblood of the city. Facilitated by the maritime environment in which the port was situated, oceanic movement and commerce shaped its built environment, the composition of the population, and the productive lives of its residents. Enslaved and free residents pioneered strategies of mobility, survival, and empowerment on the waterborne frontier of the Portuguese empire, and Africans and their descendants experimented with and collected knowledge about the natural world in which they lived. They acquired a deep understanding of local Bahian geography, its currents and winds, while pioneering routes of navigation within the bay, its tributaries, and the larger Atlantic littoral. Their lives in Bahia, as in West Africa, came to rely on both fresh and saltwater geographies. Drawing on environmental expertise gleaned from the many rivers, lagoons, and estuaries that comprised the landscapes of their homelands, enslaved inhabitants of colonial Brazil developed techniques for extracting valuable ecological resources from their maritime milieu.[30]

---

navigators also discovered how to exploit the circular wind systems of the eastern Atlantic—which propelled sailing vessels vast distances from shorelines—and were the first to employ the astrolabe to discern latitude south of the equator by using the sun as a reference point. See N. A. M. Rodger, "Atlantic Seafaring," in Nicholas Canny and Philip D. Morgan, eds., *The Oxford Handbook of the Atlantic World: 1450–1850* (Oxford, 2011), 73–74.

29. Because sailing windward was extremely dangerous in early vessels, emerging sea routes worked with, not against, the wind patterns that dominated the Atlantic. Currents in the South Atlantic circled counterclockwise from the Central African coast, across the Atlantic, and south along the South American coastline. These features propelled Portuguese vessels to navigational routes that favored sea travel along the South American coast to the Río de La Plata, as well as circular routes between West Africa and the northeast of what was to become the colony of Brazil (ibid.).

30. Victor Bulmer-Thomas, John H. Coatsworth, and Roberto Cortés Conde, eds., *The Cambridge Economic History of Latin America*, I, *The Colonial Era and the Short Nineteenth Century* (Cambridge, 2006), 156; Dawson, *Undercurrents of Power*, 2.

In 1549, forty-eight years after European navigators first explored the Bay of All Saints, Salvador da Bahia was established as the colonial capital of Brazil. Located on a rocky outcrop on the northern side of the bay, the city served as the seat of the governor-general of Brazil and quickly became one of the most active commercial ports in the Portuguese empire. The crown established an *alfândega,* or customhouse, to extract wealth from any taxable commerce moving through the coastal settlement. Royal ministers had hoped to reap profits from the colonial outpost by endowing twelve *sesmarias,* or land grants, to noblemen as proprietary captaincies in 1533, with the expectation that they would improve the land and begin extracting valuable natural resources. This strategy did not succeed. The largest export during the first half of the sixteenth century remained brazilwood, which failed to raise sufficient profits in tax revenue to cover the struggling colony's expenditures in salaries and defense.[31]

During the same period, however, a number of self-directed noblemen introduced sugar cuttings to the three areas of Portuguese settlement on the South American coast: São Vicente, Pernambuco, and the Bay of All Saints. Appropriated from established sugar plantation colonies in the Atlantic islands of Madeira and São Tomé, these cuttings eventually flourished in Pernambuco and then Bahia.[32] As explosive slave rebellions rocked São Tomé in 1595, incinerating most of the island's sugar-processing infrastructure, senhores de engenho looked to reestablish lucrative cane fields elsewhere. In the following hundred years, Portuguese sugar mill owners located in the Recôncavo—the primary sugar-producing region in Bahia—solidified their dominance in the commodity's production for newly expanding European markets.

Sugar did not harvest or refine itself, however. It required extensive, backbreaking, dangerous labor. Though not an immediate nor inevitable development, the consolidation of a Bahian slave trade oriented toward the West African coast depended on a number of factors. Enslaved indigenous Tupí-Guaraní-speaking laborers, who had dominated the landscape of Bahian cane fields in the first one hundred years of settlement, were battered by

31. Metcalf, *Go-Betweens and the Colonization of Brazil,* 76–78; Stuart B. Schwartz, *Sovereignty and Society in Colonial Brazil: The High Court of Bahia and Its Judges, 1609–1751* (Berkeley, Calif., 1973), 97.

32. Pernambuco amassed sixty-six sugar mills by the 1580s, whereas Bahia gained around forty mills during the same period. See Schwartz, *Sugar Plantations,* 17–18.

European disease and high mortality rates.[33] The subsequent economic pressures caused by the lack of an easily controlled labor force induced slaving merchants to reorient coastal trading routes they had pioneered between polities on the West African coast toward the Americas. In turn, the Portuguese crown further incentivized this new strategy, implementing a tax exemption in 1554 for the building of sugar mills and subsequently decreasing importation taxes to one-third the normal rate for any mill owner who trafficked 120 enslaved Africans to Brazil.[34]

Transatlantic slave trading linked the burgeoning ports of West and West Central Africa with the still-embryonic plantation settlements of northeastern Brazil, forming the backbone of the South Atlantic system. To strengthen this new transatlantic economic orientation against Dutch piracy and to satisfy the Portuguese crown's wish to reap greater profits from mercantile trade, an armed Brazilian fleet system emerged in 1649 to protect commercial vessels traveling from the colony to the metropole. The Portuguese crown also created a chartered company, the Companhia Geral do Comércio do Brasil, to offer military protection to merchant fleets in exchange for a monopoly on the trade of Portuguese wine, flour, olive oil, and codfish to the colonies.[35]

In the century following its establishment in 1549, the settlement of Bahia had evolved from a constellation of rustic trading outposts to a sprawling complex of sugar plantations reaching along rivers and streams on the Bay of All Saints into the interior. Over the course of the sixteenth century, sugar surged to become Brazil's most important export, a position it would hold

33. In addition, the Catholic Church's increasingly paternalistic protection of indigenous vassals envisioned them as potential converts to Christianity and as settled, rural peasants as opposed to chattel slaves. A series of local revolts involving indigenous agricultural hands pressed into labor left plantation proprietors in search of alternative sources of field hands—without which sugar cultivation was impossible. See Alida C. Metcalf, "The Entradas of Bahia of the Sixteenth Century," *Americas*, LXI (2005), 373–400; Metcalf, *Go-Betweens and the Colonization of Brazil*, 195; Schwartz, *Sugar Plantations*, 28–50.

34. Winning the *asiento*, or monopoly contract, to provide Spanish American colonies with enslaved Africans between 1594 and 1640 during the unification of the Portuguese and Spanish crowns further stimulated transatlantic traffic from the central African slaving ports of São Salvador (the capital of Kongo) and Luanda (a coastal entrepôt in the Ndongo-dominated territory that would become Angola, first contacted in 1483). See Alencastro, *Trade in the Living*, trans. Adams and Alencastro, 28; Linda Heywood, *Njinga of Angola: Africa's Warrior Queen* (Cambridge, Mass., 2017), 25–34.

35. Boxer, *Portuguese Seaborne Empire*, 222–224.

until the middle of the nineteenth century. The crop's cultivation spurred not only intensive imperial expansion but an unquenchable thirst for enslaved Africans to plant, harvest, process, and transport cane. A reliance on enslaved labor seeped into every ensuing extractive and agricultural venture in the expansive American colony: sprawling tobacco plantations that emerged in the early seventeenth century, remote gold and diamond mines following discoveries in the interior in 1692, and expansive cattle ranches and small farms. Even as Bahia's sugar economy declined temporarily in 1680, by the dawn of the seventeenth century, one thing was clear: Portuguese empire and African slavery went hand in hand.[36]

BLACK BAHIA'S AQUATIC PROVISIONING GROUNDS

Over the course of the seventeenth and eighteenth centuries, the ebb and flow of Brazil's sugar plantation economy continued to propel slaving vessels toward the West African coast. Despite the serial dislocations of the transatlantic slave trade, those who were forcibly resettled on the plantations of Bahia utilized waterborne environments to achieve a range of objectives. African people's harnessing of aquatic resources blunted the ravages of enslavement while providing a space for communal and laboring autonomy. Paradoxically, however, the Black maritime geographies forged by enslaved people's mobility also fostered the rapid development of Salvador's plantation economy. Just as Portuguese merchants and sea captains had exploited the environmental knowledge of seafarers in West Africa, in Bahia the maritime acumen of Africans and their descendants became a cornerstone of imperial expansion. In Portugal's most important Brazilian colony, the maritime forces shaped the terrestrial, and vice versa.

On arrival in Bahia, enslaved Africans might have glimpsed miles of sandy beaches, crystalline blue waters, a landscape dotted with palm trees, and a series of forts (each named for a Catholic saint) that were tasked with defending the city from naval attacks. The enslaved men, women, and children from West Africa who disembarked in the harbor of Salvador were emaciated, disoriented, and socially alienated. But they found themselves in the midst of a city defined by a vibrant waterscape that was, in many ways, as significant as

36. Schwartz, *Sugar Plantations*, 160. Most sugar engenhos were located on the northern shores of the Bay of All Saints; in the open lands north and west from the Paraguaçu River, near Cachoeira, planters began to cultivate tobacco for export at a more moderate scale. See Barickman, *A Bahian Counterpoint*, 13; Schwartz, *Sugar Plantations*, 163.

its expanding rural environs. Indeed, these two geographies were intimately connected in the lives, practices, and work of the city's enslaved inhabitants.[37]

Facing the harsh realities of their own survival, newly arrived enslaved and free people pioneered efforts to capitalize on this oceanic-oriented environment and developed a number of subsistence strategies within and around the bay.[38] This environment afforded enslaved arrivals the opportunity to supplement the meager provisions provided by slaveholders with protein-rich aquatic resources, including fish, shrimp, crab, oyster, and whale flesh, extracted through methods they themselves had devised. The waterfront in Salvador continued to be one of the most important sites of commodity and food production in the colony, a setting of community, and a locus of a fragile Black autonomy.

Indeed, because many of the enslaved men and women disembarked in colonial Bahia were from West Africa, it is likely that at least a portion of the displaced Africans who came to populate the city encountered an environment similar to the many rivers, lagoons, and estuaries that defined the coastal environs of their homelands. Relying on processes of translation, re-creation, adaptation, and invention within the spaces of the Bay of All Saints, Bahia's Black population wove together the maritime and the terrestrial through exploration, navigation, extraction, and, ultimately, mastery. Like enslaved Africans who independently converted marginal lands on sugar plantations into small garden plots or provisioning grounds, enslaved individuals living and working near bodies of water generated a multitude of innovative techniques for gathering precious resources.[39]

As the transatlantic trade in slaves drove Salvador's economic and population growth, a two-way commercial exchange between Salvador da Bahia and

37. APEB, Seção de Arquivo Colonial Provincial, maço 132, Registro de correspondência expedida do Senado da Câmara de Salvador para o rei, ano 1742–1822, 1757, "Relação topográfica da cidade da Salvador Bahia de Todos os Santos, Antônio Jozé de Fonseca Lemos."

38. This analysis owes much to the work of Emmanuel Kwaku Akyeampong, whose study of the increasing maritime orientation of the Anlo people of West Africa during the same period animated my theorization of enslaved people's interactions with the aquatic environment of Salvador and its surroundings. See Akyeampong, *Between the Sea and the Lagoon: An Eco-social History of the Anlo of Southeastern Ghana, c. 1850 to Recent Times,* Western African Studies (Athens, Ohio, 2001).

39. Ben Vinson III and Herbert S. Klein, *African Slavery in Latin America and the Caribbean* (Oxford, 2007), 155. For more on the interwoven nature of maritime and land-based activities in the Black Atlantic, see Dawson, *Undercurrents of Power,* 2.

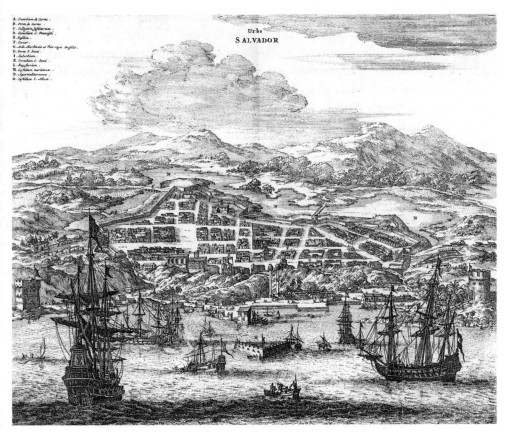

FIGURE 3. *"Urbs Salvador." In Arnoldus Montanus,* De Nieuwe en onbekende
Weereld: of Beschryving van America en 't zuid-land . . . *(*The New and Known World;
or, Description of America and the Southland . . .) *(Amsterdam, 1671). A depiction of
the Bay of All Saints and the city of Salvador da Bahia, highlighting the dominance of
commercial sailing vessels in the port. Retrieved from the Library of Congress*

the Bight of Benin was consolidated by the end of the seventeenth century,
bypassing metropolitan influence and the "triangular" organization of slaving
commerce that characterized the traffic of other empires. Salvador's status as
the busiest port in the South Atlantic in large part stemmed from the bay's
accessibility. As visitor François sieur Froger noted, it was "one of the largest, finest, and most convenient" harbors in the world. William Dampier, an
English captain, marveled that the harbor was "full of Ships" and was a place
defined by its integration into an Atlantic commerce in commodities. Salvador
was "a Place of great Trade" where "small Vessels . . . carry out from hence

Rum, Sugar, the Cotton-cloaths of St. Iago, Beads, etc. and bring in Return, Gold, Ivory, and Slaves; making very good Returns."[40]

Facilitating the creation of this increasingly dynamic commercial world was, once again, African maritime labor. Following the 1550 creation of a royal shipyard in Bahia, which initially constructed smaller, more rudimentary merchant vessels, Salvador's shipbuilding operations expanded and acquired the capacity to build larger ships for trade, as well as warships and naus da Índia for the Asian trade. Portuguese master artisans—including carpenters, coopers, caulkers, tinsmiths, saddlers, pulley makers and sailmakers—constructed vessels in the shipyards. But, as in all dimensions of maritime life and labor in Bahia, people of African descent soon became integral to its operation. Throughout the seventeenth and eighteenth centuries, the crown owned a number of slaves employed in the royal shipyard (Ribeira das Naus). There, master artisans trained the men in carpentry, caulking, and the operation of sawmills; other workers were *escravos de ganho*, or skilled, wage-earning slaves hired from local colonial administrators. By the beginning of the eighteenth century, Salvador was already home to a large cohort of enslaved laborers trained in various trades by their owners, including the key skills required to keep sailing vessels operational. Such laborers were employed with the crown's approval to expedite ship construction in the absence of a sufficient number of white, metropolitan-trained artisans. In the sixteenth century, Salvador's shipyard operated with sixteen enslaved laborers, but by the eighteenth century, there might have been six hundred slaves working in Bahia's various shipyards. The crown conserved funds by eschewing free laborers and hiring enslaved ones, who worked for cheaper wages; sometimes, their owners complained, the shipyard avoided paying them altogether. Atlantic trade and transportation would become the way of life for the majority of the city's population: those who directly engaged in these pursuits, such as

---

40. [François] sieur Froger, *A Relation of a Voyage Made in the Years 1695, 1696, 1697, on the Coasts of Africa, Streights of Magellan, Brasil, Cayenna, and the Antilles, by a Squadron of French Men of War, under the Command of M. de Gennes* (London, 1698), 108; William Dampier, *A Collection of Voyages, in Four Volumes*, III, *A Voyage round the World* (London, 1729), 34, 39. The triangular trade refers to the three legs of slaving journeys: the first, from various ports of Europe to the African coast; the second, from Africa to the Americas; and the third, the return journey. See Alencastro, *Trade in the Living*, trans. Adams and Alencastro, 20–22; Pierre Verger, *Trade Relations between the Bight of Benin and Bahia from the 17th to 19th Century*, [trans. Evelyn Crawford] (Ibadan, Nigeria, 1976), 11; James Walvin, *Crossings: Africa, the Americas, and the Atlantic Slave Trade* (London, 2013), 65.

merchants and ship captains, as well as those who indirectly enabled ocean travel, such as sailmakers, stevedores, and ironsmiths.[41]

In addition to constructing maritime vessels, African and creole laborers were crucial in connecting oceanic trade to Salvador's agricultural hinterland. In 1612, a visitor to the Recôncavo named Diogo de Campos Moreno asserted, "All the activity of this people is by water." Many sugar plantation proprietors positioned their estates close to streams, rivers, or seashores to harness water power for the running of their mills and to more easily transport their provisions and crops to Salvador by watercraft. Small vessels including boats (*saveiros*), canoes, and rafts (*jangadas*) connected plantations around the bay to Salvador. As early as 1587, Portuguese colonist Gabriel Soares de Sousa observed that every plantation in the Recôncavo possessed at least four vessels to convey its goods to the Atlantic entrepôt of Salvador. Well-capitalized planters found they could more easily control transportation costs by creating small fleets of boats. They also calculated that giving a handful of bondsmen greater autonomy by employing them as boatmen to navigate vessels on the many rivers flowing into the Bay of All Saints was a risk worth the reward. As was the situation for other enslaved artisans, the monetary value of these watermen remained higher than that of enslaved field hands on the same estate.[42]

Over time, Bahian elites' transportation infrastructure for moving plantation commodities to market became a central sinew of Black maritime life and culture in the region. It is unclear precisely when Africans and creoles

41. Russell-Wood, "Ports of Colonial Brazil," in Knight and Liss, eds., *Atlantic Port Cities*, 205, 206; Boxer, *Portuguese Seaborne Empire*, 211; AHU, CU, Bahia, caixa 26, documento 2406, June 8, 1726, "Carta de conde de Sabugosa ao rei"; José Roberto do Amaral Lapa, *A Bahia e a Carreira da Índia* (São Paulo, 1968), 51–55, 60, 113. Drawing on locally produced resources, such as Brazilian hardwoods, cotton for sails, embira and piassava fibers for making cordage, and resin for tar, master shipbuilders from Portugal (*patrão mors*) oversaw the construction of an estimated forty-five vessels during the colonial period (ibid., 112). Dampier noted, "All these Trades-men buy *Negroes*, and train them up to their several Employments, which is a great Help to them; and they having so frequent Trade to *Angola*, and other Parts of *Guinea*, they have a constant Supply of Blacks both for their Plantations and Town" (*Collection*, 42).

42. Schwartz, *Sugar Plantations*, 78, 150–151, 220. Dampier described enslaved labor as essential for conveying goods from the port into the city: "These Slaves are very useful in this Place for Carriage, as Porters; for as here is a great Trade by Sea, and the Landing-place is at the Foot of a Hill, too steep for drawing with Carts, so there is great need of Slaves to carry Goods up into the Town. . . . But the Merchants have also the Convenience of a great Crane that goes with Ropes or Pullies, one End of which goes up while the other goes down"

(both enslaved and free) became the dominant labor force in this enterprise and were given primary responsibility for powering and navigating such small watercraft. In the mid-sixteenth century, many of the watermen who plied the coasts of the northeastern region of Brazil were indigenous Tupinambá people who inhabited the region when Portuguese settlers arrived. Traversing the open sea close to the littoral, Tupinambá fishermen utilized a vessel that the Portuguese dubbed the jangada but indigenous watermen called *piperis*. The jangada was composed of "five or six round logs, thicker than the arm of a man, and tied with twisted vines (Lianas)." Indigenous navigators who operated these vessels would sit "in these rafts, with their legs extended to direct them to where they want to go with a flattened piece of wood serving as a paddle. As this piperis boat is only one foot long and two feet wide, and poorly resist storms and can barely hold a man."[43]

By the first quarter of the eighteenth century, the crown had increasingly turned to enslaved watermen to navigate these crafts, employing them to make passages from the interior to Salvador while extracting fees for the service. One pastor in 1725 stated that he relied on canoes and jangadas to transport him from the rural settlement where he resided in Santo Amaro da Pitanga to the parishes where he administered sacraments. The advantages of the crude craft were its light weight and maneuverability, two characteristics that made it ideal for traversing the waters around the Bay of All Saints. The vessels also did not take on water and were capable of voyages of several hundred miles along coastal or riverine waters. Such boats were also important for coastal deepwater fishing activities, and many jangada navigators alternated between selling fish and providing passage.[44]

(Dampier, *Collection*, 42). By the end of the seventeenth century, a single plantation generally employed several enslaved boatmen and a helmsman to navigate barges of sugarcane from the property to the mill. See André João Antonil, *Brazil at the Dawn of the Eighteenth Century*, trans. Timothy J. Coates (Dartmouth, Mass., 2012), 62.

43. In the following centuries, the form of the jangada evolved, eventually incorporating technologies derived from European sailing vessels, including sails, a crude anchor made of a stone and connected to a cord, a steering paddle, and a seat for the navigator. Though the basic construction method of lashing together several logs of light wood remained, the size of the jangada also grew to accommodate two or three men. See Luiz Geraldo Silva, *A faina, a festa e o rito: Uma etografia histórica sobre as gentes do mar (sécs. XVII ao XIX)* (São Paulo, 2001), 50–52.

44. João Rodrigues de Figueiredo estimated that he expended 30$000 réis annually on transportation this way (AHU, CU, Bahia, caixa 19, documento 1683, May 2, 1724, "Consulta do Conselho Ultramarino sobre a petição feito pelo vigário da igreja matriz de Santa Amaro

FIGURE 4. *A fishing canoe traverses waters in Pernambuco. In Henry Koster,*
Travels in Brazil *(London, 1816), facing p. 175.* © *John Carter Brown Library*

Canoes were vital to all forms of colonial communication, transportation, and passenger travel in Bahia. During the colonial period, two distinct kinds of canoes plied Brazilian seas and rivers: one for shallow waters, manned by one waterman and navigated by steering pole, and one for deepwater navigation, propelled by multiple paddlers. In Olinda, observers noted the prevalence of the first type: "The canoes used here are of a different form of those constructed for deep water. They are navigated almost entirely by the aid of setting-poles. The canoeiros are generally large and powerful negroes, each one of whom navigates his own canoe singly." Deceptively simple canoes, crafted out of a single tree trunk, required considerable ingenuity to build. Watermen of African descent deployed dugout canoes both for riverine transportation and subsistence fishing.[45]

de Pitanga João Rodrigues de Figueiredo"). On the boats' capabilities, see James Henderson, *A History of the Brazil: Comprising Its Geography, Commerce, Colonization, Aboriginal Inhabitants, Etc. Etc. Etc.* (London, 1821), 357–358; Dampier, *Collection*, 32.

45. Daniel P. Kidder, *Sketches of Residence and Travels in Brazil, Embracing Historical and Geographical Notices of the Empire and Its Several Provinces*, II (Philadelphia, 1845),

In the flourishing commercial atmosphere of Salvador, small vessels piloted by enslaved and free Black watermen were vital to the local navigation, anchorage, and loading of long-distance sailing vessels. French mariner François sieur Froger wrote that, upon arriving at the Bay of All Saints in 1697, his ship was met "all along the Coast a great Number of Barks, and the Negro's Piperies, as they are called, being no other than three or four pieces of Wood made fast together, whereon two Men go out a fishing to the extent of two Leagues." The pilots of these vessels, being well acquainted with the geography of the port, were desirable navigators to bring larger vessels into the mouth of the bay and to anchor. The pilot aboard Froger's vessel attempted to contract local jangada operators to navigate the ship, but they refused, "alledging, they were forbid to do it; but I believe it was because they would not leave their fishing." Eventually, Froger and his men contracted the captain of a small sailing vessel to steer his ship inside the bay. There, passengers and goods had to be ferried back and forth between ship and shore on smaller vessels. Again, most were navigated by men of African descent.[46]

Black mariners were also essential to extractive oceanic commerce in this period. By the early eighteenth century, commercial fishing and whaling conducted by enslaved people had become an important aspect of the urban economy. In 1730, the Bahia-born historian Sebastião da Rocha Pita noted the prevalence of fisheries devoted to the capture of the tropical black jack, or *xaréu*, between May and December, a fish he described as "always fat and delicious." Pita identified the staple as crucial to the "sustenance of slaves and poor people of Bahia." The labor-intensive process of harvesting xaréu began with giant nets cast over the ocean's surface by enslaved men and then hauled by fifty or sixty people to the fishing village of Itapuã, four leagues from Salvador. The owners of fishing boats, along with the proprietors of the *trapiches,* or coastal warehouses where the fish were stored, gained ample profit from their slaves' maritime labor, according to Pita. Local enslaved

---

153. Such vessels became more elaborate over time, and by the mid-nineteenth century most canoes in the Northeast were "not less than seven feet wide by about twenty-five in length . . . these canoes are worth from five to twelve hundred milreis each." Each canoe, navigated by three men, consisted of "a short deck at each end, forming beneath, what I will call the fore and after cabins, midships being entirely open for cargo. This canoe carried an immense triangular sail and a jib, and had on each side an *embono,* or buoy, made of two large trunks of the jangada wood fastened together, and lashed to the upper edge to prevent capsizing" (ibid., 159–160).

46. Froger, *A Relation,* 102–103.

watermen's self-directed labor required little oversight, as they conducted their aquatic duties independently from their owners. Whaling operations also departed from the Bay of All Saints. During the harvesting season, William Dampier observed, the mammals "are very thick on this Coast. They come in also into the Harbours and inland Lakes, where the Seamen go out and kill them. The Fat of them is boiled to Oil; the Lean is eaten by the Slaves and poor People: And I was told by one that had frequently eaten of it, that the Flesh was very sweet and wholsome." The profitability of whaling quickly piqued the interest of the Portuguese crown, which taxed these enterprises as a means of expanding colonial revenue streams.[47]

Black maritime laborers also sailed far beyond the immediate surrounds of Salvador. By the end of the seventeenth century, African and creole seamen had become vital to the cabotage, or coastal trade. As Dampier observed, "The small Craft that belong to this Town are chiefly imployed in carrying *European* Goods from *Bahia,* the Center of the *Brasilian* Trade, to the other Places on this Coast; bringing back hither Sugar, Tobacco, etc. They are sailed chiefly with Negro-Slaves." At all levels of commodity transportation, Black maritime labor had become fundamental. The diverse uses to which planters, captains, and other Bahian residents put Black watermen's labor denoted the profound flexibility of enslavement. Bondage often demanded, rather than prohibited, extreme mobility in the service of productive and commercial ventures in and around Salvador. For their part, bondspeople began to leverage coercive movement to their benefit, pioneering a number of strategies of craft building, aquatic extraction, and local navigation that dominated Bahia's waterscapes in the early colonial period.[48]

A "NEW GUINEA" IN BAHIA

By the beginning of the eighteenth century, the growth of transatlantic slaving and Bahia's plantation-based economy had transformed the city of Salvador into a markedly African space. The continuous influx of ships housing hundreds of *boçais*, or "unacculturated" Africans unfamiliar with Portuguese language or Catholic worship, profoundly shaped the cultural landscape and political economy of the city. Though many enslaved men, women, and children inhabited Salvador only temporarily, some remained permanently.

47. Sebastião da Rocha Pita, *História da América Portuguesa* ([1730]; rpt. Rio de Janeiro, 1965), 32–33; Dampier, *Collection,* 39–40.

48. Dampier, *Collection,* 39.

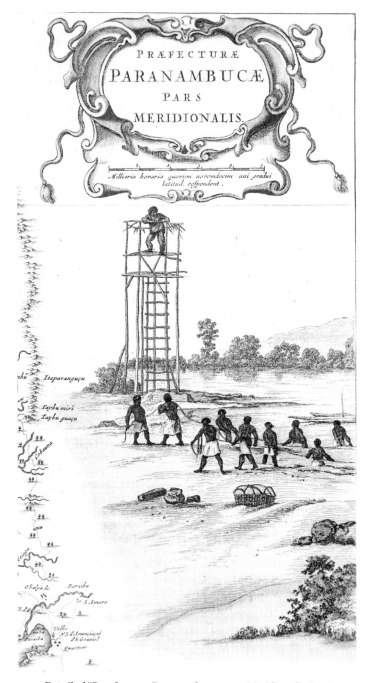

FIGURE 5. *Detail of "Praefecturae Paranambucae pars Meridionalis." In Joan Blaeu,*
Atlas maior, sive, Cosmographia Blaviana: Qua solum, salum, coelum, accuratissime
describuntur, *XI (Amsterdam, 1662), between 243 and 245. Black fishermen
(likely enslaved) fish by net in Pernambuco. D10:D12. Slaveryimages.org*

Slavery touched every aspect of urban life. Arrivals from the Old World were confronted by a disorienting proliferation of African languages, foods, music, and dance on the city's streets. One recent arrival insightfully remarked that Salvador resembled "a new Guinea."[49]

By the early 1700s, Salvador's status as a preeminent entrepôt for captive Africans was assured. The growth and Africanization of Salvador da Bahia reflected its status as a vital way station in an elaborate chain of human commodification and transatlantic enterprise that linked the hinterlands of West Africa to the shores of Brazil. Bahian slavers' demands for enslaved African labor were multiple. Though sugar plantations drove a significant degree of demand for captives, enslaved Africans were also highly prized by miners looking to exploit tributaries of gold that had been discovered in 1695. In the first decades of the eighteenth century, as miners rushed to the captaincy of Minas Gerais in search of gold, the price of slaves skyrocketed. Bahia was a key entrepôt for the thousands of enslaved Africans who eventually panned for gold and diamonds in the region's frigid mountain streams and riverbeds. The colony was also home to many of the private entrepreneurs who secured royally administered mining grants by demonstrating ownership of a sufficient number of enslaved laborers to exploit alluvial deposits. Overall, Bahian slavers sought to maintain a steady stream of African captives for a variety of purposes. In the second half of the seventeenth century, the Atlantic port received an average of approximately 4,660 enslaved Africans annually.[50]

By the dawn of the eighteenth century, slaving had become one of the city's most important commercial ventures, and Salvador was well on its way to becoming the second-largest slave-trading port of disembarkation in the Atlantic world. Until approximately 1750, it remained the busiest slave-trading center in the Portuguese colony of Brazil, when its merchant activity was surpassed only by Rio de Janeiro's trade to West Central Africa. In the 1790s,

49. Amédée François Frézier, *Relation du voyage de la mer du Sud aux côtes du Chily et du Perou, fait pendant les années 1712, 1713 et 1714* (Amsterdam, 1717), quoted in Verger, *Trade Relations,* [trans. Crawford], 69 n. 30.

50. Kathleen J. Higgins, *"Licentious Liberty" in a Brazilian Gold-Mining Region: Slavery, Gender, and Social Control in Eighteenth-Century Sabará, Minas Gerais* (University Park, Pa., 1999), 27–31, 33, 35–36; Miller, *Way of Death,* 282; Antonil, *Brazil at the Dawn of the Eighteenth Century,* trans. Coates, 112, 194. The domestic slave trade between Bahia and Minas Gerais as much as doubled the price paid per enslaved individual in the colony's northeast.

TABLE 1. *Growth of Bahia's Transatlantic Slave Trade, 1576–1875*

Years	Number of enslaved persons transported to Bahia from Africa
1576–1600	6,644
1601–1625	54,449
1626–1650	81,218
1651–1675	110,416
1676–1700	117,932
1701–1725	207,845
1726–1750	263,584
1751–1775	191,993
1776–1800	239,489
1801–1825	279,918
1826–1850	175,436
1851–1875	1,146
TOTAL	1,730,070

Source: *Voyages*, Estimates of the Trade,
http://www.slavevoyages.org/tast/database/index.faces.

Bahia's slave trade would surge once more, as slaving continued to increase in volume until the 1830s.[51]

Despite the growing importance of sugar production and precious metal mining for Bahian merchants, not all captive Africans arrived to be immediately removed to Brazil's hinterlands. Many came to shape the social and economic fabric of Salvador da Bahia itself. Although estimates of Salvador's population were sporadic and often formed through casual observance rather than precise calculation, they demonstrate that Africans and their descendants comprised a sizable proportion of the city's residents in the colonial period—and, frequently, they encompassed a majority.[52]

51. David Eltis and David Richardson, "A New Assessment of the Transatlantic Slave Trade," in Eltis and Richardson, eds., *Extending the Frontiers: Essays on the New Transatlantic Slave Trade Database* (New Haven, Conn., 2008), 1–62, esp. 45; Estimates of the Trade, *Voyages*, http://www.slavevoyages.org/tast/database/index.faces.

52. Most population estimates for the early colonial period are unreliable. But several early attempts at counting the population include one estimate from 1584 that tallied 3,000 Portuguese, 8,000 indigenous residents, and 4,000 enslaved individuals, whereas in 1714 one observer argued that 19 of 20 of Salvador's residents were enslaved. In 1759, José Antônio Caldas estimated half of the population was enslaved, out of 40,000 residents. By 1775, the census listed 33,635 inhabitants of the city spread among 7,345 households. Among this

Enslaved adolescents, for instance, would have been highly sought after in the maritime occupations that animated the economic life of the city, particularly because of their presumed facility in learning specialized skills. But in general, recently arrived Africans furnished urban Salvador with every manner of service and labor. Enslaved men and women earned wages from their trades and small-scale vending of goods. Many also lived in separate accommodations from their owners and engaged in various forms of autonomous sociability within the city, such as membership in Catholic brotherhoods, work gangs, and participation in urban religious festivals and celebrations. Moreover, many could earn wages from their independent labor, providing their owners with a daily minimum wage and retaining any surplus profit for themselves.[53]

The prevalence of various gradients of "freedom" among the city's Black population defined the city as an ostensible "new Guinea." There were obvious reasons for this. Once engaged in an urban trade, wage-earning activities, or small-scale commerce, some enslaved people would eventually be in a position to self-purchase their manumission. Enslaved individuals could accumulate capital by growing crops, fishing, producing small crafts and house-

---

population, 10,720 were listed as white (in addition to 277 members of the clergy), 4,213 as free *pardos,* or mixed race, 3,730 as free *pretos,* or Black, and 14,695 as enslaved. See Frézier, *Relation du voyage de la mer du Sud,* quoted in Verger, *Trade Relations,* [trans. Crawford], 69 n. 30; Russell-Wood, "Ports of Colonial Brazil," in Knight and Liss, eds., *Atlantic Port Cities,* 221–222; "Mappa geral no qual se vêem todas as moradas de casas que ha na cidade da Bahia," Bahia, June 20, 1775, in Edmundo de Castro e Almeida, *Inventario dos documentos relativos ao Brasil existentes no Archivo de Marinha e Ultramar de Lisboa* (Rio de Janeiro, 1914), II, no. 8813, 296; AHU, Conselho Ultramarino–Bahia, Eduardo de Castro e Almeida, caixa 47, documentos 8810–8815.

53. For examples of the sociability of enslaved residents of Salvador, see Katia M. de Queirós Mattoso, *To Be a Slave in Brazil: 1550–1888* (New Brunswick, N.J., 1991), 106–124; Luis Nicolau Parés, *The Formation of Candomblé: Vodun History and Ritual in Brazil,* trans. Richard Vernon (Chapel Hill, N.C., 2013); Mieko Nishida, *Slavery and Identity: Ethnicity, Gender, and Race in Salvador, Brazil, 1808–1888* (Bloomington, Ind., 2003); Lucilene Reginaldo, *Os Rosários dos Angolas: Irmandades de africanos e crioulos na Bahia setecentista* (São Paulo, 2011); João José Reis, *Slave Rebellion in Brazil: The Muslim Uprising of 1835 in Bahia* (New York, 1995). Nishida notes that, by the early nineteenth century, enslaved wage laborers (escravos de ganho) provided a standard *pataca* (minimum daily wage) of between 240 and 320 réis to their owners or the sum of 6 patacas on Saturday, though no standard sum was codified by Brazilian authorities and the amount could vary from owner to owner (Nishida, *Slavery and Identity,* 20).

hold goods in their spare time, and selling the products of these labors to fellow inhabitants of the city. Such initiatives were also frequently put toward larger social or emancipatory goals. Commonly, enslaved men and women combined their resources to create collective funds for manumission. Sometimes facilitated by Catholic brotherhoods or other, less institutionalized social organizations, access to Salvador's market allowed some to purchase the freedom of their clients and loved ones. Such arrangements were frequently exploitative, however, with owners charging above-market prices for their slaves' self-purchase despite their simultaneous desire to present themselves publicly as charitable. Nonetheless, access to a vital monetary economy in the city—one that was, to a significant degree, articulated toward maritime life—created a sizable class of liberated former slaves in the city. By 1775, there were an estimated 7,837 freed people of African descent in Salvador.[54]

Black mariners, in particular, asserted an integral role in the public religious life of the port city. Built on the waterfront at the end of the seventeenth century by a Spanish captain, the chapel of São Frei Pedro Gonçalves, popularly known as Corpo Santo, was established, "where Boats commonly land, and the Seamen go immediately to Prayers." In 1735, a Catholic brotherhood housed in the Corpo Santo petitioned the crown for a license to erect a hospital for ailing mariners next to the building, though the project was never undertaken. During the same century, the Nossa Senhora da Conceição da Praia was also erected in the lower city. Both locations were popular places of worship where seafaring congregants engaged in social networking and mutual aid. By the middle of the eighteenth century, African mariners and other tradesmen were prevalent in the ranks of congregants at both churches. Seamen laboring on royal vessels were also frequent visitors to the São

54. Mary E. Hicks, "João de Oliveira's Atlantic World: Mobility and Dislocation in Eighteenth-Century Brazil and the Bight of Benin," in Lawrence Aje and Catherine Armstrong, eds., *The Many Faces of Slavery: New Perspectives on Slave Ownership and Experiences in the Americas* (London, 2019); Stuart B. Schwartz, "The Manumission of Slaves in Colonial Brazil: Bahia, 1684–1745," *HAHR*, LIV (1974), 603–635; Mattoso, *To Be a Slave in Brazil*, 155–176; A. J. R. Russell-Wood, *The Black Man in Slavery and Freedom in Colonial Brazil* (New York, 1982), 48–49; Verger, *Trade Relations*, [trans. Crawford], 457–459; AHU, Conselho Ultramarino–Bahia, Eduardo de Castro e Almeida, caixa 47, documento 8810–8815. Black Catholic brotherhoods had a long-term commitment to purchasing the freedom of members. In 1686, a clause within the Brotherhood of Nossa Senhora do Rosário's charter enabled enslaved brothers to petition for loans to self-purchase their liberty, with the permission of the viceroy. By 1779, the king allowed another of Salvador's brotherhoods, São Benedito, to purchase the freedom of members. Nishida discusses urban "savings as-

Christóvão hospital housed in the Santa Casa da Misericórdia, which was administered by the local Catholic brotherhood of the same name beginning in 1556. Mariners traveling from India and Africa often suffered from communicable diseases and malnourishment contracted during their passages, and some voyages ended with hundreds of seamen requiring medical treatment provided by the Misericórdia hospital, to which sailors paid annual dues in return for care.[55]

Beyond receiving support from a handful of colonial institutions that provided a semblance of security, Black residents of Salvador lived in the crosshairs of norms that denigrated their work and status while placing limits on their often fragile forms of social privilege and economic independence. Suffused with a hierarchical ethos, Bahian society inherited a Portuguese ideology in which the ideal social structure was defined by the separation of estates, or corporate orders, including the hereditary nobility, the clergy, and the military, which in principle afforded membership only to freeborn white colonists. Privileges, including the ability to serve in public administrative positions such as the municipal council or in the colonial militias, were allocated on the basis of social status—which, in a colonial slave society, was demonstrated by possession of a *pureza de sangue* (purity of blood) testimonial that confirmed one's ownership of an untarnished line of European Christian ancestry. Slavery and imperial ideologies of racial categorization espoused the inherent superiority of those born in the metropole to the colonized; these tenets emphasized the differences between colonial inhabitants of indigenous, African, and European heritage, as well as between those colonial subjects born as Christian and those born as pagans, even after the latter converted. Freeborn subjects enjoyed greater legal privileges than either the enslaved

sociations," or juntas, through which enslaved and free African residents of Salvador pooled money in order to advance loans to members in the nineteenth century. See Russell-Wood, *Black Man in Slavery and Freedom*, 38–39; Nishida, *Slavery and Identity*, 55. For a discussion of Catholic brotherhoods and manumission funds, see Mariza de Carvalho Soares, *People of Faith: Slavery and African Catholics in Eighteenth-Century Rio de Janeiro*, trans. Jerry D. Metz (Durham, N.C., 2011), 211.

55. Dampier, *Collection*, 35; Luis Nicolau Parés, "Militiamen, Barbers, and Slave-Traders: Mina and Jeje Africans in a Catholic Brotherhood (Bahia, 1770–1830)," *Revista Tempo*, XX (2014), 2; AHU, CU, Bahia, caixa 54, documento 4616, Nov. 26, 1735, "Requerimento do Juiz e mais irmãos da confraria do Corpo Santo da Igreja da praia da cidade da Bahia ao rei"; A. J. R. Russell-Wood, *Fidalgos and Philanthropists: The Santa Casa da Misericórdia of Bahia, 1550–1755* (Berkeley, Calif., 1968), 86–87, 286–287.

or the manumitted, whereas the nobility and wealthy landholders—who abstained from manual labor and acted as patrons to a range of dependents, including spouses, children, kin, slaves, and itinerant laborers—possessed greater social prestige than all those who lived by their industry. Local administrators went to great pains to emphasize racial distinctions through the creation of sumptuary laws that restricted dress for people of African descent, separate military orders for whites, *pardos* (men of mixed European and African ancestry) and *pretos* (men of full African ancestry), restrictions on carrying arms, and targeted public curfews. A 1749 royal decree codified this distinction by prohibiting "apprentices of mechanical trades, lackeys, hunchbacks, sailors, boatmen, bargemen, blacks and other people of similar or inferior standing" from carrying swords—a mark of honorable manhood. Despite legal efforts, however, widespread liaisons between Portuguese men and indigenous and African women led to the growth of a considerable mixed-race population that confounded such categorizations.[56]

As a result of such prevailing notions, the colonial city often struggled to care for its vulnerable mariner population. Sailors were turned away at local charitable hospitals, forcing them to convalesce in the streets, where many became alcoholics and died destitute. If the Catholic mutual aid organizations tasked with caring for the multitude of impoverished residents of the city of Salvador failed in this mission, it was not for lack of motivation, as care for the poor was one of the central purposes of the Santa Casa da Misericórdia. It was the highly stratified nature of Salvadoran society, in which wealth was largely concentrated in the hands of a small number of merchants, planters, and sugar mill owners, that left the remainder of the population to suffer from chronic poverty. At the start of the eighteenth century, life for Black residents of Salvador was defined simultaneously by exploitation, precarity, and possibility. Black maritime life exemplified this fact as perhaps no other occupation could.[57]

56. Schwartz, *Sugar Plantations*, 246–247; Russell-Wood, *Black Man in Slavery and Freedom*, 37, 67–69; Silvia Hunold Lara, *Fragmentos setecentistas: Escravidão, cultura e poder na América portuguesa* (São Paulo, 2007), 87–91; A. J. R. Russell-Wood, "Black and Mulatto Brotherhoods in Colonial Brazil: A Study in Collective Behavior," *HAHR*, LIV (1974), 567–602, esp. 598–599. In addition to the difficulty in accurately determining the ancestry of an itinerant population, the crown faced a shortage of metropolitan-born whites who could fill all the necessary administrative positions required to govern a growing populace, requiring them to appoint mixed-race men (Russell-Wood, *Black Man in Slavery and Freedom*, 70).

57. Luís dos Santos Vilhena, *Recopilação de noticias soteropolitanas a brasilicas* (Salvador, Brazil, 1921), 134; Russell-Wood, *Fidalgos and Philanthropists*, 281.

FIGURE 6. *"Carta topográfica do porto de Pernambuco." 1690.*
In Cartográfica e iconografía, caixa 15–Pernambuco, documento 886.
Canoemen navigate between plantation landscapes and the Atlantic littoral in
Pernambuco. Cedida por Portugal, Arquivo Histórico Ultramarino

On one of Salvador's humble watercraft, one figure was integral to the effective operation of the city's port. João de Brito, likely a freed African man and "fisherman on a jangada," received a royal patent in 1718 to act as the commander of all the watermen within the Bay of All Saints. As the newly titled captain of the jangadas, Brito was responsible for helping to navigate deep ocean vessels to Salvador da Bahia's shore, a task that required recognizing vessels at sea and guiding them to the governor-general. In order to fulfill such a function, colonial authorities required local watermen to "honor, and respect" Brito, "following quickly whatever [was] commanded by him."[58]

Despite his royal title and African heritage, João de Brito was not an exceptional figure in the Portuguese waterborne empire. His work bestowed him with expertise and authority while facilitating larger imperial commercial

58. Cândido Eugênio Domingues de Souza, "'Perseguidores da espécie humana': Capitães negreiros da cidade da Bahia na primeira metade do século XVIII" (Ph.D. diss., Universidade Federal da Bahia, 2011), 54.

processes in ways that he, as an early modern Black mariner, was perhaps uniquely suited to do. Though the specifics of his career are unclear, many men like Brito, on the coast of West Africa and increasingly in seventeenth- and eighteenth-century Bahia, provided the maritime skills and knowledge that enabled commercial oceanic transportation to blossom in the South Atlantic. Enslaved and freed African seafarers crafted vessels, steered watercraft, pioneered navigational routes in Portugal's nascent colony, and populated deepwater sailing vessels. As the transatlantic slave trade fed the labor demands of Brazilian planters and miners, they became part of a larger African community displaced to the harsh shores of Bahia. The stark inequalities of Salvador's urban landscapes, however, spurred a range of survival strategies, including Catholic mutual aid, manumission, and mastery of the local aquatic environment. Tasked with moving at the behest of others, waterborne bondsmen began to discover ways to derive some small benefit from their new surrounds.

{ CHAPTER 2 }

A Bahian Commerce
in Flesh and Blood

Gripped by terror and confusion, a young African captive was forced by sailors into a slim dugout canoe. He would traverse the tumultuous Atlantic Ocean for the first, but not final, time in his life. As the crashing waves tossed the boat up and down, causing sickness and disorientation, pungent sea air filled his nostrils. Cries from fellow enslaved Africans, their despair mounting, punctuated the monotonous sound of paddles cutting through the water. Some desperate soul might writhe free of their restraints to jump over the canoe's side, hoping to swim to shore—or return home in death. The canoe's destination was a dark ship that loomed three to five miles in the distance, crested with billowing white sails. Its cavernous hold would be the site of his captivity for at least the next several weeks. In a space that Olaudah Equiano famously described as "this hollow place," the child would experience a transatlantic journey filled with uncertainty, fear, and deprivation, eventually concluding on the distant coastline of Brazil.[1]

Born around the turn of the eighteenth century, this adolescent would carry little with him on the voyage. During the long seaborne passage, he would have been haunted by memories of his homeland, particularly his recent seizure by what he called "countrymen" younger than himself in the politically fractured Yoruba- and Fon-speaking regions of West Africa. On his face, he bore the marks of his homeland, the scars on his cheeks attesting to the natal community from which he was now severed. His language, still-immature knowledge of the world, and youthful capacity to adapt to radically new environments, however, accompanied him to alien shores. In the 1710s,

1. The description of the canoe journey is derived from Jean Barbot's and Thomas Phillips's characterizations of the coastlines of Cabo Corso and Lagos in the late seventeenth and early eighteenth centuries. See Robin Law, Adam Jones, and P. E. H. Hair, eds., *Barbot on Guinea: The Writings of Jean Barbot on West Africa, 1678–1712*, 2 vols. (Surrey, U.K., 2010), II, 398, 665–666; Phillips, *A Journal of a Voyage Made in the Hannibal of London, Ann. 1693, 1694, from England . . .* (London, 1732), 198–201, 219; Shelly Eversley, ed., *The Interesting Narrative of the Life of Olaudah Equiano; or, Gustavus Vassa, the African* (New York, 2004), 36.

the boy was sold to a Brazilian slaver bound for Pernambuco, just north of Bahia. As a sign of his radically transformed identity, he was rechristened as João de Oliveira. But in an era marked by an accelerating expansion of the transatlantic slave trade, the young man's South Atlantic odyssey was by no means over.[2]

Oliveira would again experience captivity in 1770, albeit in a very different context. This time, he was incarcerated by colonial authorities as a free man and accused of violating Portuguese mercantile policy. Oliveira was the quintessential captive cosmopolitan, and his life's unusual but not completely anomalous trajectory was a product of his long-standing proximity to maritime commerce. By the time of his arrest, not only was Oliveira no longer enslaved; he had become a successful trader in captive Africans himself. His career likely began as a mariner in Brazil; later, he became a diplomat, merchant, and *cabeceira* (head trader) on the eastern portion of the Mina Coast. Before his resettlement near his former homeland in the Bight of Benin, Oliveira undertook dramatic social and cultural transformations including converting to Catholicism, professing his loyalty to the Portuguese empire, and securing manumission by self-purchase. His life vividly illuminates the contours of Black maritime self-making and the possibilities for individual social transformation in the early modern maritime South Atlantic.[3]

Oliveira's participation in Brazilian and West African maritime commerce over the first three-quarters of the eighteenth century was coextensive with a critical period in the development of Bahian slave society. His was a life—lived

2. Oyo, the political center of Yoruba-speaking West Africa, conquered the Fon-speaking kingdom of Allada, turning it into one of its political tributaries after nearly two decades of hostilities. At the same time, Dahomey, another polity, attacked and subdued several Fon- and Yoruba-speaking communities from the 1690s to 1720s. The young boy could have been a victim of one of these conflicts, as they fed slave trading routes to the coast. Alternatively, he could have been the target of local slave raiders who flourished in the environment of violence and instability. See AHU, CU, Bahia–Eduardo de Castro e Almeida, caixa 44, documento 8246; I. A. Akinjogbin, "The Oyo Empire in the 18th Century—A Reassessment," *Journal of the Historical Society of Nigeria,* III (1966), 449–460, esp. 451; Akinwumi Ogundiran, *The Yorùbá: A New History* (Bloomington, Ind., 2020), 245. From the years 1701 to 1725, an estimated 121,301 men, women, and children disembarked in the port of Recife as slaving rapidly expanded in the 1720s. See Daniel Barros Domingues da Silva and David Eltis, "The Slave Trade to Pernambuco, 1561–1851," in Eltis and David Richardson, eds., *Extending the Frontiers: Essays on the New Transatlantic Slave Trade Database* (New Haven, Conn., 2008), 119; and *Voyages*.

3. AHU, CU, Bahia–Eduardo de Castro e Almeida, caixa 44, documento 8246.

in motion at all stages—that was shaped in decisive ways by the evolving structures of Bahian merchant capitalism, interimperial conflict, and the growing dependence of transatlantic slaving on the work and initiatives of Black
mariners such as himself. In an era largely defined by the labor demands of
expanding sugar production in Brazil, commercial instability and increasing
political turmoil on the West African coast threatened slaving merchants' ability to procure enslaved workers. Satisfying Bahian slavers' interests required
the creation and re-creation of new trading relationships with willing partners
on the Mina Coast. As this chapter argues, geographically mobile and culturally dexterous African-born cosmopolitans such as Oliveira were vital to the
consolidation of commercial connections between West Africa and Brazil
during the eighteenth century. Oliveira's life offers a prism through which
to view the evolving structure of South Atlantic slavery and the deepening
cultural and economic connections that increasingly bound together Bahia
and the Mina Coast.

Driving this process was sugar. The commodity powered imperial expansion and, in turn, the demand for enslaved Africans to cultivate, process,
and transport it. Over the course of the eighteenth century, a sugar-driven
transatlantic slave trade remade the colony of Brazil into one of most prolific importers of enslaved Africans and one of the largest slave societies in
the Atlantic world. The king of Portugal extolled the necessity of producing
the crop, upon which "the common commerce of all my vassals" depended.
Without Black slaves—the so-called "hands and the feet" of the Brazilian
plantations and mines—the Portuguese empire would cease to exist, or so its
agents and advocates claimed. Bahian slave society in the eighteenth century
required a constant replenishment of bodies capable of wrenching physical
toil. Laboring conditions on rural *fazendas* (plantations) suppressed birth
rates and led to staggering levels of mortality; a seemingly endless demand
for working hands could be satiated only through importation, or the "mercantile reproduction" represented by securing captives in African markets.[4]

4. Eltis and Richardson, "A New Assessment of the Transatlantic Slave Trade," in Eltis
and Richardson, eds., *Extending the Frontiers*, 1–62, esp. 15–22; Estimates of the Trade,
in *Voyages*, http://www.slavevoyages.org/tast/database/index.faces; Kathleen J. Higgins,
*"Licentious Liberty" in a Brazilian Gold-Mining Region: Slavery, Gender, and Social Control
in Eighteenth-Century Sabará, Minas Gerais* (University Park, Pa., 1999), 33; Luiz Felipe
de Alencastro, *The Trade in the Living: The Formation of Brazil in the South Atlantic, Sixteenth to Seventeenth Centuries*, trans. Gavin Adams and Alencastro (Albany, N.Y., 2018),
146–147. According to André João Antonil, an Italian Jesuit residing in Bahia from 1681

Portuguese and Bahian slavers' enduring ability to purchase enslaved men, women, and children on African coasts was not the product of traditional military or mercantile advantages. They were hindered by a number of significant disadvantages: a lack of monetary capital, the absence of a monopoly-holding trading company to provide long-term credit or absorb short-term financial losses, few fortified trading posts within which they could accumulate commercial goods on the West African coast, and insufficient means of military protection against hostile European competitors.[5] Preferring not to be controlled by the edicts of the Portuguese crown, by the seventeenth century Bahian merchants began to pioneer their own maritime infrastructure on the West African coast and solidify relationships with coastal African slaving merchants and potentates. The key to the success of this project lay in commercial adaptations designed to counteract these disadvantages, including the utilization of African intermediaries on both sides of the Atlantic, collective investment in lieu of corporate or individual financial backing for voyages, and access to those commodities preferred by West African merchants, all of which allowed them to tap into extensive slaving networks reaching far into the African interior.

In particular, the relative paucity of liquid capital in the Brazilian colonies required merchants to utilize alternative methods of financing voyages.[6] In Bahia, the financial instruments essential to slaving in the North Atlantic—

---

until his death, "the slaves are the hands and the feet of the planter, for without them it is impossible in Brazil to create, maintain, and develop a plantation, or to have a productive [sugar] mill." See Antonil, *Brazil at the Dawn of the Eighteenth Century,* trans. Timothy J. Coates (Dartmouth, Mass., 2012), 39.

5. In counterpoint to the slaving powers of England, France, and the Low Countries, which mounted slaving voyages from metropolitan centers, Brazilian-based merchants organized their own transatlantic ventures in colonial ports, drawing capital, labor power, and commercial expertise from their immediate surroundings (Pierre Verger, *Trade Relations between the Bight of Benin and Bahia: From the 17th to 19th Century,* [trans. Evelyn Crawford] [Ibadan, Nigeria, 1976], 76–79).

6. Other nations favored a reliance on elite merchant families and houses as well as royally sponsored joint-stock monopoly companies to accumulate sufficient capital. See Herbert S. Klein, *The Atlantic Slave Trade* (Cambridge, 1999), 79; William A. Pettigrew, *Freedom's Debt: The Royal African Company and the Politics of the Atlantic Slave Trade, 1672–1752* (Williamsburg, Va., and Chapel Hill, N.C., 2013), 59; Johannes Menne Postma, *The Dutch in the Atlantic Slave Trade: 1600–1815* (Cambridge, 1990), 14–17; Filipa Ribeiro da Silva, "Crossing Empires: Portuguese, Sephardic, and Dutch Business Networks in the Atlantic Slave Trade, 1580–1674," *Americas,* LXVIII (2011), 7–32, esp. 27; Hugh Thomas, *The Slave Trade: The Story of the Atlantic Slave Trade, 1440–1870* (Riverside, N.J., 2013), 202–203.

especially the bill of exchange and the joint-stock company—existed alongside alternative models of managing credit scarcity and financial risk.[7] The
common undercapitalization of transatlantic voyages in the South Atlantic
thus produced a profound historical irony: it enabled and incentivized even
the humblest residents of Salvador, including captive cosmopolitan mariners
and a variety of other enslaved people, to invest in the enterprise. Bahian
slaving came to rely economically on an assemblage of small-scale investments purchased on credit with the promise of small-scale returns. Black
seafarers exploited both the commercial operations of the slaving ship and
the economic organization of Bahian slaving itself to assert trading privileges
on board. Although ships' officers were the most likely to make small-scale
investments in cargoes on slaving vessels, crew members occupying the lower
rungs of the shipboard hierarchy (including sailors and cabin boys) also invested in a variety of trade goods.[8] In granting the enslaved access to what
were euphemistically labeled "liberty chests," Bahian slavers enabled Black

7. Bills of exchange developed in the North Atlantic by English merchants to extend
long-term lines of credit to slave traders became the exclusive means by which voyages whose
profit return was often delayed for eighteen months or more could be successfully mounted
in cash-poor environments. See Pat Hudson, "Slavery, the Slave Trade, and Economic
Growth: A Contribution to the Debate," in Catherine Hall, Nicholas Draper, and Keith Mc-
Clelland, eds., *Emancipation and the Remaking of the British Imperial World* (Manchester,
U.K., 2014), 45–46; Kenneth Morgan, "Liverpool's Dominance in the British Slave Trade,
1740–1807," in David Richardson, Anthony Tibbles, and Suzanne Schwarz, eds., *Liverpool
and Transatlantic Slavery* (Liverpool, U.K., 2007), 14–42, esp. 32–33.

8. As Leif Svalesen has described for the Norwegian slaving ship *Fredensborg* and Richard B. Sheridan had noted for English vessels, only officers were permitted the privilege to
invest in European goods to trade in West Africa. In addition, two historians of British slaving voyages—Emma Christopher and Marcus Rediker—have argued that common sailors
labored for paltry wages that were subject to arbitrary reductions. In this North Atlantic
characterization, sailors comprised the Atlantic world's first proletariat. Their economic
interests remained antagonistic to authoritarian and exploitative labor regimes enforced
by ship captains. There is some evidence to suggest, however, that in the North Atlantic
and Caribbean, sailors also invested in both local commerce and the transatlantic slave
trade, though they were not explicitly permitted to do so by law. A 1729 ship sailing from
Charleston to Africa featured multiple mariner investments in "privilege slaves." One man
owned fifteen slaves on the vessel, whereas the second mate owned another, and the master,
another. In mid-eighteenth-century Cap Français, sailors erected marketing stands along the
wharves on Sundays to trade with local residents, presumably in goods. See Christopher,
Slave Ship Sailors and Their Captive Cargoes, 1730–1807 (Cambridge, 2006), 23–24; Rediker,

mariners to secure a measure of monetary and intellectual independence. Over time, this arrangement deepened captive cosmopolitans' status as independent commercial interlocutors on both sides of the Atlantic.

The commercial initiatives of such historical actors exist in sharp contrast to scholarly depictions of the transatlantic slave trades of other empires. Much of the literature has focused its attention on a small coterie of investors, insurers, and merchants whom many—perhaps with good reason—have assumed to be the economic engines of slaving capitalism. The demographic profile of this group of commercial actors has been overwhelmingly male, European or of European descent, wealthy, and upwardly mobile. But attending to the specificities of Bahia's African trade financing, as this chapter argues, reveals a more complete portrait of the diversity and what Joseph C. Miller has called the "operational complexity" of the early modern slave trade.[9]

João de Oliveira's arrest in 1770 by agents of the Portuguese crown was illustrative of both the larger structural organization of the Bahian-oriented slave trade and the changes to it that had occurred over the course of the eighteenth century. His ability to participate in the trade in the first place was the product of the decentralized nature of Bahia's slaving financing. And his arrest—for the crime of contraband trading widely practiced by Bahian merchants—indicated the weakening of the Portuguese crown's control over the mechanisms of trading within the putative boundaries of its own empire by the latter half of the century. African born and formerly enslaved, Oliveira had prospered in the face of royal opposition while sustaining the slaving operations upon which the Portuguese empire depended. Working within, and at times profiting from, the dark

The Slave Ship: A Human History (London, 2007), 230; Rediker, *Villains of All Nations: Atlantic Pirates in the Golden Age* (Boston, 2004), 24; Julius S. Scott, *The Common Wind: Afro-American Currents in the Age of the Haitian Revolution* (London, 2018), 43; Richard B. Sheridan, "The Guinea Surgeons on the Middle Passage: The Provision of Medical Services in the British Slave Trade," *International Journal of African Historical Studies*, XIV (1981), 610; Svalesen, *The Slave Ship "Fredensborg,"* trans. Pat Shaw and Selena Winsnes (Bloomington, Ind., 2000), 110; Lee B. Wilson, *Bonds of Empire: The English Origins of Slave Law in South Carolina and British Plantation America, 1660–1783* (Cambridge, 2021), 146–147.

9. Joseph C. Miller, "The Slave Trade in Congo and Angola," in Martin L. Kilson and Robert I. Rotberg, eds., *The African Diaspora* (Cambridge, Mass., 1976), 76. For studies of slave trading merchants, see Robert Harms, *The Diligent: A Voyage through the Worlds of the Slave Trade* (New York, 2002); Miller, *Way of Death: Merchant Capitalism and the Angolan Slave Trade, 1730–1830* (Madison, Wis., 1988); Linda A. Newson and Susie Minchin, *From Capture to Sale: The Portuguese Slave Trade to Spanish South America in the Early Seventeenth Century* (Boston, 2007).

underbelly of Atlantic commerce, Oliveira and his more prosaic contemporaries were able to capitalize on their position as economic and cultural intermediaries on the West African coast. Many leveraged their proximity to Atlantic commerce to accumulate a modicum of wealth, gain greater independence from their owners, and even secure their own freedom. This historically unique commercial opening allowed some enslaved mariners not only to transform their own lives but, in turn, shape the contours and operation of South Atlantic slaving.

FORGING A TRADE ON THE MINA COAST

When Oliveira retuned to the Mina Coast in 1733 as a free man, he disembarked as an agent of a slave society committed to ensuring continued access to enslaved people like his former self. Bahian merchants' access to stable markets for enslaved Africans was not guaranteed, however, and their efforts to satisfy their own economic interests frequently ran up against the objectives of the Portuguese crown. In an attempt to circumvent royal edicts, Bahian merchants began to pioneer their own maritime infrastructure on the West African coast and solidify relationships with coastal African slaving merchants and potentates. As a result, their South Atlantic slaving initiatives followed a bilateral rather than a triangular pattern, entailing two crossings—to the African coast and back—in lieu of three legs between Europe, Africa, and the Americas.[10] Bahian slaving interests consistently operated throughout the eighteenth century from a position of economic, political, and military weakness, however. João de Oliveira's career is inexplicable outside of this context. The reconsolidation of trading between Bahia and the Mina Coast—a long-standing process that made Bahia into one of the New World's most important slave societies—reveals how the improvisational nature of slaving in the South Atlantic depended on, and at times incorporated, the work and ambitions of men such as Oliveira. As Bahian slave traders were pushed eastward on the West African coast by both compulsion and choice, they were forced to establish new commercial relationships with often unfamiliar local polities and potentates. This crucial dynamic elevated the value of Oliveira and cosmopolitans like him, who were exceptionally situated to consecrate new ties of exchange.

Despite their early commercial advances on the upper Mina Coast in the late fifteenth century, the expulsion of Portuguese traders by Dutch forces

10. Alencastro has argued that the bilateral connections between Brazil and Africa coalesced at the same time that Portuguese commercial and naval power was waning (*Trade in the Living,* trans. Adams and Alencastro, 21).

from São Jorge da Mina Castle and their other established *feitorias* provoked a reconfiguration of merchant activity in Africa. Portuguese merchants were barred from trading on the Mina Coast in 1641 and were only allowed to return in the wake of an agreement with the Dutch West India Company in 1689, whereby each slaving vessel agreed to a 10 percent tax of its entire cargo (usually tobacco) at São Jorge da Mina Castle under penalty of ship seizure for failure to pay. This was a decisive moment in the evolution of South Atlantic slaving, a period that marked a transition to what Pierre Verger has termed the "Angola Cycle," or the intensification of a Bahian slave trade to the central African port of Luanda in the colony of Angola. The Portuguese crown desired that colonial purchasers of enslaved Africans destined for Brazilian plantations concentrate their efforts on Luanda, where royal authorities were exclusively capable of levying tax revenue on all commercial activities. Bahian trade on the Mina Coast quickly declined, with commerce articulated toward not only Angola but also Cacheu, Cabo Verde, and Gabon.[11]

Bahian merchants' absence from the Mina Coast was short-lived, though. They were driven back, in part, by Brazilian slaveholders' demands for slaves from the Mina Coast rather than from Angola. Crude stereotypes circulated among merchants, heralding enslaved Africans from the Mina Coast as "much tougher" and the "best and most capable for the Gold Mines" of Minas Gerais. Some buyers in Brazil were willing to pay double for captives from that region over those from Angola, who were thought to be "useless for extracting gold." Bahian traders' return to the Mina Coast at the end of the seventeenth century, however, occurred without the material support or endorsement of the Portuguese crown. The colonial apparatus there remained miniscule, largely leaving private traders to their own devices.[12]

---

11. Verger, *Trade Relations,* [trans. Crawford], 21, 44–46, esp. 46. In 1726, the ship *Santa Rita e Almas,* while in port at Ouidah, was boarded by the Dutch under the accusation that the ship's captain had failed to secure a passport to trade there at Elmina. It was the sixth vessel taken by Dutch warships in the course of several years. See AHU, CU, São Tomé e Príncipe, caixa 5, documento 578, "Carta do Capitão do Navio Santa Rita e Almas, José Ferreria, ao Governador"; ibid., documento 565, "Requerimento de José Fernandes Braga ao Rei"; Postma, *Dutch in the Atlantic Slave Trade,* 156; Thomas, *Slave Trade,* 76.

12. AHU, CU, São Tomé e Príncipe, caixa 6, documento 635, Nov. 13, 1731, "Carta do Governador da Ilha de São Tomé ao Rei sobre o mau estado em que encontrou a Ilha." In contrast to the Mina Coast, slaving markets in Luanda functioned under the careful supervision of an omnipresent cadre of Portuguese administrators who levied taxes and permeated the inner workings of the trade (Miller, *Way of Death,* 284–318).

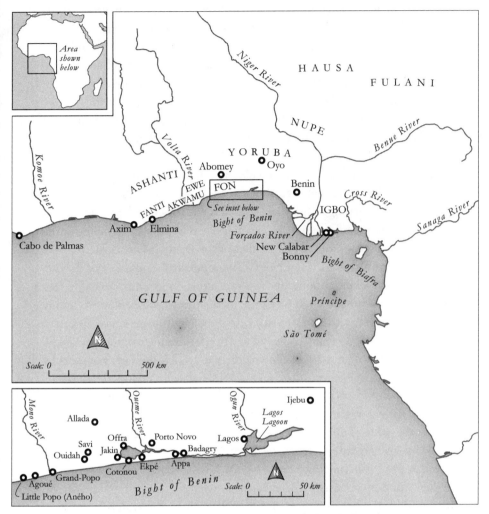

MAP 2. *West Africa's Mina Coast. Drawn by Jim DeGrand*

Rather than return to Dutch-controlled Elmina, slaving merchants set their eyes eastward. Reasserting their presence on the Mina Coast, they forged trading relations with the polities dotting the coast to the east of Ouidah. The resurgence of Bahian traders on the Mina Coast coincided with surging political turmoil as polities dissolved in the face of internecine conflicts and new settlements arose from the ashes of destroyed communities, often populated by refugees. The ability to attract willing trading partners within a politically fractious milieu became a paramount concern for Bahian merchants. Because of initial difficulties, especially a lack of access to cowry shells (a commodity preferred by merchants in the two major trading ports of the time, Allada and Ouidah), slaving ship captains hailing from Salvador pushed eastward to smaller, more marginal ports, such as Little Popo. As a newly established settlement, Little Popo was populated by canoemen from Elmina who had relocated to the shores of an inland lagoon that stretched approximately four hundred miles along the Atlantic coast. Refugees from Accra and the Ladoku kingdom—a polity that had collapsed after a conquest by the Akwamu at the end of the seventeenth century—soon joined Fanti residents.[13]

As Bahian slaving moved farther eastward, efforts to procure enslaved Africans became increasingly connected to maritime-oriented trading partners. Portuguese slavers also established trade relations with Grand-Popo, located on the opening of the same coastal lagoon to the Atlantic. Inhabited by Gbe-speaking Hula people, Grand-Popo was a tributary to the powerful Tado polity in the interior. Deriving their name from the Fon word for "sea," the Hulas were reputed to have been worshippers of the ocean since the polity's founding. Their community was one among a patchwork of different ethnic groups who subsisted on the rich aquatic environment surrounding the serene freshwater lagoon. They relied on waterborne communication and transportation to export fish and salt to neighboring communities. Specialized ecological knowledge allowed them to exploit their environment by fashioning dugout canoes and fishing with cast nets; they navigated the calm, shallow inland waters by propelling themselves with setting poles. In nearby Ouidah, fishing was so pervasive that in the 1690s the king was rumored to extract the value of one hundred slaves annually through taxation of fishermen. One visiting European observed that the growing settlement was entirely populated by "fishermen and canoemen" who distributed fish as far as Benin in their wooden canoes. Extensive local knowledge of aquatic extraction and transportation would serve the Portuguese well on the eastern portion of the Mina Coast, as maritime life helped to integrate these communities into Portugal's commercial sphere.[14]

13. Robin Law, "Trade and Politics behind the Slave Coast: The Lagoon Traffic and the Rise of Lagos, 1500–1800," *Journal of African History*, XXIV (1983), 323; Silke Strickrodt, *Afro-European Trade in the Atlantic World: The Western Slave Coast, c. 1550–1885* (Suffolk, U.K., 2015), 75–78. Cowry shells were the primary medium of exchange in Allada and Ouidah (Law, *The Slave Coast of West Africa, 1550–1750: The Impact of the Atlantic Slave Trade on an African Society* [Oxford, 1991], 135).

14. Strickrodt, *Afro-European Trade*, 42, 46–54; Robin Law, "Between the Sea and the Lagoons: The Interaction of Maritime and Inland Navigation on the Precolonial Slave Coast,"

Bahian merchants were compelled to establish trading relationships with coastal African communities to elude Dutch control of trading on particular parts of the West African coast. This development demanded more elaborate navigational routes than earlier voyages and pushed Bahian-based vessels into new forms of "contraband" trade.[15] "Contraband" was deemed by royal authorities as a broad category of unsanctioned commercial behavior that included trade between Portuguese subjects and other Europeans, the smuggling of prohibited goods such as gold and tobacco to non-Portuguese buyers and African slave traders, and nonpayment of the royal tenth, or 10 percent import tax. All of these commercial activities violated the crown's mercantilist conception of political economy. Trade, in this vision, explicitly represented the national interest, and private traders were required to abide by state regulations of economic transactions. Under these restrictions, certain Bahian commodities could be traded directly with African merchants. Brazilians could also purchase reexported goods from Britain or France in the Portuguese metropole. But they could not deal directly with foreign traders. Surreptitiously, however, merchants of all nations conspired to subvert royal prerogatives by trading with foreign rivals for their own private benefit.

Simply put, many Bahian slavers viewed the Portuguese crown's policies as financially disadvantageous. Slaving ship captains preferred to be flexible in their trading routes to maximize the profitability and efficiency of their voyages. Most would first anchor at Dutch-controlled Elmina before trading, securing a passport, and paying a 10 percent tax on their total ship holdings to officials before navigating to a string of ports along the coast until their cargoes were completed. During the first half of the eighteenth century, fifteen Brazil-

---

Cahiers d'études africaines, XXIX (1989), 220; Law, *Ouidah: The Social History of a West African Slaving "Port," 1727–1892* (Athens, Ohio, 2004), 45. Fon is part of the Gbe language group (Strickrodt, *Afro-European Trade,* 40–42).

15. Whereas São Jorge da Mina Castle had acted as the main buyer of enslaved West Africans on the Mina Coast, as well as a base within which to house African goods for reexport and the principal military outpost in the region, slaving merchants reconfigured their commercial strategies after the Dutch seizure of the fortress. Ships of all nations faced confiscation of their entire cargoes if they visited the ports of Aquitá, Grand- or Little Popo, Ouidah, Jakin, or Apa without first visiting São Jorge da Mina. See AHU, CU, São Tomé e Príncipe, caixa 5, documento 578, "Carta do Navio Santa Rita e Almas, José Ferreria ao Governador sobre a viagem à Costa da Mina"; Filipa Ribeiro da Silva, "The Slave Trade and the Development of the Atlantic Africa Port System, 1400s–1800s," *International Journal of Maritime History,* XXIX (2017), 138–154, esp. 145.

ian ships a year paid the duty to the Dutch West India Company, with some years seeing as many as thirty vessels arriving at the port. Unsurprisingly, the payment of such fees to a rival imperial power was not met with metropolitan approval. Ship captains' acquiescence to paying the levies precipitated a rift between slave traders from Bahia and Portuguese authorities. Metropolitan administrators preferred that colonial vessels reroute their trade to the more remote ports of Jakin and Apa.[16]

Despite this, Bahian slavers continued to pay the substantial duty and regularly engaged in "contraband" trade. In some instances, transactions categorized as illicit were merely part of unavoidable prerequisites necessary to conduct trade on the Mina Coast, such as the payment of tobacco duties at São Jorge da Mina Castle and the sale of gold at Elmina to contract Fanti canoemen. After the Dutch merchant vessels conducted raids of fourteen ships in 1687, during which several seamen were shot and their bodies tossed into the sea, Bahian slavers eagerly complied with paying tobacco duties when they ventured to the western part of the region.[17] Bahian captains also frequently exchanged gold for captives with both English and West African Huedan merchants, especially during the first two decades of the eighteenth century, when gold extraction was at its peak in Brazil.[18] Most of the contraband conducted on the Mina Coast, however, stemmed from attempts to avoid paying

16. Postma, *Dutch in the Atlantic Slave Trade,* 77. Manoel Pimentel's *Arte de navegar* identified the ports of Little Popo, Grand-Popo, Ouidah, Jakin, Allada, Arda (other European nations designated the port Offra), Benin, and the Forçados River (Warri) as part of the "Mina Coast route" and the best locations to purchase slaves. See Pimentel, *Arte de navegar, em que se ensinam as regras praticas, e o modo de cartear pela carta plana . . .* (Lisbon, 1712), 255–259; Robin Law, "The Slave Trade in Seventeenth-Century Allada: A Revision," *African Economic History,* XXII (1994), 59–92, esp. 59.

17. Verger, *Trade Relations,* [trans. Crawford], 63–65; AHU, CU, São Tomé e Príncipe, caixa 3, documento 375, Dec. 20, 1687, "Carta dos moradores de São Tomé ao rei queixando—se os navios da Companhia de Holanda."

18. Gold from slave-operated mines in Minas Gerais traveled to the Bight of Benin on slaving vessels. As one of the most pervasive items of contraband trade, eight or nine *onças* of gold could be bartered for one enslaved person, who would fetch an even higher price in the Americas. The viceroy of Brazil estimated in 1721 that five hundred thousand *cruzados* of gold were smuggled to the Mina Coast on Bahian vessels annually. By 1787, the illicit trade in gold had continued unabated, with administrators estimating that each ship arriving on the Mina Coast from the northeast of Brazil paid approximately six thousand to seven thousand cruzados to the Dutch at São Jorge da Mina Castle. Bahian slavers often paid a portion of

the royal tenth as well as to bypass the inflated costs of goods reexported from the metropole by purchasing items directly from other European traders.[19]

Bahian traders working on the West African coast—a group that, by the 1730s, included African cosmopolitans like João de Oliveira—regularly acquired contraband goods as they operated in the interstices of multiple imperial trades. As captains followed up their preliminary stops at Elmina with opportunistic landings in port communities stretching along the coast, they engaged both African and European trading communities. Bahian merchants chased rumors of advantageous prices per *peça,* or one prime-aged adolescent male slave, across various Mina Coast ports. There, they hoped to access abundant local markets and tap into West African trading networks to partially divert them into the Atlantic.

Like the Portuguese, Dutch, French, and English, Bahian traders constructed lightly fortified trading posts with the consent of local communities to abet their initiatives. By the dawn of the eighteenth century, at ports east of the Volta River, slavers were omnipresent in the trading forts of various nations, often sectioned off in one part of the multiethnic communities of the West African coast. This proximity, as the Portuguese crown's continuing displeasure acknowledged, led to ample opportunities for contraband or interimperial trading relations. Such activity on the West African coast, according to Carl Hanson, "accounted for a significant share of contraband foreign goods entering" the Brazilian colonies. Portuguese authorities understood renegade trading activities as a profound threat to royal coffers that relied on crown agents' ability to act as middlemen between the trade in

---

the 10 percent tax to the Dutch in Elmina in gold rather than tobacco. An onça was a unit of trade on the Mina Coast; the value of slaves was usually figured in onças. A cruzado was a unit of currency equal to four hundred réis. See AHU, CU, São Tomé e Príncipe, caixa 6, documento 635, Nov. 13, 1731, "Carta do Governador da Ilha de São Tomé ao Rei sobre o mau estado em que encontrou a Ilha"; ibid., caixa 21, documento 1771, Oct. 1, 1787, "Relação de Documentos e Informações sobre os Procedimentos dos Holandeses contra os Navios Portugueses na Costa da Mina"; Verger, *Trade Relations,* [trans. Crawford], 110, 118.

19. Bahian slavers, much to the dismay of the Portuguese crown, often stocked their West Africa–bound ships with first- or second-grade high-quality tobacco that had already been legally restricted for sale in metropolitan markets, selling it to English merchants or losing it at sea to foreign vessels (AHU, CU, São Tomé e Príncipe, caixa 7, documento 770, Nov. 24, 1739, "Carta do D. José Caetano Souto Maior, ao Rei sobre a Falta de um Selo na Alfândega").

manufactured goods produced in Europe (such as textiles) and Brazilian agricultural commodities.[20]

As they moved east of Elmina, Bahian slaving captains encountered polities already deeply engaged in various commodity trades. Port communities east of the Volta River were part of a lagoon-based network of trade, migration, and communication through which circulated textiles, produce, fish, salt, and slaves; these places had already pioneered adaptations to waterborne trade upon which the Portuguese would come to depend. Travel between the lagoon-side settlements of Keta in the west to Lake Cradoo east of Lagos relied on waterborne routes. Deterred by fierce ocean currents and surf, as well as a large sandbar that blocked access to the shore, captains relied on Fanti canoemen from Elmina who could navigate along the perilous section of coast. Because indigenous aquatic travel tended to occur in the safer waters of the lagoon, many of the communities located within the eastern Mina Coast, like their counterparts to the west, relied on aquatic commercial and subsistence strategies. These techniques were easily translated to the logistical demands of the transatlantic slave trade. As John Atkins noted, "A dangerous double Barr upon the Coast, is rendered impassable sometimes (by the alteration of the Winds) for a fortnight together; the *Negroes* only know how to paddle thro' it, and when they think it safe, a Signal is made to the Ships, from those Tents, by hoisting their Flags." Drawing on local navigational expertise to surmount these environmental challenges, European traders utilized the lagoon to conduct their trade in slaves, textiles, ivory, and other West African goods as well as communicate with administrators in Elmina and other European factories farther up the coast, relying on African canoemen to carry out these tasks.[21]

20. Kenneth J. Banks, "Financiers, Factors, and French Proprietary Companies in West Africa, 1673–1713," in L. H. Roper and B. Van Ruymbeke, eds., *Constructing Early Modern Empires: Proprietary Ventures in the Atlantic World, 1500–1750* (Leiden, 2007), 79–117, esp. 92–98; William A. Pettigrew and George W. Van Cleve, "Parting Companies: The Glorious Revolution, Company Power, and Imperial Mercantilism," *Historical Journal,* LVII (2014), 617–638, esp. 620–621; Ribeiro da Silva, "Crossing Empires," *Americas,* LXVIII (2011), 7–32, esp. 27; Carl A. Hanson, *Economy and Society in Baroque Portugal, 1668–1703* (Minneapolis, 1981), 259. With prohibitions on purchasing and selling foreign goods not yet taxed by the crown in Lisbon, any direct commerce conducted between Bahian traders and other nations was illegal under imperial law (ibid.).

21. Strickrodt, *Afro-European Trade,* 38; Law, "Between the Sea and the Lagoons," *Cahiers d'études africaines,* XXIX (1989), 209–237, esp. 222–224; John Atkins, *A Voyage to Guinea, Brasil, and the West Indies in His Majesty's Ships, the "Swallow" and "Weymouth"* . . . (London, 1737), 172–173.

Expanding Atlantic trade on the eastern portion of the Mina Coast was further assisted by the flourishing commercial prosperity of Ouidah, the largest slaving port on the coast in the eighteenth century, which exported one-third to one-half of all goods from the entire region. Ouidah—from the European distortion of the ethnonym of the Huedan inhabitants of the city— was the quintessential slaving middleman, or brokerage community, selling men, women, and children enslaved in Allada to Atlantic maritime merchants. Initially, English and French merchants—attracted by the local ruler's lower duties—monopolized the trade with Ouidah. Yet, by 1713, Bahian traders had reestablished their prominence on the coast, in large part because of their possession of two of the most prized trade goods in Ouidah: tobacco and gold. Both commodities were produced in Salvador's hinterlands; sensing an opportunity, slaving merchants came to an agreement with planters and miners, who would extend much-needed credit with the expectation of repayment in enslaved labor. As the viceroy of Brazil, Vasco Fernandes César de Menezes, boasted in 1721:

> Ajuda [Ouidah] is the most famous port along this entire coast,
> through the abundance and the great number of slaves which are
> traded there. Tobacco is the product which they esteem the most
> and without which they cannot live. It is clear that, since we are the
> only ones capable of bringing this merchandise, we are also the best
> welcomed among all nations. Experience proves this, for the ships
> of all the other nations bring iron and powder which the inhabitants
> of this coast can do without, but they cannot do without the tobacco
> which we bring them.[22]

22. Law, *Ouidah*, 46, 125; Law, "Slave Trade in Seventeenth-Century Allada," *African Economic History*, XXII (1994), 56; Verger, *Trade Relations*, [trans. Crawford], 111. These nonmonetary arrangements, in which goods were advanced by local investors on a very small scale, mirrored the credit arrangements that more prominent slave traders used to secure *fazendas* (trade goods) produced in the plantation-dense region of the Recôncavo. Often, traders conducted transatlantic exchanges exclusively on credit advanced by agricultural producers in the interior, whose products were then sold for slaves and other West African goods on the coast. In September 1743, the Trade Committee of Bahia, a local organization that represented the interests of the merchant community of Salvador, argued that a monopoly trading company would not have the same flexibility to secure goods on credit from planters in the interior. Directly linking the continuation of advances in goods from producers in the interior with the profit and longevity of the trade, the committee asserted, "The company will not be able to trade with the sugar mill owners nor with the sugarcane

Menezes was integral in solidifying Bahian commercial primacy in Ouidah and oversaw the construction of a trading fort following an invitation by the ruler of the city in 1698. This initiative at first was blocked by the Conselho Ultramarino (overseas council), who did not want to encourage ships flying Portuguese colors to travel to portions of the coast where they could be targeted by Dutch ships for seizure. The fort was finally constructed in 1721 under the direction of merchant Joseph de Torres, with the support of Menezes. The viceroy's directive, which came from Bahia instead of Lisbon, established the precedent for the affairs of the feitoria in Ouidah, São João Baptista de Ajudá, to be directed by administrators in Salvador and staffed with personnel from Bahia rather than Portugal.[23]

Viceroys such as Menezes would endeavor to balance Bahian merchants' insistence on a liberalized West African trade with the metropole's demands to create tighter imperial regulations, though they increasingly came to believe that only drastic metropolitan intervention could maintain the viability of Salvador's transatlantic trade. In an early attempt at commercial regulation, Portuguese merchants proposed the formation of a monopoly trading company. Brazilian merchants similarly advocated for the formation of a slave-trading company in 1743, albeit one based in Bahia to administer the trade to the Mina Coast. Such companies represented a popular solution to the metropole's two central goals regarding its Brazilian possession. Firstly, such a measure could structure the maritime trade and, administrators hoped, reinforce prohibitions against the Bahian merchants' illicit but commonplace transimperial commerce in Brazilian gold for European textiles and luxury goods. Secondly, metropolitan authorities believed a monopoly company would sustain and strengthen the slave trade by curbing inflation in the price of enslaved Africans on the coast, which they considered imperative for the continued vitality of gold mining and tobacco and sugar cultivation.[24]

---

or tobacco planters, as practiced by some individual traders who agree on long term credit and receive payment in kind, that the resources provided by those who lend their money at such risk will dry up, whilst the cargoes they provide will end" (Verger, *Trade Relations,* [trans. Crawford], 98 n. 9).

23. Verger, *Trade Relations,* [trans. Crawford], 47–49, 109–113. In 1746, for instance, a Bahian slaving ship captain named Felix José de Gouvea was appointed as the fort's director. During the same period, all correspondence from São João Baptista was directed to the governor of Bahia (ibid., 159).

24. Verger, *Trade Relations,* [trans. Crawford], 52–53, 98 n. 9. André Marques, along with eleven other Bahian traders, crafted a proposal for the monopoly company, which, they argued, would promote greater centralization and routinization of the trade through

Meanwhile, in West Africa, the need to fashion lasting bonds of cooperation with local potentates became even more pressing following the Dahomean king Agaja's conquest of Allada in 1724. This upheaval ushered in a period of growing hostilities between slave-trading Dahomey and surrounding polities. From the 1720s through the 1770s, Dahomey and its rivals' battles for regional supremacy periodically diminished trade on that portion of the Mina Coast, as did the increasing taxes levied by the king of Dahomey, requiring each ship captain to pay one slave to "open," or commence, the trade, as well as ten additional slaves paid to the king upon completion of a cargo. After Agaja's death, subsequent rulers of Dahomey were just as bellicose, at least according to the Atlantic merchants and Portuguese administrators stationed on the Mina Coast. One such representative went so far as to chastise the "boldness and imprudence of the petty barbarian king." The rising military powerhouse of Dahomey created persistent commercial instability in the region, even as its conquests sporadically replenished slaving markets with the polity's exiled war captives.[25]

---

the use of ships with larger cargo-holding capacities and precisely scheduled dispatches. These measures, he hoped, would increase the value of tobacco from the twelve, fifteen, or twenty rolls required for the purchase of one slave to instead require only five or six rolls per head. In the same vein, by May 1743, the Royal Court in Lisbon had approved a reduction in the number of ships allowed to trade on the Mina Coast; a squadron of three ships with a three-month interval between voyages, they reasoned, would guarantee equitable prices and a steady supply of enslaved labor from the West African coast. One month later, the Conselho Ultramarino advised the viceroy to begin soliciting guidance from Bahian merchants and administrators on the formation of a monopoly trading company based in the port. The council also limited commercial houses to owning one vessel each, looking to weaken the monopoly of the transatlantic slave trade held by a combination of thirteen merchants and commercial houses who together owned all of the twenty-four Bahian ships that regularly traveled to Mina Coast in midcentury. Bahian merchants resisted the crown's commercial reforms, arguing for a reliberalization of trade during the following years (Verger, *Trade Relations,* [trans. Crawford], 78, 81, 98–99 n. 9).

25. Verger, *Trade Relations,* [trans. Crawford], 164. The eleven-slave duty was much higher than the six slaves paid to the king, and two to his cabeceiras, or lead traders, that the Huedan ruler had mandated before his expulsion (Law, *Ouidah,* 127). Though Europeans and Brazilians perceived all political power in Dahomey to be concentrated in the hands of the king (*ahosu*), as Edna G. Bay argues, royal power was in fact corporate: the king represented to outsiders the clout of a coalition of individuals and lineages whose support was necessary to secure any Dahomean king's claim to the title of leader (Bay, *Wives of the Leopard: Gender, Politics, and Culture in the Kingdom of Dahomey* [Charlottesville, Va., 1998], 7).

As a result of Dahomey's quest to control and monopolize the slave trade in the region, Atlantic commerce on the Mina Coast was continually paralyzed. The most dramatic example was Agaja's conquest of Ouidah in 1727, which drove out Huedan king Hufon and led to the burning of the Portuguese feitoria to the ground. Nor did Dahomey limit its aggression to other West African trading polities; slave traders, captains, and their crews were regularly embroiled in such violence, sometimes imprisoned or killed. In the decades following the sacking of Ouidah, Dahomey would carry out its own series of blockades. By monopolizing slaving routes from the interior to Atlantic seaports, Dahomey quickly assumed the mantle of ascendant regional power. Though conflict between Dahomey and Hueda cooled in 1732, Bahian merchants continued to complain that the slave trade had slowed to a halt, with some ships returning to Brazil empty and others having their voyages delayed for more than a year. Agaja's local conquests were part of a grand strategy to elevate prices by concentrating all slave trading on the Mina Coast in Dahomean-controlled Ouidah. To the detriment of Bahian slavers' economic interests, the strategy was extremely successful.[26]

The unrelenting turmoil on the West African coast was a double-edged sword for the representatives of the Portuguese empire. On the one hand, hostilities between Hueda and Dahomey—which lasted until 1775—continued to produce numerous war captives, many of whom Dahomey sold to transatlantic slaving merchants for handsome profits despite the attendant price inflation on the Mina Coast.[27] On the other hand, political and military

26. Ouidah was a relatively peaceful polity, and the port was a desirable entrepôt for European captains and merchants to purchase slaves. Following a successful drive to the coast—which included an attack on Savi months earlier, during which thousands were killed and enslaved—Agaja and his army conquered the city, sparing the remaining European trading forts and gaining access to Atlantic trade. He claimed the Hueden king had "forbidden" him to trade, precipitating Dahomey's hostilities. See Bay, *Wives of the Leopard,* 43; Law, *Ouidah,* 50–54; Verger, *Trade Relations,* [trans. Crawford], 122, 125–126. Attacks on Jakin in 1732 and Badagry in 1737 followed. Each of these cities were rivals to Dahomey in the Atlantic trade, and they continued to be targets of the powerful polity's aggression, along with the newly opened ports of Porto Novo (Àjàṣẹ́ in Yoruba) and Ekpe, until the end of the century. See Ogundiran, *The Yorùbá,* 246; Verger, *Trade Relations,* [trans. Crawford], 131–141.

27. The sacking of Ouidah resulted in Dahomean forces' taking an estimated 11,000 individuals as captives; the destruction of Jakin led to the imprisonment of 4,528 residents (Luis Nicolau Parés, *The Formation of Candomblé: Vodun History and Ritual in Brazil,* trans. Richard Vernon [Chapel Hill, N.C., 2013], 30).

instability also endangered personnel stationed within the São João Baptista de Ajudá fort, the Portuguese crown's only territorial foothold on the coast.[28] In these difficult decades, the Conselho Ultramarino debated closing down the outpost, reasoning that the value derived from the taxes paid by slave trading there were inadequate to reimburse the costs of maintaining its military preparedness. The destruction of São João Baptista fort in 1743 prompted other European traders on the coast to assess their own vulnerability, with the director of the French fort in Ouidah exclaiming after the incident, "If the Dahomeans (fierce people) once began to cut the throats of the whites, this country would become a slaughter house for us, and with the slightest discontent which these people might pretend to have, they would kill us like sheep." On March 30, 1756, the Portuguese crown opened the slave trade to private traders, who could legally bypass the São João Baptista de Ajudá fort. Pierre Verger argues that this shift led to an overall decline of trade at Ouidah and an expansion of Bahian merchants' slave-trading activities to the port's east.[29]

Forced once again to relocate their trading activities, enterprising Bahian merchants turned to more culturally effective forms of commercial engagement to secure their economic goals. Indeed, the disreputable "liberty and disorder" that Portuguese administrators ascribed to the Mina Coast trade stemmed from the remote region's de facto function as a free-trade zone for European and American merchants long before the official movement of European imperial policy away from mercantilist restrictions in colonial ports. Foreign ships commonly anchored at nearby São Tomé after leaving the African coast to procure provisions of wood, water, flour, fowls, and other foodstuffs for their westward journey to the Americas. While these foreign vessels were stationed in port, the residents of the island—including Capuchin priests—purchased forbidden goods from their ships. Local waters were teeming with fishermen who approached visiting vessels in their dugout

28. The first attack on Ouidah saw the storekeeper of São João Baptista fort, Simão Cardoso, decapitated, with his head then reportedly delivered to Agaja. In 1743, the director of the feitoria, João Basílio, was taken prisoner by Agaja's successor, Tegbessu, under suspicion of colluding with the exiled Huedan king by supplying him with weaponry to attack Dahomey. A Dahomean siege of the fort on the same day as Basílio's arrest led to its destruction: the African "head servant" tasked with running it in Basílio's absence blew up the building with a keg of powder after most of the Huedan refugees housed inside had been slaughtered. The fort was rebuilt in 1744. See Verger, *Trade Relations*, [trans. Crawford], 125, 147–154; Law, *Ouidah*, 60.

29. Verger, *Trade Relations*, [trans. Crawford], 130, 147, 162, 179.

canoes to sell local produce, such as limes, in exchange for European commodities. These small-scale contraband practices existed side by side with a more lucrative clandestine interimperial trade in European luxury goods. As a result, slave-trading ships laden with untaxed commodities from West Africa arrived in large numbers on Bahia's shores.[30]

As Bahian merchants continued to exercise their autonomy from the Portuguese crown's prohibitions on interimperial commerce, mastery of the intricacies of coastal trading became paramount. To comfortably bear the risks of the transatlantic trade, sea captains and merchants needed to be confident of their ability to engage African traders on the coast. Interacting with a wider array of trading partners required attention to local commodity preferences, language, and custom. Moreover, the ability to participate in coastal trade demanded a heightened level of cultural sophistication and facility on the part of supposedly humble slaving ship captains. One administrator writing in 1763 stressed that intimate knowledge of "dealing with the trade and the people" of Mina Coast was a precursor to successful commerce there. The volatile politics of West African conquest, population displacement, and community formation required captains to navigate an evolving political landscape. Indeed, Sargento-Mor José Gonçalves da Silva noted that the style of commerce on the Mina Coast was best characterized as an "experimental science," emphasizing the ad hoc nature of most interactions between African merchants and Europeans. Familiarity with local languages, customs, material desires, and methods of negotiation became an increasingly salient aspect of slave trading. In the decades ahead, seasoned, cosmopolitan Black merchants,

30. Ibid., 166. The Portuguese island of Príncipe had become a locus of contraband trade by 1739. Bahian slaving vessels frequently transported luxurious textiles to the island, including silks and striped cloth, on the pretext of using them to exchange for slaves on the Mina Coast. They instead purchased *dendê* oil and soap produced on the island, both of which "conduct[ed] a great trade" in Bahia, and refused to pay taxes on the grounds that such intraimperial transactions were privileged. The porosity of trade on the Mina Coast riled the governor of Bahia, Marquis de Valença. He proclaimed that transatlantic commerce had "two different branches, one licit, legal and useful which was the slave trade, the other illegal, pernicious and prohibited, which was trading in all sorts of foreign cloth which they took to Bahia, under cover of trading in Negroes." See Verger, *Trade Relations,* [trans. Crawford], 79, 102 n. 74; AHU, CU, São Tomé e Príncipe, caixa 7, documento 777, Jan. 14, 1740, "Carta do D. José Caetano Souto Maior, ao Rei Respondendo à ordem de 10 de Julho 1739"; ibid., caixa 11, documento 1138, Oct. 15, 1766, "Memória do Gaspar Pinheiro da Câmara Manuel Sobre o Clima, a Geografia."

captains, and traders would prove more able to contend with the complex dynamics of slaving on the eastern Mina Coast.[31]

A BLACK MARITIME MIDDLEMAN

In the context of pervasive interimperial conflict, continual political violence, and commercial disruption, João de Oliveira became a pivotal actor on the Mina Coast and decisively altered the trajectory of Bahian slaving. As a laborer in the transatlantic trade—initially as the slave of a merchant from Pernambuco involved in the West African trade—he would have become intimately acquainted with the complexities of slaving commerce on the Mina Coast. The lasting irony of his life was that, in his social and economic ascent, Oliveira abetted, at first involuntarily and then of his own volition, the very slave trade that had severed him from his kin and community. For the next thirty-eight years, Oliveira remained on the West African coast as a cabeceira "among his [former] countrymen."[32]

Despite, or perhaps because of, the vulnerabilities innate to Atlantic slavery, the West African–born Oliveira would become an ideal maritime broker for the larger project of Bahian slaving. His cosmopolitanism enabled him to develop durable transatlantic ties. Oliveira drew on his cultural flexibility—his fluency in both Portuguese and West African language and custom—to engage Bight of Benin merchants and potentates in diplomacy, securing Brazilian access to new slave-trading routes. As Bahian slaving merchants would later attest, his "unwavering contributions to Portuguese navigation" entailed not only establishing commercial relations in new ports but expediting the embarkation of ships through the collection of cargoes and safeguarding Brazilian trade goods from robberies ordered by African potentates. Oliveira was instrumental in opening the slave trade at Porto Novo in 1758, as Bahian merchants tried to elude Dahomey's tightening grasp over Ouidah by navigating to more profitable ports.[33] Pioneering a new slave-trading route required significant diplomatic negotiations with the local ruler there, allowing Oliveira

31. AHU, CU, São Tomé e Príncipe, caixa 11, documento 1124, Dec. 6, 1763, "Requerimento do Sargento-Mor Assistente na Bahia, José Gonçalves Silva ao rei, solicitando ser provido no lugar de Director Geral."

32. Verger, *Trade Relations*, [trans. Crawford], 467; AHU, CU, Bahia–Eduardo de Castro e Almeida, caixa 44, documento 8246.

33. AHU, CU, Bahia–Eduardo de Castro e Almeida, caixa 44, documento 8245. In 1775, Porto Novo's ruler attempted to further cement ties between his port and Brazilian

to put his familiarity with the region's language and customs to use. Under his initiative, Porto Novo became the preferred outlet for slaving caravans emanating from the powerful Oyo empire, located in the interior of the Bight of Benin. By securing this new stream of captives, Oliveira managed to realize significant trading advantages for Bahian merchants in comparison to Ouidah, including lower prices and reduced time to complete cargoes. As a growing sign of Oliveira's commercial success through slaving, he accumulated sufficient wealth to establish commercial relations in Porto Novo "with his own labor and money."[34]

The cultural and commercial expertise of intermediaries like Oliveira remained paramount in facilitating the day-to-day functioning of Brazilian commerce on the Mina Coast. As Robin Law and Kristin Mann have argued, the imperative to create "efficient, reliable commercial networks" required "business and social relationships that spanned the Atlantic and linked political and commercial elites along the coast [of Africa]." Indeed, Oliveira himself insisted that he had "helped [Brazilian merchants] to affect their business with the most kindness." For his service, he gained a measure of their esteem. When Oliveira returned to Salvador in 1770, the governor declared him an official cabeceira "of letter" of the king, "one of the greatest favors of the Portuguese nation."[35]

----

merchants by requesting that the king of Portugal build a trading fort in his city. In his letter to the crown, he made a veiled reference to the domineering role Dahomey's king had played in Ouidah: "I am unable to personally look after everything that touches on the slave trade which is carried out by these ships . . . from the absence of someone who takes care of all their needs." Portuguese administrators never responded, and private traders continued to be solely responsible for managing trade in Porto Novo. See Verger, *Trade Relations,* [trans. Crawford], 180.

34. As the king of Dahomey periodically closed routes connecting slavers in the interior to Ouidah in 1758, the value of each slave sold rose from eight to twelve rolls of tobacco to thirteen to sixteen rolls. In Porto Novo, meanwhile, one enslaved man cost eight to twelve rolls of tobacco. Cargoes could also be completed 30 percent faster at Porto Novo than at Ouidah, which prevented the spoilage of Brazilian tobacco before it could be sold for slaves. See AHU, CU, Bahia–Eduardo de Castro e Almeida, caixa 44, documentos 8244, 8246; Law, "Trade and Politics behind the Slave Coast," *Journal of African History,* XXIV (1983), 328; Verger, *Trade Relations,* [trans. Crawford], 167–168.

35. Robin Law and Kristin Mann, "West Africa in the Atlantic Community: The Case of the Slave Coast," *WMQ,* 3d Ser., LVI (1999), 307–334, esp. 315–320; AHU, CU, Bahia–Eduardo de Castro e Almeida, caixa 44, documentos 8244, 8246.

In the years after 1758, Oliveira also pioneered Brazilian trade connections in Lagos—a port community located on the Lagos River that was conquered and governed by descendants of the royal dynasty of Benin, though it would not become a major site of Bahian slave-trading activity until the 1790s. Unlike in Ouidah, however, Porto Novo and Lagos contained no royally sponsored Portuguese feitorias, so the logistical work of collecting slaves and goods for cargoes, as well as securing provisioning and transportation for visiting slaving ships, had to be improvised by private traders on the ground. Achieving this once again demanded significant diplomatic skill and direct negotiations with African potentates. Oliveira's success in establishing efficacious relationships with rulers on the Mina Coast was evident by the four West African cabeceiras the leader of Lagos sent to accompany Oliveira on his 1770 return journey to Bahia.[36]

Overall, Oliveira's commercial initiatives produced a major transformation on the Mina Coast and a permanent reorientation to Yoruba-speaking eastern ports that would become the center of slaving for Bahian merchants. After several decades in West Africa, he had accumulated extensive property holdings and fabulous wealth, including luxury goods from diverse global origins such as finely painted English porcelain, Geneva brandy, and French silver spoons. Perhaps most notably, the formerly enslaved African man also returned to Salvador as the owner of seventy-nine captive males and forty-three captive females—a reminder of how tightly his social ascent was tied to transatlantic slaving.[37]

36. Law, "Trade and Politics behind the Slave Coast," *Journal of African History*, XXIV (1983), 328; Kristin Mann, *Slavery and the Birth of an African City: Lagos, 1760–1900* (Bloomington, Ind., 2007), 36; Ogundiran, *The Yorùbá*, 247; Verger, *Trade Relations*, [trans. Crawford], 167. They were identified as "free men" and acting as ambassadors to Portuguese commercial interests in the slaving ports of Recife and Salvador da Bahia in the northeastern region of colonial Brazil (AHU, CU, Bahia–Eduardo de Castro e Almeida, caixa 44, documento 8246).

37. The luxury goods included a serving plate decorated with red paint and gold gilding; others were from Asia, such as a set of fine china from India and packets of fine teas. Oliveira was also the owner of a dizzying assortment of fabrics from all over the world. Indeed, he carried embroidered silk, damask, a taffeta gown embroidered with gold, another of velvet, three British shirts, fine table linens, yellow satin pants, green- and red-striped satin pants, silk scarves and belts, blue-striped woolen cloth, blue flannels, decorated hats of taffeta, and various chambrays (AHU, CU, Bahia–Eduardo de Castro e Almeida, caixa 44, documentos 8249, 8250). In addition to captives, Oliviera returned to Bahia as the owner of bundles

A COLLECTIVE SLAVING ENTERPRISE

Over the course of the eighteenth century, Bahian merchants contended with a multitude of challenges—primarily political and military—on the Mina Coast. Their commercial ambitions were also circumscribed by the financial viability of their transatlantic slaving operations. João de Oliveira's eventual return to West Africa was indicative of Bahian slavers' solution to persistent problems of risk and undercapitalization. In fact, Oliveira's commercial endeavors represented the apex of a larger structure of slaving finance in the South Atlantic, in which a wide array of subaltern subjects were incentivized to harness their social and economic aspirations to the successful functioning of the trade in human flesh and blood. In doing so, merchants ensured their ability to raise sufficient capital to launch transatlantic voyages while also inducing those who labored on those same voyages to act in the protection of the ship's, and thus their own, transatlantic investments. Uniquely among slaving ships in the Atlantic, cargoes on many Bahian vessels tended to be collectively structured legal partnerships held by a diverse group of stakeholders, including slaving ship captains and crews, residents of Bahia—and even, in rarer cases, enslaved men and women on shore.

This distinctive investment structure had roots in Portuguese merchants' earliest forays into the business of transatlantic slave trading. Sailors laboring on the route between Guiné and Cabo Verde in the fifteenth to the seventeenth centuries were active purchasers of slaves. In the fifteenth century, because Portuguese slave-trading voyages were "organised on a share basis, the initial capital did not have to be high." This essentially medieval structure of trade mitigated the disadvantages inherent to Portuguese slaving, allowing for distribution of risk in the absence of a royally sponsored trading company that could provide long-term credit or absorb short-term financial losses. Collective finance enabled ship captains to cobble together sufficient capital to fund voyages, and such short-term legal partnerships also endowed penniless sailors with the ability to accumulate enough wealth to become independent traders in a matter of years.[38]

---

of gold. The value of these bundles amounted to four *milréis,* 709.200 milréis, and 7.640 milréis respectively (ibid.).

38. Ivana Elbl, "The Portuguese Trade with West Africa, 1440–1521" (Ph.D. diss., University of Toronto, 1986), 343. On the vessels that plied that particular trading route, dozens of residents of Santiago Island (in the Cabo Verde archipelago) individually invested in slaving voyages. Merchants in Portugal often employed representatives in West Africa to invest

In the eighteenth century, Bahian slaving ships' investment structure continued to owe its form to the medieval Mediterranean *commenda* contract,
or the "basic legal instruments to pool capital and to bring together investors
and managers." Such short-term contracts "determined the relationship between parties on several levels, including investment, agency . . . risk allocation, profit allocation, and creation of a separate pool of assets." They proved
remarkably durable in colonial Bahia, where poorly capitalized slaving voyages took on a multiplicity of investors from varying social strata to achieve
viability. In addition, the limited circulation of gold and silver in Salvador's
economy encouraged short-term, collective investment in bartered agricultural commodities, particularly tobacco and *aguardente* (liquor), and only
rarely specie. These nonmonetary arrangements, in which local investors
advanced goods on a very small scale, mirrored the credit arrangements more
prominent slave traders used to secure *fazendas* (trade goods) produced in
the plantation-dense region of the Recôncavo.[39]

To achieve financial viability, ship merchants relied on the same form of
medieval contract that had dominated an earlier Mediterranean trade struc-

---

in slaving voyages for them. See Trevor Paul Hall, "The Role of Cape Verde Islanders in
Organizing and Operating Maritime Trade between West Africa and Iberian Territories,
1441–1616" (Ph.D. diss., Johns Hopkins University, 1993), 139, 232, 250–256.

39. Robert S. Lopez and Irving W. Raymond, trans., *Medieval Trade in the Mediterranean World: Illustrative Documents* (New York, 2001), 174; Ron Harris, "The Institutional Dynamics of Early Modern Eurasian Trade: The *Commenda* and the Corporation,"
Journal of Economic Behavior and Organization, LXXI (2009), 606, 610; Miller, *Way of
Death,* 470–473; B. J. Barickman, "'A Bit of Land, Which They Call Roça': Slave Provision
Grounds in the Bahian Recôncavo, 1780–1860," *HAHR,* LXXIV (1994), 653. Access to a
continuous supply of African captives enabled the residents of Bahia to secure commodities emanating from South American, European, and Asian ports. Inferior-quality Bahian
tobacco—called *soca*—was dried and soaked in molasses, then rolled into large units for sale
on the African coast, though merchants evaded metropolitan dictates and sold first-grade
tobacco to African merchants as well. Ships carried an average of three thousand rolls in the
mid-eighteenth century. Bahian merchants also acquired gold from Minas Gerais after 1702
and silver from the Río de La Plata port of Montevideo after 1791 through their reexporta-
tion of enslaved Africans. Because Portuguese merchants required payment in gold or silver
coinage, much of the specie that entered Bahia was eventually shipped to Lisbon, especially
by 1739. Miller has found a very similar pattern for Rio de Janeiro. See Alex Borucki, "The
Slave Trade to the Río de la Plata, 1777–1812: Trans-Imperial Networks and Atlantic Warfare," *Colonial Latin American Review,* XX (2011), 81–107; Miller, *Way of Death,* 471; Verger,
Trade Relations, [trans. Crawford], 4, 12–14, 26, 32.

ture. The bilateral commenda consisted of an agreement between a "sedentary" investor who remained in port and a "traveling" manager (potentially, a sea captain) who accompanied the mobile investment. Both partners received a portion of the voyage's profits. This basic structure could be adapted to include multiple investing parties with divided shares of a single cargo (called *loca navis, partes,* or *sortes* in the medieval Mediterranean, and *praças* or *lotes* in the early modern Portuguese Atlantic); at times, even individual items held in cargoes could be divided by several owners. Because investors in overseas voyages conceptualized their involvement as participation rather than the extension of credit to an independent party, they supplied goods or services instead of contributing loans to trading ventures in currency values. Collective commercial practices existed concurrently with attempts by Bahia's merchant community to maintain a de facto monopoly on the trade in the face of metropolitan opposition to such trade arrangements. In their quest to assure that Salvador's slaving ships controlled the Portuguese trade on the Mina Coast, Bahian merchants relied on interwoven familial and patronage ties among a diverse cross-section of the city's population to raise commercial capital for voyages. Instead of depending solely on the rigid financial structures of chartered trading companies or merchant firms, merchants and captains leveraged their informal relationships. These interpersonal commercial arrangements meant that mariners, both enslaved and free, as well as other humble residents of Bahia, could become an integral part of the financing of Bahian slaving ships.[40]

To extract a measure of wealth from transatlantic voyages, mariners drew on both medieval and more recent imperial precedents that endowed seafarers the right to stow cargo free of freightage costs. While sea captains' granting of cargo privileges as a form of labor compensation faded in the North Atlantic, Portuguese merchants traversing the Atlantic and then Indian Ocean extended mariners the option to continue the customary privilege. Royal ships navigating on the Carreira da Índia between Lisbon, Goa, and Ceylon offered prospective seafarers access to a liberty chest (*caixa de liberdade*),

40. M. M. Postan, E. E. Rich, and Edward Miller, eds., *The Cambridge Economic History of Europe,* III, *Economic Organization and Policies in the Middle Ages* (Cambridge, [1942?]), 58; Max Weber, *General Economic History,* trans. Frank H. Knight (Mineola, N.Y., 2003), 225–226; Lutz Kaelber, "Max Weber and Usury: Implications for Historical Research," in Lawrin Armstrong, Ivanna Elbl, and Martin M. Elbl, eds., *Money, Markets, and Trade in Late Medieval Europe: Essays in Honour of John H. A. Munro* (Leiden, 2007), 59–86. *Commenda* in Italian means "to entrust or give."

or an allotment of space within a ship's cargo hold to store personal trading goods, a gambit to attract laborers for the deadly, protracted voyage. On routes to India, each crew member was allowed a standardized bundle or chest of goods allocated on a sliding scale according to their shipboard rank. In Goa and Ceylon, mariners purchased spices, cotton, silk textiles, and hardwoods that could be sold for handsome profits in Lisbon's markets. Salvador's long-standing status as a layover in the Carreira da Índia route likely provided inspiration for the practice on local and transatlantic voyages. Mariners on Indiamen who disembarked on Salvador's shores could have informed local seafarers of the lucrative investment goods they had managed to secure during their distant travels.[41]

Collective investment spread the benefits of transatlantic slaving among Bahia's population more broadly than in other Atlantic ports; however, financial decentralization, in the minds of some contemporaries, was tantamount to "disorder." In the early eighteenth century, the director of the French-held Saint-Louis de Grégoy fort in Ouidah complained that Portuguese trading arrangements were "disorganized" and had thus devalued tobacco and gold on the African coast. Director Louis Du Coulombier proclaimed, "The slave trade has become increasingly bad due to the large number of vessels engaged in it . . . which has ruined business, combined with the confusion and disorder of the Portuguese which has always been characteristic of this nation carrying out their slaving." As Du Coulombier further observed, slaving vessels granted "permission which captains and sailors have to embark as many slaves as they like for their own profit and that of their friends, paying the freight and the food to the shipowner." Such an arrangement, he believed, contributed to captains' decreasing authority over crews. During moments

41. C. R. Boxer, *From Lisbon to Goa, 1500–1750: Studies in Portuguese Maritime Enterprise* (London, 1997), 52–53; Chandra Richard de Silva, *The Portuguese in Ceylon, 1617–1638* ([London], 1967), 200. Maryanne Kowaleski notes that mariners on the Bordeaux wine route from Exeter were allowed to carry a volume of wine without paying freightage; in Devon, during the early fourteenth century, 13 percent of shipmasters claimed porterage, whereas 7 percent of mariners did. See Kowaleski, "The Shipmaster as Entrepreneur in Medieval England," in Ben Dodds and Christian D. Liddy, eds., *Commercial Activity, Markets, and Entrepreneurs in the Middle Ages: Essays in Honour of Richard Britnell* (Woodbridge, Suffolk, U.K., 2011), 165–182, esp. 174–175. By the end of the seventeenth century, caixas de liberdade dwarfed other forms of investment on the Carreira da Índia, comprising 90 percent of the volume of all cargoes on Indiamen. See Roquinaldo Amaral Ferreira, "Transforming Atlantic Slaving: Trade, Warfare, and Territorial Control in Angola, 1650–1800" (Ph.D. diss., University of California, Los Angeles, 2003), 53–54.

of negotiation, "after the captain has finished his slave trading, the rest of the crew in order to hurry often give up to twice the usual price to be able to have handsome captives. Thus, seven or eight ships (Portuguese) being all together at one time have spoilt everything."[42]

In 1736, a Bahian colonial authority named Wenceslão Pereira da Silva made a similar point in lamenting the precipitous decline of slaving on the Mina Coast. The reason only half as many slaving ships were at that time making the journey, he contended, was the predictable consequence of the innate "disorder" of Bahian vessels' trading practices. Ships landed on the coast "sometimes one atop the other without ensuring a sufficient amount of time between them for the smooth flow of their cargo," causing inflation in African prices as captains and seamen flooded markets with tobacco. In contrast, better-organized Dutch merchants utilized the stability of monopoly trading companies to maintain profitability, promote coordination, and discipline self-interested slaving merchants. Bahian traders elided such mechanisms of control. As a result, the Dutch secured greater access to West African commodities, later "re-selling them [slaves] to our Portuguese in exchange for gold."[43]

Despite administrators' objections, permitting mariners access to transatlantic investment was desirable for slaving ship captains. Like all managers of labor, these captains faced the perennial question of compelling worker obedience. They relied on mariners who could not only perform routine manual tasks but also execute duties that required technical expertise and precision, and captains endeavored to secure mariners' loyalties to the central mission of the ship: delivering cargo safely in a cost-effective manner. Black mariners, even when enslaved, required more than violence to motivate them. By allowing mariners to negotiate for trading privileges as well as wages, captains and merchants created an incentive structure to carry out duties well, which strengthened seafarers' commitments to the voyage's success.

Liberty chests were not just a tool of labor management, however. Black mariners struggled to acquire the privilege. In 1725, sailors aboard the *Nossa Senhora do Paraíso,* based in Luanda, requested the ability to secure a liberty chest as sailors on routes destined for Brazil and seamen laboring on the Carreira da Índia had done.[44] Their legal petition hinted at the expansive infor-

---

42. Verger, *Trade Relations,* [trans. Crawford], 77–78, 108.

43. Ibid., 77–78. The viceroy of Bahia noted in 1741 that unfavorable rates of exchange on the West African coast had increased the price of enslaved individuals in Brazil (ibid.).

44. AHU, CU, Angola, caixa 24, documento 2436, Oct. 19, 1725, "Requerimento dos mainheiros da Nau Nossa Senhora do Paraíso, de viagem para o reino de Angola."

mational networks among sailors in different ports, who communicated about the privileges accorded to seafarers across the lusophone Atlantic world. Such concessions were more than wealthy shipowners' instruments of co-optation; they became a necessity for the viability of the trade. Mariners' confident legal assertions that their trading privileges should be enshrined as a right revealed their own sense of investment in the operation of transatlantic commerce.

Collective investments in the financing of transatlantic slaving were not solely the preserve of shipboard mariners. A range of Salvador's residents— including numerous enslaved men and women—sought to utilize the slaving ship as a means to secure transatlantic commercial opportunities for themselves. Indeed, colonial authorities remarked upon this diversified investment activity as crucial to the economic foundations of the city. In March 1731, the colony's viceroy, Vasco Fernandes César de Menezes, asserted, "All of the inhabitants of Bahia live on the trade with the Mina Coast," echoing the sentiments of earlier travelers who had observed that the transatlantic trade was the source of the coastal entrepôt's prosperity. The viceroy further stated, in a letter to the secretary of state in Lisbon, "They [the inhabitants] are engaged in sending freight, or have an interest in the sale they make with owners of shipments and other people who ship from there." The trade seemed "their sole resource today, particularly the civil servants as well as the poor, who have no work to live on; or those who not even being able to have a little Negro for their domestic work, invest their twenty-five to thirty thousand reis in tobacco to send to the said coast, thus finding a remedy for their needs." Enslaved individuals purchased on the West African coast could easily be put to work on Salvador's streets as *escravos de gahno,* earning their owners an attractive daily stipend for little supervisory effort, or they could be promptly resold for a profit.[45]

Relying on mariners' trading privileges as well as the customary rights masters granted enslaved persons to own private property, African-born men who returned to the Bight of Benin as captive seamen insinuated themselves into local commodity exchanges for their own benefit. Enslaved seamen's success in capturing a sliver of slaving profits was epitomized by the activities of nine enslaved sailors laboring on the *Nossa Senhora da Esperança e São José.* The slaving vessel, captained by Antônio da Costa Basto, left the port of Salvador da Bahia for the Mina Coast in 1767, carrying a cargo of tobacco, aguardente, sugar, silk, and *buzios* (cowries). A few months after its departure, Dutch pirates in Cabo Lau violently seized the ship and imprisoned and interrogated

45. Verger, *Trade Relations,* [trans. Crawford], 14.

the mariners in nearby São Jorge da Mina Castle. As the *Nossa Senhora da Esperança*'s trade goods were appropriated, the ship's owner, Jozé de Souza Reis, petitioned the Dutch government for restitution of the lost cargo, which he estimated to have a value of 14:831$836 réis. De Souza Reis, however, was not the only party that stood to be inconvenienced by the confiscation. The ship's papers revealed a total of thirty-six individual investors in the cargo, as well as two Catholic brotherhoods. These organizations—the Irmandade do Sacramento da Matriz de Nossa Senhora da Conceição da Praia and the Irmandade do Senhor do Bonfim—collectively owned twenty-six rolls of tobacco valued at 73$288 réis. In the mid-eighteenth century, these Catholic brotherhoods were populated by a membership that was Black and largely of West African origin. Additionally, there were the nine enslaved African mariners, seven of whom were sailors and two of whom were barbers. The ship's manifest listed "one cargo of the owner of the ship, Senhor Jozé de Souza Reis for the account of his African mariners that comprises 40 rolls of tobacco at a total value of 480$000 *réis*." De Souza Reis had invested a further sixteen rolls of tobacco at a value of 192$000 réis on behalf of his slaves. The men's investment amounted to a substantial sum for a group of enslaved African mariners: 4.5 percent of the vessel's total cargo.[46]

As the manifest of the *Nossa Senhora da Esperança* indicates, Africans in Bahia were collectively investing in transatlantic commerce as early as 1767. The captain facilitated the enslaved seamen's material ambitions, sending ten rolls of tobacco worth 120$000 réis on shore in the care of the ship's enslaved African sailors so they could "purchase what was necessary" for De Souza Reis, the proprietor of the vessel. Because most of these sailors were from the Mina Coast, where the ship was conducting its trade, they would have been ideal brokers to secure provisions. While ashore, these mariners, having trade goods

46. For more on the slave-held peculium, or savings funds possessed with the approval of their owners, see Stuart B. Schwartz, *Sugar Plantations in the Formation of Brazilian Society: Bahia, 1550–1835* (Cambridge, 1985), 252; Roger A. Kittleson, *The Practice of Politics in Postcolonial Brazil: Porto Alegre, 1845–1895* (Pittsburgh, 2006), 86–87; Carl N. Degler, *Neither Black nor White: Slavery and Race Relations in Brazil and the United States* (Madison, Wis., 1971), 42. Aguardente is liquor distilled from sugarcane juice; buzios, or cowry shells from the Indian Ocean, were frequently used as currency in slave-trading polities in West Africa, including Dahomey, Ouidah, and Lagos (Law, *Ouidah*, 82–24). Both the Irmandade do Senhor do Bonfim and the Irmandade do Sacramento da Matriz de Nossa Senhora da Conceição da Praia had at least some West African–born members (Josildeth Gomes Consorte, "Sincretismo e Africanidade em terreiros Jege Nagô de Salvador," in Ana Amélia da Silva and Miguel Chaia, eds., *Sociedade, cultura e política: Ensaios críticos* [São

of their own aboard, could have easily engaged in commerce for their private benefit. That such opportunities for trade endowed enslaved mariners with a considerable degree of commercial agency and financial autonomy from their owners might seem paradoxical. In the context of eighteenth-century Bahia, however, this was not the case. Collective partnership investment strategies proved attractive not only for residents of Bahia with minimal access to wealth or capital but for elites, as well. Slaving ship captains and merchants mitigated economic risk by spreading their own transatlantic investments among voyages, even investing in ventures they did not directly manage. For the sailors, the perils of such a cosmopolitan milieu existed alongside vulnerability, however— as the men aboard the *Nossa Senhora da Esperança* experienced when the Dutch stripped them of their goods and, for a time, their physical freedom.[47]

A DECENTRALIZED WEST AFRICAN TRADE

Building on the entrepreneurial successes of João de Oliveira, at the end of the eighteenth century, Bahian traders permeated the West African coastal communities of Badgary, Porto Novo, and Lagos. The volume of trading from those ports increased dramatically from the 1760s to the 1780s. In response, Dahomey's leader, Kpengla, initiated a strategy of militarily subduing trading competitors on the coast and making escalating demands of Portuguese traders. Hoping to shift trade back to Ouidah, the *ahosu* (king) took dramatic action, sacking Porto Novo in 1787 and taking French and Portuguese slavers as well as eighty canoemen from Elmina prisoner. In addition to these men, nine Brazilian sailors, both free and enslaved, had already been held in Dahomey as hostages for several years. That same year, Dahomey's Bahian captives petitioned the crown to pay for their ransom, lamenting in a letter that they

---

Paulo, 2004], 195–203, esp. 197–198); and see AHU, CU, Bahia, caixa 50, documento 4440, Mar. 11, 1735, "Consulta do Conselho Ultramarino ao rei D. João V."

The manifest lists the men's names as follows: Matheus, Gege, sailor; Manoel, Angola, sailor; Christovão, Angola, sailor; Joaquim, Gege, barber; Tomas, Gege, sailor; Felippe, Gege, sailor; Ignacio, Gege, barber; Joaquim, Gege, sailor; Domings, Gege, sailor. "Gege" refers to Fon-speaking Africans transported from Ouidah during the mid- to late eighteenth century (AHU, CU, Bahia, caixa 164, documento 12423, Jan. 4, 1770, "Carta do Conde de Povolide ao rei sobre a carta do desembargador, Provedor-Mor da Fazenda Real da Bahia").

47. AHU, CU, Bahia, caixa 164, documento 12423, Jan. 4, 1770, "Carta do Conde de Povolide ao rei sobre a carta do desembargador, Provedor-Mor da Fazenda Real da Bahia"; ibid., documento 12420, Jan. 2, 1770, "Extrato da Carregações que o Capitão António da Costa Basto Levara da Bahia."

had been "imprisoned by the King of Dahomey for seven years, living in misery . . . and solely by the alms of the governors of the forts, [all] foreigners be they English or French." In absence of any actions by the Portuguese crown, they were freed by the director of the French fort in Ouidah, who charitably funded their release. The director of the Portuguese fort bemoaned that he did not have the necessary money to ransom the men and urged the crown to repay the French administrators, who had exchanged twenty-six *onças* in trade goods for each white sailor released and twenty-four onças for each Black sailor—indicative of the racial hierarchies of value that appraised these laborers' supposed worth.[48]

Despite Dahomey's attacks against slaving personnel and mariners, fort administrators attempted to salvage operations in Ouidah, which remained a major source of enslaved men, women, and children.[49] Violence perpetrated by Dahomey continued in the later part of the century and was matched by European vessels' sporadic acts of piracy. Both imperiled the business of Bahian slaving and the lives of seafarers. In 1778, a Dutch vessel attacked the Bahian ship *Nossa Senhora da Conceição e São Jozé,* seizing its cargo and imprisoning sixteen enslaved sailors owned by Ignacio Baptista Lisboa, the ship's captain, including both *"pardos* and *pretos."* As a consequence,

48. Ibid., São Tomé, caixa 21, documento 1755, "Requerimento de Antônio Barbosa Pereira"; ibid., documento 1780, Apr. 6, 1788, "Ofício do Director da Fortaleza de São João de Ajudá, Francisco Antônio da Fonseca Aragão"; Verger, *Trade Relations,* [trans. Crawford], 187. Mann, drawing from research by David Eltis, David Richardson, Stephen D. Behrendt, and Manolo Florentino, estimates that slave exports from Lagos were approximately 269 in 1761–1765, rising steadily for the next twenty years and reaching 14,077 in 1786–1790 (*Slavery and the Birth of an African City,* 38–39). The prisoners included Innocêncio Marques, a *pardo* pilot from the ship *Diana;* Manoel Luiz, a pardo slaving ship captain of the same vessel; Manoel da Silva Jordão, the white pilot of the *Socorro;* Manoel de Magalhaens, a pardo quartermaster of the same vessel; Domingos Braga, a creole man; Gonçalo de Christo, a freed creole, and Luiz Lisboa, a slave of Captain Felix da Costa Lisboa, who both voluntarily surrendered to the king of Dahomey (Verger, *Trade Relations,* [trans. Crawford], 245 n. 35).

49. The administrators argued in a report that it was "one of the best and most principal of all the Ports of trade on that coast, due to the great number of slaves, that are bought there, as well as for the kindness of them, that exceeds all the other nations, not only on that Coast but in Mozambique, Angola and Cabo Verde." In the years following, the fort's director argued that efforts should be made to fortify the feitoria to prevent the "repeated assaults of your enemies, and . . . of other nations, who invite some of the disorders [violence], and

traders moved even farther east from what had been Portugal's preferred slaving port.[50]

Bahian slavers—as well as those based in São Tomé—looked to heretofore unexploited ports to conduct trade without molestation, moving as far down the coast as the Gabon River estuary. Building on their long history of diversifying and expanding slaving markets on the West African coast, they sought less-frequented ports to regain a commercial advantage. Receiving less support from the crown than their counterparts operating in established trading ports, these ship captains and their crews focused on forging peaceable negotiations. In these volatile moments, the cosmopolitan diplomacy of captains and crews alike would be paramount. In 1773, merchant André Gonçalves Santiago of São Tomé sent his schooner to Gabon to buy forty captives. The inhabitants of the region were adept fishermen and conducted a "shipboard" trade in wax, ivory, and "red and black woods" with Atlantic merchants. Upon the ship's arrival, local pirates killed the captain, two white sailors, and four enslaved Black sailors and seized the cargo. One of the mariners escaped by jumping overboard in spite of his injury. Miraculously, he floated more than a league to safety, where he was taken aboard by a Dutch ship trading in a nearby port.[51]

---

robberies, that the merchants are accustomed to by the caboceers and potentates of that Coast"—plans that Dahomeans resisted. As administrators from São Tomé left pieces of lumber and artillery on the beach near the São João Baptista de Ajudá fort, Dahomeans confiscated them, likely as an effort to prevent the Portuguese from exercising the same level of military power in Ouidah as the Dutch and English did on the western Mina Coast (AHU, CU, São Tomé e Príncipe, caixa 16, documento 1533, Nov. 2, 1778, "Memória do Sargento-Mor da Praça da Ilha do Príncipe, Francisco Joaquim da Mata, sobre o porto de Ajudá na Costa da Mina").

50. Ibid., documento 1494, Feb. 9, 1778, "Requerimento do Sargento-Mor José Gonçalves da Silva, Morador da Ilha do Príncipe, negociante da cidade de São Salvador da Bahia à rainha". Between 1795 and 1797, French pirates infested the ports of Ouidah and Porto Novo, attacking two Bahian slavers and stealing their cargoes, which included eighty slaves (Verger, *Trade Relations,* [trans. Crawford], 209–210). The governor of São Tomé wrote in 1783, "Because of the continuing wars between the African kings on that coast, fewer ships come from Bahia" (AHU, CU, São Tomé e Príncipe, caixa 20, documento 1713, Dec. 13, 1784, written on Apr. 22, 1783, "Ofício do Cristóvão Xavier de Sá, ao Martinho de Melo e Castro").

51. AHU, CU, São Tomé e Príncipe, caixa 15, documento 1384, Oct. 8, 1773, "Ofício do Capitão-Mor das Ilhas de São Tomé e Príncipe, Vicente Gomes Ferreria, ao Secretário de Estado da Marinha e Ultramar, Martinho de Melo e Castro." William Bosman described

Developing new trading relationships was a fraught project. In the absence of a powerful African potentate to ensure relatively peaceable trade between European slavers and African residents, crews were left vulnerable when approaching leaderless coastal communities. In 1783, Gregorio Alves Pereira, a *coronel* of São Tomé, sent his ship to Gabon and then on to Lisbon with a crew of mostly enslaved sailors to trade peaceably in wax, ebony, cinnamon, pepper, and soap—all items of "great utility," according to his description. Pereira's gamble was a risky one, considering a violent attack on visiting mariners ten years earlier. This portion of the coast was often conceived of as a place of danger. The governor of São Tomé identified the ports of Cabo Lopes, Gabon, Benga, Benbe, Camarão, Old Calabar, Bonny, New Calabar, Warri, and Benin as being home to "hostile inhabitants." In these locales, he warned, it was not rare for Portuguese trading vessels to be attacked by "40–50 boats and canoes of war, which are carrying some 40 to 80 men deploying muskets, spears and swords." Local communities, without a unifying ruler, felt emboldened to mobilize against any approaching foreign vessel with whom they did not want to bargain. Bahian slavers' negotiation tactics, developed with a mind toward centralized polities like Dahomey, were often of little use farther east on the Bight of Biafra.[52]

Administrators representing the Portuguese crown advocated that slaving vessels rely on diplomacy over force, touting the strategic utility of doing so.[53]

---

a vibrant, canoe-based maritime culture already in the region during the early eighteenth century: "The *Negroes* manner of Fishing here, is very diverting: For passing along the River side in a Canoa, and perceiving a Fish, they instantly dart an Assaguay at him; which is so certain a way, that by means of their Dexterity, it very seldom missed" (Bosman, *A New and Accurate Description of the Coast of Guinea, Divided into the Gold, the Slave, and the Ivory Coasts* [London, 1705], 407).

52. After Pereira's ship anchored in Lisbon, the enslaved mariners aboard petitioned for their freedom, which Pereira contested (AHU, CU, São Tomé e Príncipe, caixa 19, documento 1668, June 14, 1783, "Requerimento do Coronel da Praça de São Tomé, Gregório Alves Pereira, Residente na Ilha de São Tomé, à Rainha"). In the same year, Pernambucan merchant and captain Fernando Jozé da Silva reported that he had opened the trade at Bonny, marking the beginning of a favorable commercial relationship between Brazilian traders and a region of Africa "very rich in slaves and ivory." The area was controlled by a powerful monarch who could facilitate greater efficiency than the commerce at Old Calabar (AHU, CU, São Tomé e Príncipe, caixa 44, documento 47C, Oct. 15, 1810, "Recebi o Real Avizo de 18 de Abril do Corrente").

53. They were responding to a history of hostilities and dishonest dealings endangering commercial transactions with West African communities on the coast. One ship captain, for

By 1801, the crown required captains to "place great attention to preserve friendship and peace that you have with the Kings of the Coast and Rivers of your jurisdiction." The law admonished any vessel that "mistreated" African merchants, damaging the ability of other Portuguese captains to engage in future trade. Such royal edicts, far from revealing metropolitan dominance in the remote oceanic outposts of Portuguese mercantilism, instead point to the profound commercial autonomy of Bahian ship captains and the recession of royal management of the West African trade during the latter half of the eighteenth century. In the easternmost ports of Mina Coast, Bahian ship captains, both white and pardo, continued to spearhead new trading relationships with a growing frequency, constructing their own small trading feitorias and corresponding with local African merchants and rulers. Ineffectual metropolitan policy coalesced with surging campaigns of conquest and enslavement by centralizing powers in the interior of the Bight of Benin to make transatlantic slaving more accessible and profitable for enterprising merchants than ever before. Metropolitan Portuguese merchants' marginality to the bilateral South Atlantic economy positioned the quotidian operations of the transatlantic slave trade, where captive cosmopolitans were essential, far beyond the metropole's grasp.[54]

———

instance, blamed the bad faith negotiating of slave traders from São Tomé and Príncipe for the hostile reception of Portuguese traders at Old Calabar. He noted that, one hundred years earlier, a captain illegitimately abducted a local "prince" being held as a pawn, sowing mistrust between the trading clans there—whom he identified as "civilized"—and Portuguese captains (AHU, CU, São Tomé e Príncipe, caixa 44, documento 8, Apr. 27, 1810, "Carta de Francisco Xavier Alvares de Mello Primeiro Tenente honorário da Armada Real").

54. Jeremy Adelman, *Sovereignty and Revolution in the Iberian Atlantic* (Princeton, N.J., 2021), 68–77; Alencastro, *Trade in the Living,* trans. Adams and Alencastro, 250, 324–325, 354; Gabriel Paquette, *Imperial Portugal in the Age of Atlantic Revolutions: The Luso-Brazilian World, c. 1770–1850* (Cambridge, 2013), 34. The crown proposed that all ships visiting the Bight of Biafra should require their sailors and officers to testify to the good conduct of the captain while in port; if his conduct was found lacking, the man should be "imprisoned, if he is found guilty and sentenced in conformity" (AHU, CU, São Tomé e Príncipe, caixa 34, documento 2, Jan. 2, 1803, "Avizo de 23 de Dezembro de 1801"). Following the crown's abandonment of the São João Baptista de Ajudá feitoria in 1803, independent traders—most notably Francisco Felix de Souza—took up the responsibility for managing the trade and ushered in an era of slaving that was even more decentralized and intensive than the centuries preceding it. See Verger, *Trade Relations,* [trans. Crawford], 209.

CAPTIVE COSMOPOLITAN CAREERS
IN THE NINETEENTH CENTURY

For Bahian merchants, the eighteenth century had been an era of challenges and upheaval. By the dawn of the nineteenth, however, captive cosmopolitan mariners had fashioned autonomous and, at times, lucrative lives from the unique organization of the Bahian slave trade. Beneficiaries of these arrangements existed at all rungs of shipboard hierarchies and from all sectors of Bahian society.

The early nineteenth century saw the rise of a prosperous group of African and creole traders whose wealth was intrinsically tied to the violent accumulations of slaving. For a growing cohort of already-free pardo men, this period offered unprecedented opportunities to attain positions as slaving ship captains and sometimes even shipowners. For most of the eighteenth century, Salvador's slaving ship captains were uniformly white, earning incomes equivalent to other professionals engaged in various forms of artisanal labor. The position of ship captain was one of significant social prestige that often included membership in colonial military orders and Catholic brotherhoods. By the late eighteenth century, however, a handful of Africans and creoles with ties to the slave trade had begun to enter the profession and achieve levels of social recognition and economic prosperity that were likely unmatched among their African-descended peers.[55]

Only one of these seafaring elites, the pardo slaving ship captain Innocêncio Marques de Santa Anna, left substantial records with which to reconstruct the trajectory of his maritime career. Santa Anna first gained the notice of Bahian governor Francisco da Cunha Menezes in February 1805, after he accompanied two Dahomean ambassadors to Salvador as their interpreter. A native of Bahia, Santa Anna had fallen captive to Dahomey's ahosu Adandozan after a military assault on neighboring Porto Novo, where he conducted slave trading as part of the crew of the Bahian ship *Diana*. Santa Anna's utility both in the Dahomean court as an interpreter and later as a source of information

---

55. Cândido Eugênio Domingues de Souza, "'Perseguidores da espécie humana': Capitães negreiros da cidade da Bahia na primeira metade do século XVIII" (Ph.D. diss., Universidade Federal da Bahia, Salvador, 2011), 91. These white captains were likely to be old Christians of Portuguese descent, and some were married to Portuguese women, all critical precursors to elite social status in colonial Brazil. Salvador's elite was a small group in the early eighteenth century: six families accounted for 58.43 percent of the city's wealth (ibid., 87–107).

pertaining to West Africa's trade and politics led Cunha Menezes to appoint him captain of Salvador's fourth militia regiment of pardo men.[56]

Soon after this recognition, Santa Anna achieved the position of captain aboard the Bahian brigantine *Nossa Senhora das Necessidades São José Desforço*. In 1807, this ship transported 207 captives from the Mina Coast to Bahia. Its owner was the wealthy and well-connected merchant José Tavares França; he employed Santa Anna as a captain on an additional slaving voyage to the Mina Coast in 1809. After leading six more such voyages between the years of 1811 and 1816, Santa Anna purchased his own slaving vessel, the *Santana Flor de África*, which he also captained. He later acquired the *Juliana*, making him one of the preeminent slavers in Salvador at the time and a respected inhabitant of the city's exclusive Pilar parish.[57]

Santa Anna's remarkable social ascent was not only a result of his intelligence, which had impressed both Adandozan in Dahomey and authorities in Bahia. His success was also a function of the possibilities for accumulating wealth that the transatlantic slave trade opened up for such opportunistic individuals. Another ambitious pardo slaving ship captain was the navigator André Pinto da Silveira. Though he declared himself to be of unknown parentage, his humble origins did not ultimately thwart his career advancement. Pinto da Silveira worked on three occasions as navigator for the brigantine *Scipiao Africano*, which voyaged to the Mina Coast for owner Francisco Nicolau da Costa between 1813 and 1814. In subsequent years, he established his own feitoria in Porto Novo on the Mina Coast, where he was actively trading in 1820. By 1824, he was master of both the *União* and *Crioula* before becoming the owner of the schooner *Três Manoelas*, which completed two voyages between Havana and Lagos between 1834 and 1836, as well as the *Empreendedor*, which was captured off the Mina Coast in 1839 and condemned. Silveira's final recorded endeavor in the slave trade—now under suppression by both British and Brazilian authorities—was the acquisition of the brig *Paquete Africano*, which was captured and condemned after leaving Lagos in 1840. Silveira continued his commercial activities in a different capacity, however, as a merchant of West African goods in Lagos and Ouidah, where he had settled.[58]

---

56. Verger, *Trade Relations*, [trans. Crawford], 231–234.

57. Voyage IDs 2924, 40476, 48831, 40477, 51525, 51851, 51556, 7312, 7332, 7367, 7636, 7598, 900095, *Voyages*, http://www.slavevoyages.org/tast/database/index.faces; Verger, *Trade Relations*, [trans. Crawford], 393.

58. In addition, the pardo slaving ship captain Caetano Alberto da França navigated seven voyages for the West African trade between the years 1818 and 1824. See AHI, Coleções

Slaving ship captains like Santa Anna and Silveira would prove critical in creating a new trading infrastructure on the eastern portion of the Mina Coast in the early decades of the nineteenth century. They erected rustic, private trading forts after the crown abandoned Portugal's trading fortification São João Baptista de Ajudá in 1803. And, in the tradition of Black maritime middlemen, they solidified trading relationships with willing West African potentates on the coast. Sensing the potential to take advantage of the military decline of Dahomey and Oyo, African potentates sought to establish working relationships with Bahian slaving captains as a foundation of political and economic power, even if slaving commerce drove the very chaos that continued to destroy communities around them. To this end, rulers from Ouidah, Porto Novo, and Lagos made direct entreaties to slaving ship captains, both white and pardo. They invited Bahian slavers to build feitorias on their lands to regularize commerce.[59]

Lagos's *oba* (local ruler) enthusiastically sought to establish diplomatic ties with visiting merchants. In 1821, Osinlokun, who had just wrested the title of oba from his rival and brother, Adele, initiated a correspondence with pardo slaving ship captain Vicente Ferreira Milles and his Bahian partners across the Atlantic to ensure that merchants honored long-standing agreements to purchase captives from him and not neighboring Porto Novo. Signing his name "King Ajan"—expressing pretensions to a title of sovereignty he did not, in fact, possess—Osinlokun requested that Brazilian merchants send him "coraes grossos" (large corals), "silks of diverse colors," as well as a "capable man who understands the business and customs of my port." Such luxury commodities enhanced African potentates' prestige and authority and provided a major inducement to participate in slaving commerce.[60] Osinlokun

---

Especiais, Comissão Mista, lata 9, maço 2, pasta 1, Papers of the *Crioula*, 113; ibid., lata 13, maço 14, pasta 1, Papers of the *Emília*, 277; Voyage IDs 476, 1323, 1398, 2939, 3080, 3084, 3489, *Voyages*, http://www.slavevoyages.org/tast/database/index.faces; Verger, *Trade Relations*, [trans. Crawford], 405. Innocêncio Marques de Santa Anna also acted as captain of the ship in 1816 (Voyage ID 7695, *Voyages*).

59. Law, "Trade and Politics behind the Slave Coast," *Journal of African History*, XXIV (1983), 344.

60. AHI, Coleções Especiais, Comissão Mista, lata 13, maço 14, pasta 1, Papers of the *Emília*, 277; Mann, *Slavery and the Birth of an African City*, 45–47. Such goods, when locally distributed in return for ties of loyalty, extended their networks of dependents, as increasing numbers of clients indebted to potentates with Atlantic connections expanded these strongmen's "wealth in people." As theorized by Jane I. Guyer, the precolonial African

accompanied his letters of request with gifts of two West African cloths (*panos da costa rebuços*) and three canes made of "rich bamboo"—one embellished with a gold tip and another with ivory—hoping to formalize an exclusive exchange between himself and Milles through the circulation of prized goods.[61] He also approached the merchant, whom he referred to as "friend," with personal matters, pleading to receive a Bahian remedy for the pains that vexed him at the advanced age of forty-eight. Osinlokun's commercial initiatives additionally led him to send an envoy to Bahia on the ship *Emília*, a man simply referred to as Pedro by the Brazilians, more than likely on a mission of reconnaissance in the slaving port. The Lagos potentate's insistence on appropriate personnel indicated the improvisational nature of trade on the eastern part of the Mina Coast, where Bahian merchants were required to be attuned to the specific material desires of local rulers who controlled access to the captives they fervently sought.[62]

---

concept of "wealth in people," or the imperative to invest in social relations, meant that material wealth was accumulated to secure dependents. As she explains, in "pre-colonial Africa . . . the ultimate purpose of material wealth was to transform it into personal allegiances." In "Equatorial Africa, currency valuation in exchange created the singularity of persons rather than pools of money or material wealth that conferred or represented power in themselves." This ethic of value could coexist with other forms of controlling and distributing material resources. See Guyer, ed., *Money Matters: Instability, Values, and Social Payments in the Modern History of West African Communities* (Portsmouth, N.H., 1995), 16–23; Guyer, *Marginal Gains: Monetary Transactions in Atlantic Africa* (Chicago, 2004), 10.

61. Ship captains also paid West African potentates customs to "open the trade," such as when the brig *Conceição Conde dos Arcos* gave thirty rolls of tobacco, two pieces of damask, two hats, and twelve barrels of gunpowder to the Oba of Lagos, along with cowry shells that the Oba had purchased. The ship also paid customs to the "King of Minna" and the "Cabeceira of Popo" in the form of gunpowder and tobacco, as well as paying nearly one hundred rolls of tobacco to secure canoemen in Elmina and Popo and twenty rolls of tobacco for customs at the fort at Elmina. See ANRJ, fundo 7X, Junta do Comércio, Fábricas e Navegações, caixa 375, pacote 1, Papers of the *Conceição Conde dos Arcos*.

62. AHI, Coleções Especiais, Comissão Mista, lata 13, maço 14, pasta 1, Papers of the *Emília*, 250. Pedro might have been a pawn that Osinlokun had offered up as collateral for debts to Bahian merchants. Milles referred to such a "boy" entering his feitoria for the account of Domingo Jozé de Almeida Lima. According to the captain, the "English system" of offering an African pawn as collateral for an advance of foreign goods meant that a debtor could not leave the creditor's house without paying. If no payment was offered, the pawn could legitimately be taken by the creditor and sold as a form of debt collection (ibid., Papers of the *Emília*, 290, 353).

The dealings of Milles, who was stationed in a privately owned feitoria in Lagos, were emblematic of such African-descended men's skill in acquiring enslaved adults and, increasingly, children in the early nineteenth century to be forced onto Salvador's slaving ships.[63] As João de Oliveira had done five decades earlier, Milles functioned as a key interlocutor of both African and Bahian merchants on the coast. Men like Milles and Osinlokun, through their protracted interactions, spearheaded a lasting material exchange between West Africa and Brazil, one profoundly invested in transatlantic bondage and concerned with the circulation of meaningful but exotic luxury goods—Indian, European, Chinese, and Yoruban cloth, beads, cowry currency, hats, arms, fine jewelry, strong alcohol, and potent, sweet tobacco.[64] Milles also acquired knowledge of preferred local currencies and ways to expedite transportation of captives from local merchants to slaving vessels.[65] As part of his diplomatic role, he reported back to slaving ship captains in Bahia about the state of trade, frequently warning of the continuous wars between Osinlokun

63. The declining age of captives loaded aboard Bahian slavers was partly the result of dwindling numbers of adults in spaces of intensive slaving violence. But it also reflected merchants' preference. In 1812, the owner of the *Prazeres* advised the ship's captain to procure adolescent boys and particularly girls, who were cheaper and fled less readily than adults. The merchant was especially attracted to Ouidah because of the "quality of its people," including the great number of "boas moleconas," or "good young women," that slavers such as himself attempted to acquire. Categorical thinking about the relative profitability and commercial desirability permeated slave traders' attitudes toward the individuals who had been caught up in the transatlantic trade, as their imputed characteristics became signs of assumed marketability in Salvador (ibid., lata 26, maço 6, pasta 2, Papers of the *Prazeres*).

64. On the ship *Dezengano,* luxury textiles included green and red velvet, damask, and gingham, as well as velvet boots with tassels and red velvet shoes embroidered in gold. Silver-handled knives, a gold cord and pouches of gold pieces, various hats and silver rings, fine sugar, candies, and patterned sheets all traveled to West Africa. The *Feliz Americano* held calico, likely from India, as well as satin and silk pieces, likely from China. The *Lindeza* held both large and "fine" corals, an assortment of cloth, including some checkered items of English origin, and pouches of beads. See ibid., lata 10, maço 3, pasta 2, Papers of the *Dezengano;* ibid., lata 15, maço 4, pasta 2, Papers of the *Feliz Americano;* ibid., lata 19, maço 3, pasta 2, Papers of the *Lindeza.*

65. He reported that the "people of the country," i.e., Lagosians, rejected a parcel of handkerchiefs sent to sell to local merchants. He recommended instead sending "beautiful, cheerful and fine" striped cloths, perhaps of chintz, or blue verbetina, which would be more marketable on the coast. This appraisal of "merchandise" operated in the other direction, as well, as Milles secured for buyers in Bahia two enslaved women whom he believed

and Adele, who had fled to Badagry. Owing to the "ambition and reticence of the ruler of the port," Milles lamented, "everyday there is something new" to bring coastal commerce to a halt.[66]

Even as he was unhappily stationed in Lagos, Milles continued to implement the labyrinthine financial arrangements that had structured the transatlantic trade from Bahia for a century. He kept accounts for the numerous individuals who invested in each slaving voyage and supervised a group of enslaved mariners owned by various residents in Salvador, who used the value of their bondsmen's wages to secure a return on their investment in those same mariners' initial purchase price—adding another possibility for investing in the transatlantic slave trade. When Milles reached West Africa, he probably also contracted with African canoemen to facilitate the transportation of people from his dilapidated feitoria to the holds of slaving vessels.[67] Captains like Milles also took pains to deal with *ladinos*, or "acculturated" Africans, as they conducted their business affairs on the West African coast.

---

to be "good to help . . . in the service of the kitchen." In 1812, the owner of the *Prazeres* specified the use of cowries in ports such as Popo and Ouidah. Iron bars and cloth were also frequently used as currencies on various parts of the Mina Coast. See AHI, Coleções Especiais, Comissão Mista, lata 13, maço 14, pasta 1, Papers of the *Emília*, 276, 286; ibid., lata 26, maço 6, pasta 2, Papers of the *Prazeres*.

66. Just ten years earlier, in 1812, the owner of the *Prazeres* attested to the "abundance of captives" at Lagos and Badagry, indicating how rapidly warfare caused conditions to deteriorate on that strip of the coast. During the period in which Milles was writing, hostilities were driven by Adele's attacks on Lagos, which occurred several times between 1821 and 1835. Traffic to Lagos did not abate during this period, likely owing to the inexpensive cost of enslaved individuals there, with a standard price of eight onças per "head," or person. Captain Santa Isabel affirmed that each captive cost eleven onças at Ouidah. Meanwhile, other captains estimated in 1812 that in Porto Novo one captive cost five to seven onças, though barter could raise the price as high as ten onças. See ANRJ, fundo 7X, Junta do Comércio, Fábricas e Navegações, caixa 410, pacote 1, Papers of the *Divina Providência* and *São Miguel Triunfante;* AHI, Coleções Especiais, Comissão Mista, lata 26, maço 6, pasta 2, Papers of the *Prazeres;* ibid., lata 13, maço 14, pasta 1, Papers of the *Emília*, 265, 271, 276; Mann, *Slavery and the Birth of an African City*, 46–47.

67. Though captains commonly hired canoemen in ports west of Lagos, these watermen were essential to every slaving voyage, navigating along the coast with their intimate knowledge of its geography and their ability to surmount the strong currents and surf. In Grand-Popo and Badagry, some ships deployed "A few Fantee sailors hired on the Gold Coast, and who can return home in the canoe when the ship's loading is completed, will be found of infinite service in navigating the large boat, and be the means of saving the lives of

Ladinos' presence on the coast was spurred, in part, by the labor demands of Atlantic commerce there. Brazilian and Portuguese traders hired them as commercial assistants, employing them as interpreters and messengers and requiring them to learn Portuguese. When Milles paid thirty rolls of tobacco to the oba so he could commence trading activities, he also handed over two rolls of tobacco to hire a *"ladino* boy to accompany me." The many Portuguese and Brazilian traders lodged in West African ports regularly interacted with local cosmopolitans as they pursued the purchase of commodities, provisions, medicine, and other items on shore. In hiring an array of laborers, these merchants greatly expanded the number of Africans residing on the Atlantic littoral who were acquainted with Portuguese language and culture. Some of these young men might have ended up in the holds of slaving ships destined for Bahia.[68]

Milles also enabled the economic aspirations of his own bondsmen. Just as captains facilitated transatlantic investments by family members, they permitted their own enslaved property to access slaving markets, as well. Like other accumulating material assets, enslaved mariners did not require direct supervision to make their owners a tidy sum. Their labor itself would provide regular financial returns with little daily direction from Milles himself. Mirroring the behavior of many other slaveholders in urban Bahia, he adopted a distant approach to managing his bondsmen, allowing them to participate in transatlantic commerce for their own advantage as an inducement to steadfast conduct. Such negotiations over the terms of their labor and attendant privileges could financially empower the enslaved while advancing their owner's interests.

One of his bondsmen, Ventura Ferreira Milles, had completed multiple journeys to the West African coast, becoming a sophisticated dealer of Bahian

---

many of the ship's crew." They also personally negotiated with captains to define the terms of their labor. The *São Benedito* contracted a canoe navigated by "25 free negroes" in the port of Acará. The captain compensated them with food and forty-eight rolls of Bahian tobacco for their joint services. The men also brought along boxes containing their clothing and personal property (AHI, Coleções Especiais, Comissão Mista, lata 28, maço 4, pasta 1, Papers of the *São Benedito;* John Adams, *Sketches Taken during Ten Voyages to Africa between the Years 1786 and 1800* . . . (London, 1822), 110.

68. ANRJ, fundo 7X, Junta do Comércio, Fábricas e Navegações, caixa 375, pacote 1, Papers of the Brig *Conceição Conde dos Arcos*, 3; Filipa Ribeiro da Silva, *Dutch and Portuguese in Western Africa: Empires, Merchants, and the Atlantic System, 1580–1674* (Leiden, 2011), 148–155.

goods himself. The Gege man's participation in the transatlantic trade had dark underpinnings, however. Several years earlier, in November 1810, the brigantine *Divina Providência* suffered the devastating loss of sixty-five captives in the wake of an undisclosed catastrophic event during the return voyage to Salvador da Bahia. The episode of mass death—which miraculously did not take Ventura's life—exposed the complexity that underlay the ship's finances and the reliance on a multitude of investors to achieve an economically viable cargo. The sixty-five captives had thirty-five separate owners; in addition, nine individuals residing in Bahia possessed portions of the ship's cargo of *panos da costa*. Ventura was among the investors on this ill-fated voyage. As the ship's second barber, he carried a sizable 49 of the ship's 391 panos da costa in his liberty chest. Two other captive cosmopolitans on the ship— Manoel Teles de Brito and Custódio dos Santos—had jointly purchased four slaves in Lagos. Each barrel or sack of goods on the ship had been branded with its owner's insignia, and the same brand marked the enslaved's bodies, providing a chilling illustration of how such complicated, multi-investor property claims establishing legally legible ownership were materialized on the human cargo's very flesh.[69]

Vicente Ferreira Milles's continued sponsorship of Ventura's commercial initiatives revealed that their relationship operated, in part, as one of patronage. As the enslaved African mariner of a pardo captain, Ventura likely spent much of his time on the Mina Coast as Vicente's trading assistant, considering his linguistic abilities and skills as a barber. Operating in such a capacity would have introduced the enslaved man to the intricate negotiations of slave and commodity trading and might have helped him to secure relationships with trading partners. In the decades following the loss of his cargo, Ventura continued to exercise a remarkable degree of commercial independence from

69. APEB, Seção Colonial e Provincial, no. 568-1, "Termos dos Cativos Mortos 1810–1811." One captive (a young adolescent) had earlier died while the *Divina Providência* was waiting to disembark from the African coast. Included among the proprietors were eight of the ship's crew members: the *Divina Providência*'s captain recorded his father, Jozé Joaquim de Santa Anna, as the owner of an adolescent male; the pilot, Francisco de Madereira Barboza, claimed the loss of one adult male, two adolescent males, and two adolescent females; the second pilot, Domingos Francisco Roza, jointly owned one adult female captive along with the ship's owner, Lieutenant Colonel Ignacio Antunes Guimarães. In addition, the quartermaster owned two captives; and the ship's barber, Manoel Ana, owned an adolescent female and an adult female captive. See APEB, Secção Colonial e Provincial, no. 568-1, "Termos dos Cativos Mortos 1810–1811."

his owner. In 1828, he placed one box of goods aboard the *Penha de França,* using the commodities held within to purchase three enslaved men and three enslaved women. Ventura did not travel to the Mina Coast himself in this instance; instead, he relied on the ship's second pilot, Jozé Alexandre de Almeida, to buy the captives on his behalf. Ventura's profit-making strategies were not unique for a man of his social status. Through the course of a lifetime, an African-born sailor could acquire a measure of wealth through small-scale transatlantic trading and ultimately pay for his manumission.[70]

MARITIME LIBERTY CHESTS

Ventura was but one of many enslaved and freed mariners who took advantage of trading privileges to build personal wealth. The use of liberty chests continued well into the nineteenth century as captains leveraged mariners' trading privileges to enhance seafarers' compensation, augmenting their paltry wages. Approving of liberty chests, in lieu of increasing mariner pay, kept capital costs down. Because of these profit-enhancing incentives, the commercial methods Black mariners deployed to achieve social mobility often found sanction and even assistance from more senior members of the crew. In July 1811, when the *Lindeza* left the port of Salvador, Captain Antônio de Cerqueira Lima owned two enslaved sailors laboring on board: Joaquim "of the Mina Nation" and Jozé, also a Mina. Cerqueira Lima invested 228$000 réis of trading goods, including denim and British printed cloth, "for the account of my two slaves." Two more enslaved men also invested in the voyage: Luiz, a Mina sailor who was owned by the ship's proprietor, Jozé Cardozo Marques, and Bernardo, who was not employed on the ship in any capacity. On the same voyage, six more members of the *Lindeza*'s crew and officers owned a portion of the cargo, including the freed African cooper Joaquim Gomes Rosa. Rosa's investment was substantial at 246$566 réis, more than double what he received in wages. Marques found it in his interest to make investment in his venture accessible for a range of individuals.[71]

---

70. BNA, FO 315/41/42, Papers of the *Penha de França*, no. 32.

71. The ship carried 12:867$106 réis in its principal cargo. Trade goods included 1,706 rolls of tobacco and 2,226 *canadas* of aguardente, as well as an array of textiles, hats, and household goods. The value was estimated as worth 3,766 onças on the Mina Coast; at the time, an adult male slave cost approximately eleven onças. See AHI, Coleções Especiais, Comissão Mista, lata 19, maço 3, pasta 2, Papers of the *Lindeza*. Luiz and Bernardo invested 45$700 and 14$050 réis' worth of tobacco and aguardente, respectively. See ANRJ, Junta do

Another ship apprehended in 1812, the brigantine *São Miguel Triunfante,* displayed a similar pattern of mariner investment. She left Bahia in August 1811 with a principal cargo of popular intoxicants and stimulants (including sugarcane liquor, rolled tobacco, and snuff), goods recognized as currency on the Mina Coast (such as cowry shells and iron bars), and a multitude of other commodities.[72] The *Triunfante's* captain, forty-four-year-old João da Silveira Villas Boas, left the port of Salvador with a 204$000 réis investment in aguardente. In addition to the ship's owner, Joaquim Francisco Carneiro, investors included several inhabitants of Salvador. Notable among these was an African identified as Joaquim Nagô, who had invested 12$622 réis; three unnamed slaves of Joaquina Jozé Maria dos Campos, who collectively owned 31 *canadas* of aguardente; and Maria da Conceição, who was identified as *preta,* or African, and had invested 21$600 réis. A declaration of the ship's cargo claimed 608 rolls of tobacco upon embarkation and demonstrates the diversity of small-scale investors in the transatlantic voyages launched in the period.[73]

The ship hosted investments from at least forty-two individuals of diverse racial and legal statuses. Captain Villas Boas possessed the largest tobacco investment on the ship at 39.5 percent of the total tobacco cargo. Carneiro owned only 3.3 percent of the tobacco rolls aboard. The ship's officers and crew—excluding the captain—collectively owned 19.1 percent. All told, a majority of the ship's officers and crew members owned small portions of trade

---

Comércio, Fábricas e Navegações, caixa 410, Papers of the *Divina Providência,* 5. Rosa's salary for the roundtrip voyage was 100$000 réis.

72. The vessel had a crew of forty-one mariners that contained twenty-two enslaved men, twenty-four African-born mariners, and two indigenous crew members (Indios). All told, Africans and Brazilian-born Blacks made up 70 percent of the crew. The cargo held 2,750 rolls and 18 barrels of tobacco worth 11,285$400 réis, 31 leather sacks of cowry shells worth 1,167$379 réis, 114 iron bars worth 163$687 réis, and aguardente worth 351$000 réis. See ANRJ, fundo 7X, Junta do Comércio, Fábricas e Navegações, caixa 410, pacote 1, 5–14.

73. Ibid., pacote 1, May 2, 1819, "Relação das quantidades." Others on the voyage included Joaquim Gomes Pereira, Victorino dos Santos Pereira, Jozé Joaquim da Santa, Nicolão da Silveira e Souza, Anna Joaquina de Assumpção, Maria de Assumpção, André de Madeiros, Anna Maria, Ignacia Maria do Rozário, Joaquim da Costa, Manoel João dos Reis, Domingues Francisco de Oliveira, João Luís de Abreu, Maria Victoria Carolina, Jozé Antônio de Cerqueira Braga, Maria Victoria, Bernardo da Piedade, Dona Ambulina Clara, Joanna Maria, Manoel Francisco Ramos, João da Silveira and son, Dona Francisca Massado do Sacramento e Sá, Felipe Rodriguez, and João Joaquim, Jozé Antônio, and Antônio Martins.

goods as the ship left the Bay of All Saints. The first cooper, Joaquim de Santa Anna, a freed pardo man from Bahia, held 25$600 réis in aguardente. Sailors Jozé Joaquim and Felipe Fernandes, both from Santa Catarina, jointly owned 12$000 réis of aguardente. Finally, a freed man from the "Mina nation," Francisco Alves de Carvalho, possessed 3$200 réis of aguardente, whereas Joaquim dos Reis, slave of Manoel João dos Reis, owned 4$800.[74]

Beyond the ship's crew, investors included nineteen enslaved individuals, fifteen of whom belonged to the ship's owner. Five of these investors are identified as Africans—one from Angola and four from the "Mina nation"—although it is probable that two of Carneiro's slaves who were not crew members on the *Triunfante* (Joaquim da Costa and Maria) were African, as well. Cosme, Miguel Maciel, and Marcaro, enslaved investors whose owners were not part of the crew nor investors in the voyage, were also likely to have been born in Africa. All told, enslaved investors accounted for fifty-eight rolls, or 9.4 percent of the voyage's tobacco cargo. Not all enslaved Africans and creoles residing in Bahia had such access to investment in transatlantic trade, as personal connections to ships' owners, investors, captains, and other officers largely determined who could participate.[75]

The twenty-three African men laboring on the *São Miguel Triunfante* were illustrative of mariners' pivotal role in directing West African goods to Bahia. Though the acquisition of enslaved men, women, and children was the *Triunfante*'s primary objective, many of the ship's enslaved investors were intent on purchasing goods in lieu of captives. When seizure at sea cut its journey short, the ship held 132 African captives, 28 rolls of tobacco, and 8 pipes of aguardente, as well as 454 panos da costa and 34 barrels of palm oil. As Carneiro's subsequent legal petition for restitution revealed, unnamed members of the *Triunfante*'s crew had been conducting trade on shore at Ouidah during the

---

74. ANRJ, fundo 7X, Junta do Comércio, Fábricas e Navegações, caixa 410, pacote 1, Papers of the *São Miguel Triunfante,* 15. The second barber, Ignacio Rodrigues Ferreira (identified as a freed creole from Bahia) owned—together with two enslaved sailors, Angolan Manoel and Antônio from the "Mina nation"—22$950 réis' worth of aguardente. Caetano, a slave of Gualter Martins who is also identified as Mina, invested 22$950 réis in aguardente. Alexandre, a slave of Carneiro, jointly owned 9$565 réis in aguardente with Domingos do Rozário, the ship's barber and Brazilian-born slave of Francisco Luiz de Souza. Rozario also individually owned 10$400 réis' worth of aguardente. The first pilot, Manoel Patricio da Santa, had invested 95$200 réis in sugar and cloth. The ship's second pilot, Jozé Antônio, possessed 23$715 réis in aguardente; the quartermaster, Jozé da Silva Guimarães, held 21$420 réis in liquor, as well.

75. Ibid.

ship's capture. Their negotiations had been primarily with Francisco Félix de Souza, the nineteenth century's wealthiest and most prominent merchant engaged in the slave trade on the Mina Coast. Félix de Souza, in conjunction with *"negros da terra,"* or local African commercial agents who worked for or with the Portuguese trader, was in the midst of selling slaves and panos da costa in return for 95 onças of tobacco, aguardente, and other goods, including various textiles.[76]

Mariners' ability to act as important commercial agents on the West African coast played a key role in enabling many to achieve manumission. As the slaving brig *Comerciante* invited West African merchants aboard to drink and trade with the crew in 1822, a freed Gege barber named Leandro Jozé da Costa saw an opportunity for profit.[77] He received a 200$000-réis salary for his labor on a roundtrip voyage from Salvador, but his employer, Francisco Ignacio de Siqueira Nobre, also agreed that as part of his compensation he would be allowed to transport one enslaved individual on the ship from the African coast without paying freight. One of da Costa's crewmates, Antônio Joaquim—an enslaved Angolan cooper owned by Siqueira Nobre—received no pay for the voyage but had the privilege of waived freight costs for the transportation of a small boy he had jointly purchased on the African coast "from his own account." Together with one of Siqueira Nobre's other enslaved sea-

76. Ibid. See David Eltis, and Lawrence C. Jennings, "Trade between Western Africa and the Atlantic World in the Pre-colonial Era," *American Historical Review*, XCIII (1988), 936–959, esp. 942; Miller, *Way of Death,* 709.

77. The ship anchored near Camarão, located on the river of the same name. After several African merchants approached the ship in canoes to conduct business, the captain reported that the crew had opened a cask of aguardente to drink with the African merchants as a precursor to trade, characterizing it as customary to begin with an initial offering of aguardente to sellers on the coast. Also noteworthy was the captain's contention that these unnamed African merchants were conversing, drinking, and trading with the "members of the ship's crew," which he also depicted as a routine practice. John K. Thornton draws a distinction between "shipboard trading," in which all commercial transactions and negotiations were conducted on board vessels anchored off the West African coast, and "factory trade," which was performed within the confines of a permanent or temporary post located on the coast. Usually one type of trade was more prominent in certain regions; in the Bight of Biafra, shipboard trading was more common than in more established slave trading ports such as Ouidah. Relationships between African merchants and European and American crews in shipboard forms of trading tended to be more fleeting and anonymous. See AHI, Coleções Especiais, Comissão Mista, lata 7, maço 5, pasta 1, Papers of the *Comerciante, 3,* 64; Thornton, *A Cultural History of the Atlantic World, 1250–1820* (Cambridge, 2012), 248–249.

men, Antônio Jozé, Joaquim grasped an opportunity to convert their own un-savory work into a chance to double their investment. Siqueira Nobre clearly had no objections to his bondsmen's ownership of private property, even if that property was another enslaved person. Perhaps Joaquim and Antônio Jozé had negotiated with Siqueira Nobre to assure that they could buy the enslaved boy as part of their private savings (peculium) in place of earning wages—surmising that they could secure more profit from the former.[78]

Investing in transatlantic slavery became a means of securing upward mo-bility for some enslaved mariners. In 1839, for example, on the *Firmeza*, Jozé, an enslaved seaman belonging to the captain, purchased an adolescent boy from an African merchant in Agoué. This purchase was conducted with the approval of his owner for thirteen onças of trade goods, including one onça of gunpowder and one shotgun. Another sailor on the *Firmeza*, Adolfo— from the "Benin nation"—had three years earlier secured manumission by substituting, for his own captivity, an adolescent Nagô boy that he had pur-chased on the West African coast. Adolfo's former owner, Manoel Jozé Dias, also recognized his twenty years of "fidelity and friendship" as a contribut-ing factor in freeing him. The ship's captain, Antônio da Cruz Baptista, was aware of these transactions, even requesting to receive a barrel of palm oil for the account of another enslaved man, Antônio de Almeida, from the port of Lagos. The investment of enslaved individuals in slavery (*servus vicarius*) dated at least as far back as ancient Rome, though it remained rare in most of the nineteenth-century Americas. The exception was urban Salvador, where between 1 percent and 2.7 percent of all enslaved people baptized in the city had enslaved owners. Enslaved mariners would have been familiar with cus-tomary arrangements between owners and their bondspeople. In a society as deeply tethered to slavery as Bahia, purchasing a captive while enslaved could offer a rare opportunity to improve one's own legal status at the cost of

78. Siqueira Nobre was a Portuguese merchant residing in Bahia; the *Comerciante* was captured while returning from the West African coast in 1822 while holding 612 captives, ivory, palm oil, and coffee. See AHI, Coleções Especiais, Comissão Mista, lata 7, maço 5, pasta 1, Papers of the *Comerciante*, 21; João José Reis, "Slaves Who Owned Slaves in Nineteenth-Century Bahia, Brazil," *Mecila: Working Paper Series*, no. 36 (2021), The Maria Sibylla Merian International Centre for Advanced Studies in the Humanities and Social Sci-ences Conviviality-Inequality in Latin America, São Paulo, http://dx.doi.org/10.46877/reis .2021.36. On the *Não Lêndia*, an enslaved cook acquired one captive, just as each of the ship's other officers had. On another vessel, Domingos and Alexandre, two enslaved sailors, used their jointly owned tobacco to purchase a young boy in Ouidah estimated to be worth

another's misfortune. Captive mariners only rarely acquired bondsmen and -women on the African coast, however. Other commodities proved far more affordable and thus economically desirable.[79]

Enduring financial connections between captain and crew and between shipmates and family members had significant ramifications for the dynamics of Salvadoran society. Enslaved African and creole mariners utilized their access to the lucrative transatlantic trade to purchase their liberty at a higher rate than enslaved individuals employed in other professions, augmenting the growing free-African and creole population in the city. *Coartação* was the practice whereby enslaved men and women purchased their own liberty by offering regular payments to the parties to whom they were legally bound as property. Often the price was agreed upon before the enslaved individual could legally secure manumission, and the long, uncertain process was costly and could take many years of commitment. Those with the financial wherewithal to sustain lengthy periods of payment for their liberty illustrated the attractiveness of legal manumission for the enslaved. Unlike those who chose fugitivity, coartação eventually conferred legal liberty and all the protections it entailed, including the right to hold property, initiate litigation, and move freely with less fear of reenslavement. The incentive of coartação thus bonded enslaved mariners even more tightly to slave-trading commerce. Captives who allowed mariners to participate in the material advantages of slaving could engender loyalty and obedience during perilous transatlantic voyages. At the same time, liberty chests became, for many, the most viable avenue to accumulate money and secure their individual freedom.

João de Oliveira returned to Bahia in 1770 to begin retirement; he expected to receive "the prize for the good service that he had always rendered for the [Portuguese] nation and the Crown" as a loyal vassal. Instead, he was arrested

---

90$000 réis. See ANRJ, fundo 7X, Junta do Comércio, Fábricas e Navegações, caixa 410, pacote 1, Mar. 23, 1813, "Conta de Venda de 222 Cativos vendos da Costa da Minna," 86; BNA, FO 315/45/24, Papers of the *Não Lêndia*.

79. BNA, FO 315/45/24, Papers of the *Não Lêndia;* ibid., Papers of the *Firmeza*, no. 185; Orlando Patterson, *Slavery and Social Death: A Comparative Study* (Cambridge, Mass., 1982), 185; Reis, "Slaves Who Owned Slaves in Nineteenth-Century Bahia, Brazil," *Mecila: Working Paper Series,* no. 36 (2021), 2; Daniele Santos de Souza, "'Preto cativo nada é seu?': Escravos senhores de escravos na cidade da Bahia no século XVIII," in Giuseppina Raggi, João Figueirôa-Rego, and Roberta Stumpf, eds., *Salvador da Bahia: Interações entre América e África, séculos XVI–XIX* (Lisbon, 2017), 55–75.

by the *provedor* of the customhouse and placed in the public jail, charged with
the possession of contraband cotton and linen textiles. All the goods he had
brought with him from the Mina Coast, including his enslaved property, were
sequestered by royal authorities, causing "irreparable loss and ruin." After a
two-month imprisonment, Oliveira petitioned the city's appellate judge (*desembargador*) and general magistrate of crime (*ouvidor geral do crime*) for his
release and, he hoped, the restoration of his impounded goods. Denying the
charges against him, he drew on his biography and the endorsement of other
prominent merchants in the city to justify his release. His petition exemplified
not only the factual outlines of a life forged between two continents but also
the strategies he had undertaken to forestall his forced dislocation. Though
Oliveira began his life as the consummate displaced outsider, the rhetoric
he employed in his petition of his detention highlighted his self-professed
identity as an "insider" in the Portuguese Atlantic world.[80]

Oliveira's defense affirmed his desire to leave pagan lands and to live as
a good Christian and emphasized the value of his service to the Portuguese
crown. He implicitly portrayed slaving as central to the king's commercial and
political interests in the South Atlantic, maintaining that no one had been of
greater service to the crown in West Africa than he. Oliveira simultaneously
pointed to his commercial kinship with the Brazilian merchant community
and his indispensable work on its behalf. At other times, he feigned innocence
of his supposed crimes. Despite his acumen securing commercial contacts on
the West African coast that the Portuguese crown would have deemed part of
a contraband trade, Oliveira described himself as an "ignorant" and "rustic"
individual incapable of misleading royal officials. Such a characterization of
his life belied his history as a consummate transatlantic cosmopolitan. After
he was placed under arrest in front of colonial authorities, the only legible
identity he could offer was that of an unsophisticated, racialized subject of
Portugal's empire.[81]

Oliveira's imprisonment and the confiscation of his goods cut short his
trajectory of social ascendancy, and the aftermath of his detention is scantily
documented. He was eventually freed but suffered significant losses: ten of
the enslaved individuals he owned perished in detention, whereas authori-

80. AHU, CU, Bahia–Eduardo de Castro e Almeida, caixa 44, documento 8246; ibid.,
documento 8244; Mariana P. Candido, "African Freedom Suits and Portuguese Vassals Status: Legal Mechanisms for Fighting Enslavement in Benguela, Angola, 1800–1830," *Slavery
and Abolition*, XXXII (2011), 447–459, esp. 448.

81. AHU, CU, Bahia–Eduardo de Castro e Almeida, caixa 44, documento 8247.

ties manumitted four additional captives and sent two more to serve a local church. How Oliveira spent his final days is unclear. Just as he had begun life as a young boy forced from his homelands, living at the whims of others, so did his life likely end. Nonetheless, his remarkable journey complicates binary distinctions between master and slave, trader and chattel, African and Brazilian. His life also demonstrates the possibilities available to captive cosmopolitans over the course of the eighteenth century, particularly as Bahia became an ever more important part of transatlantic slaving. Because of the multiple roles they inhabited, African and creole mariners of the South Atlantic were more akin to the Central African "brokers" described by Robert Harms than the proletarian sailors depicted by Marcus Rediker. Such brokers, or middlemen, connected distant merchant communities and were often defined by their ability to convert their cultural and linguistic flexibility and expertise into commercial capital. Slaving in the South Atlantic during the eighteenth century had been sustained by such men.[82]

Oliveira successfully negotiated everyday life by exploiting the specific contours of Bahian slaving capitalism to improve his individual life chances. He took advantage of the diffuse and often contradictory nature of power relations and status in the South Atlantic, where race, wealth, and imperial vassalage intersected but remained fluid. After integrating himself into the same merchant community that had made him a slave and displaced him from his homeland, he pioneered—through his own commercial, cultural, diplomatic expertise—new trading relationships on the West African coast that assured the profitability and continuation of a transatlantic trade in enslaved labor that, throughout the eighteenth century, remade Brazil into one of the world's largest slave societies. His ability to acculturate, move freely within South Atlantic spaces, and utilize Portuguese institutions to his own advantage, however, remained fragile. Therein lay the central paradox of his life: the same commercial acumen that had made him successful on the Mina Coast, particularly the capacity to trade across boundaries of territory, culture, and language, made him vulnerable to prosecution by a mercantilist colonial state in Bahia still committed to policing imperial boundaries.

<hr>

82. Harms's work analyzes the commercial strategies of Bobangi canoemen who connected merchants to upriver suppliers through waterborne travel. See Robert W. Harms, *River of Wealth, River of Sorrow: The Central Zaire Basin in the Era of the Slave and Ivory Trade, 1500–1891* (New Haven, Conn., 1981), 82–85. For more on brokers, see James F. Searing, "Brokers," in Joseph C. Miller et al., eds., *The Princeton Companion to Atlantic History* (Princeton, N.J., 2015), 68–70; Verger, *Trade Relations,* [trans. Crawford], 468.

Oliveira's story was a spectacular example of a captive cosmopolitan life. But that life was also reflective of a broader—if often more prosaic—lived experience among a multitude of African and Afro-Brazilian sailors and trading auxiliaries whose lives spanned the vast Atlantic Ocean. Like Oliveira, many other Black mariners accessed forms of transimperial and collective investment that animated the finances of slaving vessels in the eighteenth century. As important for the story of captive cosmopolitans, however, were their day-to-day experiences on board transatlantic slaving vessels, a space where both their labor and culture were foundational to the effectiveness and profitability of the Bahian slave trade. It is to the floating world of Black maritime labor in the late eighteenth and early nineteenth centuries that this book now turns.

CHAPTER 3

A Black Maritime
Working World

The Bahian–Mina Coast Middle Passage remained one of the most traveled saltwater voyages of the eighteenth century, and it was insatiable in its demand for mariners and maritime expertise. To satisfy this demand, ship captains, merchants, and slaveowners in late-eighteenth- and early-nineteenth-century Bahia relied, to a large extent, on the everyday labor of enslaved and freed men of African descent. Within the diverse laboring communities aboard transatlantic slaving vessels, rugged seamen from coastal Portugal worked alongside enslaved adolescents recently arrived from Africa, seasoned maritime creoles, and even a handful of indigenous inhabitants from Brazil's interior. They toiled atop primary decks, scrambled up masts, and disappeared into dark, cavernous holds. From the top to the bottom of this elaborate shipboard world, Black seafarers' labor was central to the operation of the Bahian slave trade.

In the early decades of the nineteenth century, nearly half of all mariners in Bahia's transatlantic slave trade were of African descent, and approximately a third were enslaved.[1] As this chapter shows, the biographical contours of this cohort—including their registered ethnic identity, occupation, wages, age, and legal status—marked the Bahian maritime labor force as distinct in the larger Atlantic world.[2] These years were coextensive with the peak of the slave trade to and from Salvador, a period when an estimated 748 voyages

1. This is based on a quantitative analysis of the ships' papers from fifty-one Bahian vessels between 1811 and 1839. A list of vessels is included in Appendix 1, below.

2. Black sailors, for example, comprised only a "tiny" proportion of slaving ship crews in Liverpool, with the small minority of African laborers lingering on the "fringes" of shipboard society, according to Emma Christopher. Black mariners made up an estimated 3 percent of all slaving ship crews sailing from Britain, particularly Liverpool and Bristol, at the end of the eighteenth century. A study by Mariana P. Candido has argued that, between 1767 and 1832, only 3 percent of crew members on registered Portuguese vessels were enslaved. See Candido, "Different Slave Journeys: Enslaved African Seamen aboard Portuguese Ships, 1760–1820s," *Slavery and Abolition,* XXXI (2010), 399; Stephen D. Behrendt, "Human Capital in the British Slave Trade," in David Richardson, Suzanne Schwarz, and Anthony

disembarked 243,294 individuals to the port city.[3] As key actors in the Bahian merchant capitalist project, Black mariners underpinned an expansion of the transatlantic slave trade that accrued substantial economic rewards for slavers, even amid mounting antislavery political pressures.

There was one obvious reason for Black mariners' predominance in the work of South Atlantic slaving: profitability. Enslaved mariners and freed Black seamen were most capable of fulfilling slavers' demands for flexible, highly skilled, and inexpensive workers. Employing Black mariners enabled slavers to maximize their profits because they necessitated lower capital outlays for the duration of voyages. Their labor was more easily exploitable, particularly in comparison to white sailors. Captains were not the only beneficiaries of this arrangement, however. Many nonseafaring residents of Salvador hired out their bondsmen to labor on transatlantic voyages, even though this meant relinquishing their authority or supervision over their property for the duration of the voyage. Such landbound slaveholders willingly exchanged the prospect of receiving handsome financial rewards for the risk that enslaved sailors would escape. In fact, Bahian slaveowners who hired out their enslaved property earned an average of 10 to 20 percent profit on their initial investment, making it a very lucrative form of slaveholding in Brazil's urban centers.[4]

Tibbles, eds., *Liverpool and Transatlantic Slavery* (Liverpool, U.K., 2007), 78–79; Christopher, *Slave Ship Sailors and Their Captive Cargoes, 1730–1807* (New York, 1976), 57–58.

3. As a sign of the slave trade's deadliness during the same period, an estimated 266,466 enslaved people left African shores on Bahian ships. Slave trade estimates courtesy of *Voyages*.

4. In some ways, enslaved mariners' independence from their owners was comparable to the autonomy experienced by other wage-earning slaves for hire (*escravos de ganho*)—who worked as artisans, including barbers, carpenters, and shoemakers, within urban Salvador. Many of these wage earners lived self-sufficient lives, occupying residences apart from their owners and meeting only periodically with their masters to pay a fixed portion of their earnings. As British vice-consul James Wetherell noted, for escravos de ganho in mid-nineteenth-century Bahia, the "Master [will] direct the slave to pay him at the rate of, it may be, about one shilling a day; this frequently is the case, and all the slave can raise above that sum which his master demands, belongs to himself. In the process of time those who are industrious raise sufficient money to pay the price their master values them at, and when such is the case, the slave can claim his freedom." See Mieko Nishida, *Slavery and Identity: Ethnicity, Gender, and Race in Salvador, Brazil, 1808–1888* (Bloomington, Ind., 2003), 20–21; Herbert S. Klein and Francisco Vidal Luna, *Slavery in Brazil* (Cambridge, 2009), 109–112; João José Reis, "'The Revolution of the Ganhadores': Urban Labour, Ethnicity, and the African Strike of 1857 in Bahia, Brazil," *Journal of Latin American Studies*, XXIX (1997), 355–393; Luiz Carlos Soares, "Os escravos de ganho no Rio de Janeiro do século

Black mariners' value, however, was not just a product of slaveowners' ability to exploit their enslaved status. In centering the often brutal and wrenching complexities of such work both on deck and in the holds of slaving ships, this chapter argues that Black mariners' seafaring expertise was valuable in a multitude of ways beyond their condition as bondsmen. In particular, African-born men were prized for their cultural dexterity, a vital asset in Bahia's shipping sector, which was heavily reliant on African traffic. Ethnic identity and cultural facility became marketable characteristics and a source of value for both slaveowners and enslaved mariners who were a key part of the port city's laboring classes.[5] In addition, enslaved mariners' supposed ability to manage enslaved men and women held in cargoes, and their ability to facilitate trading arrangements on the West African coast, were recognized as imperative to the project of Bahian slaving.[6]

XIX," *Revista Brasileira de História*, V (1988), 107–142; James Wetherell, *Brazil: Stray Notes from Bahia; Being Extracts from Letters, etc., during a Residence of Fifteen Years*, ed. William Hadfield (Liverpool, U.K., 1860), 16–17.

5. Contemporary social scientists have explored the question of ethnic segmentation within labor markets, in which one ethnic group earns lower wages than another, diminishing total costs to employers but generating interethnic antagonisms. The origins of such analysis lie in split labor market theory. Through a quantitative analysis of wages during the antebellum period in the United States, sociologists have attempted to understand whether varying occupational skills, one of the key drivers of wage stratification in modern free labor markets, also depressed wage rates for enslaved contract laborers. Edna Bonacich argues that both free and enslaved Black laborers received lower wages than whites in the same labor market, regardless of occupational skills or rates of productivity. Furthermore, she asserts that ethnic differentiation within labor markets gave capital greater control over all laborers by allowing employers to turn to enslaved laborers "whenever other workers are too costly or demanding." Martin Ruef finds age and gender to have been important variables influencing the average wages of enslaved and then free laborers in the antebellum- and Reconstruction-era U.S. In his study, the accumulation of occupational skills did little to lift wages for hired-out enslaved workers before emancipation. See Bonacich, "Abolition, the Extension of Slavery, and the Position of Free Blacks: A Study of Split Labor Markets in the United States, 1830–1863," *American Journal of Sociology*, LXXXI (1975), 601–628, esp. 608; Bonacich, "A Theory of Ethnic Antagonism: The Split Labor Market," *American Sociological Review*, XXXVII (1972), 547–559; Ruef, "Constructing Labor Markets: The Valuation of Black Labor in the U.S. South, 1831 to 1867," ibid., LXXVII (2012), 970–998.

6. For more Black mariners' experiences of Brazilian ships as spaces of both refuge and violent, hierarchical discipline, see João José Reis, Flávio dos Santos Gomes, and Marcus J. M. de Carvalho, *The Story of Rufino: Slavery, Freedom, and Islam in the Black Atlantic,*

Black mariners' working lives—defined to a significant degree by movement and cross-cultural exchange—were radically different from the modal experiences of enslaved men and women on New World plantations. Slaving vessels were a cosmopolitan laboring environment shaped both by economic incentives as well as the working and cultural knowledge of Black mariners themselves. Along these trading routes, Black mariners remade sailing vessels into dynamic, transcultural spaces that were structured, but not completely bound by, the racial and occupational hierarchies of the larger slaving society that depended on them. This development was distinct from the experience of Black mariners in the North Atlantic, who scholars have argued were "among the ranks of the earliest and most virulent attackers of the institution of slavery."[7] Inextricably bound to slaving commerce, Black mariners in the

trans. H. Sabrina Gledhill (New York, 2020); Beatriz Gallotti Mamigonian, "José Majojo e Francisco Moçambique, marinheiros das rotas atlânticas: Notas sobre a reconstituição de trajetórias da era da abolição," *Topoi*, XI, no. 20 (January–June 2010), 75–91; Zachary R. Morgan, *Legacy of the Lash: Race and Corporal Punishment in the Brazilian Navy and the Atlantic World* (Bloomington, Ind., 2014); Álvaro Pereira do Nascimento, "Do cativeiro ao mar: Escravos na marinha de guerra," *Estudos Afro-Asiáticos*, XXXVIII (2000); Jaime Rodrigues, "Circulação atlântica: Idade, tempo de trabalho e funções de escravos e libertos na marinha mercante luso-brasileira, séculos XVIII e XIX," *História*, XXXIV (2015), 128–145; Marley Antonia Silva da Silva and Cristiane Pinheiro Santos Jacinto, "Trabalhando nos mares: Marinheiras e marinheiros africanus nos navios da Companhia de Comércio do Grão pará e Maranhão," *Revista Maracanan*, no. 29 (January–April 2022), 16–30. The scholarly literature on quotidian maritime life aboard slaving vessels tends to emphasize Black mariners' marginality; see Christopher, *Slave Ship Sailors;* Ray Costello, *Black Salt: Seafarers of African Descent on British Ships* (Liverpool, U.K., 2012); Robert Harms, *The Diligent: A Voyage through the Worlds of the Slave Trade* (New York, 2002); Marcus Rediker, *The Slave Ship: A Human History* (New York, 2007); Joseph C. Miller, *Way of Death: Merchant Capitalism and the Angolan Slave Trade, 1730–1830* (Madison, Wis., 1988); Gregory E. O'Malley, *Final Passages: The Intercolonial Slave Trade of British America, 1619–1807* (Williamsburg, Va., and Chapel Hill, N.C., 2014); Jaime Rodrigues, *De costa a costa: Escravos, marinheiros e intermediários do tráfico negreiro de Angola ao Rio de Janeiro (1780–1860)* ([São Paulo], 2005); Rodrigues, "Cultura marítima: Marinheiros e escravos no tráfico negreiro para o Brasil (sécs. XVIII e XIV)," *Revista Brasileira de História*, XIX (1999), 15–53; Stephanie E. Smallwood, "African Guardians, European Slave Ships, and the Changing Dynamics of Power in the Early Modern Atlantic," *WMQ*, 3d Ser., LXIV (2007), 679–716.

7. Christopher, *Slave Ship Sailors*, 82–83. For more on Black sailors' antislavery activity, see Julius S. Scott, "Crisscrossing Empires: Ships, Sailors, and Resistance in the Lesser Antilles in the Eighteenth Century," in Robert L. Paquette and Stanley L. Engerman, eds., *The Lesser Antilles in the Age of European Expansion* (Gainesville, Fl., 1996), 130–131.

South Atlantic provided owners with far more than the fruits of their physical toil: they offered their vital cultural and intellectual expertise.

This chapter explores quotidian life aboard slaving vessels, an existence that revolved around both routines of labor and recurring rituals of collective worship and workmate bonding. Black mariners' participation in the religious and communal aspects of seafaring life contributed to a novel racial dynamic at sea that did not depend on rigid occupational segregation or intractable Black-white antagonism as a cornerstone of shipboard hierarchy and labor control. Though racially motivated violence and abuses against African and creole sailors were far from rare, they were blunted by the necessity for collaborative action aboard ships where vulnerable laborers worked to preserve both their own lives and the lives of the enslaved. In moments of crisis, crew members—Black, white, Brazilian, African, and European—had no choice but to work together to preserve the safety of all. In repeated moments of precarity, Black mariners' cosmopolitanism proved a key asset for merchants and slaveowners alike. Cultural flexibility and dexterity buoyed the project and profitability of Atlantic slaving, but it also assisted Black mariners in forging ties of solidarity across lines of social difference. The stratified structure of labor and social relations on sailing vessels also fostered a sense of interdependence between Black and white crew members, creating a real but fragile shipboard fraternity across lines of race and enslaved status.[8]

A WORLD OF "BLACK PORTUGUESE" MARINERS

By the late eighteenth century, African and creole mariners' place within the South Atlantic maritime economy had been cemented. When Bahia's governor, Manuel da Cunha Menezes, conducted a general census of ships and mariners in the city of Salvador in 1775, he noted the prevalence of Africans and their descendants as laborers on both long- and short-distance seafaring voyages. The census revealed the Blackness of Bahian maritime slaving labor. Cumulatively, the eighty-eight ships based in the port at that time, which engaged in either cabotage (along the Brazilian coastline) or transatlantic voyages, employed 1,096 registered sailors, 443 of whom were identified as *preto,* or African, and 392 as enslaved. Of the preto sailors, 61.6 percent, along

8. The concept of cross-racial interdependence among maritime crews is derived from Henry Trotter, "Sailing beyond Apartheid: The Social and Political Impact of Seafaring on Coloured South African Sailors," in Carina E. Ray and Jeremy Rich, eds., *Navigating African Maritime History* (St. John's, NL, 2009), 203; Rediker, *Slave Ship,* 230.

with 63.5 percent of the port's enslaved sailors, worked in the transatlantic slave trade.[9]

The census posited that, regarding the ships traveling to the "countries which are observed, with the exception of those to the Court [Lisbon] and Porto, the majority of all of their crews are composed of many enslaved Blacks due to the great lack of white sailors." Menezes, however, could not deny the degree to which African and African-descended mariners had become pivotal to the labor of South Atlantic slaving. Ships operating on the routes to the Mina Coast, Angola, and Benguela were, as the census revealed, especially prone to employing African and enslaved sailors. Menezes's data suggested that such ships were "accustomed to equip with a small number of 4 or 6 white sailors, supplying the Black captives with the rest of the majority that go."[10]

Not everyone was happy with this state of affairs. A number of ship officers from the Companhia Geral de Pernambuco e Paraíba opined that enslaved mariners recruited from various owners in Brazil "knew very little of their office, and do not perform duties as they ought to perform them." These deficiencies, such captains argued, had led to dangerous accidents at sea, such as when the ship *Gloria* began to take on water because its enslaved caulker was ineffective. The 1775 census identifying the majority of mariners in Bahia as African and creole concurred with this claim, characterizing Black sailors as "all unable, and clumsy in navigation . . . but [they] serve due to the necessity of the new ships." In addition, the census argued that local Black fishermen demonstrated "little aptitude for the exercise of sailors" and were "entirely ignorant of the maneuver of mariners."[11]

Elite critiques notwithstanding, the predominance of Black mariners in Bahian slaving ventures reflected the demographics of Salvador. Though estimates from the time vary, people of African descent were observed to outnumber white residents of the city by nearly two to one. The pool from which to draw available laborers for the city's growing maritime demands

9. AHU, CU, Bahia, caixa 47, documento 8812, July 3, 1775, "Mapa geral de toda a qualidade de embarcações que ha na capitania da Bahia e navegam para a costa da Mina, Angola."

10. Ibid. The census notes that not every parish was represented; Rua do Paso was excluded, as were three corvettes.

11. ANTT, Companhia Geral de Pernambuco e Paraíba Copiador, Letter from Intendant and Deputies, Lisbon, Aug. 11, 1773; AHU, CU, Bahia, caixa 164, documento 12425, May 27, 1775, "Mapas de carga, relações e listas e outros documents relativas a embarcações vindas da Bahia."

was thus predominantly Black and enslaved. This fact was not just a matter of demographic convenience or necessity, however. Black mariners were also explicitly recognized, at times, for their contributions to the larger project of transatlantic slaving. In 1777, for instance, the Junta do Comércio informed Félix José da Costa, captain of the *Portilhão*, that upon arriving in Benguela he should "get rid of white sailors and substitute them with black sailors who are more experienced with this kind of trip and dealing with slaves." In addition, a 1761 royal decree by the Portuguese crown identified enslaved seamen as "able sailors, . . . and experts [who] facilitate[d] navigation, and promote[d] commerce."[12]

The proportion of Black mariners on any given vessel was at least in part determined by its destination. In the sample of all preto seamen based in Salvador, 36.8 percent of all Black mariners labored on ships traveling within Bahia or to other Brazilian ports, whereas only 1.6 percent of the Black seafaring population navigated to Lisbon or Porto. By contrast, nearly 19 percent worked aboard vessels destined for the major slave-trading ports of southwest Africa (including Benguela and Luanda), with the remainder, more than 41.3 percent, principally navigating between Bahia and West Africa. Of the eighty-eight ships registered in the port, twenty-four regularly traveled to the West African coast (ten to the Mina Coast alone), a figure that was more than double the eleven ships that navigated to Portugal.[13]

Demographic realities in Salvador da Bahia had larger Atlantic maritime reverberations. By the late eighteenth century, the archetype of the "Black Portuguese" mariner had become a recognizable identity in ports both within and outside the South Atlantic. On the North American seaboard in Annapolis, Maryland, an enslaved seaman and cooper named Toney spoke English

12. A. J. R. Russell-Wood, "Ports of Colonial Brazil," in Franklin W. Knight and Peggy K. Liss, eds., *Atlantic Port Cities: Economy, Culture, and Society in the Atlantic World, 1650–1850* (Knoxville, Tenn., 1991), 222–223; ANTT, Companhia Geral de Pernambuco e Paraíba Copiador, July 4, 1777; Cristina Nogueira da Silva and Keila Grinberg, "Soil Free from Slaves: Slave Law in Late Eighteenth and Early Nineteenth Century Portugal," *Slavery and Abolition*, XXXII (2011), 436. In Pernambuco, enslaved and African mariners also comprised a majority of the seafaring labor force. A census of Recife conducted in the same year registered a total of 7 ships engaged in the slave trade, 52 in cabotage, 227 in riverine travel, and 208 fishing vessels. The city boasted 186 free sailors, 108 of whom labored on ships traveling to Rio de Janeiro and "almost all of whom were old," and 423 enslaved seafarers (AHU, CU, Pernambuco, caixa 120, documento 9196, "Ofício do José César de Meneses").

13. AHU, CU, Bahia, caixa 47, documento 8812, July 3, 1775, "Mapa geral de toda a qualidade de embarcações que ha na capitania da Bahia e navegam para a costa da Mina, Angola."

fluently but "pretend[ed] to be a Portu-guize." In 1754, he and two white convicts (his shipmates) were suspected of killing their captain and stealing the sloop *Hopewell,* finally escaping with the ship and goods aboard, along with another enslaved man. Several decades later, the *Anna,* which embarked from Liverpool in 1789, had recruited three "Portuguese Blacks" for its slaving voyages: Silvin Buckle, Jack Peters, and James Drachen. The last man had also been employed on a previous voyage to Havana. Though it is unclear what these men's origins were from their identification—whether they were born in Portugal or Brazil or whether they had African backgrounds—it is clear that they had spent some time in the Portuguese Atlantic as mariners before making their way to England. In other instances, Bahian captains recognized the value of this archetype and contracted their enslaved mariners out to foreign captains to profit from the assumed proficiency of "Black Portuguese" mariners. In the fluid maritime spaces of the Atlantic, such circulations between port cities, empires, and vessels were unsurprising.[14]

Though Black mariners were a common sight on the decks of every kind of Bahian ship, at the beginning of the nineteenth century, they were especially prevalent on transatlantic slaving vessels. The cultural hybridity of such men made them highly desirable in the eyes of ship captains and merchants seeking to reduce costs and employ seafarers with the requisite skills for the translation and cultural brokerage that slaving demanded. Enslaved and freed men of African descent had long served on Bahian ships, but an analysis of the composition of ship crews reveals the centrality of such men in seafaring well into the nineteenth century. Between 1811 and 1839, fifty-one Bahian ships captured by British antislaving forces on Africa's western coast had all or a portion of their ships' papers confiscated by British authorities. The rare surviving crew registers (*matrículas*) of these vessels reveal that, of the 1,414 men laboring on these ships, 45.8 percent were of African descent. Of this group, 35.5 percent were African born, and the remaining 10.3 percent indicated they were born

14. "Fifty Pistoles Reward," *Boston Weekly News-Letter,* May 23, 1754, [4], *Freedom on the Move,* https://freedomonthemove.org; Suzanne Schwarz, ed., *Slave Captain: The Career of James Irving in the Liverpool Slave Trade* (Liverpool, U.K., 2008), 38. Manoel da Graça was a Bahian *pardo* captain who encountered a shipwrecked French vessel in Fernando Po. The French slaving vessel was navigating to Saint-Domingue and requested Graça's aid in transporting the slaves held in the cargo to Bahia to avoid losing profits. Graça agreed and also allowed a French ship to take a number of his enslaved sailors for additional labor. See AHU, CU, São Tomé e Príncipe, caixa 23, documento 1944, Jan. 7, 1792, "Carta do Conselheiro Francisco da Silva Corte Real, à rainha dando parecer sobre a carta do governador."

outside Africa but of full or partial African descent. Of the total Bahian slave-trade labor force, 27.1 percent were enslaved. This documentary record offers clear evidence that the workers of the Bahian slave trade constituted an exceptionally Black maritime labor force, particularly in comparison to other ports and trade routes in the Atlantic. In Rio de Janeiro, one estimate placed the number of enslaved mariners serving on slaving ships between 1795 and 1811 at 16.8 percent, and another sample, from 1812 to 1863, also in Rio de Janeiro, tabulated enslaved mariners as comprising 17 percent of crews.[15]

This group of maritime laborers was also exceptionally ethnically diverse. Anyone setting sail on a slaving vessel hailing from Bahia would have been inundated with the sounds of multiple languages and the sight of figures marked with distinctive facial scarifications from a range of African origins. Such men represented a wide array of proclaimed ethnicities, though they predominantly originated from the Mina Coast region (see Table 2).

Because biographical details entered into crew registers by ship captains and owners—including birthplace, nationality, and marital status—were provided by seamen, this information indicates in particular how many mariners identified themselves. Of 502 African-born sailors, 399, or 79.6 percent, were from the Bight of Benin region, where most slaving voyages were destined, whereas a smaller proportion originated from communities in the Bight of Biafra (2.0 percent), Upper Guinea coast (1.9 percent), West Central Africa (13.7 percent), and Southeast Africa (2.8 percent).[16]

15. Herbert S. Klein, *The Atlantic Slave Trade* (Cambridge, 1999), 85–86; Rodrigues, *De costa a costa,* 187; and see Appendix 1, below. The very practice of creating matrículas was an attempt to discipline supposedly unruly maritime laborers. In 1799, naval authorities complained of the regularity with which mariners escaped from their ships—especially if punishment was imminent. Seafarers who traveled to Pernambuco demonstrated a penchant for "working only for one passage" before fleeing to the hinterlands to become robbers and "infesting" the colony with indolence. The Junta do Comércio argued that vessels should employ crews that were "unfailingly registered" so fugitive seamen could be more easily located should they "scatter" into the captaincy (ANTT, fundo 7X, Junta do Comércio, maço 10, caixa 38, "Para Vossa Excellencia seja servido o mande-lo dar por dezempedido e secendiado para seguir viagem para o Porto de Lisboa").

16. The supposition that African seamen provided information about their own origins and ethnic identifications is supported by a crew registry that noted Pedro, a free steward on an 1828 ship, could not provide his biographical details because he was "a dumb [mentally incapacitated] man who does not know his homeland." See BNA, FO 315/42, Papers of the *Bella Eliza,* no. 12; and see Appendix 1, below.

TABLE 2. *African and Creole Mariners by Birthplace or Ethnicity*

Origins	# of men	Percentage
Africa		
Mina	267	40.9
Nagô	35	5.4
Hausa	33	5.1
Gege	31	4.7
São Tomé and Príncipe	21	3.2
Calabar	7	1.0
Tapa (contemporary Nupe)	6	0.9
Camaroons (Camarão)	3	0.5
Benin	3	0.5
Acará	2	0.3
Ouidah (Ajudá)	1	0.2
Cabo Verde	9	1.4
Angola	35	5.4
Cabinda	14	2.1
Benguela	12	1.8
Congo	4	0.6
Loango	1	0.2
Gabon (Gabão)	1	0.2
Branom / Bronon (contemporary Borim)	3	0.5
Mozambique	14	2.1
Africa / unspecified	3	0.5
AFRICA TOTAL	502	76.9
Europe		
Lisbon	3	0.5
Europe total	3	0.5
Other	5	0.8
Brazil		
Bahia	97	14.9
Pernambuco	9	1.4
Rio de Janeiro	9	1.4
Santa Caterina	6	0.9
Alagoas	3	0.5
Sergipe	4	0.6
Espírito Santo	4	0.6
Rio Grande do Norte	3	0.5
São Paulo	4	0.6

Origins	# of men	Percentage
Paraíba	1	0.2
Maranhão	1	0.2
Ilha Grande	1	0.2
Minas Gerais	1	0.2
Brazil total	143	21.9
GRAND TOTAL	653	

Source: Figures are derived from a compilation of slaving ships listed in Appendix 1.

The ethnic composition of Bahia's maritime labor force was a reflection, in part, of Salvador's population as a whole. Though always a majority, the African and creole population of Salvador grew as a prolonged period of economic depression gave way to a boom in sugar production in the 1790s. Burgeoning labor requirements on sugar plantations in the northeast in the late eighteenth century were mostly met by the importation of captives from the Bight of Benin.[17] This produced a greater ethnic homogeneity among workers on Bahian slaving vessels. From 1800 to 1830, more than 131,762 enslaved men and women arrived in Salvador from the region. From 1820 to 1835, men and women with origins on the Mina Coast represented a peak 57.3 percent of the African population in Bahia. On board slaving vessels, however, the proportion of free and enslaved mariners from the Mina Coast was overrepresented when compared to the demographics of Salvador's general population. In part, this was because captains and shipowners showed a marked preference for employing crew members from the same regions in which they conducted their slaving activities. In addition, freed mariners born in this region who had been manumitted in Brazil sometimes chose to labor

17. Figures on the racial composition of Bahia's population in the early nineteenth century vary; according to Kátia M. de Queirós Mattoso, pretos, pardos, and *cabras* comprised 78.3 percent (43 percent free and 35.3 percent enslaved) of the population of Bahia in 1808. As Luis Nicolau Parés has argued, after the intensification of the transatlantic slave trade in the 1790s, Bahia's Black population experienced significant Africanization. In the tobacco-growing town of Cachoeira in Bahia's interior, between 1780 and 1800, the estimated number of Geges had reached 20.5 percent, whereas Minas comprised 24.7 percent and Nagôs, 17.5 percent. See Mattoso, *Bahia: A cidade do Salvador e seu mercado no século XIX* (São Paulo, 1978), 82, 97, 119; Parés, *The Formation of Candomblé: Vodun History and Ritual in Brazil*, trans. Richard Vernon (Chapel Hill, N.C., 2013), 35–36.

on vessels returning to ports near their homelands, despite associations with memories of their enslavement and experiences of the perilous Middle Passage. Such men could have sought familiar geographies or were lured by the commercial opportunities particularly associated with the Mina Coast. Other men might have sought to serve on ships where it was more likely their native Fon or Yoruba language was spoken by crewmates. Paradoxically, mariners' birth ties to the regions of the Mina Coast that had experienced the most intensive slaving compelled at least some to return as freed men.[18]

African-born mariners' choice to adopt the Brazilian ethnic signifier of "Mina" or being from the "Mina nation" revealed their already creolized, but undoubtedly African-influenced, sense of identity. Slightly under half of all Black mariners (40.9 percent) claimed this ethnicity. Though no ethnically, linguistically, or politically analogous group existed in West Africa, in Bahia the broad category became a means to identify enslaved Africans who were purchased from various ports on the heterogeneous Mina Coast, which, by the late eighteenth century, included a number of Gbe-speaking groups—namely, Gen or Hula people from Grand-Popo and Little Popo (Aného), those born in Allada and Ouidah, as well as Fon or Ewe people from Dahomey. Africans self-identifying in this way in Bahia were claiming a meta-ethnicity with no equivalent in Africa. Adding further complication to the emergence of dynamic West African ethnic identities in Brazil was the tendency for Africans to assert multiple, dynamic, and overlapping identities in different contexts. At various points, Mahi identities were subsumed under the identifier Mina. So too was Gege, a signifier claimed by thirty-one seamen, 4.7 percent of all Africans laboring in the Bahian slave trade. Mariners' preference to identify as Gege receded as the nineteenth century wore on, in part a result of Bahian slaving ships' movement to the eastern ports of the Mina Coast, which re-

---

18. Slave trade estimates courtesy of *Voyages*. Stuart B. Schwartz also marks the period from 1780 to 1820 as the peak of transatlantic trade from the Bight of Benin; see Schwartz, *Sugar Plantations in the Formation of Brazilian Society: Bahia, 1550–1835* (Cambridge, 1985), 341; João José Reis, *Slave Rebellion in Brazil: The Muslim Uprising of 1835 in Bahia* (Baltimore, 1993), 139–140; Ana Lucia Araujo, *Public Memory of Slavery: Victims and Perpetrators in the South Atlantic* (Amherst, N.Y., 2010), 103. During this period, Bahian slavers transported a growing number of enslaved Africans from the West Central ports of Luanda and Benguela. Prohibitions on slaving north of the equator after 1815, along with lower prices per head, led Brazilian merchants to reestablish their commercial dominance in slave trading there after a period of French and English incursions (Mariana P. Candido, *An African Slaving Port and the Atlantic World: Benguela and Its Hinterland* [Cambridge, 2013], 164–168).

ceived far more Yoruba-speaking captives than any other group. It was also a sign, however, that the designation had been supplanted in enslaved people's consciousness by other more expansive identities such as Mina.[19]

Though such ethnic signifiers remained intentionally broad and could connote origins from geographically expansive regions of Africa, African mariners' self-identifications also suggest many maritime workers were born in port communities with strong ties to maritime transatlantic trade. In 1820, two African seamen named Jorge and Joaquim de Moraes identified themselves as "Geges" and declared that they had been born in Ouidah, but after living several years in Bahia, the men claimed Portuguese subjecthood. On the one hand, Jorge and Joaquim's declarations illustrate the salience of the Gege ethnic signifier for African individuals in Bahia. Though Jorge and Joaquim did not elaborate whether they were from Ouidah proper or its hinterlands, the town's location three kilometers from a lagoon system that linked it to the Atlantic Ocean as well as to other coastal communities east of Ouidah (including Lagos and Little Popo) meant that the two men hailed from an area where riverine navigation played an important role in both local subsistence and trade. Many inhabitants of Ouidah labored as canoemen, ferrying goods and people to and from European ships, whereas others worked as porters and fishermen. A large portion of the population was involved in some form of maritime activity. By 1776, European and Brazilian merchandise was already widely available in local markets, where many Ouidah residents would have become familiar with Atlantic commerce. Given the depth of maritime activity in Ouidah, it seems probable that Jorge and Joaquim de Moraes had already been to some extent exposed to Atlantic navigation or commerce before they had been enslaved and transported to Brazil. By the early nineteenth century, such men were just one example of a long-standing

19. James H. Sweet, "Mistaken Identities? Olaudah Equiano, Domingos Álvares, and the Methodological Challenges of Studying the African Diaspora," *American Historical Review*, CXIV (2009), 285–288. Robin Law argues that, because of migrations within West Africa's Slave Coast (eastern Mina Coast) during the same period as well as the prevalence of bilingualism, discrete linguistic and political communities in West Africa merged into new "African" ethnicities in American contexts (Law, "Ethnicities of Enslaved Africans in the Diaspora: On the Meanings of 'Mina' [Again]," *History in Africa*, XXXII [2005], 257, 267). Both Parés and Carvalho Soares have traced a similar process in Salvador and Rio de Janeiro by focusing on the evolution of Gege and Mina ethnic identities. See Parés, *Formation of Candomblé*, trans. Vernon; Mariza de Carvalho Soares, *People of Faith: Slavery and African Catholics in Eighteenth-Century Rio de Janeiro*, trans. Jerry D. Metz (Durham, N.C., 2011).

TABLE 3. *African and Creole Mariners by Racial Category*

Black mariners by racial category	Number of mariners
Preto	502
Creole	67
Pardo	71
Cabra	7

Source: Figures are derived from a compilation of slaving ships listed in Appendix 1.

dimension of the transatlantic slave trade: its tendency to incorporate existing forms of African cosmopolitanism into its operation.[20]

Just as the ethnic identifiers selected by enslaved and free mariners illustrated the complex evolutions of individuals' varied sense of communal affiliation and heritage, mariners of African descent also came to be identified by an array of racial categories. Unlike the self-identification of place of birth, racial ascription could be externally assigned and frequently conveyed elite assumptions of inferiority. Of the 653 men identified as African or of African descent, 76.9 percent were labeled preto, which implied both African birth and enslaved status, though the word literally translated to "black." Racial identities did not merely signify skin color, as a number of scholars of Afro-Brazil have observed, but also implied parentage and social status. Individuals could potentially move between racial categories within their lifetimes or be ascribed differing racial identities depending on the social context. On Bahian slaving vessels, a proportion of men were labeled *crioulo*, or of full African descent but born in Brazil or other Portuguese colonies. The designation *cabra* indicated someone of mixed race but with a greater proportion of African parentage, whereas the label of *pardo* referred to someone of roughly equal European and African descent. Mirroring the general population of Salvador, the crews tasked with performing the arduous labor aboard slaving vessels were significantly more African than creole (see Table 3). The preponderance of pretos laboring aboard slaving vessels served as a visible reminder of the deep connections between slave labor, enslaved status, and African birth.

20. AHI, Coleções Especiais, Comissão Mista, lata 13, maço 14, pasta 1, Papers of the *Emília*, 345; Robin Law, *Ouidah: The Social History of a West African Slaving "Port,"* *1727–1892* (Athens, Ohio, 2004), 26–29, 84, 135, 148.

Overall, those on the lowest rung of Bahia's social and racial hierarchy were most likely to populate transatlantic crews.[21]

Ship captains and merchants also relied upon the labor of so-called *ladino* African mariners, whose cosmopolitan cultural fluencies were in part harnessed to manage the enslaved individuals held in cargoes. As the designation of ladino, or "acculturated" African, suggested, however, it was equally important that such mariners were fluent in Portuguese language and custom. For instance, in 1811 the Bahian vessel *Venus* lost two *"ladino* sailors" named Caetano Congo and Antonio Mina to British forces. The men's surnames testified to both their African origins as well as their assimilation into Brazilian society. Moreover, the *Dezengano* labeled all of the eight African-born sailors who toiled aboard "ladinos" in 1812. Though most ladino mariners became acquainted with Portuguese language and culture in Brazil following their enslavement and passage across the Atlantic, some West Africans purchased by Brazilian merchants were already "acculturated" before even arriving in the Americas. In 1819, for instance, the Rio merchant Francisco Carlos da Costa Lace registered his purchase of ten "good and acculturated slaves" in the Cape of Good Hope. A slaving vessel sailing from Bissau to São Luis de Maranhão in 1814 recorded three *"ladino* young adolescents" as part of its enslaved cargo.[22]

Slaveholders in Bahia recognized the import of such cosmopolitan fluency and in effect crafted a commodity market for enslaved maritime labor that assigned value not only to work experience but to such cultural expertise and dexterity. In 1827, for instance, José de Cerqueira Lima—the owner of twelve enslaved ladino sailors on the *Independência*—valued the men at an exorbitant five hundred *milréis* each because each was "expert in the practice of the

21. Nishida, *Slavery and Identity,* 7–8; see also Mary C. Karasch, "Guiné, Mina, Angola, and Benguela: African and Crioulo Nations in Central Brazil, 1780–1835," in José C. Curto and Paul E. Lovejoy, eds., *Enslaving Connections: Changing Cultures of Africa and Brazil during the Era of Slavery* (Amherst, N.Y., 2004), 163–184, esp. 173; João José Reis and Eduardo Silva, *Negociação e conflíto: A resistência negra no Brasil escravista* (São Paulo, 1989), 45; C. R. Boxer, *Race Relations in the Portuguese Colonial Empire, 1415–1825* (Oxford, 1963), 73–74.

22. ANRJ, fundo 7X, Junta do Comércio, caixa 372, pacote 1, Papers of the *Venus,* 19; ibid., caixa 445, Petição de Izabel Catherina Guedes e Vicente Guedes de Souza, 7; ibid., caixa 371, no. 1. The ship *Feliz Americano* also labeled its African mariners as "ladinos"; see AHI, Coleções Especiais, Comissão Mista, lata 10, maço 3, pasta 2, Papers of the *Dezengano,* 1; ibid., lata 15, maço 4, pasta 2, Papers of the *Feliz Americano;* ibid., lata 18, maço 3, pasta 1, Papers of the *Independência.*

sea." Slaveowners in Rio de Janeiro also deliberately highlighted enslaved sailors' knowledge of maritime professions, as well as their ability to speak Portuguese, as a selling point. With a keen sense of how to monetize a bondsman's acquired cosmopolitanism, one advertisement identified "a slave from Mozambique for sale, with extensive experience as a sailor." Another owner characterized his young enslaved man as a "good sailor, and ordinary cook . . . who sailed for nine years with his owner," whereas another slaveholder advertised "an Angolan, with a fine figure, young and robust, occupation baker, and also can serve as a sailor because he has already been employed on a ship." Such descriptions assumed that occupational flexibility as well as physical appearance would increase a bondsman's sale value.[23]

A demographic portrait of Salvador's maritime labor force from the 1770s through the 1830s reveals captains' persistent reliance on Black mariners to perform multifaceted labors on the transatlantic slave trade. While Black "Portuguese" seamen could be found across the Atlantic world, and in every branch of maritime navigation, their unique skills were assumed to be particularly suited to the dangerous, cosmopolitan labor demanded on slavers. At moments of both hire and sale, captains and slaveowners in Bahia regularly touted African seafarers' cultural acumen, which augmented their market value. In this context, their cosmopolitanism became a commodity. Men from the Mina Coast proved to be the most sought after for captains. Their facility with Fon and Yoruba languages, their familiarity with West African geographies, as well as their acculturation to Portuguese language and culture, made them ideal, but often coerced, brokers between captains and captives on Bahia's slaving ships.

THE WORK OF CAPTIVE COSMOPOLITANS

If Black mariners were in part valuable to slavers for their cosmopolitan sensibilities, the growth of transatlantic slaving traffic also made their everyday labor increasingly essential. As the stream of captive Africans crossing the Atlantic grew, so did the numbers of enslaved mariners. Slave-trading vessels employed the largest crews in the Atlantic in relation to their size, as additional men were first and foremost needed to potentially subdue enslaved men and women held on board. By one estimate, slaving vessels traveling from Luanda to Pernambuco carried one crew member for every four to seven tons, com-

23. AHI, Coleções Especiais, Comissão Mista, lata 18, maço 3, pasta 1, Papers of the *Independencia; Jornal do commercio* (Rio de Janeiro), Nov. 26, 1827, 2, 3; Dec. 12, 1827, 3.

TABLE 4. *Distribution of Proprietors of Enslaved Mariners Employed in Bahia, 1811–1839*

Owned by	Number of enslaved mariners
Captain	40
Other officer	38
Owned "by the ship"	7
Shipowner	94
Other / unspecified	322
TOTAL	501

Source: Figures are derived from a compilation of slaving ships listed in Appendix 1.

pared to other merchant vessels, which employed one seaman for every 12 to 20 tons. This ratio amounted to roughly 1 crew member per 19.3 enslaved individuals. The median South Atlantic vessel weighed roughly 120 to 160 tons and carried between 300 and 400 slaves. Even as ships became smaller and more efficient in the early nineteenth century, transatlantic trade continued to generate greater labor requirements than other segments of Bahia's merchant marine.[24]

Mariners both enslaved and free were contracted before ships set sail, either by the vessel's owner or the captain. On Bahian vessels, captains and shipowners were often one and the same. Before setting sail, sailors and captains negotiated pay according to the length of voyage and the level of experience of the employed seaman, whereas an enslaved mariner's wages were usually negotiated by his owner. Enslaved mariners often labored under the control of owners who worked as captains or pilots aboard slaving vessels; indeed, 36 percent of enslaved mariners in Bahia were owned by investors or officers aboard slaving vessels. For these men, negotiations for pay and terms of employment were less complicated than for enslaved mariners hired out as wage laborers by more distant, landlocked owners. Because of their ability to supervise their bondsmen directly, maritime masters also had less cause for concern that their enslaved property would attempt to escape while at sea.[25]

In some instances, however, negotiations around compensation could be-

24. Miller, *Way of Death,* 356, 370. Slave trading vessels' size was measured by tonnage. This estimate is for midsized brigantines. In the 1810s, the midsized *bergantim* became slavers' ship of choice. Its size made it the most labor-efficient vessel of the era; see ibid., 371.

25. Rodrigues, *De costa a costa,* 161.

come contentious. Such was the case for preto cook Antônio de Carvalho, who was contracted to work aboard the *Saibu* on its voyage from Pernambuco to Lisbon with a layover in Rio de Janeiro in 1800. Carvalho's owner agreed to lease out his personal cook to the *Saibu*'s owner for 60$000 réis for the roundtrip voyage, receiving 9$920 réis before the voyage commenced and the remainder once it had concluded. Upon reaching Lisbon, however, Antônio de Carvalho suffered a head injury that necessitated care at a local hospital. After waiting five days for the captain to retrieve him as he had promised, Carvalho concluded that he had been abandoned in port and lost the remainder of his promised remuneration. In Antônio's case, his enslaved status helped him lodge a civil case for libel, demanding restitution of wages with the help of his owner. Owners of enslaved seamen also had legal standing to initiate complaints for failure by captains to pay wages, and because maritime masters were so often personally involved in seafaring themselves, they were familiar with the legal options available to sailors.[26]

Once captive cosmopolitans were contracted on board, their labor was instrumental to the successful functioning of the deep-sea sailing vessel that Marcus Rediker has called one of the early modern world's most complicated machines. Like enslaved men and women working in artisanal occupations on land, seafarers accumulated their specific skills through practice and apprenticeship. Occupational divisions aboard slaving ships tended to be racialized, though not rigidly so. African-born seamen were concentrated

26. Portuguese maritime law empowered men such as Carvalho with the capacity to litigate for restitution, allowing sailors to lodge legal petitions against captains who they felt had unlawfully withheld wages. The Portuguese Commercial Code prevented mariners from doing so before arriving at their destinations, however: "The officers and crew people, cannot bring litigation against the captain or ship before the end of the trip, under penalty of loss of their entire salary. However, finding the ship in a good harbor, the officers or people of the crew or mistreated persons, or those whom the captain has not given necessary support may demand a resolution of their contract before the consul, and in the absence in front of the magistrate of the place." The code also compelled captains to pay crews within a speedy twenty-four hours of arrival on shore. This gave mariners in the Luso-Atlantic equivalent legal protection to their counterparts in the Anglo-Atlantic. See George F. Steckley, "Litigious Mariners: Wage Cases in the Seventeenth-Century Admiralty Court," *Historical Journal*, XLII (1999), 315–345; BNA, FO 315/44, Papers of the *Emprehendador*, no. 32, "Obrigações Mandadas Trasladar Neste Lugar Pelo Artigo 1442 do Codigo Commercial Portuguez"; ANTT, Feitos Findos, Juízo da Índia e Mina, maço 40, caixa 40, no. 9, "Acção de Libello em que he com Autos Antonio de Carvalho homem preto Contra Manoel Jozé de San Bernardo Capitão do Brigue, 1800."

in the lowliest occupations on slaving vessels but also nearly monopolized several skilled positions such as cooper, cook, and medical practitioner. Some mariners labored exclusively in maritime service, whereas others were merely journeymen passing through one profession among many that they would work in during their lives. Enslaved mariners, however, were distinctive for the diversity of their occupational experience. Such men had practiced multiple professions throughout their working life as they circulated from owner to owner and became regularly exposed to new roles to which they would be required to adapt. Like other artisans, enslaved mariners refined their craft over the course of multiple voyages and the many years of experience necessary to practice their trade well.[27]

Slaving ships leaving Salvador's harbor would have assembled an intricately ordered floating world before embarking on their dangerous journeys. Carrying aboard sizable crews of approximately forty men, each vessel featured an archetypal division of labor, with occupational hierarchies largely mapped onto the racial hierarchies of Bahian slave society. In command was a captain, who acted as the first, or most senior, pilot. Below him were a chaplain, a second pilot, a third pilot (who was also the ship's scribe), a quartermaster, a barber, coopers, and regularly dozens of sailors, most of whom were African born.[28] Some vessels might also have carried carpenters, cooks, clerks (who managed the ship's trading cargo), and cabin boys, who served the ship's officers. Each occupation carried unique responsibilities and privileges, and crews divided their labor hierarchically. Skilled seamen who practiced a craft garnered greater wages and exercised more authority. Officers, including captains, pilots, and quartermasters performed highly skilled and supervisory forms of labor. Because of their expertise, they comprised the upper strata of a sailing vessel's floating society.

Common sailors were also skilled laborers, though they made up—along with cabin boys—the lower rungs of the shipboard order. Captains and mer-

27. Rediker, *Slave Ship,* 57. Several Black seamen registered themselves as "sailors for the ports of Africa" on the *São João Segunda Rosalia* in 1826, indicating they specialized in navigating to West African ports specifically. On the opposite end of the spectrum, other Black mariners could labor in the transatlantic slave trade for a short time before leaving the maritime profession altogether. See AHI, Coleções Especiais, Comissão Mista, lata 28, maço 5, pasta 1, Papers of the *São João Segunda Rosalia;* Reis, Gomes, and Carvalho, *Story of Rufino,* trans. Gledhill, 63.

28. On English ships, second and third officers were called "mates," answering to first officers; see Rediker, *Slave Ship,* 58, 225; ANRJ, fundo 7X, Junta do Comércio, caixa 410, pacote 1, Papers of the *São Miguel Triunfante.*

chants tended to assign Black seamen to these most menial and worst-paid roles. As enslaved cabin boys gradually gained sailing proficiency at sea, however, their occupational capabilities and thus monetary value would grow, a development that primarily accrued to the benefit of their owners. Among all common sailors laboring aboard Bahian vessels, 44.8 percent were Black, whereas Africans and creoles comprised 45.6 percent of all cabin boys. Common sailors formed the nucleus of any crew. Paramount among their responsibilities was manipulating sails and anchors by providing taxing physical labor. Fully rigged ships housed hundreds of lines, blocks, and tackles. Only experienced sailors would have extensive knowledge of techniques for taking-in, steering, and trimming sails. Part of this work required brute strength, but to practice what seamen themselves termed the "art of the sea," sailors needed practical and in-depth knowledge that could be acquired only through experience. Often, cabin boys labored aboard ships for the explicit purpose of learning these skills as unpaid apprentices, a role African and creole seamen frequently inhabited.[29]

Although many African and creole mariners filled positions requiring the least seafaring experience, many enslaved Africans also served in a number of formally skilled occupations, a stark contrast to the composition of the North American ships during the same period. Maritime artisans, unlike common sailors and cabin boys, normally endured multiple voyages and were the most wedded to life at sea. The position of cooper—who was responsible for building and maintaining the barrels used to transport water, oil, and other goods and provisions—was an overwhelmingly Black occupation on Bahian vessels. Black mariners made up 77.6 percent of all those registered in that position. In addition, Africans made up nearly 90 percent of barbers, *sangradores,* and surgeons; of medical practitioners on board in this sample, only one was white. Africans and creoles furthermore comprised the majority of cooks, at 70 percent.[30]

Among all the artisans who labored aboard slaving vessels, it was perhaps the ships' carpenters who held the most responsibility. The charge of keeping

29. W. Jeffrey Bolster, *Black Jacks: African American Seamen in the Age of Sail* (Cambridge, Mass., 1997), 78. On slaving vessels, 54.5 percent of all African and creole seamen were registered as sailors and 13.8 percent served as cabin boys. An additional 17.6 percent labored as "slaves" and performed unspecified labor, though most were likely employed as personal servants for officers. See Appendix 1, below.

30. Bolster argues that African American sailors never rose to the rank of ship's officer (ibid., 77).

TABLE 5. *Mariners by Occupation and Race*

Occupation	White	African or of African descent	Unidentified	Indian
Captain	45	1	0	0
Pilot	68	3	0	0
Chaplain	9	0	0	0
Apprentice	15	1	0	0
Clerk	2	0	0	0
Scribe	7	2	0	0
Quartermaster	42	0	0	0
Medical practitioner	1	51	0	0
Carpenter	6	3	1	0
Cooper	8	38	2	0
Cook	3	14	1	0
Sailor	372	355	15	1
Cabin boy	73	90	7	0
Other	0	1	1	0

Source: Figures are derived from a compilation of slaving ships listed in Appendix 1.

slaving vessels afloat was a complex one, as the surprisingly delicate watercraft required constant maintenance. Mariners reinforced the hull with oakum and wooden plugs when planks separated during the voyage, repaired vital components including the masts and yards, and outfitted the ship to confine enslaved men and women in the hold during the return voyage. Their work was also integral to preventing rebellious urges on the part of recently enslaved Africans, as captains entrusted them to erect barricades on the main deck that provided a physical barrier between the crew and potentially hostile captives in the event of an escape. While anchored on the West African coast, carpenters went to work constructing platforms on the lower deck to provide extra space to accommodate a greater number of enslaved individuals in the hold. Finally, they helped to safeguard the security of the entire crew by ruthlessly containing the newly boarded captives in demarcated spaces.[31]

The health of the crew and enslaved cargo alike was also frequently in the hands of enslaved maritime healers. Barbers and sangradores tended to injuries and illnesses, managed ships' medical stores, administered cures, and performed acts of minor surgery and bloodletting. Like the other skilled

31. Rediker, *Slave Ship*, 59.

artisans aboard the ship, they received greater compensation and trading privileges than their crewmates.

Crucially, mariners' labors were not solely physical. The linguistic and cultural knowledge West African mariners utilized made them especially valuable. In contrast to their Brazilian- and European-born counterparts, they could converse with captives, issue commands, and quell acts of resistance and rebellion that occasionally erupted belowdecks. As some of the few crew members who ventured on shore into West African ports, they could also act as trade auxiliaries to ship captains. One such African mariner, Antônio Lopes, demonstrated the dual role that such men played on slaving vessels. When he petitioned a shipowner for recuperation of wages in 1784, he argued he had worked as both a "barber and interpreter [*lingoa geral*] in the slave trade." African seamen like Antônio remained acutely aware of the multifaceted intercultural value they brought to slaving vessels. They were also likely cognizant of the key role they played in pacifying enslaved men, women, and children held belowdecks. Their deployment of familiar African words to those held aboard slaving ships could alleviate some of the profound emotional distress of captivity and help maintain a semblance of tranquility at sea. The irony of the ship's healer being tasked with such a coercive mission would probably not have been lost on the men themselves. Unlike medical practitioners on land, their objective was to preserve the market value of enslaved bodies by preventing physical illness or suicidal distress, rather than heal the wounded for the benefit of their patients.[32]

Cooks also played an essential role in the management of slaving vessels. Tasked with feeding the two hundred to four hundred slaves twice daily, as well as the captain and crew, the cook was critical in maintaining the health of those on board. Some Bahian ships like the *Desforço* even employed two cooks: one to prepare the captain's meals and one for the rest of the captives and crew. Though not all ships employed a dedicated cook, the job remained a pivotal one. Cooks often worked in the small enclosure designated the galley, toiling over a wood-burning hearth for most of the day and preparing gruel in large cauldrons. Difficulties arose for cooks not only in making stale and often spoiled provisions palatable but also in stretching a voyage's meager food supply through daily rationing. Voyages could also last longer than anticipated due to weather conditions or other delays, further exhausting supplies. Cooks

32. Rodrigues, *De costa a costa*, 160–161; ANTT, Feitos Findos, Juízo da Índia e Mina, maço 12, numero 1, caixa 199, "Ação cível de soldadas em que são autores Antônio Lopes e Manuel da Cruz, homens pretos e réu Nicolau Antônio de Sousa Trovão."

also often dealt with faulty equipment, making their task even more arduous. Ideally, ships provided cooks with cauldrons fashioned from copper. Captains attempting to reduce their costs stowed cooking vessels made of inferior materials, such as tin, which, as one Portuguese doctor observed, resulted in "poisoned food, and many African slaves [who] died poisoned from the lack of cleanliness of the cauldrons from stomach pains and diarrheas." In order to avoid such calamities, slaving ship cooks had to be vigilant in maintaining a clean galley. An astute cook would make meals to placate captives held below decks in an attempt to forestall rebellious violence. Despite the essential role they played, their relationship to the rest of the crew was rarely smooth. The often paltry allotments they were forced to serve could raise objections among other sailors, marking the position of cook as particularly contentious.[33]

Although African and creole mariners made up the majority of many slaving crews, they could be excluded from certain occupations aboard. Quartermaster and other supervisory positions were typically reserved for white seamen. As secondary navigators under the captain, such men managed the sailors and cabin boys, directed their labor, distributed provisions among the crew, kept ledgers, watched enslaved men and women in the cargo, and ministered to sick slaves. They enforced shipboard routine by signaling the changing of the watch. Pilots were also much more likely to be white, though they were not exclusively so. Like quartermasters, they were second mates to the captain, taking over his duties during night watches or permanently, in the event the captain perished during the voyage. Pilots were divided into first, second, and third tiers in accordance with their level of experience and seniority. Principally charged with navigating the ship, they utilized complex instruments, including maps, astrolabes, inclinometers, nautical rings, Jacob's staffs, Davis's quadrants, and protractors in conjunction with knowledge of

33. ANRJ, fundo 7X, Junta do Comércio, caixa 369, Papers of the *Desforço;* Christopher, *Slave Ship Sailors,* 109–112; ANTT, Junta do Comércio, maço 10, caixa 36, Mar. 12, 1799, Letter of Miguel de Mello Antonio. Though the majority of cooks were men of African descent, because of the absence of strict occupational segregation in the Bahian slave trade, only 2.5 percent of all Black seamen were registered in the occupation. In comparison, Bolster reports, 24 percent of all African American seamen in Philadelphia were cooks in 1803, whereas 51 percent in Providence, Rhode Island, were registered for that occupation seven years later. These numbers highlight that, in the North Atlantic, Black seamen were more occupationally segregated to one or two roles aboard ships than they were in the South Atlantic (*Black Jacks,* 33). On the frequently tense relationship between cooks and other crew members, see ibid., 81–82. For a discussion of the poor quality of provisions and inadequate rationing on Brazilian slaving ships to Angola, see Miller, *Way of Death,* 352–355.

points of destination, trade winds, and currents. Pilots needed to master basic principles of geometry, astronomy, cartography, and geography.[34]

The pilot's rank and authority were second only to that of the captain, and both of them were most often white. Nonetheless, three pardo mariners served as pilots in the fifty-one ships sampled. Though navigational expertise was sometimes assumed to require both literacy and academic study, by the early nineteenth century, a number of mixed-race men were employed as either pilots or captains aboard Bahian slaving vessels.[35] In part, this phenomenon reflected slave traders' willingness to incorporate or defer to particular forms of African-derived expertise where necessary. The English slaving ship captain Hugh Crow recorded the hiring at Bonny of an African pilot locally called "My Lord," a man whose familiarity with geography of the coast and commercial ports located in the Bight surely made him an attractive navigator for Crow's vessel. Likewise, during the early nineteenth century, British slavers in the Bight of Biafra temporarily hired Black pilots to cross the turbulent waters of that stretch of coast, even if they were not an official part of the crew. African navigators could, at times, exercise immense control over the fate of voyages on European sailing vessels.[36]

34. Bolster, *Black Jacks*, 14; Leif Svalesen, *The Slave Ship "Fredensborg,"* trans. Pat Shaw and Selena Winsnes (Bloomington, Ind., 2000), 54–55, 110, 134; Charles R. Foy, "Ports of Slavery, Ports of Freedom: How Slaves Used Northern Seaports' Maritime Industry to Escape and Create Trans-Atlantic Identities, 1713–1783" (Ph.D. diss., Rutgers University, 2008), 298; Rediker, *Slave Ship*, 58, 232. All those registered as quartermasters on Bahian slaving vessels were white. Ships' registers identified only seamen of African descent by racial designation; those mariners of European ancestry did not have a racial ascription in the register. On navigation, see Manoel Pimentel, *Arte de navegar, em que se ensinam as regras praticas, e o modo de cartear pela Carta plana . . .* (Lisbon, 1712), 15–22.

35. The relative prevalence of men of partial African descent in the position of lead navigator and ship's master on Bahian vessels was less common in other Atlantic ports outside of Africa. Christopher has argued that, on North Atlantic trading routes, sailors of African descent were marginal figures who "were overwhelmingly confined to the lowest positions aboard ship." Likewise, Bolster states that, in the Anglo-Atlantic, outside of the pirate ship, "a skilled black sailor had little authority." Black navigators, however, appear to have been common in São Tomé. In 1826, for instance, Jozé Váz, identified as a preto born on the island of Príncipe, labored as a "second pilot for the ports of the coast of Africa." See AHI, Coleções Especiais, Comissão Mista, lata 27, maço 1, pasta 1, Papers of the *Príncipe de Guiné*, 68; Bolster, *Black Jacks*, 15; Christopher, *Slave Ship Sailors*, 83.

36. Kevin Dawson has highlighted the centrality of Black and enslaved ship pilots in the Caribbean and southern United States, where such men navigated deepwater vessels

Narrow navigational expertise was not the only value African pilots brought to slaving vessels. Crow noted that African pilots "considered it indispensable to the safety of the ship to perform certain ceremonies" before embarking, which included communicating with the spiritual forces that governed the success or failure of voyages traversing the sea. African navigators—like many of their Iberian counterparts—understood maritime environments not merely in scientific or technical terms as rationalized manipulations of predictable earthly forces, but in supernatural or spiritual dimensions, as well. The willingness of white merchants and crews to cede control of deepwater sailing vessels to African and pardo mariners suggests not only the expertise of such men but the degree to which captains of slaving ships cruising along the African coast embraced, or at least tolerated, such heterodox navigational practices out of necessity.[37]

At the apex of shipboard hierarchy, captains prepared and managed the commercial aspects of each voyage. On Bahian vessels, the occupation of captain was on occasion inhabited by men of African descent. This required an extensive knowledge of navigation, West African commerce, and experience in the management of shipboard personnel. Slaving ship papers identify a number of pardo captains working regularly during the late eighteenth and early nineteenth century. Antônio de Santa Isabel, Innocêncio Marques, Vicente Ferreira Milles, Caetano Alberto de França, Joaquim Marques Loureiro, and Prudêncio Vidal de Albuquerque Viana all recorded their profession as "captain" for ships traveling to West Africa.[38]

The captains performed myriad duties before, during, and after the voyage. Before leaving Salvador, captains recruited crewmembers and were responsible for the loading of trading cargoes onto ships. At sea, they endeavored

through harbors from the open sea to docks and storehouses. In the late eighteenth century, Olaudah Equiano learned vital navigational skills from his ship's second mate as well as from his captain and owner while still an enslaved sailor in the Caribbean, even though many believed that "it was a very dangerous thing to let a Negro know navigation." See James Walvin, *An African's Life: The Life and Times of Olaudah Equiano, 1745-1797* (New York, 2000), 70; Dawson, "The Cultural Geography of Enslaved Ship Pilots," in Jorge Cañizares-Esguerra, Matt D. Childs, and James Sidbury, eds., *The Black Urban Atlantic in the Age of the Slave Trade* (Philadelphia, 2013), 163–184.

37. Hugh Crow, *Memoirs of the Late Captain Hugh Crow, of Liverpool . . .* (London, 1830), 35.

38. Loureiro's father, Manoel Marques Loureiro, was himself a slaving ship captain in the mid-eighteenth century.

to safely and efficiently navigate to the West African coast. Once anchored, captains ventured ashore, setting up temporary lodges on coastal beaches or staying in small, crude trading forts erected by Brazilian merchants within West African communities. Along with a clerk and apprentice who sometimes accompanied them, captains would distribute duties to local rulers, porters, and canoemen, trade with coastal merchants, and attempt to secure the most beneficial terms possible. Upon completion of their trade, captains oversaw the loading of enslaved men, women, and children aboard the ship and attempted to achieve an uneventful return voyage, avoiding slave revolts, storms, shipwrecks, and other catastrophes. Captains made the final navigational decisions and delegated labor tasks among various members of the crew. As the most skilled and best-compensated member of each sailing crew, their authority superseded all others. The presence of African-descended captains in the historical record suggests the degree to which Black maritime labor and expertise were not confined to the most wrenching, menial, or taxing jobs but were present at all levels of the shipboard working world.[39]

COMPENSATING COSMOPOLITAN LABOR

Despite the widespread presence of Black mariners on slaving vessels, the distribution of wages was one area in which the hierarchies of the broader slave society were apparent. Variations in average wages for slaving ship crew members correlated strongly with occupation and the corresponding level of skill, experience, and responsibility that it was presumed to entail. During a round trip from Bahia to the Mina Coast, captains made an average of 1695.5 milréis, or more than forty times what cabin boys did for the same voyage (see Table 6). Wages paid to officers were markedly higher than those for common

39. Rediker argues that, as the merchant marine grew to comprise a greater part of the English economy, the captain's authority became more fearsome and absolute. A strict hierarchical ideology he labels "disciplinary paternalism" organized shipboard labor, in which crews treated superiors with total deference. Captains' ability to demand almost absolute obedience from crew members was derived, in part, from their capacity to employ the lash and other forms of corporal punishment. This characterization of the relations between captain and crews—while holding some correlation for Bahian vessels—was a more accurate description of labor relations in the North Atlantic, born as it was from the very specific relations between workers and capital in early modern England. Brazil, by function of its status as a slave society, operated under very different modes of social conduct and interaction. See Rediker, *Between the Devil and the Deep Blue Sea: Merchant Seamen, Pirates, and the Anglo-American Maritime World, 1700–1750* (Cambridge, 1989), 207–216, esp. 209 n. 10.

TABLE 6. *Average Wage by Race, Legal Status, and Occupation in 1$000* Réis

	White	Black	Free and freed	Enslaved
Captain	1391	2000	—	—
Clerk	800		—	—
Pilot	355.8	223.3	—	—
Chaplain	366.7	—	—	—
Apprentice	44.3	0	—	—
Scribe	85	50	—	—
Quartermaster	248	—	—	—
Medical practitioner	250	135.2	137.4	132
Cooper	132.5	99.8	115.2	77.7
Carpenter	101.25	130	—	—
Cook	155	64.3	92.3	26.7
Sailor	80.9	49.3	74.7	43.2
Cabin boy	53.3	45.8	48.8	45.8
Slave	—	43.3	—	—

Source: Figures are derived from a compilation of slaving ships listed in Appendix 1.

sailors and servants (including cabin boys and slaves), though there was wide variation among officers, as well.

An analysis of wages on Bahian slaving vessels suggests that in significant ways racial discrimination imposed restrictions on the kinds of occupations African and creole seafarers could enter and the wages they would earn for such work. Though mariners of all stripes made paltry wages, their race and legal status, whether born free, manumitted, or enslaved, influenced their remuneration.[40] African or African-descended mariners received, on average, less than their white counterparts in all occupations except those of carpenter and captain. Enslaved mariners regularly collected lower average wages than their legally free counterparts, even those with whom they shared a racial identity. All Black common sailors, for instance, averaged 49.3 milréis per roundtrip voyage, but free Black sailors earned 58.7 milréis—significantly more than the 43.2 milréis paid to enslaved sailors. The average wage for white sailors, meanwhile, was 80.9 milréis, substantially more than either group.

40. Sailors' wages in the early nineteenth century were often not sufficient to sustain a comfortable living, leading many to a life of poverty. In 1812, sailor Vicente Ignacio petitioned for his lost wages of five months at 12$000 réis per month, because, as he attested, he was "a poor sailor." See ANRJ, fundo 7X, Junta do Comércio, caixa 371, pacote 1, documento 15, Papers of the *Paquete Volante*.

TABLE 7. *Average Wage by Rank in* Milréis *(One Thousand* Réis*)*

Occupation	Average wage
First pilot	429.7
Second pilot	324.6
Third pilot	140
First cooper	124
Second cooper	68.1
Surgeon	225
First barber / *sangrador*	147.4
Second barber / sangrador	69.3

Source: Figures are derived from a compilation of slaving ships listed in Appendix 1.

This was a matter of more than racial animosity or prejudice, however. Ship captains' choice to pay mariners of African descent lower wages than their white counterparts substantially reduced the initial capital outlays required for voyages. When the *São Lourenço* left port in June of 1812, the captain had contracted four white common sailors and twenty-eight common sailors of African descent. Though the Black mariners included both Brazilian-born and African-born seamen, freed and enslaved, all earned 50 milréis for the roundtrip voyage to Ouidah, significantly less than the 60 milréis earned by white seafarers inhabiting the same shipboard position.[41]

This pattern of racially stratified wages was repeated on many other ships. Yet despite this tendency, racial identity and enslaved status did not exclusively determine financial compensation. Rank and experience were also influential in shaping compensation, with seasoned mariners usually commanding higher wages.

African and enslaved seamen more commonly occupied the lower ranks as mates or assistants, and they reached the status of first officer less frequently than white mariners. Despite considerably lower rates of advancement within the shipboard hierarchy, however, those African and enslaved mariners who did secure a post as an officer regularly received higher pay than white seafarers who labored as common sailors or cabin boys. Enslaved sangradores earned substantially more than even some white officers, including scribes and apprentices. Captains also regularly paid Black or enslaved coopers, cooks, and carpenters more than white mariners in lower-status occupations. The sheer variety of skills required to run a slaving vessel provided ample

41. Ibid., caixa 411, Papers of the *São Lourenço*.

opportunities for specialization and professional advancement, even for en-slaved African mariners. But perhaps more important, the stark conditions of shipboard life made recruiting white mariners for slaving voyages a perpetual challenge. It was this labor vacuum that opened a space for large numbers of skilled and experienced African seamen to earn wages and access trading opportunities that were comparatively rare in a colonial slave society.

Even for those who were not compelled to toil on slaving ships, the mon-etary inducements of joining a voyage often proved powerful for impoverished free men and the formerly enslaved alike. Either through earning wages or se-curing trading privileges in liberty chests, seafarers, both enslaved and freed, could accumulate financial benefits from their maritime labors. Meanwhile, captains and merchants maintained their voyages' profitability by contracting a mix of free and enslaved laborers; though occupation, experience, race, and legal status could shape levels of remuneration, ships' utilization of unfree labor allowed them to depress aggregate wages and increase profits.

THE RHYTHMS OF EVERYDAY MARITIME LIFE

As the volume of the Bahian slave trade intensified, observers in the port of Salvador would have witnessed an ever more commonplace ritual. On the bay's docks, Black mariners, alongside land-bound dockworkers, undertook the arduous work of loading cargo into ships. Mariners were noted to per-form this task while singing, a clever technique to coordinate the motions of multiple laborers engaged in a repetitive, collective task. Songs called *salomas* that were accompanied by drums, trumpets, and fifes floated through the air as sailors hoisted heavy bales of *fazendas,* or trading goods, on rudimentary pulley systems. Once cargoes were completed, merchant ships ceremoniously departed from the Bay of All Saints, accompanied by music performed by roving bands of Black musicians stationed on launches, who serenaded ships on the first days of taking on cargo as well as during their departures and arriv-als. These ceremonies of embarkation, common in many seafaring traditions, were intended to pacify the mysterious, life-threatening forces symbolized by the sea and marked the passage from the distinct realm of the land to that of the ocean. Collective rituals, mariners hoped, would augment the probability of a successful voyage and endow seamen with a greater sense of control over their unpredictable journeys.[42]

42. Rodrigues, *De costa a costa,* 206; Thomas Lindley, *Narrative of a Voyage to Brasil* (London, 1805), 71; Emmanuel Kwaku Akyeampong, *Between the Sea and the Lagoon: An*

FIGURE 7. Disembarkation. *By Johann Moritz Rugendas. Ca. 1835.*
Black mariners transport newly arrived Africans on lighters in Rio de Janeiro's harbor
in the 1820s–1830s. © *Historical Picture Archive/CORBIS/Corbis via Getty Images*

Black mariners were about to embark on a journey that was defined by both
the mundane and the unexpected. Quotidian life aboard deep-sea sailing vessels was highly regimented and varied according to maritime routes, type of
vessel, and form of commerce. For those who navigated between Bahia and the
Mina Coast, the return voyage typically lasted a brief forty to fifty days. During the course of a roundtrip voyage, slaving vessels commonly first landed
on the shores of the Mina Coast, then cruised southward trading for slaves

Eco-social History of the Anlo of Southeastern Ghana, c. 1850 to Recent Times, Western
African Studies (Athens, Ohio, 2002), 18; John J. Poggie, Jr., and Carl Gersuny, "Risk and
Ritual: An Interpretation of Fishermen's Folklore in a New England Community," *Journal
of American Folklore,* LXXXV (1972), 66–72. Most porterage occurred within Salvador's
warehouses, where workers received and packed sugar, tobacco, and other goods arriving at
and leaving from the city's port. Located on the city's waterfront, these buildings were home
to a crucial element of Bahia's maritime infrastructure. Warehouse owners tasked enslaved
individuals with performing the backbreaking work of loading, unloading, and weighing
heavy boxes, barrels, and sacks of freight. During the sugar harvest (*safra*), enslaved maritime
laborers could be found in this "unstoppable service" working "day and night, most of them
until one or two o'clock in the morning." Deepwater sailors would have also assisted in this

TABLE 8. *Average Length of One-Way Voyage between Africa and Bahia by Region in Days, 1790–1824*

Years	West Africa	West Central Africa	Southeast Africa
1760–1794	46	37	—
1795–1799	45	40	—
1800–1804	47	37	—
1805–1809	46	36	—
1810–1814	41	35	47
1815–1819	40	28	62
1820–1824	—	35	63

Source: Alexandre Vieira Ribeiro, "The Transatlantic Slave Trade to Bahia, 1582–1851," in David Eltis and David Richardson, eds., *Extending the Frontiers: Essays on the New Transatlantic Slave Trade Database* (New Haven, Conn., 2008), 149.

in towns east of the River Volta, including Porto Novo, Badagry, and Lagos, stopping for provisions on São Tomé or Príncipe and then returning directly to Bahia (see Table 8). Unlike sailors who embarked in European entrepôts, Bahian-based mariners were spared the augmented risk that accompanied a triangular voyage between Europe, West Africa, and the Americas.[43]

Once they departed from port, each mariner began the repertoire of duties specific to his role. Effective maintenance of the vessel required repetitive tasks to be performed at specific times each day, including setting and managing the sails under the guidance of the captain or pilot, dropping and raising anchor, manning the guns, and preserving the soundness of the ship by repairing rigging and sails, spinning cordage, and caulking and cleaning the decks and hull. Stores of trading goods, including perishable items such as tobacco, gunpowder, and provisions, were tended in order to prevent spoilage

---

"tireless, rigorous work," which was so intense and violent that it shortened their lives and led many enslaved workers to the "unfortunate experience of their deaths" (ANTT, fundo 7X, Junta do Comércio, maço 10, caixa 38, "Petição dos Donos do Trapiches desta cidade, 1809"). For a description of the rituals of baptism performed by seamen upon first crossing the equator, see Jaime Rodrigues, "A New World in the Atlantic: Sailors and Rites of Passage cross the Equator, from the 15th to the 20th Centuries" ("Um mundo novo no Atlântico: Marinheiros e ritos de passagme na linha do equador, séculos XV–XX"), *Revista Brasileira de Historia,* XXXIII (2013), 236.

43. Rediker, *Between the Devil and the Deep Blue Sea,* 89; Rodrigues, *De costa a costa,* 170. In comparison, a slaving ship passage originating in Liverpool at the end of the eighteenth century lasted, on average, one year. See Stephen D. Behrendt, "Crew Mortality in the

from humidity. Even mealtime was regulated, as captains organized the crew into messes for the allocation of provisions.[44]

Despite efforts to control all aspects of life at sea through strict regimentation, unpredictable and terrifying events punctuated shipboard labor. Violent storms caused by northward movements of high-pressure systems, or *pamperos,* from the Antarctic plagued voyages in the months of May, June, and July. Encountering storms could prove catastrophic in a number of ways. Masts could snap in half, or "cut away," rendering vessels difficult to control and compromising the soundness of the hull. Waterspouts were common on the West African coast, striking quickly and driving ships eastward. One Portuguese slaving ship captain sailing off the coast of Mozambique attested to the powerful feeling of being at the "mercy of the winds" during oceanic storms. In these moments of horror, mariners witnessed "the clanking of the irons, the moans, the weeping, the cries, the waves breaking over one side of the ship and then the other . . . the whistling of the winds, and the continuous roar of the waves." The dangers for those held on the slaving deck were even more intense, as "many slaves break their legs and their arms, while others die of suffocation." On the primary deck, attempting to salvage what remained of the cargo, sailors shouted as they pushed food provisions overboard, hoping that alterations to the balance of the ship would prevent it from breaking apart or capsizing. In such situations, mariners lost nearly all control. They could do no more than wait with their fellow crew members for the storm to cease, furiously expelling water that had breached the ship's hold and hoping for survival. Conversely, becoming "becalmed" following the loss of all wind—the climatic opposite of a storm—could also profoundly disrupt a voyage by bringing vessels to a halt. Sailors often turned to divine intercession during such moments.[45]

Outbound voyages vacillated between tedium and turmoil, routine and risk. Abrupt changes in weather could also greatly increase the length of slaving voyages, further imperiling the health and safety of the inhabitants of

———

Transatlantic Slave Trade in the Eighteenth Century," in David Eltis and David Richardson, eds., *Routes to Slavery: Direction, Ethnicity, and Mortality in the Transatlantic Slave Trade* (Abingdon, U.K., 1997), 49–71, esp. 54.

44. Rediker, *Slave Ship,* 232–233.

45. Miller, *Way of Death,* 322; William Reid, *An Attempt to Develop the Law of Storms by Means of Facts . . .* (London, 1850), 491–492, 500; Hugh Thomas, *The Slave Trade: The History of the Atlantic Slave Trade; 1440–1870* (Basingstoke, U.K., 1998), 426. During one such weather event, a ship traveling from the Bight of Benin to Bahia in the late seventeenth

this floating, wooden world. The possibility of running out of provisions, primarily water, was an especially dangerous prospect for slaving voyages carrying hundreds of individuals. Portuguese law attempted to forestall such an outcome through regulation. One 1684 royal edict mandated water rations at 1 *canada* (1.4 liters) per day for each enslaved individual held in cargoes, though this rate fluctuated in each following 140 years. Even so, captains were known to understock the number of water casks in cargoes to maximize the number of captives ships could hold. Mohommah Gardo Baquaqua recalled that, in the mid-nineteenth century, as an enslaved young man transported across the Atlantic on the slaving deck of a Brazilian ship, he suffered from excruciating thirst and was allotted only a pint of water a day.[46]

Food was no less vital in the success of slaving expeditions, often becoming a locus of conflict and an important signifier of status aboard vessels. Bahian ships such as the *Nossa Senhora da Esperança e São José* in the mid-eighteenth century carried provisions from Salvador with the intention of feeding captives on the return journey. The ship carried 76 *alqueires* (1,048.8 liters) of "good beef from the Bahian hinterland" and 1,579 alqueires (21,790.2 liters) of flour from Bahia, to be made into something minimally palatable by the ship's cook. Captains also acquired a significant proportion of a voyage's provisions when passing along the West African coast. While anchored near the island of Príncipe, a common port for provisioning, the *Nossa Senhora da Esperança*'s captain, Antônio da Costa Basto, purchased an additional 40 alqueires of beans, 30 alqueires of corn, 2 barrels of *dendê* oil, 2 barrels of sweet oil "better than brought from Bahia," 1 barrel of fish, 1 pipe of vinegar, and 1 barrel of fish oil. The schooner *Paquete Volante*, traveling from Bahia to Cabinda in 1811, arranged to bring a small amount of *aguardente* (sugarcane liquor), sugar, and powdered tobacco for the enslaved men and women on board. Cooks divided provisions on these vessels between those designated for the captain and officers and those for the "captives on board." The brig

---

century experienced a complete halt to the voyage's progress after a lack of wind for several days. The desperate crew resorted to kneeling and praying to a figure of Saint Anthony affixed to the ship's deck. South Atlantic trade winds, though, were much more reliable than their northern counterparts, making journeys from Brazil to West Africa less disposed to delay (ibid., 428).

46. Miller, *Way of Death*, 419–424; Robin Law and Paul Lovejoy, eds., *The Biography of Mahommah Gardo Baquaua: His Passage from Slavery to Freedom in Africa and America*, 2d ed. (Princeton, N.J., 2009), 154.

Conceição Condê dos Arcos also procured food native to the West African coast and stocked beans, corn, dendê oil, 100 chickens, 500 yams, and clothing "for the slaves" while in port at Grand-Popo in 1813.[47]

Like the ethnic composition of laborers and captives aboard, a ship's provisions were also strongly influenced by the particular West African ports at which it called. Such efforts were, in fact, a crucial part of managing the enslaved cargo, as Portuguese doctors often advised feeding enslaved Africans familiar foods to stave off "melancholia" and death. Captains (and sometimes crews), by contrast, typically ate costlier fare, sometimes imported from Europe. Captain Antônio da Costa Basto kept 2 large bags of pork, 12 bottles of aguardente, 6 *arrobas* of noodles, 3 barrels of fish, 2 barrels of flour from Lisbon, 7 arrobas of biscuits, 2 arrobas of pounded barley, 4 arrobas of butter, 1 bag of imported "Moorish cabbage," 1 barrel of olive oil, 5 arrobas of ham, 4 arrobas of chickpeas, and 1 copper pot for his own use in his personal stock. The *Nossa Senhora da Esperança* even carried separate cauldrons to prepare food for the captives held belowdecks and for sick slaves and crew members. Other descriptions, however, suggest that Brazilian slaving crews commonly ate "a very thin gruel and a kind of meal, or rather, small grain (called *farine*), with a small piece of smoked meat or fish as accompaniment." The enslaved received the same. In terms of provisions, both crews and captives occupied a status inferior to captains and officers yet shared at least some of the deprivations inherent to shipboard life.[48]

Captains', officers', crew members', and captives' daily experiences diverged not only in the food and water provided to them but also in living conditions, especially in the ways they were able to occupy the minimal space of the slaving vessel. Captains and other officers had the privilege of secur-

47. Other Bahian ships, including the *Comerciante, Desforço,* and *Paquete Volante,* also carried a substantial amount of provisions in flour and dried beef from Bahia for the provisioning of African captives. Each alqueire was officially 13.8 liters. See Miller, *Way of Death,* 709; AHU, CU, Bahia, caixa 164, documento 12420, Jan. 2, 1770, "Extracto de carga de Capitão Antônio da Costa Basto." The provisions cost a total of 1:046$600 réis (ANRJ, fundo 7X, Junta do Comércio, caixa 372, pacote 1).

48. ANTT, Junta do Comércio, maço 10, caixa 36, Mar. 12, 1799, "Dom Miguel Antonio de Mello"; AHU, CU, Bahia, caixa 164, documento 12420, Jan. 2, 1770, "Extracto de carga de Capitão Antônio da Costa Basto." An arroba equaled fifteen kilograms, whereas a barrel equaled eighty-five liters. See Miller, *Way of Death,* 709. *"Farine"* was likely manioc flour made into porridge. See H. C. Monrad, "A Description of the Guinea Coast and Its Inhabitants," in Selena Axelrod Winsnes, ed., *Two Views from Christiansborg Castle* (Accra, Ghana, 2009), II, 224.

ing their own cabins on larger ships, whereas common sailors and cabin boys sometimes were relegated to sleeping in hammocks on the lower decks with the captives or on the upper deck in open air during the return voyage from West Africa. Below primary decks, crewmembers divided enslaved men, women, and children into separate compartments, with male captives remaining shackled through most of the voyage while women were allowed to move more freely. Lower decks carrying enslaved men and women often retained humidity, causing rampant skin infections among the captives; they were also rarely cleaned and accumulated the stench of human waste, blood, sweat, and the smell of the recently deceased. Visual depictions of Brazilian slavers during the mid-nineteenth century emphasized the confined space allotted to captives and the suffocating conditions brought by an absence of sufficient ventilation.[49]

Beginning with their employment negotiations on the Bahian coast, free and enslaved mariners alike faced constant reminders of the vexed nature of their status. They performed the backbreaking task of loading goods on the ship while preparing to undertake the complex, collective labors needed to attend to the machinery of a sailing vessel. They suffered from the same aspects of life at sea as other sailors, such as dangerous weather, insufficient provisions, and claustrophobic working and living spaces. Life on a slaver, however, posed the additional risks of revolt. In this demanding environment, they had to form durable but at times unstable bonds with crewmates to perform the duties required during the forty or more days they were at sea. In the hierarchical and sometimes hostile world of the slaving ship, they devised social strategies to minimize their own vulnerability on board.

SOCIALITY AT SEA

Black maritime laborers also profoundly shaped the social organization and communal elements of shipboard life that, however tenuously, bound crew members of diverse racial and ethnic origins together. Their maritime cosmopolitanism facilitated not only their ability to forge a sense of community among crew members of various backgrounds and legal statuses but also their efforts to control enslaved men, women, and children on behalf of captains. Social ties between crew members, though at times empowering, also required individual Black mariners to subordinate their own interests—

49. ANTT, Junta do Comércio, maço 10, caixa 36, Mar. 12, 1799, "Dom Miguel Antônio de Mello."

and their thoughts about the enterprise of transatlantic slaving—for the benefit of the crew as a whole.

Though labor demands largely governed Black mariners' experiences at sea, seafaring life consisted of more than monotonous routine. Writing at the beginning of the nineteenth century, the Danish clergyman and abolitionist H. C. Monrad emphasized the central role that Catholicism played in the daily lives of slaving ship crew members, both Black and white. On nearly every Brazilian ship calling at Accra on the western Mina Coast, "There is a priest, and as soon as the slaves come aboard they are christened, and a crucifix is hung around their necks. Then they are good Christians who must be treated tolerably." In addition, Catholic mores were thought to dissuade captains and crews from sexually abusing "Christianized" African women.[50]

Catholic ritual permeated shipboard life, reflecting widely held beliefs that divine forces could deliver crews to safety in dangerous circumstances. Scholars have argued that the tendency to name slaving vessels after saints reflected an attempt to render slaving "respectable" by evoking "patron saints of slavers, their ships and the merchandise they carried." But the practice was much older than the slave trade and had roots in Iberian sailors' request for intercession by patron saints to obtain safe passage for their ships. Saints understood as particularly miraculous, such as São Francisco de Paula, were venerated by African sailors, who took their names to conjure their protective powers.[51]

Illustrative of the widespread identification of seafarers with Catholic ritual is Jean-Baptiste Debret's depiction of a group of sailors' "devout gratitude" to the patron saint who, as the men saw it, had saved their lives at sea: they crossed the city to light a votive candle at the Nossa Senhora dos Navegantes (Our Lady of the Navigators) Church. Seamen also expressed their Catholic faith by giving alms to religious institutions in their home communities. Sailors on the *Nossa Senhora da Guia,* which left Bahia for Cabinda with nineteen crew members, including six African men, donated to a local Bahian church in 1829. Sailors from the *Firmeza* contributed to the Santa Barbara Church in 1838, whereas the crew of the *Não Lêndia,* both Black and white,

50. Monrad, "A Description," in Winsnes, ed., *Two Views from Christiansborg Castle,* II, 223.

51. Pierre Verger, "The Orishás of Bahia," *Os deuses africanos no Candomblé da Bahia,* ed. Carybé (Salvador, Brazil, 1993), 235–261, esp. 235; Montserrat Barniol, "Patrons and Advocates of the Sailors: The Saints and the Sea in Catalan Gothic," *Imago Temporis, Medium Aerum,* VI (2012), 252.

FIGURE 8. *Detail of "Ex-vote de marins échappés d'un naufrage." In J[ean] B[aptiste] Debret,* Voyage pittoresque et historique au Brésil . . . , *I (Paris, 1834), title page. Sailors visit Nossa Senhora dos Navegantes in Rio de Janeiro in the 1810s–1830s. The Miriam and Ira D. Wallach Division of Art, Prints and Photographs: Print Collection, The New York Public Library. New York Public Library Digital Collections*

gave alms to the Senhor do Bomfim Church for "salvation." Both on land and at sea, religious sociability suffused mariners' lives, with many belonging to mutual aid organizations or Black and Brown Catholic brotherhoods in Salvador. Some enslaved mariners even escaped to hospitable ones while stationed in Lisbon.[52]

Many captains encouraged Catholic practices, stocking ships with religious paraphernalia. Accordingly, Mass became a regular part of shipboard routine, as did veneration of the ship's patron saint. The Bahian slaving vessel *Nossa Senhora da Esperança* left the Bay of All Saints carrying "one chest with all the ornaments necessary for mass" and three images of the altars: one of Jesus Christ, one of Our Lady of Hope, and one of Saint Joseph. Such articles, besides being a significant investment, constituted a crucial aspect of a ship's communal life. When French corsairs attacked a Bahian slaving vessel off the western Mina Coast in 1795, the pirates—while taking the ship's aguardente, provisions, tobacco, gold, and sailors' clothing—also "destroy[ed] the ornaments of their Mass, their images, the priests gowns, etc and taking their silver cup, drinking out of it Brandy, wine and then beating it

52. BNA, FO 315/43, Papers of the *Nossa Senhora da Guia,* no. 25; ibid., FO 315/45, Papers of the *Firmeza,* Papers of the *Não Lêndia.*

with a hammer and then throwing it overboard." Their blasphemous actions riled the ship's crew.[53]

Enslaved mariners frequently participated in religious rituals while aboard, and most were characterized by their owners as loyal Catholics. When Dutch pirates seized the above-mentioned *Esperança*, two of the ship's nine enslaved mariners escaped, and another was taken prisoner by the Dutch ship. A subsequent letter penned by the *Esperança's* owner demanded the return of the missing men and made the case on purely religious grounds, arguing that the men, all "acculturated" Catholics, "should not remain in unholy and heretical lands." In the event that they had already died, however, he required the return of their value. One of the escaped mariners had been owned by the archdeacon of Bahia, who likely provided him with religious instruction.[54]

In fact, the Portuguese crown endorsed the importance of Catholic ritual aboard slaving vessels, requiring them to employ a chaplain as one of the ship's officers. These men were tasked with directing shipboard religious practice. In addition to ministering to crews, chaplains baptized slaves as they arrived on the ship, though captains' adherence to this edict was intermittent. A 1799 petition to the crown by thirty-eight of Salvador's merchants characterized the requirement to hire a chaplain as "burdensome." Though ships calling at Angola were required to carry chaplains, captains often avoided carrying clergymen, as they also had the responsibility of reporting to the crown the number of slaves that died during the voyage—deaths that captains could be held financially responsible for. Recruiting chaplains remained difficult, as most white priests took pains to avoid service on dangerous slaving vessels, even going so far as to escape into the Angolan hinterlands when a ship approached port in Luanda. Chaplains might also cause other tensions aboard. In the early nineteenth century, Monrad noted, "Portuguese captains are often dissatisfied with their padres . . . and accuse them of, instead of instructing the slaves, intriguing and causing unrest among the crew." Fears of insubordination notwithstanding, a chaplain was the one officer aboard who could regulate the behavior of the captain: "The true reason [for this dissatisfaction], undoubtedly, is that these padres keep a sharp lookout on the captains, and, when they have returned home, can report them, and have them punished if they have treated the slaves

53. AHU, CU, Bahia, caixa 164, documento 12420, Jan. 2, 1770, "Extracto de carga de Capitão Antônio da Costa Basto"; Pierre Verger, *Trade Relations between the Bight of Benin and Bahia from the 17th to 19th Century*, [trans. Evelyn Crawford] *(Ibadan, Nigeria, 1976)*, 196.

54. AHU, CU, Bahia, caixa 164, documento 12420, Jan. 2, 1770, "Extracto de carga de Capitão Antônio da Costa Basto."

inhumanely." In the midst of such conflicts, the captain's absolute authority on board could be diminished. Despite the demands of the law, only nine voyages between 1811 and 1839 listed a chaplain on the crew manifest.[55]

The prevalence of Catholicism on long-distance slaving vessels facilitated a key imperative of shipboard life: developing fraternal relations among crew members. The specific nature of maritime labor, which sometimes required dozens of men to work in concert to accomplish a particular task, necessitated an integrative social climate that mitigated established notions of racial difference or division along lines of occupational hierarchy. Indeed, in their own testimonies, African and creole sailors often expressed a sense of camaraderie with their fellow crew members that was so intense it often superseded other rhetorical forms of identification such as race, nation, or ethnicity.[56]

With the potential for disaster and ruin looming over every voyage, the imperative for crews to work together to stave off mortal threats heightened the necessity of subordinating individual interests to the security of the entire ship. This ethos was also, in part, a product of Portuguese laws governing maritime conduct. The Portuguese Commercial Code required all crew members to rally and assist the captain in the case of "attack of the ship or [if] disaster befalls the ship or cargo." Such guidelines augmented the captain's authority but also encouraged common sailors and other mariners at the lower end of the shipboard hierarchy to understand obedience, subordination, and collective action as a necessity to maintain everyone's safety. The governing principle that underlay the chain of command effectively concealed the personal power of captains under the guise of the need to act for the vessel's defense by submitting to his orders. The law framed such entreaties reciprocally, as the loyal seamen who did come to the aid of their seafaring brethren were offered guarantees they would be taken care of if harm should befall

55. Verger, *Trade Relations*, [trans. Crawford], 95; Miller, *Way of Death*, 407; Kalle Kananoja, *Healing Knowledge in Atlantic Africa: Medical Encounters, 1500–1850* (Cambridge, 2021), 174; Monrad, "A Description," in Winsnes, ed., *Two Views from Christiansborg Castle*, II, 223.

56. Christopher, for instance, has argued that English mariners' relationships with one another constituted a form of "fictive kinship" and that, though white seamen might not have treated Black mariners as equals, "they regarded them as fellow members of the crew, trusted them as co-workers and, on occasion, rebelled with them against a ship's officers" (*Slave Ship Sailors*, 16). For Black sailors on British and American slaving vessels, "[their] cultural ties and professional identity in some ways cut across the divisions of skin colour, even in the highly divisive setting of a slave ship." See ibid., 16–17; Bolster, *Black Jacks*, 82.

them. By law, "every one of the crew who falls ill in the course of the journey, both in the service of the ship, or in a fight against the enemy, or pirate, was wounded or mutilated, will be paid their wages, treated and cured, and in the case of mutilation, damages will be paid at the discretion of the judge."[57]

In the event of conflict with outside forces, Bahian mariners both Black and white mobilized in the service of their captains, defending the ship even if they elevated their own risk of capture. In 1777, an English captain, Mr. Chalmers, invited the captain of a Bahian slaving brig, Jozé Gonçalvez Marques, to his cabin while anchored off the Mina Coast, for the purpose of exchanging his goods for Brazilian tobacco. In the wake of the men's peaceable exchange of goods between ships, a roll of tobacco was lost at sea. The missing item quickly became a flashpoint for violent disagreement. To settle the conflict, Chalmers boarded Marques's vessel, causing the Brazilian captain to accuse Chalmers's men of theft. Marques subsequently ordered his ship's mate to fire his musket at the Englishmen. On the mate's order, three enslaved sailors "immediately came, and seized hold [of Chalmers]; and throwed [him] overboard." The mate continued to fire at Chalmers as he swam away. Chalmers quickly retaliated; twenty-four hours later, he put Marques in irons and confined the "three Negroes for the Villainous attempt they made to murder [him]." In exacting his retribution, Chalmers ordered the "beating and ill using [of] many of the Bahian [crew]" and detained the Brazilian vessel. The English captain demanded the three slaves as recompense for the damage done to him at Marques's hands. The English mariner's treatment of the enslaved seamen revealed their position as property who could be traded for financial losses at sea. Soon after the event, the Bahian brig sailed away, with the three enslaved seamen still in English custody, stranding the men and indicating their disposability.[58]

Threats to the safety of maritime laborers, of course, also came from below-decks, amid the ranks of the enslaved. But in the case of the Bahian slave trade, where ships employed a high proportion of African-born seafarers, such vessels tended to depend less on the perpetual physical incarceration of recently enslaved Africans than on comparable Atlantic routes. Monrad wrote that enslaved men and women on Portuguese vessels from Brazil were "treated the most mildly." He noted that "only very few of [them] are chained in the hold; most of them are on deck, and, to a degree, mingle with the crew." Brazilian

57. BNA, FO 315/44, Papers of the *Emprenhendedor,* no. 32, "Obrigações Mandadas Trasladar Neste Lugar Pelo Artigo 1442 do Codigo Commercial Portuguez."

58. Letters of Jan. 27, 31, 1778, BNA, SP 89/85, 363–365.

ships were less prone to slave revolts as a result of more humane treatment; as a passenger on a Brazilian slave ship, "never did I see anyone actually flog the slaves; they scarcely thrust them away with mockery and disdain. Rather, I often saw the sailors make as much of the small Negro children as if they had been their own." "What surprised me most," Monrad added, "was that slaves were not even imprisoned at night, but that most of them slept on deck with a sail spread over them," though he did observe that physical punishment was meted out occasionally following arguments between enslaved individuals.[59]

Monrad's travelogue—though undoubtedly rose-tinted—suggests that African crew members working on Bahian slaving vessels contributed to the relative placidity of transatlantic trading routes emanating from Salvador. In this moment, slaving merchants and officers deployed Black mariners' cosmopolitan expertise, in concert with incarceration and the threat of violence, to maintain a delicate peace on board ships during the taxing transatlantic voyage. Monrad was clear on the Bahian vessels' distinctiveness. He argued that enslaved individuals held in cargoes "who know the method of treatment on the Portuguese ships, show little fear . . . they see that their comrades [Africans] often come back to the Coast as sailors, and conclude that the condition of all of them is equally fortunate."[60]

Monrad's observation that "a freedom and equality holds sway on the Portuguese ships which I have met nowhere else among the other nations" sanitized to a significant degree the conflicted relationship between captives and crew members. But in general, his writing demonstrated little appetite for whitewashing the realities of the transatlantic trade. His first-person account remained highly critical of the slave trade's general brutality, in contrast to the pro–slave trade voices of the era. He highlighted the cruelty and casual acts of violence that characterized French and Dutch captains' and crews' interactions with African captives, but he characterized Brazilian slavers as exceptions, and his suggestion that African mariners were more adept at controlling enslaved men and women in the cargo without extreme violence echoed earlier contentions by Portuguese merchants and administrators. The historical record suggests a degree of validity to his claims, as Brazilian ships featured a comparatively low rate of insurrection among captive Africans during the Age of Revolution. In this period, there were only twelve recorded instances of slave revolt on Brazilian vessels, and only one of these originated

59. Monrad, "A Description," in Winsnes, ed., *Two Views from Christiansborg Castle,* II, 223.
60. Ibid.

in Bahia. On ships traveling to the Caribbean, the enslaved led an estimated 305 revolts and attempted uprisings.[61]

Despite the relative paucity of recorded slave rebellions on Bahian vessels, the specter of lethal violence nonetheless shaped their social and working environment. The possibility of slave revolt on board demanded a degree of crew cohesion that bound enslaved African and creole common sailors together with their white counterparts and superiors. First and foremost, captains and shipowners took a number of precautions. The expectation that violence could suddenly materialize on any slaving voyage led many Bahian vessels to carry large caches of arms, including shotguns, knives, and swords, in addition to the pieces of artillery mounted on the deck. Weapons were available for enslaved crew members to use in the event of pirate attack or slave revolt, though such eventualities were rare. Captains also tasked sailors with monitoring enslaved men, women, and children with the goal of preventing attacks, uprisings, or suicides spurred by the desperate conditions of life at sea.[62]

A pervading sentiment of a shared interest among shipmates also worked against the development of any bonds of resistance between enslaved Black mariners and enslaved Africans held in cargoes, despite potential commonalities of enslaved status, birthplace, language, or ethnic identity. Enslaved African seafarers overwhelmingly related to enslaved individuals in a supervisory sense. Patterns of resistance on Bahian slaving routes also suggest this was the case.

61. Ibid., 223–224; Voyage IDs 3068, 3192, 3433, 4035, 4563, 7071, 8119, 8898, 11265, 40302, 48583, 49378, *Voyages*. A more probable catastrophe was a violent attack by pirates seeking to strip a lonely vessel of its goods, captives, and even the lives of its crew. Though piracy by the mid-eighteenth century was less of a threat than it had been in the seventeenth, the possibility that such an assault might transpire lingered in the minds of many merchants and seamen. During this period, two attempted or actual revolts occurred on slaving vessels navigating to Europe, whereas twenty-seven occurred on voyages to North America and ten to Spanish South America (*Voyages*).

62. The *Esperança Feliz* traveled with six muskets, five cutlasses, sixteen pounds of gunpowder, and several cannonballs in 1821. The *Dezengano* traveled to the Mina Coast with sixteen enslaved mariners aboard and four barrels of knives in the principal cargo. Investor Antônio de Espírito Santo also carried three shotguns, two blunderbusses, and two silver-tipped knives in his personal trading cargo, presumably to exchange for slaves on the African coast. The *Terceira Rosalia* carried five hundred shotguns and fifty barrels of gunpowder. See AHI, Coleções Especiais, Comissão Mista, lata 15, maço 1, pasta 1, Papers of the *Esperança Feliz;* ibid., lata 10, maço 3, pasta 2, Papers of the *Dezengano;* and ibid., lata 28, maço 2, pasta 1, Papers of the *Terceira Rosalia*.

The only recorded incident of an enslaved crew member joining in a shipboard revolt by men and women imprisoned in the cargo occurred in 1812 on the *Feliz Eugenia,* traveling from Benguela. As the voyage left African shores, sailors and enslaved seamen attacked the quartermaster and a white sailor, administering several wounds to the men before tying them up. Escape from the ship seemed to be the objective: after subduing the other seamen, the Black mariners fled for shore on the ship's rowboats, along with enslaved men and women who had just been placed in the hold. Black mariners' connections of aid and cooperation with their shipmates as a means of preserving their well-being amid the slaving ships' dangerous atmosphere likely played a role in forestalling similar incidents, precluding both freed and enslaved mariners from forming more subversive bonds of resistance with the unfortunate men, women, and children held on their ships who had fallen victim to the slave trade.[63]

SOLIDARITY AND CONFLICT AT SEA

Even though ships operated according to the ideal of a cohesive, well-ordered crew, conflicts between mariners could boil over at any moment. Slaving commerce held inherent contradictions as it brought together men of different statuses, cultural backgrounds, and positions in the chain of command amid the slave ship's claustrophobic atmosphere. Sometimes such tensions could only be resolved through violence. Strife could be sparked by matters of money, trade, and wages as well as the perceived transgression of shipboard hierarchies. Moments of friction often reflected the dynamics of power at sea, which favored the interests of merchants over laborers, officers over common sailors, free over enslaved, and white over Black. The subjects of shipboard aggression were frequently those of lesser status. Hostility was an omnipresent part of the seafaring life that Black mariners were forced to navigate. Sailors' cultivation of fraternal bonds was mediated by the stark racial and occupational divisions that defined the maritime working world, as well as the volatil-

63. AHU, CU, Angola, caixa 125, documento 5, "Ofício de Antônio Rabelo de Andrade Vasconcelos a José de Oliveira Barbosa, governador de Angola"; Miller, *Way of Death,* 409–410; Jaime Rodrigues, "Escravos, senhores e vida marítima no Atlântico: Portugal, África e América portuguesa, c. 1760–c.1825," *E-a Revista Almanack,* no. 5 (2013), 155. In the few instances when African and creole mariners collectively mobilized while aboard slaving ships, it was almost never in support of the plight of the enslaved men, women, and children who perhaps shared their language, ethnicity, or birthplace. It was for the well-being of their maritime brothers and superiors.

ity of that work. Interpersonal violence, often spurred by racial animus, sexual desire, or the will to dominate others, could challenge supposedly egalitarian relations—even among sailors of the same rank.

Conflicts between crew members could become lethal, with common sailors conscripted into the deadly schemes of their captains. In 1823, on the Portuguese schooner *Sinceridade,* a clerk was murdered in a plot involving the captain and two members of the crew. The clerk, while stationed ashore on the West African coast, had allowed the "king of the country"—likely a local commercial agent—to steal "a great many long coats and other articles." The captain quarreled with the clerk and placed him in irons, seized his goods and an enslaved individual he had already purchased, and sent him back to the *Sinceridade* to be confined to the hold until the return to Bahia. Soon after, the captain ordered the boatswain, Manoel Justino da Silva, who had been reprimanded for insubordination—ignoring orders and thinking "himself as good as the captain"—to be sent ashore in irons. After several days, Manoel Justino returned to the *Sinceridade* alongside another seaman, who possessed a foreboding letter sent by the captain. According to Manoel Justino, the letter demanded that two sailors aboard—Juan de Silva and Manoel the Spaniard— kill the clerk, threatening that, if they did not, "the captain [would] come on board with a number of Black men and kill us all." The same evening the letter was delivered, the clerk left the hold, still in chains, to sleep on deck along with the creole cook and three other crew members. At about eleven o'clock, Manoel Justino and Manoel the Spaniard, after initially hesitating to kill the clerk, struck him in the head with an ax, stabbed him in the stomach, and threw his body overboard, along with his bloody mattress and bedclothes. They told the other members of the crew that the clerk had jumped overboard. For their deed, their lives were spared, and they received the captain's gratitude. The clerk's gruesome end darkly illustrates the "casual violence of all kinds" that punctuated shipboard life. The crux of the conflict between the captain and crewmembers, although aggravated by lack of adherence to the chain of command, was ultimately about the loss of valuable trading goods, which had crippled the purpose of the voyage.[64]

Violence between shipmates of equal rank also plagued life at sea, especially when mariners were divided by race, legal status, and even sexuality. In another bloody encounter one evening in 1833, Domingos Jozé, a twenty-three-year-old preto sailor born in Cachoeira, Bahia, lay in his bed on the

---

64. ANTT, Junta do Comércio, maço 62, caixa 203, Sierra Leone, Apr. 21, 1823, Testimony of the British Portuguese Mixed Commission; Rediker, *Slave Ship,* 7.

naval ship *Dom João VI*. Six white sailors approached, hurling insults at him. Among them were Paulo Alves and Antônio Maria. One of these two, unprovoked, struck Domingos's face with a shoe. The other stabbed the unsuspecting Black sailor a total of four times in both arms. Defending himself, Domingos slashed both Antônio and Paulo in the face, leaving wounds deep enough to require immediate medical attention in a local hospital. Naval authorities were baffled by the motive for the attack. Once shackled and placed in custody, Domingos identified the cause as racial animosity. The men, whom he identified as his "comrades," were "angry with him for being black." All three were charged with assault. The Auditor General, however, questioned Domingos along with several shipmates, some of whom revealed that Domingos's breach of the boundaries of honorable behavior was what had led to the confrontation. He had taken to bed with him a young white man, allegedly for "bad ends." Domingos rejected any sexual connotation to seafarers' bedding together, identifying the unnamed youth as "his oldest comrade" and nothing more. His reticence about confessing to a romantic relationship with another man was a shrewd calculation, as such "immoral acts" could subject sailors to harsh corporal punishment, including the lash.[65]

It is impossible to discern whether Domingos's race or his same-sex intimacies had been responsible for the vicious reaction among his white shipmates. Authorities largely accepted his account of self-defense but questioned whether he could have escaped Paulo and Antônio's wrath without wielding a knife. Another Black sailor, Lourenço Antônio Joaquim, was the only one among his shipmates to confirm that Domingos was lying prone at the time and could not run away to forestall an escalation of violence. Paulo and Antônio denied that they had attacked Domingos at all, claiming that he had randomly struck them before turning the knife and wounding himself. Authorities did not deny that the white sailors had initiated the altercation; nonetheless, Domingos was sentenced to four years in the galleys for what was presumably a consensual sexual rendezvous. This punishment could have been tacit condemnation on account of his race or for undertaking a homoerotic encounter in public view. Notably, Domingos's attackers received a lighter but not-insignificant sentence of three years each. His victimization by Paulo Alves and Antônio Maria, and later the Royal Navy, exposed free Black seamen's vulnerability to brutality at the hands of their white peers as

65. ANTT, Feitos Findos, Processos-Crime, letra D, maço 19, no. 62, caixa 51, "Continuação do Processo Verbal feito aos Réus Domingos Jozé, de côr preto, Paulo Alves e Antonio Maria, marinheiros da Nau Dom João Sexto"; Morgan, *Legacy of the Lash*, 109.

well as the authority of a larger state disciplinary apparatus that targeted free Black men branded as rebellious. For Black mariners like Domingos, responsible performance of their duties at sea was insufficient to protect them from perceived transgressions of masculine ideals about race and sexuality.

The homosocial atmosphere of shipboard life could also be marred by acts of sexual aggression between crew members that could mirror the widespread intimate violence visited upon enslaved captives. On one such voyage from Rio de Janeiro to Luanda, an enslaved pardo man, Lourenço da Rosa, faced constant harassment from his owner, the ship's pilot, Antônio Francisco Ferreira. One night, Ferreira forced himself into Rosa's bed and lay on top of him. The youth, "fearful in [Ferreira's] midst," suffered a series of sexual assaults perpetrated by Ferreira during the remainder of the voyage. While at sea, he had little recourse to halt the pilot's predatory behavior. Once Rosa arrived in Lisbon, he pleaded for his own sale. Though Ferreira's power over Rosa was underpinned by physical force, the violence Rosa experienced was also the result of asymmetries in their age, race, and status, all of which left Rosa particularly vulnerable. The enslaved man was able to escape his terrifying predicament once on land. In the metropole, he confessed to the sin of sodomy before inquisitors in the Holy Office. Such forced sexual relations between men at sea, because of their stigma, were rarely recounted to religious authorities. In addition to fear, Rosa's testimony also revealed a profound degree of shame. Shipboard working environments were places where norms of universal, albeit male, fraternity coexisted with regular violations of that same moral and laboring order. The sheer physical intimacy of shipboard life fostered homosocial relations that were desirable for the sense of community and protection they afforded seafarers; but those same proximities could provoke volatility.[66]

In addition, the more mundane need to protect property and the imperative to maintain the profitability of voyages also frequently incited internal

66. Sowande' M. Mustakeem, *Slavery at Sea: Terror, Sex, and Sickness in the Middle Passage* (Urbana, Ill., 2016), 90, 113. The Holy Office of the Inquisition, which operated from 1536–1821, adjudicated potentially heretical conduct by Portuguese subjects. Ritualized confessions of sinful acts were a key part of its procedures, as were denunciations detailing the "deviant behaviour" of others. See ANTT, Portugal, Torre do Tombo, Tribunal do Santo Ofício, Inquisicao de Lisboa, 28 processos, caixa 1611, documentacao dispersa, no. 15486, Denúncia Contra Lourenço da Rosa; Toby Green, Philip J. Havik, and F. Ribeiro Da Silva, *African Voices from the Inquisition*, I, *The Trial of Crispina Peres of Cacheu, Guinea-Bissau (1646–1668)* (Oxford, 2021), xxii–xxiv.

disagreements among crew members. Captains and shipowners quarreled with subordinates over the commercial prerogatives allowed sailors during slaving voyages, in large part because they were suspicious that these privileges impinged upon the financial interests of shipowners and financiers. On one such occasion, Jozé Pereira Inácio, a quartermaster on the *São Lourenço*, traveling from Bahia to the Mina Coast, testified that he had stowed several casks of aguardente in his cabin and disagreed that he should pay freight fees to the ship's owner. Inácio was also promised a portion of his pay in trading goods, namely thirty rolls of tobacco, when the ship arrived in West Africa.[67] While on the coast, however, the captain of the ship used eight rolls to pay duties to Portuguese slave trader Francisco Félix de Souza in Little Popo, a tax that enabled the ship to finally leave port. Inácio sued the *São Lourenço's* owner, Joaquim Jozé de Andrade, asking for restitution of the lost ten rolls of tobacco as well as additional slaves, West African textiles, and other goods that the owner claimed were destroyed in a fire in Lagos. In his defense, Andrade argued that Inácio had stolen gunpowder and firearms from the cargo of the *São Lourenço*, and thus he owed the quartermaster no additional compensation.

Though outmatched against Andrade in terms of wealth and relative resources, Inácio drew on the fraternity of his fellow crewmates to substantiate his own account. In his suit, Inácio solicited the testimony of thirteen of his fellow crew members, including several African and creole sailors. All of them corroborated the quartermaster's story and vouched for the honesty of their companion mariner. Freed African Benedicto Luiz Teixeira, aged twenty-four, argued that Inácio was a "truthful man, and incapable of lies," whereas the Reverend João Antonio Ferreira claimed that he was an "honorable man" and that the gunpowder he allegedly stole was in fact used to defend the *São Lourenço* against an English ship of war during a firefight. Despite the support of his fellow crew members, Inácio's suit was unsuccessful in securing restitution. The Board of Trade, Industry and Navigation (Real Junta do Comércio, Fábricas e Navegações) ruled that, by illegally carrying trade goods without

67. ANRJ, fundo 7X, Junta do Comércio, caixa 411, "Libello Cível de Jozé Pereira Inácio por Joaquim Jozé de Andrade e Silva Menzes," 34–41. A *pipa* was a cask of approximately fifty liters in volume (Miller, *Way of Death*, 712). Bahian tobacco was twisted into ropes and wound into rolls that were then soaked in molasses and encased in leather; each roll weighed approximately eighty to ninety-six pounds. See Schwartz, *Sugar Plantations*, 85; G. A. Robertson, *Notes on Africa: Particularly Those Parts Which Are Situated between Cape Verd and the River Congo* . . . , I (London, 1819), 281.

paying freights, the quartermaster had "defraud[ed] the owners of the ship." Clearly, however, the other mariners aboard the *São Lourenço* interpreted the parameters of mariners' customary rights to stow and trade goods differently than the board's officials.[68]

Inácio's case demonstrates both the willingness of mariners to seek legal redress for wrongs by their superiors as well as the strategic use of solidarity with shipmates to mount such challenges. Camaraderie was one of the few resources available in such asymmetrical relations of power. Though shipboard life was punctuated by tension and violence produced by hierarchy, crews could either defend or challenge their captains' will in this context. When doing the latter, they often turned to their close bonds with crewmates to mitigate their structural disadvantages.

Key to Inácio's rhetorical strategy was his emphasis on his identity as a mariner and his loyalty to maritime professions as an iteration of his own honor. He insisted that he was capable of fulfilling any occupation on board, and no one could do it better:

> Since an early age [Inácio] had engaged in seafaring, due to having a natural propensity to be "a nautical," he has exercised this profession for more than 30 years, and has already conducted ten or eleven voyages to the Mina Coast, once as a captain, and others as a First and Second Pilot, and has not only navigated to the Mina Coast, [but] to different ports, many in America and Europe, arriving in France, England, always working on Ships, where we transported, and therefore did not become a Cooper, Shoemaker, or Tailor, like others, always exercised maritime professions, at the age, he cannot learn another office or second Art.

Like many seamen, Inácio avowed loyalty not only to his shipmates but to seafaring life as well. Such protestations of identity were central to how he represented himself in a judicial context.[69]

For African and creole sailors, language also revealed the depth of such fictive kinship bonds with other mariners, particularly of the same rank. Antônio Neves, a freed Gege man who labored as a barber on a Bahian slaving vessel, referred to his shipmates as his "companion sailors." Likewise, the twenty-year-old Manoel da Silva, a free pardo man, attested to British authorities that

68. ANRJ, fundo 7X, Junta do Comércio, caixa 411, "Libello Cível de Jozé Pereira Inácio por Joaquim Jozé de Andrade," 34–41.
    69. Ibid.

he lived in the home of his "comrade" Bernardino, who was also a sailor. In more adverse circumstances, the brotherly affection offered by fellow mariners could be vital to survival. Such was the case for a sailor from the Cape of Good Hope, Domingos, who reported in 1857 that, five years earlier, he had been abducted by the crew of a Portuguese warship, the *Conde de Villa Flor*, as he labored aboard a local vessel on the south African coast. He was deceitfully enslaved and forced to serve aboard the ship. Domingos claimed he survived the ordeal only with the support of his "companions [also] impressed aboard various ships of war as sailors." Later revealing his story to naval officers after escaping from his "owner" to Lisbon's royal shipyards, he recalled that he had found solace with his shipmates in their shared experiences of suffering and victimization, an emotional resource that saved him.[70]

Such mutually supportive attitudes extended beyond the interactions of common sailors and enslaved mariners. Relations between captains, officers, and common sailors at times conveyed mutual respect and even collegiality. As Jaime Rodrigues points out, a moral economy of paternalism shaped the contours of interactions between subordinates and captains aboard Brazilian vessels and simultaneously necessitated the ideals of both hierarchy and reciprocity. Captains might solicit advice from crew members during storms, for instance. These suggestions, however, could just as easily be refused or ignored. Brazilian mariners' commonplace challenges to the directives of their superiors shocked foreign observers. In the early nineteenth century, British traveler Thomas Lindley characterized Brazilian sailors as existing in a state of "licentious freedom," commenting, "On board of [a] ship an order is seldom issued without the sailors giving their opinion on it, and frequently involving the whole [of the crew] in dispute and confusion." Lindley complained that captains addressed crew members as "comrade" and that such "unreserved freedom" was "productive of the most pernicious consequence; you get no command promptly obeyed." This culture of negotiation between officers and common sailors befuddled Lindley, who was accustomed to a more rigid hierarchy aboard English vessels. Such discussions struck him as pure rebelliousness. As if to reassure readers that Bahian vessels were not a world completely turned upside down, Lindley noted that corporal punishment was not totally absent, as officers at times carried walking sticks on deck to "use as occasion requires."[71]

70. Ibid., caixa 369, Papers of the *Desforço;* ACML, caixa 311-1, no. 368, Inspeção do Arsenal da Marinha do Pará, Mar. 31, 1857.

71. Rodrigues, *De costa a costa*, 193–194; Lindley, *Narrative of a Voyage to Brasil*, 69–70. Morgan has found that corporal punishment in the Brazilian navy was commonplace by the

Corporal punishment could be seen as a necessary tool for preserving the chain of command, which, to captains' minds, underlay the smooth functioning of the ship's working world. Its semiregular deployment, however, was also a sign that seamen challenged occupational hierarchies from below. In 1839, aboard the *Firmeza,* the ship's cook, Zé, insulted the quartermaster after the officer had issued a command. The captain questioned Zé (short for Jozé) after the incident and reprimanded him for the "disgrace" of a superior. The mariner explained that "on board he only knew of the captain's ability to issue reprimands" and that "he was not lame nor a dwarf"—indicating that Zé believed the quartermaster had little right to issue orders to him and was not, in fact, his superior. The captain reiterated Zé's "lack of respect" and reminded him that "sailors were subject to officers, and sailors did not have the right to act as officers."[72]

Like the enslaved people held in cargoes, seamen—both enslaved and freed—could face exacting forces of corporal discipline if they failed to follow orders.[73] Balancing external threats and internal unrest, insubordination, conflict, and revolt required captains to walk a fine line between the violent coercion of enslaved and free crew members and a cultivation of loyalty. Enslaved seamen, like their free shipmates, were subject to both and had fewer avenues of recourse for abuse and disregard from captains or shipmates. For Black seamen, the intrinsic risks of seafaring life were heightened, as they could be kidnapped and even reenslaved by enemies at sea or just by unscrupulous captains. Black skin, even within the socially fluid brotherhood of the sea, could mark one as commodifiable and ultimately disposable. In the face of these persistent laboring hardships, ties of solidarity between mariners of similar rank could, at times, provide solace and even a path to challenging the paternalistic power of captains.

---

end of the nineteenth century. The lash had become the principal method of disciplining seamen understood as the "dregs" of imperial society, even after its use had been outlawed in 1889. See Morgan, *Legacy of the Lash,* 79–84.

72. BNA, FO 315/45, Papers of the *Firmeza,* no. 370.

73. For instance, on Portuguese-owned slaving vessel the *Liberal,* apprehended by British antislaving forces in 1841 while traveling from Havana to the Bight of Benin, carried aboard "four or five shackles for the crew." See "Enclosure in No. 79, Report of the Case of the Brigantine 'Josephina' Manoel Antonio dos Santos Perreira, Master: Sierra Leone, May 24, 1841," in House of Commons, *Parliamentary Papers: Accounts and Papers,* 20 vols., XLII, *Slavery: Session 3, Feburary-12 August 1842* (London, 1842), 83.

WATERBORNE POSSIBILITIES FOR FREEDOM

Despite its vicissitudes, Black mariners' working world was also one of potential opportunities. Through their negotiations with officers, many attempted to maximize their own personal and commercial autonomy by resisting orders, securing trading privileges, or banding together with crewmates to refute their captain's depiction of events at sea. These quotidian tumults, however, rarely erupted into incidents that had the potential to derail entire voyages. The integrative aspects of shipboard life helped to perpetuate slaving's profitability. Slaving captains sought the capacity to exploit cheap labor power but resisted meting out excessive mistreatment, which could push mariners to either flee or, in some cases, take legal action. Like all mariners, captive cosmopolitans used the opportunities presented by the mobility of shipboard life to access an alternative and, in their eyes, superior status for themselves.

Maritime fugitivity was the most immediate form such emancipatory pursuits could take. Sometimes, Black mariners fled on the spur of the moment with the help of shipmates. In 1833, a fourteen-year-old enslaved sailor from Cabinda escaped his owner in the company of "another boy from Cabinda, wearing an English sailor's cap." Fugitive seamen did not, however, always abandon maritime life completely. On one occasion, an African mariner named Antônio, who was born in Angola, fled from his owner while serving on a ship. His owner speculated that Antônio remained in the seafaring profession after his escape, guessing that "he ran away aboard some ship, or boat in this port, because he very much enjoyed the maritime life." In a similar vein, a sixteen-year-old enslaved escapee named Satiro, who was born in Bahia and worked as a tailor and sailor, was deemed by his former owner to have likely retained his profession because he was "very keen on the service of the sea." Enslaved sailors also took advantage of crises on board, such as pirate attacks or capture by foreign vessels, to flee. In 1768, a Bahian slaving ship attacked by Dutch pirates lost several enslaved mariners when they escaped to shore on the West African coast during the chaotic event. Some mariners wished to remain at sea, even if the impetus for their fleeing was a desire to evade the tyrannical behavior of owners or supervisors. Enslaved sailor Jorge escaped from his master, Joaquim Pedro de La Faria, pilot of the ship *São João Baptista,* to work on another ship, the *Vasco da Gama,* as a "freed" man. Jorge's escape prompted La Faria to petition the Portuguese crown for his return in 1819 after spying the Black sailor in port. The possibility of escape was also enabled by realities on the West African coast, where captive mariners moving between slaving forts, beaches, and vibrant port city markets mingled with a diverse assortment of people. Moreover, interimperial conflicts in the region incentivized mariner desertion, as fugitives used the cover of the heavy international traffic to run away. In 1777, a slave, "still unacculturated," escaped from a French sailing vessel to the island of São Tomé. Three years later, while navigating from the port of Benin, two enslaved mariners owned by Captain João Ferreira de Souza ran away alongside three soldiers from a colonial regiment stationed in Príncipe. The men eventually absconded to the ship of David Wilson, an English captain and imperial rival.[74]

The vast majority of enslaved sailors, however, decided against the option of fugitivity as a pathway to freedom. The British merchant John Luccock noted in the early nineteenth century that, on sailing vessels traveling from Brazil to West Africa, a "number of Seamen, employed on board Slave Ships, are themselves Negro Slaves, born in Africa; and though frequently going over to their own country, they do not leave the vessel there." The phenomenon of African slaves serving on slaving vessels struck Luccock as an enigma, contradicting his own understandings of how the slave trade operated in his native England, a trade that required almost exclusively white crews to brutally manage hostile African captives.[75]

Captive seamen seeking emancipation had complex agendas that distinguished between various forms of liberation and autonomy. Freedom as a fugitive proved less attractive for many than legal liberation and the moderate protections it entailed. Preferring manumission over flight was, in part, a function of the economic structure and incentives of the Bahian slave trade itself—specifically, the accessibility of small-scale trading privileges that encouraged many seamen to defer freedom until it could be purchased. Shipboard sociability, like the economic incentives of the slave trade, also bound enslaved and free Black mariners to the prerogatives of crews and even captains. Integrated into maritime social networks, such men faced the difficult

74. Another enslaved African seaman escaped from the Brazilian vessel on which he served because of "poor treatment" at the hands of the ship's quartermaster. See BNRJ, *Jornal do commercio*, Mar. 7, Mar. 20, Apr. 12, 1833, 4; AHU, CU, Bahia–Avulsos, caixa 164, documento 12423, Jan. 4, 1770; ibid., São Tomé e Príncipe, caixa 15, documento 1437, Oct. 28, 1775, "Ofício do Capitão-Mor das Ilhas de São Tomé e Príncipe, Vicente Gomes Ferreira"; ibid., Brasil-Pernambuco, caixa 281, documento 19117; ACML, caixa 311–1, no. 368, Inspeção do Arsenal da Marinha do Pará, Mar. 31, 1857.

75. John Luccock, *Notes on Rio de Janeiro, and the Southern Parts of Brazil* (London, 1820), 392.

option to escape to alien environments—sometimes to legal jurisdictions that did not recognize their enslaved status—or to persist in attempting to achieve a measure of social advancement and community in Bahia.

Enslaved and freed mariners laboring in and beyond Bahia's transatlantic slave trade experienced a life defined by various tensions. Representing the least expensive form of maritime labor, such men were the most exploited by slaving merchants. Their employment resolved two omnipresent dilemmas for captains: recruitment and control. Because they were more easily corralled into maritime service and paid less than white sailors for performing equal work once aboard, their cosmopolitan expertise could be commodified by merchants looking to maximize profits from slaving voyages. With a penchant for hiring enslaved and freed men born on or near the Mina Coast, slavers employed culturally dexterous mariners who were fluent in the languages and customs of the regions from which their ships purchased captives. In addition to performing the countless tasks required to navigate a sailing vessel, mariners also managed enslaved individuals confined in cargoes. African seafarers were identified as particularly skilled in this regard. Though concentrated on the bottom of shipboard hierarchies, these men performed nearly every role aboard, and their myriad skills remained fundamental to the slave trade's operation.

At sea, slaving merchants and captains ordered Black seamen to attend not only to the physical soundness of enslaved individuals held on board but to their emotional stability, as well. Hoping to sell the highest-valued captives on the other side of the Atlantic, slaving merchants employed mariners who they believed would arouse less fear and resistance on the part of the men, women, and children held belowdecks. Captive cosmopolitans, they wagered, would reduce costly and dangerous instances of revolt, suicide, and depression. For slavers, the regulation of captive laborers' movement, both of captive Africans and slaving ship seafarers, acted as a key technology of merchant-driven globalization.

Though their cosmopolitanism proved instrumental to merchants' and captains' accumulation of profits, seamen could also use their cultural flexibility subversively. On slaving vessels, Black mariners looked to create empowering ties of solidarity with other crew members, even if they were ephemeral or unreciprocated. Through communal ritual practice, shipmate bonding, and collective challenges to maritime superiors, Black mariners integrated themselves into the rhythms of seafaring life. The ethos of the shipboard community was predicated on the insistence that crew members—regardless of legal status, station, or race—shared an interest in maintaining order, safety, and discipline on transatlantic voyages. Along with disciplinary violence perpetrated by superiors, it bound African seamen to their crewmates and dissuaded them from encouraging or joining slave revolts initiated by enslaved Africans held in the cargo. In lieu of open rebellion and in the face of harsh exploitation, Black seamen often turned to solidarities with crewmembers of equal status, providing mutual support and a strong sense of occupational identity. But when those same ties failed Black seamen, they could be subjected to heinous acts of violence or take it upon themselves to escape such abuses. Difficult decisions about how to best minimize vulnerability and mistreatment confronted Black mariners daily. The evolving legal and geopolitical landscape of the South Atlantic in the Age of Abolition, however, would provide enslaved mariners with new choices regarding liberation, escape, Black community, and abolition.

CHAPTER 4

A Port of Black Sanctuary

Thousands of miles from home, speaking a language that was not his own, Juan Jozeph approached members of Lisbon's Conselho Ultramarino (Overseas Council) to appeal to the "piety and clemency" of the king of Portugal. A free-born Black mariner—originally from Havana but residing in São Tomé—Jozeph laid out a dramatic tale of deceit, greed, and exploitation. Claiming status as "one of [the king's] vassals," Jozeph implored royal officials to rectify an "insult" he believed had been committed against him. Expressing pathos and indignation in equal measure, he demanded to be reimbursed for the "pains and injuries" inflicted on him by a man named Domingos Luis Coelho who had, Jozeph believed, usurped the "liberty that he had always possessed" by illegally taking Jozeph as his slave. Although fragmentary, Jozeph's 1739 petition preserves a remarkable personal odyssey through the Caribbean, West Africa, and the landscapes of imperial Europe. His story illuminates the fragility of freedom for people of African descent and the ceaseless need for vigilance against the threat of illegal enslavement for those whose Black skin marked them as presumptive captives.[1]

Jozeph's self-advocacy in front of the Conselho Ultramarino also demonstrates that his was a life not defined solely by vulnerability. As this chapter shows, the geographic mobility of enslaved mariners—and particularly their ability to navigate from an array of colonial ports to Lisbon, Portugal's imperial metropole—indicated a larger historical phenomenon. In Lisbon, captive cosmopolitan mariners regularly sought access to what they perceived as receptive legal forums where, as Jozeph did, they could challenge their enslaved status. Jozeph's petition is only a slight document, conveying a complicated series of events that culminated in his reclamation of freedom. His story, however, highlighted a broader Luso-Atlantic process in which numerous enslaved Black mariners demonstrated their fluency with Portuguese legal

1. AHU, São Tomé, caixa 7, documento 753, July 23, 1739, "Requerimento do homem preto, João José."

principle and reinterpreted it for their own ends. During the decades before abolitionism became a transformative political force in the Atlantic world, petitions initiated by Black mariners articulated an increasingly expansive notion of freedom that anticipated later abolitionist currents.[2] The traces left from these contentious legal proceedings reveal the political possibilities of enslaved people's cosmopolitan intellectual worlds forged at sea and demonstrate how concepts of legitimate and illegitimate slavery circulated between maritime spaces and evolved over time.

Juan Jozeph's 1739 petition antedated a larger number of similar but reformulated manumission efforts in the late eighteenth and early nineteenth centuries. A close reading of two dozen petitions authored by captive cosmopolitans in the South Atlantic from the 1760s onward exposes the ways in which a subsequent generation of enslaved mariners crafted their own lay theorizations of jurisdiction, liberty, and imperial subjecthood.[3] Captive cosmopolitan subjects seeking their freedom straddled a profound historical divide between an ancien régime definition of manumission as a royal favor for the deserving and an early modern emphasis on the universality of natural rights. By the end of the eighteenth century, fugitive Black mariners fused these two ideas, characterizing their bondage as unnatural and there-

2. Black people's legal activism anticipated the demands of many abolitionist movements. As José Lingna Nafafé points out, in 1684, Angolan elite Lourenço da Silva Mendonça argued an "ethical and criminal" case before the Vatican courts to advance the cause of abolition, the gradual end of New World slavery, and the suspension of Portugal's conquest of Angola. He charged the empires involved in slaving—Italy, Portugal, Spain, and the Vatican itself—with crimes against "Divine or Human law." Importantly, Mendonça chose to use ecclesiastical rather than civil legal processes to challenge African slavery. He said the slave trade was not only a moral abomination that caused widespread human suffering and death but a political problem that eroded African sovereignty (Nafafé, *Lourenço Da Silva Mendonça and the Black Atlantic Abolitionist Movement in the Seventeenth Century* [Cambridge, 2022], 1–6). Manisha Sinha posits that, in the North Atlantic, abolitionist movements were preceded by freedom suits initiated by people of African descent beginning in the early eighteenth century. Following the 1772 *Somerset v. Stewart* decision in Britain, a multitude of enslaved people hoped to escape from the American colonies to the European metropole, which was popularly conceived of as home to a free-soil principle (Sinha, *The Slave's Cause: A History of Abolition* [New Haven, Conn., 2016], 16–23).

3. It is also likely that the legal petitions initiated by enslaved seamen far outnumber the surviving cases, or *processos,* that are currently housed in metropolitan archives. And it is probable that the petitions predating 1776 left no paper trace, since they were not contested by slaveowners under strict interpretation of the law.

fore unjust in the eyes of royal law while arguing that their maritime service was a distinctive justification for freedom.[4] Escapee mariners harnessed juridical concepts, including Catholic sanctuary, descent from a free womb, *prescripción* (a statute of limitations on claiming a free man or woman as a slave), and free soil. Simultaneously, however, they offered their own novel interpretations of those precepts, articulating a vision of liberty that, at times, found a sympathetic reception with the Portuguese authorities responsible for adjudicating them.

Following the Portuguese crown's *alvará* (royal edict) of September 19, 1761, the trickle of enslaved mariners' petitions swelled to a flood. At its core, the principle of free soil—which theoretically liberated any enslaved person who stepped foot on Portuguese soil—laid bare Portugal's contradictory relationship with those non-European subjects who overwhelmingly populated its empire. On one hand, the Portuguese crown's insistence that enslaved people be able to access imperial law legitimized claims of sovereignty over a geographically expansive empire by securing subaltern actors' loyalty to the monarch, bringing them under the legal authority of the crown's benevolent justice. On the other hand, to successfully make freedom claims through such laws, the enslaved were obliged to represent themselves as loyal imperial subjects. As one of the most important technologies of colonial control, Michelle A. McKinley notes, law "provided the basis for empire itself."[5]

4. Word of the free-soil law superseded the territorial confines of the Portuguese empire. On the ethnically diverse Atlantic waterfronts where enslaved seamen labored, vessels frequently housed multinational crews, enabling non-Portuguese-speaking mariners to become aware of its prospective benefits, as when two Black sailors arrived in Lisbon on a French ship seeking manumission in 1791. Even during the era of the French Revolution and increasing abolitionist pressures in France, these enslaved men chose Portuguese jurisdictions as most conducive to making their escape from legal bondage. See Cristina Nogueira da Silva and Keila Grinberg, "Soil Free from Slaves: Slave Law in Late Eighteenth- and Early Nineteenth-Century Portugal," *Slavery and Abolition,* XXXII (2011), 435.

5. Michelle A. McKinley, *Fractional Freedoms: Slavery, Intimacy, and Legal Mobilization in Colonial Lima, 1600–1700,* Studies in Legal History (New York, 2016), 13; Mariana P. Candido, "African Freedom Suits and Portuguese Vassal Status: Legal Mechanisms for Fighting Enslavement in Benguela, Angola, 1800–1830," *Slavery and Abolition,* XXXII (2011), 447–459; Mariana Armond Dias Paes, "Shared Atlantic Legal Culture: The Case of a Freedom Suit in Benguela," *Atlantic Studies,* XVII (2020), 432; Sherwin K. Bryant, *Rivers of Gold, Lives of Bondage: Governing through Slavery in Colonial Quito* (Chapel Hill, N.C., 2014), 3. As Stuart B. Schwartz notes, the administrative structures of Iberian American colonies tended to be "curiously legalistic" in their approach to government and life (Schwartz, *Sover-*

Numerous captive cosmopolitans in the South Atlantic recognized an opportunity, however. Rather than accept the putative logics of imperial law—which aimed to discipline them—they sought legal openings that could challenge their enslaved status. Moreover, free-soil petitions initiated by the enslaved contested the property-holding control of owners and utilized the rhetorical power of "liberty" against those who sought to circumscribe their autonomy. Unlike other processes of manumission, access to free soil almost always entailed bypassing their owners' consent and appealing directly to imperial authorities. The records of these petitions demonstrate the depth and sophistication of some Black mariners' legal knowledge, which combined legal and rhetorical precedents with new forms of freedom argumentation. Enslaved petitioners' testimonies and legal arguments were undoubtedly mediated by colonial scribes, *procuradores* (legal representatives), and religious advisors to whom they turned for aid. Though polyvocal in nature, each petition reveals that enslaved seamen possessed—in consort with land-based interlocuters—a remarkable level of cosmopolitan knowledge about the 1761 alvará's liberatory potential that was inseparable from the South Atlantic maritime world in which they operated.[6]

The accumulation of petitions by enslaved mariners suggests another degree to which such men were central to a geographically expansive subaltern legal culture that connected the colony and metropole.[7] Though the particular legal mechanisms by which enslaved people secured manumission have long been of interest to scholars of the Atlantic world, this chapter emphasizes the key cultural, social, and institutional influences on Black mariners' legal imaginaries. Arriving in Lisbon from the edges of imperial geographies, runaway sailors did not act simply as individuals but rather as part of a larger network of enslaved and free Black people that spanned the Atlantic.[8] This

---

eignty and Society in Colonial Brazil: The High Court of Bahia and Its Judges, 1609–1751 [Berkeley, Calif., 2018], xv). See also Candido, "African Freedom Suits and Portuguese Vassal Status," 450–452.

6. McKinley, *Fractional Freedoms*, 14.

7. This refers to the circulation of "legal norms, legal categories, and arguments" between lusophone Africa and Brazil in the mid- to late nineteenth century. For an example of a similar process, see Paes, "Shared Atlantic Legal Culture," *Atlantic Studies*, XVII (2020), 419–440, esp. 420.

8. Such networks operated similarly to the informal informational linkages among the enslaved sailors, maroons, and market women that Julius S. Scott details for the late-eighteenth-century Caribbean. Scholars of the Spanish Caribbean have also uncovered the

chapter centers the role of Black Catholic brotherhoods in Lisbon, revealing how those institutions provided the monetary and intellectual resources that enabled captive cosmopolitan mariners' legal claims-making and sometimes even physical escape.[9] Lisbon itself was home to nine Black Catholic brotherhoods.[10] After the 1761 alvará, they would be key in organizing the resources to launch free-soil petitions before civil legal bodies, often relying on vernacular notions of Catholic spaces as sites of protection coupled with the new perception of Portugal itself as a liberty-conferring jurisdiction. Sanctuary for the enslaved entailed more than a consecrated space that promised to offer immunity from prosecution—the ecclesiastical definition; it also entailed an understanding of Catholic churches as sites of liberatory aid and inspiration.[11]

-----

word-of-mouth networks that linked those islands to Jamaica and other British colonies. Fugitives seeking freedom from British slavery in Spanish territories often relied on such transimperial informational networks. See Scott, *The Common Wind: Afro-American Currents in the Age of the Haitian Revolution* (London, 2018), 3, 12, 27, 39; Fernanda Bretones Lane, "Free to Bury Their Dead: Baptism and the Meanings of Freedom in the Eighteenth-Century Caribbean," *Slavery and Abolition*, XLII (2021), 449–465.

9. Candido, "African Freedom Suits and Portuguese Vassal Status," *Slavery and Abolition*, XXXII (2011), 447–459; José C. Curto, "Struggling against Enslavement: The Case of José Manuel in Benguela, 1816–20," *Canadian Journal of African Studies/Revue Canadienne des Études Africaines*, XXXIX (2005), 96–122; Roquinaldo Ferreira, "Slave Flights and Runaway Communities (17th–19th Centuries)," *Anos 90*, XXI, no. 40 (2014), 65–90; John C. Marquez, "Witnesses to Freedom: Paula's Enslavement, Her Family's Freedom Suit, and the Making of a Counterarchive in the South Atlantic," *HAHR*, CI (2021), 231–263.

10. For more on the global circulation of rituals of Catholic devotion between Black brotherhoods and the creation of "distinct spaces for black community" in the churches of Brazil and Portugal, see Erin Kathleen Rowe, *Black Saints in Early Modern Global Catholicism* (Cambridge, 2019), 1–12, 63; Lucilene Reginaldo, *Os Rosários dos Angolas: Irmandades de africanos e crioulos na Bahia setecentista* (São Paulo, 2011), 14.

11. Michelle A. McKinley analyzes the use of Catholic "sanctuary" spaces for escaping slaves in colonial seventeenth-century Lima, in the Spanish viceroyalty of Peru. Much as in Lisbon, enslaved people's claims-making redefined the content of legal statutes that had initially excluded slaves from sanctuary protections during the period. In 1707, a synod held in Bahia codified religious guidelines pertaining to slaveholding in the Constituições primeiras do arcebispado da Bahia. The code, adopted throughout Brazil, barred enslaved fugitives from using the right of sanctuary. See Schwartz, "The Manumission of Slaves in Colonial Brazil: Bahia, 1684–1745," *HAHR*, LIV (1974), 610–611; McKinley, "Standing on Shaky Ground: Criminal Jurisdiction and Ecclesiastical Immunity in Seventeenth-Century Lima, 1600–1700," *UC Irvine Law Review*, IV (2014), 141–174, esp. 149.

Seafarers escaping to one of these spaces of Black Atlantic religiosity were more often than not dependent on the legal acumen, monetary resources, and advocacy of Black Catholic brothers to advance their freedom claims.[12] By 1825, the political work of Lisbon's Black Catholic institutions as an insistent pressure group bore fruit, as Portuguese authorities came to accept enslaved people's freedom claims after many years of denying them.

The act of legal petitioning expressed more than enslaved litigants' basic awareness of formal legal principle; their maritime *marronage* also provides a dramatic illustration of how Black mariners came to exploit the legal possibilities of their movement through Atlantic spaces.[13] Because mobility was a defining part of their profession, enslaved seamen were frequently in a position to access alternative legal jurisdictions while traveling abroad.[14] As this chapter argues, the lived experience of captive cosmopolitanism facilitated the development of a spatially rooted legal imaginary—a jurisdictional consciousness—that prompted some enslaved people to gravitate toward Portugal, a jurisdictional realm they hoped might recognize their desires to be freed from

12. For more on Catholic spaces, particularly churches, as spaces of refuge for the enslaved in colonial Latin America, see Jorge L. Chinea, "A Quest for Freedom: The Immigration of Maritime Maroons into Puerto Rico, 1656–1800," *Journal of Caribbean History*, XXXI (1997), 51–87; Elena A. Schneider, "A Narrative of Escape: Self Liberation by Sea and the Mental Worlds of the Enslaved," *Slavery and Abolition*, XLII (2021), 484–501.

13. The concept of "maritime marronage" was first elaborated by N. A. T. Hall in "Maritime Maroons: 'Grand Marronage' from the Danish West Indies," *WMQ*, 3d Ser., XLII (1985), 476–498. For more on maritime marronage in the Caribbean, see Hilary Beckles, "From Land to Sea: Runaway Barbados Slaves and Servants, 1630–1700," in Gad Heuman, ed., *Out of the House of Bondage: Runaways, Resistance, and Marronage in Africa and the New World* (London, 1986), 79–94; Lane, "Free to Bury Their Dead," *Slavery and Abolition*, XLII (2021), 449–465; Kevin Dawson, "A Sea of Caribbean Islands: Maritime Maroons in the Greater Caribbean," ibid., 428–448; Justin Dunnavant, "In the Wake of Maritime Marronage," ibid., 466–483; Chinea, "Quest for Freedom," *Journal of Caribbean History*, XXXI (1997), 51–87; Charles R. Foy, "Seeking Freedom in the Atlantic World, 1713–1783," *Early American Studies*, IV (2006), 46–77; Jeppe Mulich, "Maritime Marronage in Colonial Borderlands," in Lauren Benton and Nathan Perl-Rosenthal, eds., *A World at Sea: Maritime Practices and Global History* (Philadelphia, 2020), 133–148; Linda M. Rupert, "Marronage, Manumission, and Maritime Trade in the Early Modern Caribbean," *Slavery and Abolition*, XXX (2009), 361–382; Schneider, "Narrative of Escape," *Slavery and Abolition*, XLII (2021).

14. Because of their unique occupational position in the Atlantic world, enslaved seamen, like free mariners, constantly traversed political boundaries and, in the process, became

bondage.[15] Though this form of spatially informed legal consciousness relied on an understanding of codified law, in the decades following 1761, mariners and their Black allies also generated their own, distinctive rationales for freedom that did not fully comport to the law. Far more than mere passive "readers" of legal precepts, Black fugitives would eventually compel the crown to use the free-soil law as a tangible tool of manumission, despite its original design solely as an abstract measure to dissuade slaveholders' transportation of their enslaved property to the metropole. Their imaginative, and often collective, legal strategies would transform the law's function and meaning as mariners' self-advocacy clashed with the conservative counterarguments of slaveholders. Over the course of seven decades, enslaved litigants and their Black Catholic supporters would craft ideologically sophisticated arguments and ultimately push the crown, against its original intention, to apply the law with a measure of regularity.

In exploring Black sailors' free-soil legal claims in Lisbon in the late eighteenth and early nineteenth centuries, this chapter challenges commonplace assumptions about the flight from slavery, revealing how maritime marronage in the South Atlantic entailed a confrontation with, rather than evasion from, Portuguese imperial power and law. In their efforts to escape slavery, Black maritime sailors critically utilized seaborne passage *toward* the metro-

---

acutely aware of jurisdictional divisions. Their cognizance was expressed through what Lauren Benton has termed "forum shopping," or the strategic effort to access favorable legal bodies to adjudicate cases of piracy and military seizure at sea. See Benton, "Legal Spaces of Empire: Piracy and the Origins of Ocean Regionalism," *Comparative Studies in Society and History,* XLVII (2005), 700–724, esp. 718.

15. My conceptualization of "jurisdictional consciousness" is distinct but related to other historians' theorization of enslaved people's "geographic literacy." Historians have also analyzed the "counter-hegemonic Caribbean geograph[ies]" constructed by the enslaved through maritime movement and freedom claims. My term also draws on Herman L. Bennett's concept of "legal consciousness," or the awareness of "rights and obligations" developed by enslaved Africans in Mexico who accessed colonial legal institutions and utilized litigation to further their aims. This concept extends enslaved people's legal perceptions to their spatial politics. See Bennett, *Africans in Colonial Mexico: Absolutism, Christianity, and Afro-Creole Consciousness, 1570–1640* (Bloomington, Ind., 2003), 1–7; Philip Troutman, "Grapevine in the Slave Market," in Walter Johnson, ed., *The Chattel Principle: Internal Slave Trades in the Americas* (New Haven, Conn., 2004), 203–233; Rashauna Johnson, *Slavery's Metropolis: Unfree Labor in New Orleans during the Age of Revolutions* (Cambridge, 2016), 7; Schneider, "Narrative of Escape," *Slavery and Abolition,* XLII (2021), 485.

pole rather than fleeing *from* the domain of colonial authorities.[16] Arriving in Lisbon to contest their enslavement was emblematic of their cosmopolitan political sensibility. Instead of escaping to the remote hinterlands of Brazil, where a hidden web of fugitive slave communities, or *quilombos,* had been established, such seamen chose to engage the colonial state itself. Rather than flee its sphere of authority, captive cosmopolitan mariners used the empire's mechanisms for amelioration of legal status instead of risking criminalization or even death by pursuing alternative means of freedom.[17]

JUAN JOZEPH IN BLACK LISBON

Though Lisbon was a relatively marginal destination within the broader landscape of the transatlantic slave trade, Africans had long arrived in the port city to fulfill urgent urban labor needs by toiling as washerwomen, fishermen, servants, cooks, artisans, vendors, musicians, and coachmen. As the currents of commerce carried enslaved people into the city from the fifteenth century onward, their numbers swelled. By the mid-eighteenth century, such men

16. For instance, Schwartz defines manumission as "a juridical action in which property rights were surrendered and in which the former slave assumed a new legal personality and new legal responsibilities." He argues that enslaved individuals in urban spaces achieved higher manumission rates in late-seventeenth- and early-eighteenth-century Bahia. Furthermore, liberated women (*libertas*) prevailed over liberated men by a ratio of two to one during the period. Mixed-race Brazilians also were more likely than African-born enslaved people, or *crioulos,* to achieve manumission. The cases that Schwartz analyzes involved enslaved people manumitted with their owners' consent (Schwartz, "Manumission of Slaves in Colonial Brazil," *HAHR,* LIV [1974], 603–635, esp. 608–612).

17. The late eighteenth and early nineteenth centuries were an intensive period of militarized state repression against rural and suburban quilombos in Bahia. Escape by the enslaved to fugitive slave communities could become a capital crime. Another possibility was forced relocation. As the residents of the captaincy of Pará, in the peripheral northern region of Brazil, complained in 1790, recently arrived *boçais*—unacculturated enslaved Africans who, they claimed, were often "disease-ridden"—arrived from Bahia, Maranhão, and Pernambuco alongside those enslaved *ladinos* deemed criminals. Residents feared the "disorders" and violence that resulted from the importation of criminalized slaves, reporting that these outsiders perpetrated "robberies, murders, and continuous escapes to the many Mocambos [quilombos]," and encouraged other members of the local enslaved community to do the same. The subversive threat from these newly arrived ladinos was typified by the "six black slaves of the Captain of the Auxiliaries, Ambrozio Henriques, that he has kept for years by the authority of [the] Justice in the jail of this city," who were on trial in the wake of "being

and women made up approximately 15 percent of the population of Lisbon. A sizable number of free Black inhabitants also populated the urban landscape. Black neighborhoods or parishes such as Mocambo (the Kimbundu word for "hideout") were established and became havens for a racially marginalized population in the imperial metropole.[18]

This urban milieu, one often associated with poverty and criminality by local officials, fostered informal sociocultural ties among free and enslaved Black inhabitants. At the core of this social world were Black and Brown Catholic brotherhoods *(irmandades pretos e pardos)* that exemplified a longstanding tradition of Catholic antislavery legal action. As José Lingna Nafafé argues, the first Atlantic abolitionist movement—pioneered in the 1680s—was rooted in Black Catholic brotherhoods in Angola, Brazil, the Caribbean, Portugal, and Spain. In this early transatlantic abolitionist effort, Black litigants wedded evidence of slavery's violence to an argument that neither natural nor divine law could discriminate on the basis of enslaved status or race. Instead, some Catholics argued, a common humanity had endowed Africans with a "right to justice," like their white Catholic brethren.[19]

---

caught running away, after having robbed and murdered some of his other good slaves, who opposed them . . . even [trying] to kill their own master." In lieu of imprisonment and deportation, those enslaved individuals and the communities they inhabited could be targeted for destruction. The quilombos of Oitizeiro, Orobó, and Andrah were razed following the crown's 1799 order requiring immediate assaults on them until they were completely "extinguish[ed]" and no "shadow" of them remained. Bahia's royal governor after 1805, João de Saldanha de Gama Mello e Torres Guedes de Brito, the count of Ponte, executed this task expeditiously. See ANTT, fundo 7X, Junta do Comércio, maço 10, caixa 38, "Reprezentão a vossa excellencia os homens de negocios da praça desta cidade do Pará"; João José Reis, "Slaves and the Coiteiros in the Quilmbo of Oitizeiro, Bahia, 1806," in Reis and Flávio dos Santos Gomes, eds., *Freedom by a Thread: The History of Quilombos in Brazil* (New York, 2016), 288–325, esp. 288–289; Gomes, *A hidra e os pântanos: Mocambos, quilombos e comunidades de fugitivos no Brasil (séculos XVII–XIX)* (São Paulo, 2005), 396–415; Stuart B. Schwartz, *Sugar Plantations in the Formation of Brazilian Society: Bahia, 1550–1835* (Cambridge, 1985), 479–483.

18. Didier Lahon, "O escravo africano na vida económica e social potuguesa do antigo regime," *Africana studia*, no. 7 (2004), 73–100, esp. 79; James H. Sweet, "The Hidden Histories of African Lisbon," in Jorge Cañizares-Esguerra, Matt D. Childs, and James Sidbury, eds., *The Black Urban Atlantic in the Age of the Slave Trade* (Philadelphia, 2013), 233–247, esp. 236.

19. Sweet, "Hidden Histories of African Lisbon," in Cañizares-Esguerra, Childs, and Sidbury, eds., *Black Urban Atlantic in the Age of the Slave Trade*, 237–240. Black Catholic

Juan Jozeph arrived in Lisbon at the end of a long and tumultuous journey. As he recounted in his 1739 petition to the Conselho Ultramarino, though he was born to a "free womb" (a free woman of African descent) and lived peaceably as a sailor in Havana, Jozeph had been enslaved by an English ship while on a voyage from the Caribbean to Corsica. Eventually, he escaped to Portuguese São Tomé "in order to be in a Catholic kingdom, [because the Catholic faith] which he's always professed . . . has always kept him safe." Jozeph's fugitive state was short-lived, however. Quickly imprisoned by local officials, he was delivered to resident pastor Manoel Luis Coelho, who held Juan Jozeph's *carta de alforria*, a letter demonstrating his legal freedom. But Coelho's death soon after left Jozeph alone, with his status once again arbitrarily transformed by the winds of fate. According to his own telling, he remained living in his home "in liberty," "without the dependence of a captive" and leading a financially independent life.[20]

The arrival in São Tomé of Manoel Luis Coelho's brother, Domingos, disrupted Jozeph's deceptively secure existence. With abundant "ambition and little fear of God," according to Jozeph, Domingos hid Juan's carta de alforria

----

brotherhoods' longer history of antislavery action included seeking the patronage of the crown, as they incorporated African members into their ranks and undertook the mission of catechizing and manumitting them. These brotherhoods particularly worked to secure manumission for enslaved members who had been granted freedom by will or those who were in danger of being sold outside of the kingdom. Creating a rift between white patrons and Black members, "insubordinate" Black brothers mastered legal strategies to sequester enslaved fugitives from their owners by "removing their slaves from their control" and placing them in the hands of legal authorities while the brothers litigated against slaveholders' claims. See Didier Lahon, "Black African Slaves and Freedmen in Portugal during the Renaissance: Creating a New Pattern of Reality," in T. F. Earle and K. J. P. Lowe, eds., *Black Africans in Renaissance Europe* (Cambridge, 2005), 268; A. J. R. Russell-Wood, *The Black Man in Slavery and Freedom in Colonial Brazil* (New York, 1982), 153; Reginaldo, *Os Rosários dos Angolas,* 86. While living in exile, Mendonça engaged with local members of Black Catholic brotherhoods, first in Salvador and then in Lisbon. In the Portuguese capital, he worked on behalf of the Nossa Senhora do Rosário Brotherhood. See Nafafé, *Lourenço Da Silva Mendonça,* 6–7, 20, 220, 379–390, 412.

20. AHU, São Tomé, caixa 7, documento 753, July 23, 1739, "Requerimento do homem preto, João José." Jozeph implicitly referenced the Spanish legal principle of prescripción, or a statute of limitations for claiming one's fugitive slave if said slave "believed himself to be free and acted as if he were free for a period of ten years." In Spanish America, where Jozeph was born, the medieval legal code Las Siete Partidas governed slave law and stipulated, "Where the slave of any person goes about unmolested for the space of ten years, in good

on the pretext of guarding it and imprisoned him in a private cell in his home, claiming that Jozeph was his property. Jozeph's vulnerability to reenslavement and the "paper thin" status of his freedom became crystal clear in the following four months. Without the legal protections of his manumission document, Jozeph's claims to free status had little value. After his capture, he existed in a state of "continuing torment," as Coelho's treachery resulted in repeated attempts to sell the man to various buyers. Jozeph always protested that he was free, a gambit that was initially successful in thwarting Coelho's plans. Eventually, however, he was sold to a French captain and for the two following years found himself subject to various "jobs and sales" before arriving in the "ports of the Kingdom of France." There, he secured the advice of local Catholic "confessors," whose guidance enabled his escape to London and, finally, to Lisbon. In a bid to once more secure his freedom, he returned to São Tomé. He petitioned the crown to punish Coelho, who had since returned to Rio de Janeiro, with the help of the colony's *ouvidor* (special magistrate), João Coelho de Souza, who corroborated Jozeph's story.[21]

------

faith and thinking that he is free in the country where the master resides . . . he becomes free for this reason." The principle had taken root in the Americas through deployment by a variety of enslaved litigants. Indicative of a deeper ambiguity in the law, the statute revealed the extent to which legal property rights only existed for slaveholders insomuch as they were capable of exercising control over their bondspeople. See McKinley, *Fractional Freedoms*, 145; William D. Phillips, Jr., "Manumission in Metropolitan Spain and the Canaries in the Fifteenth and Sixteenth Centuries," in Rosemary Brana-Shute and Randy J. Sparks, eds., *Paths to Freedom: Manumission in the Atlantic World* (Columbia, S.C., 2009), 31–50, esp. 35; Rebecca J. Scott, "Under Color of Law: *Siliadin v France* and the Dynamics of Enslavement in Historical Perspective," in Jean Allain, ed., *The Legal Understanding of Slavery: From the Historical to the Contemporary* (Oxford, 2012), 152–164, esp. 163.

21. Rebecca J. Scott argues that freedom was a specified condition for people of African descent in the Atlantic world, one that required documentary proof. This was particularly true for those who crossed legal boundaries. See Scott, "Paper Thin: Freedom and Reenslavement in the Diaspora of the Haitian Revolution," *Law and History Review*, XXIX (2011), 1061–1087, esp. 1063; Rebecca J. Scott and Carlos Venegas Fornias, "María Coleta and the Capuchin Friar: Slavery, Salvation, and the Adjudication of Status," *WMQ*, 3d Ser., LXXVI (2019), 727–762. On his return to São Tomé, see AHU, São Tomé, caixa 7, documento 753, July 23, 1739, "Requerimento do homem preto, João José." Interestingly, Jozeph did not attempt to secure his freedom in France, which had a long history of free-soil claims-making; but, by 1738, the king greatly limited who could legally petition for freedom using the free-soil principle (Sue Peabody, *"There Are No Slaves in France": The Political Culture of Race and Slavery in the Ancien Regime* [Oxford, 1996], 37–40).

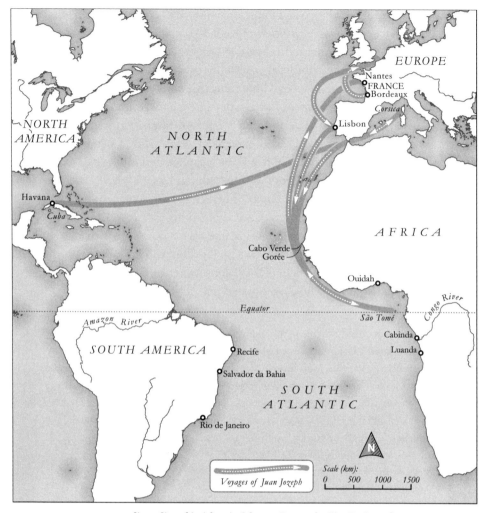

MAP 3. *Juan Jozeph's Atlantic Odyssey. Drawn by Jim DeGrand*

FIGURE 9. *Detail of "Requerimento do homem preto, João José."*
July 23, 1739. Juan Jozeph's signature on his petition to royal authorities,
demonstrating Black legal literacy. In Concelho Ultramarino, São Tomé,
caixa 7, documento 753, Arquivo Histórico Ultramarino. Photo by author

The outcome of Juan Jozeph's petition is absent from the historical record. After giving a haunting account of his plight, his voice disappears. His surviving plea, however, illustrates how seamen of African descent imaginatively navigated competing imperial administrative jurisdictions and geographies through a reliance on semipublic religious networks. Several times, Juan invoked his instrumental attempts to gain access to Catholic kingdoms and contact fellow Catholics. And, like a subsequent generation of runaways, Jozeph continued to perceive Catholic spaces and social networks as particularly receptive to aiding the cause of his manumission. Though a public embrace of Catholicism had long been linked to integration into a "community of faith" in the Iberian Atlantic world, by the end of the seventeenth century, conversion secured insider status and thus aided "foreigners" in their quest for naturalization. Jozeph framed his adoption of Catholicism in the language of religious devotion, but it was also tied to an assertion of his own imperial belonging through the construction of himself as a loyal, Christian vassal with bonds to both church and king. As such, his effort also revealed the multitude of overlapping strategies and rhetorical devices that Juan Jozeph himself saw as best assuring his "liberty."[22]

22. For a discussion of competing imperial claims of jurisdiction, see Lauren A. Benton, *A Search for Sovereignty: Law and Geography in European Empires, 1400–1900* (Cambridge, 2010). On the relationship between Catholic conversion and belonging, see Nafafé, *Lourenço Da Silva Mendonça*, 377–380; Tamar Herzog, *Defining Nations: Immigrants and Citizens in Early Modern Spain and Spanish America* (New Haven, Conn., 2003), 122–124. In Castilian legal thought, vassalage "was a personal tie created by virtue of mutual consent" between a

Jozeph's petition also suggests he understood the benefits of claiming status in Catholic realms that allowed baptized enslaved men and women some measure of "legal personhood," including the right to own personal property with their owner's consent, a degree of personal security, and the de jure ability to stand before legal bodies and authorities. Jozeph's ability to argue his case to the Conselho Ultramarino with the backing of the colonial magistrate attests to the fact that many occupants of the maritime Atlantic saw Catholic Portugal as a favorable venue. His strategies were effective—staving off being sold by protesting to potential buyers that he was free and escaping to a territorial domain that recognized his free status. Jozeph navigated a maritime Atlantic world comprised of competing jurisdictional realms, eventually arriving in Lisbon, where his freedom claims—couched in the language of religious and imperial fidelity—were recognized.[23]

Unfolding in the 1730s, Juan Jozeph's experience was a critical antecedent of the legal and political upheavals of the free-soil era, providing an early window into the meaning of movement for those who traversed imperial boundaries in the name of freedom and refuge. In a world soon to be remade

------

king and his vassals, reinforced through mutual obligations and demonstrations of loyalty. The notion that enslaved people should be excluded from vassalage was far from universal. John C. Marquez argues that enslaved people in eighteenth-century Brazil generated a body of legal thought through myriad royal petitions that sought to assert their vassalage. They precipitated the codification of manumission through self-purchase into a legal right. Anthony Pagden concludes that Africans residing in the Americas were not considered vassals of Spain during the same period. See Herzog, *Defining Nations,* 133–134; Marquez, "Afflicted Slaves, Faithful Vassals: *Servícias,* Manumission, and Enslaved Petitioners in Eighteenth-Century Brazil," *Slavery and Abolition,* XLIII (2022), 91–119; Pagden, *The Fall of Natural Man: The American Indian and the Origins of Comparative Ethnology* (Cambridge, 1982), 33.

23. Mariana Armond Dias Paes states that the legal code Ordenaçoes filipinas (1603) recognized the legal personhood of the enslaved but not their civil capacity. Thus the right to stand before legal bodies and offer testimony was not an absolute privilege for the enslaved, and often it was conditioned on their owners' consent ("O tratamento jurídico dos escravos nas ordenações manuelinas e filipinas," *Anais do V Congresso brasileiro de históriado diretio* [Curitiba, Brazil, 2013], 523–536, esp. 529). For analysis of the absence of legal personhood for Black mariners in the Anglo-Atlantic, see Lee B. Wilson, *Bonds of Empire: The English Origins of Slave Law in South Carolina and British Plantation America, 1660–1783* (Cambridge, 2021), 155; Saidiya V. Hartman, *Scenes of Subjection: Terror, Slavery, and Self-Making in Nineteenth-Century America* (New York, 1997), 7; and Ariela J. Gross, *Double Character: Slavery and Mastery in the Antebellum Southern Courtroom* (Princeton, N.J., 2000).

by the Portuguese crown's free-soil edict, Black mariners forged a new trans-atlantic intellectual network—one rarely visible in the current literature—that reshaped the experience of slavery and the act of petitioning for freedom in the broader South Atlantic world. Such physical and informational networks were not infallible, however; whispered suppositions about what constituted the most favorable legal venue or the contention that free soil represented broad emancipatory principle for the enslaved at times reflected falsehood, conjecture, and aspiration. The speculative legal advice that circulated among the enslaved could lead litigants astray in their quest for manumission.[24] This was especially true during the eighteenth century, when the legal landscape of the Atlantic itself underwent profound transformations. Nonetheless, such earlier visions of freedom and liberty rooted in protestations of Catholic iden-tity, fidelity to the Portuguese crown, and imperial belonging lived on—if increasingly recalibrated—in a new political context.

A WORLD REMADE BY FREE SOIL

Though the 1761 alvará's immediate origins lay in the modernizing aspira-tions of the Portuguese crown, the formative legal principle of free soil in Europe stretched back to at least the fourteenth century. Such statutes built on customary practices that attempted to delineate certain territories as "free" from slavery. In effect, free-soil edicts legally freed from bondage any enslaved person who crossed particular state borders. Drawing from medieval French and Dutch precedents, by the late seventeenth century, Spain had begun to employ free-soil laws to attract enslaved fugitives from rival imperial pow-ers to the frontier spaces of its Caribbean colonies. The first Spanish *real cédula* (royal order) to encourage transimperial marronage was issued in 1680, granting freedom to runaways from the Windward Islands (Martinique, St. Vincent, Grenada) and other "foreign countries" who arrived in the sparsely populated colony of Trinidad and agreed to be baptized. A dozen similar royal decrees followed, including the real cédulas of 1733 and 1750, which led to a substantial migration of fugitives from the British, French, and Dutch Atlantic to Spanish colonies, particularly Florida and Venezuela. Premised on notions of Christianization and religious sanctuary, these laws expressly forbade the freeing of runaways from Spanish imperial possessions. Notwithstanding Spanish sanctuary laws' explicit invocation of sacred faith, the royal orders

24. Jozeph's petition for freedom would have likely found greater success in Spanish courts.

served largely political—rather than spiritual—objectives, helping the empire fortify its territories during moments of intra-European warfare and conflict.[25]

Portuguese free-soil laws were also instrumental to larger imperial goals. Ultimately, the law sought to encourage the importation of slaves to colonial territories by decreasing the number of African-descended people residing in the metropole, in turn stimulating colonial agricultural production, generating taxable wealth, and buttressing the empire's declining economic fortunes.

The Portuguese crown issued the alvará of 1761 as a means to limit the migration of enslaved people of African descent to the kingdom, in effect segregating enslaved populations to the colonies to preserve their economic viability. When José I ascended to the throne in 1750, he—along with his chief minister, Sebastião José de Carvalho e Melo, count of Oeiras (known as the marquês de Pombal)—sought to rationalize and modernize the empire by diverting a greater flow of enslaved individuals to commodity-producing colonies, where they could be more productive. The free-soil law was but one piece of a larger reform project to reverse the empire's declining fortunes, in the context of declining gold importations from Brazil, by stimulating economic growth in overseas colonies. With Pombal's help, José I's court tried to minimize the influence of British merchants in the kingdom, established the Junta do Comércio (Board of Trade) to restore domestic industries, and attempted to revive the cotton economy in Brazil. José I noted that the royal decree of 1761 was a result of the

25. The first jurisdiction that recognized the free-soil principle in France was Toulouse (Sue Peabody and Keila Grinberg, "Free Soil: The Generation and Circulation of an Atlantic Legal Principle," *Slavery and Abolition*, XXXII [2011], 331–339, esp. 331–333). On Spain's use of free-soil laws, see ibid., 334; Linda M. Rupert, "'Seeking the Water of Baptism': Fugitive Slaves and Imperial Jurisdiction in the Early Modern Caribbean," in Lauren Benton and Richard J. Ross, eds., *Legal Pluralism and Empires, 1500–1850* (New York, 2013), 199–231, esp. 200, 201; Chinea, "Quest for Freedom," *Journal of Caribbean History*, XXXI (1997), 62, 65–66; Jane Landers, "Spanish Sanctuary: Fugitives in Florida, 1687–1790," *Florida Historical Quarterly*, VI (1984), 296–313; Landers, *Black Society in Spanish Florida* (Urbana, Ill., 1999), 32–34; John J. TePaske, "The Fugitive Slave: Intercolonial Rivalry and Spanish Slave Policy, 1687–1764," in Samuel Proctor, ed., *Eighteenth-Century Florida and Its Borderlands* (Gainesville, Fl., 1975), 1–12. Slaves in British-held American territories continued to take advantage of these edicts, which inspired the Stono Rebellion in 1739. Fifteen years later, a group of Havana-born slaves attempted to sail from Charleston, South Carolina, to Cuba in search of freedom. See Landers, *Atlantic Creoles in the Age of Revolutions* (Cambridge, Mass., 2010), 22; see also Rupert, "'Seeking the Water of Baptism,'" in Benton and Ross, eds., *Legal Pluralism and Empires*, 202; Hall, "Maritime Maroons," *WMQ*, 3d Ser., XLII (1985), 484.

great inconveniences, and the resulting excess, and debauchery, that contrary to the Law, and customs of other [European] courts which prohibit the annual transportation from Africa, America and Asia to this Kingdom [Portugal] such an extraordinary number of black Slaves, that are making My Overseas Dominions susceptible to a lack of [workers] for the cultivation of Lands, and of Mines, and [they] only come to this Continent to work as domestic servants.

Such a measure was necessary for the "zealous service of God, Myself, and the Common Good." The edict, however, inadvertently presented a number of contradictions for the metropole by attracting enslaved fugitives to Lisbon instead of deterring them.[26]

In theory, the 1761 alvará granted freedom to any enslaved individual who arrived in Portugal from beyond its borders. In reality, those who gained freedom through the 1761 law were also heavily regulated. The alvará required manumitted individuals, after a six-month grace period following its passage, to carry with them their *carta de liberdade* or *alforria* (manumission letter) when traveling to Portugal. Upon arrival, free people of African descent also had to provide a declaration of the places they had come from, the ship they traveled on, and the day, month, and year in which they disembarked. Following the edict's adoption, Portugal's Royal Court tasked the Supreme Court of the Desembargo do Paço (a subsidiary of the Casa da Supplicação, which housed the High Court of Appeal), the Conselho de Real Fazenda (Council of the Royal Treasury), the Conselho Ultramarino, the Mesa de Consciência e Ordens (Board of the King's Conscience and of the Military Orders), the Junta do Comércio, colonial viceroys, governors, and *capitaes geraes* (captains general) with enforcement. The raison d'être of this increasingly elaborate bureaucracy was to secure Portugal's imperial interests throughout the Atlantic world. Unbeknown to the crown, the law's intentions would be reimagined in the coming decades by the enslaved themselves.[27]

26. Nogueira da Silva and Grinberg, "Soil Free from Slaves," *Slavery and Abolition* XXXII (2011), 431–446; ANTT, fundo Leis e Ordenações, Serie Coleção de Leis, maço 6, documento 40-2, "Alvará com força de lei de D. José I proibindo o transporte de escravos pretos de ambos os sexos dos portos da América, África e Ásia para Portugal."

27. The Mesa de Consciência e Ordens housed a mixture of civil lawyers and ecclesiastical authorities who "advised the crown on Questions affecting the Church, the military orders, and the University of Coimbra. It was also the responsibility of the *Mesa* . . . to provide all benefices and bishoprics, to ransom captives, and to administer the property of persons who died intestate, and to see generally to the state of the royal conscience." See

The mid-eighteenth century was already a period of growing mariner litigiousness. Even enslaved mariners could choose to pursue legal strategies as a remedy for what they perceived as injustices against them, sometimes preferring official channels over outright violent rebellion or escape. Mariners from across the Portuguese empire also had access to the Juízo da Índia e Mina—a judicature created to hear lawsuits, or *processos,* of civil and criminal cases as well as litigation involving commercial shipping disputes. Legal claims-making became an increasingly integral part of Black mariners' tactical repertoire for advancing their labor interests. Though only sporadically, enslaved and free sailors appealed to Portuguese imperial law by petitioning for unpaid wages, which, at times, undermined the authority of their owners and employers.[28] Mariners' confidence in litigation as an effective form of redress helped inspire a growing number of appeals for unpaid wages in the

---

Schwartz, *Sovereignty and Society in Colonial Brazil,* 13; Nogueira da Silva and Grinberg, "Soil Free from Slaves," *Slavery and Abolition,* XXXII (2011), 431–446.

28. Shipboard cooks predominated in lawsuits for unpaid wages during the period, owing perhaps to the regularity with which they were undercompensated by captains. Racial discrimination could have also factored into salary disputes, as maritime cooks were often men of African descent. Despite these obstacles, Black mariners regularly utilized the Juízo da Índia e Mina to recover lost wages. One of the earliest recorded suits is from 1772, involving free Black cook Elias Ximenes. He sought 33$000 réis in deficient wages from the captain of the *Nossa Senhora dos Prazes,* Manoel Lazaro Leitão, after the ship had sailed from Pernambuco. According to Ximenes, he had carried out tasks beyond the duties of a shipboard cook, demanding higher compensation from Leitão. In 1782, Joaquim Vicente, a Black cook, sailed on a galley from Bahia to Lisbon. Once he arrived in port, he mounted a civil action against his captain, Jozé Rodrigues, for failure to pay 6$000 réis of the 40$000-réis wage the men had agreed upon before the voyage had left Salvador. Another Black cook, Francisco Xavier, also was paid for insufficient wages after laboring on a ship traveling from Rio de Janeiro to Lisbon during the same period. He petitioned the Juízo da Índia e Mina to receive 50$000 réis for the voyage and 10$000 réis for the layover in Maranhão. Xavier highlighted his occupational experience, noting that he "always performed the same job of cook." His familiarity with customary pay rates according to shipboard occupation was also a commentary on his sense of the value of his own labor, which he insisted was equivalent to that of other experienced, able-bodied seamen aboard his ship, attesting to the "laborious" nature of his service. Even royal vessels were not immune to such breaches of agreement between employers and mariners: in 1788, Francisco da Piedade, a cook, filed a legal action against a *capitão-de-mar-e-guerra* on the royal ship *Golfinho* for failure to pay 14$670 réis in wages. Similarly, Sebastião Rodrigues, a Black sailor, was ordered by his captain to care for a sick passenger ashore. The additional duties lasted three months, after

court from across the empire and litigation quickly became a routine part of maritime life.[29]

Though litigation was becoming a key avenue for accessing manumission and protecting one's livelihood, the parameters by which enslaved litigants were eligible for its application remained restricted. The text of the 1761 alvará unambiguously declared that it was not intended to free enslaved men and women already residing in Portugal. The law included no explicit articulation of a broad freedom principle. But enslaved subjects of the crown increasingly interpreted it as holding the opposite intent. Owners hoping to relocate with their captives began petitioning for personal exceptions to the law almost immediately. As Cristina Nogueira da Silva and Keila Grinberg argue, metropolitan authorities "were apparently surprised at the volume of manumission requests that were filed and granted, especially by sailors" in the wake of the law's adoption. Additional emancipatory laws, including the alvará of January 16, 1773—which introduced the so-called "free-birth law"—reinforced popular notions of the Portuguese crown as a benevolent dispenser of justice for the enslaved. A measure of gradual emancipation, it freed any enslaved person whose family had been in captivity in Portugal for four generations, as well as the children of enslaved women.[30]

---

which his captain refused to pay Sebastião for his labor. Citing the customary wage for such care work, Sebastião sued the captain for 21$000 réis, or a wage of $200 per day, in 1789. See ANTT, Feitos Findos, Juízo da Índia e Mina, maço 40, no. 9, caixa 40, "Acção Civil de Joaquim Vincente Contra Jozé Rodrigues"; ibid., Conservatória da Companhia Geral de Pernambuco e Paraíba, maço 6, no. 10, caixa 8, "Acção cível de Juramento de Alma em que é autor Elias Ximenes e réu Manuel Lazaro Leitão"; ibid., Juízo da Índia e Mina, maço 34, no. 11, caixa 221, "Acção Cível Sumária de soldadas em que é autor Francisco Xavier e réu João Rodrigues Pomuceno"; ibid., maço 48, no. 5, caixa 235, "Acção Cível de Soldadas Reduzida a Condenação de Preceito em que é autor Franciso da Piedade e réu Manuel da Cunha Souto Maior"; ibid., maço 19, no. 17, caixa 206, "Acção Cível Sumária de Salários em que é autor Sebastião Rodrigues e réu Domingos Luís das Neves."

29. The Juízo da Índia e Mina held jurisdiction over the Atlantic islands, Angola, São Tomé and Príncipe, Benguela, Cabo Verde, the Mina Coast, Macau, India, China, Ceylon, and Brazilian colonies—including Bahia, after 1700.

30. AHU, CU, Brasil, Bahia, caixa 156, documento 11923, "Requerimento de Narcisco Marins da Costa Guimarães ao rei"; Nogueira da Silva and Grinberg, "Soil Free from Slaves," *Slavery and Abolition*, XXXII (2011), 434–435. The law read: "It is not my intention, neither with respect to the black men and women who are already present in these Kingdoms as well as to those who come here within the aforementioned terms, to change anything through this law; nor for slaves to leave my overseas domains under the pretext

Though such edicts suggested the possibility that royal justice had widened legal avenues for enslaved people to petition for their manumission, several other restrictions soon followed. Crucially, modifications of the law were targeted at captive cosmopolitan mariners and aimed to resolve a central conundrum of the Portuguese empire: the dependence of South Atlantic slaving and commerce on Black mobility and labor. Under Pombal's direction, in 1776, José I amended the alvará with several "notices" that excluded enslaved "professional sailors" from gaining manumission upon arrival on Portuguese soil, stipulating that they had been registered as part of their ship's crew before leaving their port of embarkation. In a feat of cognitive dissonance, the amendment recognized the vital role that enslaved African and creole mariners played in imperial commerce: "Due to a lack of free white sailors, the crews are composed of slave sailors, it would be a blow to navigation in these ports of Brazil or the other colonies if the slaves who make up the crews of these ships became free as soon as they arrived in the port of this capital." The exception for mariners highlighted the alvará's purpose as an instrument of imperial economic development, not a measure for widespread emancipation. Enslaved mariners could not be afforded freedom, or so they were told by the crown. In the face of this legal shift, however, many continued to insist that the law allowed them to claim manumission.[31]

---

of this law. Much to the contrary, I order that all free black men and women who come to these Kingdoms to live, trade or serve, using their full freedom to which they are entitled, necessarily bring the papers from the respective Chambers from which they left showing their sex, age, and figure, so that their identity is given and that state whether they are black, freed, and free. And if any come without these papers as stated, they will be arrested and fed and sent back to the places from whence they came, at the expense of the people in whose company or the ships came or are." See Nogueira da Silva and Grinberg, "Soil Free from Slaves," 432. The understanding of the crown as dispenser of justice for the enslaved was, in part, influenced by the crown's own self-presentation. Encouraging an ethos of "patrimonial control" in which "the ruler embodied legitimacy and authority," the Portuguese crown defended its prerogatives through the invocation of the king as the ultimate symbol of the arbiter of justice. See Schwartz, *Sovereignty and Society in Colonial Brazil,* xx. For more on the reception of the 1773 law in Brazil, see Marquez, "Afflicted Slaves, Faithful Vassals," *Slavery and Abolition,* XLIII (2022), 91–119; Luiz Geraldo Silva, "'Esperança de liberdade': Interpretações populares da abolição ilustrada (1773-1774)," *Revista de história,* CXLIV (2001), 107–149.

31. ANTT, Cada dos Cantos do Reino e Casa, Erário Régio, Alfândega de Lisboa, Alfândega Grande do Açucar, livro 7419, "Registo dos Avisos"; AHU, CU, Brasil, Maranhão,

Despite these intrepid attempts to use legal argumentation to forge new possibilities of freedom, the likelihood of achieving manumission through petitioning waned over the course of the eighteenth century. Imperial law forged in the shadow of the crown's modernizing machinations tended to deny mariners' freedom claims on the basis of being contrary to the state's economic interests. But mariners' expansive visions of liberty lived on in popular understandings of free soil—and, indeed, became increasingly universal—despite limits of royal jurisprudence and its emancipatory potential.

TRANSATLANTIC INSTITUTIONS
OF BLACK SANCTUARY

The necessity of amendments to the 1761 law were, in fact, a dramatic indication of the frequency with which enslaved sailors had begun to utilize the alvará to gain legal access to manumission. But they did not do so alone. Crucial to the cultivation of the language used in free-soil petitions were Lisbon's Black Catholic brotherhoods, which offered institutional support and expertise for fugitives as well as a social base for expressing an emergent, oppositional politics to slavery. In the final decades of the eighteenth century, Black mariners regularly drew on such institutions' legal expertise, fusing the strategic efficacy of transatlantic networks of Black sociability with medieval Catholic custom and eighteenth-century imperial slave law to create a novel pattern of legal claims-making that redefined the meaning and application of the free-soil law of 1761.

------

caixa 50, documento 4903, "Ofício do governador Joaquim de Melo e Póvoas para o secretário de estado da Marinha e Ultramar"; "Decree of 7 January 1788," in Sílvia Lara, "Legislação sobre escravos africanos na América portuguesa," in José Andrés-Gallego, ed., *Nuevas aportaciones a la historia hurídica de Iberoamérica* (Madrid, 2000), 362 n. 528, quoted in Nogueira da Silva and Grinberg, "Soil Free from Slaves," *Slavery and Abolition,* XXXII (2011), 435, 436. Many of these early petitions for free-soil manumission did not produce a lasting paper trail. In part, the resilience of popular ideas regarding royal jurisprudence was indicative of a broader legal culture, forged by the enslaved in the eighteenth century, that sought extrajudicial redress through direct appeals to the monarch. The majority of free-soil petitions appealed to metropolitan officials, such as the General Administrator of the Customhouse, the Secretary of State, or the Juiz da Índia e Mina, not the king himself. See A. J. R. Russell-Wood, "'Acts of Grace': Portuguese Monarchs and Their Subjects of African Descent in Eighteenth-Century Brazil," *Journal of Latin American Studies,* XXXII (2000), 307–310.

Within a dense network of religious institutions in the city, the Irmandade de Nossa Senhora do Rosário dos Homens Pretos, the Real Irmandade de Jesús Maria Joseph, and the Irmandade de Nossa Senhora de Guadalupe e São Benedito dos Homens Pretos e Pardos, as well as other religious organizations, provided advice and monetary resources to fashion legal petitions.[32] As vital champions of enslaved people's legal strategies, Lisbon's Black brotherhoods also constituted one node of a larger, transatlantic socioreligious network that traversed the Portuguese empire, connecting enslaved Africans in Lisbon to those in Brazil and Africa.[33] These organizations had long been fixtures in both Lisbon and Salvador, providing spaces of aid, acculturation, ethnic identification, circulation of African cosmological beliefs, and social autonomy for their enslaved members. Popular understandings of Black religiosity grounded in Catholic sociability inspired enslaved people from around the Portuguese empire, but particularly from Brazil, to flee to sanctuary churches that dotted the urban landscape. Each of the city's nine exclusively Black and Brown irmandades augmented their visibility through participation in public Catholic festivals and the dispensing of largesse to enslaved and freed members. Black mariners arriving in Lisbon could have been availed of such institutions in a variety of ways: through happenstance, through an awareness of the longer history of Black Catholic abolitionism, or perhaps through more mundane ways. A newly arrived mariner could have spied a street procession with brightly costumed members perform-

32. These Black Catholic brotherhoods were dispersed throughout the city. The Irmandade de Nossa Senhora do Rosário dos Homens Pretos, for instance, had several chapters, one housed in the Convent of Santa Joana and another in the Convent of Nossa Senhora da Graça. The Real Irmandade de Jesús Maria Joseph was housed in the Covent of Nossa Senhora do Monte do Carmo, whereas the Irmandade de Nossa Senhora de Guadalupe e São Benedito dos Homens Pretos e Pardos was located in the Convent of São Francisco da Lisboa.

33. Enslaved mariners fleeing from Bahia would have been aware of the existence of Black brotherhoods. As Carlos Ott has said, by 1703–1704, the enslaved members of the brotherhood Nossa Senhora do Rosário dos Pretos do Pelourinho had constructed their own chapel. Within this space, West African brothers acculturated newly arrived Africans and attended to Christian burials for members. Meanwhile, Catholic missionaries' presence in West and West Central Africa reached back to the sixteenth century. Luanda, Mozambique, and São Tomé were also home to several confraternities by the eighteenth century. In West Central Africa, most confraternities were concentrated in Luanda. See Ott, "A Irmandade de Nossa Senhora do Rosário dos Pretos do Pelourinho," *Afro-Ásia* [S.I.], nos. 6–7 (1968), 119–126, esp. 121–123; Reginaldo, *Os Rosários dos Angolas*, 51–53, 60–69; Rowe, *Black Saints*, 70–71.

ing as "kings" and "queens" during a Portuguese saint's festival or relied on information gathered from other Africans living in the city.[34]

One such beneficiary was Francisco da Silva Martinho, who arrived in Lisbon from Pernambuco with the intent of protesting his enslavement. In February 1777, Francisco disembarked from the *São Jozé e Remédio* with his owner, the vessel's quartermaster, Manoel da Silva Martinho. With the aid of the judge and officers of the Irmandade de Nossa Senhora do Rosário dos Homens Pretos, he lodged a *requerimento,* or petition for his manumission letter, with the Juízo da Índia e Mina in May. Though it is unclear how or when Francisco made it to Nossa Senhora do Rosário, it was one of the oldest and best known of all the city's irmandades. Its members had become enmeshed in local freedom claims as they offered resources to enslaved members in danger of being sold outside of Portugal as well as those who faced mistreatment by their owners. Due to these liberty-seeking activities, Nossa Senhora do Rosário developed a reputation across the empire as a font of protest and as a defender of the interests of the enslaved. Francisco's faith that the brotherhood could provide a fundamental source of support for his cause was correct, as the brothers granted him the legal counsel and funds to formally protest his enslavement.[35]

Black Catholic brotherhoods in Lisbon also proved integral in helping sailors craft legal arguments against the alvará's mariner exemption clause. Standing before legal authorities—and likely acting on the advice of Rosário's Black brothers—Francisco testified that he was not a sailor and alleged that his owner had fraudulently registered him on the ship's *matrícula* (muster roll). Because of this, he insisted he should not subject to the crown's 1776 exception. Francisco's denial of his status as a mariner was not unusual; numerous petitioners arriving in Lisbon claimed either not to be mariners or to have only a transient or temporary relationship to maritime life. Evaluating the

34. Reginaldo, *Os Rosários dos Angolas,* 85. Due to these liberty-seeking activities, the Brotherhood of Nossa Senhora do Rosário developed a reputation across the empire as a font of protest and defender of the interests of the enslaved. See Lahon, "Black African Slaves and Freedmen in Portugal during the Renaissance," in Earle and Lowe, eds., *Black Africans in Renaissance Europe,* 268; Reginaldo, *Os Rosários dos Angolas,* 88–92; Mariza de Carvalho Soares, *People of Faith: Slavery and African Catholics in Eighteenth-Century Rio de Janeiro,* trans. Jerry D. Metz (Durham, N.C., 2011); Elizabeth W. Kiddy, "Congados, Calunga, Candombe: Our Lady of the Rosary in Minas Gerais, Brazil," *Luso-Brazilian Review,* XXXVII (2000), 47–61.

35. ANTT, Feitos Findos, Juízo da Índia e Mina, maço 6, numero 13, caixa 373, "Translado de justificação em que é autor Irmandade de Nossa Senhora do Rosário dos Homens Pretos"; Reginaldo, *Os Rosários dos Angolas,* 88–92.

FIGURE 10. *Altarpiece in the chapel for the Brotherhood of Nossa Senhora do Rosário in the Igreja da Graça (Lisbon). Our Lady of the Rosary stands on top, flanked by four Black figures: Saint Elesbão, Saint Efigénia, Saint Antônio de Notto, and Saint Benedito. Saint Raphael stands to her left, and the Archangel Saint Michael, with his scales of justice and protection, to her right. Photo by author*

truthfulness of their claims is impossible. But information about such updates to the 1761 alvará undoubtedly spread through the maritime informational networks that captive cosmopolitans traversed and pioneered. Francisco's petition was a case in point. He alleged that his owner, before leaving port in Brazil, had consulted with the governor of Pernambuco, who had notified him that when "slaves arrive in Lisbon they become freedmen, except if they are sailors on the ships that come." As a sign of the other crew members' solidarity, or perhaps as an illustration of the general confidence in Francisco's claims, the other men aboard the *São Jozé e Remédio* supported his statement. The ship's pilot testified that the governor of Pernambuco had summoned all maritime officers and sailors to his palace and notified them that any slave who stepped foot on Portuguese soil was legally free, with the exception of enslaved mariners. If Francisco knew that maritime labor disqualified freedom claims, it is likely other captive cosmopolitans did, too.[36]

36. ANTT, Feitos Findos, Juízo da Índia e Mina, maço 6, numero 13, caixa 373, "Translado de justificação em que é autor Irmandade de Nossa Senhora do Rosário dos Homens Pretos."

FIGURE 11. *Nossa Senhora do Rosário Church in Salvador, center of Black religiosity in Bahia. Photo by author*

As the royal officials and shipowners of Brazil conspired to circumvent the letter of the law, the enslaved covertly mobilized their own channels of communication. Francisco himself was not present at the meeting with the governor, but he had likely learned of it through his social contacts. As general knowledge of the 1761 law spread, mariners drew upon rumors emanating from private conversations to cast their owners as cynically attempting to undermine the spirit of free soil through legal technicality. Francisco's crewmates offered a variety of arguments in support of his position. One argued that the enslaved man had been purchased in the port of Recife shortly before embarkation and was therefore not a mariner. Pedro Jozé, a freed Black cabin boy, agreed that Francisco had never labored as a sailor before the voyage but was a simple *jangada* fisherman in the port. Manoel da Silva Martinho, he claimed, had convinced the captain to substitute a white sailor with Francisco on the *São Jozé e Remédio*'s voyage as a means to traffic his slave to Portugal illegally. Despite this supporting testimony, Francisco's petition for liberty was denied.[37]

It is also likely that transatlantic connections between Black Catholic brotherhoods in both Portugal and Brazil were central in disseminating awareness of free-soil laws far beyond the geographic boundaries of the imperial metropole. These nodes of social connection, community, and religiosity help explain why a number of enslaved mariners arrived in Portugal already familiar with imperial law's emancipatory possibilities. The case of escaped mariner Luiz João Jozé Ozare, for instance, hints at a transatlantic sense of affiliation and collaboration between Portuguese and Brazilian branches of the Nossa Senhora do Rosário Brotherhood. Employed in the Royal Armada, Luiz escaped to the Irmandade do Rosário, located in the Trinidade Convent. Like Juan Jozeph decades earlier, Ozare also experienced a circuitous path to his appearance before Portuguese legal bodies. He had already traveled to India and the Americas, living for a time in Bahia, where he might have joined a well-established chapter of Nossa Senhora do Rosário dos Homens Pretos. In Lisbon, Ozare sought respite from the punishing treatment of his owner, Lieutenant João Baptista. The sailor asserted not only that he was a member of the Portuguese irmandade but that his services were "necessary" to the religious community. The extent of Ozare's participation in the daily life of Lisbon's Black Catholic brotherhoods remained unspecified, but he presented his relationship to the free Black community as a stalwart one. Baptista,

37. Ibid.

in turn, disputed his bondsman's religious membership, and the Desembargo do Paço ultimately agreed. Ozare was unsuccessful in his manumission suit.[38]

PUSHING THE LIMITS OF FREE-SOIL LAW

Ozare was but one of numerous captive cosmopolitans in the late eighteenth century who sought to apply the 1761 alvará in increasingly creative ways. Their legal efforts included attempts to elude the edict's mariner exception while articulating a broader interpretation of its applicability vis-à-vis the status and predicament of the enslaved. In 1779, a group of five enslaved men from Benguela attempted to claim their liberty after arriving in Lisbon on a slaving vessel hailing from Rio de Janeiro. African-born Vicente Ferreira, Ambrozio Roque, Manoel Pereira, Ventura Gomes, and Caetano Jozé did not deny that they served as mariners but rather accused their owners, Manoel Gomes Cardoso (a slaving merchant) and Jozé Luis Viana (the captain of the ship on which they labored), of mistreatment and cruelty. Cardoso countered their petition and denied the charges, claiming it was pretext for the mariners to free themselves and return to their African homelands.[39]

Connections to Lisbon's local Black community also appear to have facilitated the men's daring escape from their ship. As Cardoso alleged, the enslaved men's "disobedience" was "sinisterly induced and encouraged" by "free Blacks" in the city, who "encouraged them to reject the power and authority of their owners." Though it is unclear how Vicente, Ambrozio, Manoel, Ventura, and Caetano first contacted these "free Blacks," it was they, Cardoso contended, who had made the African mariners aware of the free-soil provision, a communication that eventually allowed them to plead their case before the secretary of state. To Cardoso, the subversive potential of informational networks involving both free Black residents of Lisbon and arriving mariners was apparent. In response, slaveholders like him warned about the dire economic consequences of unfettered free-soil privileges. Cardoso's challenge to the sailors' petition hinged on a defense of his property rights in slaves. Mirroring the logic of the 1776 mariner exclusion, Cardoso

38. Candido, "African Freedom Suits and Portuguese Vassal Status," *Slavery and Abolition,* XXXII (2011), 451; Lauren Benton, "The Legal Regime of the South Atlantic World, 1400–1750: Jurisdictional Complexity as Institutional Order," *Journal of World History,* XI (2000), 48; Reginaldo, *Os Rosários dos Angolas,* 88–89.

39. AHU, CU, Brasil, Rio de Janeiro, caixa 110, documento 9172, "Requerimento do commerciante da praça do Rio de Janeiro, Manoel Gomes Cardoso."

asserted that the crown had to recognize his own "goods and rights" first and foremost.[40]

In doing so, however, he inadvertently reiterated the importance of Black mariners to transatlantic slaving, noting that such men were "indispensable" to the commerce between Benguela and Rio de Janeiro. According to Cardoso, the alvará's freeing of enslaved African sailors would disrupt imperial Portuguese commerce on the entire African coast because they served as "linguists for the unacculturated *[boçais]* slaves that are extracted from those [African] nations." In Cardoso's telling, captive cosmopolitanism—with emphasis placed on both elements—was vital to Portuguese mercantile interests. Once they were freed, he feared Black mariners would abandon their essential maritime profession. For Cardoso, enslavement was a source of moral cultivation that would promote the "virtues of civilization," an allusion to slavery's promise as a source of Christian tutelage and European acculturation. His confidence in slavery's innate Catholic virtue was ironic, given the role that religious sentiment had played in inspiring Vicente, Ambrozio, Manoel, Ventura, and Caetano's petition for liberty. Regardless of the creative legal arguments advanced by the enslaved litigants, royal officials found Cardoso's claims more persuasive. Agreeing that the mariners had unfairly taken advantage of the latitude allowed seafarers, officials concurred that Cardoso's rights as a slaveholder superseded any claims to liberty the men had offered—a tendency to favor property rights over claims to free status that would complicate the cases of subsequent enslaved petitioners. Despite their legal ingenuity, the five men were ordered to return to Cardoso and Viana. The ruling was but one sign of the narrowing possibilities of free soil for mariners and indicated the growing priority royal judicial bodies placed on slaveholders' property rights—as well as the empire's commercial interests—over enslaved individuals' assertions of their rightful liberty.[41]

In addition, the saga of the five enslaved men suggested the subversive impact of solidarities between African- and Portuguese-born men and the degree to which awareness of free-soil laws had spread beyond the metropole. Legal claims-making was accessible enough in both urban Brazil and Portuguese-speaking West Central Africa that many enslaved mariners arrived on Portugal's shores carrying with them a nascent theory of the law and its regulation of enslavement. This legal imaginary had the potential to be re-

40. Ibid.
41. Ibid.

shaped by interactions with free men and women of African descent that they encountered in a new, decidedly cosmopolitan landscape.[42]

In the same year, another group of four enslaved African men and one woman aboard the ship *Santissimo Sacramento e Nossa Senhora da Arabida* petitioned the royal Junta do Comércio in Lisbon to "claim their freedom." The group had arrived in Lisbon under contested circumstances. The unnamed *preta*, or Black woman, had been brought as a domestic servant for her owner, Captain Teodorio Gonçalves, who also owned the four African men. Beyond this, it is unclear what bound the five individuals together, other than a desire and collective strategy for freedom. According to the men, they were not mariners in Bahia, where the *Santissimo Sacramento* had traveled from. Rather, they claimed that two of their group—Amaro and Sebastião—labored as sedan chair carriers and domestic servants, whereas Antônio knew "a bit of the profession of a tailor" and Pedro had sailed on only one voyage from Bahia to the Mina Coast. The men maintained that the ship's register listed them as "servants," and aboard the *Santissimo,* they "only pulled some cables on deck, but never . . . caulked, unfurl[ed] or hoist[ed] sails, or govern[ed] the helm." At its core, their petition argued that a mere matrícula should "not be enough to hold them in bondage." Their owner had forced them to participate in a charade by making them change into mariners' clothing at the finish of the voyage, though they had little experience in the profession.[43]

The fugitives' petition also expressed a sophisticated reading of the 1761 alvará. On the one hand, they recognized that the law sought to restrict enslaved people's ability to travel to Portugal. Directly quoting the original text, they argued, "This Alvará had as its object curbing the excesses and debauchery that are against the laws and customs of other civilized Courts." Tacitly agreeing with—or at least strategically endorsing—the mercantilist logic of the edict, they noted, "Transported annually from Africa, America and Asia, to this Kingdom are an extraordinary number of African slaves . . . in doing so the Overseas kingdom significantly lacked [slaves] for cultivation of the land, [and] mines." As a result, the escapees suggested, transatlantic slaving traffic was a source of moral decline: the enslaved "only came to [Europe] to occupy the jobs of domestic servants, to escape into the streets . . . to indulge

42. Candido, "African Freedom Suits and Portuguese Vassal Status," *Slavery and Abolition,* XXXII (2011), 451; Benton, "Legal Regime of the South Atlantic World," *Journal of World History,* XI (2000), 48.

43. AHU, CU, Bahia–Avulsos, caixa 180, documento 13437, "Consulta da Junta do Comércio do Reino, December 19, 1780."

in idleness . . . and participate in vices." In turn, the fugitives reframed the purpose of the law by contesting the proslavery objectives of the 1776 alvará, which codified the mariner exemption. They remarked that, "aside from all these ends, [the law] also addressed the benefit of the Liberty of slaves . . . for the benefit that they become freed." The five enslaved petitioners expanded the implicit legal significance of the original 1761 law, insisting that its true purpose was to aid enslaved fugitives in securing liberty. The assertive language they used likely revealed more than their personal beliefs: Black Catholic brothers, having closely followed the law's application in local cases, might well have introduced them to this nuanced reading of the 1761 alvará. Rather than an expression of individual legal consciousness, the processo claim of Amaro, Sebastião, Antônio, Pedro, and the unnamed woman was polyvocal—encompassing not only their own imaginaries and expressions of just law but also those of the Black Catholic brothers.[44]

The capacious nature of their lawsuit's rhetoric indicated a shifting sense among both Lisbon's Black residents and its recent arrivals that slavery was categorically, not situationally, illegitimate. Far from envisaging manumission as a private affair governed by the whims of slaveowners, they averred that there was a public interest in the assurance that the enslaved could secure liberty. Turning the moral valence of the original law on its head, they reconceptualized a narrowly proslavery law as an expansive antislavery judicial principle. Their petition also reinterpreted the 1776 alvará, stating that it was "not only conceived in the same spirit" as the alvará of 1761 but also "in no way opposes the favor of Liberty of slaves, which are transported to these Kingdoms." In addition, the freedom principle included "enslaved mariners of any quality of ship" and, barring some exemptions, should include slaves who were listed in the matrícula and earned wages from the voyage. The enslaved "seamen's" petition argued that Teodorio Gonçalves had merely registered them as part of the ship's crew to avoid obeying the alvará of 1761, and his true purpose was to transport them back to Bahia to labor as personal servants. In doing so, he had partaken in a "fraudulent pretext" to subvert the ideals of royal justice. In contrast to Gonçalves, who had conformed to the formal letter of the law while subverting its spirit, the enslaved petitioners' legal arguments positioned them as loyal subjects and the true interpreters of the king's royal justice.[45]

44. Ibid.

45. AHU, CU, Bahia–Avulsos, caixa 180, documento 13437, Consulta da Junta do Comércio do Reino, Dec. 19, 1780. Enslaved petitioners were also making similar arguments

The five enslaved litigants' legal creativity in stretching the alvará's intent to include an implicit, royally supported principle of liberty for slaves did not ultimately bear fruit. The members of the Junta do Comércio denied the four men's petition but freed the woman. Their decision was not unanimous, however, with the *vice provedor*, Francisco Nicolão Roncon, favoring freeing all the seamen save for Pedro. The deputies, who voted to allow the four men to remain enslaved, did so with the explicit language of preventing a disruption in commercial navigation between Portugal and the colonies. They reiterated the importance of the 1776 alvará to remedy the deficiencies of the 1761 law, which had "impeded the increase in the number of people necessary for the sailing of ships of that continent [Europe], [by] not being able to bring slaves, even in the profession of sailor, which is very useful and necessary for [commercial] Navigation." They also contended that they had found no evidence of Gonçalves's fraud. Rather, in keeping his enslaved mariners as servants before a return voyage to Bahia, he was acting no differently than many other slaveowners. In short, the Junta do Comércio declared that enslaved mariners hoping to secure manumission by landing on the "free soil" of Portugal could not expect to substantiate their cases and circumvent the law by bringing the slaveholders' deceptions to light.[46]

Black mariners' arguments also showed that the proscriptions of free soil could be wedded to broader pro-manumission arguments that challenged imperial administrators' efforts to exclude them from the applicability of the law. In contrast to enslaved litigants who obscured their maritime work, other fugitive seamen emphasized the breadth of their maritime service as an essential basis of their freedom claims. Francisco de Paula—an enslaved mariner in Rio de Janeiro—appealed to the Portuguese Royal Court to free him under the auspices of the 1761 law by arguing that his owner, Colonel Arielino da Fonseca Coutinho, had realized "five or six times his [own] value" in the twenty-plus years he had served as a mariner. Captive cosmopolitanism, in his telling, was not only a value to be harvested by owners; it was an asset that should be recognized by legal authorities as a basis for manumission. De Paula's petition emphasized that, during his long career, he had labored on diverse vessels and traveled often to America, Asia, and Africa, highlighting

---

about the volubility of slaveholders' property where freedom was concerned in Brazil during this period (Marquez, "Afflicted Slaves, Faithful Vassals," *Slavery and Abolition*, XLIII [2022], 91–119).

46. AHU, CU, Bahia–Avulsos, caixa 180, documento 13437, "Consulta da Junta do Comércio do Reino, December 19, 1780."

his own cosmopolitanism and the worth of his skilled labor to Portuguese imperial commerce. De Paula protested that he should be "cut" from his master or be allowed to pay for his own freedom. The mariner's emphasis on his financial independence echoed Juan Jozeph's insistence thirty-seven years earlier that he was free because he did not depend on others for his own subsistence. Invoking a "right over himself," the mariner's contention that he was monetarily capable of purchasing his liberty alluded to his ability not only to survive but also to accumulate a small reserve of wealth and embody a state of independence. Like many such petitions, De Paula's case has no recorded resolution; however, his cosmopolitanism enhanced his ability to gain knowledge of Portuguese free-soil laws and utilize such awareness in pursuit of his own aspirations.[47]

By the end of the eighteenth century, fugitive mariners such as De Paula increasingly characterized their bondage as unnatural and unfair. In this vein, four enslaved seamen approached the Portuguese royal navy in 1797 for their manumission. Joaquim Thomas, Francisco Pedro, Jorge Joaquim, and Joaquim Corrêa de Brito appealed for their freedom by invoking the alvará of 1761. They emphasized their honorable naval service, testifying that they had, several years earlier, labored as enslaved mariners aboard a ship based in Pernambuco before being captured by a French vessel, where they remained for three years as enemy captives. After the French vessel was taken by an English one, the men were transported to London, where they sought the protection of the Portuguese consul, eventually returning to Lisbon and lodging their petition. In addition to appealing to the free-soil alvará to "regain . . . their natural liberty," the mariners averred that they would continue to serve in the Royal Armada as seamen after receiving their manumission letters.[48]

Their written legal arguments challenged the dominant view of human bondage as a universal and natural feature of civilizations around the world. Such arguments also functioned as claims about what the law *should be* as well as about the nature of freedom itself. By framing their freedom as "natural," the four mariners contended that natural law should justly supersede the

47. Biblioteca Nacional Rio de Janeiro, C420, 49, "Requerimento de Francisco de Paula," Jan. 16, 1776; Bianca Premo, *The Enlightenment on Trial: Ordinary Litigants and Colonialism in the Spanish Empire* (Oxford, 2017), 207. The idea of being "cut" from one's master is a reference to *coartação,* or the process whereby enslaved men and women purchased their own liberty by offering regular payments to their masters over a set period of time.

48. AHU, CU, Brasil, Pernambuco, caixa 198, documento 13635, Nov. 20, 1797, "Requerimento dos negros e ex-escravos na capitania de Pernambuco, Joaquim Thomas, Francisco Pedro, Jorge Joaquim, e Joaquim Corrêa de Brito"; Herzog, *Defining Nations,* 134.

law of nations—which held them in slavery—and that liberty was imparted by inclusive legal right, not by the discrete dispensation of individual acts of royal benevolence. The men also drew on a gendered discourse of masculine service to the Portuguese crown's military and commercial interests. Rhetorically constructing themselves as Portuguese subjects through their military service, they drew on assertions of seafaring acumen and proposed that their status as loyal and valuable vassals should result in their manumission, echoing the legal principle that vassals who served the king in times of war merited favored status.[49] Such a justification also contradicted the mariner exemption to free soil, as they argued that their maritime skills qualified rather than excluded them for liberty. And as Juan Jozeph had done decades earlier, they advanced the notion that the lived experience of personal independence should qualify them for legally recognized freedom.[50] Each petitioner sought to stretch the 1761 alvará's meaning far past the law's initial purpose, either by proclaiming their exceptional value to the empire or by invoking new, and sometimes universal, rationales for their liberty. Such rhetorical maneuvers

49. Proslavery arguments advanced by the Concelho Ultramarino a mere four years later highlighted slavery's commonality in history and argued against the notion that manumission or freedom was a right of the enslaved (Marquez, "Afflicted Slaves, Faithful Vassals," *Slavery and Abolition*, XLIII [2022], 91–119). At the end of the eighteenth century in Spanish America, enslaved litigants increasingly highlighted slavery as an unnatural state and espoused a universal natural rights notion of their liberty that eclipsed other forms of positive law, such as the law of nations (Premo, *Enlightenment on Trial*, 209–214).

50. The emphasis on the free-soil law's universality was often circumvented by slaveholders entering Portugal. During this period, owners took steps to subvert the letter of the law by smuggling their enslaved property into Portugal without notifying the proper authorities. When Friar Raimundo de São José fled Bahia without even a passport or license, he decided to clandestinely enter Lisbon. To conceal the presence of the enslaved man he brought with him, Alberto de Santa Anna, São José avoided declaring his own arrival in the port. His ploy did not remain hidden long. Upon becoming aware of São José's fraud, the customhouse's general administrator, Diogo Inácio de Pina Manique (also the kingdom's police intendent), endeavored to bestow upon Alberto his freedom letter, in accordance with the 1761 law. But when the Carmelite friar learned that his bondsman would be freed, he provoked the local civil magistrate to have the enslaved man arrested to prevent his emancipation. In 1783, Manique appealed to Maria I on Alberto's behalf, asking for a royal writ of protection for the "miserable vassal" who had lived in "desolation" while jailed for the last six months. Manique stressed the desperate nature of Alberto's plight and the necessity of royal intercession. Alberto, twenty-six years old and originally from the Mina Coast, had lived in Bahia before his arrival in Lisbon. His unwarranted imprisonment attracted the

would continue to become more complex, presenting a profound challenge to the operation of imperial commerce in the coming years.

COSMOPOLITAN LEGAL IMAGINARIES AND IMPERIAL CRISIS

Ongoing alarm about the application of the free-soil principle in the early decades of the nineteenth century revealed persistent fears among both Portuguese and Brazilian officials about the destabilizing effects of enslaved mariners' mobility. Sanctioned movement underpinned Atlantic slavery, commodity production, and the colonial economy. The specter of unsanctioned movement, however, threatened the core of the imperial system. Beyond the disruption to the maritime labor force, as enslaved seamen escaped to Portuguese ships and waterfronts, the royal navy faced potential liabilities from slaveowners seeking restitution. This was a period of intensifying inter- and intraimperial conflict generated by the Age of Revolutions; the attendant political uncertainty afforded new strategic and rhetorical possibilities for enslaved mariners in making their freedom claims.[51]

---

support of a Black religious brotherhood, who hoped to legally contest his desperate situation. Manique meanwhile argued that Alberto should be removed from prison and given his freedom papers. At the core of the customhouse administrator's logic was São José's string of deceptions. The enslaved man was not a mariner serving on a royal warship, nor was he registered in any ship's crew manifest: the 1776 mariner exception did not apply. His case was unequivocal—he was not legally enslaved. Critically, Manique had asserted Alberto's vassalage, despite his enslaved status, evoking the law's essential purpose as freeing bondspeople under the auspices of the queen's protective justice. Black petitioners who directly appealed to the crown as an "impartial arbitrator of justice" often evoked the language of social contract between moral monarch and humble subject. Even a Portuguese functionary such as Manique recognized that the law should be justly applied, regardless of the objections of conniving slaveowners like São José. See AHU, CU, Brasil–Avulsos, caixa 25, documento 2133, "Ofício do administrador-geral da Alfândega e intendente da Policia [do Reino], Diogo Inácio de Pina Manique, ao [secretário de estado da Marinha e Ultramar], Marinho de Melo e Castro"; Russell-Wood, "'Acts of Grace,'" *Journal of Latin American Studies*, XXXII (2000), 309.

51. In 1821, João Antonio, enslaved mariner, escaped his owner, Captain José Joaquim Pinto Cascáes, master of the brig *Marques de Cascáes*, to another naval vessel, the *São Sebastião*, prompting a request for restitution and the return of the fugitive bondsman. Maritime slaveowners lodged further petitions for restitution in the following years. See ACML, caixa 311–1, Aug. 22, 1821, Dec. 10, 1821, Aug. 5, 1822, Aug. 22, 1822, Feb. 28, 1824.

Enslaved sailors sometimes mobilized their status as prisoners of war to advocate for their own legal manumission, even if they had not been legally free before they were taken. In 1802, for instance, Luis da Silva—the former bondsman of a Bahian slave trafficker named Francisco Jozé de Souza—petitioned the Portuguese crown to issue his carta de liberdade after he had been captured by a Spanish ship of war while traveling from Bahia to Pernambuco with a cargo of more than one hundred other enslaved individuals. Da Silva, along with the other crew members, was taken to Buenos Aires. There, his owner eventually collected him. The creole mariner testified that, upon his release, the Spaniards had declared him free as a prisoner of war and endowed him with a manumission letter and passport, the former of which was confiscated by his owner when the two arrived back in Bahia, "returning him to captivity." In addition to referencing the alvará of 1761, Da Silva—like many other enslaved mariners who petitioned for manumission—highlighted his seafaring service as a justification for his freedom, claiming that, as a liberated man, it was "his destiny to pursue maritime life" within any port of the Portuguese empire. His words provided a commentary not only on the nature of freedom but also on his perceptions of his own labor. Though the fate of the petition is unclear, Da Silva's allusion to his occupational identity and his innate value to the empire as a skilled laborer articulated a logic for freedom that far exceeded what the letter of the law prescribed. Although the 1776 law presumed that Black mariners required coercion to toil within the empire's merchant marine, Black seafarers themselves highlighted their agency by invoking the worthiness and voluntary nature of their service.[52]

Captive cosmopolitans' exploitation of free-soil law did not go unnoticed by colonial authorities, who lobbied the Secretaria de Estado dos Negócios da Marinha e Domínios Ultramarinos (Secretary of State of the Navy and Overseas Domains) in Lisbon to restrict its application. As Bahia's governor, Dom Fernando José de Portugal, explained in 1796, the "real intention" of the law was being distorted by enslaved mariners, who he argued traveled to Portugal merely to desert their ships. To support his assertion that the 1761 alvará encouraged illegal fugitivity, Dom Fernando related the case of Bernardo, who—without a passport or the knowledge or permission of his mistress, the widow of a prominent local merchant—had escaped to Lisbon's customhouse. There, he was able to secure freedom papers once he presented himself before the general administrator. Elevating Bernardo as a symbol of

52. AHU, CU, Bahia, caixa 224, documento 15554, Mar. 4, 1802, "Requerimento de Luis da Silva."

free soil's socially unseemly effects, the governor revealed that the fugitive man had abandoned his enslaved wife and children in the colony.[53]

Imperial administrators' growing alarm stemmed from what they perceived as the undue application and scope of the free-soil law. Dom Fernando insisted the law could be applied only to those who had been illegally taken to Portugal and that it excluded runaways who had traveled to Lisbon for unlawful ends. The order's intention was not to reward disobedience, and the governor argued that the liberality with which it was being applied in the metropole had unjustly weakened slaveowners' authority in the colonies. Bernardo was one of many who, in the governor's mind, had taken advantage of the "law of liberty" to "escape from [Bahia] to the Kingdom [of Portugal] and obtain their freedom with such ease." Both men and women *("Pretos* e *Pretas")* had used it to elude the control of their owners and migrate to the imperial capital.[54]

This maritime rebelliousness, Dom Fernando believed, had generated ongoing conflicts between Lisbon's legal imperatives and the sanctity of Bahian property holding, particularly in enslaved men and women. The governor urged a reevaluation of free-soil law and expressed particular disdain for mariners' ability to represent themselves in potentially emancipatory legal processes. He lamented that mariners "even defended themselves against their own masters by seeking asylum" in front of officials who, in his view, were often too sympathetic to their cause. Finally, the intercession of the São Benedito Brotherhood was another cause for complaint. Although the brothers had offered to compensate Bernardo's former owner to guarantee his emancipation, the governor deemed the amount an insignificant sum. Reform of this counterproductive law was imperative, given its "disastrous consequences" for "commerce and agriculture" in Portugal's overseas domains. This final statement—framed in such dramatic, if not hyperbolic, terms—suggests the degree to which imperial authorities sincerely believed that free soil's application had been far more widespread than the number of surviving legal disputes suggests.[55]

Portuguese mercantilist authorities, convinced by the protestations launched on behalf of Brazilian slaving interests, began to critique the law's broad application. A growing consensus emerged in the early nineteenth century that, despite royal intentions to use free soil as an instrument of economic growth, the alvará posed a grave threat to Portugal's mercantile interests. As

53. Ibid., caixa 84, documento 16501, "Ofício do Governador D. Fernando José de Portugal para Luiz Pinto de Sousa."

54. Ibid.

55. Ibid.

maritime marronage continued largely unabated, the crown—under mounting pressure from the colonies—issued modifications to the law in 1800 and
1802 to reiterate that enslaved mariners were exempted from accessing the
liberatory possibilities of free soil. These notices not only excluded mariners
from the free-soil principle but also prescribed that the enslaved men return
aboard the same ships on which they had traveled to Portugal. However, the
amendments did little to ebb the tide of enslaved individuals who were laboring in other capacities and applying the law.[56]

Thus, when an enslaved Bahian man, Vicente Antônio Telles, appealed
to the crown for manumission under principle of the law in 1804, the Portuguese secretary of state, viscount of Anadia (João Rodrigues de Sá e Melo
Meneses), used the opportunity to lament the ill effects of free-soil law that
he believed had produced "ruinous consequences" for the colonies. The
viscount elaborated that "slaves [were] the most important property held
by settlers in Brazil, [especially] when they are taught and know a trade . . .
and when they are not available in the complicated sugar and tobacco mills,
an entire harvest is lost." He also noted the link between cosmopolitanism
and fugitivity: "The sugar masters, cauldron stirrers, carpenters, and other
[enslaved] artisans . . . are the most acculturated *[ladino]* and most attentive,
with the greatest propensity to run away." As a consequence, the Brazilian
colonies were losing the skilled labor that was vital to their primary commercial activities.[57]

56. During this period, the Concelho Ultramarino engaged in vigorous debates about the
right of enslaved people to gain manumission. Enslaved litigants had successfully pressured
the crown to make manumission by purchase more accessible in the decades preceding 1801,
but by that year, an increasingly conservative attitude toward the matter prevailed. Under
the influence of royal advisors, the crown revoked an earlier edict allowing the enslaved to
secure manumission by purchase without their owner's consent, instead premising access
to self-purchase on an owner's will. See Marquez, "Afflicted Slaves, Faithful Vassals," *Slavery and Abolition,* XLIII (2022), 91-119; Nogueira da Silva and Grinberg, "Soil Free from
Slaves," ibid., 435-436; ANTT, Arquivo do Arquivo, Avisos e Ordens, maço 4, numero 88,
"Aviso para quardar no real arquivo, o alvará para os escravos dos domínios ultramarinos
poderem ser ocupados na marcação dos navios de comércio que vierem aos portos deste
reino não ficando por isso compreendidos no benefício do alvará de 19 de setembro de 1761";
ibid., Chancelaria Régia, Núcleo Antigo 34, folha 125v, "Alvará declarando e amplianto o de
19 de Setembro de 1761 para que os Escravos que Viessem ao Porto de Lisboa"; *Gazeta de
Lisboa,* no. 14, Apr. 8, 1800, n.p.

57. AHU, CU, Bahia–Avulsos, caixa 233, documento 16095, Sept. 17, 1804, "Aviso do
Visconde de Anadia."

The costs of such edicts were high, according to the viscount. Portuguese law had created an irrational set of incentives wherein enslaved fugitives frequently sought their manumission before metropolitan legal bodies while their owners were absent, with some owners never receiving so much as an explanation for the freeing of their bondsmen. Anadia's description was itself a sign that enslaved individuals often planned their course of escape and litigation at moments in which owners would be absent and unable to offer countervailing arguments to their manumission claims. This, Anadia believed, "rewarded a crime" and promoted disorder in the colonies by "importing slaves from the coast of Africa, and then declaring them free without hearing from their owners." Indeed, enslaved sailors and other tradesmen had been so successful in utilizing the alvará that the viscount accused Portuguese law as demonstrating "benign love to the slaves," to the "detriment of their masters," and warned that, for slavery and thus agricultural production to flourish in Brazil, "it [was] necessary to support the rights of slave masters" above the legal claims of slaves. The viscount's objections to the law's application in Portugal starkly revealed royal administrators' focus on labor control as a key mode of mercantilist economic policy. The ills produced by free soil were clear if the empire's prosperity was intrinsically tied to the wealth created by slavery and the transatlantic slave trade. His pleas implicitly conveyed the proslavery conviction that emancipatory law successfully applied by the enslaved was in danger of becoming a decisive source of imperial decline. Anadia's emphasis on the sanctity of slaveholders' property rights as the cornerstone of a prosperous economy would ironically become commonplace in the period after Brazilian independence.[58]

By the turn of the nineteenth century, the concerns of Bahian slaving interests—and their critiques of metropolitan law and policy—had only grown deeper as Portuguese authorities continued to be approached by numerous escapees from the colony. One such case was that of Francisco da Costa, who pursued freedom from his owner, a militia *coronel* on the island of Itaparica (located across the bay from Salvador) as a result of cruel treatment and an unreasonable refusal to allow Costa to self-purchase manumission. In 1799, Costa, who was perhaps a mariner but certainly engaged in military service due to his owner's occupation, sought the assistance of the São Benedito Brotherhood. In supporting him, the Catholic brothers revealed their awareness of enslaved people's evolving legal tactics in the colonies. Costa's assertions of mistreatment as a justification for manumission, in fact, drew on

58. Ibid.

a set of customary claims enslaved litigants in Brazil had made since 1700. *Servícia,* or the legal principle that a pattern of cruelty by one's owner could be the basis for a petition of self-purchase, suffused enslaved people's legal argumentation in the eighteenth century. Imperial authorities in Bahia began to cast blame widely for such instances of fugitivity. Enslaved mariners had been emboldened not only by the furtive networks of communication that connected escapees and Black Catholic brothers, they argued, but also by customhouse officials in Lisbon who had been indiscriminately bestowing freedom papers on enslaved arrivals and producing "bad consequences" in the colonies. These "consequences," they claimed, had entailed an upsurge of fugitivity and the prospect that imperial law and its broad application could imperil the resurgent slave-based sugar economy in Brazil's northeast.[59]

Ignoring such internecine imperial arguments, Black mariners persisted in interpreting the "true" meaning of the 1761 alvará, not as a penalty for slaveholders trafficking their bondsmen to the metropole, but as a beneficent promise of royally granted liberty. In response, state authorities and slaveholders increasingly turned to both litigation and imprisonment of fugitives to regain control of rebellious captive arrivals in the city. In 1810, Jozé Antônio Pereira approached the Desembargo do Paço to initiate a libel against his bondsman, Luis Pereira, for falsely "claiming to be free." As Pereira indignantly explained, he had purchased Luis in Mozambique in 1801, trafficking him to Maranhão, where he sent Luis to learn the trade of mariner. For the next eight years, Luis had labored on the slaving ship *São José Indiano* until his arrival in Lisbon. Once he stepped foot in the metropole, Luis "fled and deserted the ship, living as a vagabond" outside his owner's supervision until he was arrested and incarcerated in the *cadeia do Castelo,* a local jail. Once there, Luis shrewdly convinced the customhouse administrator to issue him a manumission letter, which would free him unless Pereira demonstrated dominion over him. Objecting to this requirement, Pereira lamented that it would create an inducement to escape for the "other [seafaring] slaves on

59. Da Costa allegedly offered his owner, José da Costa Mirales, 270$000 réis for his freedom (ibid., caixa 98, documento 19190, "Ofício do Governador D. Fernando José de Portugal para D. Rodrigo de Sousa Coutinho"). The legal principle of servícia had been established in Las Siete Partidas, which required owners convicted of mistreating their slaves to sell them. Accusations of owners' cruelty and mistreatment suffused a diverse array of enslaved litigants' petitions in eighteenth-century Spanish America, as well. See Bryant, *Rivers of Gold, Lives of Bondage,* 115–119, 137–138; Premo, *Enlightenment on Trial,* 194, 199–204; Marquez, "Afflicted Slaves, Faithful Vassals," *Slavery and Abolition,* XLIII (2022), 91–119.

which Navigation depended so much" while arguing that the manumission letter was unlawful according to the alvará of March 10, 1806, which precluded freeing enslaved mariners.[60]

Such cases laid bare the expansive and variegated ways in which the enslaved, slaveholders, and imperial authorities alike could interpret free-soil law. More particularly, Luis's suit indicated a disparity between the customhouse's interpretation of free soil's applicability and that of other legal bodies in the city. Luis's name had clearly been registered in the *São José Indiano*'s muster roll, disqualifying him under the terms of the 1761 law. Pereira advocated for his bondsman's return to Brazil, and officials required the escaped mariner to "acknowledge [Pereira] to be his legitimate owner and provide services to him as long as he remained in slavery." Pereira's claims over Luis apparently needed no corroboration, as the enslaved man's perspective on his escape, imprisonment, and potential manumission were not recorded or

60. ANTT, Feitos Findos, Juízo da Índia e Mina, maço 4, no. 15, caixa 324, "Acção Cível de Libelo em que é autor José António Pereira e réu Luís Pereira." Luis was far from unusual in his detention. By this period, the numbers of jailed people of African descent was high in Lisbon. Many were pressed into forms of maritime labor as part of the terms of their sentencing. In 1795, three out of seven men sent to the galley in the Naval Arsenal were men of African descent, each arrested for a variety of crimes, including burglary and stabbing. In 1798, a Black man named Jozé Francisco was detained and sent, at least initially, to the Cadeia (jail) de Belém. From there, he was confined in the Real Fábrica de Cordoaria (Royal Rope Factory) and conscripted to perform forced labor. The factory, created through an order by the marquis de Pombal in 1771, produced cables, ropes, sails, and flags for Portuguese sailing ships. Francisco believed his imprisonment to be unlawful, launching a petition against the Real Junta da Fazenda da Marinha, or the naval authorities who oversaw his case. Local jails also became a means to limit Black mobility in the city as well as prevent Black mariners from jumping ship. João Antônio, an eighteen-year-old *pardo* sailor, was condemned to the galleys for five years for carrying a knife in 1801, after which he would serve on a Portuguese warship destined for Asia. Antônio de Roza, another pardo seaman who had labored in the Royal Armada, was sentenced to three years in the city's galleys for an unknown crime; he was also eventually deported to Asia. In 1805, an enslaved man, upon escaping from an English frigate that had been seized on the island of Martinique by a French ship, boarded the Portuguese frigate *Minerva* and escaped to Portugal. Once there, he was apprehended in the Navy Arsenal Galley. Naval authorities planned for him to be delivered to the French chargé d'affaires. See ACML, Presos, caixa 384, annos 1759–1800, Arsenal Real da Marinha, Dec. 23, 1795, "Prezo da Galle"; ibid., "Requeirmento de Jozé Francicao, homem preto, prezo na Real Fábrica de Cordoaria," Mar. 24, 1800; ibid., "Diz Antonio de Rosa," n.d.; "Diz João Antônio, marujo," Aug. 2, 1806; ibid., Feb. 19, 28, 1805.

likely even sought by the officials of the Desembargo do Paço. Pereira, like Juan Jozeph's captor several decades earlier, might have utilized legal mechanisms to fraudulently enslave Luis, a man who had ceased to live under his control. The murky truth of what had occurred, however, was subordinated to the imperatives of maritime commerce. As the petitioner himself argued, Luis "cannot be considered free, not only because of the provisions of the Law" but because the loss of enslaved mariners would be damaging to the present "circumstances of lack of manpower to crew the ships."[61]

These sorts of arguments did little to stem the tide of freedom-seeking litigants from all corners of the empire. In 1805, José Ignácio Joaquim— a slave of Joaquim da Costa, a merchant from Maranhão, Brazil—and an unnamed Black woman petitioned for their cartas de alforria. The two enslaved litigants contended that they were no longer enslaved because Costa had failed to secure a passport for either, and by disembarking with them in the city without following proper procedure, he designated them legally free. After depositing a carta de alforria with the unnamed enslaved woman, Costa had absconded to Brazil, leaving the two to live, as they told it, in increasing desperation. Despite their intervening hardships, particularly the struggle to subsist in an alien city, the pair marshaled the support of the Irmandade de Nossa Senhora do Rosário, which likely paid the $278 réis fee for a scribe to craft their petition. They also gained the confidence and perhaps friendship of two Black Lisbon residents, Luis Jacob and Francisco Luis, identified as a laborer and a cook, who corroborated their story to the Juízo da Índia e Mina. In absentia, they argued, Costa had relinquished his legal claim on them, and they were owed their legal freedom. Ultimately, they were successful in their litigation, as the mariner exception did not apply to them.

The legal consciousness and acumen of American- and European-born enslaved and free people shaped the strategies of ladino Africans who had recently become ensnared in bondage. The benefits—and subversive potential—of such cross-cultural alliances are evident in one free-soil marronage case from 1812, when Cipriano, a twenty-two-year-old enslaved mariner from Rio de Janeiro, escaped alongside Pedro, an Angolan man. Manoel de Abreu Lima, a ship captain from Pernambuco, owned both men and maintained that he had correctly registered them at the customhouse when he arrived in Lisbon. Once there, the two men escaped to the Irmandade de Nossa Senhora

---

61. ANTT, Feitos Findos, Juízo da Índia e Mina, maço 4, no. 15, caixa 324, "Acção Cível de Libelo em que é autor José António Pereira e réu Luís Pereira."

do Rosário dos Homens Pretos e Pardos, causing Lima to petition the Juízo da Índia e Mina for their release.[62]

In a similar vein, the Bahian-based mariner Silvestre Maria e Freitas successfully petitioned for his freedom in 1814. Freitas explained that he had been born on the African island of Príncipe, the colony where his owner, João Resende Tavares Leote, served as governor. Despite living there in "good circumstances," the young man was sent to Lisbon to learn the "art of hairstyling and barbering." Francisco Pereira, the captain of the ship on which he traveled, was expected to return Freitas to the island. During their layover in Salvador, however, his owner died, allowing the ship's owner, Innocêncio José da Costa, to capture Freitas as his slave. After several years, Pereira sold the young man to a local merchant, who hired him out as a sedan chair carrier. Freitas accompanied his new master on a ship traveling to Lisbon. Arriving there in 1811, he swiftly petitioned for his carta de liberdade, protesting the illegal circumstances in which he had been enslaved in Brazil. He sought out his former mistress, Leote's wife, Dona Luiza Angelica Victoria de Andrade, requesting from her a manumission letter. He also secured Leote's last will and testament, which verified that he had indeed been the governor's human property. Andrade reported that she had naively entrusted Freitas to Costa, but in the five years that her bondsman had been absent, she had heard little from him. Freitas argued that his spontaneous escape had been necessary to "repair his freedom." The initial act of false enslavement meant that the then-thirty-year-old Freitas, despite being registered on the ship that carried him from Bahia to Lisbon, was protected by the 1761 law.[63]

The relative speed at which those recently torn from African homelands became acquainted with the principle of free soil suggests how effectively enslaved seafarers—in consort with land-based informational networks in Black religious spaces on both sides of the Atlantic—circulated ideas about emancipatory imperial law. The Lisbon-based brotherhood Real Irmandade de Nossa Senhora de Guadalupe e São Benedito dos Homens Pretos e Pardos petitioned the Casa da Índia in 1814 on behalf of their brother João

62. Ibid., maço 11, numero 17, caixa 331, "Acção civil de requerimento em que e autor Manuel de Abreu Lima e réu Irmandade de Nossa Senhora do Rosário dos Homens Pretos e Pardos." Lima's success in recapturing the two men remains unclear.

63. Ibid., maço 39, numero 9, caixa 359, "Acção civil de embargos á primeira em que é autor Silvestre Maria e Freitas e réu Bento José de Freitas"; ANTT, Feitos Findos, Juízo da Índia e Mina, Justificações Ultramarinas, Brazil, maço 287, numero 8, "Autos de justificação de José Ignácio Joaquim."

Antônio for his liberty, as well as back pay from his owners, Father José Luis Coutinho and Manuel Luis Coutinho. As early as 1778, the same brotherhood had sought to emulate the Rosário Brotherhood by acquiring the same emancipatory privileges as their predecessor. The brothers of Guadalupe e São Benedito petitioned the Desembargo do Paço, requesting "not only to exercise the meritorious works of freeing their brothers who lived in captivity, paying their masters [for] their just value, but for all the others, of which the privileges were composed." Likewise, a chapter of the Irmandade Nossa Senhora do Rosário, located in the Convent of Santa Joana da Graça, collectively sued Captain Luis Barbalho to free Manoel Barbalho, who traveled to Lisbon from Pernambuco with his owner. But churches were not the sole resource for maritime fugitives. Anselmo José da Cruz was an example of a Black man who sought a different source of help in securing freedom. Born in Sabará, Minas Gerais, Cruz traveled from Rio de Janeiro to Lisbon in 1818; when he arrived in port, he chose not to escape to a sanctuary church but instead petitioned the general administrator of the customhouse for his manumission letter—and was successful.[64]

THE POSTCOLONIAL AFTERLIVES OF FREE SOIL

Brazil's independence from Portugal in 1822 prompted new uncertainties about the 1776 law's applicability to enslaved mariners traveling on Brazilian ships to Lisbon. As the geopolitics of fugitivity abruptly shifted, it remained unclear whether the cessation of Portugal's mercantile interest in the maintenance of colonial slavery would spell the end of the mariner exception. The growing pressures produced by mariners' escape could have compelled the Portuguese crown to suspend the 1776 and 1800 laws exempting mariners from the newly created sovereign territory of Brazil. Though no rationale was given for an extension of the mariner exception, royal authorities lacked commitment to universal abolition and continued to take a conservative position

---

64. ANTT, Feitos Findos, Juízo da Índia e Mina, maço 33, numero 4, caixa 157, "Acção civil de Liberdade e embargos a primeira em que a autora a Irmandade de Nossa Senhora de Guadalupe e São Benedito dos homens pretos e pardos e réus o padre José Luis Coutinho e Manuel Luis Coutinho"; ibid., Juizo da Chancelaria, maço 334, numero 23, "Autos de execução de dizima em que e réu o capitão Luis Barbalho e autores os mesários da Irmandade do Rosário dos Homens Pretos da Graça"; ibid., Juízo da Índia e Mina, maço 8, numero 5, caixa 132, "Autos civeis de requerimento e despacho para julgar por sentença a Liberdade de Anselmo José da Cruz"; Reginaldo, *Os Rosários dos Angolas,* 87.

about the limits of the free-soil law. A royal notice reiterated the stance of the 1800 alvará exempting mariners from attaining freedom by arriving in Portugal. Furthermore, administrators argued, "This legislation has much more reason to be applied to slaves in the Empire's ships coming from Brazil, which today forms an independent and foreign nation." Such decisions endeavored to stabilize the kingdom's commercial interests in the midst of political disruption, given that enslaved maritime labor still helped sustain long-distance trade to the Americas and Africa. The crown also hoped to revitalize a mutually beneficial commercial relationship with its former American colonies, and infringement on slave ownership in Brazil would have imperiled that goal.[65]

From the standpoint of enslaved mariners, however, Brazilian independence left the promise of Portuguese free soil unscathed, and jurisdictionally oriented maritime marronage remained a popular freedom-seeking strategy. In 1822, twenty-five-year-old José Manoel, an African sailor from Cabinda, arrived in Porto on a ship hailing from Bahia. He escaped his vessel and traveled to Lisbon, making his way to the Real Irmandade de Nossa Senhora do Rosário housed in the Igreja do Salvador. The enslaved man and his Catholic allies claimed he had escaped in order "to be catechized and baptized there." His owner, José Manoel Fernandes, argued that the enslaved man had not escaped because of spiritual motivations but because the seaman "only wanted to be free from his slavery." An official at the church countered that José, a "miserable black man . . . did not want to return to his pagan existence . . . [and] this was his primary, true motivation." His petition wove together religious motifs of salvation with an appeal to royal benevolence as he "implored justice" from the monarch, requesting freedom under the 1761 law.[66]

José Manoel's wish to be catechized also strategically drew on notions of Catholic sanctuary, which did not explicitly guarantee freedom for enslaved fugitives who "access[ed] consecrated ground." Nonetheless, his evocation of Catholic ideals of protection and mercy illustrates that, just as in the preceding decades, enslaved men and women could and did seek ecclesiastical immunity. José Manoel was not successful in attaining his manumission, however; the Casa da Índia ruled that it was "impractical to free" him and endorsed the principle that slaveholders immigrating from Brazil should be able to retain

---

65. Joaquim Pedro Celestino Soares, *Additamentos aos quadros navaes e epopeia naval portugueza, dedicados e offericidos, a sua magestate el-rei o Senhor d. Luiz* . . . , IV (Lisbon, 1869), 161–162; Gabriel Paquette, *Imperial Portugal in the Age of Atlantic Revolutions: The Luso-Brazilian World, ca. 1770–1850* (Cambridge, 2013), 142–143, 194–195.

66. ACML, caixa 311–1, Casa da Índia, Apr. 10, 1822.

their enslaved property. Emphasizing the benign piety of the kingdom, the administrative body ordered that the man "be instructed in the dogmas of your Holy Faith" before being delivered back to his ship and owner.[67]

In the wake of independence, numerous slaveholders in Brazil—many of whom were Portuguese and motivated by a growing anti-Portuguese sentiment in the former colony—made hasty waterborne escapes, often with their enslaved property in tow. When they landed on Portuguese shores, they pursued the crown's sanctification of their absolute property rights, beseeching royal authorities to ignore the 1761 law. Enslaved individuals, laboring as domestic servants, mariners, and artisans, displaced once more, quickly became aware that they could exploit the political uncertainty of the moment to litigate the lawfulness of their bondage. In response to slaveholders' attempts to circumvent the law, Black Catholic brotherhoods again mobilized to ensure its application. The brothers of São Benedito were particularly ambitious in their attempts to apply the free-soil law in a moment of imperial crisis that saw a sharp rise in the number of appeals. In 1824, they petitioned naval commander Jozé da Costa Corto to release and free three enslaved individuals: a Mozambican man named Jozé da Costa, an Angolan man named Antônio Maria, and an unnamed Black woman who served Corto in his home. The two men had traveled to Lisbon on the war brig *Infante Dom Sebastião* from Rio de Janeiro, presumably as either mariners or Corto's personal servants. The commander curtly denied that the three enslaved individuals were eligible for manumission under the 1761 law.[68]

Free-soil law in the wake of independence was not only an issue for former plantation owners. As imperial military personnel returned to the metropole

67. McKinley, "Standing on Shaky Ground," *UC Irvine Law Review,* IV (2014), 149; ACML, caixa 311–1, Casa da Índia, Apr. 10, 1822. The year 1824 hosted a particularly large number of petitions using the free-soil law. Also that year, Antônio Jorge, another enslaved Black man from Rio de Janeiro, successfully appealed to metropolitan law to secure his freedom from his owner, Miguel Inácio Machado. See ANTT, Feitos Findos, Juízo da Índia e Mina, maço 18, numero 12, caixa 142, "Acção civel de embargos á primeira em que e autor Antônio Jorge, homem preto e réu Miguel Inacio Machado"; ACML, caixa 311–1, Casa da Índia, Mar. 27, 1824.

68. ACML, caixa 311–1, Real Irmandade de São Benedicto, sentada na Igreja de São Francisco desta cidade, Feb. 7, 1824. Jozé Machado Pinto, the admiral of the Royal Navy Arsenal in Bahia, petitioned the secretary of state to allow him to legally transport eight of his slaves, five young women and three men, to Lisbon in violation of the 1761 law. See ibid., "Tendo Jozé Machado Pinto de voltar á Capitania da Bahia de Todos os Santos," Feb. 20, 1824.

from Brazil, the legal status of their slaves became a particularly complicated matter for Portuguese naval authorities. At stake once again was the question of whether enslaved men laboring on royal vessels would be subject to the mariners' exception, even if they were not in the service of the trading ships that were the focus of the 1776 law. In 1824, Jozé Mozambique, a sailor on the royal ship *Venus,* tested the limits of the 1800 amendment to the free-soil principle. After taking several voyages on the same naval vessel in the preceding years, including to Cabo Verde and Madeira, he arrived in Lisbon. There, with support from an unnamed Catholic brotherhood, Jozé fled the dominion of his owner, Commander Costa Coito. According to the letter of the law, Jozé did not qualify for the mariners' exception, as he was not a "preto do comércio," or a part of the empire's merchant marine. This did not satisfy authorities, who had the man imprisoned in an effort to ascertain his legal status. After launching inquiries into the legitimacy of Jozé's free status, including contacting his owner, the secretary of state verified that Jozé was indeed registered on the *Venus.* What transpired next is unclear. One thing was evident: Brazilian independence signaled an opportunity, however fleeting or unlikely, for men like Jozé to seize the prospect of a new, liberated life in the former metropole. Their aspirations collided with a Portuguese military administration dealing with the loss of its most prosperous colony, skeptical about expanding access to manumission and willing to use the coercive powers of the state to forestall enslaved individuals' attempts to achieve their freedom.[69]

Despite such bureaucratic obstacles to the application of the original alvará, the tradition of legal claims-making pioneered by captive cosmopolitan mariners inspired a new generation of enslaved litigants who often labored outside of maritime professions. After 1822, women and children represented a growing portion of freedom petitions, reflecting the increasing diversity of returnees to the metropole and the continuing strategic relevance of the legal foundation that captive cosmopolitan mariners had developed. In 1823, the brothers of São Benedito, acting on behalf of Marianna and her two daughters, Carlota and Henriqueta, addressed the king himself after the family fled from Rio de Janeiro. Her owner had taken Marianna (originally from the Mina Coast) as well as another slave, José (from Benguela), to Lisbon following Brazil's declaration of independence. Marianna and her daughters were all granted freedom in accordance with the law of 1761, and their former owner,

---

69. Ibid., Feb. 28, 1824, "Tenho a honra de enviar a V. Ex.a a Representação incluza do Administrador Geral d'Alfândega Grande de Lisboa."

Jacinto de Araújo, was ordered to pay court costs to the brotherhood. Families escaping together faced enormous vulnerabilities and unique risks, as mothers attempted to secure better lives not only for themselves but also for their young children. Maria Luiza, an enslaved woman originally from the Mina Coast, fled her owner in 1824. With her son, Custódio, in hand and carrying a small bundle of possessions with her, she relied on the intercession of the Irmandade de Jesús, Maria, e José, which appealed to the Juízo da Índia e Mina on the young family's behalf. Six years later, the same brotherhood, nestled in the Convent of Nossa Senhora do Monte do Carmo, aided an enslaved woman from Angola, Anna, in securing her freedom from her owner, Lourenço da Costa Dourado, in the name of "royal Justice in the Cause of liberty." Clearly, women such as Maria Luiza and Anna would not have been subject to the mariner exception.[70]

As the rhetorical power of the idea of liberty spread across the Atlantic world, appeals made by Black Catholic brothers on behalf of the enslaved also became both more confident and more ambitious in argumentation and scope. They began embracing a broad principle of freedom beyond individual deeds of Christian charity and singular acts of liberation for the particularly deserving. Emphasizing protection for the weak and vulnerable, the Irmandade de São Benedito's assistance proved vital to João Caetano da Costa, an enslaved man from Mozambique, who obtained his freedom after his owner had left him penniless in a hospital. The Irmandade Jesus Maria José, meanwhile, rescued Pascoal Pires Alves de Carvalho after he had been falsely enslaved by Manuel Ribeiro da Silva, who was planning to kidnap him and take him to Pernambuco. The brotherhood insisted that Carvalho was but a

70. Nogueira da Silva and Grinberg, "Soil Free from Slaves," *Slavery and Abolition,* XXXII (2011), 436. The court costs totaled 5$723 réis. See ANTT, Feitos Findos, Juízo da Índia e Mina, maço 12, numero 12, caixa 136, "Execução de sentença em que é autora a Irmandade de São Benedito e réu Jacinto de Araujo e José de Sá." On Maria Luiza's case, see ibid., maço 33, numero 16, caixa 157, "Acção civil de embargos a primeira em que a autora a Irmandade de Jesus, Maria, José, erecta no Convent do Monte do Carmo, por Maria Luiza e seu filho Custódio, e réu Custódio José Ribeiro Guimares, 1824." In the same period, Luciano, an enslaved Congolese man, alongside Carolina, a creole woman, escaped from their owner with the assistance of the Irmandade de Nossa Senhora do Rosário and acquired their cartas de alforria. See ibid., maço 2, numero 1, caixa 126, "Autos cíveis de requerimento para embargo em que é requerente Joaquim José da Costa Portugal e réu Luciano, homem preto"; ibid., Cartório do escrivão Bernardo José Saraiva da Guerra, maço 31, numero 1, caixa 155, "Acção sumária de liberade em que e autora a Irmandade de Jesús, Maria, e José e réu Lourenço da Costa."

"tender creature" who was "brotherless" and alone in the city. The collective argued that they were working for the "cause of securing the *Alforria* of all our Black Brothers" in order to bring "all that is for the good of our Justice" within Portugal. Openly proclaiming their ambitious aims, a cohort of the city's brotherhoods stressed the culmination of their efforts to be the freeing of all members. Invoking an eminently Catholic sensibility, the brothers of São Benedito were adamant that a wave of free-soil manumissions would lead to the universal achievement of "Justice" in the kingdom, a stance that flew in the face of the original free-soil law's argument that social disruption and the spread of vice would ensue.[71]

In fashioning themselves as sources of legal aid for the enslaved, many Black Catholic residents of Lisbon came to articulate radical ideas about liberty as man's natural state. These self-appointed guardians of their enslaved "brothers," in conversation with fugitive mariners who sought protection among their ranks and with legal authorities, grew to embrace an expansive vision of manumission that would eventually include everyone of African descent. Conceptualizing legal processes as an effective means for achieving general freedom, they worked on a case-by-case basis to liberate those in need. By denying a boundary in worth and status between free and enslaved Catholics, Black and white parishioners, the brotherhoods' legal activism articulated a universal Christian humanity that called into question the very legitimacy of slavery itself.[72]

71. Ibid., maço 33, numero 12, caixa 157, "Acção cível de embargos a primeira em que é autora a Irmandade de São Benedito erecta no Convento de S. Francisco por José Caetano da Costa, homem preto e réu Constantino Guelffi"; ibid., maço 38, numero 8, caixa 162, "Acção cível de liberade e embargos a primeira em que a autora a irmandade Jesus Maria José, erecta no Convent de Nossa Senhora do Carmo, representante de Pascoal Pires Alves de Carvalho, homem preto, e réu Manuel Ribeiro da Silva." The brothers' pursuit of a universal "Justice" challenged proslavery views that held that "on the other side of liberty lay disorder and lawlessness" (Premo, *Enlightenment on Trial*, 192).

72. Ideas about racial hierarchy within the Portuguese empire were tied to evolving notions about slavery's legitimacy and broader processes of manumission. For instance, the 1773 alvará, part of a larger set of Pombaline reforms, linked emancipatory law to an elevation in freedmen's social status by terminating rules that excluded free Black inhabitants of Portugal from certain professions, trades, privileges, and honors. During this period, free Black inhabitants of the Portuguese Atlantic, utilizing the language of royal dispensation of privileges and mercy, argued that the enslavement of their ancestors should not mark them with permanent social stigma. See Luis Geraldo Silva and Priscila de Lima Souza, "'Sem a

For administrators, liberty still had its limits. Beyond the disruption to the maritime labor force, as enslaved seamen escaped to Portuguese ships and waterfronts, the royal navy faced potential liabilities from slaveowners seeking restitution.[73] In 1825, however, a sea change in Portuguese policy occurred. The customhouse of Lisbon began to issue cartas de liberdade for Black bondsmen on Portuguese ships of war. Critical of Brazilian immigrants who had surreptitiously stowed their slaves on naval vessels to circumvent the 1761 edict, customs officials disembarked and issued certificates of freedom for individuals unlawfully held in bondage. It is not possible to read this decision in isolation, however. The spate of manumissions came after years of determined pressure by the Black Catholic brotherhoods, who regularly challenged the legal limits of the 1776 alvará and subsequent directives restricting the free-soil principle's application. In contesting the illegal maneuvers of slaveholders, royal officials established their own independent legal prerogatives in upholding the letter of the 1761 law. Though drawing on the long-standing principle of the king's right to "intervene in and govern matters concerning relations between subjects," even in contradiction of the wishes and property-holding rights of slaveowners, the rigorous and consistent execution of the 1761 law only crystallized after a protracted period of legal advocacy by fugitive mariners with the crucial assistance of free Black inhabitants of Lisbon. Though free soil did not evolve into a universal legal principle of freedom in the period, it did survive a barrage of challenges by slaveowners themselves, successfully inscribing legal limits on their paternal power over bondspeople and creating spatial restrictions on property-holding rights in slaves.[74]

The vernacular significance of Portugal's free-soil principle continued to inform the maritime marronage strategies of enslaved people across the Luso-Atlantic world. In 1839, Joaquim Antônio da Costa, a Black cabin boy, arrived

---

nota de libertos': Mudanças nas petições de afrodescendentes livres da América portuguesa ao longo do século XVIII," *Taller de la Hisotria,* IX (2017), 28–56, esp. 33.

73. In 1821, João Antônio, enslaved mariner, escaped his owner, Captain José Joaquim Pinto Cascáes, master of the brig *Marques de Cascáes,* to another naval vessel, the *São Sebastião,* prompting a request for restitution and the return of the fugitive bondsman. Maritime slaveowners lodged further petitions for restitution in the following years. See ACML, caixa 311–1, Aug. 22, 1821, Dec. 10, 1821, Aug. 5, 1822, Aug., 22, 1822, Feb., 28, 1824.

74. Ibid., caixa 311–1, "Constando-me que o Preto Pedro, que veio a esta Capital na qualidade d'escravo," Aug. 17, 1825; ibid., "Constando-me, que alguns Emigrados do Brazil," Aug. 25, 1825; ibid., caixa 311–1, Dec. 24, 1825, Feb. 14, 1829; Marquez, "Afflicted Slaves,

in Lisbon and attempted to take advantage of the law of June 6, 1776, which, he argued, "favor[ed] the liberty of man, which has always existed as a presumption of the law." This rhetoric, echoing that of petitioners four decades earlier, voiced the sentiment that Portuguese imperial law favored the cause of enslaved people's freedom, despite its explicit restrictions. Such language points to how captive cosmopolitans pioneered a capacious and multivalent tradition of legal argumentation that undergirded an expansive understanding of laws such as the alvará of 1761 and subsequent "emancipatory" decrees. Never content with merely applying the strict letter of the law, enslaved individuals had repeatedly sought, sometimes successfully, to expand its meaning and scope. Their efforts revealed a sophisticated knowledge of colonial law and reflected the ways highly mobile enslaved individuals constructed networks of information that disseminated knowledge of metropolitan legal principles throughout the Portuguese empire and beyond. Such networks—rooted in the associational, religious, and social life of Black Lisbon—contributed to a perceived crisis among colonial administrators about the economic and political stability of the Portuguese empire itself.[75]

The elaboration of these new social geographies and ties of cooperation came to threaten—particularly in the minds of colonial administrators—the stability of slavery in Brazil. Seeking immunity from their owners' claims of possession, many mariners returned to Brazilian colonies, where they circulated information about emancipatory Portuguese law.[76] Enslaved peoples' furtive channels of person-to-person communication produced subversive but ephemeral informational networks. The transatlantic transmission of rumor in turn encouraged additional fugitivity in the colonies, as a diverse

Faithful Vassals," *Slavery and Abolition*, XLIII (2022), 93. The order reprimanding immigrant Brazilians for hiding their bondspeople on ships of war in "contravention" of the 1761 law referred to both enslaved men and women; however, only men were manumitted by name in the following years. See ACML, caixa 311–1, "Constando-me, que no Brigue Escuna Luiza," Dec. 24, 1825.

75. ACML, caixa 311–1, Lisbon, July 22, 1839.

76. Like European free-soil provisions, the emancipatory laws crafted during the Haitian Revolution also fostered a groundswell in enslaved people's maritime networks of political communication and rumor; see Ada Ferrer, *Freedom's Mirror: Cuba and Haiti in the Age of Revolution* (Cambridge, 2014), 44–82; Ferrer, "Haiti, Free Soil, and Antislavery in the Revolutionary Atlantic," *American Historical Review*, CXVII (2012), 40–66; Cristina Soriano, *Tides of Revolution: Information, Insurgencies, and the Crisis of Colonial Rule in Venezuela* (Albuquerque, N.M., 2018), 185–188.

array of enslaved people—not merely seamen—increasingly pursued metropolitan legal claims-making as an avenue to secure individual liberation.

The protestations of the viscount of Anadia at the start of the nineteenth
century highlighted the effectiveness with which enslaved men and women
were able to achieve individual manumission using the principle of free soil,
and how maritime journeys to the metropole facilitated marronage in the
decades after the free-soil principle took effect. The impetus for desertion
and fugitivity provided by the 1761 alvará drew on a long history of the judicial sanctioning of transjurisdictional escape from slavery in the Spanish and
Portuguese colonial Atlantic. That said, the law was also one of the earliest
to make freedom, as Edlie Wong has argued, "coextensive with . . . territorial
and jurisdictional boundaries." As one of the first spaces to "territorialize,"
or geographically define, freedom in the Atlantic, Portugal faced mounting
challenges in controlling the mobility and thus legal status of an indispensable
group of laborers as they traversed borders. Capitalizing on administrative
designs intended to modernize the empire, enslaved men and women utilized
knowledge of the law as well as strategies to represent themselves as "insid-
ers"—Portuguese imperial subjects, vassals, Catholics, or members of the
royal navy—to strengthen their appeals to royal authority. In asserting the
limits of slaveholders' power over them, litigants invoked the authority of the
Portuguese imperial state and its legal prerogative to intervene in master-slave
relations. In the process, they also produced evocative commentaries on their
experiences of bondage, shedding light on their understanding of their own
labor, relationships, and religious affiliations.[77]

The freedom claims made over seven decades by enslaved Afro-Brazilian
mariners and others revealed an evolving Black Atlantic legal imaginary shaped
by the tumultuous politics of the Age of Revolutions and post-independence
period. Notions of natural rights encountered personal experience and Catholic sociability to forge new forms of cosmopolitan consciousness for seafaring
captives. For many enslaved mariners, the agency and mobility afforded by
maritime life led to a dramatic divergence between the proprietorship of legal
freedom and their quotidian experiences of self-possession and independence. Although the physical mobilities fostered by seafaring offered myriad
possibilities for clandestine escape to legal jurisdictions that did not recognize
one's slavery, mariners preferred to flee to ports that housed legal bodies ca-

77. Edlie L. Wong, *Neither Fugitive nor Free: Atlantic Slavery, Freedom Suits, and the
Legal Culture of Travel* (New York, 2009), 2; Candido, "African Freedom Suits and Portuguese Vassal Status," *Slavery and Abolition*, XXXII (2011), 447–459.

pable of conferring legal freedom; in the process, they cultivated new methods of political and legal agency. The longer enslaved mariners dwelled in the cosmopolitan milieu of the port city, the more their proliferating social ties and varied interactions with both free and enslaved Black individuals nourished an increasingly complex legal imaginary. The pervasiveness of cultural and intellectual exchange in these maritime communities enabled such subalterns to draw on diverse sources of legal knowledge and strategy, facilitating their own creative interpretations of Portuguese imperial law. In conjunction with Catholic brotherhoods in the metropole, who converted religious spaces into places of refuge and redemption for fugitives, mariners remained steadfast in their free-soil claims. Their actions highlighted the longevity of vernacular conceptions of the law's emancipatory promise within both Black maritime communities and religious enclaves across the larger South Atlantic world as seafaring slaves spread information across the Atlantic. Free soil enabled mariners to seize freedom on their own terms. It provided a path to manumission that granted them a semblance of legal rights within Portuguese realms—a form of freedom in stark contrast to the much more circumscribed iteration of liberty conferred by the forced emancipations of the era of British abolition at sea beginning in the early nineteenth century.

CHAPTER 5

Black Mariners in the Age of Abolition

In 1812, while anchored off the coast of Ouidah, the enslaved mariner Jozé Angolla had his life turned upside down. Officers of the British navy boarded his ship, the *São Miguel Triunfante,* and detained all on board for conducting illegal slaving—at least, as it was understood by British law. Jozé was subsequently imprisoned and taken to Freetown, Sierra Leone, where he would likely have been detained in the colony's "captured Negro yard." There, the archival record of his life concludes. But his was a story with larger resonances for similarly situated captive cosmopolitans in the Age of Abolition. Black mariners had a front-row seat to momentous transformations in the South Atlantic beginning in the late eighteenth century, an era defined by both intensified slaving activity and countervailing abolitionist challenges. At stake for men such as Jozé was the threat of assaults to both their lives and livelihoods. In fundamental ways, abolitionism raised questions about the quality of their captive existences. In contrast to those who sought out manumission and sanctuary in Lisbon, the essential maritime workers of the Bahian slave trade experienced increasing vulnerability and turmoil during the rise of British antislavery. In the ports of Portugal, enslaved seamen had taken a measure designed to deepen slavery's dominance in the colonies and remade it into a tool of liberation; but on the high seas near West Africa and later Brazil, they found British antislavery's effects to be far from emancipatory. Conditional freedom, as conferred by white British abolitionists in West Africa, could be a kind of reenslavement, at least for men like Jozé. For a multitude of enslaved mariners in the South Atlantic, British emancipation held far less appeal than the forms of liberation Black religious communities and mariners had collectively envisioned in Portugal during earlier decades.[1]

---

1. Padraic X. Scanlan, *Freedom's Debtors: British Antislavery in Sierra Leone in the Age of Revolution* (New Haven, Conn., 2017), 99. As Briton James Prior noted, "Jealousies of course exist on many points; African slavery is one of the principal; for the trading part of the people, perhaps I may add every class, affected by it in some way or another, cling to this object as if it were their last stake. All other considerations give way to it. Portugal and

This chapter charts how captive cosmopolitans navigated the shifting political culture of freedom in the larger Atlantic world. It also examines Bahian captains' and merchants' responses to British antislavery, which included the outright violation of diplomatic agreements and the articulation of a distinctive vision of liberalism that enshrined the legal sanctity of slaveholders' property rights. Indeed, centering the lived experiences of enslaved mariners suggests the impossibility of disentangling these two overlapping processes. It was a revolutionary moment on both sides of the Atlantic. As the Haitian Revolution upended an entire slave society and inaugurated the Age of Revolutions, elites and even some enslaved residents of Bahia expected that stunning example of radical emancipation to inspire similar upheavals in Brazil. In Bahia, however, such liberatory violence remained only intermittent. In response to the precipitous decline of plantation production in Saint-Domingue, the waning sugar sector in Bahia rapidly expanded and created an exploding demand for enslaved labor, intensifying the volume of the Bahian slave trade, which peaked between 1801 and 1825. Simultaneously, British abolitionist pressures in West African slave trading ports and on the high seas placed the lives of Black mariners in an ever more precarious position. British vessels frequently targeted Bahian slaving ships, leading in some instances to the imprisonment of enslaved captive cosmopolitans. Black mariners' working lives thus increasingly functioned to satisfy the voracious demands of Bahian planters in a context of growing vulnerability and risk.[2]

The structure of the Bahian slave trade had also afforded captive cosmopolitans their own set of commercial prerogatives, which were threatened by the possibility that British ships would confiscate not only enslaved Africans

Spain, England and France, Wellington, Bonaparte and the Prince, may all go headlong to the shades, provided their darling traffic—the subject of their waking and sleeping dreams, be but permitted to remain" (Prior, *Voyage along the Eastern Coast of Africa, to Mosambique, Johanna, and Quiloa; to St. Helena; to Rio de Janeiro, Bahia, and Pernambuco in Brazil, in the Nisus Frigate* [London, 1819], 99).

2. For a discussion of the Haitian Revolution's reverberations throughout the Atlantic, see Ada Ferrer, *Freedom's Mirror: Cuba and Haiti in the Age of Revolution* (New York, 2014); Ashli White, *Encountering Revolution: Haiti and the Making of the Early Republic* (Baltimore, 2010); Alfred N. Hunt, *Haiti's Influence on Antebellum America: Slumbering Volcano in the Caribbean* (Baton Rouge, 1988); Julia Gaffield, *Haitian Connections in the Atlantic World: Recognition after Revolution* (Chapel Hill, N.C., 2015); Rashauna Johnson, *Slavery's Metropolis: Unfree Labor in New Orleans during the Age of Revolutions* (New York, 2016); David Geggus, "Slave Rebellion during the Age of Revolution," in Wim Klooster and Gert Oostindie, eds., *Curaçao in the Age of Revolutions, 1795–1800* (Leiden, 2011); Cristina

but the trading goods held in ships' liberty chests. As Black mariners were thrust into these tense, labyrinthine legal and military dramas, they formed alliances with their employers, even as these same captains reduced seafaring bondsmen into expendable commodities whose monetary value far outweighed their human worth. The tumultuous interimperial politics wrought by abolition at sea heightened Black mariners' vulnerability, leaving them with the limited option to accept circumscribed emancipation in a new imperial context or an uneasy—and likely desperate—loyalty to slaving ship crews as the mariners made calculations about their own lives, their economic futures, and the possibility of achieving tangible forms of social mobility.

Slave traders and their allies also experienced the Age of Abolition as a remade world defined by peril and instability. By 1815, Bahian slaving ships were coming face-to-face with perhaps their greatest-ever threat: the British empire's military mobilization to suppress the transatlantic slave trade, spearheaded by the Royal Navy. Much of the literature on the era of the trade's global suppression has focused on the intricate diplomatic and national political strategies of metropolitan actors in Britain and Portugal, but the project of abolition also unfolded in arenas located far from European parliaments and courts. By exploring the dynamics of abolition on slaving vessels on the West African coast, this chapter emphasizes the interwoven dilemmas that the suppression of the slave trade posed for both slaving merchants and maritime laborers.[3]

British abolitionism at sea and its attendant violence severely tested solidarity among shipmates. The intimacies of shipboard life played a seminal role in helping crews escape detection by the Royal Navy's antislaving forces.

Soriano, *Tides of Revolution: Information, Insurgencies, and the Crisis of Colonial Rule in Venezuela* (Albuquerque, N.M., 2018). The slave trade to Bahia peaked in the years 1801 to 1825 as an estimated 258,736 Africans were disembarked in the port. Between 1811 and 1819, enslaved people from the Bight of Benin swelled the city's population, with Nagôs representing 15 percent of the enslaved population, Hausas 17 percent, and Geges 20.4 percent. See Maria José de Souza Andrade, *A mão de obra escrava em Salvador, 1811–1860* (São Paulo, 1988), 189. Slave trade estimates courtesy of *Voyages*.

3. A number of scholars have explored the political, ideological, diplomatic, and legal dimensions of Britain's suppression of the transatlantic slave trade beginning in 1808 and Portuguese efforts at containing abolitionist advances. They include Leslie Bethell, *The Abolition of the Brazilian Slave Trade: Britain, Brazil, and the Slave Trade Question, 1807–1869* (Cambridge, 1970); Christopher Leslie Brown, *Moral Capital: Foundations of British Abolitionism* (Williamsburg, Va., and Chapel Hill, N.C., 2006); João Pedro Marques, *The Sounds of Silence: Nineteenth-Century Portugal and the Abolition of the Slave Trade,* trans.

Sentiments of solidarity also assisted captains and mariners in constructing coherent legal defenses after being apprehended, enabling them to provide (often fraudulent) justifications for their breach of international treaties. Yet this intimacy could do little to save individual enslaved and free sailors from imprisonment or even death inflicted by British ships. As high-stakes diplomatic clashes within the royal courts of Europe and later Brazil reverberated throughout the Atlantic, they inadvertently amplified the bodily insecurity of Brazilian mariners at sea, who became subject to apprehension and forced relocation to Sierra Leone. As Britain deepened its antislavery quest, it sought to curtail the transatlantic slave trade through force, seizing and searching ships with the aid of superior firepower and ethical resolve. Clandestine slaving became a far more dangerous prospect for crews and captives than legal slaving had once been. But despite its intimidations, Britain's military assertiveness failed to substantively quell transatlantic slaving to Bahia.

Messy maritime battles largely played out on the western coast of Africa, bringing a capitalist slaveholding power into irrevocable conflict with a capitalist abolitionist one. This "war between the whites," as one West African potentate termed it, hardened Bahian merchants' proslavery resolve. Contentious interactions with British military and legal officials appointed to Sierra Leone's Mixed Commission Court, which was responsible for adjudicating suspected traffickers, not only evoked feelings of indignation but inspired Bahian elites to formulate complex schemes to evade the letter of the metropolitan law. Though slavers rarely recorded the violence they themselves committed against enslaved individuals imprisoned on their vessels, mer-

Richard Wall (New York, 2006); Jenny S. Martinez, *The Slave Trade and the Origins of International Human Rights Law* (Oxford, 2012); Scanlan, *Freedom's Debtors*. For interpretations of mariners' and "liberated" Africans' experiences of the perils of suppression, see João José Reis, Flávio dos Santos Gomes, and Marcus J. M. de Carvalho, *The Story of Rufino: Slavery, Freedom, and Islam in the Black Atlantic,* trans. H. Sabrina Gledhill (New York, 2019), 128–186; Walter Hawthorne, "Gorge: An African Seaman and His Flights from 'Freedom' Back to 'Slavery' in the Early Nineteenth Century," *Slavery and Abolition,* XXXI (2010), 411–428; Hawthorne, "'Being Now, as It Were, One Family': Shipmate Bonding on the Slave Vessel *Emília,* in Rio de Janeiro and throughout the Atlantic World," *Luso-Brazilian Review,* XLV (2008), 53–77; Martine Jean, "The Slave Ship 'Maria da Gloria' and the Bare Life of Blackness in the Age of Emancipation," *Slavery and Abolition,* XLII (2021), 522–544; Christopher Lloyd, *The Navy and the Slave Trade: The Suppression of the African Slave Trade in the Nineteenth Century* (London, 2012); Siân Rees, *Sweet Water and Bitter: The Ships That Stopped the Slave Trade* (London, 2009); Beatriz G. Mamigonian, *Africanos livres: A abolição do tráfico de escravos no Brasil* (São Paulo, 2017).

chants and captains wrote and testified in exhaustive detail about the real or imagined violence perpetrated against themselves and their property by British antislaving crews. In the process, they elaborated ideas about the sanctity of their own commercial prerogatives, contesting the notion that diplomatic constraints could be placed on international merchant capitalist exchange.[4]

THE WINDS OF REVOLUTION IN BAHIA

In late-eighteenth- and early-nineteenth-century Bahia, an influx of enslaved Africans and the movement of Black residents through revolutionary hot spots in the Atlantic world aroused suspicions among slaveholders. The Revolt of the Tailors (Conjuração dos Alfaiates) in 1798 proved their fears were far from baseless. Fomented by free mulatto artisans and some enslaved Africans in the city, the revolt seized on the radical ideas of the French Revolution. The rebels hoped to upend the colonial social order by establishing Bahia as a separate nation, independent of Brazil. They also endeavored to abolish slavery, challenging the rigid racial hierarchies that kept them politically disenfranchised and impoverished. The uprising was quickly suppressed; in the years following, the conservative, slaveholding class that dominated Salvador's political fortunes watched with paranoia for signs of seditious activity, particularly by recently arrived enslaved Africans, who launched successive but failed revolts in 1807, 1814, and 1822. Palpable fears of violent uprisings from below mingled with concerns about shadowy conspiracies involving suspicious elites.[5]

4. On British capitalists' support of abolition, see Eric Williams, *Capitalism and Slavery* (Chapel Hill, N.C., 1994). On Brazilian slaving merchants' capitalism, see Fernando A. Novais, *Portugal e Brasil na crise do antigo sistema colonial (1777–1808)*, 4th ed. (São Paulo, 1986), 106–109. Originally, captured slaving ships were tried before the British vice admiralty court, but on July 28, 1817, a convention established an Anglo-Portuguese court in both Sierra Leone and Rio de Janeiro. See Marques, *Sounds of Silence*, 46.

5. João José Reis, *Slave Rebellion in Brazil: The Muslim Uprising of 1835 in Bahia*, trans. Arthur Brakel (Baltimore, 1993), 40–45. Independence movements spearheaded by the popular classes continued to be an omnipresent feature of the late colonial period. In 1817, just north of Bahia, the Pernambucan Revolution expressed antiroyalist sentiment. While occupying Recife, rebels seized royal symbols and disavowed hierarchy and onerous taxes. Several years later, widespread anti-Portuguese violence perpetrated by the popular classes followed Brazil's declaration of independence in 1822–1824. See Javier A. Galván, "Tailors' Revolt (1798)," in Junius Rodriguez, ed., *Encyclopedia of Emancipation and Abolition in the Transatlantic World*, 3 vols. (London, 2007), 518–519; Reis, *Slave Rebellion in Brazil*, trans.

Salvador's status as a culturally and demographically porous port city—one inundated by new arrivals—did little to mitigate the worries of those most committed to the stability of Bahian slave society. In their darkest, most anxious moments, Bahian slavers fixated on what they saw as the conjoined threats of "jacobinite" revolution, subaltern political activity, and foreign influence. In the uncertain period following the French and Haitian revolutions, Bahian elites began to think of Jacobinism and abolitionism as politically indistinguishable. Anti-French conspiracies tied together fears of antiroyalist insurrection and antislavery subversion, and suspected French influences became the target of authorities' surveillance. Freemasons, in particular, came to embody the spirit of French revolutionary fervor in the minds of the empire's elite, but enslaved and freed populations more broadly were also considered potential vectors of revolutionary contagion. In the same period, several free Black and *pardo* militiamen were apprehended in Rio de Janeiro sporting medallions with portraits of Jean-Jacques Dessalines, the revolutionary leader and new emperor of Haiti. Such an image would have suggested to Bahian slaveholders, in no uncertain terms, what the new era of abolitionist sentiment could mean for their social and economic authority.[6]

Slaveholding elites viewed ports as the spaces most susceptible to the infiltration of foreign strains of political radicalism. Such fears were undoubtedly acute in Salvador da Bahia. In a city defined by a proximity to water and well-established connections to the larger Atlantic world, the continuous movement of people, profound social and cultural differences, and ravages of

Brakel, 23–25; Gabriel Paquette, *Imperial Portugal in the Age of Atlantic Revolutions: The Luso-Brazilian World, c. 1770–1860* (Cambridge, 2013), 105–106; Richard Graham, *Feeding the City: From Street Market to Liberal Reform in Salvador, Brazil, 1780–1860* (Austin, 2010).

6. Luiz R. B. Mott, "A revolução dos negros do Haiti e o Brasil," *Mensario do Arquivo Nacional,* XIII, no. 1 (January 1982), 3–10. A 1798 letter from Dom Rodrigo de Souza Coutinho to the king of Portugal informed the crown that various inhabitants had been denounced for expressing "Jacobinite principles." He advised that the crown should counteract these political currents with the "greatest severity" so they did not spread. Such rapid measures must have failed to materialize, since a year later he warned that royal administrators needed to be vigilant because the "contamination" of "Jacobins and revolutionaries" had invaded Brazilian provinces, including his own. During this period, printed materials from France were banned in the colony. See APEB, Cartas Régias, LXXXV, documento 13; ibid., LXXXIX, documento 95. The prince regent, João VI, sovereign of the Brazilian colonies after 1815, remained vigilant about the city's three masonic lodges, whose membership included the governor, archbishop, and local elites, fearing they secretly nurtured a spirit of "treason and jacobinism." See Prior, *Voyage along the Eastern Coast of Africa,* 104–105.

inequality guaranteed that a specter of rebellion hung over the heads of local elites. A dramatic example of the latent possibilities for violent political sedition arose in 1814 out of occupational bonds forged on the Bahian seafront. Two hundred fifty enslaved insurgents who had traveled from a suburban *quilombo* (community of enslaved fugitives) converged on the fishing marina and made common cause with local Black watermen. After burning their fishing nets, the crowd moved through Itapuã, a village near Salvador, executing not only white merchants but also a number of enslaved men and women who refused to join their cause. Animated by a desire for freedom, a proclaimed love for a king who they insisted was an abolitionist, and a goal of killing whites and pardos, they were violently suppressed by Bahian militiamen after setting several sugar plantations aflame.[7]

This was a relatively spectacular example of revolutionary unrest, but forms of social disorder on Salvador's waterfront could spring from mundane, everyday conflicts. Contests over masculine honor and public reputation sparked by interactions between the multinational, multiethnic seamen who populated Salvador's pulsating waterfront heightened elites' sense of peril. In 1816, a sailing ship anchored in Bahia after a long voyage from another slave society, Jamaica. As the English crew from the *Portsmouth* disembarked in the lower city from longboats, one of the foreign mariners traded insults with local Black seamen stationed nearby. Perhaps a misunderstanding—or, more likely, the result of a clash between two distinct colonial ideologies of race and hierarchy—the war of words did not end there. Seeking revenge, a number of Black seamen sought out "the first English official they saw" the following day. By chance spying Lieutenant John Calthorpe, a mariner on another ship, the men turned violent, resulting in Calthorpe's death. His lifeless body, a testimony to the aggressions that could quickly materialize at such watery international crossroads, was returned to Europe aboard the same vessel it had arrived on.[8]

7. Reis, *Slave Rebellion in Brazil,* trans. Brakel, 46–47. Fears of violent uprisings from below mingled with outlandish theories of shadowy conspiracies involving moneyed elites, and the city's merchants were far from unanimous in their suspicion of revolutionary activity. For instance, Bahian pardo slaving ship captain Jozé Dias ventured south to the Río de La Plata in 1810 to participate in anticolonial conflict in Spanish America and publicly expressed "great happiness" at the triumph of the May Revolution in Buenos Aires—the first successful battle for independence in South America. See APEB, Cartas Régias, CXII, documento 3; ibid., CXI, documento 137.

8. BNRJ, *Idade d'Ouro do Brazil* (Bahia), Nov. 8, 1816, no. 90.

Salvador's status as a city connected to the larger, increasingly revolutionary Atlantic world shaped Bahians' fears about the contagion of rebellion. Twin suspicions persisted in the minds of propertied Bahians: that Black seamen, in particular, would become vectors of insurrection and that waterfronts, in general, were dangerous environments where radical ideas could infect local servile populations with defiant aspirations. The enslaved residents within the fluid spaces of slaving ports, unlike those confined on the slaving ship, were less easily managed and more prone to engage in acts of disobedience. In 1817, a year after Calthorpe's death, planters from the town of São Francisco in Bahia's interior complained that "the spirit of insurrection is seen among all types of slaves, and is fomented principally by the slaves of the city [of Salvador], where the ideas of liberty have been communicated by black sailors coming from Saint Domingue." Salvador's merchants even went so far as to protest to the Portuguese crown, identifying the rising sense of "insolence" by the enslaved. Unregulated mobility and African and creole watermen's resulting translocal sociability would, they feared, ignite rebellion.[9]

Such suspicions were largely unwarranted, however. Underpinning the social order of Bahia's slave society was always the shadow of violence, and resistance remained dangerous for those who challenged authority. Though slaveholding elites continued to be dismayed by the prospect of violent insurrection by the enslaved and the chance that radical republican ideas could penetrate the colony, such skirmishes never credibly endangered the region's dense network of plantations. Waterfront urban life in Salvador remained unpredictable and treacherous, feeding anxieties about the potential for transgressive politics to emerge from a radicalized local population. The Age of Revolutions and its circulating ideals of freedom, equality, and the increasing legitimacy of political violence would place the significance of these eruptions in a new light. Slaveowners also began to understand their enslaved mariners' mobility in new and more threatening ways. However, other, more existential threats to the enterprise of Bahian slaving were on the horizon.

SLAVING AND ABOLITION AT SEA

The trepidations of Bahian elites notwithstanding, it was British abolitionism—rather than the Haitian Revolution—that upended the day-to-day existence of both slave traders and captive Black mariners. In the wake of Britain's criminalization of its own transatlantic slave trade in 1807, Bahian slaving

9. George Reid Andrews, *Afro-Latin America, 1800–2000* (New York, 2004), 67–68.

vessels navigating to the Mina Coast were placed on a collision course with the Atlantic's most powerful empire. Emboldened by a sense of moral and civilizational superiority, the British government endeavored to create a series of bilateral agreements with the purpose of compelling foreign nations to incrementally conclude their own trade in captive Africans. Leveraging Portugal's political and commercial dependence on Britain in the wake of the Napoleonic Wars, the Strangford Treaties of 1810 forced significant concessions from the obstinate slaving power. The British placed limitations on traders' activities to "the African dominions of the Crown of Portugal," which excluded the Mina Coast from legal Bahian slaving due to its position north of the equator. The diplomatic covenant was followed by a mobilization of Britain's Royal Navy to enforce its evolving legal arguments. The British began a decades-long campaign to capture any vessel engaged in slaving and navigate it to Freetown in Sierra Leone for adjudication and condemnation. British vessels aggressively undertook the role of an oceanic policing force, often acting in advance of explicit legal authorization. Though initially targeting suspected British slavers, the ambiguous parameters of enforcement soon ensnared a spate of Brazilian vessels in antislaving conflict.[10]

10. Brown, *Moral Capital,* 22–23, 26; Seymour Drescher, "Whose Abolition? Popular Pressure and the Ending of the British Slave Trade," *Past and Present,* no. 143 (May 1994), 136–166; Bethell, *Abolition of the Brazilian Slave Trade,* 9; Mary Wills, *Envoys of Abolition: British Naval Officers and the Campaign against the Slave Trade in West Africa* (Liverpool, U.K., 2019), 15–20; Marques, *Sounds of Silence,* 37. The British interpreted the Slave Trade Act of 1807 as a broad mandate to police African ports that hosted the British merchant community. Though principally tasked with suppressing the British trade, royal ships turned to vessels flying the colors of foreign nations, including the Bahian ships using Portuguese flags. The Slave Trade Act was heavily influenced by prize law, but, as Lauren Benton argues, the act built upon a longer tradition of adjudicating captured vessels in the courts of their captors and indicated an expansion of imperial legal power—particularly that of the British empire. A string of seventeen ships, most from Bahia, seized in 1811 and 1812, revealed the ambiguity of the 1810 treaty. The British navy assumed that ports in West Africa fell outside the parameters of Portuguese colonial possessions, with all ports north of the equator deemed illegal for slave trading, whereas Bahian slavers insisted that these active entrepôts were part of Portuguese territory. See Benton, "Abolition and Imperial Law, 1790–1820," *Journal of Imperial and Commonwealth History,* XXXIX (2011), 355–374, esp. 356; Bethell, *Abolition of the Brazilian Slave Trade,* 10; AHU, CU, São Tomé, caixa 45, documento 24, Sept. 28, 1811; ANRJ, fundo 7X, Junta do Comércio, caixa 410, pacote 1, Papers of the *São Miguel Triunfante.*

When the *São Miguel Triunfante* left the port of Bahia for its third-ever voyage, Captain João da Silveira Villas Boas had no awareness it would be the ship's last. The vessel ventured to the port of Ouidah seeking enslaved individuals who would secure the "best price" in Salvador's markets. On April 5, 1812, an English schooner, the *Quiz,* sent an official aboard the Brazilian ship as it anchored off the West African port city. Looking to register the slaver, he requested the ship's royal passport, possibly as a pretext. Several officers from the *Quiz* then boarded the *Triunfante,* followed by more of the crew, who pillaged the ship's goods with what one Brazilian mariner lamented was "manifest violence and force." The invading skeleton crew then navigated the *Triunfante* to Freetown, Sierra Leone, a British-held port in West Africa. Ultimately, the British vice admiralty court in Sierra Leone stripped the *Triunfante* of an array of West African goods, including cloth and palm oil, crew members' nautical instruments, the ship's tackle, guns, and furniture, as well as 132 captives held in the cargo. Those enslaved men, women, and children taken with ships could then be "apprenticed, enlisted in the military, or compelled to work for the colonial government" in Sierra Leone. It was a process that was repeated hundreds of times over the next several decades.[11]

This skirmish at sea stemmed from disagreement about the boundaries of British naval authority in international waters, a conflict that would have profound ramifications for enslaved mariners involved in the transatlantic slave trade. The British asserted that Villas Boas was acting counter to the Strangford Treaties between the crowns of Britain and Portugal. Because the *Triunfante* had sailed north of the equator, the captain of the *Quiz* asserted

11. ANRJ, fundo 7X, Junta do Comércio, caixa 410, pacote 1, Papers of the *São Miguel Triunfante,* 14. The enslaved's "best price" is in comparison to enslaved individuals coming from ports farther south (ibid., 30). The law made slaving ships into legal "prizes" to be taken by any British ship, with the vessel and goods aboard to be auctioned for the private profit of crew members of the capturing vessel if the slaving ship were judged by British vice admiralty courts to be operating in breach of the law. The "right to visit" any ship on the seas gave British ships pretense to execute impromptu searches, whereas the promise of monetary rewards incentivized the taking of ships operating outside of the British empire. Captains and crews received a portion of the profits from seized vessels auctioned after condemnation. In the years following the seizure of Bahian ships, their goods, and enslaved individuals held in cargoes, slaving ship owners staunchly rebuked the Royal Navy's interpretation of the treaty and launched legal petitions demanding restitution of ships and goods that had been confiscated. The information they provided in these legal documents was comprehensive and illuminates the daily operation of these vessels, providing a key body of evidence for my study (Scanlan, *Freedom's Debtors,* 98–101).

his right to detain the *Triunfante* and its crew. Alongside the ship's goods, however, fifteen enslaved mariners were also "condemned." Judged no longer to be the property of their owners, these mariners faced a fate determined by the same legal procedure that had been applied to the ship and its goods. All were held in Freetown, likely alongside other recently confiscated enslaved individuals in the colony's "captured Negro yard." The procedures of the British vice admiralty courts threw captive mariners' status as both laborers and property into sharp relief. The men's fate after their removal to Sierra Leone went unrecorded, however, suggesting their relatively minor place among the priorities of British abolitionism.[12]

Following the proceedings, the *Triunfante*'s proprietor, Francisco Joaquim Carneiro, asserted the illegality of these actions to Portuguese royal authorities: as "Portuguese vassals," the ship's investors were entitled by law to buy and sell "goods," including slaves, on the West African coast. Echoing the logic of the law of nations, which endowed sovereign states with autonomy in commercial relations, he insisted that the licensed vessel, flying Portuguese colors, was acting legally. As Carneiro sought the recovery of his property, the loss of the fifteen enslaved seamen remained a paramount concern. This was not because Carneiro sought their return; rather, he petitioned the British crown for their market value, 200$000 réis, an appropriate sum considering their "age, service and disposition." Like the enslaved individuals held on the ship's lower deck, their worth was now merely monetary in Carneiro's eyes. As a consequence of a formal legal process initiated by British abolitionist commitments, the mariners' value had been reduced to that of commodi-

12. George Macaulay, the marshal of the vice admiralty in Freetown, condemned the vessel in June (ANRJ, fundo 7X, Junta do Comércio, caixa 410, pacote 1, Papers of the *São Miguel Triunfante*, 70). In 1812, pardo ship captain Antônio de Santa Isabel testified that the ports of the "Gold Coast" stretching from Cabo de Palmas to Lagos, where "it was always practice for Portuguese vessels to conduct business," constituted spaces of legal Portuguese trade. Constructing an appeal for the legitimacy of slaving commerce in the region based on precedent, he claimed the heritage of Portuguese dominion over the São Jorge da Mina Castle allowed Brazilian ships to anchor there unmolested by the "acts of violence of the English Vice Admiralty" (ibid., caixa 411, Papers of the *São Lourenço*, 45–47). The fifteen enslaved mariners included six owned by the ship's proprietor, Francisco Joaquim Carneiro (Caetano, Francisco, Custodio, Bento, Estevão, and Felippe), two owned by the ship's captain (Tomaz and Felippe), and seven others belonging to other owners (Joaquim Angola, Gonçalo, Joaquim Gege, Jozé Angolla, Jozé Gabão, Benedito, and Felippe Marinheiro). See ibid., caixa 410, pacote 1, Papers of the *São Miguel Triunfante;* Scanlan, *Freedom's Debtors,* 99.

ties in a ledger, obliterating firmly established distinctions of experience and expertise between maritime workers and enslaved cargoes on Bahian slaving vessels. This result reflects the fundamental irony of British abolitionism: though intended to liberate the enslaved, the work of abolition at sea prioritized punishing the slave trade's perpetrators—including the owners of enslaved mariners—and extracting a semblance of value from captured ships and the Africans they found aboard. In order for Britain to underwrite antislavery's military and legal costs and to provide indentured African labor for the fledgling colony of Sierra Leone, the wishes of captive cosmopolitans, such as the men aboard the *Triunfante,* remained a much more distant concern.[13]

British diplomats continued their attempts to extend their empire's abolitionism internationally. In 1814, they corralled allies at the Congress of Vienna with the hopes of forcing Portugal to acquiesce in ending its transatlantic trade. By 1815, they had achieved a partial victory. The Anglo-Portuguese treaty of that year clarified ambiguous requirements in the earlier agreement to halt the transatlantic slave trade to Brazil: it banned all slaving north of the equator while offering a financial incentive of £300,000 paid to previously seized ships. Such a prohibition, although it would preserve the more lucrative subequatorial trade from Rio de Janeiro to Cabinda, Luanda, and Benguela, would be particularly detrimental to slavers in Bahia and Pernambuco, whose routes operated farther to the north. In spite of this deterrent, Bahian captains still flocked to the West African coast—particularly Elmina, Cabo Corso, Ouidah, Porto Novo, and Lagos—ignoring the terms of the diplomatic agreement that had rendered their enterprise illegal. Many felt confident in their ability to elude British suppression efforts; they continued to utilize the same, profitable routes they had relied on for decades. Indeed, the price of enslaved Africans continued to rise during the era of abolition at sea. In response, Britain dispatched its newly formed West Africa squadron, composed of a motley assortment of royal vessels, to extinguish the trade in international waters.[14]

13. Carneiro's argument on vassals was in keeping with classical pre-Enlightenment defenses of slavery, which justified the taking of foreigners as slaves during war under the law of nations. See Martinez, *Slave Trade and Origins of International Human Rights Law,* 18; ANRJ, fundo 7X, Junta do Comércio, caixa 410, pacote 1, Papers of the *São Miguel Triunfante,* 3, 33.

14. Martinez, *Slave Trade and Origins of International Human Rights Law,* 67–68, 83. For the ambiguities preceding the 1815 treaty, see note 10, above. The treaty also included other financial inducements, such as the cancellation of a £600,000 Portuguese debt to

An evolving series of diplomatic treaties in the following two decades permitted the capture and adjudication of Bahian slaving vessels under varying conditions. Initially, only ships with captives already aboard could be taken. Suspected slavers apprehended by British mariners were navigated to the Mixed Commission Court of Sierra Leone, where they faced judges from both Portugal and Britain. Although the procedures of the courts were in flux during their early months, with proceedings held in secret, eventually each bilateral body was comprised of a commissioner or judge from both nations as well as an arbitrator. Each trial required the presentation of a repertoire of evidence, including ships' papers; an affidavit, submitted by the captain of the British vessel, explaining the circumstances of the ship's capture; and interrogations of officers and mariners from both sides, conducted by the court's registrar. Only rarely were the testimonies of the captives sought. Both the captain and owner of the captured slaving vessel as well as the captain of the naval ship that had detained the slavers were entitled to representation in court, but often the guilt of involved vessels was cut-and-dried, and judgments were not subject to appeal. The verdict had the power to "condemn" all enslaved people held in cargoes as well as the enslaved mariners serving on board ships, making both effectively crown property.[15]

The diplomatic tensions between former and current slave-trading powers in the Atlantic roused suspicions, recriminations, and charges of hypocrisy on all sides. Bahian merchants resented the incursion of the more militarily and economically powerful British, interpreting the Royal Navy as a surreptitious neocolonizing force. As one British observer noted, slaving merchants had "caused considerable clamour against our country [Britain]; this, however, is but the usual bitter animosity felt by all commercial men, who, being detected

----

Britain. See Marques, *Sounds of Silence,* 40–43. Their seizures were premised on the right to search and capture vessels suspected of crimes on the high seas, such as piracy. See Richard Huzzey, *Freedom Burning: Anti-slavery and Empire in Victorian Britain* (Ithaca, N.Y., 2012), 42; Rees, *Sweet Water and Bitter,* 37–42; Scanlan, *Freedom's Debtors,* 101–102; Wills, *Envoys of Abolition,* 10–12, 15–19.

15. Martinez, *Slave Trade and Origins of International Human Rights Law,* 68–73. An 1817 decision in the British courts limited the Royal Navy's ability to search and capture vessels illegally engaged in trade. After the adoption of an additional Anglo-Portuguese treaty in 1817, which restored the right of search, the Royal Navy began to again seize slaving vessels in West Africa. See Bethell, *Abolition of the Brazilian Slave Trade,* 16–17, 52. On January 26, 1818, the law prohibiting the slave trade north of the equator was finally published (Marques, *Sounds of Silence,* 46).

adventuring in speculations contrary to treaties or national law, complain of tyranny and injustice, when galled by the loss of their property; as well might thieves complain of officers of justice."[16]

The new illegality of transatlantic slaving prompted Bahian-based captains and merchants to pioneer numerous strategies to evade detection and capture. Salvador produced a large share of the illegal traffic, but captains and merchants in the city also mobilized to become a hub for disseminating materials designed to aid the clandestine slave trading of other nations by "furnish[ing] false contracts, colours, and papers to foreign speculators in human flesh." As slaving devolved into greater levels of criminal conspiracy, slavers responded by relying on the same strategies that had buttressed commercial endeavors in previous decades. They marshaled collective capital for investment, established trading relations with a diverse and growing array of West African potentates, navigated smaller vessels that could rapidly traverse the Atlantic and launch multiple voyages a year, and relied on low-cost forms of maritime labor, particularly that of the enslaved, to increase profits. Indeed, as Britain's abolitionist efforts wore on, authorities stationed in Sierra Leone noted with exasperation that the widespread participation in such an "odious commerce" by residents in both Bahia and West African ports represented a "serious obstacle to the extinction of this [transatlantic slave] trade." When authorities captured the Bahian ship *Providência* in 1827, while it was traveling from Lagos with 198 enslaved men, women, and children aboard, the measures that the ship had taken to avoid detection were revealed to be truly extreme. As their British captors noted, the vessel had not only used false colors and an erroneous passport, perhaps furnished by authorities in Bahia; the captain had also assumed a false identity. While stationed off the island of Príncipe to purchase provisions, he further attempted to hide his illegal purchases from Lagos by labeling recently embarked captives as "passengers." The ship's cook confirmed that the enslaved individuals held aboard were to be unloaded to a remote port in Bahia, Rio Real, to avoid alerting British vessels. Though the captain's deceptions proved to be insufficient—the *Providência* was condemned, and all enslaved individuals aboard were confiscated—the complexity of his strategy to evade capture reveals how suppression made the

16. A British visitor to the region added, "It is remarkable, that many of the people believe Great Britain has a longing eye to the possession of Brazil. The origin of this opinion is not easy to trace, except it be to the general jealousy entertained of English influence in the affairs of the government." See Prior, *Voyage along the Eastern Coast of Africa,* 106; Brown, *Moral Capital,* 11.

quotidian operations of slaving more unpredictable and dangerous during the first decades of the nineteenth century than they had been throughout the century before.[17]

ABOLITION'S VIOLENCE

Bahian slave traders' increasingly evasive tactics also put captive cosmopolitans in positions of ever-greater peril. In the ensuing years, British suppression efforts became more forceful and relied on the violent seizures of people and property at sea as the principal mechanism of abolition. This development not only subjected enslaved seamen to protracted firefights and chases but also exposed the affected West African communities to eruptions of abolitionist-motivated force. This violence was not only bodily; as the records of British abolitionist efforts show, there was a violence to the ways living, breathing mariners were reduced to commodities in the moment of a slaving vessel's capture. As owners and colonial authorities sought to litigate illegal slaving, captive Black mariners were often defined and valued in legal proceedings by their supposed basic form: as property.

In 1812, the same year as the *Triunfante*'s capture, the British ship *Amelia* managed to seize the *Destino* as it left one of Bahian slavers' most frequented ports, Porto Novo. Commander Fredrick Foley apprehended 10 *ladino* enslaved mariners alongside the 316 enslaved individuals held in the cargo. The Royal Navy's impetus for confiscating the enslaved sailors serving aboard the *Destino* was murky. All African born and originally from the same coasts that they now returned to as seamen, the mariners possibly shared the same facial scarifications as the men, women, and children trafficked on the *Destino*, making their status on the vessel ambiguous to the British crew.[18] Foley and his men, however, must have appreciated that the men communicated in Portuguese and sported the traditional sailor's dress of denim pants and woolens. Some seamen might have also worn a Phrygian cap, or liberty cap, popular in Brazil. These corporeal details would have marked them as distinct from the barely clothed and disoriented people forced aboard the *Destino*. Like the *Triunfante*'s owner, the *Destino*'s proprietor lamented, in a petition for restitution from the British crown, the "truly lost value in goods" of 200$000

17. Prior, *Voyage along the Eastern Coast of Africa,* 106; ANTT, PT/TT/MNE-ASC/I/C224, caixa 228, "Dispatch from Sierra Leone to Viscount Palmerston, 14th July, 1837."

18. All the men were labeled as from the "Mina nation" (AHI, Coleções Especiais, Comissão Mista, lata 10, maço 2, pasta 2, Papers of the *Destino,* 1–7).

réis that each man represented. In both ships' cases, Black mariners' value was revealed to be purely monetary in slaving merchants' eyes.

Repeating this coldly materialist sentiment was the owner of the *Feliz Americano,* a ship that was also overtaken near Porto Novo in the same year. The twelve enslaved seamen aboard, like the men captured on the other two vessels, were seized and imprisoned in Freetown. The ship's captain and owner, Manoel Izidoro Cardoso, claimed they represented a "real" financial loss. He exercised "his right to demand their value" before the Mesa da Inspeção (Board of Inspection) in Bahia, where he requested monetary restitution but not the return of his mariners. Cardoso evoked his status as a Portuguese vassal, arguing that the goods held on the ship, including its enslaved African-born sailors, were not subject to legal seizure by a foreign nation's military. Fellow slaving ship captain Joaquim Jozé de Sampaio attested to his own maritime slaves' broadly accepted "good" commodity value in Salvador's market, which he argued was "ordinarily 200$000 *réis.*" These two complaints obscured enslaved mariners' embeddedness in particular working and social relationships both on board vessels and on the West African coast and devalued their unique intellectual and laboring contributions to the operation of the trade itself. Their elevated value as cosmopolitan laborers would have likely enhanced Sampaio's financial claims, but he chose to ignore it.[19]

Clashes between Brazilian crews and British ships could also lead to deadly results. In 1815, royal ships seized five more Bahian vessels, resulting in an arms race as surviving slavers heavily equipped their ships in response. An escalation of violent encounters ensued. A year later, the brig *Temerário*'s owner refused to abide by a ban on the northern slave trade and secured its passage by stowing guns aboard. Once it had embarked six hundred enslaved individuals at Ouidah, a deadly battle at sea led to carnage on both sides. Similarly, the *Leal Portuguez* found its fortified defenses inadequate to stave off British firepower, and eventually it was sunk in the midst of its transatlantic voyage. In 1821, the slaver *Volcano* was captured by a British antislaving vessel in West Africa; a British prize crew boarded the vessel and navigated it to Sierra Leone for adjudication. Six weeks into the voyage, a midshipman named Castles, who had been given command of the *Volcano,* was attacked by the Portuguese captain with a cutlass and thrown overboard. Shortly thereafter, the Bahian crew shot and killed the British quartermaster. Two African sailors who were part of the British crew jumped overboard, and the Bahian ship's Black cook

19. Ibid., lata 15, maço 4, pasta 2, Papers of the *Feliz Americano;* ibid., lata 10, maço 2, pasta 2, Papers of the *Destino,* 3.

and another Portuguese sailor killed the remainder of the British crew aboard. Two more African Kroomen, or contracted canoemen working with the British, were captured on the slave deck and taken to Bahia before being sold to plantations in the interior. One of the captured men—identified as "Quashie Sam"—escaped to the coast and was able to board a British ship of war stationed in Bahia, eventually making his way back to Freetown.[20]

The Black sailors who mobilized to take back the Bahian ship might have been motivated by loyalty to their captain or by economic self-interest. However, they could also have experienced British antislaving policing as a moment of violent social and cultural dislocation. Enslaved African sailors captured on Brazilian slavers were customarily taken to Sierra Leone and "liberated," where they would serve as apprentices for fourteen years in settlements in and around Freetown. Even though many had resided in Brazil for years, established social relationships there, and considered themselves Portuguese subjects, their new home would be, for the time being, on the west coast of Africa. Seamen seeking to avoid such a fate could have thrown their lot in with their rebelling crew members, even if that action meant they would remain enslaved for the foreseeable future. Mariners whose vessels were captured by pirates or other hostile groups lost their wages for such interrupted voyages, and owners were not financially responsible for any instruments, freights, or other goods lost by seafarers. Regardless of their motives, during such conflicts on the high seas, violence could easily flow in both directions.[21]

Enslaved mariners bore additional risks during the uncertain moments leading up to the boarding of slaving vessels as well as in the early days of a return voyage. In 1821, when the sailors began to load enslaved individuals aboard the *Esperança Feliz* from shore "all in irons," a British ship patrolling the coast suspected its illegal activity. As enslaved men and women seized from the ship later testified to Mixed Commission authorities, the vessel was taken so quickly after their embarkation, they had not even been served a meal

20. Mariners could also die from disease or other causes during the perilous journeys along the West African coast to Sierra Leone in the wake of capture. Ship captain Joaquim Marques Loureiro perished in uncertain circumstances on the return voyage of the *Divina Providência* from Príncipe in 1812. See ANRJ, fundo 7X, Junta do Comércio, caixa 410, Papers of the *Divina Providência;* Marques, *Sounds of Silence,* 44; Rees, *Sweet Water and Bitter,* 57; Anthony Sullivan, *Britain's War against the Slave Trade: The Operations of the Royal Navy's West Africa Squadron, 1807–1867* (Barnsley, U.K., 2020), 81.

21. Hawthorne, "Gorge," *Slavery and Abolition,* XXXI (2010), 413; ANRJ, fundo 7X, Junta do Comércio, caixa 445, Acção de Padre Jozé Dias Alvares, Aug. 3, 1811.

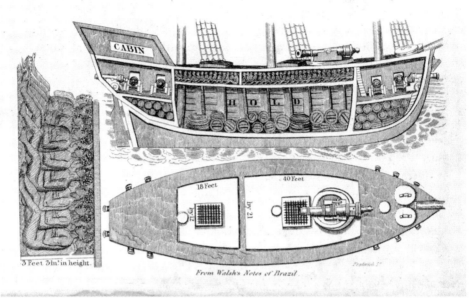

FIGURE 12. *"Sections of a Slave Ship. From Walsh's Notes of Brazil." In M[athew] Carey,*
Reflections on the Causes That Led to the Formation of the Colonization Society . . .
*(Philadelphia, 1832). Confinement of captives within the slave deck. Schomburg Center
for Research in Black Culture, Manuscripts, Archives and Rare Books Division,
The New York Public Library. New York Public Library Digital Collections*

aboard.[22] Such subterfuges and exigencies required of illegal slaving were
not uncommon, as shipboard circumstances were significantly degraded in
the wake of British attacks on the trade. As abolitionists Robert Walsh and
Lieutenant Meynell both portrayed, captives on Brazilian slave ships during
this era were perpetually chained belowdecks. Where once captive women
and children remained on the primary deck, the physical confinement so associated with slaving-ship passages became even more pronounced during the
era of suppression. Captains attempting to elude British surveillance on the

22. The enslaved individuals in question, whose names were registered by commissioners
as Omaroo Chiloo, Alasa, Ajosay, Abyoma, Masaga, and Ajaiare, were interrogated by two
Black interpreters associated with British authorities in Freetown. These interpreters were a
seaman aboard H.M.S. *Iphigenia,* William Pascoe, an African mariner from Hausaland, and
Ali, a "constable of Lichfield," who spoke a dialect of Yoruba common in Oyo. Their testi-

West African coast would have eschewed allowing captives to remain visible during their return voyages. While British abolitionists remained steadfast in their conviction that military suppression was the only way to eradicate the abomination of the transatlantic trade, the resulting violence of slaving continued to escalate in the long decades it would take to finally accomplish their goal.

PRISONERS OF THE BRITISH

Tense struggles in the halls of the vice admiralty and then Mixed Commission Courts of Sierra Leone and Rio de Janeiro further illuminate the degree to which enslaved mariners' variegated loyalties and commitments—occupational, economic, imperial, and racial—shaped their response to British abolitionism. During the course of such protracted legal proceedings, a key question loomed for enslaved seamen: would they participate in the collective fictions that sustained clandestine slaving by claiming no knowledge of wrongdoing and thus non-culpability? Or would they contradict the testimonies of their shipboard brothers? Such mariners gave a variety of responses, from faithful adherence to clandestine slaving to—at times—outright rejection of the defenses levied by slaving merchants and slave ship captains. In the records of cases involving dozens of Bahian ships captured and adjudicated in the 1810s, 1820s, and 1830s, Black seamen offered a spectrum of responses to these questions, indicative of their own fractured interests while participating in slaving at sea.

Mariners' testimonies before Mixed Commission Courts tended to support the claims of merchants and captains, suggesting a pervasive of sense of fealty—or at least obedience—to their superiors, who of course were hoping to evade sanction for their illegal slaving activities. An array of tactics were available for evading antislaving laws: deceptively flying foreign colors, carrying royal passports with falsified destinations, and recounting implausible stories involving strong winds and storms that had pushed vessels off course to forbidden ports.[23] Fabrications spun by captain and crew alike in the wake of these subterfuges attempted to forestall legal censure and concomitant loss of

---

mony pertaining to their experiences of being trafficked is brief but reveals that the Mixed Commission Courts at times challenged assertions made by slaving ship captains with the testimony of captive Africans themselves. The six men and women were later emancipated in the Freetown colony (AHI, lata 10, maço 2, pasta 1, Papers of the *Destimida*).

23. These attempts at evasion were supported by colonial authorities in Bahia, as well,

property after adjudication. The consistency of testimony in such accounts implies the strength of vertical as much as horizontal lines of solidarity, as lowly seamen mobilized to defend their superiors in court.

Such responses were not only shaped by the avoidance of violence or fealty to fellow mariners, however. Many enslaved mariners had significant financial investments in slaving voyages, and upon these investments hinged much of their economic and social aspirations. Bonds of shipboard fraternity were deeply enmeshed in shared or reciprocal notions of economic interest. At times, Black seamen even went so far as to act as guardians of shipowners' property. For instance, Jozé Egido, a barber on the *Tentadora*, and Antônio Joaquim, the ship's cook, testified before the Mixed Commission that they had alerted their employer to the nefarious activities of the British crews that had captured their ship at São Tomé. Egido spotted a group of sailors boarding the mostly vacant ship under the cover of night. Using their long-boat, they escaped with a range of supplies, including pork, beef, flour, tar, brass stanchions, two copper cauldrons, African baskets, silver utensils, and dishes that had formerly been used to feed captives. Also part of the theft were a group of local "maroon women": they boarded the ship under the guise of performing necessary washing but left with a collection of pans and other goods belonging to the vessel. Jozé and Antônio Joaquim were two of many Black mariners who corroborated their captains' accounts of what they saw as British corruption and injustice during ship seizures and subsequent sequestration of Brazilian property in port.[24]

On rare occasions, enslaved seamen dramatically broke with their captains' falsehoods, condemning a handful to legal censure and financial loss. In one of the few instances of dissent, an enslaved Gege sailor named Jorge, laboring on the *Emília*, testified before the Mixed Commission Court in Rio de

---

especially by governors and members of the Mesa da Inspeção, who issued passports to slaving vessels falsely claiming they were navigating to Molembo instead of their more likely destinations on the Mina Coast—a favored set of slave markets for Bahian captains. The *Príncipe de Guiné*'s captain claimed in 1826 that "powerful currents and storms" had directed his ship from its intended destination of Molembo to Oudiah. He also claimed ignorance of Anglo-Brazilian antislaving treaties. See AHI, Coleções Especiais, Comissão Mista, lata 13, maço 14, pasta 1, Papers of the *Emília*, n.p.; ibid., lata 27, maço 1, pasta 1, Papers of the *Príncipe de Guiné;* Pierre Verger, *Trade Relations between the Bight of Benin and Bahia from the 17th to 19th Century,* [trans. Evelyn Crawford] (Ibadan, Nigeria, 1976), 368.

24. AHI, Coleções Especiais, Comissão Mista, lata 30, maço 1, pasta 1, Papers of the *Tentadora*.

Janeiro that, despite the shipowner's insistence that the captives held on the vessel hailed from Cabinda, they had been illegally loaded in Lagos. Jorge had come before the bilateral court after a series of ordeals. His first brush with British military authority had occurred several years earlier, in 1816, when the *Bann* apprehended the aforementioned *Temerário,* a slaving ship on which he was laboring and that was subsequently navigated to Freetown. There he remained, in his words, a "prisoner" of the British, alongside his enslaved crewmates and the ship's pilot, Manoel Patricio, who ultimately "handed [him] over" to his owner, Joaquim Carneiro de Campos, upon their return to Bahia. Before his seizure, Jorge had lived in Bahia for nine years. A twenty-six-year-old ladino, he spoke Portuguese and claimed the king of Portugal as his sovereign. Forcibly relocated to an adversarial imperial space, Jorge held an ambiguous status during his ten months in Sierra Leone. According to his later recollection, no British official conferred freedom onto him, though an unnamed bureaucrat had noted Jorge's name and personal details in a logbook—part of the usual process British authorities used to emancipate captured enslaved Africans. He remained in Freetown, laboring for the British Macaulay Company, probably as a stevedore, on the settlement's crude waterfront. As he would later testify, his months-long captivity in Sierra Leone did little to loosen his master's hold over him. Campos denied his emancipation, asserting his ownership of Jorge through Patricio, who would later escort him back to slavery. Perhaps making the injustice of his own, unaltered status even more agonizing, Jorge watched across the settlement's main square as his African crewmates sported the uniform of colonial troops to attain a kind of half-liberation in the British colony. It appeared their fourteen-year indenture would be served in the local African Corps in exchange for freedom, where they became conscripts in yet another perilous imperial project, while Jorge returned to Brazil.[25]

The enslaved man's confusion about his status, freed or enslaved, illustrates the ambivalence of abolitionism on the coast of West Africa. Anti-slavery's entanglement in age-old interimperial rivalries meant that diplomatic

25. Ibid., lata 13, maço 14, pasta 1, Papers of the *Emília,* 345, 351–352; ANTT, PT/TT/ MNE-ASC/I/C224, caixa 228, Letter to Rio de Janeiro Mixed Commission; Martinez, *Slave Trade and Origins of International Human Rights Law,* 77; Hawthorne, "Gorge," *Slavery and Abolition,* XXXI (2010), 413, 418, 419; AHI, Coleções Especiais, Comissão Mista, lata 13, maço 14, pasta 1, Papers of the *Emília,* 351–352. Jorge's loyal vassalage to the king of Portugal was preceded, according to his own words, by his alliance to a king in Ouidah, where he was born and lived before he was "sold to the whites." See ibid., 351.

and legal imperatives superseded the well-being of the Atlantic's Black mariners, whose status could become a mere afterthought for both sides. Jorge's second fateful encounter with military representatives of the British empire further confirmed the precarious position of enslaved individuals caught up in the uncertainties of the Age of Abolition. As a sailor aboard the *Emília,* he left the coast of West Africa, sailing for several days, when the *Morgiana* spotted the slaving ship and overtook her 180 miles south of Lagos in February 1821. The British crew confronted a shocking scene upon boarding: 396 men, women, and children were crowded onto the vessel, some already ravaged by disease and close to death. Captain Servero Leonardo attempted to evade liability for breaching the Anglo-Portuguese treaty. Presenting the ship's royal passport, which listed the central African port of Molembo as the destination, he claimed the enslaved individuals had been taken aboard at Cabinda, which was located south of the equator, near the Congo River. The absence of emptied water casks as well as the recent signs of branding on the flesh of captives belied Leonardo's assertions that the ship had been at sea long enough to have embarked from there. Once Captain Finlaison of the *Morgiana* verified the *Emília*'s obfuscation, he removed the crew and a portion of the captives, swiftly navigating the ship to Freetown as a prize. More than half of the 28 mariners shuffled aboard the *Morgiana* were African-born and enslaved, like Jorge. Much like his previous experience of detention at the hands of the British, his status following his second apprehension remained unclear. Were he and his comrades to become prisoners, or "condemned" property, as earlier captive seamen had? In the years between Jorge's first and second capture, Anglo-Portuguese treaties endeavored to clarify the murky status of such men. In 1818, the Portuguese crown adopted an edict that allowed enslaved crewmembers to be confiscated if they were "the property of persons implicated in the crime of the illicit trade in slaves," such as slaving ship owners, captains, or mariners. Because Jorge was not owned by an investor or participant in the voyage, this directive did not apply to him, and he returned to Bahia with the other members of the crew.[26]

26. Sullivan, *Britain's War against the Slave Trade,* 80; AHI, Coleções Especiais, Comissão Mista, lata 13, maço 14, pasta 1, Papers of the *Emília,* 18; Hawthorne, "Gorge," *Slavery and Abolition,* XXXI (2010), 412. Jorge's testimony slightly differs from this account. According to the enslaved seaman, it was the presence of a large cauldron aboard that revealed that the ship was outfitted for slaving, leading to its detection as an illegal vessel. See Sullivan, *Britain's War against the Slave Trade,* 80; AHI, Coleções Especiais, Comissão Mista, lata 13, maço 14, pasta 1, Papers of the *Emília,* 23–25, 351.

Just as the disruptions of abolition at sea had done little to challenge Carneiro's earlier assertions of paternalistic responsibility over Jorge, they did little to unilaterally curtail the property claims of the *Emília*'s proprietor to the ship's enslaved cargo. The surviving captive adults and children seized from the ship had to be navigated to Rio de Janeiro in insalubrious conditions for the *Emília*'s adjudication before they were finally freed in late July. During the process, numerous individuals fell ill and died. By the time the ship arrived in the imperial capital, forty-two individuals had perished. While commissioners debated the legality of the ship's seizure, a key part of the legal proceedings attempted to deduce the status of the captives held aboard. Were they fungible commodities that had been illegally seized or persons wrongly enslaved and legitimately emancipated by the *Morgiana?* Meanwhile, the enslaved remained in squalid conditions in a guarded warehouse. Those who endured such legal processes became *emancipados*. This status included profound limitations on individual autonomy. Just as those freed in Sierra Leone were forced to labor for years following their formal liberation, exercising little control over their own working and social lives, individuals freed by the Mixed Commission Court in Rio de Janeiro were subjected to harsh labor demands and persistent neglect during their period of "apprenticeship." Some were even rumored to have been surreptitiously reenslaved.[27]

The futures of those seized from the *Emília* in part depended on the evidence offered by men such as Jorge. Whereas the other seamen escaped when the ship docked in Salvador before arriving in Rio de Janeiro to face legal proceedings, Jorge was left to testify to his captain's guilt or innocence. The African seaman's testimony before the Mixed Commission, alongside that of freed African *sangrador* Jozé Joaquim de Moraes, became instrumental in securing the *Emília*'s condemnation and the emancipation of the captives housed aboard. Neither man accepted his captain's account of events. Like most captive cosmopolitans, Jozé was multilingual. In the seven years since Brazilian merchants had first trafficked him from West Africa, Jozé had acquired a basic comprehension of the Yoruba language, in addition to Portuguese and his native Fon. Both men testified that the *Emília*'s enslaved cargo had illegally been taken at Lagos alongside textiles *(panos da costa)*, *dênde* oil, and cowry shells. Both mariners had been told, when they first boarded the

---

27. Hawthorne, "Gorge," *Slavery and Abolition,* XXXI (2010), 423. The Portuguese commissioner at the court in Sierra Leone was no longer available to hear cases, meaning that the closest available venue for a bilateral hearing was the newly created Court of Mixed Commission in Rio de Janeiro. See Sullivan, *Britain's War against the Slave Trade,* 80–81.

Emília in Bahia, that the vessel was headed to Molembo; but when Jozé—who was also ethnically Gege—inquired as to his whereabouts upon arrival in West Africa, the "blacks of the land" informed him that he was in Lagos. Jorge's growing realization that the *Emília* was acting illegally on the West African coast might have sprung from another, unacknowledged source. As Leonardo directed shackled enslaved men, women, and children aboard the *Emília* after they had been ferried through perilous waters in dugout canoes, did Jorge recognize the stifled cries of mourning and terror, some of which would have been uttered in his native Fon language? Only Jozé explicitly referred to the language of the captives as a sign of identification. Both men, however, confidently asserted that no enslaved individuals from Cabinda had ever stepped foot on the *Emília*, rebutting the claims of their captain that the ship's slaving had occurred south of the equator.[28]

Although Jorge's and Jozé's dexterous verbal skills likely facilitated their ability to form their own, opposing understanding of the ruse in which they had unwittingly participated, both men's agency remained constrained by their vexed embeddedness in the project of transatlantic slaving. Jorge relinquished an opportunity for legal emancipation by failing to claim to be a subject of the British crown, yet he incriminated the *Emília* in front of com-

---

28. AHI, Coleções Especiais, Comissão Mista, lata 13, maço 14, pasta 1, Papers of the *Emília,* 345, 357. In the passage from Sierra Leone to Rio de Janeiro, the *Morgiana* and *Emília* stopped in Salvador to refresh their provisions. While in port, Leonardo, the white officers and crew members, as well as two enslaved mariners escaped. Antônio and Caetano, the Black sailors, jumped ship together. See Hawthorne, "Gorge," *Slavery and Abolition,* XXXI (2010), 422; Scanlan, *Freedom's Debtors,* 100, 118–127; Beatriz G. Mamigonian, *Africanos livres: A abolição do tráfico de escravos no Brasil* (São Paulo, 2017); Robert Conrad, "Neither Slave nor Free: The *Emancipados* of Brazil, 1818–1868," *HAHR,* LIII (1973), 50–70; Luciano Raposo Figueiredo, "Uma Jóia Perversa," in Figueiredo, *Marcas de escravos: Listas de escravos emancipados vindos a bordo de navios negreiros, 1839–1841* (Rio de Janeiro, 1989), 1–28. Jozé furthermore noted that he did not recognize the language spoken by the captives aboard as "Cabinda," indicating he had some working knowledge of the Kikongo dialect of Bantu. The ethnically plural grouping of the nearly four hundred men, women, and children aboard included a mixture of Nagôs, Hausas, Tapas, and Geges, a linguistically and politically diverse set of individuals from a variety of city-states inland from the Mina Coast. The *Emília*'s human cargo offered a potent symbol of the waves of ongoing political turmoil, warfare, and resulting displacement that plagued the region during the period. See AHI, Coleções Especiais, Comissão Mista, lata 13, maço 14, pasta 1, Papers of the *Emília,* 355.

missioners. Though both men were participants in transatlantic slave trading, when called upon to testify under oath, they rejected their captain's deception. Perhaps as a slight to his owner, Jorge further confirmed Leonardo's duplicitous behavior to commissioners by revealing that he had witnessed the captain tossing the ship's papers, likely containing incriminating details, into the ocean.[29]

Captains and owners frequently corroborated each other's testimonies in an attempt to exonerate themselves. They also expected mariners to act in complicity with their erroneous defenses. Notably, however, they often condemned the Mixed Commission Court's utilization of witness statements by Black mariners despite the mariners' propensity to substantiate the slavers' defense. Manoel Joaquim de Almeida, captain of a ship also under prosecution by the Mixed Commission Court but testifying on behalf of the owners of another slaving vessel, protested to commissioners about the "violence done by the English frigate of war" to his ship. But his belief in British abolitionism's illegitimacy was also aimed at the evidentiary standards of the court. Perhaps as a veiled reference to Jorge's participation in mounting a persuasive case against the *Emília,* Almeida bemoaned the use of incriminating testimony by enslaved and freed Black sailors. These men, he argued, offered false statements because they lacked any financial interest in the ships on which they sailed. They were not to be trusted. His statement was a telling example of the continuing perception that African-born sailors were unreliable allies in Brazilian battles against abolitionism. Moreover, it ignored the complex economic and investment realities aboard such clandestine slaving vessels. Almeida's accusations were emblematic of the dangers faced by Black mariners caught up in competing imperatives of abolition at sea—torn between a constrained liberation in Sierra Leone or slavery in Brazil, between loyalty to shipmates and captains and the possibility of divulging their own, truthful account of the horrors they had witnessed at sea. Even while ship merchants and captains utilized Black mariners as instruments to perpetuate covert slaving activities, they treated them as an expendable asset rather than a trustworthy part of crews.[30]

29. Hawthorne, "Gorge," *Slavery and Abolition,* XXXI (2010), 413; AHI, Coleções Especiais, Comissão Mista, lata 13, maço 14, pasta 1, Papers of the *Emília,* 354.

30. AHI, Coleções Especiais, Comissão Mista, lata 21, maço 2, pasta 1, Papers of the *Minerva,* 51, 220.

CONTESTED SOVEREIGNTY AND
ENSHRINED PROPERTY RIGHTS

Disdainful of British abolitionism, Bahian slavers continued to take advantage of tensions on both sides of the Atlantic to illegally transport enslaved Africans. The Age of Abolition was also characterized by the Atlantic's rapidly shifting political landscape, which presented opportunities to evade commitments made in diplomatic agreements. Brazil's declaration of independence from Portugal on September 7, 1822, was seized upon by some opportunistic merchants and captains as a cover for slaving. For instance, in November 1823, the *Minerva* diverged from its proposed route to Molembo. The ship's captain, the aforementioned Manoel Joaquim de Almeida, claimed that its slaving activities north of the equator were merely an unhappy accident. Despite his best intentions, Almeida insisted, his ship sailed north of its intended route to escape a Portuguese ship of war near Angola. The prospect of Portuguese hostilities precluded the *Minerva* from going to São Tomé or Elmina, and Lagos presented the only viable option for refreshing the ship's depleted rations, according to Almeida's reasoning before the Mixed Commission. Even the ship's Black crewmembers endorsed this characterization of events. Bento da Silva, a pardo sailor who lived in Santo Antônio Além do Carmo—above Salvador's harbor, alongside several other seamen—claimed that, because Portugal was "disputing Brazil's independence," the *Minerva* had been forced to navigate north of colonial strongholds like Luanda. White sailors João Jozé de Souza and Manoel Pereira dos Santos echoed Silva's wording almost exactly, as did the freed African barber Felipe Serra.[31]

The *Minerva*'s captain and his men had been ashore for fourteen days in Lagos, dealing in tobacco and *aguardente* for palm oil and textiles alongside the captains from two other Bahian ships, when a British frigate investigated

31. After a two-year conflict with Portugal, Dom Pedro founded the empire of Brazil, and Britain looked to reinstate its anti–slave trade agreement. In 1825, as Britain agreed to recognize Brazil as an independent nation, they leveraged the new sovereign polity to sign a treaty that would abolish the slave trade and establish a Mixed Commission Court, composed of British and Brazilian judges, to adjudicate captured vessels in Rio de Janeiro, in addition to the one already in operation in Sierra Leone. Portugal did not recognize the independent sovereignty of the empire of Brazil until the Treaty of Rio de Janeiro was signed in 1825. Almeida's claim of low provisions specifically mentioned beans and beef, intended to sustain a cargo of captives on the return voyage to Bahia. See AHI, Coleções Especiais, Comissão Mista, lata 21, maço 2, pasta 1, Papers of the *Minerva*, 99, 120, 222.

but failed to uncover any signs of slave trading. The following day, on January 3, four British ships—including the *Bann* and the *Swinger*—arrived in port and anchored in front of a trading factory inhabited by an Englishman who had entered the waters surrounding Lagos under a false American flag, presumably to illegally trade in slaves. The arrival of the British vessels, carrying forty men and two officers armed with artillery and muskets, aroused the suspicions of Bahian traders. The *oba* (ruler) of Lagos, Osinlokun, whose economic and political fortunes increasingly relied upon transatlantic slave trading, sent for the British officers later that night to inquire about their intentions. Upon arrival, the officers implored the oba to "deliver up the Slaves that the Portuguese had bought." Osinlokun replied that he had only textiles, ivory, palm oil, and provisions to trade. The African potentate, as a participant in the Brazilian slavers' attempts to circumvent British antislavery activity, was likely aware that, before slaving vessels could be seized, enslaved individuals needed to be on board. Slavers cognizant of this requirement avoided loading slaves unless British ships were absent. Unconvinced by this explanation, the officers then offered to pay the oba for half of the slaves in return for delivering them to the British.[32]

After leaving the oba's home, the officers visited Almeida's *feitoria*. Noting the illegality of his passport to Molembo, they demanded to know if slaves were being embarked. Almeida replied that only textiles were for trade in the port. The officers again returned to speak to the oba, threatening to fire on land if enslaved Africans were not delivered to them by the next morning. The oba "wanted to know why there was a war between the whites"—the Brazilians and British—and maintained that he did not have slaves to deliver to anyone. He implored the British officers "to do no harm to their land, as he had not offended them before, but rather treated them well, as he had done with all the whites that came to his Port." The officers responded "that they knew very well what [the Brazilian traders and the oba] were going to do" and threatened to fire on "not only the inhabitants of the country . . . but the [Brazilian] *feitorias*" if slaves were not delivered the next morning. Again, they left unsatisfied.[33]

The freed African barber, Felipe Serra, became an unwilling participant in

32. Kristin Mann, *Slavery and the Birth of an African City: Lagos, 1760–1900* (Bloomington, Ind., 2007), 42–43; AHI, Coleções Especiais, Comissão Mista, lata 21, maço 2, pasta 1, Papers of the *Minerva*, 123.

33. AHI, Coleções Especiais, Comissão Mista, lata 21, maço 2, pasta 1, Papers of the *Minerva*, 123.

this tense standoff. Born on the Mina Coast, Serra was indispensable to the *Minerva*'s commercial dealings. Having accompanied Captain Almeida and other officers to shore, Serra became a firsthand witness to the random eruptions of violence that attended efforts to enact abolition on the West African littoral. The following day, British soldiers disembarked and fired on the three manned pieces of artillery guarding the port. The hostile fire destroyed the port's battlements and "kill[ed] and wound[ed] a great quantity of Blacks." British soldiers retreated to the *Bann* and commenced firing on the Brazilian slavers anchored nearby, leading to "real naval combat" that lasted three hours. During this time, Serra recalled, the *Minerva* and two other ships were approached and captured, even though they held no slaves on board. The British officers sent an African interpreter to inform the three Brazilian captains that the crews of their ships had been put in chains, "in spite of the Protests, and Proclamations" of the men, and were in naval custody aboard the *Bann*. The vessels were navigated to Sierra Leone, where they were found guilty of illegally engaging in the slave trade, and the ships were auctioned as lawful prizes.[34]

The example of the *Minerva* reveals the impossible choices that faced those Black mariners who became ensnared in Britain's abolitionist efforts. As a freed barber of relative prestige aboard the *Minerva*, Serra likely wanted his livelihood to continue unmolested. British abolitionism—a project he condemned in his testimony for its violence and disregard for West African sovereignty—was an immediate and visceral threat to both his life and his work.

The conflict surrounding the *Minerva* also illustrates an emergent tendency in the ways Bahian slavers articulated a defense of their enterprise. Through the legal process of the Mixed Commission Courts, Bahian slave traders contested the "arbitrary and violent" nature of British seizures at sea as well as the sincerity of their abolitionism and claimed that such efforts were a violation of their property rights. This defense of slaving was part and parcel of a capricious liberalism that both legitimized Brazilians' separation from Portugal in the era of Latin American independence and enshrined their desire to participate in foreign slaving commerce unimpeded. Black mariners could easily become casualties of Bahian slavers' insistence on illegally pursuing trade on the Mina Coast amid repeated acts of British naval aggression.[35]

---

34. Ibid., 121, 123; *British and Foreign State Papers, 1825–1826*, XIII (London, 1848), 116.

35. AHI, Coleções Especiais, Comissão Mista, lata 27, maço 2, pasta 1, Papers of the *Providência*. For more on the conservative nature of Brazilian liberalism in the early nineteenth century, see Emilia Viotti da Costa, *The Brazilian Empire: Myths and Histories* (Chapel Hill, N.C., 2000), xxii–xxiii.

As violence on slaving ships and in port cities mounted, Bahian slave traders fashioned countervailing arguments to undermine the legality of antislaving measures on the West African coast. In a number of petitions lodged by the
Cerqueira's owner, José de Cerqueira Lima, against British actions in Lagos,
the Brazilian trader stressed the unprecedented nature of the altercation,
claiming that "the Commander and Officers of the [British] Corvette" had enacted "the most violent and unheard of attempts, against the Chief and Inhabitants of the Country, who they rashly pretended to force to deliver to them the
Slaves, which they supposed had been purchased for the Brig of the Claimant,
when, in fact, none had been bought." Furthermore, they had attempted "to
intimidate the said Chief and Inhabitants, first with promises, and then with
threats of force, which in effect they employed, discharging on the shore both
artillery and musketry; with other gross insults, which it is unnecessary that the
Claimant should relate, as well as against the several Brazilian Vessels." Such
actions, Lima asserted, had denied sovereign Portuguese subjects "all power
and means to substantiate their rights being denied to the captured Vessel, of
which certainly it will not be easy to find a similar Case, in the maritime annals
of any civilized Nation, even supposing the Parties in a state of open War." He
furthermore criticized the "illegality and injustice" of what had occurred.[36]

At first glance, Lima's petition appears to be the self-serving justification
of an unrepentant slave trader who brazenly ignored Brazil and Britain's
antislaving treaty. After all, the wealthy and powerful merchant had been a
staunch opponent of the additional acts that limited Bahian slaving north of
the equator. He was correct, however, that Britain's use of force and its ability to legally impede trade between two self-proclaimed sovereign "nations"
were largely unprecedented. The British crown's lack of oversight of its West
African squadron and the presence of financial incentives for captains and
crews to apprehend foreign vessels carrying slaves had, in fact, led to increasing violence in port cities and a growing disregard for African sovereignty,
which diminished potentates' ability to freely engage in slave trading.[37]

36. *British and Foreign State Papers, 1825–1826,* XIII, 116, 118.

37. Verger, *Trade Relations,* [trans. Crawford], 396–397. These military tactics were
precursors to the 1839 blockade of the River Galinas and the destruction of several barracoons used to store slaves, which Commander Matson advised could be done even without
the consent of local rulers. Naval blockades of slaving ports, including Lagos in 1851 and
Dahomey in 1851–1852, further eroded local West African control of ports and riverine passages. Between 1830 and 1835, an average of ten ships were taken annually; in 1836, thirty-
five were taken as a result of newly established treaties with Portugal and Spain, which was

During Bahia's independence era, transatlantic merchants also embraced an emphasis on the imperative of diplomacy and national law to ensure the protection of property and deepen global commitments to the free flow of goods between commodity markets. Throughout this transitional period, local authorities in Salvador largely echoed the view of powerful slaving merchants and other commercial interests. Animated by French and British economic theory, the 1824 Constitution for the newly formed empire of Brazil guaranteed rights in property, which, as Emilia Viotti da Costa has noted, worked to safeguard the economic interests of landholding classes as well as those of slaving merchants. The politics of the independence era in Brazil's northeast remained fractious, with nonroyalist and royalist factions articulating contrasting theories of the new empire's emergent liberalism. From the vantage point of Bahian elites, however, a drive for greater equality of rights remained compatible with the territory's traditional commitment to the sanctity of slavery and property holding. An emphasis on the liberalization of trade and the eradication of colonial monopolies intensified the demand for enslaved labor as new markets opened up for Brazilian agricultural goods internationally. As manufacturing imports from Europe grew and commodity exports rose, Brazilian politicians articulated a liberal vision that emphasized free trade and restraint in the use of state policy to regulate production. Slave-trade advocates argued that the traffic was vital to imperial trade and industry and thus should not be impeded by any diplomatic agreement.[38]

---

still a small portion of the total number of slaving vessels leaving West Africa. Many British abolitionists, such as Thomas Fowell Buxton of the African Civilization Society, argued that the transatlantic slave trade would cease only when the supply of slaves from West African polities was halted. In 1841, British administrators formed treaties with leaders at Abo and Ida that stipulated the rulers agree to prohibit their subjects from engaging in the slave trade as well as from constructing forts for that purpose. In addition, the treaties gave British officers the right to use force within West African territories in order to prevent slave trading. The Admiralty further advised British officers negotiating similar treaties with other rulers to encourage West Africans to participate in the suppression of the trade, but also instructed, "In the event, however, of ultimate failure of the negotiation . . . Her Majesty's Officers have orders to liberate Slaves when found embarked in boats of his subjects for that purpose." See *Instructions for the Guidance of Her Majesty's Naval Officers Employed in the Suppression of the Slave Trade* (London, 1844), 20; Robin Law, "Abolition and Imperialism: International Law and the British Suppression of the Atlantic Slave Trade," in Derek R. Peterson, ed., *Abolitionism and Imperialism in Britain, Africa, and the Atlantic* (Athens, Ohio, 2010).

38. Cândido Eugênio Domingues de Souza, "'Perseguidores da espécie humana': Capitães negreiros da cidade da Bahia na primeira metade do século XVIII" (Ph.D. diss.,

In this context, military and legal restrictions on the transatlantic slave trade appeared to be contrary to a liberalism that depended on unfettered commerce. The legal arguments mounted by owners of condemned vessels also reveal how little legitimacy British abolitionist efforts had in the eyes of propertied Brazilian citizens. Their fundamental rejection of the British legal right to enforce abolitionist measures internationally had several inter-related rationales that emphasized Brazilian sovereignty and minimized any sense that the natural rights of Africans seized from slaving vessels superseded their own right to hold enslaved people as merchandise. As the widow of the owner of the apprehended ship *Providência* argued, the "incoherencies and illegalities" of the Mixed Commission stemmed not only from the overrep-resentation of biased British judges but the hypocrisy of Britain's abolition-ism itself. Labeling abolition a false "philanthropy," Dona Anna Jozefa do Bomfim e Oliveira contended that the antislavery crusade acted as a mere "pretext" and that the British had "no right" to exercise military regulation of Brazilian commerce. While disputing the genuineness of British abolitionist international politics, she pointed out that the British empire, much like the Brazilian one, was a slave society and that those enslaved Africans "liberated" from Brazilian ships faced fourteen years of indenture in Sierra Leone—a state suspiciously akin to slavery.[39]

Brazilian slavers continued to evoke a slew of disingenuous justifications for their illegal trading activities. They asserted, in various contexts, that they were transporting "colonists" between Portuguese colonies in West Africa and Brazil; that they were only trading in African goods and not in slaves; that irons aboard ships were for crewmembers and not for captives; that they were ignorant of prohibitions against the slave trade north of the equator; and that the Mixed Portuguese and British Commissions did not have the authority to

---

Universidade Federal da Bahia, 2011), 180–185; Costa, *Brazilian Empire,* 60, 126; Marques, *Sounds of Silence,* 52. The constitution did not explicitly address slavery but did enshrine a number of individual rights as articulated in the Declaration of the Rights of Man—includ-ing the right to property. The inherent contradiction in such a position was not resolved until the end of the century. See Leslie Bethell, "The Independence of Brazil," in Bethell, ed., *Brazil: Empire and Republic, 1822–1930* (Cambridge, 1989), 24–25; Costa, *Brazilian Empire,* 126–127.

39. AHI, Comissão Mista, lata 27, maço 2, pasta 1, Papers of the *Providência*. Bomfim's assertion of British abolitionism's insincerity was echoed in the Bahian press of the period. See Marques, *Sounds of Silence,* 51–53; AHI, Comissão Mista, lata 27, maço 2, pasta 1, Papers of the *Providência*.

prosecute subjects of the sovereign Portuguese crown. In the wake of independence, merchants similarly decried the legitimacy of Mixed Brazilian and British Commissions and painted British military enforcement of abolition as an affront to national honor. Though these claims were, for the most part, disingenuous, Brazilian slavers did consistently evoke the rights of African polities to engage in the slave trade, hearkening back to eighteenth-century legal custom and reifying the status of West African polities as independent, sovereign entities. For instance, when the Brazilian ship *Providência* was captured in 1827, the captain of the ship asserted that the British had unlawfully obstructed "the trade between two law abiding nations," meaning Brazil and Lagos. The lasting irony of British abolitionism was that Bahian slaving merchants remained the starkest defenders of West African political sovereignty, insofar as that sovereignty produced an unimpeded supply of captives to be loaded onto their awaiting ships.[40]

In the two decades following Brazil's 1822 independence, conflicts over the military and legal procedures of abolition continued to rage at sea and on shore.[41] For those Black inhabitants of the South Atlantic caught in the crosshairs of these hostilities, abolitionism did not lead to a simple, linear unfolding of liberation. During the era of antislavery at sea, such men continued to toil for the benefit of the Atlantic world's preeminent slavers, whose commitment to the continuation of transatlantic traffic had transformed Bahian slaving into a dangerously clandestine affair. As partially incorporated participants in the project of South Atlantic slaving, captive cosmopolitans navigated competing social and economic incentives that did not axiomatically align them with the cause of abolition. Fearful of the violence British naval ships could bring to bear on their bodies, captive mariners also, at times, mobilized to protect the well-being of shipmates, preserve their social ties at sea and on land, and defend their own property during abolitionist offenses. With ties to captains and crews whom they were required to defend, they could view British antislavery forces as menacing military adversaries. Furthermore, the

---

40. Marques, *Sounds of Silence*, 54. On the ship *Destimida,* the captain claimed that the fifty African men held aboard were not enslaved but rather free domestic servants. See AHI, lata 10, maço 2, pasta 1, Papers of the *Destimida*.

41. The captain of the *Príncipe de Guiné* complained that he at first assumed the British ship *Hope* was a pirate because it was not flying national colors; after a lengthy chase and "naval combat" of more than three hours, his ship was taken. See AHI, Coleções Especiais, Comissão Mista, lata 27, maço 1, pasta 1, Papers of the *Príncipe de Guiné*, 1–3.

Mixed Commission's procedure of seizing all trade goods aboard suspect slavers had the potential to leave even Black mariners in a state of financial ruin, provided they had made trading investments. Once captured, they found themselves subject to the whims of both Brazilian and British seafaring abolitionists. Even when legally freed in Sierra Leone, Black mariners were still compelled to serve the interests of others as apprentices and servants enlisted in Britain's new colonial venture.[42]

Such paradoxes permeated the experience of antislavery at sea for Bahia's Black mariners. In spite of the nearly unfettered mobility and high degree of self-possession it conferred on individual seafarers, Black mariners in the South Atlantic were not in the vanguard of a broader movement for freedom as they were in other Atlantic ports. Indeed, perhaps what is most striking is that instances of fugitivity, self-purchase, and negotiation such as those detailed in Chapter 4 did not energize a fully developed abolitionist movement in Bahia. Although Britain's antislavery campaign was successful in making the transatlantic slave trade more perilous and costly than it had ever been, abolitionism in Brazil largely stalled. Despite slaveholding elites' deepest fears, the latent radicalism of mobility did not manifest itself in substantial challenges to Brazilian slavery by Black seamen and, at times, even led to a deepening commitment to it. Black mariners' experience of the Age of Abolition at sea helps explain why. Even when faced with the legal opportunities presented by belligerent abolitionist power Britain, many enslaved mariners chose an uneasy loyalty to their fellow crewmates and captains, the possibility of further economic advancement, or at least the chance to return home to Bahia—a world whose dangers and inequalities they already understood—over confronting the uncertainties of British-enforced abolition on an increasingly volatile West African coast.[43]

As men accustomed to operating in difficult and ever-changing circumstances and making situational, strategic decisions to minimize their own vulnerability, Black mariners drew on the stability offered by ties to shipmates,

42. The length of their indenture varied from seven to fourteen years. The rationale of conscripting the labor of emancipated Africans seized by royal ships was chiefly economic. To defray the costs of adjudicating suspected slavers within the Mixed Commission Courts, the labor value of those emancipated was mobilized. All nations receiving "the benefit of the labor of emancipated negroes" were charged a fee, including Brazil. See AHI, lata 10, maço 2, pasta 1, Papers of the *Destimida*.

43. W. Jeffrey Bolster, *Black Jacks: African American Seamen in the Age of Sail* (Cambridge, Mass., 1997), 211; Costa, *Brazilian Empire,* 127.

captains, and owners to navigate the many hazards of abolition at sea. Such social connections—be they of transitory convenience or of a more lasting nature—continued to mark Black mariners' strategies of survival during the Age of Abolition. They also pulled many enslaved mariners back to Bahian shores, where they were part of a larger, dynamic cultural world and community. There, Black mariners' social ties indelibly fostered the creation of new intellectual worlds that linked Africa's slaving ports with the urban landscapes of Brazil, particularly as they turned to West African ideas to guide their acts of healing at sea. Just as their cosmopolitanism had helped these men to navigate the legal and geopolitical complexities of the South Atlantic, their willingness to access diverse streams of knowledge enabled them to generate life-saving techniques to treat the physically ailing African captives transported on the ships on which they labored, further maintaining the slave trade's viability in challenging conditions. Their willingness to creatively combine various intellectual influences not only helped them to survive but allowed them to produce a new body of transatlantic medical knowledge and provided them with an avenue to secure a measure of esteem that marked them as distinct among West Africans residing in Bahia.

{ CHAPTER 6 }
Transatlantic Healers

In late 1827, the *Novo Dispique* made a routine departure from the West African coast. As 24 members of the crew toiled above decks on the bustling primary deck, 118 enslaved men, women, and children lay shackled below, in the darkness of its cavernous hold. Among the ship's crew was a formerly enslaved Gege man, Pedro Antônio de Oiteiro, who served as the ship's *sangrador* and was, by virtue of his position, chiefly responsible for the health of the enslaved individuals on board. The relative calm that characterized his first days at sea, however, abruptly turned to terror as enslaved men and women belowdecks began to display signs of illness. In the course of two weeks, an unidentified infectious disease swept through the ship, killing fourteen bondspeople; the captain, Antônio Lacerda Peixoto, speculated that the malady had been contracted while the ship was still anchored on the African coast. What captives made of their circumstances as peril, and potentially death, loomed around them is unknown. Bound together and unable to escape contact with the bodies, sweat, urine, and feces of the mortally ill, they existed in a state of extreme vulnerability. Dying captives were unceremoniously removed, one by one, from the hold. Above, the ship's crew responded with alarm as they moved to stop the infection's spread.[1]

Captain Peixoto laid the blame for the journey's disastrous beginning entirely at the feet of Oiteiro. Peixoto alleged that Oiteiro had failed to apply

1. One year later, the same vessel was recorded as having carried 449 slaves to Bahia (Voyage ID 46978, *Voyages*). The ship's owner, Antônio Pedroso de Albuquerque, was just embarking on a long career as the owner of several slaving vessels, whereas Captain Peixoto would serve on a slaving vessel only once more. Albuquerque's vessels included several whose routes went according to plan: the *Novo Brihante* (1825), the *Venus* (1827), the *Pedroso* (1829), the *Campeadora* (1830), the *Flor de Etiópia* (1830), the *Coquete* (1840), the schooner *Picão* (1841 [three voyages], 1842)—and several more that were captured and condemned by the Mixed Commission, including the *Príncipe de Guiné* (1826), the *Venturoso* (1827), the *Crioula* (1827), the *Terceira Rosalia* (1828), and the *Veloz* (also the site of a slave insurrection in 1836); see Voyage IDs 2960, 2968, 1028, 1159, 1161, 2048, 2154, 2172, 2201, 2965, 2974, 2980, 2996, 3068.

any remedies from the ship's medicine chest, improve the diets of captives with fading health, or perform treatments in keeping with the "manner of the trade." Most damningly, Peixoto alleged that the African sangrador had not even been able to diagnose the illnesses that afflicted his enslaved patients, endangering not only the prospective profitability of the voyage but the lives of the other crew members. The captain expelled Oiteiro from the ship, a drastic move that forced the other officers (including the captain) to take over his duties, despite their "lack of practice" and knowledge of medical techniques. Peixoto's accusations reveal more than simply his commitment to blaming Oiteiro for his financial losses; they also expose the centrality of Black barbers and sangradores to Bahia's slave trade. In fact, the captain's testimony delineated a repertoire of duties commonly expected of such Black medical personnel: identifying illness, formulating and dispensing effective medicines, treating wounds, and monitoring the diets and overall health of captives. In short, captains tasked them with preventing the spread of infectious diseases aboard slaving vessels, in an environment where disease-driven mortality was an endemic part of life.[2]

This contentious episode on the *Novo Dispique* reveals one of the central paradoxes of the medical cosmopolitanism that defined African-born barbers' and sangradores' experiences of slaving commerce. Peixoto's insistence that he himself, as well as the other officers, had been betrayed by the "deceitful" African man in whose abilities they had placed their "good faith" illustrated a larger phenomenon: the extent to which slavers placed immense trust in the knowledge and skill of Black medical practitioners whose expertise drew not exclusively from European medical precepts but from intellectual and material resources that originated in Africa as well as across the globe.[3] The responsibility—and corresponding power—that white captains ceded to enslaved

2. BNA, FO 315/41, Papers of the *Penha da França*, nos. 12 and 17. The mortality rate of the *Novo Dispique*'s voyage—11.9 percent—was by no means anomalous. Highly infectious conditions maintained an average of a 6.8 percent mortality rate for Bahian ships between 1776 and 1830 (Joseph C. Miller, *Way of Death: Merchant Capitalism and the Angolan Slave Trade, 1730–1830* [Madison, Wis., 1988], 428–442). Between 1831 and 1851, mortality rates of captives rose sharply and averaged 19.9 percent; thus, the period discussed above represents a nadir of captive deaths during the transatlantic voyage, as illegal voyages then began to take on greater risks to avoid detection. See David Eltis and David Richardson, *Atlas of the Transatlantic Slave Trade* (New Haven, Conn., 2010), 185–187.

3. Peixoto's statement was perhaps also intended to guarantee that the owner of the *Novo Dispique* would blame the sangrador for the lost profits caused by captives who perished,

and freed African barbers and sangradores meant that such men were often highly valued and well compensated. They comprised some of the most affluent and upwardly mobile Black mariners working both within and on the peripheries of the Bahian slave trade.

Owners and captains placed barbers and sangradores in perilous circumstances as they treated the enslaved within tight enclosures, coming into close contact with highly infectious and sometimes deadly pathogens. At times viewed by white captains as incompetent and dangerous, such men could be scapegoated if they failed to maintain the health and thus value of the precious human cargo aboard. Barbers and sangradores exercised little control over the factors that most influenced the health of captives: the quality and quantity of shipboard rations, the space allotted to each individual belowdecks, captives' health before boarding ships, and overall voyage length. Nonetheless, the necessity of the Black healers' labor and the subjectivity of assessments about the cause of mortality aboard slaving vessels meant that captains and owners would continue to depend upon men such as Oiteiro for future voyages. Indeed, Oiteiro was not banished from the Bahian trade with his reputation in ruins following the deadly episode on the *Novo Dispique*. Within two years, he was hired to work on another slaving vessel, the *Emília*, and served without incident.[4]

This chapter explores a duality at the heart of enslaved barbers' and sangradores' lives and labors. On the one hand, such men were subaltern transatlantic intellectuals whose work functioned as a vector between healers based in West African ports, the enslaved men, women, and children held aboard ships, and the African residents of Bahia who required their care. As a crucial link between these geographically distant collectivities, barbers and sangradores spearheaded a larger transatlantic circulation of medical knowledge. On the other hand, this dissemination, by virtue of sangradores' occupational status, ensconced them in a healing project that sustained the profitability of South Atlantic slaving even as they gave sustenance, comfort, and respite to those dehumanized by its practices. Such healers sought out medicines and therapies that could cure African captives for the ultimate purpose of guaranteeing the captives' market value.

Sangradores' culturally specific knowledge attended to the bodily, spiritual, and corporeal health of enslaved Africans, particularly in the urban environs

---

ensuring that Peixoto and the other officers would avoid culpability (BNA, FO 315/41, Papers of the *Penha da França*, no. 17).

4. BNA, FO 315/43, Papers of the *Emília*, no. 23.

of Salvador da Bahia. Carrying out the critical task of healing both at sea and on shore, Bahian barbers and sangradores occupied multiple roles. When employed by slaving ship captains, they pioneered creolized therapies by incorporating African and European forms of bloodletting and botanical remedies to treat ailing enslaved individuals held in cargoes. In Salvador da Bahia's variegated healing landscape, they translated the maritime therapies forged on the decks of slaving ships to improvisational spaces of recovery—the humble barbershops, quiet street corners, and busy urban squares—where the city's impoverished African population sought remedies for myriad ailments. Many of Bahia's African barbers and sangradores circulated between maritime and urban healing spaces in the course of their careers. In terrestrial environments, barbers and sangradores influenced popular understandings of corporality and healing. Their labor enabled them to become vital brokers of medicinal material exchanges between West Africa and Bahia, as they disseminated ideas about efficacious therapies gleaned from their wide-ranging interactions. By the early nineteenth century, maritime barbers' work had become central to both the medical infrastructure of Salvador da Bahia and the transatlantic slave trade.

A number of scholars have highlighted the unique medical epistemologies created by enslaved Africans in the wake of the displacement and dehumanization of the transatlantic slave trade, particularly in terrestrial environments. In order to combat the twin bodily and existential threats represented by Atlantic slavery, Africans and their descendants in the diaspora collectively fashioned durable healing practices that attended not only to the physical but also to the social and spiritual deprivations of enslavement. The exact origins of such therapies, however, has divided historians into those who foreground African influences on New World practices and those who insist on American creolization.[5] For the former, African diasporic healing existed as a subversive social and political practice with epistemological roots in West

5. James H. Sweet's study of Mahi ritual healer Domingos Álvares in eighteenth-century Brazil locates the origins of his sought-after communal medicinal techniques in African categories of knowledge, particularly in the West African political idiom of healing. His practices were drawn from *vodun* worship and its attendant use of medicinal plants, prayers, shrine construction, and ritual animal sacrifice to cure. Álvares's therapies of ritual and bodily cleansing, Sweet argues, were native to the Bight of Benin—particularly the Fon and Mahi communities where Álvares had been born, though he also incorporated healing methods he learned in Brazil. See Sweet, *Domingos Álvares, African Healing, and the Intellectual History of the Atlantic World* (Chapel Hill, N.C., 2011), esp. 5–6; Karol K. Weaver, *Medical Revolutionaries: The Enslaved Healers of Eighteenth-Century Saint Domingue* (Urbana,

Africa, as specialists restored physical ailments as well as social ties destroyed by slavery, capitalism, and empire. In contrast, scholars who emphasize New World creative adaptations focus on how Black ritual practitioners devised new, creolized methods of healing for a diverse population, arguing that they drew on incorporative and improvisational knowledge-making strategies unrooted in a particular epistemological tradition.[6] Scholars of Atlantic Africa, moreover, have highlighted how readily colonial Europeans assimilated foreign techniques and materials into their repertoires. Building on this scholarly corpus, this chapter shows that Salvador, like many port cities across the Atlantic, became a locus of medical innovations as African-born practitioners' transoceanic work transmitted ideas about bodies, healing, and medicine between the coasts of Africa and Brazil.[7]

Ill., 2006); Sharla M. Fett, *Working Cures: Healing, Health, and Power on Southern Slave Plantations* (Chapel Hill, N.C., 2002).

6. Fett and Weaver also highlight continuities between Africa and the Americas in Black healing, especially in the case of root work—or botanical therapeutics. See Fett, *Working Cures*, 113–115, 123–129; Weaver, *Medical Revolutionaries*, 67. According to Pablo F. Gómez, seventeenth-century Black ritual healers utilized an experiential style that ushered in an "epistemological revolution" in which healing drew from methods of trial and error and sensorial observation, as opposed to received wisdom. Success or failure hinged on continuous reinvention in the context of a competitive, ethnically diverse market for reliable remedies (Gómez, *The Experiential Caribbean: Creating Knowledge and Healing in the Early Modern Atlantic* [Chapel Hill, N.C., 2017], 2–11).

7. Abena Dove Osseo-Asare, *Bitter Roots: The Search for Healing Plants in Africa* (Chicago, 2014); Hugh Cagle, *Assembling the Tropics: Science and Medicine in Portugal's Empire, 1450–1700* (Cambridge, 2018); Kalle Kananoja, "Bioprospecting and European Uses of African Natural Medicine in Early Modern Angola," *Portuguese Studies Review,* XXIII (2015), 45–69; Kananoja, *Healing Knowledge in Atlantic Africa: Medical Encounters, 1500–1850* (Cambridge, 2021); Tom C. McCaskie, "'The Art or Mystery of Physick'—Asante Medicinal Plants and the Western Ordering of Botanical Knowledge," *History in Africa,* XLIV (2017), 27–62; Londa Schiebinger, *Plants and Empire: Colonial Bioprospecting in the Atlantic World* (Cambridge, Mass., 2004); Susan Scott Parrish, "Diasporic African Sources of Enlightenment Knowledge," in James Delbourgo and Nicolas Dew, eds., *Science and Empire in the Atlantic World* (London, 2007), 281–310; William J. Simon, "A Luso-African Formulary of the Late Eighteenth Century: Some Notes on Angolan Contributions to European Knowledge of Materia Medica," *Pharmacy in History,* XVIII (1976), 103–114; Timothy Walker, "Acquisition and Circulation of Medical Knowledge within the Early Modern Portuguese Colonial Empire," in Daniela Bleichmar et al., eds., *Science in the Spanish and Portuguese Empires, 1500–1800* (Stanford, Calif., 2009), 247–270.

The intellectual work of African practitioners synthesized disparate African- and European-derived medical theories into a cosmopolitan healing practice that attended to the needs of the enslaved. Barbers and sangradores, epistemically grounded in West African methods, created therapies based on long-held interrelated notions of metaphysical power and bodily integrity while incorporating elements from other intellectual traditions. As the premier cosmopolitans of their milieu, they drew on a plurality of African ethnic healing practices to fashion a shared belief in the importance of a porous body, a potent head, and the curative quality of flowing blood. The power of such ideas persisted through the first half of the nineteenth century, shaping the most common forms of medical praxis in Salvador. At the same time, the cornerstone of their healing therapies—particularly phlebotomy, or bloodletting, and botanical pharmacy, or the application of herbal remedies—was legitimized by a widely practiced European therapy: the Hippocratic-Galenic theory of humoral balance, which required the expulsion of stagnant, harmful blood.[8]

Their intellectual labor also relied on an inherited but expanding (and at times improvised) repertoire of healing techniques and principles from West Africa, where many practitioners were born. Fluency in multiple healing traditions imbued their therapies with both intellectual and social legitimacy. Such men needed to demonstrate their understanding of the physical, natural, and spiritual forces that afflicted the body. Treatments required a high degree of intimacy and concomitant trust with those who laid their healing hands on ailing bodies; and constructing socially intelligible therapies demanded a knowledge of—and faithfulness to—the bodily imaginary of one's patients as well as the successful realization of dynamic and polysemic public healing performances. Barbers and sangradores in Bahia also drew on the relative openness, borrowing, and experimentation that characterized the relationship between local and nonlocal forms of healing in coastal Africa during the era of transatlantic slaving, where Portuguese colonists and indigenous communities exchanged therapeutic knowledge in a context where supposedly discrete medical practices resembled each other more than they differed.[9] Because African medical epistemology had always been dynamic, European

8. George M. Foster, "On the Origin of Humoral Medicine in Latin America," *Medical Anthropology Quarterly,* I (1987), 355–393; Foster, "The Validating Role of Humoral Theory in Traditional Spanish-American Therapeutics," *American Ethnologist,* XV (1988), 120–135.

9. As Kananoja has emphasized, medical pluralism prevailed in the early modern Atlantic, revealing that a simple dichotomy between traditionally African and American creolized forms of medicine elides the dynamism of therapeutic practice on the continent (Kananoja, *Healing Knowledge in Atlantic Africa,* 8–11). For more on "therapeutic pluralism," see Steven

and American practitioners found it easy to derive inspiration from the healers they encountered on the African coast. Indeed, as Portuguese physicians and apothecaries in particular expanded their own pharmacopoeia knowledge, they coveted African botanical expertise because of the respective traditions' compatibility.[10]

Scholars' emphasis on diasporic creativity and improvisation, however, has tended to overshadow the degree to which West African cultures demonstrated a propensity to "adopt, adapt and innovate" independent of Europeans' influences. Though the logic underpinning Afro-Bahian therapies was derived from Africa, it was not always orthodox. Indeed, medical practices had to be malleable, given the geographic, ethnic, and cultural diversity of African-born people who arrived on the shores of Brazil. Because many disembarked with "broadly shared sensibilities," healers devised adaptive strategies of bodily restoration based on techniques they learned from each other in the multiethnic landscape of the city. An African-oriented medical cosmopolitanism emerged from practitioners' simultaneous willingness to experiment with novel healing strategies alongside their predilection to turn to a multiplicity of African-derived therapies as the most effective means for preserving life in the face of rampant illness in Salvador and on slaving vessels. The intellectual and ritual power they derived from transforming the broken bodies of enslaved patients into healthy ones imparted them with a level of social prestige, recognition, and economic advancement largely unmatched by other Africans in Salvador.[11]

Feierman, *Peasant Intellectuals: Anthropology and History in Tanzania* (Madison, Wis., 1990), 100–111.

10. Spaces where European practitioners were absent also gave birth to potent cross-cultural medical amalgamations. This is particularly true of communities that were home to Muslim ritual healers. See Ismail H. Abdalla, "Diffusion of Islamic Medicine into Hausa-land," in Steven Feierman and John M. Janzen, eds., *The Social Basis of Health and Healing in Africa* (Berkeley, Calif., 1992), 177–194; Bernard Greenwood, "Cold or Spirits? Ambiguity and Syncretism in Moroccan Therapeutics," ibid., 285–314; Thomas Lux, "Healer as Producer of Reality and Knowledge: The Examples of Blacksmiths among the Songhay," *Curare*, XVII (1994), 181–198; Philip J. Havik, "Hybridising Medicine: Illness, Healing, and the Dynamics of Reciprocal Exchange on the Upper Guinea Coast (West Africa)," *Medical History*, LX (2016), 181–205; Kananoja, *Healing Knowledge in Atlantic Africa*, 19–20, 44–45, 51; Benjamin Breen, *The Age of Intoxication: Origins of the Global Drug Trade* (Philadelphia, 2019), 57–58.

11. Joseph C. Miller, "Retention, Reinvention, and Remembering: Restoring Identities through Enslavement in Africa and under Slavery in Brazil," in José C. Curto and Paul E.

Though influenced by African epistemologies and sensibilities, such maritime medical practices were not counterhegemonic. Crucial in sustaining the longevity and profitability of the transatlantic slave trade by maintaining low mortality rates, these men's healing practices operated at the intersection of the competing imperatives of commerce, evolving medical discourses originating from Europe, and intensifying notions of racial hierarchy. Imperial prerogatives to lessen shipboard mortality rates of slaves, merchants' efforts to keep investment costs on slaving voyages low by employing inexpensive labor, and competing claims to exclusive healing knowledge by physicians all contributed to barbers' and sangradores' precarious position at sea. On land, the African residents of Bahia sought out the expertise of African-born medical practitioners, endowing them with elevated prestige and social status. But on slaving vessels, the unwilling subjects of shipboard barbers' and sangradores' treatments exercised little control over the manner of therapies used to preserve their rapidly deteriorating health. African practitioners became enmeshed in the violent mechanisms of coercion used to control captive cargoes on slaving vessels, where they imposed potentially lifesaving but intrusive therapies on patients. In maritime spaces of healing, the preferences of slaving merchants and captains reigned supreme. On Bahian slaving vessels, the preservation of enslaved individuals' physical soundness and thus commercial value motivated the application of heterodox healing therapies. Slaving vessels became sites of intellectual transmission and medical improvisation as well as spaces where the power and hierarchies of transatlantic slaving endured and constrained the work of African healers. On board such ships, barbers and sangradores fashioned themselves into key actors in the

---

Lovejoy, eds., *Enslaving Connections: Changing Cultures of Africa and Brazil during the Era of Slavery* (Amherst, N.Y., 2004), 85. Edna Bay argues that endless adaptation, invention, and modification characterizes the religious system of vodun (Bay, *Asen, Ancestors, and Vodun: Tracing Change in African Art* [Champaign-Urbana, 2008], 6). For more on New World creativity of Africans, see Sidney W. Mintz and Richard Price, *The Birth of African-American Culture: An Anthropological Perspective* (Boston, 1992); Suzanne Preston Blier, *African Vodun: Art, Psychology, and Power* (Chicago, 1995), 9. For a critique of the idea of orthodoxy in African ritual and a case for the salience of orthopraxis, see Laura S. Grillo, "African Rituals," in Elias Kifon Bongmba, ed., *The Wiley-Blackwell Companion to African Religions* (Oxford, 2012), 112–126. On the relationship between control over diagnosis of illness, the performance of acts of healing, and social authority in Africa, see Feierman and Janzen, "Introduction," *Social Basis of Health and Healing in Africa*, 18; Feierman, *Peasant Intellectuals*, 107.

maintenance of the Bahian slave trade, which continued to rely on the conscription of their creativity, knowledge, and agency to profitably function.[12]

SICKNESS, DEATH, AND HEALING IN COLONIAL BAHIA

On the punishing passages between Africa's coast and the city's harbor, slaving ship captains depended on the skills of African barbers and sangradores in lieu of formally trained white surgeons and physicians. These African practitioners emerged from a medical community based in Salvador that was overwhelmingly African born, mostly enslaved, and educated in the context of a perilous epidemiological urban landscape. Nothing contributed to the high rates of disease in Salvador da Bahia as much as the transatlantic slave trade. Slaving ships—as spaces that, by their very nature and organization, produced chronic malnutrition, infectious disease, and bodily injury—guaranteed a continuous stream of ill and malnourished captives who tested the medical capacities of local practitioners. In port, slave trafficking was widely viewed as a source of disease and death, and by the beginning of the nineteenth century, its latent dangers inspired the creation of a new public health apparatus aimed at containing the spread of diseases believed to originate in Western Africa.[13] Despite practitioners' efforts to maintain captives' health while at sea, contagions spread easily. Belated attempts at prophylaxis remained inadequate, and the overall attitude of the colonial state continued to be one of neglect. Private slaveowners in Bahia were also indifferent. Rarely willing to expend the necessary funds to contract academically trained physicians to treat their ailing bondspeople, they left the enslaved to seek therapies for themselves.

Within this lacuna of care, African and creole healers bearing specialized skills flourished. A paucity of credentialed surgeons in the Portuguese colony enabled the proliferation of skilled barbers who were trained—like

12. Sowande' M. Mustakeem, *Slavery at Sea: Terror, Sex, and Sickness in the Middle Passage* (Urbana, Ill., 2016), 45. Some scholars, such as Sweet, Weaver, and Fett, have argued that such influence was counterhegemonic, or that Africans in the Americas created a counterculture of medicine and health. See Sweet, *Domingos Álvares;* Weaver, *Medical Revolutionaries;* Fett, *Working Cures.*

13. A. J. R. Russell-Wood argues for the predominance of Africans and African descendants among barbers and sangradores throughout Brazil in the eighteenth century. In Bahia from 1741–1749, of thirty-eight registered barbers, seventeen were slaves, and twenty-one were free Blacks or *pardos* (of mixed European and African ancestry). In 1810–1822, of thirty-three barbers, thirteen were free blacks or pardos, whereas twenty were slaves. See Russell-Wood, *The Black Man in Slavery and Freedom in Colonial Brazil* (New York, 1982), 57.

other artisans—by masters. Under master barbers in barbershops, practitioners learned and performed services including cutting hair, pulling teeth, bleeding patients, and performing minor surgeries. They acquired knowledge and experience through application of their trade under supervision rather than through the abstract study of medical treatises and theories of nutrition, disease, and pharmacopoeia. Barbers, however, were distinct from the numerous African and creole lay healers (or *curandeiros*) who also roamed urban streets and squares. Barbers' work, in contrast to that of other Black healers, had been conferred with royal legitimacy through a range of temporary and permanent licenses (*provisões* or *cartas*) that were financed by their owners, slaving ship captains, master barbers, or the owners of the shops in which they were employed. As early as 1741, the law required barbers to apply for a license to practice, a process that required the payment of a fee and an examination by a panel of doctors and the chief surgeon of Portugal. Royal authorization for African (both enslaved and freed) barbers and sangradores condoned the medical therapies they performed as well as the profession itself by subjecting applicants to tests of their skills. The royal government's attempts to institutionalize and regulate the work of sangradores and barbers developed from a recognition that African medical practitioners were already an integral part of a colonial slave society where a sizable portion of the population was chronically ill and more likely to prefer therapies offered by African practitioners to the treatments provided by white surgeons and physicians.[14]

In Salvador, like other urban centers in colonial Brazil, the combination of endemic poverty, malnutrition, poor urban sanitation, frequently rancid food, and limited medical provisions generated insalubrious living conditions for

14. Mariza de Carvalho Soares, "African Barbeiros in Brazil Slave Ports," in Jorge Cañizares-Esguerra, Matt D. Childs, and James Sidbury, eds., *The Black Urban Atlantic in the Age of the Slave Trade* (Philadelphia, 2013), 218; Russell-Wood, *Black Man in Slavery and Freedom,* 56–57. On medical licenses, see Soares, "African Barbeiros," 218; Tânia Salgado Pimenta, "Terapeutas populares e instituições médicas na primeira metade do século XIX," in Sidney Chalhoub et al., eds., *Artes e ofícios de curar no Brasil* (Campinas, Brazil, 2003), 311. The predominance of African medical practitioners at sea mirrored realities in the urban landscape of Salvador. This is explicable when one considers the development of medical institutions in Brazil. Until 1808—when the newly relocated Portuguese crown created the Escola de Cirurgia da Bahia (Bahia School of Surgery)—the colony lacked medical schools and other forms of institutionalized medical knowledge. This absence forestalled the ascendance of academically trained surgeons over lay practitioners. See Pimenta, "Physicians and Surgeons in the Early Decades of the Nineteenth Century in Brazil," *Almanack,* Guarulhos, no. 22, 120–152, esp. 122.

most of the city's freed and enslaved populations. The routine recurrence of diseases such as leprosy, yellow fever, and dysentery brought by sailors, slaves, and passengers on arriving ships heightened an already dangerous epidemiological environment. Moreover, damp and unsanitary living conditions in the crowded lower city, especially during the heavy rains in the summer months of November, December, and January, exacerbated outbreaks of respiratory and pulmonary infections such as tuberculosis, rheumatic fever, and ague. Heavy rains washed animal and human waste into low-lying areas of the city, where many of the poor and enslaved lived, resulting in increased incidents of dysentery and typhoid. Humidity, rain, and pests assaulted the bodies of the enslaved, inflicting endemic parasitic ailments and contagious skin diseases. One such parasite originated in the Americas and was introduced to western Africa only through sand ballast carried by slaving vessels. Nonetheless, contemporary doctors such as Luiz Antônio de Oliveira Mendes associated the sand flea and its accompanying skin disease with indigenous Angolans and newly arrived enslaved Africans. Mendes's interpretation of the malady's origin both echoed and reinforced a broader impression of the enslaved—and especially of the newly arrived *boçais* (unacculturated) Africans—as particularly disease ridden (*bichados*).[15]

In response to the pervasive devastation of illness in the city, healers, therapists, and patients collectively created culturally independent spaces of healing. African curandeiros, midwives, barbers, and sangradores specialized in treating other Africans in the city and carved out niches in the broader urban medical landscape, offering specific therapies for specific ailments. Throughout the eighteenth and early nineteenth centuries, traveling barbers roamed

15. A. J. R. Russell-Wood, *Fidalgos and Philanthropists: The Santa Casa da Misericórdia of Bahia, 1550–1755* (Berkeley, Calif., 1968), 260–271, 288–290. Russell-Wood notes that, in November and December 1742 and the first eight months of the following year, there were more than five thousand deaths from respiratory illnesses in the city (ibid., 289). Scabies (an infestation of skin-burrowing mites), yaws (painful bacterial lesions), "guinea worm" (*Dracunculus medinensis*), parasites in the legs (*bicho de pé*), a painful skin disease caused by the penetration of sand fleas (*Tunga penetrans*) into the feet, and boils afflicted much of the enslaved population. See Jean Baptiste Debret, *Viagem pitoresca e histórica ao Brasil*, I (São Paulo, 1972), 268; Miller, *Way of Death*, 429; Russell-Wood, *Fidalgos and Philanthropists*, 289; Weaver, *Medical Revolutionaries*, 24; Jorg Heukelbach, "Tungiasis," *Revista do Instituto de Medicina Tropical de São Paulo*, XLVII (São Paulo, 2005), 307–313. For Luiz Antônio de Oliveira Mendes's observations, see his *Memórias econômicas da Academia Real das Sciencias de Lisboa . . .*, IV (Lisbon, 1812), 56. An account from 1847 described the symptoms and treatment of the infamous and pervasive bicho: "It first appears as a slight spec, and is

Salvador's streets and squares, attending to wage-earning slaves who labored as porters, food and textile vendors, sailors, errand boys, and artisans. Elsewhere, barbers worked in small shops as "master[s] of a thousand talents," where they utilized a broad range of tools to perform barbering, bleeding, tooth extraction, and the application of leeches. The clientele of stationary barbers were more varied and included middle-class urban residents as well as impoverished or enslaved Africans. Another category of healer, identified by one visitor as "African surgeons" (a group who likely considered themselves to be curandeiros or sangradores), diagnosed illnesses, provided medications and talismans, applied blistering cups, and bled patients in bustling public spaces. They offered "comfort" and solutions to men and women with no alternate means of treatment, including those whose owners neglected to provide medical care or freed individuals who were too poor to afford the attention of a white or *pardo* surgeon. Sometimes labeled "popular healers," these men and women provided vital medical attention for those who, owing to malnutrition, poverty, overwork, and heightened exposure to pathogens, were most vulnerable to disease and injury. In return, medical practitioners were accorded respect and deference by the community of enslaved and freed Africans because of their unique and superior practical (as well as spiritual) knowledge. Far from the gaze of elite Bahians, African medical practitioners served an almost exclusively Black clientele. Trusted by African patients for their widely recognized expertise, they derived their legitimacy from the preferences of Salvador's popular classes.[16]

---

surrounded shortly by a livid colour. It soon increases and forms a bag, filled with young, which requires to be skilfully removed, otherwise, if the bag be broken there may be some left in the skin. From constant practice, the blacks are the best operators. After extraction, snuff, or lime scraped from the white-washed walls, is generally put into the wounds to kill the embryo bicho, should such be left. Erisypelas has been known to supervene in cases where the bicho has been carelessly taken out, and blacks are occasionally met with who have lost their toes consequent upon unskilful extraction." See James Wetherell, *Brazil: Stray Notes from Bahia; Being Extracts from Letters, etc., during a Residence of Fifteen Years,* ed. William Hadfield (Liverpool, U.K., 1860), 19; Russell-Wood, *Fidalgos and Philanthropists,* 261–262.

16. Russell-Wood, *Black Man in Slavery and Freedom,* 56–57; Debret, *Viagem,* 151, 268; Zephyr L. Frank, *Dutra's World: Wealth and Family in Nineteenth-Century Rio de Janeiro* (Albuquerque, N.M., 2004), 109; Pimenta, "Terapeutas populares," in Chalhoub et al., eds., *Artes e ofícios de curar no Brasil,* 323. As Kananoja notes, in Central Africa, individuals with medical expertise often wielded political power. In short, "those who controlled healing, controlled people" (*Healing Knowledge in Atlantic Africa,* 215).

SLAVING SHIP HEALERS

Many of Bahia's healers circulated between land and sea. On slaving ships sailing from Salvador between 1810 and 1839, African-born men comprised 82 percent (43 of 52) of medical practitioners, and Brazilian-born men of at least partial African descent made up an additional 16 percent. In contrast to the cultural milieu of Black Salvador, however, slaving vessels were spaces where the inclinations of merchants and captains, not patients, prevailed. There, captains and owners of ships contracted freedmen, or *escravos de ganho,* whose owners resided in Salvador. Other Black practitioners were the property of captains or prosperous slaving merchants. The captains assumed that African-born medical practitioners were better suited to treating other Africans. As Susan Scott Parrish has argued, for British inhabitants in the early modern Atlantic, Portuguese merchants "constructed African expertise spatially, topically, and temporally rather than in an essential hierarchy of superior and inferior." Instead of insisting on the universal superiority of European physicians and methods of medical treatment, Europeans on the West African coast deferred to the greater experience of indigenous medical practitioners in treating local diseases. In Brazil, acceptance and even endorsement of heterodox medicinal practices was facilitated by the European perception of African familiarity with ailments particularly widespread in the enslaved African population, as well as the treatments to cure them.[17]

Because of shipowners' belief that African practitioners were best suited to treat enslaved individuals held in cargoes, they employed such men at a high rate. Although Africans made up 35.5 percent of all maritime personnel on slaving vessels in the same period, they virtually monopolized the positions of barber, surgeon, and sangrador. When the British and Portuguese crowns

17. Rana A. Hogarth, *Medicalizing Blackness: Making Racial Difference in the Atlantic World, 1780–1840* (Chapel Hill, N.C., 2017), 8–9; Parrish, "Diasporic African Sources of Enlightenment Knowledge," in Delbourgo and Dew, eds., *Science and Empire in the Atlantic World,* 286; Weaver, *Medical Revolutionaries,* 68–69; Kananoja, *Healing Knowledge in Atlantic Africa,* 105; Havik, "Hybridising Medicine," *Medical History,* XL (2016), 181–205. These statistics are derived from ships adjudicated by the Mixed Commission Courts in Freetown, Sierra Leone, where the birthplace of crew members was recorded between 1811 and 1829. See Chapter 4, above, for more details. Joaquim de Moraes, a freed African and sangrador on the *Emília,* testified that he was appointed by the ship's owner, Manoel Francisco Moreira (AHI, Coleções Especiais, Comissão Mista, lata 13, maço 14, pasta 1, Papers of the *Emília,* 345).

agreed to a partial abolition of the slave trade in African ports north of the equator in 1817, an amendment to the treaty enacted in 1818 stipulated that

> If Surgeons do not sail on board such Vessels, on account of the
> impossibility of procuring them, or for some other reason equally
> conclusive, the Owners shall be obliged to carry with them black
> Sangradores, experienced in the treatment of the diseases with which
> the Slaves are commonly afflicted, and in the remedies proper for
> curing them.

Superficially, the treaty—articulated in the language of enlightened humanism characteristic of abolitionist legal culture—expressed a preference for academically trained surgeons. The impulse to substitute African-born practitioners for European ones in the treatment of the enslaved, however, had a deeper rationale than mere expediency. Assumptions about the proper division of medical expertise in the preceding century emphasized geographic more than racial difference. The belief that certain diseases—particularly fevers—were unique to tropical "torrid zones" such as Africa and Brazil meant that locally born people were more familiar with the constitutions of those stricken with such diseases as well as how to treat them. Many merchants with this belief embraced medical heterodoxy as a matter of necessity, deferring to African therapists and caretakers to treat their enslaved property.[18]

Slavers viewed captives' health and healing options through the lens of a balance between presumed efficacy and cost and were inclined to provide some semblance of health provisioning aboard their vessels. Between 1811 and 1839, the vast majority of African captives transported by Bahian ships had access to some form of specialized medical care. A survey of fifty-one ships originating from Salvador reveals that forty-five employed at least one medical practitioner, and seven employed two. By the beginning of the nineteenth century, therefore, more than 88 percent of slaving vessels carried surgeons, sangradores, or barbers, with the latter the most commonly employed. The duties of barbers and sangradores remained in large part interchangeable. In 1827, freed African sangrador Francisco Joaquim dos Santos listed the specialties of his "art" as "bleeding, scarifying, applying cups and leeches." These duties match those required of barbers in 1782 by the royal Junta de Proto-

18. *British and Foreign State Papers, 1820–1821* (London, 1830), 23; José Pinto de Azeredo, *Ensaios sobre algumas enfermidades d'Angola* (Lisbon, 1799), viii. For a discussion of competing conceptualizations of global "torrid zones," see Cagle, *Assembling the Tropics*, 54. For the tabulation of slaving ship papers, see Appendix 1, below.

TABLE 9. *Wages Listed by Occupation (Rounded to Closest Full 1$000* Réis *Value) and Year*

Years	Profession	Average wage / pay	Median wage / pay
1811–1813	Barber	87$000	80$000
	Sangrador	N/A	N/A
	Surgeon	N/A	N/A
1821–1826	Barber	200$000	200$000
	Sangrador	163$000	165$000
	Sangrador or barber	180$000	180$000
	Surgeon	200$000	200$000
1827–1831	Barber	N/A	N/A
	Sangrador	175$000	175$000
	Surgeon	250$000	250$000

Source: Figures are derived from a compilation of slaving ships listed in Appendix 1.

medicato (Board of Physicians). The prevalence of sangradores in the later period reflected a mere change in title rather than a shift in tangible medical practice. The wages of barbers, surgeons, and sangradores likewise remained commensurate, though wages for all medical practitioners aboard slaving ships gradually increased during the initial decades of the nineteenth century (see Table 9). Medical personnel continued to be the highest-paid African and creole crew members aboard slaving ships, receiving the same compensation as other officers (including quartermasters and coopers), though lower than mariners engaged in navigational duties.[19]

Black barbers not only treated valuable human commodities; they were valuable laborers and commodities themselves. If they were enslaved, their owners regularly appraised medical practitioners' market worth above other

19. Pimenta, "Terapeutas populares," in Chalhoub et al., eds., *Artes e ofícios de curar no Brasil,* 307; Jean Luiz Neves Abreu, *Nos domínios do corpo: O saber médico Luso-Brasileiro no século XVIII* (Rio de Janeiro, 2011), 26. Slaving merchants overwhelmingly favored contracting barbers to treat their crews and enslaved cargoes, with only 9 percent of the twenty-two barbers registered in the years after 1815. In the period from 1815 to 1829, twenty-eight sangradores were registered on Bahian ships, indicating a shift to slaving merchants, employing almost exclusively bloodletters on their vessels. In 1826, on the ship *Venturoso,* Vicente Francisco Camaxo's registered occupation was listed as "barber or *sangrador,*" indicating that the two titles were indeed interchangeable. See AHI, Coleções Especiais, Comissão Mista, lata 31, maço 7, pasta 1, Papers of the *Venturoso.*

TABLE 10. *Age Distribution of Barbers and* Sangradores
Employed in Bahia, 1811–1839

Number of mariners identified by age

10S	20S	30S	40S	50S	TOTAL
1	4	4	3	2	14
7.14%	28.57%	28.57%	21.43%	14.29%	100%

Source: Figures are derived from a compilation of slaving ships listed in
Appendix 1.

---

enslaved men working in skilled trades. In 1827, the prominent Bahian slaving merchant and shipowner José de Cerqueira Lima argued that his enslaved sangrador Barilio was worth 800$000 réis because of the man's "fine figure" and "great expertise at his art." Twelve other enslaved crew members, all common sailors and all "expert in the practice of the sea," were valued significantly lower, at 500$000 réis. Moreover, enterprising owners would often purchase newly arrived adolescent Africans for the express purpose of training them in the vocation of barbering, hoping to elevate the value of their human property through mechanical education while exerting a degree of intellectual control over their bondsmen. Unlike barbers and sangradores instructed on land, slave-trade medical personnel either trained under a primary barber as a "second," or steward, or did not receive any formal training at all. Young men dominated the ranks of slave-trade barbers and sangradores, with 64.3 percent below the age of forty (Table 10). The youngest sangrador was the tender age of seventeen. Indeed, the paucity of middle-aged barbers and sangradores in crew manifests reflected their upward social trajectory. Initially, their inexperience and enslaved status could depress their wages, making them more affordable for merchants looking to cut costs. Multiple successful voyages, however, could allow barbers to quickly amass sizable personal wealth—acquired through both trade and wages—sufficient to purchase their own manumission. Fully 39.6 percent of African and creole barbers were identified as freed.[20]

20. AHI, Coleções Especiais, Comissão Mista, lata 18, maço 3, pasta 1, Papers of the *Indêpendencia*, 11. Lima's estimates were inflated for the period, however. The seasoned slaving merchant, whose ships were regularly seized by British antislaving forces, most likely attempted to claim restitution at higher rates in order to profit. Owners at times trained enslaved individuals in multiple "professions"; for example, in 1811, an unnamed slaveowner sold a young creole adolescent who labored as a "captain, a barber and knew something of

The career arcs of African healers suggest how complex such competing incentives could be. Once they escaped the bonds of slavery, some African healers left the slave trade altogether, preferring to labor in less perilous circumstances. The high retention of freedmen in the ranks of slaving ship crews, however, illustrates that the lucrative nature of seafaring work continued to lure medical practitioners to the trade. In 1822, African sangrador Joaquim de Moraes had lived in Salvador for seven years. He had already secured manumission, pointing not only to the frequency of manumission for medical practitioners but its rapidity as well. Like many seafaring barbers, Moraes responded to the potent combination of monetary incentives and a lack of alternative means of support at the end of his own enslavement, deciding to continue laboring in the infamous trade. Overall, 34 percent of barbers and sangradores working on the fifty-one vessels were identified as enslaved, though the true number was likely higher. The slave trade was a common starting point for enslaved medical practitioners forced to take a less desirable post before they had accumulated significant healing experience.[21]

ASSESSING BODIES AND PROCURING PROFITS

Barbers' and sangradores' relative privilege vis-à-vis other enslaved Bahians could obscure the harrowing and dangerous nature of their labor. As an essential part of the brutal merchant capitalist machinery that transformed African men, women, and children into fungible Atlantic commodities, barbers and sangradores assessed and maintained the commercial value of enslaved individuals held in cargoes, often in the most intimate ways. After weeks or even months at sea en route to the west coast of Africa, the grim work of slaving ship barbers and sangradores began in earnest. Within bustling commercial ports and rustic *feitorias* and on the exposed beaches of the Mina Coast, their

---

the profession of cook." See *Idade d'Ouro do Brazil* (Bahia), Nov. 1, 1811, no. 50. The percentage of freed Africans working in the slave trade in Salvador was also much higher than what Soares found for the trade in Rio de Janeiro ("African Barbeiros," in Cañizares-Esguerra, Childs, and Sidbury, eds., *Black Urban Atlantic,* 221).

21. AHI, Coleções Especiais, Comissão Mista, lata 13, maço 14, pasta 1, Papers of the *Emília,* 345. This aspect mirrors the British trade, which commonly employed barber-surgeons who could not find jobs in England or Scotland because of lack of experience. See Richard B. Sheridan, "The Guinea Surgeons on the Middle Passage: The Provision of Medical Services in the British Slave Trade," *International Journal of African Historical Studies,* XIV (1981), 611.

intellectual labor reconfigured vulnerable, displaced individuals into bodies with a quantifiable market value that could be inscribed into the balance books of ship clerks and captains.[22] African medical practitioners were tasked with appraising the eyes, teeth, skin, height, and genitals for age, "imperfections," or visible signs of infectious disease. This grim responsibility made them central actors in the contentious negotiations that played out between the West African brokers who supplied captives and the Brazilian slaving captains who endeavored to pay the lowest price for them.

Crucially, African medical practitioners' examinations helped to determine enslaved people's value at the moment of purchase. Captains also tasked them with assessing captives' suitability for surviving the arduous transatlantic voyage and the likelihood of their ultimate resale in Bahia. Because the price assigned to enslaved bodies on both sides of the Atlantic largely determined the profitability of any given voyage, market preferences forged in Bahia for age, gender, health, and bodily fitness reverberated across the ocean. Portuguese traders pioneered methods for physically examining and evaluating the enslaved, labeling the practice *palmeo,* in reference to the desired height of "seven palms" for those they attempted to purchase. Brazilian and Portuguese merchants remained notorious among European peers for their preference of adolescent male slaves (*molecãos*) and young boys (*moleques*). Adolescent females (*moleconas*) were deemed less commercially desirable. Within the broader category of preference, captains sought out the enslaved individuals they imagined had the longest potential working life as well as the greatest cultural and linguistic malleability and best physical adaptability to arduous agricultural labor. To meet this demand, African merchants sometimes shaved older captives and rubbed their faces with pumice stone to create a beardless appearance; buyers or barbers would lick the cheeks of young male captives to discern their true age. Aging skin was massaged with palm oil, and gray hairs were shaved off to produce "ideal slaves." Observant barbers and sangradores attempted to detect these ruses in order to negotiate lower prices or refuse purchase.[23]

22. African ports with a more regularized trade with Portuguese and Brazilian merchants (such as Ouidah, and later Porto Novo, Lagos, Badagry, and Agoué) usually contained small feitorias owned by individual traders or slaving ship captains. In less-frequented ports, captains, clerks, and other personnel erected short-term camps on the port's beach, from which they could conduct business transactions.

23. Hugh Thomas, *The Slave Trade: The Story of the Atlantic Slave Trade: 1440–1870* (New York, 1997), 395; Robert Harms, *The Diligent: A Voyage through the Worlds of the Slave Trade* (New York, 2002), 247–248; Robin Law, *Ouidah: The Social History of a West*

For those caught in the midst of such high-stakes negotiations—the enslaved men, women, and children offered for sale—a sense of bewilderment and extreme deprivation accompanied the series of displacements that had forced them to the West African coast. Compulsory medical examinations were preceded by a prolonged march to Atlantic shores in small groups at the hands of local brokers. These strenuous journeys were rife with hunger, exposure, exhaustion, pain, and disease. At times, such treks led to the loss of as many as half of all enslaved individuals by escape or death. In addition, the logistical considerations of West African coastal brokers required extended periods of confinement in rudimentary barracoons before the enslaved embarked for Brazil. While in port, the enslaved lingered in horrific conditions. In Savi, for instance, merchants kept slaves in irons within European-held "trunks," or huts, before they could be carried aboard sailing vessels. One European visitor in the eighteenth century complained of the "horrid stench" resulting from the absence of latrines and of the inadequacy of provisioning, which amounted to little more than bread and water.[24]

The time spent in these coastal enclaves highlighted the profound liminality of enslaved individuals awaiting transatlantic sale. Ripped from their natal communities, with their previous ties of kinship severed, these human beings were being transformed into anonymous chattel. The application of violent surveillance and the cultivation of fear staved off rebellion and attempted flight at this sensitive moment. As former slave Joseph Wright explained of his detention in Lagos in the 1820s, after a "strict examination" by a "white Portuguese" buyer, slavers held him for two months "with a rope around my neck. All the young boys had ropes round their necks in a row, and all the men with chains in a long row, for about fifty persons in a row, so that no one could

---

African Slaving "Port," 1727–1892 (Athens, Ohio, 2005), 141. As Mustakeem has argued, "The motivating force for negotiations hinged on obtaining those physically and psychologically capable of enduring the hardships of bondage" (*Slavery at Sea,* 44; see also 48).

24. Law, *Ouidah,* 137, 140. On the slave trade as an experience of serial displacement, see Alexander X. Byrd, *Captives and Voyagers: Black Migrants across the Eighteenth-Century British Atlantic World* (Baton Rouge, 2008); Sharla M. Fett, "Middle Passages and Forced Migrations: Liberated Africans in Nineteenth-Century U.S. Camps and Ships," *Slavery and Abolition,* XXXI (2010), 75–98. The distinction between the Bight of Benin and Angola is clear in the size and length of captives' trek from the interior. In Angola, sizable caravans of as many as one thousand slaves required captives to be coffled, or placed in gangs in fetters at the hand or ankle, and marched to the coast. Such journeys could cover twenty miles per day and last several months (Thomas, *Slave Trade,* 383–387). "Half of all enslaved individuals" comes from Raymond Jalamá's observations in late-eighteenth-century Luanda (ibid., 386).

escape without the other." His isolation intensified as his captors led him to the sea. "We were all very sorrowful in heart," Wright recounted, "because we were going to leave our land for another . . . [and] we had heard that the Portuguese were going to eat us when they got to their country." Tormented at the thought of irreversible separation from his homeland, Wright experienced an existential rupture. For Africans who defined themselves socially, the prospect of permanent removal from kinship networks represented no less than a death of the self. Moreover, his fear of white cannibalism revealed his critique of the moral abomination perpetrated by rapacious slaving merchants who metaphorically consumed the bodies of African captives in pursuit of individualistic monetary reward. Echoes of Wright's particular sense of dread were common in testimonies from other enslaved people, who frequently feared slavers had designs to lure them to the land of the dead.[25]

Though slave traders and merchants have, for good reason, been placed at the center of this ordeal, Black maritime workers also participated in the emotionally fraught process of detention. Their medical labor remained critical to enslaved people's transformation into fungible commodities for sale and transport. In the early nineteenth century, freedman and abolitionist Mahommah Baquaqua described his captivity in Little Popo before embarking to Pernambuco: "Whilst at this place, the slaves were all put into a pen, and placed with our backs to the fire, and ordered not to look about us, and to insure obedience, a man was placed in front with a whip in his hand ready to strike the first who should dare to disobey orders." With his visibility constrained, disoriented, and unsure of what lay ahead, Baquaqua had little defense against what was to come next. "Another man," Baquaqua recalled, "then went round with a hot iron, and branded us the same as they would the heads of barrels or any other inanimate goods or merchandize." For Baquaqua, this moment married literal and symbolic violence and was a forceful illustration of slavers' objectification of him.[26]

Though not explicitly noted, the act of branding—a routine part of the Bahian slave trade—would likely have been performed by sangradores and barbers. If they were part of the ship's onshore crew, such men would have

25. Thomas, *Slave Trade,* 714; Jared Staller, *Converging on Cannibals: Terrors of Slaving in Atlantic Africa, 1509–1670* (Athens, Ohio, 2019), 6; Roquinaldo Ferreira, *Cross-Cultural Exchange in the Atlantic World: Angola and Brazil during the Era of the Slave Trade* (New York, 2012), 157–159; Miller, *Way of Death,* 5, 425.

26. Robin Law and Paul Lovejoy, eds., *The Biography of Mahommah Gardo Baquaqua: His Passage from Slavery to Freedom in Africa and America,* 2d ed. (Princeton, N.J., 2009), 149–150; Miller, *Way of Death,* 441–442.

been responsible for marking the backs, shoulders, chests, and arms of the enslaved with up to fifty distinctive signs representing the diverse investors on individual voyages. Merchants' insistence on the practice stemmed from their conviction that it was a defense against commercial fraud aboard their vessels. Without it, they feared, captains and crewmembers would substitute their surviving captives for African individuals they had purchased who had succumbed to disease before landing in Bahia. In facilitating this process, barbers and sangradores drew on their expertise, lubricating hot irons with palm oil to prevent them from sticking to the skin. For the enslaved, the trauma of skin disfigurement lingered long past this initial moment of violence, as scarification, tattooing, and other skin modifications signified various forms of social belonging in West African communities. Slavers' marks, identical to the symbols charred into boxes, barrels, and pipes containing trade goods, indicated a new reality: the transformation of human beings from socially embedded individuals to interchangeable, disposable, and enslaved commodities.[27]

Sequestering enslaved people on shore immersed slaving crews in volatile and often contagious circumstances. In 1807, the Bahian brig *Intrepido* left Lagos with six hundred slaves waiting on land under the eye of the brig's quartermaster. Suddenly, the sequestered captives fell prey to an aggressive sickness that swept through the barracoon housing them. According to the captain, "no one escaped death" during the onslaught, save the thirty-odd slaves who remained alive, though gravely ill. The insalubrious conditions in barracoons—which most often was defined by an absence of adequate nutrition and clean water, exposure to feces, and close contact with other contagious captives—made such epidemiological catastrophes all the more likely. As Joseph C. Miller has argued, the squalid atmosphere enslaved individuals were held in for several weeks while they awaited embarkation from Luanda had an adverse effect on shipboard health, claiming the lives of 10

27. Tania Andrade Lima, Marcos André Torres de Souza, and Glaucia Malerba Sene, "Weaving the Second Skin: Protection against Evil among the Valongo Slaves in Nineteenth-Century Rio de Janeiro," *Journal of African Diaspora Archaeology and Heritage,* III (2014), 103–136. In 1813, royal regulation sought to replace branding with the more humane forms of identification, including metal bracelets or collars. Five years later, branding by hot iron was made illegal in favor of branding with silver carimbos, though Baquaqua's experience demonstrates that this prohibition was often ignored during the period of the illegal slave trade. For an example of brands, see APEB, Secção Colonial e Provincial, no. 568-1, "Termos dos Cativos Mortos 1810–1811." By the early 1800s, British slaving vessels were no longer using brands. See Marcus Rediker, *The Slave Ship: A Human History* (New York, 2007), 268; *British and Foreign State Papers,* 22; Miller, *Way of Death,* 404–408, esp. 405.

to 15 percent of all slaves captured and bound for the Americas. Though no exact estimate exists for the Mina Coast, anecdotal evidence suggests a similar prevalence of epidemic disease.[28]

Such an environment necessitated vigilance. Captains and medical practitioners alike had to carefully watch for any signs of disease present before embarkation. In 1820, pardo captain Vicente Ferreira Milles received five enslaved men and five enslaved women in his feitoria located in Lagos, where he quickly observed an almost undetectable smallpox mark on the face of an enslaved woman. He quarantined her to prevent the disease from spreading to the other slaves before sending her to be treated by Senhora Janinha Gomes, likely a local medical practitioner. The long months spent on land trying to collect captives, material goods, medicines, and provisions also were a period of acute bodily insecurity for mariners, particularly for captains, who had the closest contact with slaves during this segment of the voyage. Indeed, Captain Ferreira contracted a vicious fever that left wounds on his legs while he was in residence at his feitoria. Ferreira claimed this kind of ailment was common on what he termed the "pestilent" coast. He treated the illness by imbibing laudanum and quinine (*agua de inglaterra*), which proved effective after five days. Domingos Jozé de Faria, a pilot who was working on the ship *Emília* and called at Ferreira's feitoria to collect slaves, also fell ill, likely contracting the same fever. The *Emília*'s sangrador, freed Gege man Lourenço Domingos dos Santos, found the onboard medicines inadequate and went on shore to obtain a cure. Shortly after his departure, the *Emília* was taken by British antislaving forces, during which time three more enslaved sailors ran away, though Faria survived and was taken into custody by the British. As for Santos, he never returned to the ship, either having abandoned it—or fallen ill himself. His fate is unknown, his disappearance a reminder of the dangers inherent in his labor.[29]

MIDDLE PASSAGE MEDICINE

The journey across the Atlantic formed the core of maritime healers' work. As ships traversed the ocean, the imperative to maintain the health of captives and thus their monetary value spurred the development of medical cosmo-

28. ANRJ, fundo 7X, Junta do Comércio, caixa 411, pacote 1, Acção Civil de Libelo, 7; Miller, *Way of Death*, 440.

29. AHI, Coleções Especiais, Comissão Mista, lata 13, maço 14, pasta 1, Papers of the *Emília*, 236, 261, 343.

politanism at sea, as Black healers creatively synthesized both African and European health epistemologies and practices. This cosmopolitanism was in part a matter of expediency and access, as captive medical practitioners were in a unique position to utilize botanical healing substances from the far-flung corners of the world. Drawing on what Parrish calls "slave knowledge," Brazilians of European descent frequently looked to their chattel as well as those they encountered on the African littoral to solve and address some of their most intractable medical problems. African-derived remedies and ingredients began to appear in the medicine chests of Bahian slaving ships, supplied by captains who had purchased them from local apothecaries. In acquiring therapeutic substances from a range of sources, apothecaries, as exponents of medical cosmopolitanism, legitimized African-derived medical knowledge for captains and slavers, who were committed to maximizing the profitability of transatlantic slaving voyages. Barbers and sangradores themselves accessed an array of medical substances as they cobbled together the materials of healing on land while traveling between Bahia and the African coast. These improvised cures also found their place on Bahia's slaving vessels.[30]

Barbers and sangradores were charged not only with healing but also with the management of enslaved cargoes. Captive cosmopolitans' linguistic and cultural facilities could be utilized to forestall violent rebellion on slaving vessels. In 1812, Luiz Jozé Gomes, the owner of the *Prazeres,* explained in his letter of orders to the ship's officers that the quartermaster and barber should take care of any uprisings that "ordinarily occurred." Gomes argued that captives treated without much "care and love" by officers were more prone to rebellion. Crew members should attempt to convince all captives that they belonged to one owner by treating them equally; such an artifice, he hoped, would not only prevent slave conspiracies but would also ensure a speedy departure from the West African coast.[31]

The first order of business for most slaving crews, however, was to prevent illness. Once they embarked, the unpredictability of life on African littorals gave way to the daily routines of shipboard life. At sea, crews began their work by stripping the enslaved of their clothing (a precaution to prevent uprisings as well as the spread of typhus, which was carried by lice) and separating them

30. For more on "slave knowledge," see Susan Scott Parrish, *American Curiosity: Cultures of Natural History in the Colonial British Atlantic World* (Williamsburg, Va., and Chapel Hill, N.C., 2006), 259–306; Londa Schiebinger, *Secret Cures of Slaves: People, Plants, and Medicine in the Eighteenth-Century Atlantic World* (Stanford, Calif., 2017), 13–17.

31. AHI, Coleções Especiais, Comissão Mista, lata 26, maço 6, pasta 2, Papers of the *Prazeres,* 64–68.

by sex. Men were placed in the claustrophobic slave deck, which Mahommah Baquaqua remembered as "that horrible place [that] will never be effaced from my memory," whereas women and children usually remained above, on the primary deck. Throughout the voyage, sailors periodically removed captives from the hold for exercise and feeding. Women—perceived as less of a physical threat—could be compelled to cook, clean the decks, and mend crew members' clothing. Officers also forced enslaved Africans of all genders and ages to sing and dance on deck, a strategy to ostensibly improve health and spirits but also provoke amusement and arousal among members of the crew. In 1813, Vicente Ferreira Milles, captain of the *Conceição Conde dos Arcos*, purchased three drums (*tambores*) and two African instruments called *"gomgoms* for the captives."[32]

Small moments of physical activity punctuated otherwise stagnant conditions that took a lasting toll on captives, weakening their already tenuous health. In the face of these debilitating circumstances, sangradores and barbers struggled to maintain the deteriorating condition of captives. Mealtimes provided one small source of relief for the confining life of the slave deck. Two or three times a day, crews led captives above in small groups to eat a thin porridge of manioc and palm oil. Rations provided little in the way of nourishment, however, and water was in short supply throughout the oceanic passage. Baquaqua characterized life belowdecks as profoundly taxing: "The hold was so low that we could not stand up, but were obliged to crouch upon the floor or sit down; day and night were the same to us, sleep being denied us from the confined position of our bodies, and we became desperate through suffering and fatigue." For medical officers, the charge of providing treatment meant that, unlike most of the other crew members, they had to go belowdecks into the hostile and dolorous world of the captives. James Barbot described the difficulties of ministering to sickly slaves in this environment: "They cannot do [it] leisurely between decks, because of the great heat that is there continually, which is sometimes so excessive that the surgeons would faint away, and the candles would not burn."[33]

32. Law, *Ouidah*, 145–146; Sheridan, "Guinea Surgeons," 606; Law and Lovejoy, eds., *Baquaqua*, 153; Thomas, *Slave Trade*, 716; Rediker, *Slave Ship*, 268–269, 332; Katrina Dyonne Thompson, *Ring Shout, Wheel About: The Racial Politics of Music and Dance in North American Slavery* (Urbana, Ill., 2014), 44; ANRJ, fundo 7X, Junta do Comércio, caixa 375, pacote 1, Papers of the *Conceição Conde dos Arcos*.

33. Miller, *Way of Death*, 413; Law and Lovejoy, eds., *Baquaqua*, 153; James Pope-Hennessy, *Sins of the Fathers: A Study of the Atlantic Slave Traders, 1441–1807* (New York, 1967), 13.

Medical practitioners frequently received significant resources and assistance from slaving ship captains and merchants, who had the most to lose from an outbreak of ill health. Ship barbers had access to a diverse and costly array of medicines at sea. Manoel José Freire de Carvalho paid a *boticário* (apothecary) in Salvador 77$140 réis for "drugs and vaccines" to stock his ship, the *Esperança Feliz,* during its voyage to Lagos in 1821. Unlike many slaving vessels, the *Esperança Feliz* employed a surgeon. Twenty-three-year-old, Bahian-born Joaquim José Baptista served as the ship's medical practitioner. He identified himself as pardo, married, and living in Arcal de Lima. The brigantine *Venus* paid an apothecary named Manoel Joaquim Dias e Sampayo 115$510 réis for the contents of its *botica* (medicine chest), to be used by the ship's two barbers. The first barber was Manoel dos Reis, a freed African man from the Mina Coast; the second barber was identified as Pedro Pereira, a freed *cabra* man from Bahia. The cost of the ship's botica was greater than Reis's and Pereira's salaries combined, indicating both a substantial investment in healers' work and, perhaps more important, a significant degree of trust in the efficacy of cosmopolitan healers' treatments.[34]

Enslaved healers' boticas were creolized medical objects shaped by ship captains' desires to protect the value of enslaved cargoes, the preferences of enslaved healers, as well as the intellectual labor of men of color in Salvador and the African practitioners Europeans encountered while anchored on the slaving coasts. The boticário who supplied the medicine chest of the *Venus* was probably of African descent and possibly enslaved.[35] The diversity of items in these chests also reveals slaving ship practitioners' capacious and

34. The Bahian *Comerciante,* which left for the west coast of Africa in 1822, invested 212$320 reis in a botica, provided by boticário Agostinho da Costa, which comprised 5.6 percent of the total investment made for the voyage. The expense was greater than the amount spent on water barrels and almost equivalent to what owner Francisco Ignacio de Siqueria Nobre spent on the 800 iron shackles he had purchased for the ship. Freed Gege barber Leandro Jozé da Costa would have used the contents of the said chest in his treatment of the 112 slaves aboard. See AHI, Coleções Especiais, Comissão Mista, lata 7, maço 5, pasta 1, 27; ibid., lata 15, maço 1, pasta 1, Papers of the *Esperança Feliz.* The schooner *Paquete Volante,* going from Bahia to Angola, recorded spending the sum of 192$400 réis on its botica. See ANRJ, fundo 7X, Junta do Comércio, caixa 371, pacote 1; ibid., caixa 372, pacote 1, Papers of the *Venus,* 3.

35. Apothecary shops were bustling entities where an array of assistants synthesized medical preparations for sale; they became informal meeting spaces for political discussion and leisure. Within these spaces, lay apothecaries (*práticos de botica*) and apothecaries' boys (*moços do boticário*) were frequently enslaved. At the beginning of the nineteenth century,

complex healing knowledge. Slavers expected their enslaved medical practitioners to be familiar with European- and American-derived *materia medica*
(pharmacology), medicinal formulation (pharmacopoeia), and treatment, as
well as African-derived therapies. The material culture of the slave ship barber and sangrador included both botanical and mineral medicines as well as
instruments for treating wounds, blistering, and bleeding.

Responsibility for assembling healing provisions in boticas was a complicated matter. In 1727, the British barber-surgeon John Atkins argued that slaving ship medical personnel ought to have "considerable" influence in choice
and quantity of medicine to be taken aboard. Despite this long-standing ideal,
the owner of the slaving vessel was most commonly responsible for acquiring the contents of medicine chests. On Bahian vessels, these were likely in
part assembled by an apothecary, including equipment for measuring, syn-
thesizing, and applying medical compounds. Sometimes, African medical
practitioners supplied their own equipment. Barber Domingos do Rozário
carried the "implements of his profession" with him as he boarded the *São
Miguel Triunfante*. In the Bahian trade, however, barbers and sangradores
were often forced to work with whatever was supplied. Three surviving descriptions of the diverse contents of medicine chests found on Bahian vessels
suggest the wide array of medical resources barbers and sangradores utilized.
On a ship sailing from Salvador to Badagry in 1812, the captain supplied
medical practitioners Manoel dos Reis and Pedro Pereira with a total of forty-
six medical ingredients and compounds as well as implements for fabricat-
ing and applying medicines, including a spatula, a mortar and pestle, glass
bottles, sacks, and boxes, with which they could perform their healing "art."
Upon opening the ship's chest, barbers would have a variety of treatment
options: tonics to treat respiratory and digestive ailments and astringents
to desiccate open wounds, sores, and ulcers; electuaries (surgery syrups)
composed of many ingredients; poultices made of a flour base and applied
to skin for soreness and inflammation; and ointments used to treat burns,
wounds, blisters, skin inflammation, and infection. In addition, plasters—
applied externally but used to treat internal fractures or dislocations and
external wounds—would likely have been present, alongside mercury-based
elixirs to treat syphilis and the common shipboard ailment yaws, aromatics to

---

at least one of Salvador's apothecaries, João Gomes, was pardo. See João José Reis, Flávio
dos Santos Gomes, and Marcus J. M. de Carvalho, *The Story of Rufino: Slavery, Freedom,
and Islam in the Black Atlantic,* trans. H. Sabrina Gledhill (Oxford, 2020), 14–15; Lycurgo
de Castro Santos Filho, *História geral de medicina brasileira,* II (São Paulo, 1991), 368.

make medicines more palatable, and analgesics such as laudanum and opium to provide comfort to ill slaves. Each of these remedies had multiple variations and could consist of a diversity of ingredients, depending upon the ailment and what materials were available.[36]

The contents of such medical chests reveal both the global reach of European trade and the degree to which African practitioners as medical cosmopolitans learned to harness a diversity of treatments from around the world. Practitioners utilizing rich apothecary chests both at sea and on land were materially and intellectually enmeshed in an imperial botanical network. Captive healers used medicines derived from rosemary, poppies, elderberry, cinnamon, lavender, saffron, and parsley that had been widely available in Iberia since the medieval period, where they were cultivated in gardens and used to treat common illnesses. Some "European" botanicals housed in medicine chests were directly imported from Europe, though many others had already been introduced to New World environments during the sixteenth century and were grown locally. In the sixteenth and seventeenth centuries, indigenous people introduced botanical substances such as cocoa, marcela, jalapa, quina (used to fabricate quinine), ipecacuanha, and simaruba bark to Europeans, leading them to become essential New World imports to Europe. Medicines labeled "quina," present in various forms on all Bahian slaving ships, were, despite their name, not the same botanical antimalarial from Peru first introduced to Jesuits by Andean people. They were produced from a

36. John Atkins, *The Navy-Surgeon; or, A Practical System of Surgery* (London, 1734), v. These instruments were quite costly, valued at 17$000 réis. See ANRJ, fundo 7X, Junta do Comércio, caixa 410, Papers of the *São Miguel Triunfante,* 25; ibid., caixa 372, pacote 1, Papers of the *Venus.* Early-nineteenth-century academic pharmacology divided materials used to synthesize medicinal compounds into botanical and mineral branches, with the majority of remedies being plant based. Apothecaries further subdivided medical materials into "simple" ingredients combined to create specific remedies and compounds that were already fabricated in shops and could be applied without additional preparation. Both boticários on land and barbers and sangradores at sea regularly encountered and concocted a set repertoire of remedies (Jacinto da Costa, *Pharmacopea naval, e castrense: Offerecida ao illustrissimo senhor . . .* [Lisbon, 1819], II, 1–2). The contents of the *Venus* and two additional slaving vessels from the years 1824 and 1839 (see Appendix 3) reveal a marked continuity in the types of medicine employed aboard slaving vessels during the period. Indeed, a majority of therapies used to treat African captives in the early nineteenth century were also employed by barbers to treat European sailors and soldiers laboring on eighteenth-century Portuguese ships engaged in the India trade (C. R. Boxer, *From Lisbon to Goa, 1500–1750: Studies in Portuguese Maritime Enterprise* [London, 1997], 124–130).

variety of local trees thought to have the same properties as quinine because of their bitter character and success in treating fevers. Sarsaparilla, with origins in Central and South America, was carried on both the *Venus* and the *Dois Amigos Brasileiros* and had become a popular treatment for syphilis, pox, yaws, and gonorrhea for Dutch barbers working in the slave trade during the seventeenth century. Local people on the Gold Coast were avid consumers of a sarsaparilla-infused ointment favored by the Dutch and procured it for slaving vessels to treat yaws and smallpox as well. In West Central Africa, Portuguese physicians adapted from African practitioners the use of *kikongo* and cobra wood for treating fevers. Europeans also appropriated Asian therapeutics during this period, introducing asafetida, camphor, and senna into their medicinal repertoires.[37]

Crucially, enslaved and freed healers incorporated African botanicals into an evolving vocabulary of medical practice aboard slaving vessels. One such resource was gum arabic, which was commonly harvested from the trunks of the acacia tree, prevalent in the Sahel region on the southern littoral of the Sahara. The substance was first identified as a medicament by local people; Portuguese physicians then began utilizing the substance to treat ulcers and diarrhea, prepare medicinal gums, and make viscous solutions. It became one of the first major West African exports to the metropole.[38] In addition, tamarind pulp—extracted from the fruit and made into syrup—was incorporated

---

37. Robert A. Voeks, *Sacred Leaves of Candomblé: African Magic, Medicine, and Religion in Brazil* (Austin, 1997), 22–23; John Baptist von Spix and Carl Friedrich P. von Martius, *Travels in Brazil, in the Years 1817–1820, Undertaken by Command of His Majesty the King of Bavaria*, 2 vols. (London, 1824), I, 213–214; Lycurgo de Castro Santos Filho, *História geral da medicina brasileira*, I (São Paulo, 1977), 122; Johannes Rask, "A Brief and Truthful Description of a Journey to and from Guinea," in Selena Axelrod Winsnes, trans., *Two Views from Christiansborg Castle*, 2 vols. (Accra, Ghana, 2009), I, 112; De-Valera N. Y. M. Botchway, "A Note on the Ethnomedical Universe of the Asante, an Indigenous People in Ghana," in Effie Gemi-Iordanou et al., eds., *Medicine, Healing, and Performance* (Oxford, 2014), 162; J[ohn] Kost, *Domestic Medicine: A Treatise on the Practice of Medicine, Adapted to the Reformed System, Comprising a Materia Medica, with Numerous Illustrations* (Cincinnati, 1859), 556–557; Kananoja, *Healing Knowledge in Atlantic Africa*, 53–55.

38. By the eighteenth century, the area around the mouth of the Senegal River was the sole supplier of the substance to Europe. In the early nineteenth century, local peoples extracted gum for export to Europe for "manufactures and medicine" and ate it "in a crude state." See James L. A. Webb, Jr., "The Trade in Gum Arabic: Prelude to French Conquest in Senegal," *Journal of African History*, XXVI (1985), 149–168, esp. 149; Jean Baptiste Léonard Durand, *Voyage to Senegal* . . . (London, 1806), 141–142, 157.

into Portuguese medical practice for its ability to soothe fevers and act as a laxative. The Portuguese first encountered it in western Africa and on India's Malabar Coast in the sixteenth century, where local populations employed it as a medicinal plant. Later transplanted to South America by colonists, it supplied slavers in Bahia such as those on the *Dois Amigos Brasileiros*.

Tamarind's effectiveness as an antiscorbutic made it indispensable in the Bahian slave trade, an environment in which many suffered from an acute vitamin C deficiency that often led to scurvy. The disease was so prevalent that one contemporary barber-surgeon believed it to be a communicable disease originating in Angola and dubbed it *mal de Loanda,* or Luanda sickness. The symptoms appeared slowly, often only revealing themselves well into the transatlantic journey, afflicting sufferers with ulcerated gums, lips, throat, and nose, loose teeth, fatigue, respiratory distress, and bruising. As early as 1741, Portuguese barber-surgeons treating enslaved Brazilians touted the efficacy of changes to diet to prevent mal de Loanda and advocated for the inclusion of fresh vegetables and meats in the rations for the enslaved. Tamarind pulp, however, presented the most effective means of treating the severe malnutrition many enslaved men and women suffered from during the transatlantic voyage. In fact, slaveowners had learned of tamarind's utility from enslaved peoples themselves, as they imitated the medical techniques of Africans who, as one slaveowner observed, utilized the fruit to "make a Drink . . . mixed with Sugar, or Honey, and Water. They also preserve it as confection to cook and quench Thirst; and the Leaves chewed produce the same Effect." Captains stocked tamarind alongside other vitamin C–rich botanicals such as "scurvy grass," which was integral to preventing the disease when no fresh fruits or vegetables had been procured for the voyage.[39]

39. Junia Ferreira Furtado, "Tropical Empiricism: Making Medical Knowledge in Colonial Brazil," in Delbourgo and Dew, eds., *Science and Empire in the Atlantic World,* 144–145; Miller, *Way of Death,* 383; Sowande' M. Mustakeem, "'I Never Have Such a Sickly Ship Before': Diet, Disease, and Mortality in 18th-Century Atlantic Slaving Voyages," *Journal of African American History,* XCIII (2008), 483–485. Miller has emphasized that most of the ailments from which enslaved people suffered during the transatlantic voyage were the result of poor nutrition in the months leading to sea travel, as enslaved men and women were often the victims of drought and famine in their native communities and were further malnourished during their trek to the Angolan coast (*Way of Death,* 424–426). Slavers also used the fruit to improve the taste of stagnant water (Judith A. Carney and Richard Nicholas Rosomoff, *In the Shadow of Slavery: Africa's Botanical Legacy in the Atlantic World* [Berkeley, Calif., 2009], 70).

Tamarind's utility on transatlantic slaving vessels also indicated one critical environmental reality that shaped the development of Black mariners' medical cosmopolitanism: in humid climates, herbs and other botanical medicines tended to decay during the first half of slaving journeys, rendering them unusable. The biotic reality of the tropics frequently forced medical personnel to procure substitutes in West African port towns. And given their ignorance about local flora, Europeans and their crew often relied on local Africans and their environmentally specific botanical expertise to provide otherwise unseen treatment options. Once enslaved medical practitioners had demonstrated the efficacy of "foreign" forms of medical knowledge, Europeans readily incorporated them into their repertoire of medicines, particularly herbal applications. British surgeon John Atkins, who traveled widely in Africa during the early eighteenth century, claimed he had found near-equivalents to the medicines he was accustomed to using in large quantities on the African coast. In turn, other European descriptions of medical practice on the West African littoral suggested a pronounced desire to incorporate African-procured medicinal substances. Jean Baptiste Durand, a French author who lived in Senegal at the end of the eighteenth century, insisted that the biodiversity of the fertile areas surrounding the Senegal River was home to a variety of effective plant-based cures for common diseases. He identified a class of medical practitioners in the area—"apothecaries," as he put it—who synthesized remedies from local natural substances such as tree bark.[40]

Young African-born barbers and sangradores encountered familiar medical resources in their medicine chests. By the eighteenth century, European medical personnel recognized these substances as beneficent and worth carrying in apothecaries' shops, but it was in the hands of African healers that they were applied to ailing bodies. Although African botanicals had been incorporated into larger global networks of pharmacology, African practitioners still determined the specific method of their usage. One example of African-oriented medical hybridity was the medical substance with perhaps the most expansive Atlantic circulation and greatest number of applications: dendê (palm) oil. Used to treat wounds, epidermal infections, and bruises, it was lauded by Europeans as the "most excellent medical agent" on the Gold Coast. In the late eighteenth century, Brazilian physicians also advocated using a mixture of palm oil, lead carbonate, and corn flour to make a plaster to treat scabies or painful boils caused by bacteria. Palm oil treated skin ailments broadly in West and West Central Africa; it also reputedly rendered

40. Atkins, *The Navy-Surgeon,* iv; Durand, *A Voyage to Senegal,* 157.

"joints supple" and eased the pain of gout. Various communities in the area cultivated aloe, which local healers employed as a cathartic (purgative), providing effective treatments for dysentery to foreigners—though they preferred to prevent rather than treat the infection through "a medium between excess and privation." Calumba, a bitter root used in Mozambique to treat venereal disease, dysentery, and diarrhea (and carried in the medicine chest of the *Dois Amigos Brasileiros*), was introduced to the Portuguese as early as the seventeenth century, when it became a staple export, and later transplanted to a number of British colonies in the Indian Ocean.[41]

Treatment of Europeans stationed on African shores was common and became another source for the dissemination of African-derived therapies into the wider Atlantic world. Indigenous people living near the recently established colony of Freetown, Sierra Leone, introduced the English to "virtues" of a "new kind of Peruvian bark" in the treatment of fevers as well as the kola nut, already a familiar trading good for the Portuguese. Like so many other Atlantic botanical substances, with the help of indigenous African bioprospecting, by the end of the eighteenth century, this wondrous "new Peruvian bark" had already been spirited away to London laboratories for scientists to deduce additional medicinal properties.[42]

On shore and at sea, African healers' manipulation of such botanical medicines continued to pique the interest of European slavers, scientists, and physicians. They practiced their healing techniques in the context of an active exchange of botanical medical materials between Africa and Brazil. In their boticas, they employed dozens of medicines that had originated from every corner of the world. Their medical training required them to understand these substances' medical properties, deduce proper dosages, and choose the best manner of application. Though captains and apothecaries on land (many of whom were men of African descent as well) exercised the most influence, barbers and sangradores also procured botanical medical materials while stationed in West Africa and worked with their own instruments carried from Bahia. They provided therapies in a creolized medical world, but they also

41. Rask, "Brief and Truthful Description," in Winsnes, trans., *Two Views from Christiansborg Castle*, I, 56; Durand, *Voyage to Senegal*, 109, 157–168, esp. 167; William Woodville, Sir William Jackson Hooker, and G. Pratt, *Medical Botany: Containing Systematic and General Descriptions, with Plates of All the Medicinal Plants, Comprehended in the Catalogues of the Materia Medica*, V (London, 1832), 23.

42. Durand, *Voyage to Senegal*, 91. For more on the European appropriation of indigenous American knowledge as an imperial project, see Parrish, *American Curiosity*, 215–258.

exercised discretion over their own medical choices. Because of sangradores' and barbers' agency, the influences of West African therapeutic techniques would prove critical to their improvised therapies.

A TRANSATLANTIC THERAPEUTIC PRACTICE

African mariners were central conduits for the transmission of materials, ideas, and practices that transcended the physical limits of slaving vessels and came to inform not only maritime medical cosmopolitanism but the medical culture of Bahian slave society itself. African-influenced medical cosmopolitanism could be found far into Bahia's interior, on remote, rural plantations. Robert Voeks has argued that African horticulture had been introduced to colonial Bahia as early as the sixteenth century, as enslaved people transplanted and cultivated species that had been used for food as well as sacred healing rituals in West Africa.[43] Slaving vessels' consistent practice of procuring local healing plants on the African coast for return journeys suggests that seafaring African medical practitioners facilitated a portion of these transplants. Just as Europeans procured substitutes for European botanical substances with which they were familiar on African coasts, enslaved people displaced to Brazil discovered and utilized local flora with healing properties analogous to species they knew at home.

On both sides of the Atlantic, healers employed nearly identical techniques for applying botanical medicines. The utilization of herb-based teas could be found in medical repertoires of both Bahians and Africans. Brazilian physicians came to recommend that ill slaves imbibe hot teas infused with herbs on transatlantic voyages, a practice that African lay healers employed on land to treat various ailments. In Angola, Francisco Damião Cosme prescribed herbal teas to treat indigestion, stomach pain, cholera, and more generally "illnesses of this country," though it is unclear whether he incorporated local medicinal practices when making this recommendation. Herbal teas had long been a common therapy along the West African coast. Examples included the preparation of a mixture of lime juice and malagueta pepper to treat colic in Accra and the creation in the same region of a tonic made from the bark of the "Tandoorue" (Tannuro) tree and pepper for stomach pains and constipation. Osifekunde, a man originally from Ijebu who was enslaved and trafficked to

43. Transplanted species include the dendê palm, or *Elaeis guineensis;* "akoko," or *New-bouldia laevis;* kola, or *Garcinia kola Heckel;* malagueta pepper, or *Aframomum melegueta* (Voeks, *Sacred Leaves,* 23-32, 169-191).

Brazil around 1810, reported that, in his community, a class of men called *olouchigou,* or doctors, treated fever by "building a large fire and drinking hot infusions of a plant called *Ewe eloukeze*." Osifekunde lamented that he had found no substitute in Brazil, indicating that he sought out medical equivalents of West African substances he was familiar with.[44]

A number of African-derived therapeutic practices were also central to both shipboard medical practice and land-based treatment cultures in Brazil. By the end of the eighteenth century, bathing in frigid seawater had become a common method of disease prevention and treatment on Brazilian slaving vessels. West Africans had extensive experience with this technique, as curative herbs were commonly administered through hot and cold baths. In the Bight of Biafra during the mid-nineteenth century, healers near Bonny and New Calabar utilized "heated sand-baths, ablutions of hot water, and . . . vapour-baths" to treat fevers, where the patient was "held over [the bath], water being slowly dropped thereon, so that the steam, as it ascends, may act on the affected portion of the body." In Brazil, African curandeiros utilized a wide variety of herbs infused in baths to treat muscular ailments, wounds, inflammation, and "nervous fevers." Some of these herbs had African origins, such as the "Raiz de Pipi," a plant described as originating in "Guinea" that lay healers used to treat paralysis in the early nineteenth century. European naturalists noted the popularity of *guiábo* (okra) in Brazilian healing methods, which John Baptist von Spix and Carl Friedrich von Martius noted was "introduced by the negroes from Africa." Guiábo leaves were boiled and used to make a "softening" poultice for internal wounds and fractures.[45]

44. Furtado, "Tropical Empiricism," in Delbourgo and Dew, eds., *Science and Empire in the Atlantic World,* 144; Francisco Damião Cosme, "Tractado das queixas endêmicas e mais fataes nesta conquista," *Studia,* XXII (1967), 189; William Bosman, *A New and Accurate Description of the Coast of Guinea, Divided into the Gold, the Slave, and the Ivory Coasts . . .* (London, 1705), 225; Botchway, "A Note on the Ethnomedical Universe of the Asante," in Gemi-Iordanou et al., eds., *Medicine, Healing, and Performance,* 162–163; Philip D. Curtin, ed., *Africa Remembered: Narratives by West Africans from the Era of the Slave Trade* (Madison, Wis., 1968), 260.

45. On the use of baths in the slave trade, see Harms, *Diligent,* 311; Cosme, "Tractado das queixas endêmicas," *Studia,* XXII (1967), 185, 197. For a description of herbal baths in Afro-Bahian healing practice, see Voeks, *Sacred Leaves,* 98–100. In West Central Africa, Kongolese male and female healers utilized baths, herbs, and roots to treat myriad diseases, as did Mbundu "surgeons" in Luanda (Kananoja, *Healing Knowledge in Atlantic Africa,* 44–45). William F. Daniell notes the use of baths and sudorifics to treat fevers, which he believes the local people adopted from Europeans whom they came in contact with dur-

Like the enslaved, many Europeans were convinced of the value of this medical cosmopolitanism, even to treat their own ailments. British physician William Daniell, for instance, asserted the superiority of African treatments over commonly used European remedies such as bloodletting, saline purgatives, and large doses of calomel (mercury chloride) for foreign visitors to the African coast. In addition, Danish clergyman H. C. Monrad described what he believed were efficacious treatments for "Coast fever" and yellow fever performed on the Gold Coast in the early nineteenth century. For the former, he observed, "The Negroes use nearly boiling herb baths into which the patient is lowered during his paroxysms, and is covered with a *kente* or sheet. Sometimes they smear the entire body, from top to toe, with finely ground Spanish pepper, which causes a burning heat." When Monrad contracted yellow fever, he sought out a local practitioner for treatment. The man, he explained, "cured [me] both simply and rapidly" by washing his body three times a day "in water in which a number of both nicely scented and bitter herbs had been soaking for a long time. In addition, I had to drink three handfuls, each time, of the same water in which I was being bathed." The therapy continued for three days. While providing a treatment with baths, the "doctor called upon his fetish very frequently, and forbade me to eat palm oil or legumes during the cure, which, he told me very seriously, his fetish had forbidden."[46]

Despite Monrad's endorsement of the outcome of his treatment, his experience suggested the limited ways European observers understood efficacious African healing practices while benefiting from them. Like slaving merchants, Monrad was appeased because his treatment was effective, and he saw no reason to question the underlying principles of his African healer. For his Fanti caretaker, however, Monrad's recuperation was not so much a matter of the isolated potency of medical substances and their biological properties. It depended on the informed manipulation of a metaphysical world by a qualified practitioner in tandem with medicinal applications to the body. Such botanical substances reached their full healing potential only if accompanied by the proper ritual acts. Though Monrad was largely incognizant of the larger intellectual world on which his treatment depended, his experience anticipated a

_____

ing the course of trade; however, his explanation for the therapy's origins is unclear. See Daniell, *Sketches of the Medical Topography, and Native Diseases of the Gulf of Guinea, Western Africa* (London, 1849), 120; von Spix and von Martius, *Travels in Brazil in the Years 1817–1820,* II, 98.

46. Daniell, *Sketches,* 120; H. C. Monrad, "A Description of the Guinea Coast and Its Inhabitants," in Winsnes, trans., *Two Views from Christiansborg Castle,* II, 205, 206, 426.

developing shift. For those looking to modernize and economize the operation of transatlantic slaving in the early nineteenth century, healing practices that they could not see and, increasingly, did not understand justified attacks on the position and status of captive cosmopolitan barbers and sangradores.

The creation of a cosmopolitan medical knowledge that bridged the worlds of the slave ship and colonial Bahia was ultimately a product of the intense commercialization spurred by the transatlantic slave trade. Tasked with staving off the physical deterioration of enslaved men, women, and children to maintain the profitability of voyages, captains and merchants at least agreed that such medical practitioners were largely successful. Over the course of the eighteenth and nineteenth centuries, their therapies moderated the effects of shipboard scurvy, smallpox, yaws, dysentery, and fevers. Black barbers' historical ascendance in the operation of the Bahian slave trade overlapped with a decline in mortality rates.

But even with effectual, innovative treatments, epidemic catastrophes were still commonplace. In 1810, the brigantine *Ligeiro* was traveling from the Mina Coast to Salvador when 84 of 466 enslaved individuals on the ship died from a contagious illness, which eventually killed the captain and a portion of the crew. Seventeen years later, a ship leaving Cameroon lost its mast in a storm, slowing the voyage considerably. After illness struck both the captives and crew, slaves refused ship provisions of manioc and salted beef. The unnamed epidemic disease spread like fire throughout the ship, eventually killing 178 of the 440 slaves who had departed the African coast—resulting in a mortality rate of 40.5 percent. Such epidemics remained unpredictable, and although therapeutic practices often successfully alleviated symptoms, they were also often ineffective against the spread of disease on tightly packed, poorly ventilated ships.[47]

47. Miller estimates that slave ship mortality declined precipitously early in the nineteenth century. This situation was driven by the popularization of the *bergantim* (brigantine), which allowed captains to carry more provisions in larger holds, and the introduction of copper-sheathed hulls to speed ships' passage as they eluded British antislaving patrols. Mortality for enslaved people registered at an estimated 25 to 30 percent at the beginning of the eighteenth century; by the end, it had fallen to 10 to 15 percent; and by 1820, it had reached a nadir of 5 to 10 percent. See Miller, *Way of Death*, 436; Herbert S. Klein, *The Atlantic Slave Trade* (Cambridge, 2010), 139; Alexandre Vieira Ribeiro, "The Transatlantic Slave Trade to Bahia, 1582–1851," in David Eltis and David Richardson, eds., *Extending the Frontiers: Essays on the New Transatlantic Slave Trade Database* (New Haven, Conn., 2008), 147. A description of the Bahian slaving vessel the *Feloz* revealed that 562 slaves were held belowdecks with only three feet of space for clearance. Allowed no space to shift positions,

In many instances, barbers and sangradores failed to cure enslaved individuals subjected to unrelenting contagious disease and acute deprivation during transatlantic passage. If medical practitioners were unable to remedy enslaved individuals before arriving in port, slavers treated them as they would any other damaged piece of cargo, labeling them as "defective captives" or "refuse" slaves to be sold below market value. On a voyage in 1813, twenty-one slaves were labeled as "refuse," including one African man with a head injury; nine men and adolescent boys suffering from stomach injuries; one man "bleeding from the mouth"; two men afflicted with scurvy; one man and woman labeled "dumb," or mentally incapacitated; and one adolescent boy who suffered from inflamed lymph glands, leaving him "very thin." These slaves were sold for half the value of their healthier counterparts. Perversely, such human devastation could become a private opportunity. Sometimes barbers and sangradores would purchase sick slaves at lower prices in the city's market before treating them and then selling them for a profit. Alternatively, they might keep such afflicted slaves as their own. In other cases, Bahian slavers sent "refuse" slaves to the distant and sparsely populated Brazilian province of Maranhão—including slaves "infected with epidemic illnesses and smallpox"—where buyers had little choice, as the volume of the slave trade was much smaller.[48]

Increasingly, blame for the unsound epidemiological environment of Bahian slaving became a matter of concern for colonial administrators. They were quick to find an obvious scapegoat. As early as 1793, the Bahian-born Luiz Antônio de Oliveira Mendes, a member of the Portuguese Royal Academy of Science who had attended medical school in Coimbra, argued that Black sangradores employed in the slave trade were "awful surgeons."

---

captives were packed so tightly, they sat between each other's knees. The only ventilation consisted of a grated hatchway, which made the temperature of the cargo hold unbearable. Fifty-five bondspeople perished from dysentery and other diseases, along with eight or nine crew members, though no sign of disease had been present when the ship set sail seventeen days earlier. Six additional slaves occupied hammocks on deck as they were treated for fevers, whereas the remaining captives belowdecks were so incapacitated that few could stand. See Robert Walsh, *Notices of Brazil in 1828 and 1829*, 2 vols. (London, 1830), II, 479–485.

48. ANRJ, fundo 7X, Junta do Comércio, caixa 411, Papers of the *São Miguel Triunfante*; Claudio de Paula Honorato, "Valango: O mercado de escravos do Rio de Janeiro, 1758-1831" (Ph.D. diss., Universidade Federal Fluminense, Niterói, 2008); Walter Hawthorne, *From Africa to Brazil: Culture, Identity, and an Atlantic Slave Trade, 1600-1830* (New York, 2010), 127.

Motivated by a desire to monopolize healthcare, in the late eighteenth century, a number of European physicians employed in Angola endeavored to influence crown policy on the (often ignored) standards of medical care and nutrition in slaving ports. In particular, they implored officials to more rigorously regulate how slavers housed captives before their forced departure from Africa and improve captives' treatment once aboard slaving vessels. In 1809, the royal government created the Provedoria-Mor da Saúde, an agency that regulated public health and required health agents to visit arriving slaving vessels. Though widespread acceptance of medical heterodoxy had historically characterized Bahian slavers' attitudes, the establishment and growth of academic institutions for training white physicians, as well as the rise of miasma theory in the late eighteenth and early nineteenth centuries, challenged Bahia's improvisational, heterogeneous, and multiethnic healing landscape and allowed blame for the structurally produced mortality of the transatlantic slave trade to be placed at the feet of African and creole healers in racialized language.[49]

The rise of miasma theory in particular—which contended that illness was the result of unhealthy environments and the inhalation of noxious vapors produced by decomposing matter—provided a new theoretical solution to the long-standing, mortality-based inefficiencies of slaving capitalism. Viewed in this new light, African and creole medical practitioners could be construed as deficient or deviant healers. As reformers latched onto this new framework, a central irony of their project became clear: ostensible humanitarianism toward enslaved Africans and racialized degradation toward African healers increasingly went hand in hand. Angola's governor, Miguel de Mello Antônio, advocated for sweeping reforms of the inhumanity of the slave trade from Luanda, where he believed the "sordid ambition" and greed of slaving ship owners had led them to disregard the high mortality rates within the slave trade. Such arguments dovetailed with critiques of Black healers. Physicians, in particular, questioned not only the legitimacy of barbers' therapies but also the supposed innate ability of African people to provide effective medical care. In 1828, the British abolitionist Robert Walsh blamed the *Feloz*'s medical practitioner for

---

49. Mendes, *Memórias econômicas da Academia Real das Sciencias de Lisboa,* IV, 29–30; Soares, "African Barbeiros," in Cañizares-Esguerra, Childs, and Sidbury, eds., *Black Urban Atlantic,* 217 n. 30; Miller, *Way of Death,* 434–435. The Provedoria-Mor da Saúde also quarantined newly arrived African slaves and crews for forty days before they could enter the city, aiming to sequester any arriving diseases away from the city's general population (Ribeiro, "The Transatlantic Slave Trade to Bahia," in Eltis and Richardson, eds., *Extending the Frontiers,* 147).

the loss of fifty-five slaves and eight crew members, claiming the "mortality did not arise from want of medicine. There was a large stock ostentatiously displayed in the cabin, with a manuscript book, containing directions as to the quantities; but the only medical man on board to prescribe it was a black, who was as ignorant as his patients." By 1831, the newly formed Sociedade de Medicina (Society of Medicine) in Rio de Janeiro sought to disqualify sangradores and barbers from licensed status altogether, complaining that "these professions . . . are not only for free men, [but for the] still ignorant, without principles, and are made up of unacculturated [African] slaves, on commission from their owners, thereby giving rise to unpleasant and inconvenient and very sad . . . infractions of the laws that exist." The organization depicted the profession of barbering as a bastion of illegality while demeaning it by virtue of the racially and socially inferior status of its practitioners. Another critic of captive cosmopolitan healing lamented that the ranks of sangradores were filled by "ordinary stupid Africans," who, in lieu of formal academic training, "learn to blood-let on the stocks of sprouts and then armed with sharp lancets"—which led to "disastrous consequences for patients."[50]

A new hierarchy of knowledge was taking shape. Physicians arguing that African medical practitioners had failed to conform to these self-consciously "empirical" forms of therapy, however, elided the rich history of hybrid, African-informed intellectual networks in Brazil that had appropriated both European and African precedents to foster both healing and community for those men

50. By the late eighteenth century, miasma enthusiasts had identified slaving ships as among the world's most abhorrent environments. One such proponent of miasma theory, Governor Miguel de Mello Antônio, argued for a number of reforms to slaving practices: that the quality and quantity of provisions had to be improved, the length of voyages shortened, and the tight packing of bondspeople in the cargo hold abandoned. He also advocated that slave decks be washed every day with water and vinegar, ventilated to reduce humidity, and smoked with herbs, and that captains and surgeons should take care to bring each captive above decks every day. In lieu of giving them a ration of liquor, captains and surgeons should rinse slaves' mouths with vinegar and water to lessen the spread of disease. Mello also bitterly criticized Black sangradores and barbers, whom he dismissed as "ignorant" and lacking the skills to accurately diagnose disease or apply the appropriate medicine for treatment. Instead, they "only knew how to bleed, apply blistering cups and scarify." See Manuel Barcia, *Yellow Demon of Fever: Fighting Disease in the Nineteenth-Century Transatlantic Slave Trade* (New Haven, Conn., 2020), 11, 37–39; ANTT, Junta do Comércio, maço 10, caixa 36, Mar. 12, 1799, "Carta de Miguel de Mello Antônio"; Walsh, *Notices of Brazil in 1828 and 1829*, II, 484–485; Pimenta, "Terapeutas populares," in Chalhoub et al., eds., *Artes e ofícios de curar no Brasil*, 319, 320.

and women whose lives had been radically reshaped by enslavement. A lasting irony of the Age of Abolition's progressive humanitarianism was medical professionals' increasing contempt for their expertise and the validity of African-influenced healing methods. In this regard, Black medical practitioners' experience was similar to other captive cosmopolitans who experienced abolitionist progressivism as dislocation, vulnerability, and marginalization.

CIRCUITS OF BLOOD-LETTING KNOWLEDGE

Despite growing opposition to Black healers' medical work aboard slaving vessels, one key African-derived therapeutic method—bloodletting, or bleeding and purging—remained central to both maritime and terrestrial healing practices in the early nineteenth century. Brought to medieval Iberia by Moorish intellectuals, the practice of bloodletting, like other forms of purging, rested on a Hippocratic-Galenic, or humoral, model of physiology. Popularized by Francisco Morato Roma's influential 1664 medical treatise *Luz da medicina, pratica racional, e methodica, guia de enfermeyros, directorio de principiantes (The Light of Medicine, Rational and Methodological Practice, a Nurse's Guide and Beginners' Directory)*, Catholic missionaries administering colonial hospitals and colleges applied humoral theory in their educational and therapeutic practice in Portuguese and Spanish America. The Portuguese were also noted to be enthusiastic bloodletters. Bloodletting was a fundamental part of Salvador's medical landscape, with physican José Pinto de Azeredo noting at the end of the eighteenth century, "The abuse of blood-letting . . . is extraordinary in the Cities of America, particularly Bahia." There, however, such practices were primarily the result of African healing influences, which derived from a variety of West African cultural and medical contexts. And though regularly employed to treat contagious disease aboard Bahian slaving vessels, bloodletting's use and historical visibility became most pronounced on land in Salvador da Bahia.[51]

51. Cagle, *Assembling the Tropics*, 279–283; Francisco Morato Roma, *Luz da medicina, pratica racional, e methodica, guia de enfermeyros, directorio de principiantes* (Lisbon, 1664). Notorious among their European peers, the Portuguese had long been enthusiastic bloodletters. In 1702, Bosman observed that Portuguese residents on the West African coast were so fond of phlebotomy—bleeding themselves up to fifty times a year—that they appeared to be walking ghosts rather than men. In 1725, John Atkins noted that Portuguese barbers on slaving ships who "presume[d] themselves best judges in the Country distemper" treated the crew members' violent fevers with a course of six or more bloodlettings over a two-day period, twice as often as Atkins himself recommended. According to Philip D. Curtin, the

West African communities engaged in bloodletting therapies that over-lapped with, complemented, and modified European practices. In 1770, peoples in the interior of Angola practiced bleeding from the nose. Three decades later, in Luanda, Pinto de Azeredo noted that doctors were obsti-nately engaged in bleeding as treatment for a range of fevers. Barbershops were a common sight not only in Luanda but in other remote Portuguese outposts, where Mbundu subjects were trained in the art of barbering. Just north, in Kongo, male and female Kikongo practitioners applied cupping horns (*mpodi*) to "suck out" impurities from blood and restore the "balance" and "purity" necessary for health.[52] Kongolese cupping, unlike the European variety, which favored glass implements, relied on "a small calabash, a horn, or a shell, perforated on the top," applied to the "arm, leg, belly, or head" to relieve "distemper."[53] In São Tomé, locals applied ox horns to their fore-heads, temples, and shoulders to relieve fevers during cold months. On the

---

frequency of Portuguese bloodletting on the African coast derived from Iberian theories of disease prevention. Witnessing African resistance to local diseases, the Portuguese hy-pothesized that immunity to illnesses common on the coast was dependent on the bodily environment in which one's blood was formed. European visitors, influenced by a concep-tual framework of "environmental humoralism," subscribed to the conviction that blood created by the body while the patient still resided in Europe had to be removed and slowly replaced with blood produced once the patient had arrived in Africa. Profuse medical bleed-ing became a necessity for bodily adaptation and the prevention of illness. See Bosman, *A New and Accurate Description*, 414; Curtin, *The Image of Africa: British Ideas and Action, 1780–1850*, I (Madison, Wis., 1964), 83; Parrish, *American Curiosity*, 79–80; José Pinto de Azeredo, *Ensaios sobre algumas enfermidades d'Angola* (Lisbon, 1799), vi.

52. Kananoja, *Healing Knowledge in Atlantic Africa*, 30, 127–129. In 1875, another visi-tor to Angola noted that "they [local people] are also very fond of being cupped for any pain, and it is rare to see a man or woman whose back or shoulders do not bear signs of this operation." He went on to describe Bunda people as "very skillful in the use of the lancet" and remarked on the predominance of bloodletters operating in the city of Cambambe. See Azeredo, *Ensaios sobre algumas enfermidades d'Angola*; Joachim John Monteiro, *Angola and the River Congo*, II (London, 1875), 262–263.

53. Olfert Dapper's *Description of Africa* characterized common treatments for headache and fever in Kongo: "Against these they make use of the sandal wood . . . whether red or grey, tho' the former is most esteemed; this being reduced into powder, and mixed with palm oil, they make into an excellent ointment, with which they anoint the patient all over two or three times, which seldom fails of curing. But if it doth not allay the pain in the head, they have recourse to bleeding in the temples by incision and suction." He also noted that a similar treatment was utilized for "violent cholics," or *npichi* in Kikongo, which he assessed

western Mina Coast in the early eighteenth century, bleeding was believed to relieve headaches and cure rheumatism, whereas in Ouidah, cupping was performed with a calabash and used for facial scarification, which left a portion of raised flesh on the cheeks as a form of communal identification. At the beginning of the nineteenth century, bloodletting was still practiced on the Mina Coast. H. C. Monrad reported that the "Negroes and the Europeans do [it] regularly" and that he himself had sought the treatment from African practitioners.[54] As he explained, "We [Danes] sometimes place ourselves in the hands of the Negroes, who also concern themselves with treating [fever]. They use a purgative agent which is made of the bark of a certain tree; of warm baths, in which there are various bitter and astringent herbs; and of cupping." Another account identified the primary practitioners of bloodletting for the Fanti-speaking people on the coast as women, who performed it with "much dexterity."[55]

---

as effective in "prevent[ing] vast numbers dying." He criticized, however, the crudity of cupping: "They have the use of phlebotomy, but, for want of lancets and incision-knives, perform the operation in a sad butcherly manner, tho' in imitation rather of our cupping than bleeding. Instead of cupping-glasses, to which they are strangers, they use a small calabash, a horn, or a shell, perforated on the top. These they apply to an arm, leg, belly, or head, or any other part which they imagine to be the seat of the distemper, after having first made as deep a gash with a knife as the skin will admit of. They next apply their mouth to the hole of the calabash, or horn, and suck the blood thro' it till it is full. This they repeat till they have drawn a sufficient quantity of it from the patient; in some cases they will, instead of a calabash, make use of an earthen pot . . . and apply it with lighted tow, as we do our cupping-glasses." See *The Modern Part of the Universal History: Compiled from Original Writers* . . . , VI (London, 1760), 466–467.

54. Kananoja, *Healing Knowledge in Atlantic Africa*, 32; Rask, "Brief and Truthful Description," in Winsnes, trans., *Two Views from Christiansborg Castle*, I, 113, 133. Monrad's description of the procedure is very similar to others noted in the Bight of Biafra and the Kongo: "The Negroes perform cupping using a small calabash in which there is a hole about the size of an ordinary copper shilling, and which, is otherwise, hollow. The air is removed from the calabash by a dry plantain leaf which has been dipped in palm oil and then lit. This calabash is then placed over an incision that has been made in the skin and the blood is drawn out. These incisions are usually made on either side of the head, under the temples, and on the back below the neck. They then apply charcoal and citron juice to the wound, and this results in blue stains on the face, as if from gunpowder" ("A Description," ibid., II, 203–204).

55. Monrad, "A Description," ibid., II, 204; "Substance of a Communication Made by Henry Meredith, Esq. to the Secretary, Dated Winnebah," Dec. 20, 1809, in *Fourth Report*

Healers in the Bight of Biafra placed their trust in indigenous African methods of bloodletting throughout the eighteenth century to cure a variety of ailments. Olaudah Equiano recollected that, while he was a child in Igboland during the 1750s, ritual specialists practiced *atama*, or "bleeding by cupping." In a parallel to the logic of humoral medicine, which favored the purging of harmful substances from the body to restore health and balance, Equiano postulated that therapists deploying this method were "successful in healing wounds and expelling poisons." Likewise, Hugh Crow observed that in Bonny the local people "appl[ied] certain remedies, chiefly decoctions of herbs and cupping, which they perform with a small calabash, after having made incisions . . . for relief." Doctor William F. Daniell remarked that "this mode of cupping is one constantly adopted by the natives in the Bights, in all painful affections of the head." He also witnessed the creation of "a series of deep scarifications . . . bathed with hot fomentations to promote the free oozing of the blood" to alleviate the pain of rheumatism as well as to treat apoplexy and respiratory congestion. The aforementioned Osifekunde similarly recalled that, in late-eighteenth-century Ijebu, local healers performed bloodletting using "small hollowed out calabashes . . . applied over a wick made of old calabash fiber soaked in oil and lighted." In lieu of orally evacuating blood with the aid of animal horns, as was common for Bahian barbers, practitioners in Ijebu utilized heat to create a vacuum that expelled blood from precisely made cuts on their patient's flesh.[56]

On slaving vessels, African-informed bloodletting practices were sanctioned in part because they comported with both European theories of heal-

---

of the Directors of the African Institution: Read at the Annual General Meeting on the 28th of March, 1810 (London, 1810), 91. African women's therapeutic knowledge failed to find expression in the barbershops of Brazil, however. In Bahia, most medical expertise—save midwifery—was seen as intrinsically masculine. The translation of African healing forms to the Americas created a gendered division of labor and expertise that did not exist in African contexts.

56. Douglas B. Chambers, "'My Own Nation': Igbo Exiles in the Diaspora," *Slavery and Abolition*, XVIII (1997), 72–97, esp. 89. In addition, Crow revealed that the Igbos in the same region "were very subject to head ache, and in order to relieve them we sometimes resorted to cupping. They were not strangers to the operation, but told us it was a remedy [that] often had recourse in their own country." Another report from the southeast of the Niger Delta confirms the practice there, as well: "In congestion of the vessels of the brain or its membranes, accompanied by much feberile excitement, relief is experienced from the native process of cupping, which consists in making three parallel longitudinal or horizontal incisions on either temple, from ten lines to an inch in length, and about eight lines apart.

ing and the supposed profit-making mandates of slaving capitalism. Early modern European medical practitioners, whose logics significantly but not exclusively informed slavers' decisions, posited that illness resulted from a disequilibrium of the four fluid elements, or humors, that comprised the body: blood, phlegm, yellow bile (or vomit), and black bile, with blood being the dominant humor. The humoral equilibrium model was a long-held and attractive means of explaining health and illness because it offered a concrete theory of causation for most afflictions, as well as presenting an attainable cure. Further confirming the utility of bloodletting, medical treatises such as the *Tractado das queixas endemicas, e mais fataes nesta Conquista (Treatise of Endemic and Most Fatal Diseases in This Conquest)*, penned by Francisco Damião Cosme in 1770, advised barbers and surgeons to bleed enslaved patients afflicted with a number of infectious diseases. Captives kept in tightly packed holds often contracted communicable diseases such as the notorious bloody flux or dysentery. To restore health, Cosme prescribed an eclectic mixture of disparate healing methods. He argued for bleeding in conjunction with the administration of medicinal teas or tonics containing sudorifics, emetics, and purgatives. Such solutions of bodily purging, including bleeding and forced vomiting, were necessary, Cosme argued, to cleanse the body of "corruption" and reestablish the balance of the humors. Drastic steps were essential, he reasoned, if any sufferers were to combat the most "ardent" fevers common on the West African coast.[57]

Bloodletting became a privileged site for the incorporation of distinct medical traditions. As a complement to bleeding, practitioners administered

---

These incisions are performed by a sharp razor, or knife, and a small calabash is then applied, the air being then exhausted by burning paper or cotton *secundum artem*. After the abstraction of a few ounces of blood, the wounds are dressed with a black carbonaceous matter, manufactured from the oil lamps." See *Memoirs of the Late Captain Hugh Crow, of Liverpool* . . . (London, 1830), 225–227; Daniell, *Sketches,* 94, 95, 113; Curtin, *Africa Remembered,* 260.

57. According to the humoral equilibrium model, the restoration of humoral balance through cleansing one or more humors with forms of purging or through the expulsion of stagnant blood by the opening of veins, blisters, or the application of leeches was just as vital as the application of botanical and mineral substances to slaving ship healing. See Foster, "On the Origin of Humoral Medicine in Latin America," *Medical Anthropology Quarterly,* I (1987), 358–363; Foster, "The Validating Role of Humoral Theory in Traditional Spanish-American Therapeutics," *American Ethnologist,* XV (1988), 120–135. The symptoms of dysentery included inflammation, delirium, severe diarrhea, and bloody stools, alongside what Cosme called bilious or malignant fevers, which resulted in indigestion, skin rashes,

to their patients powerful emetics such as ipecacuanha; purgatives or laxatives including jalapa, castor oil, manna, senna, poppies, and cream of tartar; and diaphoretics such as elderberry—all of which were common in slaving ship medicine chests. Medical practitioners followed these treatments by giving patients food, liquids like wine or tea, and analgesics such as laudanum dissolved in vinegar, as well as water, provided it had not already spoiled at sea.[58] On transatlantic slaving vessels, both European medical impositions and the specter of slavery's ravages haunted barbers' African-derived healing strategies. Though their work at first glance might have appeared similar to European practices, the physical techniques of bloodletting favored by African practitioners diverged in key ways from those of Portuguese surgeons and European medical theorists. Moreover, they were underpinned by radically distinct ideas about the metaphysics of healing. At sea and on land, African medical practitioners formulated their own rationales and socially intelligible medical logics as they expelled blood from the heads, shoulders, and backs of weak, sickly, and dying enslaved African patients. Though few sources detailing the precise nature of barbers' healing techniques at sea survive, they likely mirrored practices of Black bloodletters in urban Brazil, as such men often sold their healing therapies in both spaces.

In terrestrial environments, sangradores employed distinctive, African-derived instruments to heal patients, including "mysterious small cone[s] made of ox horn" to evacuate blood from lacerated flesh. In an operation "most skillfully performed," according to one witness, patients bared their backs and awaited the barber's razor. After he raised the "flesh on the back between his finger and thumb, and, holding it tightly, dexterously," he "cuts the flesh several times, immediately applies the horn and exhausts the air by

---

strokes, and body pain, as well as pleurisy or inflammation of the chest and lungs. See Cosme, "Tractado das queixas endemicas, e mais fataes nesta Conquista (Luanda, 1770)," ed. Luis de Pina, *Studia*, XX–XXII (1967), 174–175, 187, 189, 252; Miller, *Way of Death*, 420–423.

58. Fresh water was often in short supply on slaving voyages as captains under-rationed water casks to make room for more slaves and other cargo; where it was sufficient, it was often contaminated. Standards of water rationing varied over time, but slaving ships often functioned with a pervasive shortage. The meager amounts they did carry were often spoiled by seawater and other contaminants, becoming a vector of disease at sea. By 1813, royal regulations attempted to standardize water rations, ensuring that each vessel secured two *canadas* (approximately 2.8 liters) per captive per day in its casks; this was still inadequate for the dangerous conditions of a slaving ship that caused enslaved individuals held in humid holds to continuously lose bodily fluids through profuse perspiration (Miller, *Way of Death*, 351–352).

FIGURE 13. *Detail of* Le chirurgien nègre. *By J[ean] B[aptiste] Debret.*
Ca. 1834–1839. An African "surgeon" at work, bloodletting on the streets of 1810s–1830s
Rio de Janeiro. He has placed ox horns over incisions on the head and back.
Schomburg Center for Research in Black Culture, Photographs and Prints Division,
The New York Public Library. New York Public Library Digital Collections

putting his mouth to the smaller end, which done, he stops the orifice, and leaves the horn; this is fastened on the back of his patient for about ten minutes." An adept bloodletter could provide gentle treatment; as one observer noted, patients "bear the operation . . . with great fortitude; and I have repeatedly watched their faces to discover signs of pain, but have only done so when the air is being exhausted from the horn, and the blood is beginning to flow."[59]

A key part of African barbers' social and intellectual power lay in their mastery not only of the human body but of the metaphysical forces they and their patients believed produced sickness and health. Visitors to Bahia were

59. Blistering cups, or *ventozas,* as well as horns would create a vacuum when heated. Though practitioners used bull horns and glass cups to expel blood, in 1694 João Ferrira da Rosa identified the latter as a hallmark of popular medical practice, claiming that blistering

often captivated by barbers' deft therapies, and descriptions of bloodletting reveal a range of techniques broadly shared by practitioners. Barbers—unlike physicians or surgeons—provided Black patients with services for corporeal maintenance, health, and appearance, creatively combining bloodletting, bodily modification, and powerful oral incantations to provide momentary relief. As one observer explained, the Bahian barber was "expert at shaving and hair-cutting, but [also drew] teeth and [bled] with leeches, besides being a musician." Their expansive set of skills required the manipulation of both flesh and the forces that afflicted it, powers that could be activated by the words and sounds of those who had knowledge of their properties. In cities such as Salvador, Black healers created distinctly African-oriented therapeutic spaces that allowed enslaved residents to seek comfort and relief among other African-born people.[60]

African healers' "musical talents" were also put to good use during bleeding therapies, a phenomenon that marked their practice as epistemically unique from the bloodletting therapies offered by white surgeons and physicians. In early-eighteenth-century Bahia, André João Antonil noted that local "witch doctors and folk healers" used "words to heal." Like other Black popular healers, barbers and sangradores made use of orality in their therapies. A century later, another visitor touted such men's vocal accompaniments, which complemented "the master [barber as he was] performing any of the operations of his profession." As the bloodletter skillfully wielded his knife, his assistants sang to "soothe the soul" of patients "or drown the cries of pain, as the *case*

---

cups were more accurate and preferred by trained surgeons. See J[ean] B[aptiste] Debret, *Voyage pittoresque . . .* , II (Paris, 1835), 142; Kananoja, *Healing Knowledge,* 32; Wetherell, *Stray Notes from Bahia,* ed. Hadfield, 4. Another description echoes the use of cupping and bleeding for pain relief and the popularity of the practice among the Black population in Rio de Janeiro: "For rheumatic pains, they use cupping, in a curious way, and a negro is generally the operator. I was one day passing through a street, in the rear of the palace, and I saw a negro doctor administering to some patients, who were sitting on the steps of a church. He bound the arm and shoulder of a woman, who seemed in great pain; and making slight scarifications in several places with the broken blade of a razor, he patted the parts with the flat, till the blood began to ooze out; he then placed small cow-horns over them, and applying his mouth to a perforation at the tip, he dexterously exhausted the air, and then stopping it with clay, it remained firmly attached to the skin. In this way he fastened seven horns from the elbow to the shoulder, where they exhibited a very extraordinary appearance. When removed, the arm was covered with blood; and the woman said she was greatly relieved" (Walsh, *Notices of Brazil in 1828 and 1829,* I, 230).

60. Wetherell, *Stray Notes from Bahia,* ed. Hadfield, 33.

may be." Though Europeans observing such healing scenes remained ignorant of the indispensable function of such melodious acts, an enduring link between music and barbering suffused Salvador. Thomas Lindley contended as early as 1805 that all of the musicians in the city were Black and "trained by the different barber-surgeons of the city, who are of the same colour, and have been itinerant musicians from time immemorial." These "swarthy sons of harmony" provided entertainment for all of Salvador's residents. Owners also leveraged African and creole men's vocational dexterity to their advantage, advertising their bondsmen as both expert barbers and musicians.[61] This urban practice was undeniably informed by African medical and cultural precedents. Healers in multiple regions of western Africa relied upon orality to heighten the effectiveness of their therapies while, across the Atlantic, African-born practitioners from culturally diverse origins continued to believe that sound was an integral part of bodily restoration.[62]

Barbers' and sangradores' focus on the head reflected deeply held West African conceptions of the body that inspired African healers' therapies. Fon and Yoruba speakers in West Africa (where many slaving ship barbers had been born) imagined the head as a unique site of power and transformation. Though evidence for the precolonial period is sparse, ethnographic descriptions of popular modes of healing suggest the extent to which bodily concepts underpinned both historical and present-day bloodletting practices. In Gbe-speaking polities that dotted the Bight of Benin in the early eighteenth century, residents configured the head as an important site of metaphysical

61. André João Antonil, *Brazil at the Dawn of the Eighteenth Century*, trans. Timothy J. Coates (Dartmouth, Mass., 2012), 26; Wetherell, *Stray Notes from Bahia*, ed. Hadfield, 33; Thomas Lindley, *Narrative of a Voyage to Brasil* (London, 1805), 71. In 1816, a nineteen-year-old creole enslaved barber was listed as a *"tocador,"* or musician; in 1824, Joaquim, "a barber, hairstylist and *serpentão* (a wind instrument) player," liberated himself from his owner. See BNRJ, Periódicos, *Idade d'Ouro do Brazil,* Oct. 22, 1816; ibid., *Grito da Razão* (Bahia), June 15, 1824. Zephyr L. Frank and Luis Nicolau Parés argue that African barbers frequently led musical bands in nineteenth-century Salvador and Rio de Janeiro. See Lindley, *Narrative of a Voyage to Brasil*, 71; Frank, *Dutra's World*, 111–112; Parés, "Militiamen, Barbers, and Slave-Traders: Mina and Jeje Africans in a Catholic Brotherhood (Bahia, 1770–1830)," *Revista Tempo,* XX (2014), 1–32.

62. Soares has hypothesized that bloodletting in early-nineteenth-century Brazil was derived from West African precedents practiced by Hausa peoples that were introduced to other Africans in the Americas. In this context, bloodletting was governed by the principle of *magani,* or "restoration," wherein treatment entailed correcting what was out of order and reestablishing *lafiya,* or well-being. *Wanzami* (medical practitioners) most commonly

power. In these regions, ritual offerings of skulls became an important funerary practice. Centuries later, in contemporary Fon-speaking West Africa, the head (*ta*) became identified with notions of "success, power, and individuation," whereas the fontanel is most closely linked with the "soul and the spiritual nourishment of life" and the forehead to "individual destiny and fortune." Proper treatment of the physical head is assumed to affect not only health but also self-actualization. In nearby Yoruba-speaking West Africa, the concept of *ori* connotes both individuality and destiny and encompasses the inner, spiritual head (*ori-inu*) as well as the outer, physical head (*ori-ode*). For this reason, as the art historian Rowland Abiodun has noted, "the head is treated with great respect and propitiated like Orí-Inú, its spiritual counterpart." As the seat of authority and *àṣẹ*, defined as power, life force, aura, or potentiality, the inner head can guide a person through life. Through ritual manipulation of the physical head, specialists seek to affect an individual's destiny. Curative bodily incisions also tend to be focused on the head, as do beautifying facial scarifications and incisions that are used to facilitate the worship of *orishas*, or deities. Such cuts aid deities in accessing the ori-inu, "opening the way" for contact between the physical world and otherworld, affecting the restoration of health through a manipulation of the physical and supernatural. The power of ritual healers lies in their ability to wield blades and knives, cutting the skin and hair with painless precision, and this prowess is linked to their veneration of Ogun, orisha of blood and iron.[63]

---

used cupping to restore lafiya. Soares's argument, though based on descriptions taken from contemporary West African ethnography, is almost identical to those described for nineteenth-century Bahia and Rio de Janeiro. Though it is clear that the modern Hausa practice of bloodletting was likely related to nineteenth-century Brazilian practice, enslaved people displaced from other parts of Africa to Bahia during the same period also utilized bloodletting in their therapies ("African Barbeiros," in Cañizares-Esguerra, Childs, and Sidbury, eds., *Black Urban Atlantic*, 225–227).

    63. The Gbe-speaking polities included Ouidah, Dahomey, Badagry, and Porto Novo. See Luis Nicolau Parés, *O rei, o pai e a morte: A religião vodum na Antiga Costa dos escravos na África ocidental* (São Paulo, 2016), 84–87; Suzanne Preston Blier, *African Vodun: Art, Psychology, and Power* (Chicago, 1995), 155. As Rowland Abiodun notes, contemporary proverbs stress the overall indispensability of the head: "When Ori is missing from the body, what remains is useless." Furthermore, ori is crucial to allowing individuals to master their environment and to overcome difficulties (Abiodun, *Yoruba Art and Language: Seeking the African in African Art* [Cambridge, 2014], 41–42, 44). An orisha is a deified ancestral ori (Henry John Drewal, "Yoruba Body Artists and Their Deity Ogun," in Sandra T. Barnes, ed., *Africa's Ogun: Old World and New*, 2d ed. [Bloomington, Ind., 1997], 247). The connec-

Barbers' reliance on herbal remedies and verbal incantations to cure enslaved Africans betrayed the influence of West African healing cultures with many similar characteristics. The curative process for Yoruba-speaking peoples, for instance, is overseen by the orisha Osanyin, who guides ritual specialists through "knowledge of the healing properties of leaves and herbs" and "offers humankind relief from physical suffering." *Babaláwo*—or healers endowed with heightened perception of the natural world and the body—are typically devotees of orisha Ogun, the deity of iron, warring, hunting, and metal tools (such as those used by barbers), and Ifá, the deity of divination. Yoruba-speaking ritual specialists combine power and knowledge imparted by these respective orishas in their healing methods. During healing rituals, babaláwo activate the power of specific herbal medicines through the performance of incantations. Puns and wordplay in such ceremonies verbally link the names of medicinal plants, the *odu* (or the sign of Ifá) under which they were classified, and the anticipated healing effect. African barbers' singing therapies suggest the importance of the "empowered word" to local healing techniques. Empowered words activate and channel the latent àṣẹ, which, according to Yoruba-speaking people's cosmologies, resides in all humans, animals, plants, hills, rivers, and orishas.[64]

Just as the Brazilian barber cut through the flesh of patients with razors, iron knives worked on the flesh of West Africans. Cutting—one of the primary therapeutic methods of the barber—plays an important role in cur-

---

tion between blades and metaphysical power is also apparent in the extent to which those who use iron tools (barbers, body artists, healers) are associated with Ogun, who is linked to regeneration, fertility, and creativity as well as blood and warfare. Barbers using razors are said to be "feeding" Ogun with hair, whereas body artists "feed" Ogun with their patients' blood (ibid.). In Porto Novo, an invocation interprets blood and hair offered to Ogun as a ritual sacrifice: "Ogun alake eats dog / Ogun of the barbers eats human hair / Ogun of the body artists drinks blood / Ogun of the butchers eats meat" (ibid., 241).

64. Bay, *Asen, Ancestors, and Vodun*, 30. *Babaláwo* also can be translated as "father of secrets" (Pierre Fatumbi Verger, *Ewé: The Use of Plants in Yoruba Society* [São Paulo, 1995], 1). Divination offers ritual practitioners a way to discern the natural or supernatural causes of illness and prescribes appropriate ritual actions. Ogun's presence in iron instruments (particularly the *opa Osanyin*, or ritual staff / altar) allowed healers to "cut through the bush and forest and gather healing plants," whereas the divinatory powers of Ifá enabled them to prepare the proper medicines from these raw materials and diagnose illnesses. Ogun's Dahomean counterpart, Gu, the god of iron and warfare, would similarly open new paths for ritual practitioners with his hot iron knife. See Sweet, *Domingos Álvares*, 123–125; Drewal, "Yoruba Body Artists," in Barnes, ed., *Africa's Ogun*, 235–260, 238; Verger, *Ewé*, 14–15.

rent Yoruba healing practices, as medical preparations (*oogun*) imagined as particularly potent can be absorbed into the body through small cuts in or around the mouth.[65] Within the Yoruba healing complex, àṣẹ must be activated by "verbalizing, visualizing, and performing the *oríkì* of those things or beings whose powers are being harnessed."[66] Hausa and Kongolese healers also utilized verbalizations and music in ritual medicinal practice to unleash ancestral powers and healing energies.[67] As barbers and sangradores interwove their acts of bloodletting with musical performance, they revealed their African epistemological influences, particularly their insistence on the intersection of patients' bodily health with the invisible forces of the metaphysical world.[68]

65. Abiodun, *Yoruba Art and Language,* 59. Mary Olufunmilayo Adekson hypothesizes that cuts made by traditional Nigerian medical practitioners on the top of the head work to prevent evil from coming into the lives of patients (Adekson, *The Yorùbá Traditional Healers of Nigeria* [New York, 2003], 86).

66. Babaláwo relied upon prayer and invocations of the gods and ancestors in the healing process, indicating that the "empowered word" continues to be an important aspect of medicinal practices in modern-day Nigeria. During these rituals, language is a "vehicle" for traditional healing. "Without Ohún ('speech,' 'voice,' or 'the performed word'), neither Èpè (the malevolent component of lifeforce), nor Àṣẹ, (the largely beneficent component of lifeforce)—two sides of the same coin—can fulfill its mission." See Abiodun, *Yoruba Art and Language,* 61; Adekson, *Yorùbá Traditional Healers of Nigeria,* 85–88; Teresa N. Washington, *The Architects of Existence: Àjẹ́ in Yoruba Cosmology, Ontology, and Orature* (n.p., 2014), 21.

67. In the northern interior of West Africa, Islamicized Mande blacksmith doctors and sorcerers cut flesh, perform secret healing speech, employ divination, and craft and administer botanical medicines to transform bodies from sickness to health, much like enslaved barbers. Islamic medicine that reached Hausaland in the fourteenth century was inspired by Hippocratic-Galenic methods of bloodletting and purging. Ritual speech played an integral role in the restoration of health during the medieval period. The association between Islam and healing can be seen in contemporary Songhay, where "sufferings of the head" are cured through treatments by blacksmiths, who are capable of transforming both material (iron) and the human body. Similarly, in early modern Kongo, ritual healers used music to activate ancestral powers. See Lux, "Healer as Producer of Reality and Knowledge," *Curare,* XVII (1994), 181–198; Patrick R. McNaughton, *The Mande Blacksmiths: Knowledge, Power, and Art in West Africa* (Bloomington, Ind., 1988), 42–70; Abdalla, "Diffusion of Islamic Medicine into Hausaland," in Feierman and Janzen, eds., *Social Basis of Health and Healing in Africa,* 177–194; Kananoja, *Healing Knowledge in Atlantic Africa,* 28.

68. For more references to Africans and their descendants' use of incantations during the course of medical therapies in seventeenth- and eighteenth-century Latin America, see

Bloodletting practices derived from a variety of western African communities converged in nineteenth-century Salvador da Bahia. On slaving vessels and in barbershops, African people from numerous origins interacted with one another, shared knowledge, and sought relief. Within the city's growing independent Black medicinal networks, patients and practitioners stitched together compatible African modes of bleeding therapy. Easily adaptable to the most hostile and insalubrious of New World settings, including the slaving ship, bloodletting inspired faith in African patients, who were familiar with the practice from their homelands. Even as bloodletters superficially adhered to Portuguese phlebotomist practices, they forged their own techniques by drawing blood from the forehead and back instead of the Iberian-prescribed foot or arm. In the transatlantic slave trade, such African-derived medical epistemologies proved attractive, effective, and profitable.[69]

CAPTIVE COSMOPOLITAN HOUSEHOLDS

In spite of the creeping diminishment of their work and value, many African-born barbers made themselves into important pillars of Salvador's economic and social fabric. Their elevated status flowed not only from their widely recognized medical expertise but their continued financial connections to the same trade that had rendered them property at the beginning of their long Atlantic journeys. Although some, no doubt, slipped away from the deadly traffic that their skills were called upon to repair, many others remained tethered to it. In the process of their social ascendance, they transformed their cultural mastery into authority and, eventually, financial capital, with some amassing sufficient wealth throughout their travels to afford propertied households in Bahia and become independent transatlantic traders in their own right.[70]

Sweet, *Domingos Álvares*, 112; Gómez, *Experiential Caribbean*, 101. For more examples of cutting, bleeding, and the application of herbs as a medical therapy by Africans in the seventeenth-century Caribbean, see ibid., 104–106, 112.

69. George James Guthrie, *Commentaries on the Surgery of the War in Portugal, Spain, France, and the Netherlands* (Philadelphia, 1862), 365; [Joachim] Le Grand, *A Voyage to Abyssinia, by Father Jerome Lobo, a Portuguese Missionary: Containing the History, Natural, Civil, and Ecclesiastical, of That Remote and Unfrequented Country . . .*, trans. Samuel Johnson (London, 1789), 417.

70. This rendering of the interplay between distinct fields of power in which African barbers and sangradores operated is partially modeled on Pierre Bourdieu's distinction between forms of capital. Social capital entails the creation of expansive networks of inter-

Such men were lured by the opportunity to convert their lucrative connections to West Africa and coveted occupational skills into a measure of material stability, Catholic sociability, and a household filled with active and loyal wives and children—or, failing that, enslaved clients. In short, they managed to build robust social networks that could counteract the intense isolation and existential volatility brought by their transatlantic displacement, but only if they continued to participate in the slave trade. Their life trajectories—from Africa to Brazil and back—as well as their individual choices expose not only the contours of slaving capitalism but the nature of freedom in the South Atlantic. For a number of manumitted mariners, freedom meant much more than formal independence from owners: it entailed the ability to act as a patron to other freed and enslaved Africans, to worship, and to gain property rights of one's own. This notion of autonomy and social status was conditioned, in part, by their existence in a highly stratified, patriarchal slave society.

Black seafarers of all stripes leveraged their indispensable skills to achieve greater economic and social mobility than their landlocked peers. With a modicum of prosperity secured at sea, many carved out spaces of social independence on land. This was particularly true of captive cosmopolitan barbers and sangradores. Such men remained cognizant, however, that in Bahia the most indispensable tool to augment one's influence was slaveholding, even for the port city's former slaves. Liberty in the early nineteenth century, at least in part, entailed the autonomy garnered by profiting from the labor of others. Black healers' subsequent commercial strategies often led to the formation of vertical ties of patronage as well as financial independence from current and former owners as they became patrons and property holders in their own right. Accumulating goods and slaves on the West African coast also allowed them to expand their households in Bahia and build coveted interpersonal ties of loyalty.

The ability to access transatlantic slaving commerce—even in the years of its illegality under Brazilian law after 1831—enabled barbers to accumulate sufficient property to free family members, a crucial aspiration that gave them control over their own domestic lives. Lino Ricardo, the barber on *Divina Providência*, registered his last will and testament with the municipal government, revealing his wealth acquisition strategies of the preceding years. Ricardo identified Jozé Ricardo Gomes as his former owner and patron-and

personal relationships as a resource, whereas cultural capital is defined as the power, prestige, and social currency that comes from specialized forms of knowledge (Bourdieu, *The State Nobility: Elite Schools in the Field of Power* [Stanford, Calif., 1996]).

noted that he had been born "on the Mina Coast" in West Africa but currently lived in domestic tranquility in Nossa Senhora da Conceição parish with his wife, Dona Thereza Francisca de Jesus. The couple had built a life together in a neighborhood that was a haven for seamen. Ricardo had, through his commercial exploits, accumulated enough capital to purchase Thereza's freedom years earlier. He was baptized as a Catholic and was the father to two children, Jozefa and Manoel, to whom he respectively left 300$000 and 120$000 réis. Ricardo's ability to fund Thereza's manumission left the couple's children legally free, a highly desirable outcome for two individuals who had been trafficked from West Africa.[71]

Building an autonomous domestic life in Bahia entailed more than securing the status of one's wife and children, however. Like many ambitious Bahians, Ricardo included in his household not only those related by blood but a substantial number of bondspeople with whom he had forged complex relationships that could not be reduced to mere ownership. The means by which Ricardo acquired the enslaved Africans laboring for him are murky. As a medical practitioner on a slaving ship, he would have had privileged access to several methods of acquiring his own slaves: he could have purchased them from a local merchant on the streets of Bahia, used his occupational connections to buy newly arrived bondspeople in port, or even procured captives on the coast of West Africa, where he had frequently traveled.

Though Ricardo benefited from labor of the enslaved men and women in his possession during his lifetime, his treatment of them implied layered ties of loyalty and even reciprocity he had developed between owner and bondsperson. After his death, he requested that four of the six slaves be freed rather than sold or inherited by his children. These included Emorgem, Maria, Romão, and Felicidade, to whom he bequeathed 20$000 réis each.[72] Romão was identified as an American-born creole, but the other enslaved individuals were likely from West Africa. Perhaps familiar geographic origins engendered a sense of identification or even fictive kinship on Ricardo's part. His extensive ownership of enslaved Africans as well as his insistence that the majority of them be freed at his death are illuminating. His mobility and that of his family were tied to slaveholding in the city and to the trade of West African goods he accessed as a part of slaving ship crews. He was no stranger to the exploitation of African labor; however, he gained these talismans of respectability only because of his status as a barber. He had once been an exploited

71. APEB, Tribunal de Justiça, Testamento do Lino Ricardo, livro 12, 34.
72. Ibid.

escravo de ganho himself, but his savvy transatlantic investments had enabled him to accumulate his own small cadre of wage-earning bondspeople who contributed to his household income. The frequency with which Ricardo manumitted his slaves indicates that he did not hold an exclusively economic conception of them. He also acted as a patron to his enslaved clients and did not seek to make them into transferable wealth upon his death.

Like Ricardo, Francisco Pires—a freed barber from the "African coast"—used slaveholding to expand his personal network during his lifetime. And like Ricardo, Pires did not seek to transfer his wealth in slaves to other proprietors after his death. He had arrived in Bahia at the age of twelve sometime in the late eighteenth century; in 1838, he noted in his will that his wife, Anna Rita Gonsalves, had passed away, and he had no natural or legitimate heirs. His household consisted of himself and, instead of children, his slaves: Antônio, Francisco, Ezequiel, and Marcelina. Pires saw to it that several of his bondspeople were trained in trades. Francisco was a cooper and Ezequiel was a bricklayer, whereas Marcelina appeared to have been a domestic servant. Such an investment hinted that Pires, like Ricardo, viewed the enslaved members of his household, not merely as property, but as loyal clients worthy of nurturing. He legally freed Antônio, Ezequiel, and Marcelina upon his death and left a donation to his Catholic brotherhood, Matriz de Nossa Senhora da Conceição da Praia. The latter was an indication of the degree to which this African man's religious community and enslaved property both comprised his most important and intimate relationships near the end of his life. Pires also requested that his bondspeople attend a proper Catholic burial for him.[73]

Other African-born barbers similarly depended on slaveholding to augment their personal wealth, prestige, and power and to provide heirs, clients, and confidants in childless households. Antônio Neiva, along with his wife, Victoria dos Prazeres, owned two bondswomen: Joanna and Rita, both Geges. Ventura Ferreira Milles, a barber whose first recorded transatlantic trading activities appeared in 1810, married a freed Hausa woman named Possedonia Maria Barboza in 1825 and settled in Conceição da Praia. The couple remained childless for the next two decades, until Ventura's 1844 death in Lagos. The barber and, later, trader had accrued an estate worth 2:610$000 réis in slaves. Ventura remained tied to nautical life in his old age, owning four boats as well as a young creole boy, Manoel, who was rented out to serve on a voyage to Pernambuco. He was also a creditor to five men, hinting at the complexity of his commercial relationships. Unlike other African barbers, he

73. Ibid., Testamento do Francisco Pires, livro 26, 48.

did not manumit his bondsmen outright upon his death. One of these slaves, João Nagô, offered Ventura's sole heir and widow one-fifth of his market value of 500$000 réis to purchase his freedom "in compliance with the law." The African man ultimately paid far more than his potential value to secure his *carta de liberdade* from Possedonia two years following Ventura's death.[74]

Possessing a diverse array of enslaved clients could enable Black barbers to build networks of patronage grounded in collective yet lucrative forms of artisanal labor. Several African barbers trained their male slaves in skilled professions, converting the owner-slave relationship into one of master-apprentice. Francisco Nazaré, an African barber and trader of West African goods, employed such a strategy when he sent his young Nagô slave, Manoel, to learn "the barber's craft in Antônio de Araujo Santana's [another freed African barber] shop." Some of the men who trained their slaves as apprentices were perpetuating their own experiences of apprenticeship. José Antônio d'Etrea, who died at the age of ninety in 1828, was originally from the Mina Coast and had been owned by the slaving ship captain Francisco Antônio d'Etra. José Antônio likely learned the craft of barbering on board the slaving ship of his owner. By the end of his life, he had acquired twenty-one slaves, fifteen of whom he freed outright, and two additional women whom he agreed to free if they paid for their own manumission by the time of his death. Many of his own bondsmen were also barbers, including Antônio and Francisco, who both served aboard Bahian slaving vessels. Like José Antônio, Gege barber Francisco Nunes de Moares owned and trained several bondsmen as barbers. Moares died married but childless in 1811 but granted his slaves Gonçalo, Leandro, and Domingos—all barbers—their freedom, alongside his two other slaves, Custodio and Manoel. Joaquim Gomes Toquinho, born on the Mina Coast, identified himself as a "Gege." Though married, he was without sons or daughters. Upon his death in 1814, he freed his slave, João Gomes Toquinho. Ignacio Sampaio, who belonged to the same African Catholic brotherhood as Toquinho, left his estate to his daughter but freed two domestic servants, Maria and Caetana, also from the Mina Coast, after he passed away.[75]

74. No mention of children was made by either of the freed Africans in the sparse documents they left behind (ibid., Escritura de Debito, livro 205, 88). João finally offered 612$000 réis for his freedom papers (ibid., Tribunal de Justiça, 05/1977/2449/10, Inventory of Ventura Ferreira Milles, 1846).

75. Luis Nicolau Parés, "Milicianos, barbeiros e traficantes numa irmandade cathólica de africanus minas e jejes (Bahia, 1770–1830)," *Revista Tempo,* XX (2014), 28; APEB, Tribunal de Justiça, Testamento de José Antonio D'Etra, livro 16, 100; ibid., Testamento de Francisco Nunes de Moraes, livro 3, 34; ibid., Testamento de Joaquim Gomes Toquinho, livro 4, 180.

The property accumulation methods of freed barbers in Salvador illustrate the ways in which African-born men utilized their participation in transatlantic commerce, including slaving and slaveholding, to expand their households and social influence. Operating within a political and commercial context in which the slave trade was increasingly subject to British suppression measures and, later, was also illegal under Brazilian law, African barbers and sangradores sought to carve out financially secure lives. They leveraged their ethnic affiliations and maritime occupations to accumulate the personal and material resources to construct large households of kin and other dependents, including African-born slaves. Their emphasis on manumitting slaves upon their deaths also reveals that bondspeople within the households of African-born slaveholders occupied an ambiguous position as neither fully transferable chattel property nor free clients. Freed African barbers, through the course of their own lives, had moved between these poles of existence as well and understood their contextual ambiguity.

In many respects, these Africans reproduced—for quite different reasons— the conditions of their original enslavement as escravos de ganho. Their former owners had understood that cultivating their enslaved property's skills, hiring them out to be wage laborers, and allowing them to access trading opportunities inspired loyalty and prevented more dramatic forms of resistance such as escape. Treating maritime barbers as clients and, at times, trade auxiliaries allowed permissive slaveholders to accumulate capital from their slaves' independent wealth, earning off their labor without resorting to more exacting forms of supervision and domination. In some ways, African freedmen might have emulated these slaveholding tactics. They were also likely, however, to expand their households—their wealth in people—through the accumulation and later mentoring of their enslaved African property. In the wake of the freedmen's own physical and social displacement, such methods built wealth, prestige, and autonomy as they sought to relieve their enforced social alienation and isolation. For them, freedom meant, not individualistic independence, but the security of a large household of male and female dependents, wives, children, and slaves with whom they could re-create a semblance of kinship relations in a radically new context.

As exponents of a medical cosmopolitanism that married Euro-American practices with African material and intellectual resources, Black barbers and sangradores were an essential part of the Bahian slave trade; they shaped the fabric of Bahian slave society and altered Atlantic landscapes of medical knowledge. In the floating world of the slave ship, Black practitioners diffused

African therapeutic forms by introducing diverse western African ideas about the nature of the human body, the environment, and illness. Even though nearly all African barbers and sangradores trained in Portuguese-influenced phlebotomy as adolescents, their subsequent working lives also immersed them in African communities where such practices existed independently. Dialogues between practitioner and patient fostered the formation of new, creolized forms of therapeutic knowledge that drew on influences from both sides of the Atlantic. Within the discrete field of healing the enslaved, their specialized knowledge predominated in both influence and value. In turn, African medical practitioners' emphasis on the therapeutic quality of flowing blood, healing plants, and empowering vocalizations found purchase with displaced and physically vulnerable communities in Brazil.

Despite academically trained theorists' dismissal of their value, Africans continued to comprise the overwhelming majority of sangradores and barbers laboring in the Bahian slave trade. This professional centrality, unique in the Atlantic world, attests to both merchants' and enslaved people's continued confidence in their medical efficacy.[76] In the South Atlantic, such cosmopolitan African medical epistemologies were lucrative. Merchants, motivated by their desire to value and commodify African bodies as cheaply and effectively as possible, hired African barbers and sangradores to contain illness on their vessels. Reciprocal exchanges between Brazilian and West African healing techniques supplied barbers with intellectual tools to combat—to an extent—the physical ravages of enslavement. But their skilled labor simultaneously sustained the slave trade's profitability. Because management of sickness was such an integral part of the slaving business, both European and African medical practitioners were compelled to produce new forms of medical knowledge in an attempt to halt the rapid and horrific spread of disease on board slaving ships, in African port cities, and in American slave societies such as Salvador. The transatlantic slave trade produced rampant, recurrent pathogenic exchanges. Africans and Europeans appropriated therapies from one another to resist these epidemic and economic threats.

76. On both French and British slaving vessels, medical practitioners were uniformly European and, by the late eighteenth century, entirely trained by the Royal College of Surgeons of Edinburgh and at Trinity College in Dublin. After the passage of Dolben's Act of 1788, British vessels were required to employ a surgeon on board. Moreover, surgeons represented the vast majority of medical personnel on British slave ships. See Sheridan, "The Guinea Surgeons on the Middle Passage," *International Journal of African Historical Studies*, XIV (1981), 611–612; James Walvin, *The Zong: A Massacre, the Law, and the End of Slavery* (New Haven, Conn., 2011), 53.

The perilous living and working conditions of many Africans and their descendants made a pluralistic landscape of medical therapy in colonial Brazil, and on slaving vessels, a necessity. The ongoing medical crisis fostered by slavery nurtured a class of medical practitioners from ethnically diverse origins who utilized manifold experimental methods of treatment to earn substantial salaries and achieve social mobility. At sea, such men's creative agency worked to heal bodies on behalf of slaving capitalism, a practice they leveraged into some measure of social status and material prosperity while on land. As they established households filled with wives, children, and enslaved clients, they became key figures within Salvador's community of African residents. Some used their social ascendance to escape the dangers of the transatlantic slave trade. Others chose to remain, even after they had achieved manumission, hiring out their labor for transatlantic voyages and sometimes investing in the transatlantic trade for their own, personal benefit. Working in such a physically and epidemiologically perilous vocation was a compromise such men were willing to accept in light of the opportunities that mobility afforded them and their growing families. As barbers and sangradores traveled between Bahia and West Africa, they came to control a flow of ideas that would medically transform both regions. Their movements would also crucially spawn an entrepreneurial culture of transatlantic exchange that would remake the material and religious landscapes of Bahia.

{ CHAPTER 7 }

Making an African
Material World in Bahia

On October 18, 1811, readers of the Salvador da Bahia newspaper *Idade d'Ouro* were notified about the recent arrival of a slaving vessel from the Mina Coast. The newspaper proclaimed that the brig *Bom Sucesso*, captained by Antonio Simões, had docked four days earlier with a cargo of "263 captives (2 died)." Many of Salvador's denizens would have traveled from the upper city, replete with commanding white buildings and "fine houses, gay people, handsome churches, and . . . good streets," down to the lower city's commercial epicenter by the water. There, they met mariners and local stevedores unloading the hundreds of enslaved men, women, and children who had been lucky enough to survive the transatlantic journey. The *Bom Sucesso's* cargo also held a product that would have brought Salvador's Black residents to the city's waterfront as excited consumers: along with four pipes of oil, the ship had returned from the African continent with "2100 cloths" to be sold. The announcement might not have been necessary, however. The primary buyers of such products—Black market women (*quitandeiras* and *ganhadeiras*)— often had well-established connections to the mariners who had brought the cloths back to Brazil from the West African coast. For these enterprising women, word of mouth had likely already alerted them to the arrival of a trove of West African commodities in the city.[1]

As the announcement in the *Idade d'Ouro* suggests, the transatlantic slave trade was about more than the forced movement of enslaved; it also encompassed the transmission of African commodities and the subsequent remaking of material worlds on both sides of the Atlantic. Illuminating the contours

---

1. BNRJ, *Idade d'Ouro do Brazil* (Bahia), Oct. 18, 1811, no. 46. Salvador's lower city was defined by its "narrow and dirty" alleyways, which jutted off from the main drag rife with countinghouses, small-scale snuff producers, brothels, rustic market stalls, and merchant firms crowded with recently landed enslaved Africans. The waterfront urban district became a hub for exchanges of all kinds. See James Prior, *Voyage along the Eastern Coast of Africa to Mosambique, Johanna, and Quiloa; to St. Helena; to Rio de Janeiro, Bahia, and Pernambuco in Brazil, in the Nisus Frigate* (London, 1819), 100–101.

of a transatlantic trade in *panos da costa* ("cloth of the coast"), *dendê* (palm) oil, and other African-derived commodities, this chapter reveals the everyday commercial agency of captive cosmopolitans and the ways in which their trading initiatives suffused the economic and cultural life of both Salvador's waterfront and the larger Atlantic world. If the commodification of enslaved Africans by avaricious merchants and ship captains was one of the central processes of the early modern Atlantic, as many scholars argue, the transatlantic trade in African commodities suggests another, equally important story. On the economic margins of transatlantic slaving, enslaved and freed people seized on the possibilities of oceanic commerce to enrich themselves, consecrate social and spiritual ties, and secure greater autonomy. In the South Atlantic, commodified people moved African commodities, both for the benefit of others and of their own volition. As autonomous producers, traders, and consumers, enslaved and freed people forged new translocal trading circuits. By the early nineteenth century, this fully elaborated exchange in West African goods had become significant enough to produce a particularly Bahian material culture, one suffused with potent symbols of African origin that threaded together past and present and helped those who lived in a slave society make sense of their place in that world.[2]

That goods from the shores of West Africa traveled to both the city of Salvador and the rural environs of Bahia suggests the degree to which captive cosmopolitans and their associates, friends, and romantic partners on both sides of the Atlantic had constructed a commodity trade defined by a steadfast preference for African-derived material cultures. Taking advantage of their ability to move through and around aquatic spaces, Africans—often of the same ethnicity—residing in both the interior of Bahia and the city of Salvador built West African commodity networks through links of sociability. Textiles and palm oil produced in the interior of the Bight of Benin made their way to the coast in the hands of merchants trafficking enslaved men, women, and children. Stepping on shore in the distant ports of Ouidah, Porto Novo, and Lagos, enslaved Black mariners bartered with local African brokers for such precious goods. Many wares would be transported across the Atlantic in

---

2. BNRJ, *Idade d'Ouro do Brazil,* Oct. 18, 1811, no. 46. On the enslaved as commodities in the transatlantic slave trade, see Jennifer L. Morgan, *Reckoning with Slavery: Gender, Kinship, and Capitalism in the Early Black Atlantic* (Durham, N.C., 2021), 80–89; Marcus Rediker, *The Slave Ship: A Human History* (New York, 2007); Stephanie E. Smallwood, *Saltwater Slavery: A Middle Passage from Africa to American Diaspora* (Cambridge, Mass., 2007).

captive cosmopolitans' liberty chests. As the swift, wooden sailing vessels of the slave trade approached the Bay of All Saints, African vendors in the city rushed to meet Black sailors, to whom they were often connected by social or ethnic bonds. On the vibrant waterfronts of Salvador, vendors' boxes and satchels containing African commodities circulated on the heads and backs of mobile Black vendors. As the lithe canoes and lighters of Bahia flowed into the port city, rural boatmen negotiated with local market women—their principal trading partners—to secure items both mundane and rare arriving from across the expanse of the Atlantic. Enterprising ganhadeiros (enslaved traders) ventured from the city on foot to sell fabric that would eventually clothe the bodies of those enslaved on rural plantations.

The acumen and access of captive cosmopolitans helped create a self-organized transatlantic commercial circuit that was largely *African*-dominated at the points of production, oceanic transportation, and consumption. Mariners, boatmen, and market women pioneered and largely controlled a chain of commodity exchange that stretched thousands of miles, from Old Oyo and Ijebu in the Yoruba-speaking African interior to the plantations of rural Brazil. Historians have demonstrated that enslaved men and women living in Bahia during the late eighteenth and early nineteenth centuries created their own economies of commodity and currency exchange by marketing surplus agricultural products cultivated on rural plantations. They were able to achieve a degree of autonomy as well as access to cash economies and property.[3] Focusing on the commercial world of Salvador, however, reveals that enslaved Bahians with access to local aquatic environments developed forms of expertise, circulation, and exchange that both provided subsistence for enslaved communities and created circuits of commerce into which a demand for goods procured in the larger Atlantic world, and specifically

3. For analyses of enslaved people's local marketing practices in Bahia, see B. J. Barickman, *A Bahian Counterpoint: Sugar, Tobacco, Cassava, and Slavery in the Recôncavo, 1780–1860* (Stanford, Calif., 1998), 57–63; Alex Andrade Costa, "Entre a morada e a roça: Escravidão no Recôncavo sul da Bahia, 1850–1888," *Politeia*, X (2010), 131–150. For additional works on slaves' marketing in the Caribbean and U.S., see Sidney W. Mintz and Douglas Hall, "The Origins of the Jamaican Internal Marketing System," *Yale University Publications in Anthropology*, no. 57 (1960), 12–13; Philip D. Morgan and Ira Berlin, *The Slaves' Economy: Independent Production by Slaves in the Americas* (London, 1991); Justene Hill Edwards, *Unfree Markets: The Slaves' Economy and the Rise of Capitalism in South Carolina* (New York, 2021); Shauna J. Sweeney, "Market Marronage: Fugitive Women and the Internal Marketing System in Jamaica, 1781–1834," *WMQ*, 3d Ser., LXXVI (2019), 197–222.

Africa, would become integrated. As this chapter argues, captive cosmopolitans aboard Bahian slaving vessels were at the heart of this process, working within Salvador da Bahia's commercial infrastructure. The composite commodity circuit they forged—weaving together individuals both enslaved and freed, rural and urban—was the product of African and Afro-Brazilian people's mobility, ingenuity, commercial expertise, and most important, their aesthetic and cultural preferences. The vitality of Bahia's transatlantic commerce from below begs the question of not just *how* the enslaved were able to construct such a trade but *why*—especially in light of their limited means.[4]

For the recently displaced Africans living in Bahia, such commodities—particularly panos da costa—functioned as a site of monetary investment and a source of social symbolism and cultural meaning–making. As people circulated between West Africa and Bahia, so did ideas, values, and cultural connotations ascribed to material goods. Understanding the multivalent significance of these commodities requires an interdisciplinary methodology. By combining economic analysis and ethnographic insights, this chapter traces the routes and roots of West African goods to historicize the emergence of a culture of commercialized material expression by Salvador's Black inhabitants.[5] Drawing on theories of African materiality from art history and anthropology, it reveals how the enslaved used material culture to communicate

4. David Hancock, *Oceans of Wine: Madeira and the Emergence of American Trade and Taste* (New Haven, Conn., 2009); Sidney W. Mintz, *Sweetness and Power: The Place of Sugar in Modern History* (New York, 1985); Marcy Norton, *Sacred Gifts, Profane Pleasures: A History of Tobacco and Chocolate in the Atlantic World* (Ithaca, N.Y., 2008). African commodities included palm oil, assorted shells, baskets, straw mats, soap, gourds, kola nuts, herbs, and peppers. See J. Lorand Matory, *Black Atlantic Religion: Tradition, Transnationalism, and Matriarchy in the Afro-Brazilian Candomblé* (Princeton, N.J., 2005), 92; *Correio mercantil* (Bahia), Feb. 7, 1847, no. 34, 3.

5. Akinwumi Ogundiran and Paula Saunders, eds., *Materialities of Ritual in the Black Atlantic* (Bloomington, Ind., 2014), 14. One pioneering effort by a scholar of Brazilian slavery to enrich historical textual evidence by employing ethnography and oral history was that of Stanley J. Stein, whose *Vassouras* utilized mid-twentieth-century observations of *caxambú* or *batuque* (drum performances with dancing and verbal accompaniment) to interpret historical ideological challenges to slavery. In deciphering recordings of *jongos,* or coded "songs of protest" that featured riddles and African linguistic expressions, Stein argued that subtle political messages were expressed through playful musicality. He also drew on the insider knowledge of Afro-Brazilian informants who still lived in the rural communities of Paraíba that he studied, a technique he devised collaborating with famed Africanist anthropologists

shared concepts and values, particularly regarding the relationships among people and between humans and spirits. Any recovery of African-derived belief systems, social values, and cosmological perspectives must involve more than the written word, and an engagement with the world of materiality can reveal previously submerged histories of consciousness in the diaspora.[6]

Through the circulation of goods, novel ideas about aesthetics and materiality were introduced to Bahia, allowing enslaved men and women to engage in innovative forms of bodily signification while earning valuable income with which to subsist in a harsh and unforgiving urban environment. Captive cosmopolitans moved not only West African materials but also seductive ideas about those products. As wearable "social documents," panos da costa enabled Bahians to express unique modes of bodily signification and empowerment, constructing notions of both community and status in a Bahian context.[7] By participating in the same commercial networks that had rendered them property, mariners helped generate new forms of African diasporic cultural expression. In the hands of West Africans and some creoles in the city, these items also became vital for the performance of public and private ritual offerings as religious devotees created material assemblages to honor powerful spirits. The material flows produced by transatlantic merchant capitalism produced new types of religious expression and community that paradoxi-

---

Melville Herskovits and Frances Herskovits. See Stein, *Vassouras: A Brazilian Coffee County, 1850–1900; The Roles of Planter and Slave in a Plantation Society* (1958; rpt. Princeton, N.J., 1985), 204–209. For a more recent example of such a mixed methodology, see James H. Sweet, "Reimagining the African-Atlantic Archive: Method, Concept, Epistemology, Ontology," *Journal of African History,* LV (2014), 147–159, esp. 148; Sweet, *Domingos Álvares, African Healing, and the Intellectual History of the Atlantic World* (Chapel Hill, N.C., 2011).

6. On commodities as products of socially and culturally specific processes, see Arjun Appadurai, "Introduction: Commodities and the Politics of Value," in Appadurai, ed., *The Social Life of Things: Commodities in Cultural Perspective* (Cambridge, 1986), 3–64, esp. 6. On the abilities of materials—particularly fetishes—to act as agents and remake human subjectivities, see J. Lorand Matory, *The Fetish Revisited: Marx, Freud, and the Gods Black People Make* (Durham, N.C., 2018), 2–4. On the circulation of objects and ideas about them in the early modern African diaspora, see Akinwumi Ogundiran and Paula Saunders, *Materialities of Ritual in the Black Atlantic* (Bloomington, Ind., 2014), 14.

7. Like panos da costa, *asen,* or ritual staff altars, acted as "social documents" inflected with socially defined, dynamic representational meanings in Dahomey. See Edna G. Bay, *Asen, Ancestors, and Vodun: Tracing Change in African Art* (Champaign, Ill., 2008), 10; Ogundiran and Saunders, *Materialities of Ritual in the Black Atlantic,* 18.

cally allowed those displaced to Brazil to re-create social fabrics that had been torn apart by the violence of slaving. Though many of these practices and ideas derived from African precedents, they evolved into something uniquely American: an expression of Afro-Brazilian consciousness and a new collective identity that linked Bahia to West Africa.

AFRICAN GOODS IN MARITIME LIBERTY CHESTS

When the *Bom Sucesso* docked in Salvador in 1811 carrying 2,100 African cloths, many mariners aboard likely carried liberty chests with them. As discussed in Chapter 2, such chests could be physical objects, but the term was euphemistic. They amounted to space in slaving vessels' cargo reserved for the personal property and goods of mariners, both enslaved and free, working on board. Captains' approval of liberty chests enhanced the value of roundtrip voyages for sailors who received meager wages, which in turn reduced capital costs for powerful merchants. Political considerations in the era of British suppression of the transatlantic slave trade were also central. Ships that purchased commodities such as palm oil and panos da costa in the ports of Ouidah, Porto Novo, and Lagos could conveniently claim they were trading in West African goods, not slaves, in the hope of evading British detection. The subsidiary trade in West African goods proved attractive to calculating captains and enterprising common seamen alike. On deepwater vessels traveling to the Bight of Benin, cosmopolitan mariners born in Africa but with personal connections to Brazil leveraged their familiarity with both sides of the Atlantic to procure African-derived commodities. In doing so, they established networks of exchange that transformed the urban spaces of Salvador da Bahia, particularly modes of dress, religious ritual, and cuisine, while crafting an inventive strategy for purchasing their freedom and accumulating property.

In 1811, the *Divina Providência*'s cargo revealed extensive investments by enslaved seamen of a value that often exceeded their wages as well as a pronounced affinity for West African material goods among slaving ship investors. British antislaving forces had captured the ship near Lagos with 235 Africans imprisoned on board and a crew of 34 men, 23 of whom were African and 17 of whom were enslaved. Deep below its teeming primary deck, the *Providência* housed 6 barrels of palm oil and 550 "diverse" panos da costa, the value of which was estimated to be 1:873$000 réis. A great variety of West African cloth included 50 "fine large" panos da costa, valued at 6$000 réis each, 100 "bed cloths" valued at 5$000 réis per piece, and 100 brocade panos and 300 *panos dos Jotós* valued at 2$000 and $960 réis each, respectively. The ship's African crew members included Lino Ricardo, identified as a barber from the "Mina nation" and earning a salary of 80$000 réis. Crucially, this African mariner also had cobbled together enough capital to possess 85$800 réis in trade goods, which included tobacco, *aguardente,* and panos da costa. The tobacco held by Ricardo was 2½ percent of the ship's total cargo. Alongside him, Elias da Matta, also a freed African sailor who hailed from the Mina Coast, owned 16$800 réis in goods, whereas Antônio Francisco, a sailor from Angola, was paid a mere 40$000 réis but supplemented his earnings with investments of 9$600 réis in goods. Caetano and Manoel, both enslaved Mina sailors aboard the *Providência,* jointly owned 19$200 réis in goods.[8]

Liberty chests were not just evidence of the entrepreneurial ambitions of Black mariners; they were also evidence of mariners' importance to the creation of material worlds and circuits of exchange that would bring Africa to the Americas in tangible forms. The presence of twenty-three African men laboring on the *São Miguel Triunfante* is also suggestive of the part that Black mariners played in directing West African goods to Bahia. The ship had not yet completed all of its trading transactions on the Mina Coast before its capture by a British antislaving vessel on April 5, 1812. As Chapter 2 details, the *Triunfante's* primary purpose was the acquisition of enslaved men, women, and children, but many of the ship's enslaved investors were instead keen on purchasing goods: when it was captured by the British, the ship held 132 African captives, 28 rolls of tobacco, and 8 pipes of aguardente, as well as 454 panos da costa and 34 barrels of palm oil. Like the *Divina Providência,* the *Triunfante* had obtained textiles of various sizes, styles, and applications. These included 400 panos of "3 lengths" valued at 1$112 réis each, 54 brocade cloths for 2$000 réis each, 1 West African "bed cloth" worth 12$800 réis, and 1 "finely embroidered" pano da costa for a handsome sum of 8$000 réis in

8. ANRJ, Junta do Comércio, Fábricas e Navegações, caixa 410, Papers of the *Divina Providência,* 5, 31–33. The meaning of *Jotós* is unclear in this context, but it could be a reference to the "guardian genius" of the ancestors and one's living relationship with one's ancestor. Thus "panos dos Jotós" could mean "ancestral cloth," or the material connection to one's ancestors in the West African Ewe language. See [Edward G]eoffrey Parrinder, *West African Psychology: A Comparative Study of Psychological and Religious Thought* (Cambridge, 2002), 62, 121; Robert D. Pelton, *The Trickster in West Africa: A Study of Mythic Irony and Sacred Delight* (Los Angeles, 1980), 114–115.

the principal cargo. Alongside these, the ship's first pilot had also acquired 30 "finely brocade crochet" cloths (*panos furos de reboço*), 5 "long cloths," and 6 "blue bed cloths." In addition, quartermaster Jozé da Silva Guimarães, barber Domingos do Rozário, cooper Joaquim da Santa Anna, second cooper Ignacio Rodrigues Ferreira, and unidentified *preto* sailors all owned a portion of the ship's palm oil cargo. Bahian-born Domingos do Rozário, of African descent, possessed 162$280 réis worth of extensive and unusual holdings, including 34 *canadas* of palm oil, 2 dozen small and 7 "large corals," and 11 straw mats, 2 large and 3 small panos da costa valued at 4$000 réis and $800 réis, respectively.[9]

The rich material world housed within the liberty chests of the *Triunfante* was just a trace of larger commercial transformations unfolding over the course of the eighteenth and nineteenth centuries that had made the trade in African goods to Bahia possible. In the Bight of Benin, the reorientation of coastal trading routes to Yoruba-speaking city-states during the late eighteenth century meant that West African brokers carried a greater array of textiles and larger quantities of palm oil to Atlantic shores alongside the enslaved individuals they trafficked. At sea, the long-standing practice of granting trading privileges to enslaved and freed African mariners reached its pinnacle during this period. At the same time, in Bahia, the emergence of a Black-dominated commercial infrastructure facilitated the distribution of such goods to urban inhabitants of Salvador and those residing on remote plantations in the interior.

9. A pipe of liquor equaled 126 U.S. gallons; a canada equaled approximately 1.4 liters. See David Eltis and Lawrence C. Jennings, "Trade between Western Africa and the Atlantic World in the Pre-colonial Era," *American Historical Review*, XCIII (1988), 936–959, esp. 942; Joseph C. Miller, *Way of Death: Merchant Capitalism and the Angolan Slave Trade, 1730–1830* (Madison, Wis., 1988), 709. In Ouidah in April 1812, 48 of these panos da costa had been purchased, alongside 95 captives, from Francisco Felix de Souza, the notorious Portuguese slave trader residing on the African coast (ANRJ, fundo 7X, Junta do Comércio, Fábricas e Navegações, caixa 410, pacote 1, Papers of the *São Miguel Triunfante*, 7, 15). The crochet pattern likely referred to an "openwork," or lace style (*Aṣọ oníhò*, in Yoruba) in which the weave was altered to create a row of holes. See Colleen E. Kriger, *Cloth in West African History* (Oxford, 2006), 20; Carolyn Marian Keyes, "Àdìrẹ: Cloth, Gender, and Social Change in Southwestern Nigeria, 1841–1991" (Ph.D. diss., University of Wisconsin, Madison, 1993), 71; ANRJ, fundo 7X, Junta do Comércio, Fábricas e Navegações, caixa 410, pacote 1, Papers of the *São Miguel Triunfante*, 7–9.

A WATERFRONT COMMERCIAL WORLD

Mariners arriving in Bahia expected to market the assorted contents of their maritime liberty chests to local African and African-descended consumers. The existence of such a market for their commodities, however, depended on the existence of a vibrant, aquatic-oriented commercial world that facilitated enslaved people's access to larger networks of transatlantic commerce. By the 1770s, Salvador's commercialized waterborne world had reached maturity, and enslaved people were at the center of its operation. Salvador's water-ways not only acted as a site of transatlantic commodity circulation; they also sustained many Bahian inhabitants' livelihoods. On an average day, sailors, fishermen, merchants, colonial administrators, market women, and dry goods vendors alike came to the city's waterfront to hawk, haggle, trade, and acquire goods. Inhabitants sought local produce, straw mats, crude household imple-ments, wines, spices, fine silks, and other exotic luxury imports for their own uses and initiatives. In addition, planters continued to rely on the enslaved to take their produce to urban markets, guaranteeing a steady stream of arrivals from the city's rural hinterlands.

Enslaved people circulated throughout the Bay of All Saints and surround-ing waterfronts, moving not only key export commodities of sugar, tobacco, and beef but also transporting merchandise and foodstuffs they themselves had produced. As local authorities noted, "Those that live and fish for their maintenance, like the Free sailors and Fishermen, and the slaves that are in every captaincy, [and] parish . . . [and] reside at the water's edge" enabled the urban settlement to provision itself and provided the means for goods of all kinds to circulate. Salvador's miles of sandy beaches, crystalline blue waters, and sinuous rivers stretching inland afforded enslaved people the opportunity to supplement the meager provisions provided by slaveholders.[10]

Waterborne traffic entering and departing Salvador came from all direc-tions. On larger *cabotage* ships, merchants engaged in the coastal trade, re-exporting European, Asian, and African goods—including textiles, manufac-tures, iron, gold, foodstuffs, and slaves—to Pernambuco and Rio de Janeiro. Agricultural commodities produced in Bahia, such as tobacco and sugar, were also shipped, whereas salted beef, hides, tallow, and other goods were imported from the captaincies of Rio Grande do Sul, Ceará, and Paraíba for consumption in Salvador. The majority of their crews consisted of free or

10. AHU, CU, Bahia–Castro Alves, caixa 47, documento 8812, May 27, 1775, "Mapa geral de toda a qualidade de embarcações que há na capitania da Bahia."

FIGURE 14. *"A Jangada." In Henry Koster,* Travels in Brazil *(London, 1816).*
Two watermen navigate a jangada. © *John Carter Brown Library*

enslaved people of African descent; of the 317 mariners registered on cabotage voyages, 51.4 percent were identified as pretos. These men provided crucial transregional commercial linkages in the late eighteenth century and likely became the means by which a number of West African textiles filtered into other colonial Brazilian centers, such as Rio de Janeiro.[11]

Just as essential to this process were local, Black-navigated small watercraft. Daily, a constellation of "country boats"—*jangadas* (rafts), barks, *lanchas* (barges), and canoes—would descend on the harbor, resembling, as one con-

11. A. J. R. Russell-Wood, "Ports of Colonial Brazil," in Franklin W. Knight and Peggy K. Liss, eds., *Atlantic Port Cities: Economy, Culture, and Society in the Atlantic World, 1650–1850* (Knoxville, Tenn., 1991), 217. Cabotage vessels accounted for a total of 32 watercraft housed in the Bay of All Saints by 1775 (AHU, CU, Bahia–Castro Alves, caixa 47, documento 8812, May 27, 1775, "Mapa geral de toda a qualidade de embarcações que há na capitania da Bahia"). Of those 317 mariners, 25 men were identified as freed Blacks and 138 as enslaved. The predominance of enslaved seamen was mirrored in nearby Pernambuco, where a 1775 census registered a total of 7 ships engaged in the slave trade, 52 in cabotage, 227 in riverine travel, and 208 fishing vessels. The city was home to 186 free sailors and 423 enslaved sea-

temporary observer commented, a "miniature fleet." This "moving medley" of commerce landed on the shores of the lower city, comprising the principal means by which commodities circulated in Salvador and beyond. Small vessels were particularly prevalent in Salvador and its hinterlands, with 188 canoes registered within the city, 61 jangadas, 43 lanchas, and 35 *saveiros* (small sailboats). Enslaved and free watermen brought goods on their small crafts to the city, where they sold them to small-scale African and creole vendors in bustling markets. Colonial administrators recognized that aquatic provisioning remained vital to the lifeblood of Salvador. As they observed in 1775, "The delivery of goods, and living that foments this commerce . . . sustains the city." Anchored ships unloaded cattle, barrels of aguardente, and empty crates to be filled with European wares at owners' or employers' behest. At the same time, boatmen peddled smaller items produced by enslaved people in rural Bahia, including palm leaf baskets full of rice, fruits, and vegetables, bales of tobacco, earthenware, manioc flour, piassava rope, wood, and coral. In addition to the hundreds of watercraft based in Salvador, a multitude of other vessels regularly streamed into the city's port, each manned with up to a dozen sailors or watermen, saturating the urban landscape with goods from all corners of the colony.[12]

The majority of those who labored locally in maritime subsistence and commodity production were of African descent. As the 1775 census enumerated, 145 free and 251 enslaved fishermen were the pilots of small vessels navigating into Salvador. In the city, "Fishermen, numbered 1267, and among them there are not 100 white men, [who for] the most part are old, and almost [everyone else are] *pardos,* and *pretos.*" Owners often tasked enslaved watermen with generating income by collecting sellable commodities such as fish or ferrying passengers and goods for a fee. For those who owned watercraft, the enslaved mariners who navigated them became themselves a piece of movable property—no different than the vessels they possessed. When one

farers. See AHU, CU, Bahia–Castro Alves, caixa 47, documento 8812, May 27, 1775, "Mapa geral de toda a qualidade de embarcações que há na capitania da Bahia"; ibid., Pernambuco, caixa 120, documento 9196, "Ofício do José César de Meneses."

12. Prior, *Voyage along the Eastern Coast of Africa,* 100; AHU, CU, Bahia–Castro Alves, caixa 47, documento 8812, May 27, 1775, "Mapa geral de toda a qualidade de embarcações que há na capitania da Bahia." In 1775, Salvador was the base for 412 of these small vessels, which comprised 19.2 percent of the total number of 2,148 in the entire captaincy of Bahia. See Appendix 1, below; James Wetherell, *Brazil: Stray Notes from Bahia; Being Extracts from Letters, etc., during a Residence of Fifteen Years,* ed. William Hadfield (Liverpool, U.K., 1860),

FIGURE 15. *"Negroes Impelling a Canoe with the Vara. and Scenery at Ponta Decho."*
In James Henderson, A History of the Brazil: Comprising Its Geography, Commerce,
Colonization, Aboriginal Inhabitants, Etc. Etc. Etc. *(London, 1821), facing p. 389.*
Black watermen ferry passengers on a canoe. SI-OB-241. Slaveryimages.org

such proprietor sold his raft, he advertised both the enslaved waterman who
navigated it and the vessel itself as a unified parcel of property.[13]

Navigators of these small watercraft helped make the local economy more
dynamic by obtaining, moving, and selling commodities. Bahia's Black
watermen specialized in navigating a variety of boats, each attuned to portage
needs and the specificities of bodies of water. Raft, or jangada, navigators—a
common sight in the Bay of All Saints—engaged in fishing and transportation of passengers and goods. The modest vessels of the early colonial period

26–27. By 1808, Salvador's waterborne commerce attracted 363 vessels to enter the port
that year. During the same period, 285 vessels left the port; see Appendix 2, Table 2, below.

13. AHU, CU, Bahia–Castro Alves, caixa 47, documento 8812, May 27, 1775, "Mapa geral
de toda a qualidade de embarcações que há na capitania da Bahia." One advertisement read,
"For sale, a boat all ready including with mariner, Father Francisco Agostinho Gomes"
(BNRJ, *Idade d'Ouro do Brazil,* Aug. 19, 1815, no. 69).

FIGURE 16. Matelots. *By Johann Moritz Rugendas. 1835. An early-nineteenth-century depiction of Bahian boatmen selling their wares to market women waterside. Schomburg Center for Research in Black Culture, Photographs and Prints Division, The New York Public Library. New York Public Library Digital Collections*

had, by the early nineteenth century, been significantly redesigned, with the influence of Black maritime expertise helping to refashion them into large, elaborate craft composed of thick trunks of tropical wood.[14] African and creole navigators also mastered the subtle art of building and manning the deepwater canoe, another essential vessel in the commercial world of Salvador's aquatic environs.[15] Black watermen's expertise in navigating these crafts included the mastery of collaborative working routines. Like singing

14. As many as twenty logs could comprise one jangada, reaching twenty feet in length. Atop these rustic rafts, a simple mast supported a three-corner sail, with a steersman's seat positioned at its back next to the rudder. If the jangada was intended for travel, a crude awning was perched above the heads of passengers, while a rush mat and bag of provisions accompanied navigators. The crew, commonly sparse, consisted of "two men, the proeiro and patrão, or the bowsman and steersmen." See Daniel P. Kidder, *Sketches of Residence and Travels in Brazil: Embracing Historical and Geographical Notices of the Empire and Its Several Provinces,* II (Philadelphia, 1845), 176–180.

15. By stripping a tree of branches, shaping its trunk, and reinforcing the interior with

porters on Salvador's streets, mariners utilized music to coordinate complex movements; such undertakings not only made physical maneuvers easier but also promoted a "framework for community integrity" aboard. Sonic rituals promoted solidarity and eased the strain of toil. Relations among canoemen evoked a more egalitarian sensibility than on larger vessels.[16]

Gleaning knowledge from local environments was not just crucial to Black watermen's abilities to move commodities; it was key in devising the most effective methods for extracting valuable resources from aquatic provisioning grounds. Black fishermen were required to master local currents and read water depths. The cultivation of such specialized environmental knowledge helped those reduced to servility secure a relatively steady living.[17] Indeed, the vibrant biodiversity of the Bay of All Saints conferred ample opportu-

---

additional wood, canoemen produced a fast, elegant vessel. Propelled by crude sails, paddles, or setting poles, these vessels required intricate choreographies involving multiple rowers as well as a mastery of the currents and winds that influenced the complex riverine networks they traversed. Canoemen stood on vessel's edge, fastened to the mast only with a cord, and thrust their bodies backward, maneuvering the canoe while suspended parallel to the water, allowing them to accelerate. Increased velocity could also be achieved by watermen who preferred paddling, as they synchronized movements by singing in a "monotonous chorus, every now and then raising the paddles completely out of the water, and striking the flat part of them with their hands, keeping time with the chorus." Though it is unclear how such a method of group navigation evolved, African and creole residents of the Bay elaborated these innovations independent of slaveholders. African watermen in South Carolina employed similar expressive forms. This shared, musically infused laboring culture points to a common origin in Western Africa. See Philip D. Morgan, *Slave Counterpoint: Black Culture in the Eighteenth-Century Chesapeake and Lowcountry* (Williamsburg, Va., and Chapel Hill, N.C., 1998), 243–244; João José Reis, "'The Revolution of the Ganhadores': Urban Labour, Ethnicity, and the African Strike of 1857 in Bahia, Brazil," *Journal of Latin American Studies,* XXIX (1997), 355–393, esp. 363–365; Kidder, *Sketches,* II, 176–180; Wetherell, *Stray Notes from Bahia,* ed. Hadfield, 97–98, 134–135.

16. One observer reported that, on a canoe captained by a "mulatto" and navigated by two more Black seamen, "the greatest harmony" prevailed among captains and crews "without any of those troublesome ideas of rank and authority which commonly prevail on salt water." Duties were delegated in a democratic manner. Distribution of labor solidified unity among small canoe crews, as "they interchanged places and duties without the least ceremony, and from the indomitable garrulity of the *proeiros,* which drowned all sounds more harmonious than their own rough voices, one would have supposed them second to no one in consequence." See Kidder, *Sketches,* II, 159–160.

17. African and creole fishermen utilized many of the same methods for fishing imple-

nities to enslaved fishermen of various kinds.[18] The coastal inhabitants in Brazil's northeast also devised novel methods of fish collection, including the construction of fish pens (*curraes*) that relied on tides to capture fish within wooden traps close to shore. In addition, *camareiros* (shrimpers) and *caranguejeiros* (crabbers) supplied urban inhabitants' diets, as they skillfully extracted maritime resources from the mangroves that bordered the bay's shores, which were also rich with oysters. Whaling was also central to maritime-based provisioning in Salvador. Man-powered watercraft trolled the waters of the bay to prey upon the local whale population, which was harvested for two commodities: baleen and fat. Enslaved labor was crucial to this enterprise: by 1775, 94.8 percent of all laborers, including rowers, harpooners, and navigators, working in the Bahian whaling industry were African or creole, and 55.5 percent of all whalers were enslaved.[19]

Food stalls (*quitandas*), largely operated by quitandeiras, or African and creole women, were important buyers for both maritime-transported and

---

mented in the interior, deploying small, circular hand nets and simple lines with hooks to feed a burgeoning urban population. See Wetherell, *Stray Notes from Bahia,* ed. Hadfield, 139.

18. Wetherell also recorded a "curious" but effective technique of canoe-based fishing that entailed complex coordination between boatmen. The method involved canoemen steering fish into a net by agitating the surrounding waters. Wetherell's interest indicated that he had not encountered similar strategies in Europe; the strategy was most likely pioneered in West Africa or Brazil (ibid., 65–66).

19. This form of maritime food production was especially advantageous to enslaved communities around the Recôncavo, as net and fish-pen forms of fishing as well as shellfish collection in the shallows could be carried out by women and children, leaving deep-sea fishing to men. Such coastal activities required little in the way of technology, navigational tools, or time and could be used to supplement agricultural production, especially on rural estates around the bay. In nearby Pernambuco, rural enslaved communities relied on proximity to water, as did their owners. On the many small streams and creeks abutting sugar plantations, "slaves [were] fed with more ease, and less expense: and the quantity of food which they themselves have the means of obtaining from the sea and from the rivulets, enables them to be less dependent upon the rations of the master than the slaves of the Mata or districts between the coast and the Sertam [hinterlands]." See Henry Koster, *Travels in Brazil,* II (London, 1817), 132; Luiz Geraldo Silva, *A faina, a festa e o rito: Uma etnografia histórica sobre as gentes do mar (sécs. XVII ao XIX)* (São Paulo, 2001), 81–87; Wetherell, *Stray Notes from Bahia,* ed. Hadfield, 40. The figure of 55.5 percent accounts for 164 mariners. See AHU, CU, Bahia–Avulsos, caixa 164, documento 12425, Lisbon, Jan. 4, 1775, "Mapas de carga, relações e listas e outros documentos relativos a embarcações vindas da Bahia."

maritime-produced commodities. First and foremost, such stalls functioned as vendors for a variety of products from the rural interior. Quitandeiras flocked to the littoral, where, as the English traveler James Wetherell observed, "large crates of fowls are borne off by the fortunate purchasers, [b]ananas and oranges are piled in golden heaps, the shore boats are quickly laden with cabbages, yams, sugar cane, pumpkins, or melons." A quitandeira lost no time "hastening to her market-stand to make the best of her bargain by retailing." Quitandeiras also provided fish oil, cooked whale meat, fish stews, herbs, produce, and rudimentary household goods. As outlets for terrestrial and aquatic resources, such women often forged strong personal and commercial relationships with local Black mariners. Female vendors exploited these social relationships for their own entrepreneurial gain, often exercising a de facto monopoly over a variety of provisions to maximize their own profits. "There is quite a monopoly kept up of articles of food," one observer remarked. "Fish is not sold at any price to any person but the customers of the fisherwomen," he added, "who are the retailers. Fruit, in the same manner, comes direct to the market-women, being supplied by regular growers, and thus high prices are supported."[20]

In the commercially dynamic lower city of Salvador, market women encountered watermen to secure the best selection of portable goods. In the midst of widespread poverty and deprivation, the entrepreneurial quitandeiras of Salvador, like the industrious watermen of the captaincy's rivers and bay, developed survival strategies to blunt slavery's ravages. In a city plagued by rotten provisions, where a sizable proportion of the enslaved had neglectful owners, independent fishing activities were crucial in sustaining enslaved people's health. One inhabitant noted with approval that Bahian shrimp "of a large size . . . caught in great numbers in the creeks and inlets, shallows and rivers of the bay" were, in the rustic pots of enslaved women, transformed into "a great article of consumption," particularly in the Afro-Bahian specialty of "*carraru*," or fish stew. Likewise, whale meat continued to feed the city well into the mid-nineteenth century. In Rio Vermelho parish, the center of

20. Wetherell, *Stray Notes from Bahia,* ed. Hadfield, 26–27; Luís dos Santos Vilhena, *Recopilação de noticias soteropolitanas e brasilicas contidas em XX cartas,* II (Salvador, Brazil, 1921), 93, 124. This monopoly could work to the detriment of enslaved urban consumers. Quitandeiras would sell goods multiple times, maximizing the number of vendors who profited from the marketing of foodstuffs but also greatly driving up the price of provisions in Salvador. See ibid., 127; A. J. R. Russell-Wood, *The Black Man in Slavery and Freedom in Colonial Brazil* (New York, 1982), 47.

the city's whale oil–rendering enterprise, Salvador's inhabitants thronged beaches to scavenge the unused whale flesh of discarded carcasses. After the megafauna had been harvested, "Vast quantities of this flesh are cooked in the streets, and sold by Quitandeiras." In the simple market stalls that populated Salvador's beaches, in the central square of Terreiro de Jesus, and on the bustling streets, mobile residents congregated daily to secure food.[21]

African and creole Bahians' ability to participate in local markets provided the much-needed means for subsistence while reshaping Salvador's cultural life into something that reflected sensibilities of the city's popular classes. The waterfront urban district, appearing to some as a "depository of commerce and filth," presented a stark contrast with the pristine, elevated part of Salvador, home to the city's propertied elite and strewn with palaces, cathedrals, monasteries, libraries, and an opera house.[22] But for those people of African descent who moved in and out of the lower city—the stevedores, palanquin bearers, sailors, militiamen, and market women—the crowded streets represented a commercial world animated less by human vice than by their own initiatives, tastes, and commercial desires. In turn, however, access to those markets integrated enslaved men and women into larger streams of Atlantic-procured, African commodities that arrived on slaving vessels in the hands of captive cosmopolitans. This fact would also have a profound effect on remaking Salvador into a city whose material cultural, intellectual, and religious life was shaped by its transatlantic African orientation.

AN AFRICAN MATERIAL WORLD IN BAHIA

The development of intricate transatlantic commercial arrangements by captive cosmopolitan mariners demonstrates that Africans could be far more than mere objects of Atlantic merchant capitalism. In manipulating the financial structures of transatlantic slaving to incorporate their own commercial needs and aspirations, such men and women forged a novel trading circuit predicated on a desire for West African goods. As the men returned to Salvador

21. Kidder, *Sketches*, II, 24–25; Vilhena, *Recopilação*, 93. Vilhena said that slaves on rural plantations received a weekly ration of a quarter pound (*quarta*) of *farinha*, and three and one-half pounds (*libras*) of dried, salted beef. See ibid., 187–188. Maritime Bahians' reliance on oceanic subsistence mirrored land-bound enslaved people's cultivation of garden plots near slave quarters (*roças*) (Wetherell, *Stray Notes from Bahia*, ed. Hadfield, 55).

22. For a visitor's description of the lower city, see Prior, *Voyage along the Eastern Coast of Africa*, 100–101; see also Chapter 2, above.

da Bahia with a rich array of wares to generate profits, they became part of a larger African commercial world bound to the autonomous waterborne circulation of commodities. On shore, many seamen fashioned multilayered relationships with other entrepreneurial Africans living in Bahia. Numerous West Africans of lower social status—agricultural hands, street vendors, and market women—were participants in this transatlantic commercial culture as both sellers and consumers. And through their aesthetic and culinary preferences for African commodities, African residents of Salvador remade the material landscape of Bahia. Through the elaboration of a shared material culture, captive cosmopolitans, alongside enslaved and freed Africans in the city and beyond, forged ties of entrepreneurship, community, and cultural regeneration.

Almost all vendors of food, household goods, and clothing in the city, as well as the owners of many small storefronts or stands in markets, had been born in Africa. Informal social and commercial networks connected predominately female mobile vendors to African mariners. Rushing to meet sailors at the waterfront, these enterprising women leveraged personal relationships—both romantic and ethnic—to procure transatlantic goods. The African mariner Lino Ricardo noted in his will that Ritta da Penha de França, his African-born wife, owned several gold coins. This was a significant asset she had likely accumulated from selling the panos da costa that Ricardo had transported from the Bight of Benin. Such cloth also appeared in humble Salvador storefronts owned by formerly enslaved African residents. In 1832, Lucinda and Raimundo, a freed African couple who resided in Bahia along with their "little American-born daughter," owned and operated a small shop, which sold various styles of cloth, beads, beaded clothing, skirts, and blouses, alongside "one new blue *pano da costa*." Though it is unclear when either Lucinda or Raimundo had been manumitted, the couple had amassed enough wealth to register several pieces of gold jewelry as part of their property holdings.[23]

The urban Black women who exercised near-complete control over the city's food supply as small-scale vendors were also the principal vendors of African goods. Portuguese observer Luís dos Santos Vilhena lamented the ease with which local Black women (both enslaved and freed) acting as mobile hawkers were able to monopolize the purchase and sale of African commodities in Salvador's busy harbor. They dotted the streets carrying "small boxes

23. APEB, Justiça, Testamento de Lino Ricardo, livro 12, 34; ibid., Inventário de Lucinda e Raimundo, 05/2006/2477/09.

FIGURE 17. Nègré et negresse de Bahia. *By Johann Moritz Rugendas. 1835.*
A market woman and a fisherman meet on Bahia's waterfront. Schomburg
Center for Research in Black Culture, Photographs and Prints Division,
The New York Public Library. New York Public Library Digital Collections

of cloth, most of it contraband, pilfered or purchased from foreign vessels . . . which leave loaded with money." Cloth from the Mina and Guinea Coasts was especially prized by the local population since they were imported free of tax for local vendors, unlike European or Asian textiles. Petty vendors, or ganhadeiras, colluded with soldiers and utilized protection from their owners to evade paying customs on imported cloth. As with mariners' trading activities, these women had obtained the tacit approval of their owners. As Santos Vilhena explained, "No one disturbs them nor demands account from them out of respect to the powerful houses to which they belong."[24]

Owing to the increased volume of the transatlantic slave trade from the 1790s through the 1820s, African foodstuffs also became materially abundant in Salvador da Bahia. Some African-derived commodities had long been a part of transatlantic commerce. In part, this was because the use of provisions such as palm oil aboard slaving ships had been born out of the practicalities of slaving. Though Portuguese slavers established an export trade in palm oil on the coast of the Bight of Benin as early as the 1570s, the oil was most significant for furnishing vessels with consumable calories for captives. African foodstuffs were also readily available and culturally familiar—even if they were not a strict necessity to keep the enslaved alive—on the premise that they could provide a small source of familiarity to fearful and desperate bondspeople.[25] Judith Carney's study of African-derived vegetation in the Americas reveals the extent to which European slavers relied on African crops (particularly rice, yams, sorghum, and millet) to provide sustenance on shore (in *feitorias*

24. Vilhena, *Recopilação,* 59.

25. On the early palm oil trade by the Portuguese, see Case Watkins, *Palm Oil Diaspora: Afro-Brazilian Landscapes and Economies on Bahia's Dendê Coast* (Cambridge, 2021), 63–66. In 1724, Bento de Arousio de Souza traded 259 ounces of gold to the Royal African Company agents at Cape Coast Castle on the Gold Coast for sixty-five slaves and provisions for the journey, which included eighty chests of corn, fifty pounds of malagueta pepper, four bushels of salt, and thirty gallons of palm oil. Decades later, on British slaving vessels, officers in the late eighteenth century provided captives held in the cargo with dried shrimp, flour, and palm oil to make a stew from their homelands. Slaving ship captain Hugh Crow claimed that, when provisioning ships, captains studied captives' "personal comfort." Crow also claimed that slaves were provided with palm oil to apply after baths, as it was "their favorite cosmetic." On occasion, slavers meted out small comforts such as tobacco and liquor in hopes of preventing violent uprisings. See *Memoirs of the Late Captain Hugh Crow, of Liverpool* . . . (London, 1830), 146–147; Pierre Verger, *Trade Relations between the Bight of Benin and Bahia from the 17th to 19th Century,* [trans. Evelyn Crawford] (Ibadan, Nigeria, 1976), 41 n. 82.

where captives were held until departure) as well as during the ocean journey. By the late eighteenth century, however, trading voyages returned from the Mina Coast bearing palm oil and textiles intended not only as provisions for captives but also for consumption and sale in Bahia. After 1815, the legal trade in panos da costa, dendê oil, and other African commodities served as a cover for illegal slaving, giving vessels a plausible motive for calling at Mina Coast ports where slave trading was forbidden. This commercial subterfuge resulted in the increasing visibility of West African textiles and palm oil as commodities at Salvador's waterfront. Sailing vessels hailing from West Africa regularly advertised shipments of these desirable commodities for sale.[26]

As palm oil imported from West Africa made its way into Bahia's interior, it was likely transported by the same boatmen who carried produce to the city. An inventory of the estate of Bahian slave trader Manuel Francisco Moreira in 1836 reveals that he had purchased 8½ canadas of dendê oil for the 120 enslaved Africans who had arrived on his plantation. The inclusion of palm oil among slave food stores—purchased rather than cultivated, imported rather than locally produced, and used as a condiment rather than as a staple—signals the possibility that African slaves residing in rural Bahia were capable of exerting some control and choice over their diets and that their owners were, in some cases, willing to accommodate their preferences.[27]

In Bahia, African-derived foods, particularly those prepared using West African oils, were dismissed by Europeans as "insignificant and vile," but such observers could not deny their importance to the cultural life of Black Salvador. Thomas Lindley wrote in 1802 that the city's enslaved population were "indulged to licentiousness, not-overworked, and enjoying their native vegetable food." In the midst of such epicurean comfort, he went so far as to claim, "The negroes are cheerful and content." African vegetation—including

26. The owner (Joaquim José de Oliveira) and captain (Joaquim José de S. Pavo) of the brig *Conde de Amarante* advertised on the pages of a local newspaper that the ship had landed "with 395 captives, 8 died and panos da Costa" (*Idade d'Ouro do Brazil,* Jan. 3, 1815, no. 1). When the *Minerva* traveled to the Mina Coast in 1823 with its destination listed as Molembo (Malembo) on the vessel's official passport, its captain, Manoel Joaquim de Almeida, diverted to Lagos to partake in an "advantageous exchange of textiles for tobacco, *aguardente* and goods." Almeida's justification for participating in slave trading north of the equator appears to have been subterfuge, and the *Minerva* likely never intended to travel to Malembo (AHI, Coleções Especiais, Comissão Mista, lata 21, maço 02, pasta 1, Papers of the *Minerva*).

27. APEB, Justiça, Inventário de Manoel Francisco Moreira, Salvador, 1836, 05/1959/2431/04.

the "African eggplant," okra, and sesame—had been present in the northeast of Brazil since the late seventeenth century, having been introduced by enslaved Angolans. The growing numbers of Africans arriving in Salvador between 1775 and 1825, however, consolidated the presence of an African-centric food culture in the city. As the nineteenth century wore on, common street foods prepared by Africans were widely consumed. Wetherell noted in the mid-nineteenth century, "'Cararú' is a dish eaten by the blacks, but is much esteemed by the whites, and is, to my taste, very delicious. It is made of fish or fowl, several kinds of vegetables cut small [principally okra] . . . all mixed with palm oil."[28]

The anthropologist Nina Rodrigues characterized the culinary culture of Africans and their descendants at the end of the nineteenth century as the dominant food source in urban Salvador, the preparation of which was still controlled by African women, who, "in shops or *quitandas* [street stalls], in the doorways of homes, or in the streets carrying trays, are the practitioners of the urban prepared food commerce, especially in African cuisine." Their work was representative of "the tastes of the population, including condiments, fruits, vegetables, and products from the African coast (xoxo, abuxo, palm oil, banha, obi)." West African provisions might have been initially prized by displaced, isolated, and newly arrived captives owing to their familiarity and centrality to culinary habits and experiences that predated personal enslavement. For many recent and not-so-recent arrivals, Bahian food culture sensorially evoked their African homelands. Rodrigues's assertion that Afro-Bahian cuisine represented the "tastes of the population" reflects a contention that food functions not merely as a commodity or as simple subsistence but rather a "cultural field" through which certain values and aesthetics are selected, asserted, and assessed by group consensus. As identity markers, food and communal choices about which foods to consume reveal food's power as an instrument in creating social investments in a community, ultimately functioning as a central means of social reproduction.[29]

28. Verger, *Trade Relations,* [trans. Crawford], 430; Judith A. Carney and Richard Nicholas Rosomoff, *In the Shadow of Slavery: Africa's Botanical Legacy in the Atlantic World* (Berkeley, Calif., 2009), 124; Wetherell, *Stray Notes from Bahia,* ed. Hadfield, 123. Such foods made with imported West African oil included "mocotós . . . carurus, vatapás, mingaus, pamonhas," alongside fritters fried in the same substance: "papas de milho, acassás, acarajées, abarás" (Vilhena, *Recopilação,* 130).

29. Nina Rodrigues, *Os Africanos no Brasil,* 3d ed. (São Paulo, 1945), 173; Priscilla Parkhurst Ferguson, *Accounting for Taste: The Triumph of French Cuisine* (Chicago, 2004),

Bahian cuisine was also, however, culturally cosmopolitan in nature. The culinary choices of West African market women, ambulant vendors, and quitandeiras suggest that they appropriated aspects of indigenous Brazilian diets and vegetation while incorporating familiar items from their homelands. Foodstuffs prepared by quitandeiras were comprised of a diversity of ingredients, origins, and methods of preparation that combined both African and American food traditions. Bahian food, including grilled meats and fish, stews, fritters, and porridges consisted of American ingredients, including manioc and corn. They were prepared with African-originating ingredients such as okra, palm oil, and rice, indicating the degree to which Afro-Bahian culinary habits cannot be characterized as mere African re-creations. Food's expressive qualities existed alongside the practical aims of providing a source of income. In Richard Graham's words, the African and creole women who pioneered advantageous relationships with fishermen and mariners of all stripes also "fed the city." Their culinary preferences included both practical and symbolic dimensions and helped to define a distinctive African identity through a tangible and visible connection to West Africa as well as a broader Salvadoran identity based on the intermingling of diverse material cultures.[30]

SOCIAL FABRICS

Perhaps no commodity was more central to the African-infused material culture of Salvador and its rural hinterlands than textiles (panos da costa). Even the most marginalized members of Bahian slave society concurred. One evening in 1807, three enslaved African men from Salvador da Bahia gathered in the humble quarters of Antônio and Jeronima, an enslaved couple who lived and worked on a plantation in the rural parish of Santa Anna do Catu. This meeting was one of both intraethnic sociability and entrepreneurial strategizing, as Antônio had invited fellow Gege men—José, Agostinho, and Benedito—to tour "the farms of his neighborhood . . . [to sell] *panos da Costa* and [buy] other Things." The meeting abruptly ended, however, when authorities entered the couple's home and charged the men with conspiracy to revolt. Antônio claimed his innocence to the parish captain while Jeronima insisted that the visiting men were honorable vendors of West African textiles

1–10; Sidney W. Mintz and Christine M. Du Bois, "The Anthropology of Food and Eating," *Annual Review of Anthropology,* XXXI (2002), 109–110.

30. Richard Graham, *Feeding the City: From Street Market to Liberal Reform in Salvador, Brazil, 1780–1860* (Austin, 2010), 41.

who slept in her home only to conduct the business that was "their liveli-hood." Benedito regarded Antônio as a "brother" and "great friend," saying he arrived at the plantation to deliver textiles to a *cabra* woman, Efigenia, who would distribute them in Sítio da Palma. The three African men proudly described their trade of panos da costa as a "good business," suggesting the significant demand for the striking blue and white strip-woven textiles of the Mina Coast in colonial Brazil's environs.[31]

Throughout the city of Salvador, brocade cloth, embroidered cloth, and solid indigo cloths of "3 lengths" as well as blue-and-white-striped varieties could be observed in the vendors' boxes of mobile ganhadeiras, who served a growing consumer demand for the product. That common sight, however, was the last moment in a much longer, more geographically expansive circuit of production and trade through which the cloth had passed. Fashioned in the West African interior by male and female artisans located in urban centers with thriving central markets, these hand-woven cotton cloths flowed into the port of Salvador in the liberty chests of sailors and African "Brazilian" transatlantic traders. These men, to a significant extent, owed the success of their expanding transatlantic commercial and social networks to the growing desire for panos da costa in Bahia, where Africans both enslaved and free built a dynamic culture of bodily signification that underpinned demand for the cloth.[32]

31. The men apparently had traveled to the plantation to sell cloth for chickens. Benedito had also been tasked by his owner, Padre Pedro Ferreira dos Santos, a resident of Lisbon, with disbursing pay to workers in the rural parish every week. See Rachel E. Harding, *A Refuge in Thunder: Candomblé and Alternative Spaces of Blackness* (Bloomington, Ind., 2000), 173-174. Gege, or *jeje,* was an ethnic signifier in Brazil that indicated peoples from Gbe-speaking regions of West Africa, which stretched from the Volta River east to Porto Novo, including Ewe, Gèn, Ajá, and Fon. See Matory, *Black Atlantic Religion,* 76. Cabra was a Brazilian designation used to identify individuals of mixed indigenous, European, and African ancestry (ibid., 173-175).

32. Visually striking cloths were produced by diverse forms of artisanal household manu-facture, with families and lineages often specializing in particular aspects and methods of production. Weavers fabricated most cloth on domestic vertical looms of varying breadths—sometimes with advances of European credit if they were intended for export. Cloth woven on horizontal treadle looms mostly by male artisans was narrower, and the resulting strips could be sewn together to make sizable pieces, whereas female weavers produced wider cloth on vertical looms. An enslaved man from Ijebu-Ode recalled that in the 1820s women harvested, spun, wove, and dyed cloth within their households. Women aided by children

FIGURE 18. *"Kanemboo Market Woman. Unmarried Woman of Soudan." Engraved by E[dward Francis] Finden. In Dixon Denham,* Narrative of Travels and Discoveries in Northern and Central Africa, in the Years 1822, 1823, and 1824 . . . *(London, 1826). Market women in the Upper Niger region. One wears a shoulder shawl. Schomburg Center for Research in Black Culture, Manuscripts, Archives and Rare Books Division, The New York Public Library. New York Public Library Digital Collections*

Cloth had long been a part of economic exchanges involving Europeans' slaving activity on the West African coast. The acquisition of African textiles began around 1607, when European merchants arriving on the shores of the Upper Guinea coast purchased cotton textiles from Wolof weavers to sell in Spain. Farther south, Iberian traders conveyed "different coloured cotton cloths" from Allada to the Kongolese capital of São Salvador in exchange for captives.[33] Woven cotton cloth was already a prevalent trade good throughout West Africa, up to the margins of the Sahara Desert, with several centers of production in Kano, Kanem, and Benin, as well as Nupe- and Yoruba-speaking city-states.[34] Though "Benin cloths"—what European traders labeled the blue indigo broadcloth and blue-and-white-striped cotton wrappers they purchased from the African polity—predominated in the coastal middleman trade during the seventeenth century, by 1800, textiles produced

---

were also purported to be the primary textile makers in Benin during this period. Conversely, Samuel Ajayi Crowther, an Anglican bishop in colonial Lagos, identified men as the principal producers of cloth in Osogun. Crowther identified weaving as a family endeavor, with expertise passed down through generations: "I am the son of a weaver, my father gradually introduced me into the trade of weaving the country cloth as well, as all his relations were of that trade." See Kriger, *Cloth in West African History,* 43; Philip D. Curtin, ed., *Africa Remembered: Narratives by West Africans from the Era of the Slave Trade* (Madison, Wis., 1968), 253, 263; Kriger, "'Guinea Cloth': Production and Consumption of Cotton Textiles in West Africa before and during the Atlantic Slave Trade," in Giorgio Riello and Prasannan Parthasarathi, eds., *The Spinning World: A Global History of Cotton Textiles, 1200–1850* (Oxford, 2009), 111; Keyes, "Àdìrẹ," 68–69.

33. Manuel Álvares observed in 1607 that Wolof producers made "very well-known cotton cloths by sowing [*sic*] from six to twelve strips together," which could fetch as much as 6$000 réis when sold in Iberia. See Kriger, *Cloth in West African History,* 34–35; Philip D. Curtin, *Economic Change in Precolonial Africa: Senegambia in the Era of the Slave Trade, 1500–1800* (Madison, Wis., 1975), 247–253; Robin Law, "Trade and Politics behind the Slave Coast: The Lagoon Traffic and the Rise of Lagos," *Journal of African History,* XXIV (1983), 321–348.

34. During this period, textiles manufactured in Benin were the most prominent in Portugal's coastal West African trade. See Kriger, *Cloth in West African History,* 39–41, esp. 40; Verger, *Trade Relations,* [trans. Crawford], 134 n. 1; Kriger, "'Guinea Cloth,'" in Riello and Parthasarathi, eds., *The Spinning World,* 109–117; Kriger, "Mapping the History of Cotton Textile Production in Precolonial West Africa," *African Economic History,* XXXIII (2005), 87–116, esp. 92–99; George E. Brooks, *Eurafricans in Western Africa: Commerce, Social Status, Gender, and Religious Observance from the Sixteenth Century to the Eighteenth Century* (Athens, Ohio, 2003), 19–20; Peggy Stolz Gilfoy, *Patterns of Life: West African Strip-Weaving Traditions* (Washington, D.C., 1987), 33.

FIGURE 19. Bahiana, negros e criança. *By J[ean] B[aptiste] Debret.*
Ca. 1820–1830. A Bahian woman in 1820s Rio de Janeiro, wearing a blouse and
skirt, with a pano da costa *wrapper (*aṣọ ìró*), head wrap, and shoulder shawl*
*(*ìborùn*). Watercolor. MEA 0402, Coleçao Museus Castro Maya–IBRAM/MinC,*
Rio de Janeiro. Photograph by Horst Merkel

in neighboring Oyo and its hinterlands had surpassed them.[35] The English
merchant John Adams reported that, in the West African entrepôt of Porto
Novo, weavers demonstrated "much practical knowledge," unraveling red
Asian- and European-imported textiles and incorporating the thread into blue
and white panos. Adams identified Oyo and Ijebu-Ode as the most prolific
producers of panos da costa, describing locally produced white, blue, or
multicolored cloth, twelve to fourteen inches wide and of "excellent quality."
For Adams, Oyo textiles were superior, "both for variety of pattern, color
and dimensions, to any made in the neighboring states." The diversity of
fabric styles revealed the complexity of regional commerce, allowing wealthy

35. Olfert Dapper, who synthesized the firsthand accounts of slavers and missionaries,
provided a number of suggestive details about the social role of cloth in the Benin kingdom,
noting its role in defining royal authority and relationships of patronage and signifying
maturity and insider status. He alleges that boys were required to enter the court of Benin

consumers to acquire a wide array of clothing styles to furnish extensive wardrobes that included apparel for specific occasions. Dutch, English, and Swedish slavers also purchased thousands of what they called "Allada cloths," the colorful striped or brocaded textiles that were not, in fact, produced in Allada. Originally from Oyo and Ijebu, these textiles had been shipped to the slaving empire via the inland lagoon that stretched along the Mina Coast. Eventually, Portuguese traders exported them to Elmina, Gabon, Angola, and São Tomé, extending an existing regional trade via new Atlantic routes.[36]

Building on these long-standing exchanges, a trade in panos da costa to Brazil had been fully established by the end of the eighteenth century. In fact, the aforementioned slaving merchant João de Oliveira might have played a pioneering role in the creation of the transatlantic trade in textiles. As early as

---

naked, a rite of passage into adulthood that included the oba, or ruler, bestowing both a wife and clothing on a young man after he had come of age. Similarly, girls remained unclothed until marriage, when their husbands conferred upon them clothing and a home. The prestige of woven textiles in Benin society was also indicated by royal funerary rites, as the oba was reputedly buried alongside his clothing, furniture, and cowry shells. See John Nutt, *For Africa: Containing What Is of Most Use in Bleau, Varenius, Cellarius, Cluverius, Baudrand, Brietius, Sanson, etc. with the Discoveries and Improvements of the Best Modern Authors to This Time*, IV (n.p., 1714), 477-478; H[enry] Ling Roth, *Great Benin: Its Customs, Art, and Horrors* (London, 1903), 24.

36. John Adams, *Remarks on the Country Extending from Cape Palmas to the River Congo, Including Observations on the Manners and Customs of the Inhabitants . . .* (London, 1823), 79, 94; Curtin, *Africa Remembered*, 232-233. Kriger argues that weaving techniques likely circulated among Benin, Ijebu-Ode, and Ifẹ in the fifteenth century. In addition to the extensive nature of markets for domestically produced cotton cloths, textiles comprised the "largest and most valuable category of commodities imported into Africa during the Atlantic slave trade era as a whole." See Kriger, *Cloth in West African History*, 32-34, 42-43; Kriger, "The Importance of Mande Textiles in the African Side of the Atlantic Trade, ca. 1680-1710," *Mande Studies*, XI (2009), 1-21, esp. 2. The lagoon system that connected Allada, Ouidah, Ijebu, and Benin by the seventeenth century hosted a vibrant regional, canoe-based trade in textiles. The earliest descriptions of Ijebu cloth in Elmina date to 1519. By 1621, Portuguese ships were acquiring slaves and textiles directly from the king of Ijebu, though, by the late seventeenth century, it appears this trade had stalled. See Kriger, "Mapping the History of Cotton Textile Production," *African Economic History*, XXXIII (2005), 102-103; Law, "Trade and Politics," *Journal of African History*, XXIV (1983), 321-326; A. F. C. Ryder, *Materials for West African History in Portuguese Archives* (London, 1965), 16; John Vogt, *Portuguese Rule on the Gold Coast, 1469-1882* (Athens, Ga., 1979), 68; Kriger, "'Guinea Cloth,'" in Riello and Parthasarathi, eds., *The Spinning World*, 122-123.

1770, records show he was responsible for shipping twenty-three West African textiles to Bahia. By 1797, a once-minute textile trade had expanded to become the third most valuable import from West Africa to Bahia after slaves and gold, with the eighteen ships that annually returned to Salvador from the Bight of Benin carrying 6:000$000 réis' worth of both commodities.[37]

Strip-woven indigo, hand-loomed, cotton textiles (*aso òke,* "cloth of the hill," or heritage cloth), and brocaded textiles (*aso olona,* or "cloth with patterns") became an everyday sight in Bahia, where they circulated among the population in the hands of enslaved African itinerant traders of all ethnicities. Enslaved people within the city chose to expend precious resources on these textiles despite their simultaneous access to rudimentary, locally produced cotton and woolen garments. African and creole women most commonly used panos as shoulder shawls, accompanied by a voluminous patterned or solid skirt in cotton or denim underlaid by petticoats, and a delicate white muslin blouse sometimes embellished with lace or embroidery.[38] The amalgam of diverse textiles worn by African and Afro-Bahian women, including muslin, lace, netting, calico, and panos da costa, indicates a marked tendency

37. Oliveira also, according to royal officials, had acquired a "large cloth of three lengths called Mandy" and four additional "painted" cloths of the same kind. These might have been Mande cloths from ports farther west such as Elmina (AHU, CU, Bahia–Eduardo de Castro e Almeida, caixa 44, documento 8244). The eighteen ships had carried 3,938 captives to Bahia from the Mina Coast, worth a sum of 392:800$000 réis, in comparison. The second largest import from West Africa in the same years was gold powder, worth 12:220$000 réis. See APEB, Seção Colonial e Provincial, no. 138, 278.

38. Robert S. DuPlessis, *The Material Atlantic: Clothing, Commerce, and Colonization in the Atlantic World, 1650–1800* (Cambridge, 2016), 141. Wetherell described the unique and elegant character of local dress for "black women": "The upper part of the dress above the petticoat is made of fine muslin. . . . The part round the bust is edged with broad lace; small armlets, richly worked, are joined with a double gold button; . . . The skirt of the dress is very voluminous forming a complete circle when placed upon the ground; the lower edge is bordered with lace or has a white arabesque pattern sewed upon it; the inner petticoat is likewise edged with lace. . . . The arms are covered with bracelets of coral and gold beads, etc. The neck loaded with chains and the hands with rings. . . . A handsome coast cloth is thrown over the shoulder. These cloths are woven into small strips of colored cotton from two to four inches wide in striped or checked patterns and the slips sewed together to form a shawl. . . . The favorite color now is bluish gray ground with dull crimson stripes. A large handkerchief of white net or lace or colored muslin with white lace border or black net is most gracefully made into a turban for the head, and curious earrings complete the costume." See Verger, *Trade Relations,* [trans. Crawford], 464.

toward appropriation of material from various origins—including West Africa, Europe, India, and Brazil—that produced a uniquely Bahian style of dress. The silhouette favored by enslaved and free women of color in the city— a circular, full skirt with several layers—referenced feminine styles prevalent in Europe, whereas the shoulder-baring muslin top and accumulation of gold bracelets indicated the availability of that precious metal in Brazil as well as the imperative to wear light clothing in the tropical city. Intermingled with gold ornamentation were coral amulets and bracelets, likely derived from the "large corals" imported from West Africa, such as those carried by Black barber Domingos do Rozário on the *São Miguel Triunfante*.

Meanwhile, men frequently wore aso òke in the form of tailored pants, a style common in Oyo and its environs, indicating a more direct translation of an African form. Not all men who did so, however, were originally from the region. In 1839, enslaved Tapa man Manoel escaped from his owner while wearing pants of panos da costa. In the same year, an American-born slave escaped from a plantation in Pernambuco carrying his small wardrobe of blue panos da costa pants, a pair of trousers made of denim, and a jacket. At sea, two enslaved mariners from Gabon escaped their brig wearing blue-striped shirts and white pants with "patches" of panos da costa. Beyond a direct re-creation of "Africa," the absorption of panos da costa into wardrobes of the enslaved suggests a process of intra-African creolization that relied on a selective and creative incorporation of African sartorial elements alongside items of American and European origin.[39]

Attesting to the centrality of panos da costa in the material and cultural life of enslaved communities, fugitive slave announcements found in Bahian newspapers between 1815 and 1850 reveal that their use was widespread across the social and ethnic spectrum. Descriptions of fugitives' dress demonstrate that the cloth was worn by both men and women, American-born and African, aged from eleven to fifty. Wearers were also identified as belonging to a wide variety of ethnicities from regions within western Africa, including Cabinda, Angola, Gabon, Mina, Calabar, Tapa, Hausa, Fulani, and Gege. Overall, Nagôs were the most prevalent wearers. Adams insisted that aso òke was highly

---

39. Enslaved man Osifekunde explained that, in early-nineteenth-century Ijebu, tailors fashioned strip-woven cloth into wrappers for women and vests and trousers for men. African men in Bahia sometimes wore panos da costa tailored into a shirt. See Curtin, *Africa Remembered,* 263; Verger, *Trade Relations,* [trans. Crawford], 449. Tapa was the Brazilian term for Africans from Nupe. See *Correio Mercantil* (Bahia), May 17, 1838, Oct. 3, 1839, Oct. 25, 1839.

esteemed by the peoples of African origin "because it is manufactured in a country which gave many of them, or their parents, birth." The claim that Salvadorans' affinity was rooted solely in cultural tradition, however, is belied by the fact that many of the ethnically diverse consumers of panos da costa would have become familiar with aso òke after their enslavement and forced dislocation to the Americas. Although some wearers of panos da costa were from the Yoruba-speaking parts of West Africa, where the cloth was produced, most were not. The diffusion of the cloth among the African population in the city and beyond suggests that panos da costa had acquired new meaning and value in the context of Bahia's slave society, and its usage in adornment became wholly integrated into the American sartorial landscape.[40]

That enslaved fugitives prioritized securing these items in their escape also suggests the extent to which wardrobes constituted a form of movable property that provided financial security to such freedom seekers. When Maria Luiza, a Bahia-based enslaved woman from the Mina Coast, made a harrowing escape from her owner while in Lisbon in 1824, she carried a young son as well as a bundle of possessions. In addition to the 100$000 réis that she "had earned from diverse sales" in Salvador, where she had likely labored as a ganhadeira, Maria carried gold, a blanket, a headscarf (*mantilha*), three blouses, three skirts, a calico dress, a pair of socks, a straw mat, and a pano da costa. Maria Luiza's relatively extensive wardrobe provided a modicum

40. Adams, *Sketches*, 25. The fugitive slave announcements appeared in such newspapers as *Idade d'Ouro do Brazil*, *Correio Mercantil*, *Grito da Razão*, and *Suplemento ao Bahiano*. Enslaved man Vicente of the "Tapa nation" escaped wearing pants made of a pano da costa (*Idade d'Ouro*, July 25, 1815). A "young boy" from Quelimane escaped wearing pants made of "thick" panos da costa (ibid., Oct. 23, [n.d.]). In 1818, a "ladino" Fulani boy named Domingos escaped wearing pants of panos da costa and a blue denim jacket (ibid., May 21, 1819). Benedita from Calabar, "still unacculturated," ran away wearing a "used" pano da costa (*Supplemento ao Bahiano*, Sept. 1, 1829). The youngest identified wearer of a pano da costa was Julieta, a "freed African girl" between eleven and twelve years old (*Correio Mercantil*, May 17, 1838). Luiza, a woman of thirty to thirty-five with filed teeth and from the "Nagô nation," escaped wearing a pano da costa (ibid., Aug. 13, 1838). A fifty-year-old creole enslaved woman named Joanna escaped wearing a skirt, cotton blouse, white head wrap, gold hoop earrings, and a pano da costa (ibid., Aug. 21, 1838). Manoel, with the facial marks of a "Nagô or Tapa," escaped wearing pants made of panos da costa (ibid., Oct. 6, 1838). David, of the "Hausa nation," also ran away wearing blue-and-white-striped panos da costa pants (ibid., Dec. 4, 1838). Constança, an enslaved woman from Cabinda, escaped with several panos da costa (ibid., Feb. 9, 1839). Felisarda, an Angolan woman, ran away while wearing a "worn-out red and blue striped" pano da costa the same year (ibid., Dec. 11, 1839).

of wealth in property to the young fugitive, as it could be resold if such a need arose.[41]

Even African men and women who were not fleeing slavery held wealth in panos. Francisco Nazaré, a freed barber from the Mina Coast who traveled to Ouidah on the *Heroina* in 1826 as the slaving ship's medical practitioner, died in the Bight of Benin in 1832 as the owner of two "ordinary *panos da costa.*" Unlike Maria Luiza, Francisco likely did not imagine that these textiles would be for his personal use; they represented a reliable investment that could be traded or sold in the future. Women who had secured sufficient incomes from their labors were the primary buyers of panos da costa. African women living in urban Bahia, such as Maria Luiza, leveraged their predominance in ambulant vending to access currency and the significant disposable income necessary for the purchase of an expensive decorative textile. Enslaved Bahians who toiled in the urban cash economy as wage laborers, sailors, mobile vendors, artisans, and healers were far more likely to accumulate the capital to purchase one. Panos da costa circulated continuously through Black-dominated commercial circuits. Salvador was also home to a market in used textiles, making them a wise investment for men and women of extremely limited means.[42]

AFRICAN COMMODITIES AND
AFRO-BAHIAN RELIGIOUS CULTURE

The region of the Mina Coast stretching from Elmina to Lagos hosted a heterogeneous patchwork of localized religious cultures that were joined together by a number of overlapping features. West African Mina-Gen *yehwe* cults and Nagô *òrìṣà* cults were important antecedents to Candomblé, a devotional Afro-Brazilian practice. In Fon-speaking areas, religious activities

41. ANTT, Feitos Findos, Juízo da Índia e Mina, maço 33, número 16, caixa 157, "Acção civil de embargos a primeira em que a autora a Irmandade de Jesus Maria José, erecta no Convento do Monte do Carmo, por Maria Luiza e seu filho Custódio, e reu Custódio Jose Ribeiro Guimaraes, 1824."

42. APEB, Justiça, Inventário de Francisco de Nazaré, 5/2011/2482/4, 14; Luis Nicolau Parés, *The Formation of Candomblé: Vodun History and Ritual in Brazil,* trans. Richard Vernon (Chapel Hill, N.C., 2013), 97–98. The intensive labor and specialized knowledge required to make panos de costa explains the considerable commercial value of these textiles in Brazil. As Wetherell revealed in 1860, one fabric cost 50$000 réis; the wearer needed access to monetary income in order to purchase one (Verger, *Trade Relations,* [trans. Crawford], 465).

took on various scales. During the eighteenth century, private forms of worship, both individual and familial, entailed the performance of rituals to affect quotidian, practical concerns, such as divination and healing. Yehwe (or spirit / *lwa* / *vodun*) cults, by contrast, were organized around public iterations of deity worship, including initiation ceremonies and complex festivals. To the east, in Yoruba-speaking regions, cults of òrìṣà worship included localized public and private ritual performance, centered on òrìṣàs ("deified ancestors"). Materiality underpinned most ritual acts, with items such as blood, botanicals, shells, animals, kola nuts, oil, feathers, and textiles facilitating rites of protection and the production of sacred medicines. These principles framed how recently displaced enslaved individuals in Bahia oriented their ritual lives and religious communities.[43]

African inhabitants of Bahia transformed imported objects into powerful signifiers for religious affiliations with Candomblé, which was influenced by Fon and Yoruba precedents and grounded in worship of one or more orixás. Viewed as spiritually potent, panos da costa and dendê oil provided the raw materials for new forms of worship and prestige. Africans in Salvador, for instance, used oil and cloth in religious applications to consecrate ties among themselves as well as to venerate individual deities. Early forms of such devotion were both social and spiritual, as initiates to the *povo-de-santo* (congregation) relied on the guidance of its more experienced members. During Candomblé's development, as Luis Nicolau Parés notes, its adherents established a repertoire of complex practices and institutional connections. These included loosely organized public "*batuques* (drumming performances), work crews, [and] Catholic Brotherhoods," which evolved into mobile, ephemeral *calundus* (musical ceremonies of healing and divination) and organizationally elaborate, socially extensive Candomblés. The term Candomblé first appeared in Bahia as late as 1807.[44]

Africans in Bahia forged the first dedicated ritual spaces (*terreiros*) of Can-

43. Luis Nicoalu Parés, *O rei, o pai e a morte: A religião Vodum na Antiga Costa dos escravos na África ocidental* (São Paulo, 2016), 92–97; Matory, *Black Atlantic Religion*, 17–19, 20–21.

44. Parés, *Formation of Candomblé,* trans. Vernon, xv–xvi, 15, 88, 117, 271; Matory, *Black Atlantic Religion*, 31, 119, 140, 233. Parés defines Afro-Bahian divination as an oracular method that allows "prediction, diagnosis, and prescription of the best strategy to be adopted when faced with a given conflict," a practice that is inseparable from ritual healing (*Formation of Candomblé,* 73–79); and see Roger Bastide, *Sociología de la religión* (Madrid, 1986), 314–316.

domblé in the late eighteenth century. Initial terreiros tended to be small and innocuous, hidden in the urban homes of African freedmen or on more remote, suburban properties. Ceremonies often adopted a clandestine character. One of the first accounts of collective ritual activity by enslaved individuals from the Mina Coast dated to the 1780s, as a royal administrator warned of "secret" gatherings wherein a "Master Negress" led the worship of an altar of idols, and participants "anoint[ed] their bodies with various oils"—almost certainly a reference to dendê oil. During the same decade, police intruded on a calundu in Cachoeira, in Bahia's interior. Those targeted included three men and three women, identified as ethnically Gege, Mahi, Dagomé, and Tapa. Among the objects recovered from their hidden ceremony was an ostensibly charmed floating arrow, coins, cowry shells, gourds, ointments, leaves, iron, liquor, feathers, seeds, and more. Though the style of ointment was not specified, it was likely produced from palm oil, which had long been used to fabricate healing remedies. In this early moment of ritual experimentation, this group of African-born men and women in Cachoeira employed materials probably of African origin in their powerful shrine to an unnamed deity.[45]

Early Candomblé practices included humble, intimate gatherings and periodic secretive festivals that featured both dance and divination. Enslaved and freed Africans, the first adherents to these communities, empowered themselves through the acquisition of diverse African materials for their clandestine "altar-offering complexes." Access to transatlantic materiality enabled Bahians to generate increasingly elaborate ritual practices that would eventually include not only individual acts of cowry-shell divination, deployment of herbal medicine, and the use of metaphysical healing but also, according to J. Lorand Matory, collective practices of spirit possession, animal sacrifice,

45. Parés, *Formation of Candomblé*, trans. Vernon, 81–83, 115–117; João José Reis, *Divining Slavery and Freedom: The Story of Domingos Sodré, an African Priest in Nineteenth-Century Brazil* (Cambridge, 2015), 88. Bahian authorities alternated between suppression and acceptance of early Candomblés. Though such religious festivities preceded a number of rebellions by the enslaved in the first decades of the nineteenth century, the count of Ponte, Bahia's governor from 1805 to 1810, demanded "systematic repression" in the name of discouraging African resistance. His successor, the count dos Arcos, considered the allowance of African batuques a useful tactic to divide African ethnic populations and prevent rebellion (ibid., 90–91). In a later period, Candomblé utilized both flowing oils and shea butter from West African rituals. In modern Candomblé, members of the community are identified euphemistically as "in the [red palm] oil" (Matory, *Black Atlantic Religion*, 128, 140–142, 233, 336).

and culinary offerings. In the early nineteenth century, as devotees congregated in domestic spaces, they created sophisticated material assemblages (including leaves, cloth, oil, gourds containing cowry shells, oil, blood sacrifice, and liquor) to venerate powerful deities that could intercede on their behalf to bring fortune and prosperity. Fundamentally, enslaved and freed Africans reestablished the ritual, religious, and social significance of palm oil. In West African Yoruba-speaking communities particularly, dendê oil cultivation was not only a key part of agricultural economies; it also fulfilled spiritual needs. The red, viscous substance produced from the ubiquitous oil palm supposedly had the awesome power to cool the heated energies of trickster deity Eshu through offerings and to evoke ancestral protection. Beyond palm oil's bodily applications, Bahia's inhabitants likely used it in their offerings for *peijis,* or shrines to individual orixás.[46]

The transatlantic trade was key to the acquisition of such materials. The contents of Domingos do Rozário's liberty chest are emblematic. As mentioned above, he carried palm oil, cowries, corals, straw mats, and panos da costa. His holdings were particularly suggestive of early Candomblé's material complexity. All of these items—especially the straw mats and shells—were crucial to Yourban Ifá divination, or the divinely informed reading of cast cowries or palm nuts to predict future outcomes. Though it is not stated, Rozário could have been an early specialist (later known as *pai-de-santo*) in a nascent urban terreiro, and his ability to accumulate such goods would have burnished his status among other West Africans in Salvador. Rozário crossed the Atlantic in 1812, a pivotal moment in the elaboration of Candomblé ritual, when access to West African liturgical materials would have been central not only to the performance of divination but to the consecration of ties to deities, the successful realization of acts of healing, and the bodily signification of one's membership in a ritual community. Though domestically produced palm oil was already available in Bahia by the late eighteenth century, worshippers likely sought out West African varieties that were seen as particularly powerful by Africans in the diaspora, stimulating transatlantic circulation.[47]

46. ANRJ, fundo 7X, Junta do Comércio, Fábricas e Navegações, caixa 410, pacote 1, Papers of the *São Miguel Triunfante,* 8–9; Robert Farris Thompson, *Flash of the Spirit: African and Afro-American Art and Philosophy* (New York, 1983), 21, 34–35; Matory, *Black Atlantic Religion,* 32; Parés, *Formation of Candomblé,* trans. Vernon, 81–87, 90–92; Watkins, *Palm Oil Diaspora,* 58–57, 150–153.

47. Watkins, *Palm Oil Diaspora,* 110–111.

Equally critical to burgeoning Candomblé ritual and social affiliations were panos da costa. These textiles had practical applications, and the durable cotton cloths were initially worn by Africans and Afro-Brazilians of all genders, ethnicities, statuses, and ages. But by the middle of the nineteenth century, such cloth became an emblem for the female leadership of Afro-Brazilian Candomblé temples. The social logics that imbued panos da costa with religious power originated in West Africa, where, as art historians, archaeologists, and anthropologists have noted, textiles have been understood as ontologically distinct from other aspects of the material world. In Yoruba culture and religion, Rowland Abiodun, Ulli Beier, and John Pemberton have argued that "the significance of cloth goes beyond body covering to express a rich and profound belief system. In its creation, the color, weave, and design of cloth reflects the aesthetic sensibilities and character of the artists as well as of the future owner." West African cloth, both historically and in contemporary contexts, conveyed a powerful social logic signifying authority while, for its wearers, imbuing life force and acting as an agent of personal empowerment. In its semiotic function, cloth not only "covers the body, but has the power to express the person." Through pattern composition, motifs, color, and texture, cloth records and articulates shared memories as well as the personal histories of the wearer and creator of the textile.[48]

By the 1830s, female Candomblé priestesses and initiates had adopted the pano da costa as a key component in what would become their *ropa de*

48. Cloth is also the material embodiment of the link to one's ancestors. See Rowland Abiodun, Ulli Beier, and John Pemberton, *Cloth Only Wears to Shreds: Textiles and Photographs from the Ulli Beier Collection* (Amherst, Mass., 2004), 7. In Yoruba-speaking West Africa, cloth inhabits the same ontological category as *oríkì*, or praise poems that celebrate òrìṣà and ancestors. Like other sacred objects, cloth is imbued with *àṣẹ*, or life force, aura, or potentiality to transform / act upon. See Abiodun, *Yoruba Art and Language: Seeking the African in African Art* (New York, 2014), 163–164. The conflation of cloth with social identity is communicated by the Yoruba proverb "My people are my cloth." See ibid., 48; John Pemberton III, "The Dreadful God and the Divine King," in Sandra T. Barnes, ed., *Africa's Ogun: Old World and New,* 2d ed. (Bloomington, Ind., 1997), 105–146. The communicative mode of West African cloth is perhaps best expressed by *adire eleko*, or indigo-dyed textiles, first fabricated in Abeokuta at the end of the nineteenth century. These hand-woven cotton textiles incorporate writing or abstract symbols that express "one's identity (including status and lineage, beliefs or set of values)." The dyeing method of adire cloth through a multistage process allows Nigerian female artisans and artists to communicate local histories and òrìṣà mythologies through motifs that only other textile artists can decipher. See Nina Sylvanus, *Patterns in Circulation: Cloth, Gender, and Materiality in West Africa* (Chicago, 2016), 2;

axé, or ritually prescribed clothing. Africans in Bahia made panos da costa into a specialized emblem of female ethnoreligious power and authority. The religious implications of cloth were clear in 1829 when a police raid of a clandestine Gege religious gathering uncovered a trove of panos da costa, money, and other, unnamed items. Practitioners of the Afro-Brazilian religion would come to view African-derived textiles as capable of empowering their wearer as well as signifying and enacting a connection to a particular orixá through a rich symbolism of color and design. The specificity of design also eventually connoted a position of prestige and authority within the hierarchy of the terreiro. On the streets of Salvador, female vendors believed that panos da costa evoked the protection of the gods and guarded against jealous competitors. Within the private confines of the temple complex, a pano draped across the shoulder became an identifiable emblem of the *iyalorixá,* or female leader, of many Nagô temples, signifying a spiritual relationship to ancestral Africa and one's ritual community. The finer the design and construction of the cloth, the more prestigious and wealthier the wearer.[49]

A primary signifier of West African heritage, prestige, and artistry, panos da costa functioned as a medium of communication and cultural transmission, not only within enslaved communities in Bahia but also between Brazil and Africa. These transatlantic exchanges produced effective translocal religious dialogues in both ideas and goods. West African goods were prized among Candomblé's earliest adherents, and their circulation was facilitated by the

---

Lisa Aronson, "The Language of West African Textiles," *African Arts,* XXV (1992), 36–41, esp. 38; Nkiru Nzegwu, "Introduction: Contemporary Nigerian Arts; Euphonizing the Art Historical Voice," in Nzegwu, ed., *Contemporary Textures: Multidimensionality in Nigerian Art* (Binghamton, N.Y., 1999), 1–39.

49. Raul Giovanni Lody, *Panos da costa* (Rio [de Janeiro], 1977), 3–7; Mikelle Smith Omari-Tunkara, *Manipulating the Sacred: Yorùbá Art, Ritual, and Resistance in Brazilian Candomblé* (Detroit, 2005), 45–48; João José Reis, *Slave Rebellion in Brazil: The Muslim Uprising of 1835 in Bahia,* trans. Arthur Brakel (Baltimore, 1993), 143; Melville J. Herskovits, "Some Economic Aspects of the Afrobahian Candomble," in International Congress of Americanists, *Miscellanea Paul Rivet, Octogenario Dictata,* II (Mexico City, 1958), 230. In the same period, a parallel practice evolved in West Africa as *itagbè,* or Ijebu-made brocade cloth, became the unique purview of female *Ògbóni* religious leaders. As with panos da costa, the textile insignia was used as a shoulder cloth (Keyes, "Àdìrẹ," 74). As Rodrigues has observed, by the beginning of the twentieth century, African women were the predominant wearers of panos da costa—which had been imported by English- and Yoruba-speaking African merchants alongside other crucial "gege-youruba cult objects" (Rodrigues, *Os Africanos no Brasil,* 127–128).

movement of a number of African-born freedmen and -women of means, some of whom traveled to Lagos for religious education while participating in the transatlantic commodity trade. West African freedmen and merchants residing in Bahia, several of whom had been active as mariners in the transatlantic slave trade, were also integral to the emergence of the organized Afro-Bahian ritual communities of Candomblé. These African men (and at times their lovers, wives, and female ritual assistants) residing in Bahia continued to make the passage to Africa to trade in sacred West African goods and solidify religious ties on the other side of the Atlantic. A handful of maritime African barbers and *sangradores* also became key participants in these early religious communities. As practitioners creating a burgeoning religious complex, they incorporated bloodletting rituals similar to those found on Brazilian slaving vessels. They applied African-derived plants to bodies in healing and initiation ceremonies, just as shipboard barbers and sangradores had done. These "healer-diviners" paid special attention to the head, a site of both physical and metaphysical power, as a way to guard against malevolent forces and manipulate benevolent ones.[50]

Many captive cosmopolitans came to inhabit the overlapping roles of African transatlantic trader, Candomblé ritual specialist, and shipboard barber or sangrador. Such occupational cross-pollinations were foundational to Candomblé. In ways that have not been fully recognized by the literature on Afro-Brazilian religious practice, Candomblé's emergence was spurred not only by the Africanization of Bahia's population after 1790 but by the transatlantic slave trade's commercial dynamics. As Chapter 6 has shown, South Atlantic slaving produced a worldly and socially powerful cohort of enslaved and freed African men with the healing skills and financial means to support

---

50. As Reis asserts, the vast majority of Candomblé's early leadership was freed Africans in Bahia. See Lisa Earl Castillo and Luis Nicolau Parés, "Marcelina da Silva: A Nineteenth Century *Candomblé* Priestess in Bahia," *Slavery and Abolition*, XXXI (2010), 1–27; Reis, "Candomblé in Nineteenth-Century Bahia: Priests, Followers, Clients," in Kristin Mann and Edna G. Bay, eds., *Rethinking the African Diaspora: The Making of a Black Atlantic World in the Bight of Benin and Brazil* (London, 2001), 116–134, esp. 121–122; Matory, *Black Atlantic Religion*, 32, 95, 130; Castillo, "Mapping the Nineteenth-Century Brazilian Returnee Movement: Demographics, Life Stories, and the Question of Slavery," *Atlantic Studies*, XII (2016) 25–52; Parés, *Formation of Candomblé*, trans. Vernon, 82–83, esp. 82; Estélio Gomberg, *Hospital de Orixás: Encontros terapêuticos em um terreiro de Candomblé* (Salvador, Brazil, 2011), 15; Flávio Gonçalves dos Santos, *Economia e cultura do Candomblé na Bahia: O comércio de objetos litúrgicos afro-brasileiros—1850/1937* (Ilhéus, Brazil, 2013), 95–98.

early ritual experiments. In particular, barbers and sangradores adapted slaving ship healing techniques for new cultural and religious purposes. Captive cosmopolitan mariners' history of routine travel to West Africa positioned them as authorities in the spiritual communities of freed and enslaved Africans who made up Candomblé's first adherents. As scholars have shown, the cult religion's early leadership was overwhelmingly African-born and freed, defined by cosmopolitanism as much as by African origins. Few, however, have emphasized the centrality of the African materials they moved to the Afro-Bahian religion's growth and increasing sophistication. Steeped in the multiethnic intellectual currents of slaving ship medicine and the commercial networks spawned by the transatlantic trade, such cosmopolitan men were well versed in the contours of oceanic commodity exchange.[51]

In fact, the earliest Candomblé terreiros counted numerous captive cosmopolitans among their members. Francisco Nazaré, who traveled to Ouidah on the *Heroina* in 1826 as the slaving ship's medical practitioner, appears to have become a member of the temple Gantois, alongside another African barber, Marcos Rodrigues Soares. Likewise, José Bernardino da Costa Faria joined the leadership of Casa Branca terreiro, and José Joaquim de Moraes transitioned from slaving ship medical practitioner to leader of the Bogum terreiro in the 1860s. Men such as Moraes would have been ideal early Candomblé ritual specialists, as they exercised what were perceived as awesome and rare powers over the body.[52]

Another example of Black transatlantic entrepreneurship's influence on Candomblé was the African merchant Manoel Joaquim Ricardo. Following the resurgence of the clandestine slave trade in the late 1830s, Ricardo employed a freed Gege man, Joaquim Antônio da Silva, whom he sent to Ouidah to surreptitiously engage in slaving while managing West African exports of

51. Matory, *Black Atlantic Religion,* 128; Reis, "Candomblé in Nineteenth-Century Bahia," in Mann and Bay, eds., *Rethinking the African Diaspora,* 121–122; Parés, *Formation of Candomblé,* trans. Vernon, 111; Parés, "Militiamen, Barbers, and Slave-Traders: Mina and Jeje Africans in a Catholic Brotherhood (Bahia, 1770–1830)," *Revista Tempo,* XX (2014), 1–32. They discovered ways to profit from the importation of ritually essential materials from Lagos, Porto Novo, and Ouidah, particularly textiles, dendê oil, kola, straw mats, baskets, beads, and gourds. See Matory, *Black Atlantic Religion,* 92; Santos, *Economia e cultura do Candomblé na Bahia,* 32, 127.

52. Parés, "Militiamen, Barbers, and Slave-Traders," *Revista Tempo,* XX (2014), 1–32 n. 59. Parés has identified thirty-seven Candomblés and twenty-eight individual practitioners of divination and healing from 1863 to 1872 (Parés, *Formation of Candomblé,* trans. Vernon, 94–95).

coral, textiles, and indigo to Bahia. Manoel Joaquim Ricardo also partnered with African-born but Bahia-based freedman and healer José Pedro Autran. Reputedly one of the founders of the illustrious Iyá Nassô Oká terreiro, Autran was the owner of another central figure in the early history of the Afro-Brazilian religion: Marcelina da Silva, a priestess, or iyalorixá, of the same temple.[53]

Ricardo's social network stretched further still into the world of Candomblé. He was also friends with Domingos Sodré, a notorious diviner and founder of a small ritual community that gathered in a house he shared with his wife and assistant, Delfina. When it was raided in 1862 by Bahian police, they found Delfina's "vendor's box of cloth." Though it is unclear whether Delfina sold panos da costa, it is likely that, as a mobile ganhadeira, she did. As contemporary oral histories of Candomblé practitioners articulate, adherents created an essential link between consumption of the cloth and belonging in the ritual community. Beyond everyday use, panos da costa became de rigueur for worshippers. The spiritual obligation to decorate one's body in West African textiles helped to support the livelihoods of freed and enslaved African women throughout the city. By the middle of the nineteenth century, their entrepreneurial initiative had transformed the social and cultural meanings ascribed to panos da costa, as their usage became markedly feminized and ritualized.[54] For sellers and consumers alike, such corporeal practices

53. João José Reis, "From Slave to Wealthy African Freedman: The Story of Manoel Joaquim Ricardo," in Lisa A. Lindsay and John Wood Sweet, eds., *Biography and the Black Atlantic* (Philadelphia, 2014), 133–134, 143. Also among this cohort of barbers / transatlantic traders was Ventura Ferreira Milles, who traveled to Lagos in March 1830 on an American brig carrying a cargo of palm oil and cloth. He was accompanied by six other freed African barbers, with whom he likely shared a business relationship, as well as numerous seamen, merchants, and artisans from Bahia. See House of Commons, *Parliamentary Papers* (London, 1831), 116.

54. Reis, *Divining Slavery and Freedom*, 95. Maria do Rosario, a freedwoman and trader, specialized in selling African goods, including *sabão da costa* (soap of the coast), *pimento da costa* (pepper of the coast), *limo da costa* (shea butter), *buzios da costa* (shells of the coast), and panos da costa, in the 1860s. Freedwoman Mariana Joaquina do Espírito Santo owned a store in Salvador specializing in West African and European textiles and, at her death in 1871, she owned several slaves, substantial capital, and lines of credit. In addition, an African woman named Sabina da Cruz became a wholesale merchant of West African goods, including soap, cowry shells, and panos. She had also consigned a variety of panos to João do Prado Carvalho, including eleven blue textiles, twenty-two *panos da costa sanhá*, or crocheted cloth, and twenty-three *panos da costa Tepolás*. Meanwhile, in 1896, Afro-Brazilian

exceeded the resistive pleasures of adornment, instead signifying a complex, West African–influenced public performance of the spiritually powerful female body. Female leadership drove Candomblé's adoption of the pano da costa, making the cloth the definitive article of the religion's iconography. Cloth—as an authenticating signifier—also elevated their individual status within the spiritual community, becoming the ultimate symbol of their place within a larger communal hierarchy.[55]

Access to these materials in Brazil spurred new forms of social identification as Africans negotiated and expressed human bonds through the wearing of Yoruban cloth and the ritual application of palm oil. The social dislocation, cultural fragmentation, and vulnerability of life for enslaved and freed Africans residing in Bahia provoked them to fashion new meanings from the wearing of panos da costa and the consumption of dendê oil. To understand the material history of Candomblé, however, requires attending to a longer commercial history connecting West Africa and Bahia that was, to a significant degree, facilitated by captive cosmopolitan mariners. The transatlantic trade in these items grew out of a smaller, regional West African trade in these commodities that predated the era of the slave trade. That Africans in the diaspora were able to successfully expand this trade with a decided paucity of resources illustrates the various ways that transoceanic consumer markets were cre-

woman Felicidade Maria de Sant'Anna imported twenty-four panos da costa worth 216$000 réis from Lagos, alongside black soap, kola nuts, and gourds. These women were among the first to specialize in African imports after the end of the slave trade. See Manuela Carneiro da Cunha, *Negros, estrangeiros: Os escravos libertos e sua volta à África*, 2d ed. (São Paulo, 2012), 159; APEB, Tribunal de Justiça, Inventário 03/1100/1569/7, 22, 85; Watkins, *Palm Oil Diaspora*, 151–152.

55. For more on dress as a form of bodily agency and resistance for the enslaved, see Steeve O. Buckridge, *The Language of Dress: Resistance and Accommodation in Jamaica, 1760–1890* (Kingston, 2004); DuPlessis, *Material Atlantic;* Tamara J. Walker, *Exquisite Slaves: Race, Clothing, and Status in Colonial Lima* (Cambridge, 2017); Lisa Ze Winters, *The Mulatta Concubine: Terror, Intimacy, Freedom, and Desire in the Black Transatlantic* (Athens, Ga., 2016). For interpretations of dress as "pleasure," see Stephanie M. H. Camp, *Closer to Freedom: Enslaved Women and Everyday Resistance in the Plantation South* (Chapel Hill, N.C., 2004), 134–135. African cloth provided both subsistence and status, enabling women such as Eugênia Anna Santos (Mãe Aninha), the founder of the Ilê Axé Opó Afonjá terreiro, to acquire personal wealth and authenticate her belonging to a Nagô religious culture—despite her Gurunsi ethnic origins. See Matory, *Black Atlantic Religion*, 118; Lody, *Panos da costa*, 3–6.

ated and sustained during the early modern period. The development of a Bahian market in West African goods points to an alternative, subaltern-oriented theory of Atlantic commercial life. The circulation of African-derived commodities depended on the economic initiatives of both maritime and terrestrially based enslaved economic actors. Enslaved people could be drivers of transatlantic *demand,* a definitive indication of their integration into Atlantic-connected forms of commercial exchange. Their commercial initiatives irrevocably shaped the growth of a transatlantic trade in African-derived commodities, inspiring and incentivizing captive cosmopolitans to seek out such materials on African coasts.

This process was not driven by acquisitive logics alone. In addition to their economic value, the socially defined value of panos da costa and dendê lay in their rarity and ritual potency. Paradoxically, African items first transported to Bahia in the festering holds of slaving ships would become fundamental to the empowering, community-building Candomblé rituals of divination and spirit possession in the next hundred years. Like many aspects of Black mariners' influence in the eighteenth- and nineteenth-century South Atlantic world, the historical significance of the African commodities that traveled in liberty chests from West Africa to Bahia broached the spatial confines of ships. The prevalence of African-derived commodities in Salvador powerfully suggests that, as Black mariners traversed the Atlantic, they also became central commercial agents in remaking the material and cultural landscape of Bahia and Afro-Brazil more generally. Though the winds of cosmopolitan agitation blew from all directions in Salvador, those from Africa—not Europe or the Caribbean—made the most profound mark on the city.

Enslaved and freed Africans residing in Bahia responded to the hardships of bondage and displacement by producing new forms of cultural creativity that could be apprehended as a distinctive Black Bahian culture. The material contours of eating, worshipping, and dressing for Salvador's inhabitants relied on commercial and intellectual ties captive cosmopolitans forged with the Bight of Benin. These practices spread beyond the nucleus of the enslaved and freed African population, becoming commonplace among all ages, ethnicities, and legal statuses of Bahia. Enslaved people thus forever remade the cultural lives of all Bahians. In the wake of their own physical and social displacement, they developed material strategies to build wealth and prestige at the same time they sought to relieve social alienation and isolation through religious communion. Their material world, sacred expressions, and social power became a legacy of the very same trade that had reduced them to property at the beginning of their long Atlantic journeys.

The Afterlives of
Captive Cosmopolitanism

You are a perfect Proteus in the way you take on every kind of shape,
twisting about this way and that, until at last you elude my grasp.
  —Plato, *Ion*, 541e

It is not, in fact, only the place that is significant but also the manner of the
journey and arrival, the eager walking, or manacled stumble, the panicked
flight, or forced or voluntary sailing toward and away from each other.
  —Hazel Carby, *Imperial Intimacies: A Tale of Two Islands*

The cosmopolitan lives of African mariners were marked by the profound
ironies of the transatlantic trade that had first violently carried them to Bahia.
By the first decade of the nineteenth century, a complex West African community had taken shape in the city of Salvador. Though the vast majority labored
without the possibility of attaining manumission, those who participated in
the transatlantic slave trade as mariners were far more likely to achieve some
measure of upward mobility. Despite failing to enjoy rights of citizenship in
the period, many freedmen managed to exert some control over their familial
and associational arrangements, the terms of their labor, and their ritual and
intellectual lives. In Salvador, Black seafarers were integral to the urban social
milieu, where their wide-ranging social connections fostered networks of commerce, healing, and patronage. Though a modicum of economic success at
sea had liberated some from the personal fetters of bondage, they remained
captive to the system of slavery even after the attainment of their own freedom.
Mirroring the constraints they experienced at sea, freed Africans in the city
faced stark legal and economic impediments to fashioning the kinds of lives
they wished to live. Slavery remained woven into every aspect of Salvador's
society, and the provincial government's need to suppress potential violent
threats against the institution amid continuing political and civil unrest created
an increasingly restrictive legal regime for African freedmen and -women.[1]

1. Plato, *Plato in Twelve Volumes*, trans. R. G. Bury, VIII (Cambridge, Mass., 1929), 447;
Hazel V. Carby, *Imperial Intimacies: A Tale of Two Islands* (London, 2019), 51; Luciana da

Indeed, after the Brazilian government finally embraced the legal abolition of the slave trade with the law of November 7, 1831, both slavers and freed Africans faced mounting legal pressures. By prescribing concrete penalties for engaging in the transatlantic slave trade, the law marked the beginning of a national effort to combat trafficking, albeit one that would not be rigorously enforced for another twenty years. The named penalties for illegal slaving included the seizure and emancipation of all African slaves entering Brazilian territory and criminal charges of piracy for captains, mates, and shipowners who engaged in slaving. The law dissuaded some slavers from attempting transatlantic journeys, and the volume of the slave trade sharply declined for eighteen months following its passage. This would be only a momentary respite, however. Brazilian naval squadrons lacked the capacity to enforce the law, and slave merchants and ship captains displayed widespread defiance, motivated by seemingly bottomless demands for enslaved labor. Slaving vessels continued to arrive on Bahian shores but no longer anchored near Salvador. Instead, cunning captains sought out hidden ports, particularly the western edge of Itaparica Island and smaller islands within the Bay of All Saints. Though the 1831 law had included an exception for emancipating enslaved seamen found aboard slavers, the anti–slave trade provision curtailed Black movement by subjecting traveling Africans to an additional layer of scrutiny by local police and justices of the peace. Although martial solutions to the persistence of the illegal slave trade would prove to be ineffectual, violent rumblings from below would prove decisive in permanently transforming patterns of slaving in the city.[2]

Cruz Brito, *Temores da África: Segurança, legislação e população Africana na Bahia oitocentista* (Salvador, Brazil, 2016), 26–28. The 1824 Constitution was largely silent on the issue of citizenship for individuals born in Africa, meaning most were de facto disenfranchised. But as Brito points out, there were a handful of freed Africans who managed on an individual basis to access Portuguese and later Brazilian citizenship. People of African descent born in Brazil, however, enjoyed civil rights and, if they met minimum income requirements, political rights. See Brito, "Sem direitos, nem cidadania: Condição legal e agência de mulheres e homens africanos na Bahia do século XIX," *História Unisinos,* XIV (2010), 334–338, esp. 334; Brito, *Temores da África,* 43; Márcia Regina Berbel and Rafael de Bivar Marquese, "The Absence of Race: Slavery, Citizenship, and Pro-slavery Ideology in the Cortes of Lisbon and the Rio de Janeiro Constituent Assembly (1821–4)," *Social History,* XXXII (2007), 415–433, esp. 416; Manuela Carneiro da Cunha, *Negros, estrangeiros: Os escravos libertos e sua volta à África,* 2d ed. (São Paulo, 2012), 69.

2. The Brazilian slave trade was formally abolished on September 4, 1850, with the passage of the so-called Queirós Law. See Leslie Bethell, *The Abolition of the Brazilian Slave*

REVOLT AND THE UNMAKING OF
CAPTIVE COSMOPOLITANISM

On October 27, 1835, thirty-five-year-old Tobias Barreto Brandão, a freed Gege man and slave trader, wrote a letter to the president of the province of Bahia. He recalled the exemplary conduct he believed he had always exhibited since arriving in Salvador at the age of seven in shackles. Despite murmurs of rebellion in the city, he himself had never been a target of suspicion. While attempting to travel to the island of Príncipe on business, however, Brandão was "unjustly arrested" after failing to have on his person the passport required by the chief of police. Though the African recorded his official occupation as a "tailor" in his documents, he was a transatlantic merchant who regularly traveled back and forth between Bahia and West Africa. Undeterred, Brandão insisted that his conduct was legitimate, and he should be released immediately.[3]

The timing of Brandão's detention was no accident; it was but one sign of the rapidly changing place of African-born sailors and traders in the web of Bahia's transatlantic commerce. Nine months earlier, a seismic event had transformed white elites' attitudes toward the city's freed African population as well as the desirability of the slave trade itself. In the dead of night on January 25, 1835, a group of fifty to sixty African rebels embarked on an elaborate plot to overtake the city by force. After a skirmish with national guardsmen, they attacked the city jail in Salvador's palace square and attempted to free African prisoners. When their initial attack proved unsuccessful, the group spread throughout Salvador, attracting additional insurgents to their cause.

Trade: Britain, Brazil, and the Slave Trade Question, 1807–1869 (Cambridge, 1970), 69–72; Mieko Nishida, *Slavery and Identity: Ethnicity, Gender, and Race in Salvador, Brazil, 1808–1888* (Bloomington, Ind., 2003), 17; David Eltis, *Economic Growth and the Ending of the Transatlantic Slave Trade* (New York, 1987), 244. As Isadora Moura Mota argues, the abolition law became a mechanism for denying entry into Brazil for free African Americans and other foreigners unconnected with the transatlantic slave trade. See Mota, "On the Imminence of Emancipation: Black Geopolitical Literacy and Anglo-American Abolitionism in Nineteenth-Century Brazil" (Ph.D. diss., Brown University, 2017), 17; Bethell, *Abolition of the Brazilian Slave Trade*, 69–71; Pierre Verger, *Fluxo e refluxo: Do tráfico de escravos entre o golfo do Benim e a Bahia de Todos-os-Santos, do século XVII ao XIX,* trans. Tasso Gadzanis (São Paulo, 2021), 372–373.

3. Tobias Barretto Brandão was one of the passengers on the Bahian ship *Gratidão*, which was seized by British antislavers off the coast of the Bight of Benin after leaving Agoué. Letters discovered on the *Gratidão* suggest the extent of Brandão's trading activities, which had lasted for at least two years, as well as the names of several of his business associates residing

Several hundred men then stormed two police barracks, but once cavalrymen joined the city's police and military defense, the tide turned against the rebels, who attempted to escape, scattering throughout the city and disappearing into the darkness. Though the Muslim men who had planned the attack predicted slaves from the rural areas surrounding the city would join their insurgency, the movement never expanded past a few hundred urban bondsmen and a handful of small rebellions on nearby plantations. The men's objectives reportedly included killing as many whites as they could and upending Salvador's racial hierarchy by establishing themselves as a new local elite.[4]

Once the dust had settled the following morning, authorities in Salvador began a massive manhunt to locate, question, and punish all conspirators. This process was accompanied by a widespread panic over the possibility of additional slave revolts. For local authorities who had strongly supported the contraband transatlantic slave trade despite its illegality after 1831, the rebellion became the just cause for its termination. Driven by the fears that Salvador was unwittingly importing an enemy population of hostile Africans, local politicians began to advocate for the slave trade's total abolition. In early March 1835, the president of the province, Francisco Gonçalves Martins, addressed the general assembly and urged for the "absolute prohibition of all direct trade with the ports of Africa." After years of local authorities' abetting illegal slaving, Martins realized the hidden dangers it posed to the white populace. He argued that the Malê revolt had laid bare the "urgent necessity of taking serious and efficacious measures to prevent [rebellion] . . . by preventing entirely the contraband of slaves, which, in spite of the prohibition and of the penalties inflicted by the law, continues to be carried on clandestinely with scandalous recklessness." Continuing the slave trade, Martins proclaimed, would ensure that "every slave disembarked on our shores is a fresh barrel of powder thrown into the mine."[5]

---

in Agoué, Ajudá, Onim, and Salvador. These included Elias Domingos de Carvalho, Antônio Caetano Coelho, Seca Medair, Agostinho de Freitas, and Antônio Vieira dos Santos. Upon his capture, Brandão had been transporting 200$120 réis' worth of goods from Bahia, including tobacco, leather, and honey, to Joaquim de Almeida, a close associate. Almeida was a freed African merchant who operated between Bahia and the Mina Coast in the first decades of the nineteenth century, leading to his peers to identify him as the "assistant of the Port of Agoué." See BNA, FO 315/48, Papers of the *Gratidão*, no. 48, Letter to Joaquim de Almeida, Bahia, Sept. 5, 1840.

4. João José Reis, *Slave Rebellion in Brazil: The Muslim Uprising of 1835 in Bahia,* trans. Arthur Brakel (Baltimore, 1993), 73–92.

5. "First Enclosure in No. 170. Extract from Speech of the President of Bahia," Bahia,

The Malê revolt—labeled as such because its leaders were African Muslims, or "Malês"—created a lasting anti-African sentiment in the city. As a wave of paranoia wracked the city's white population, police and local authorities became obsessed with possible subversive activities by the enslaved and free African populations. Mounting legal restrictions on Salvador's African population were touted as necessary in the face of potential seditious activity. In the name of public serenity and security, a xenophobic backlash boiled over into violence. Bahia's president requested the

> full authority to expel from the Brazilian Territory all free Africans who may become dangerous to our tranquility; such individuals not being born in Brazil, with a language, religion, and habits different from ours, and having by the late events shown themselves inimical to our peace, ought not to enjoy those securities which the constitution guarantees only to Brazilian citizens.

Martins, together with the chief of police, mobilized to indiscriminately arrest freed Africans throughout the city, eventually trying 301 men and women as conspirators. The penalties for those found guilty—only 28 were acquitted—ranged from flogging to prison to deportation to death. Some convicted insurgents eventually convinced authorities to allow them to travel back to West Africa, spurring a minor exodus of freed Africans from the city.[6]

The very men who had once been indispensable to the port's vibrant commercial atmosphere were now assumed to be its principal internal enemies. In addition to forbidding the practice of Islam, the sale and importation of African goods, and public gatherings of enslaved people, Black mariners soon became targets of political repression. Of all the accused Malê conspirators, seven were boatmen (including six enslaved men and one freedman) and one was a fisherman. Reputedly, enslaved boatmen had transported some insurgents into Salvador from surrounding plantations on their lighters in the days preceding the revolt, giving rise to the fear that Black mariners were fomenting sedition in the countryside. The uncontrolled mobility of local Black seamen,

---

Mar. 1, 1835, *Correspondence with the British Commissioners, at Sierra Leone, the Havana, Rio de Janeiro, and Surinam: Relating to the Slave Trade, 1835, Presented to Both Houses of Parliament by Command of His Majesty* (London, 1836), 258–259.

6. Ibid., 259; Reis, *Slave Rebellion in Brazil,* trans. Brakel, 206, 220–221; Pierre Verger, *Trade Relations between the Bight of Benin and Bahia from the 17th to 19th Century,* [trans. Evelyn Crawford] (Ibadan, Nigeria, 1976), 314–321; Cunha, *Negros, estrangeiros;* Milton Guran, *Agudás: Os "brasileiros" do Benim* (Rio de Janeiro, 1999), 9–10.

as well as their numerical dominance in the port, aroused suspicions that they could overtake one of the most important strategic locations of the city or harbor fugitives. In Bahia, the loyalties of African seamen now appeared suspect, and the use of Black maritime labor risky. On slaving vessels, such men could also signal to British antislaving cruisers that ships were engaged in contraband. The practical benefits of their labor to merchants diminished significantly during the transatlantic slave trade's decline. Plagued by the persistent lack of manpower, authorities sought to find a laboring alternative to Black mariners. By 1850, the municipal council prohibited all slaves and freedmen from employment in Salvador's port and took measures to attract whites to maritime occupations.[7]

These regulations, together with the increasing scrutiny of Salvador's African population and the gradual decline of the illegal slave trade after 1831, marked the beginnings of the dissolution of captive cosmopolitans' central role in defining the dynamic maritime culture of Salvador. Though merchants and *senhores de engenho* continued to vigorously resist abolition, and despite a brief expansion of slaving traffic in the 1840s, the transatlantic slave trade was all but extinguished by 1850. The numbers of African residents in Salvador began to decline soon thereafter. In an environment of heightened surveillance, growing restrictions on slaving and the politicization of Black mobility, the intimate ties of commerce, politics, and culture that had closely bound West Africa and Bahia—connections forged in large part by African and creole mariners—continued in markedly new ways. Ships traveling to West Africa became smaller and fewer in the decades following the Malê revolt. As the oceanic circuits animated by the need to acquire African slaves withered, merchants' demand for Black mariners and commercial intermediaries also waned. This dissolution would not prove final, however. As the transatlantic slave trade declined in regional significance, the oceanic ties that defined Salvador would be succeeded by the religious and cultural imperatives of Candomblé. A new generation of cosmopolitan travelers would again make the spaces between Bahia and West Africa their refuge, this time as they com-

7. The swift repression of Africans living in the city following the Malê rebellion built on a longer history of the "fear of Africanisation," according to Bethell. Forming one of the core abolitionist arguments of the 1830s, overt racial prejudice, and a desire to forestall an increase of Africans in the Brazilian population, some arguments against the slave trade framed abolition as a remedy to national backwardness. See Bethell, *Abolition of the Brazilian Slave Trade*, 71-72; Reis, *Slave Rebellion in Brazil*, trans. Brakel, 77, 166; Dale Torston Graden, *From Slavery to Freedom in Brazil: Bahia, 1835-1900* (Albuquerque, N.M., 2006), 37-39.

muned with their spiritual companions in the growing city of Lagos on the West African coast.[8]

THE WORLD CAPTIVE COSMOPOLITANISM MADE

In January 1940, the denizens of Salvador gathered to consecrate new beginnings. A procession through the winding urban streets celebrated Nossa Senhora da Boa Viagem, a patron saint of navigators, whose effigy sailed atop a small vessel toward the lower city's old stone Santa Bárbara wharf. On this day, the city's residents eschewed the somber respectability of Catholicism and instead embraced raucous, bacchanalian festivities. Revelers erected an arch covered in foliage and raised paper flags and pennants on masts to greet the visage of the guardian of seamen and safe voyages. The sumptuous affair, funded by Salvador's African-descended boatmen, porters, and vendors who labored in the commercial section of the city, articulated a sense of communal life in the port.

Stalls spilled over with mountains of pineapples, watermelons, cashew, and bananas. Market women hovered over bubbling pots full of African palm oil and pepper. The air was pulsating with the sounds of drums, guitars, harmonicas, and clapping. Men, women, and children circled the streets in samba and capoeira (an Afro-Brazilian martial art created by the enslaved), performing "wheels," accompanied by the sounds of the African-inspired *berimbau*. Bodies danced, sang, swayed, and assembled. The festival also signaled watermen's continuing influence in generating day-to-day productive life for all Bahians, with locally harvested and imported tropical products featured prominently in the feasting amid the devotional procession. The celebration's material world evoked the past and the waterborne ties that still linked the busy streets of Salvador to expansive local and global networks of trade and travel.

Though an ostensibly religious spectacle, the festival had become a collective ritual honoring the commercial bounty of Bahia, as traditional Catholic imagery mingled with the vibrant, African-infused material culture on teeming streets. Seamen and the abundance they brought to shores of Salvador played

8. The domestic slave trade displaced many Africans living in Bahia to the south. In the Santo Antônio parish, the number of baptized enslaved Africans dramatically declined after the 1830s. See Nishida, *Slavery and Identity*, 17; J. Lorand Matory, *Black Atlantic Religion: Tradition, Transnationalism, and Matriarchy in the Afro-Brazilian Candomblé* (Princeton, N.J., 2005), 47–57.

a key role in the veneration—with some revelers even dressing as sailors. The
following day, a statue of Nossa Senhora dos Navegantes floated through the
Bay of All Saints en route to the Church of Nossa Senhora da Conceição.
This waterborne procession was accompanied by banks of rowers comprised
of Catholic fraternity brothers, as well as sailboats, sloops, lighters, canoes,
and fishermen's *jangadas* that crisscrossed the calm waters surrounding the
religious emblem. Seamen's infectious shouts, chants, claps, and songs wafted
through the air as the patron saint made her way to a final resting place built
for the occasion. As the statue traveled through the crowds, it was greeted
with "the greatest enthusiasm . . . disorder, tumult and extreme agitation."
Celebrations continued until dawn.[9]

Though this vibrant scene above unfolded in 1940, its origins lay in the
celebrations initiated by slaving ship captains and pilots in centuries previous
as a means of assuring their own protection at sea for the new year, making
a public plea for the intercession of powerful saints. The participation of all
of Salvador's residents, however, vividly illustrated the entire community's
continuing investment in the life of the sea and the well-being of its mariners. The days of festivities also evoked the enduring nature of Salvador's
culturally hybrid urban setting. The ritual trappings of Portuguese baroque
Catholicism converged with African-derived foods, music, and sacrificial offerings. This mélange of material and expressive cultures formed the center-
piece of celebration, conveying the intense entanglements of commerce and
culture, spirituality and entrepreneurship. A colorful legacy of the complex
world that Salvador's transatlantic slave trade had made, the public rituals
reminded both participants and onlookers of the intimate historical connections between the waterscapes of the Atlantic and the urban landscape. It was
a potent symbol that the enslaved men and women of Salvador had not been
relegated to the margins of the commercial currents of the city but were, in
fact, still at its cultural and emotional center. The rich local material culture
displayed during the public spectacle revealed that enslaved watermen had
left their indelible mark on both the city and the culture of Bahia. In short,
the world of captive cosmopolitan labor lived on, a remarkable fact given the
rise of powerful forces to the contrary.

This book has demonstrated how the multifaceted labors of African mariners—intellectual, physical, social, and cultural—gave birth to a new world,

9. João da Silva Campos, *Procissões tradicionais da Bahia: (Obra póstuma)*, Publicações
do Museu do Estado, no. 1 (Salvador, Brazil, 1941), quoted in Pierre Verger, *Notícias da
Bahia–1850* (Salvador, Brazil, 1981), 76–77.

one that would live on long past their own lifetimes. The maritime Atlantic they helped generate was interconnected, fluid, and hybrid, bound together by newly forming ties of commerce and migration. Compulsion and coercion provided the impetus for the Atlantic's first maritime merchant capitalist ventures. They also provided a reason for captives of African origin to adopt linguistic, cultural, and commercial fluencies beyond those they were born with. African forced labor was pivotal, not only in the expansive sugar and tobacco plantations of the Recôncavo but on the innumerable sailing ships that ferried people and goods from Bahia to Europe, Africa, and Asia. Men of African descent often involuntarily supplied the backbreaking and dangerous work necessary to power early modern slaving ships. They conformed to our images of strenuous maritime labor as they swabbed decks, pumped water, hoisted sails, supervised enslaved individuals, and rowed longboats. Much more difficult to recognize, however, were their innumerable intellectual contributions to South Atlantic slavery. Their pioneering insights into maritime geographies, legal discourses of liberty, transcultural commercial negotiations, and methods of efficacious healing have been neglected in scholarship on early modern maritime life. These skills collectively defined theirs as a cosmopolitanism of the displaced.

Captive Cosmopolitans ultimately reimagines the historical actors capable of making empire and making capitalism. Though our inherited master narratives almost universally foreground affluent, well-connected, and European members of the first transatlantic communities, marginalized actors in the South Atlantic were instrumental alongside powerful merchants and colonial administrators in constructing the teeming, early modern commercial landscape of Salvador. Often submerged in the surviving historical record, Africans and their descendants nonetheless helped transform a fledgling colonial outpost into a thriving metropolis by mastering the very winds and currents that carried them to American shores as slaves. The navigational acumen of the enslaved, both in the Bay of All Saints and throughout the South Atlantic, functioned as a critical part of the infrastructure that enabled colonial expansion by water. Without aquatic travel, the glittering wealth derived from the precious tropical commodities that underwrote Portugal's expansionist ambitions would have perished in African and American ports. By decentering the seemingly omnipotent commercial agency of royally sponsored monopoly trading companies, insular merchant families, and sophisticated financiers, we can appreciate the actions of everyday stakeholders in Bahia's transatlantic slave trade: captains and crews, residents of Salvador, religious brotherhoods, and even enslaved men and women on shore. These individuals, located in multiple social strata, gained access to transatlantic slaving from a web of familial and patronage ties, sending small portions of locally produced goods in return for a captive or two to sustain their livelihoods in the inhospitable port community. Their modest investments in turn sustained the slave trade and made it indispensable to reproducing Bahia's strict hierarchical economic and social order.

Though their efforts ultimately prolonged slavery, they never became the pure instruments of their masters' desire. Obligated to move for the profit of others, they crafted their own diffuse communities through their sometimes-uncontrollable mobility. The movement of captive mariners' bodies and their accompanying labors constructed transatlantic circuits of commerce and bondage at the behest of owners; however, these pathways grounded in violence, domination, profit, and servility gave way to African-centered intellectual and spiritual connections forged to remake modes of belonging in slavery's wake. They, along with their families and neighbors, fashioned networks of healing and sustenance, not in opposition to, but skillfully layered on top of, the hegemonic geographies of merchant capitalism, though these alternative imaginings sometimes failed to comport with the boundaries of empire and mercantilism prescribed by colonial authorities and owners. It was in the interplay between these two extremes of conceiving the watery world of the South Atlantic—as an endless terrain for the extraction of material prosperity or as a space crisscrossed by dense but fragile networks of people, spirits, ideas, and empowered objects—that the modern world was born.

APPENDIX 1. *Bahian Slaving Vessels Whose Papers Were Included in This Study*

No.	Ship's name	Date of capture	Reference
ARQUIVO NATIONAL DO RIO DE JANEIRO			
1	*Venus*	1811	Fundo 7X, Junta do Comércio, caixa 372
2	*Urbano*	1811	Fundo 7X, Junta do Comércio, caixa 371
3	*São Miguel Triunfante*	1812	Fundo 7X, Junta do Comércio, caixa 410
4	*Divina Providência*	1812	Fundo 7X, Junta do Comércio, caixa 410
5	*São Lourenço*	1812	Fundo 7X, Junta do Comércio, caixa 410
6	*Dezengano*	1812	Fundo 7X, Junta do Comércio, caixa 369
7	*Desforço*	1813	Fundo 7X, Junta do Comércio, caixa 369
8	*Intrepido*	1812	Fundo 7X, Junta do Comércio, caixa 411
ARQUIVO HISTÓRICO DO ITAMARATY RIO DE JANEIRO			
9	*Destino*	1812	Comissão Mista, lata 10, maço 2, pasta 2
10	*Feliz Americano*	1812	Comissão Mista, lata 15, maço 4, pasta 2
11	*Flor do Porto*	1812	Comissão Mista, lata 16, maço 4, pasta 2
12	*Lindeza*	1812	Comissão Mista, lata 19, maço 3, pasta 3
13	*Prazeres*	1812	Comissão Mista, lata 26, maço 6, pasta 2
14	*Emília*	1820	Comissão Mista, lata 13, maço 14, pasta 1
15	*Dez de Fevereiro*	1821	Comissão Mista, lata 10, maço 3, pasta 1
16	*Esperança Feliz*	1821	Comissão Mista, lata 15, maço 1, pasta 1
17	*Comerciante*	1822	Comissão Mista, lata 7, maço 5, pasta 1
18	*Dois Amigos Brasileiros*	1822	Comissão Mista, lata 11, maço 2, pasta 1
19	*Crioula*	1823	Comissão Mista, lata 15, maço 1, pasta 1
20	*Heroina*	1826	Comissão Mista, lata 17, maço 4, pasta 1
21	*São Benedito*	1826	Comissão Mista, lata 28, maço 4, pasta 1
22	*São João Segunda Rosalia*	1826	Comissão Mista, lata 28, maço 5, pasta 1
23	*Tentadora*	1826	Comissão Mista, lata 30, maço 1, pasta 1
24	*Venturoso*	1826	Comissão Mista, lata 31, maço 47, pasta 1
25	*Providência*	1826	Comissão Mista, lata 27, maço 2, pasta 1
26	*Indepêndencia*	1827	Comissão Mista, lata 18, maço 3, pasta 1
27	*Príncipe de Guiné*	1827	Comissão Mista, lata 27, maço 1, pasta 1
28	*Trajano*	1827	Comissão Mista, lata 30, maço 2, pasta 1
29	*Terceira Rosalia*	1828	Comissão Mista, lata 28, maço 2, pasta 1
30	*São Antônio*	1828	Comissão Mista, lata 21, maço 2, pasta 1

No.	Ship's name	Date of capture	Reference

THE NATIONAL ARCHIVES, KEW, U.K.

No.	Ship's name	Date of capture	Reference
31	*Andorinha*	1828	FO 315/42 no. 14
32	*Bella Eliza*	1828	FO 315/42 no. 12
33	*Donna Barbara*	1828	FO 315/42 no. 15
34	*Nova Viagem*	1828	FO 315/41 no. 1
35	*Penha de França*	1828	FO 315/41 no. 6
36	*Santa Effagenia*	1828	FO 315/41 no. 5
37	*Santo Iago*	1828	FO 315/42 no. 20
38	*Sociedade*	1828	FO 315/41 no. 3
39	*Triunfo*	1828	FO 315/42 no. 11
40	*União*	1828	FO 315/42 no. 13
41	*Zepherina*	1828	FO 315/41 no. 8
42	*Emelia*	1829	FO 315/42 no. 19
43	*Emília*	1829	FO 315/43 no. 23
44	*Não Lêndia*	1829	FO 315/44 no. 24
45	*Nossa Senhora da Guia*	1829	FO 315/43 no. 25
46	*Nova Resolução*	1829	FO 315/44 no. 28
47	*Primeira Rosalia*	1829	FO 315/43 no. 26
48	*Simpathia*	1829	FO 315/44 no. 33
49	*Tentadora*	1829	FO 315/43 no. 21
50	*Umbelino*	1829	FO 315/43 no. 27
51	*Emprehendedor*	1839	FO 315/44 no. 32

Note: This list encompasses ships captured by British antislaving forces, with the exception of the *Intrepido.*

APPENDIX 2. *Supplement to Chapter 3*

Table 1. Bahian Ships by Current Port of Anchor, Type, and Number of Seamen (1775)

Port of anchor	Navios (ships)	Curvetas (corvettes)	Galeras (galleys)	Sumacas (smacks)	Total no. of ships	Officers	White sailors	Freed Black mariners (%)	Enslaved Black mariners (%)	Total officers and sailors
Lisbon	5	2	1	0	8	51	214	0	5	270
Porto	0	2	1	0	3	15	25	2	0	42
Luanda	0	6	0	1	7	22	40	9	32	103
Benguela	0	4	0	1	5	19	20	1	38	78
Rio de Janeiro	1	1	0	0	2	8	6	2	24	40
Pernambuco	0	0	0	1	1	1	3	0	4	8
Guiné and the Mina Coast	0	9	0	1	10	49	31	12	171	263
Mozambique	0	1	0	0	1	5	10	2	8	25
Pará	0	0	0	1	1	1	6	0	2	9
Rio Real, Cotinguiba, and Sertão	0	0	0	27	27	32	50	20	68	170
Alagoas	0	0	0	1	1	2	4	0	2	8
Bahia	2	12	1	6	21	26	13	3	38	80
TOTAL	8	37	3	39	87	231	422	51	392	1,096

Source: AHU, CU, Brasil–Bahia, caixa 47, documento 8812, July 3, 1775, "Mapa geral de toda a qualidade de embarcações que ha na capitania da Bahia e navegam para a Costa da Mina, Angola."

Table 2. Traffic to the Port of Salvador da Bahia in 1808

LIST OF SHIPS THAT ENTER AND LEAVE THE PORT OF THE
CAPTAINCY OF BAHIA IN 1808

Arriving from	Number	Leaving for	Number
Alagoas	16	Alagoas	6
Alcobaça	3	Alcobaça	1
Bangala	1	Angola	1
Buenos Aires	1	Bahia	4
Cabo Verde	1	Caravelas	23
Caravelas	21	Callao de Lima	1
Bahia	2	Mina Coast	17
Coruripe	4	Charleston	1
Mina Coast	22	Gibraltar	8
Cotínguiba	56	Spain	1
Island of Príncipe	1	Island of Madeira	7
Island of Madeira	7	Island of Barlavento	1
England	32	England	21
Lisbon	16	Island of Terceira	1
London	3	Lisbon	1
Macau	1	London	4
Montevideo	2	Maranhão	3
Paratí	1	Pará	1
Paranaguá	3	Paranaguá	3
Pernambuco	14	Paratí	1
Porto Calvo	1	Pernambuco	8
Porto de Pedras	1	Rio Grande	90
Rio Grande	80	Rio de Janeiro	35
Rio de Janeiro	35	Rio de São Francisco do Norte	2
Rio de São Francisco do Norte	5	Rio de São Francisco do Sul	1
Rio de São Francisco do Sul	1	Rio Real	6
Rio Real	5	Santos	5
Santa Catarina	4	São Mateus	15
Santo Antônio Grande	3	Sergipe D'El-Rey	5
Santos	2	Santa Catarina	4
São Mateus	13	Santo Antônio Grande	4
Sergipe D'El-Rey	5	Santo Antônio do Príncipe	2
Una	1	São Tomé	1
		Torre	1
TOTAL	363	TOTAL	285

Source: ANRJ, fundo 7X, Junta do Comércio, caixa 448, "Mappa dos navios que entrarão, e sahirão do porto da capitania da Bahia em 1808."

APPENDIX 3. *Supplement to Chapter 6*

Table 1. Contents of the *Botica* on the *Venus* (1812)

Camphor (*alcamfor*)	East Asian derivation, used to treat ardors of the stomach and bladder, persistent fever
Rose water (*agoa rosada*)	Used as an astringent, aromatic medium to dissolve other substances
Nutmeg (*noz moscada*)	South Asian derivation, used to make several compounds including an antiseptic, aromatic powders, oils to treat flux, cough, vomiting, diarrhea
Paxorins	Not identified
Gum arabic (*goma arabica*)	North African derivation, used to treat ulcers, prepare medicinal gums, dissolved in water to make viscous solutions, and treat diarrhea
Saffron (*açafrão*)	Mediterranean derivation, used as a component in tonics to treat dysentery, cough, fevers, infectious disease
Almond oil (*óleo de amêndoas*)	Middle Eastern derivation; used as an astringent
Spirit of vitriol / sulfuric acid (*espiríto de vitriolo*)	Used to treat smallpox
Extract of Saturn (a mixture of lead, acetate, and lead oxide)	Dissolved in water to make a sedative, to treat inflammations and ulcers
Powdered cream of tartar (*cremor de tártaro em pó*)	Used to make purgative syrups, electuaries, pastes, pills, to treat fevers, hemorrhoids
Deer antler shavings (*raspas de veado*)	Used in a variety of chemical compounds including silver nitrate, muriatic acid / marine salt added to tonics to treat infectious and contagious disease, fevers
Marcela	South American derivation, used to make infusions, to treat colic, epilepsy, nausea, and gastric problems including diarrhea and dysentery; also used as a pain reliever and anti-inflammatory

Table 1 (*continued*)

Red poppies (*papoulas rubras*)	Mediterranean derivation, used to make a syrup to treat chest afflictions, (bloody) cough, general anodyne, emollient, purgative
Flower of Sabugueiro (elderberry)	European derivation, used as diaphoretic, expectorant, to treat scarlet fever, rubella, pulmonary hemorrhages, skin ailments
Spirits of cinnamon (*espiríto de canella*)	Mediterranean, South Asian, North African derivation, used to treat typhoid fevers, digestion, uterine hemorrhage
Compound tincture (*tintura de composta*)	Alcohol to make distillations
Water of cinnamon (*agoa de canella*)	Aromatic used to make tonics
Manna (*manna novo*)	From the Mediterranean, transformed into a syrup from the manna tree or powdered, used as a purgative, to treat dropsy
Camel ointment (*unguento de camelo*)	Used to treat wounds
Alcea ointment (*unguento de alcea*)	Derived from the flower of the mallow family, found in Europe and Asia, used to treat wounds, cleansing to ulcers, used for treatment of dysentery
Caustic apple (*maçã caustica*)	Not identified
Powdered Peruvian bark / quinine (*casca peruviana em pó*)	Peruvian derivation, used to make tonics, an expectorant, to treat pulmonary infection, malaria, and fever; an anti-inflammatory and analgesic
Spirits of rosemary (*molhos de alecrim*)	European derivation, infused in water to create tonics, antiseptic vinegar to treat infectious disease, fevers
Spirits of lavender (*molhos de alfazema*)	Used as an antispasmodic
Spirits of white vitriol or zinc sulfate (*molho de vitriolo branco*)	Used to make eye drops, astringent powders and to treat ulcers

Table 1 (*continued*)

Spirits of bitter salt, epsom salt, suphate of magnesia (*espiríto de sal amagro*)	Used as a sedative in small doses or a diuretic or purgative for constipation, cramps
Pure saltpeter (*nitro puro*)	Taken orally for typhus, syphilis, tetanus, atonic dysentery, chronic hepatitis, pulmonary hemorrhage
Salt of wormwood (*sal de losna*)	Used for fevers, stomach ailments, dysentery
Powdered jalapa (*jalapa em pó*)	Brazilian and Central American derivation (from indigenous usage), powdered root, strong purgative
Powdered rhubarb (*ruibarbo em pó*)	Asian derivation, laxative
Rose honey (*mel rosado*)	Used in combination with other medicines, infused in electuaries
Basilicon ointment (*unguento bazilicão*)	Made of rosin, wax, olive oil, and burgundy pitch used on blisters, ulcers, burns, sores
White ointment (lead oxide, wax and oil) (*unguento branco*)	Used on burns, for skin ailments, cooling and drying
Linseed (*linhaça*)	Portuguese derivation, used as emollient, laxative, and diuretic
Emollient herbs (*ervas emolientes*)	Emollients
Cipó (or ipecacuanha)	Brazilian derivation, emetic, used to treat dysentery
Ervas peitoraes (pectoral herb)	Used for cough, consumption, respiratory illness
Sarsaparilla (*salcaparilha escolhida*)	Brazilian derivation, used as a sudorific, antirheumatic, diuretic, to treat buboes, syphilis
Common plaster / poultice (*emplasto comun*)	Made of flour base, applied to skin for soreness and inflammation
Gummed plaster / poultice (*emplasto gomado*)	Or *emplasto diaquilou gomado;* made of lead oxide, olive oil and water, used as an emollient

Table 1 (*continued*)

Comforting plaster (*emplasto confortativo*)	Applied to skin to heal fractures and wounds
Soapy liniment (*linimento saponáceo*)	Soap made with opium, used to treat inflammation and rheumatic pain
Liquid laudanum	Portuguese derivation, opium-based sedative, used to treat gonorrhea and fevers
Spirits of cochlearia (scurvy-grass)	European derived, used in mouthwashes to treat scurvy, bleeding gums, hemorrhages
1 spatula	Instrument to make shavings
Fuming nitrous acid (*ácido nitroso fumante*)	Used to synthesize nitric ether, to treat nervous fevers, apoplexy
1 mortar and pestle (*almofariz*)	Used to pulverize herbs and other medicinal components
Dissolution of alum stone (*agoa forte*)	Used to dissolve other elements, astringent used to dry ulcers, wounds and treat warts
Glass bottles, sacks, and boxes	Used to store and mix medicine

Sources: ANRJ, fundo 7X, Junta do Comércio, caixa 372, Papers of the *Venus*; Richard Holland, *Observations on the Small Pox; or, An Essay to Discover a More Effectual Method of Cure Than Has Hitherto Been Found Out. . . . To Which Is Added, by the Same Author, a Short View of the Nature and Cure of the Small Pox; Also, the Great Usefulness of Spirit of Vitriol, Opiates, etc, with Some Proper Reflections on the Common Practice of Bleeding in That Distemper*, 2d ed. (London, 1741); Theodoro J. H. Langgaard, *Diccionario de medicina domestica e popular . . . com 236 figuras intercaladas no texto*, II (Rio de Janeiro, 1865); J. B. Fonssagrives, *Tratado de hygiene naval; ou, Da influencia das condições physicas e moraes em que está o homem do mar* (Lisbon, 1862); Jacinto da Costa, *Pharmacopea naval, e castrense: Offerecida ao illustrissimo senhor*, II (Lisbon, 1819); *Pharmacopeia geral para o reino, e dominos de Portugal: Publicada por ordem da Rainha Fidellissima D. Maria I*, II, *Medicamentos simplices, preparados, e compostos* (Lisbon, 1794); Caetano de Santo Antonio, *Pharmacopea lusitana augmentada methodo pratico de preparar os medicamentos na fórma Galenica, e Chimica . . .* , 4th ed. (Lisbon, 1754); Francisco da Fonseca Henriques, *Medicina lusitana, soccorro Delphico, a os clamores da naturesa humana . . .* , 2d ed. (Amsterdam, 1731); Lourival Ribeiro, *Medicina no Brasil colonial* (Rio de Janeiro, 1971).

Table 2. Contents of the *Botica* on the *Firmeza* (1839)

Burnt wine (*vinho queimado*)	Used to treat fevers
English water, made of magnesium sulfate and quinine (*agua de inglaterra*)	Used to treat fever, malaria, and as an analgesic
Basilicon ointment (*unguento bazilicão*)	Used to treat blisters, ulcers, burns, sores
Tamarind pulp (*polpa de tamarindos*)	Sub-Sahara African derivation, used to treat scurvy, fever, intestinal ailments
3 syringes (*siringas*)	
1 balance (*balança*)	Used to measure medicine
Pectoral herbs	Used "to make hot tonics for cough and fever"
Emollient herbs	Used "to make a hot bath for pains"
Barley (*cevada*)	Used as a mixing agent in flour form
Marcela	South American derivation, used to make infusions, to treat colic, epilepsy, nausea, and gastric problems including diarrhea and dysentery, also used as a pain reliever and anti-inflammatory
Elderberry flower (*flor de sabugo*)	Emollient
Mustard	"For the poultice, and given with vinegar for bladder pains"
Castor oil (*oleo de recino*)	Mediterranean, Asian, and African derivation, used as a purgative or enema, to treat skin conditions
Lavender (*alfazema*)	Used to make hot tonics to treat fevers and cough
Parsley (*salsa*)	Used to infuse tonics and as a diuretic
Thread	
Blistering cups (*ventozas*)	Used for cupping, when heated and laid on skin, attracts blood to the capillaries
Deer antler shavings (*raspas de veado*)	Used to treat infectious and contagious disease, fevers
Gum arabic (*goma arábica*)	North African derivation, used to treat ulcers, prepare medicinal gums, dissolved in water to make viscous solutions, and treat diarrhea

Table 2 (*continued*)

Magnesium sulfate / epsom salt (*sulfato de guanipa*)	2–12 grams to produce vomiting or purging, treating fevers
Liquid laudanum	Analgesic
White ointment of lead oxide, wax and oil (*unguento branco*)	Used on burns, for skin ailments, cooling and drying
Arceo balm (*balsamo de arceo*)	Made of tallow, turpentine, and lemon
Ointment for scabies (*unguento para as sarnas*)	
Alvacada	Not identified
Poultice of Spanish flies (*emplasto de cantharidas*)	Used to treat ulcers, wounds and sores
Powdered ipecacuanha (*ipecacuanha em pó*)	South American derivation, powerful emetic
Powdered jalapa (*jalapa em pó*)	South American derivation, powerful purgative
Catholic balsam (*bálsamo cathólico*)	Made of castile soap, camphor, saffron and spirit of wine, used to treat pain and ulcers
Antimony potassium tartrate / emetic tartar (*tártaro emético*)	Used as an emetic
Pós de joanes	Used to treat ulcers, yaws and wounds, particularly relating to venereal disease, mixed with sweet mercury
Sweet mercury (*mercúrio-doce*)	Purgative, used to treat ulcers and wounds, particularly relating to venereal disease (syphilis)
Alum (*pedra hume*)	Used as an escharotic for diseased skin, and to treat smallpox
Lipis stone (*pedra lipis*)	Used to make liquid astringent, and treat the bloody flux (dysentery)
Verdeta em pó	Not identified
Gummed diaquilon plaster (*emplasto diaquilon gomado*)	Plaster made of lead oxide, olive oil, and water, used as an emollient

Table 2 (*continued*)

Poultice with mercury (*emplasto de bans com mercúrio*)	Not identified
Pearls of the family (*pérolas da família*)	Not identified
Powdered rhubarb (*ruibarbo em pó*)	Asian derivation, used as a laxative
Powdered Peruvian bark / Jesuit's bark / quinine (*quina em pó*)	Peruvian derivation, used to make tonic, an expectorant, to treat pulmonary infection, stomach and intestinal problems, gastric or bilious and typhoid fever; also an analgesic and anti-inflammatory
Powdered cream of tartar (*cremor de tartaro em pó*)	Used to make purgative syrups, electuaries, pastes, pills, to treat fevers, hemorrhoids
Saltpeter (*nitro em pó*)	Was taken orally for typhus, syphilis, tetanus, atonic dysentery, chronic hepatitis, pulmonary hemorrhage
Extract of Saturn (a solution of lead acetate, alcohol and lead oxide) (*extracto de Saturno*)	Used to treat burns, contusions, rheumatic pains, hernias, and inflammation
Silver nitrate (*pedra infernal*)	Used to desiccate tumors, warts, ulcers, and cauterize wounds
Camphor (*alcamfor*)	East Asian derivation, used to treat ardors of the stomach and bladder, persistent fever
Flaxseed (*semente de linhaça*)	To treat hernias, sores, oil used as an emollient and to make ointments
Almond oil (*oleo de amendoas doces*)	Astringent and emollient
White vitriol or zinc sulfate (*vitriolo branco*)	Used to treat fevers and cholera
Nutmeg (*noz moscada*)	South Asian derivation, used to make several compounds including an antiseptic, aromatic powders, oils to treat flux, cough, vomiting, diarrhea

Table 2 (continued)

Tincture of Spanish flies (*tintura de cantharidas*)	Made of powdered Spanish flies (common in Brazil) and alcohol. Used as a stimulant, rubefacient, and to raise blisters, treat asthma, tumors, some paralysis, toothache, bruises, and respiratory illness
Opodeldoc liniment (*opodeldoc*)	Liniment, mixture of castile soap, alcohol, and herbs including camphor and wormwood, to treat bruises and swelling
Asafoetida	Central Asian derivation, used to make tincture to treat abscesses and venereal disease
White lead (*alvaiade*)	Used as an astringent to treat skin abrasions
Cathartic salt / sodium sulfate / Glauber's salt (*sal catartic*)	Purgative
Burraxinha para os direr gatorios	Not identified
Sedelites	Used to treat fevers and hemorrhoids
Bitter water or emetic tartar dissolved in water (*agua amarga*)	Used to treat constipation: "Take one dose in the morning and the other at night, in intervals of thirst"

Sources: BNA, FO 315/45, no. 34, Papers of the *Firmeza;* Gabriel Grisley, *Desenganos para a medicina; ou, Botica para todo pay de familias; Consiste na declaração das qualidades e virtudes de 260 ervas, com o uso dellas, tambem de 60 agoas estiladas, com as regras da arte da estilação* (Coimbra, 1669); Theodoro J. H. Langgaard, *Novo formulario medico e pharmaceutico; ou, Vademecum medicum . . .* (Rio de Janeiro, 1868); Eugene Soubeiran, *Nuevo tratado de farmacia teorico y practico . . . ,* III (Lima, [1817]); Antonio Gomes Lourenço, *Cirurgia classica, lusitana, anatomica, farmaceutica, medica, a mais moderna* (Lisbon, 1761); Ephraim Chambers, *Cyclopaedia; or, An Universal Dictionary of Arts and Sciences . . . ,* 5th ed., 2 vols. (London, 1743); Manuel Hernandez de Gregorio, *Diccionario elemental de farmacia, botanica y materia medica . . . ,* II (Madrid, 1803); Caetano de Santo Antonio, *Pharmacopea lusitana augmentada methodo pratico de prearar os medicamentos na fórma Galencia, e Chimica . . . ,* 4th ed. (Lisbon, 1754); Jeronymo Joaquim de Figueiredo, *Flora pharmaceutica e alimentar portugueza . . .* (Lisbon, 1825); Joaõ Curvo Semmedo, *Polyanthea medicinal: Noticias galenicas, e chymicas, repartidas em tres tratados . . .* [with "Manifesto que o doutor Joam Curvo Semmedo. . . ."] (Lisbon, 1716).

Table 3. Contents of the *Botica* on the *Dois Amigos Brasileiros* (1824)

Rose honey (*mel rosado*)	Used in combination with other medicines, infused in electuaries
Turpentine oil (*óleo de terebintina*)	Used to treat strokes, convulsions, (bloody) cough, abscesses, poor blood circulation, smallpox lesions
Catholic balsam (*bálsamo cathólico*)	Made of castile soap, camphor, saffron, and spirit of wine, used to treat pain and ulcers
Powdered cream of tartar (*cremor de tartaro em pó*)	Used to make purgative syrups, electuaries, pastes, pills, to treat fevers, hemorrhoids
White ointment (lead oxide, wax and oil) (*unguento branco*)	Used on burns, for skin ailments, cooling, and drying
Spirit of sal ammoniac (*espiríto de sal amoniaco*)	Astringent
Anodyne medicines (*medicamento anódino*)	Analgesic, pain relief
Rhubarb syrup (*xarope de ruibarbo*)	Bitter, lightly astringent
Sweet mercury (*mercúrio-doce*)	Purgative, used to treat ulcers and wounds, particularly relating to venereal disease (syphilis), as well as intestinal parasites such as worms
Sulfuric mercury (*mercúrio sulfurico*)	Not identified
Nitric acid (*ácido nítrico*)	Used to dissolve mercury
Castor oil (*oleo de ricinos*)	Purgative, laxative, anti-inflammatory
Powdered rhubarb (*ruibarbo em pó*)	Bitter aromatic
Arceu balsam (*balsamo de arceu*, or *unguento elemi*)	Stimulant and digestive ointment, to dress ulcers, made with turpentine
Compound rose ointment (*unguento rosado composto*)	Used to treat venereal and herpetic ulcers
Opium (*opio*)	Analgesic
Solimão	Treatment for scabies

Table 3 (*continued*)

Pedra infernal	Not identified
Torios de Tartaro[?]	Not identified
Sheets of tin (*folhas de flandres*)	Used to make a face mask to punish slaves; prevents eating and drinking by covering the mouth of the wearer
12 cups for bloodletting (*ventozas*)	
1 pair of scissors	
1 cast (*estreito*)	
Large laces for bandages (*cadarço largo para ataderas*)	
3 volume measures	
1 mortar and pestle	
1 new balance with all of its weights and measures up to 24 grams in silver (*"balança nova com todos os seus pezos e granatarios ate 24 grams de prata"*)	
2 syringes	
2 pipes	
Ointment of althea (*unguento de althea*)	Used to treat hemorrhoids
Powdered Spanish fly (*cantharidas em po*)	Used to treat ulcers, wounds, and sores
Asafoetida (*asafetida*)	Middle Eastern and South Asian derivation, plant used as an antispasmodic, expectorant, diuretic, and to treat digestive problems
Lead salt (*sal de chumbo,* or *sal de Saturno*)	Used to cleanse and cauterize ulcers
Lipis rock (*pedra lipes*)	Astringent
Senna (*senne*)	Common in Asia, Americas, Europe, and Africa, used as a purgative, to treat fever, venereal disease

Table 3 (*continued*)

Flower of sulfur, or sulfur powder (*flor de enxofre*)	Used to treat skin diseases, scabies
Linseed (*linhaça*)	Portuguese derivation, used as emollient, laxative, and diuretic
Mustard (*mostarda*)	Middle Eastern and Indian derivation, used to treat rheumatism, sciatica
Cocoa butter (*manteiga de cacão*)	Central and South American derivation, emollient
Barley (*cevada*)	Used as a mixing agent in flour form
Gum arabic (*goma arábica*)	North African derivation, used to treat ulcers, prepare medicinal gums, dissolved in water to make viscous solutions, and treat diarrhea
Simaruba bark (*cascas de simaruba*)	South American derivation, used to treat dysentery
Alum (*alumem*)	Used as an escharotic for diseased skin, and to treat smallpox
Sarsaparilla (*salsaparrilha*)	Caribbean, Central and South American derivation, this variety likely Brazilian in origin, purgative
White vitriol (*vitriolo branco*)	Purgative
Thread (*fios*)	
Pectoral herbs (*especies peitoraes*)	Used to treat respiratory ailments
Antiscorbutic herbs (*especies antiescorbúticas*)	Used to treat scurvy
Vulnerary herbs (*especies vulnerarias*)	Used to treat wounds
"Legitimate" agua de inglaterra (*agua de* Andre Lopes)	Used to treat malaria, fevers
Quinine wine (*vinho quinado*)	Used to treat malaria, fevers
Manna	From the Mediterranean, transformed into a syrup from the manna tree or powdered, used as a purgative, to treat dropsy

Table 3 (*continued*)

Basilicon ointment (*unguento basilicão*)	Used to treat blisters, ulcers, burns, sores
Tamarind pulp (*polpa de tamarindos*)	African derivation, antiscorbutic to treat scurvy
Powdered quinine (*quina em pó*)	South American derivation, used to treat fevers
Doubled dissolution of alum (*agua forte dobrada*)	Used to dissolve other elements, astringent used to dry ulcers, wounds and treat warts
Antiscorbutic electuary (*electuario antscorbutico*)	
Bruised quina bark (*quina contuza*)	Antimalarial, used to treat fevers
Electuary of senna (*electuario de senne*)	Common in Asia, Americas, Europe, and Africa, used as a purgative, to treat fever, and venereal disease
Pós de dover	Used to treat fevers and rheumatism. A mercury-based compound used to treat gonorrhea, syphilis and yaws
Mercury chloride (*calomelanos preparados*)	Purgative, cathartic
Cinnamon water (*agua de canela*)	Aromatic, used to make tonics
Peppermint water (*agua de hortelã pimenta*)	Aromatic, used to make tonics
Mercurial ointment (*unguento mercurial*)	Used treat lesions characteristic of yaws
Visicatory plaster (*emplastro visicatorio*)	Not identified
Ointment of Saturn (*pomada de Saturno*)	To treat lesions characteristic of yaws
Epsom salt (*sal de epsom*)	Emetic
Fine turpentine salt (*sal de terebenthina fina*)	Not identified
Saltpeter (*Nitro purificado*)	Taken orally for typhus, syphilis, tetanus, atonic dysentery, chronic hepatitis, pulmonary hemorrhage

Table 3 (*continued*)

Tincture of quinine (*tintura de quina composta*)	Used to treat fevers
Liquid laudanum (*laudano liquido de Londres*)	Analgesic
Sweet almond oil (*oleo de amendoas doces*)	Emollient, astringent
Lead vinegar (*vinagre de chumbo*)	Resulting vapors used to treat colic
Copaiba balsam (*balsamo de cupaiba*)	Brazilian derivation, local to Bahia, used to treat fever and mucous inflammations, especially gonorrhea and bronchitis, yellow fever, pneumonia, tuberculosis, an appetite stimulant
Rose water (*agua rosada*)	Aromatic
Turpentine spirits (*espiríto de terebenthina*)	Used to treat smallpox lesions
2 *varas de elefante*	Not identified
Linen cloth	
1 knife	
Powdered jalapa (*jalapa em pó*)	Brazilian and Central American derivation (from Indigenous usage), powdered root, strong purgative
Powdered pink root (*lombrigueira em pó*)	Used to treat intestinal worms
Ipecacuanha em pó	Emetic
Tincture of Spanish flies (*tintura de cantharidas*)	Made of powdered Spanish flies (common in Brazil) and alcohol, stimulant, rubefacient, used to raise blisters, treat asthma, tumors, some paralysis, toothache, bruises, respiratory illness
Agua da rainha	Emetic
Papel aparado para atlacar	Not identified
Pós de Joannes	Used to treat ulcers, yaws, and wounds, particularly relating to venereal disease, mixed with sweet mercury
Emollient herbs (*especies emolientes*)	

Table 3 (*continued*)

Carminative herbs (*especies resolutivas*)	Used to relieve gas and aid digestion
Febrifuge herbs (*especies febrifugas*)	Herbs to reduce fever
Lavender (*alfazema*)	Aromatic
Marcela	South American derivation, used to make infusions, to treat colic, epilepsy, nausea, and gastric problems including diarrhea and dysentery, also used as a pain reliever and anti-inflammatory
Bitterwort, or Gentiana lutea (*genciana*)	European derivation, used to treat digestive, liver, and bladder ailments, combined with purgatives
Calumba	East African derivation, the root is used to make tinctures and infusions and used as a tonic and stomachic.
Virginia snakeroot (*serpentaria*)	North American derivation, aromatic bitter to aid digestion
Lead carbonate (*alvaiade fino*)	Luiz Antônio de Oliveira de Mendes recommended a mixture of lead carbonate, with dendê oil, and corn flour, to make a plaster to treat painful boils caused by bacteria
Common plaster (*emplastro comum*)	Made of flour base, applied to skin for soreness and inflammation
Gummed plaster (*emplastro gomado*)	Or *emplasto diaquilou gomado*; made of lead oxide, olive oil, and water, used as an emollient.
Plaster of hemlock (*emplastro de cicuta*)	Used to treat scirrhous tumors, cancers, scrofula (tuberculosis)
Stomatal plaster (*emplastro estomatico*)	Not identified
Mercurial plaster (*emplastro mercurial*)	Not identified
Nonjas[?]	Not identified
Teriaga magna	Emetic, treatment for fevers, colic, and gout in children

Nutmeg (*noz moscada*)   South Asian derivation, used to make several
                           compounds including an antiseptic, aromatic
                           powders, oils to treat flux, cough, vomiting, diarrhea

Rosemary (*alecrim*)   Aromatic

Sources: AHI, Coleções Especiais, Comissão Mista, lata 11, maço 2, pasta 1, Papers of the *Dois Amigos Brasileiros,* 77–79. The total value of the *Dois Amigos Brasileiros's botica,* including instruments, was 283$920 reís, produced by apothecary, or *boticário,* João Lourenco Seixas (ibid., 9). The ship's *sangrador* was Florencio da Silveira, a freed man from Angola (ibid.). Table based on information in C[arlos] A[ugusto] Taunay and L. Riedel, *Manual do Agricultor Brazileiro . . .* , 2d ed. (Rio de Janeiro, 1839); John XXI, *Obras médicas de Pedro Hispano,* ed. Maria Helena da Rocha Pereira (Coimbra, 1973); Alberto Pessoa, *A botica de Eusébio Macário* (Coimbra, 1934); Robert A. Voeks, *Sacred Leaves of Candomblé: African Magic, Medicine, and Religion in Brazil* (Austin, 1997); *Jornal de Coimbra,* XIII (Lisbon, 1818); *Pharmacopeia geral para o reino, e dominios de Portugal: Publicada por ordem da Rainha Fidellissima D. Maria I,* II, *Medicamentos simplices, preparados e compostos* (Lisbon, 1794); Jacinto da Costa, *Pharmacopea naval, e castrense,* I, II (Lisbon, 1819); Roberts Bartholow, *A Practical Treatise on Materia Medica and Therapeutics* (New York, 1897); C[harles] E[dward] Armand Semple, *Aids to Therapeutics and Materia Medica . . .* (London, 1878); Robert Christison, *A Dispensatory; or, Commentary on the Pharmacopoeias of Great Britain . . .* (Edinburgh, 1842); [Pierre] Pomet, [Nicolas] Lemery, and [Joseph Pitton de] Tournefort, *A Complete History of Drugs . . .,* 4th ed. (London, 1748); Pedro Luiz Napoleao Chernoviz, *Diccionario de medicina popular . . .* III, *M–Z* (Rio de Janeiro, 1851); Lourival Ribeiro, *Medicina no Brasil colonial* (Rio de Janeiro, 1971); Melvina A. M. Araújo, *Das ervas medicinais à fitoterapia* (São Paulo, 2002); Maria Beatriz Nizza Da Silva, *Cultura letrada e cultura oral no Rio de Janeiro dos vice-reis* (Brazil, 2016); J[acob] de Castro Sarmento, *Materia medica physico-historico-mechanica: Reyno mineral . . .* (London, 1758); Armand Trousseau et al., *Tratado de terapéutica y materia médica,* II (Madrid, 1863); Francisco Soares Franco, *Pharmacopéa lusitana composta pela Commissão creada por decreto da Rainha Fidelissima D. Maria II. em 5 de Outubra de 1838* (Lisbon, 1841); Joaõ Curvo Semmedo, *Polyanthea medicinal: Noticias galenicas, e chymicas, repartidas em tres tratados . . .* [with "Manifesto que o doutor Joam Curvo Semmedo. . . ."] (Lisbon, 1716); Pedro Luiz Napoleão Chernoviz, *Formulario ou guia medica . . .* (Paris, 1864).

Table 4. African and Creole Medical Practitioners Employed on Bahian Ships, 1811–1829

Name	Occupation	Year of voyage	Destination	Age	Legal status	Race	Origin/place of birth	Wage in réis	Investments in réis
Manoel dos Reis	Barber	1811	Badagry	25	Freed, single	*Preto*	Mina Nation	120$000	
Antônio Gomes	Barber	1811	Cabinda, Angola		Freed	Preto	Mina Nation	200$000	
Domingos do Rozário	Barber	1812	Ajudá		Slave of Francisco Luiz de Souza	Preto	Bahia	100$000	13 *canadas* of *aguardente*, 34 canadas of *dendê* oil, 7 large corals, 2 large *panos da costa*, 3 small panos da costa
Francisco Alvez	Second barber	1812	Ajudá						13 canadas of aguardente
Lino Ricardo Gomes	Barber	1812	Porto Novo, Badagry		Freed	Preto	Mina Nation	80$000	85$800, consisting of 10 rolls of tobacco
Domingos	Second barber	1812	Porto Novo, Badagry		Slave of Ignácio Antunes Guimares (ship's owner)	Preto	Mina Nation	50$000	4$800
Boaventura Teixeira de Souza	Barber	1812	Ajudá		Freed	Preto	Mina Nation	90$000	65$500, consisting of 36 canadas of aguardente and 10 rolls of tobacco

Name	Occupation	Year	Place	Age	Status	Color	Nation	Value	Notes
Raimundo	Second barber	1812	Ajudá		Slave of Domingos Jozé Correa		Bahia	50$000	
Joaquim de Nação Angola	Barber	1812	Porto Novo, Ajudá		Slave of Dona Francisca Maria do Sacramento	Preto	Angola	80$000	
Antônio Neves	Master barber	1813	Badagry	"30 and some"	Freed, single	Preto	Mina Nation Gege	70$000	37$750 consisting of 7 rolls of tobacco, 44 canadas of aguardente
Firmiano	Second barber and steward (*despensairo*)	1813	Badagry		Slave of Jozé Tavares Franca (ship's owner)	Creole	Bahia	50$000	15$800, consisting of 40 rolls of tobacco and 10 canadas of aguardente
Ignacio Jozé	*Sangrador*	1831	Molembo		Freed	Preto	Gege	Private	
Leandro Jozé da Costa	Barber	1822	Rio de Camarão, São Tomé and Príncipe, Molembo		Freed	Preto	Gege	200$00 and a "praça livre" to transport one slave free of freight	One young male slave
José Marques	Sangrador	1823	Onim (Lagos)		Freed	Preto	Gege	120$000	
Antônio Ribeiro Filgueira	Barber	1812	Porto Novo		Freed	Preto	Mina Nation	100$000	
Antônio de Nasção Mina	Barber	1812	Porto Novo		Slave of Reverendo Padre João Mendes	Preto	Mina Nation	50$000	

Table 4 (*continued*)

Name	Occupation	Year of voyage	Destination	Age	Legal status	Race	Origin/place of birth	Wage in réis	Investments in réis
Florencio da Silveira	Sangrador	1824	Badagry		Freed	Preto	Angola	150$000	
Jozé Joaquim de Moraes	Sangrador	1820	Ajudá, Cabo-Corso, Acará, Onim (Lagos)		Freed	Preto	Gege nation, born in Ajudá,	120$000	12 rolls of tobacco, 2 *ancoras* of aguardente, 1 adult male slave
Joaquim José Baptista	Surgeon	1821	Onim (Lagos)	23	Free, married	*Pardo*	Bahia	200$000	
Torilio Reipia	Barber	1812	Porto Novo		Slave of Francisco Luiz Reina	Preto	Mina Nation	200$000	Owned 102$704 consisting of 8 rolls of tobacco, 6 pieces of cloth, 72 canadas of aguardente
Joaquim Lopes	Second barber	1812	Porto Novo		Slave of Domingos Lopes	Preto	Mina Nation	50$000	Owned 48$352 in trade goods, consisting of 4 rolls of tobacco and 37 canadas of aguardente
Jozé de Nasção Mina	Barber	1812	Onim (Lagos)		Slave of Jozé de Souza	Preto	Mina Nation	100$000	
Francisco Nazaré	Sangrador	1826	Ajudá		Freed	Preto	Mina Nation	200$000	
Barilio	Sangrador	1827	Molembo		Slave of Jozé Cerqueira Lima (ship's owner)	Cabra	Bahia	300$000	

Name	Occupation	Year	Place	Age	Status	Color	Nation/Coast	Value	Notes
Agostinho Jozé Ricardo	Barber	1816			Slave of Manoel Jozé				1 ancora of aguardente, 18$000
Dionizio Alves Pereira	Barber	1812	Onim (Lagos)	32	Freed	Cabra	Bahia	100$000	Owned 213$108 in trade goods, consisting of 74 canadas of aguardente, containers, 9 massos of beads, textiles
Felippe Serra	Barber	1823	Onim (Lagos)	40	Freed, single	Preto	Mina Coast	100$000	
Antônio Jozé de Carvalho	Barber	1812	Cabo de Palmas, Popo, Ajudá, Cabo Corso		Freed	Preto	Mina Nation	1$000	
Raymundo Cardozo	Sangrador	1827	Ajudá				São Tomé	100$000	
Manoel Felicianno	Surgeon	1827	Ajudá	28			Bahia	250$000	
Firmiano	Sangrador	1827	Onim (Lagos)		Slave of Joaquim Jozé de Oliveira (ship's owner)	Preto	Hausa	150$000	
Antônio Mendes	Sangrador	1828	Popo			Preto	Mina	160$000	
Antônio de Aranjo de Santa Anna	Barber	1826	Ajudá	30		Preto	Mina	200$000	
Luiz Joaquim Bahia	Sangrador	1827	Molembo			Preto	Mina	120$000	

Table 4 (continued)

Name	Occupation	Year of voyage	Destination	Age	Legal status	Race	Origin/ place of birth	Wage in réis	Investments in réis
Vicente Francisco Camaxo	Sangrador or barber	1826	Badagry	50		Preto	Mina	180$000	
Ignácio Gomes João	Sota-Sangrador Sangrador	1826 1828	Badagry Molembo	50	Slave of Vicente de Paulo Silva (ship's owner)	Preto	Mina São Tomé	180$000 200$000	
Ignacio José	Sangrador	1828	Mina Coast, São Tomé, Molembo	43		Preto	Mina	180$000	
Luis Joaquim Bahia	Sangrador	1828	Cabinda, São Tomé	32	Freed	Preto	Gege	150$000	
Luiz Ignacio	Sangrador	1828	Mina Coast				Benin	140$000	
Bento Jozé Gonsolvez	Sangrador	1828		28	Freed	Preto	Angola	200$000	
Joaquim de Santa Anna	Sangrador	1828		20	Free	Creole	Bahia	Private	
Caetano Maciel	Sangrador	1829	Ambriz		Freed	Preto	Mina	Private	
Constantino da Roxa	Sangrador	1828	Cabinda			Preto	Tapa	Private	
Francisco	Sangrador	1828	Cabinda, Mina Coast, São Tomé		Slave of Joaquim Jozé de Oliveira (ship's owner)	Preto	Gege	Private	

Name	Occupation	Year	Origin	Number	Status	Color	Ethnicity	Private	Notes
Joaquim	Sangrador	1828	Cabinda	17	Slave of Antônio Santa Anna	Preto	Nagô		
Jozé	Sangrador	1828	Mina Coast, Cabinda, São Tomé		Slave of Geraldo Rodrigues Perreira	Preto	Cabinda	150$000	
Honorio	Sangrador	1829	Cabinda	20	Slave of Maria de Jezus	Preto	Mina	200$000	
Paulo (Pedro?) Antônio do Outeiro	Sangrador	1829	Mina Coast, São Tomé, Molembo	46	Freed	Preto	Gege		
Domingos Antônio	Sangrador	1829	Cabinda	36		Preto	Mina	200$000	
Jozé Egidio	Sangrador	1829	Molembo			Preto	Mina	170$000	
Ternirano	Sangrador	1839	Cabinda		Slave of Joaquim José de Oliveira (ship's owner)	Preto	Hausa	250$000	
Alberto Felis de Santa Anna	Sangrador	1829	Mina Coast, São Tomé, Cabinda			Preto	Mina	200$000	Owned 1 barrel of gunpowder, 1 canada of aguardente, 2 shotguns

Source: Figures are derived from a compilation of slaving ships listed in Appendix 1.

APPENDIX 4. *Supplement to Chapter 7*

Table 1. Census of 1775, Relative Numbers of Types of Sailing Vessels in Bahia by Parish

Location	Navios (ships)	Curvetas (corvettes)	Galeras (galleys)	Sumacas (smacks)	Barcos (boats)	Lanchas (launches)	Saveiros (barges)	Canoas (canoes)	Jangadas (rafts)
PARISHES IN SALVADOR									
São Salvador na Sé		1		1		4	1		
Santíssimo Sacramento na Rua Paso		3					4		
N.S. da Vitória						1	1	31	37
S. Pedro Velho				2		9	1	21	
N.S. das Brotas								1	24
N.S. da Conceição	2	21	1	16	1	12	21	6	
Santíssimo Sacramento no Pilar	5	12	2	9	2	17	3	23	
S. Senhora da Penha						7	4	106	
PARISHES IN THE SUBURBS OF SALVADOR									
S. Bartolomeu em Pirajá						4	2	26	
N.S. do Ó em Paripe						4	7	35	
S. Miguel em Cotegipe						4	5	24	
N.S. da Piedade em Maruim					2	6	20	75	
N.S. da Encannam em Pasé					1	2	21	20	
Santa Vera Cruz em Itaparica					1	27	14	140	
Santo Amaro em Itaparica					1	14	2	80	
São Pedro no Sauipe da Fosse				3				22	
Santo Amaro na Ipitanga								5	53

TOWN OF SÃO FRANCISCO

São Gonsalo na Vila de Santo Amaro				2	5	1	40	
N.S. do Socorro				1	8	13	53	
N.S. do Monte				5	4	1	10	
N.S. Mãe de Deus no Boqueirão					28	20	125	
TOWN OF SANTO AMARO								
N.S. da Pun. E Va. De Santo Amaro				2	17	1	50	
S. Domingos na Saubara					11	4	21	
TOWN OF CACHOEIRA								
N.S. do Rozario e Vila da Cachoeira		1		10	8		20	
São Pedro de Mortiba				6	2		32	
Santiago no Iguape					17	1	71	
TOWN OF MARAGOGIPE								
São Bartolomeu na Vila de Maragogipe				2	32	4	144	
TOWN OF JAGUARIPE								
N.S. da Ajudá e Vila de Jaguaripe				2	49		22	
N.S. de Nazareth					30			
Santo Antônio em Giquirisã					4		13	
N.S. Mãe de Deus em Parajuía					9	4	78	
TOWN OF ABADIA								
N.S. e Vila de Abadia			4				50	1
N.S. do Monte do Itapicurí da Praia			4				20	4
TOTAL	7	37	3	40	38	335	155	1,342	141

Note: "N.S." stands for "Nossa Senhora."

Source: AHU, CU, Bahia-Avulsos, caixa 164, documento 12425, Jan. 4, 1775, Lisbon, "Mapas de carga, relações e listas e outros documentos relativos a embarcações vindas da Bahia."

Table 2. Investors on the Brigantine *São Miguel Triunfante*

Name / Relationship to vessel	Rolls of tobacco
João da Silveira Villas Boas / captain of *São Miguel Triunfante*	240
Jozé Antônio / second pilot	12
João da Silveira Villas Boas, Junior / third pilot, scribe, and son of captain	20
Jozé da Silva Guimares / quartermaster	30
Joaquim de Santa Anna Penna / first cooper	16
Ignácio Roiz Ferreira / second cooper	8
Jozé Joaquim and Felipe Fernandes / sailors	5
Antônio / sailor and slave of Joaquim Jozé Maria de Campos	7
Sargento-mor Joaquim de Santa Anna Mundim / none specified	10
Jozé Francisco da Silva / none specified	3
Joaquim Francisco Carneiro / owner of *São Miguel Triunfante*	20
Manoel Vieira Mendes Leitão / none specified	20
Joaquim Jozé Maria de Campos / owner of 3 of the ship's enslaved sailors	50
Manoel João do Reis / owner of 3 of the ship's enslaved sailors	25
Francisco Domingues de Oliveira / none specified	12
Luis dos Santos Lima / none specified	10
Manoel Joaquim Alvez / none specified	15
Preto Cosme / slave of Manoel da Silva Cunha	4
Preto Miguel Maciel / slave of João Maciel de Souza	4
Preto Marcaro / slave of Boaventura Ferreira da Roxa	4
Preto João / slave of Francisco Joaquim Carneiro (owner)	5
Pretos Luiza, Ianoario, Manoel, and Antônio / slaves of Francisco Joaquim Carneiro	4
Pretos Alexandre and Domingos / sailors and slaves of Francisco Joaquim Carneiro	6
Pretos Joaquim da Costa and Maria / slaves of Francisco Joaquim Carneiro	5
Pretos Francisco and Vicente / sailors and slaves of Francisco Joaquim Carneiro	6
Pretos Caetano, Euzebio, Custodio, and Francisco / sailors and slaves of Francisco Joaquim Carneiro	6
Preto Joaquim / sailor and slave of Francisco Joaquim Carneiro	7
Anna Joaquim da Assuncam / none specified	8
Julianna Maria and Anna Rosa / none specified	12
Joaquim Jozé de Magalles / none specified	10
Andre de Medeiras / none specified	20
Anna Maria / none specified	4
TOTAL	608

Source: ANRJ, Fundo Junta do Comércio, Fábricas e Navegações, caixa 410, pacote 1, Papers of the *São Miguel Triunfante*

{ INDEX }

Page numbers in italics refer to illustrations.